# SURVIVORS

A STORY IN LETTERS OF
AN ENGLISH FAMILY'S SURVIVAL
DURING FOUR CENTURIES OF WARS

BILL
BIRCH REYNARDSON

ADWELL PRESS

Published by Adwell Press

Text © William Birch Reynardson

First published 2014

ISBN 978 0 9931071 0 8

**Copyright notice**

All rights reserved. No part of this publication may be reproduced in any form or by any means (including photocopying or storing it in any medium by electronic means and whether or not transiently or incidentally to some other use of this publication) without the written permission of the copyright owner, except in accordance with the provisions of the Copyright, Designs and Patents Act 1988 or under the terms of a licence issued by the Copyright Licensing Agency, Saffron House, 6–10 Kirby Street, London EC1N 8TS (www.cla.co.uk). Applications for the copyright owner's written permission should be addressed to the publisher at billbirchreynardson.survivors@gmail.com.

Edited by Kate Dinn
Designed by Sara Rafferty
Index: Sue Lightfoot

Typeset in Palatino

Printed and bound by Ingram Spark

Cover illustrations: (front) The Birch Reynardson coat of arms (see **Fig. B**, page 6) (back) *The Landing of the British Troops at Aboukir, 8 March 1801*, by Philip James de Loutherbourg (**Fig. 4 c**), page 94). National Galleries of Scotland

## CONTENTS

*List of Illustrations* — iv

**Foreword** by Professor Sir Michael Howard, OM, MC — 1

**Introduction** The Three Families — 2

**Chapter 1** Two Unsuccessful Courtships
*Family Letters 1680–1728* — 13

**Chapter 2** The Law, Farming and 'The Forty-Five'
*Letters from Friends and Family 1721–1750* — 36

**Chapter 3** The Three Thomases
*Letters and Diary Extracts 1759–1796* — 61

**Chapter 4** The Egyptian Campaign
*Letters and Maps 1800–1801* — 84

**Chapter 5** The Peninsular War (1) and the ill-fated Walcheren Campaign
*Letters and Diary Extracts 1802–1809* — 132

**Chapter 6** The Peninsular War (2) and the end of the Napoleonic Wars
*Letters and Eye-witness Accounts 1810–1815* — 168

**Chapter 7** The General's Family
*Family Letters 1816–1847* — 193

**Chapter 8** In the Crimea
*Letters and Diary Extracts 1854–1856* — 234

**Chapter 9** Adwell
*History, Genealogy and Reminiscences 1850–1900* — 281

**Chapter 10** The Boer War and the Great War
*Letters and Reminiscences 1900–1918* — 298

**Chapter 11** The Inter-War Years
*Reminiscences 1918–1939* — 335

**Chapter 12** Eton, North Africa and Italy
*Recollections and Letters 1939–1946* — 352

**Chapter 13** The Post-War Years
*Letters and Recollections from 1946 onwards* — 397

**Acknowledgements** — 422

**Appendix I** The Battle of Dettingen, 1743 — 424

**Appendix II** 'The Angels on Horseback' — 428

**Appendix III** Peninsular War Memorabilia — 431

**Appendix IV** The General's Napoleonic Archive — 435

**Appendix V** 'Real Home Solves Homeless Children's Problem' — 439

**Appendix VI** From *The Times* Obituaries, 2 September 1997 — 445

**General Index** — 447

**Index of Authors of Original Letters and Documents** — 460

# LIST OF ILLUSTRATIONS

*(pages 4–5)*
**Fig. A**  Family Tree.

*(page 6)*
**Fig. B**  The Birch Reynardson coat of arms.

*(page 8)*
**Fig. C**  Pages from Sir Abraham Reynardson's copy of *The Pourtraicture of His Sacred MAJESTIE in his Solitudes and Sufferings* (1648).

*(page 10)*
**Fig. D**  Sir Abraham Reynardson's house at Tottenham.
**Fig. E**  *Portrait of Sir Abraham Reynardson*, by Cornelius Janssen.
**Fig. F**  *Portrait of Eleanor Wynne, Lady Reynardson*, by Cornelius Janssen.

*(page 14)*
**Fig. 1 a)**  *Portrait of Jacob Reynardson.*
**Fig. 1 b)**  *Portrait of Frances Farnaby (Mrs Jacob Reynardson).*

*(page 15)*
**Fig. 1 c)**  List of plant ingredients from the reverse of LETTER 1: 1.

*(page 18)*
**Fig. 1 d)**  *Portrait of Samuel Reynardson as a child.*
**Fig. 1 f)**  Letter from Edward Owen to Elizabeth Phillips, dated 6 November 1699.

*(page 19)*
**Fig. 1 e)**  *Portrait of Lady Barnardiston, née Mary Reynardson.*

*(page 30)*
**Fig. 1 g)**  A 'ticket' for the hanging of Jonathan Wild at Tyburn, May 1725.

*(page 40)*
**Fig. 2 a)**  Extract from LETTER 2: 2, dated 29 September 1739.

*(page 44)*
**Fig. 2 b)**  *Portrait of Judge Sir Thomas Birch.*

*(page 45)*
**Fig. 2 c)**  Letter from Lord George Murray, dated 9 October 1745.

*(page 50)*
**Fig. 2 d)**  *The March of the Guards to Finchley*, by William Hogarth (1750).

*(page 66)*
**Fig. 3 a)**  *Portrait of Elizabeth Cust, later Mrs Philip Yorke*, by Francis Cotes.
**Fig. 3 b)**  *Portrait of Anne Cust, later Mrs Jacob Reynardson*, by Francis Cotes.

*(page 71)*
**Fig. 3 c)**  Page from Jane Birch's cashbook, September 1761.

**Fig. 3 d)**  Tailor's Bill for Servants' Livery (William Drake to James Birch), 1770.

*(page 74)*
**Fig. 3 e)**  *Portrait of Thomas Birch.*

*(page 86)*
**Fig. 4 a)**  *Portrait of Sir Ralph Abercromby*, by John Hoppner (c.1787).

*(page 91)*
**Fig. 4 b)**  *Sir Sidney Smith* (study for *The Landing of British Troops at Aboukir*, **Fig. 4 c)**), by Philip James de Loutherbourg (1802).

*(page 94)*
**Fig. 4 c)**  *The Landing of British Troops at Aboukir, 8 March 1801*, by Philip James de Loutherbourg (1802).

*(page 96)*
**Fig. 4 d)**  *Plan of Alexandria & Surroundings, showing the Disposition of British Troops & Enemy Lines*, by Thomas Birch (March 1801).

*(page 98)*
**Fig. 4 e)**  *The Battle of Alexandria, 21 March 1801*, by Philip James de Loutherbourg (1802).

*(page 121)*
**Fig. 4 f)**  *Map of the Operations of British Forces in Egypt, 8–21 March 1801*, from the plan drawn by Thomas Birch (published 1801).

*(page 126)*
**Fig. 4 g)**  Page from LETTER 4: 23, dated 1 September 1801.

*(page 134)*
**Fig. 5 a)**  *A Riding Party at Southend*, by Thomas Birch (July 1805).

*(page 145)*
**Fig. 5 b)**  *Portrait of Lieutenant-General Sir John Moore*, by Thomas Lawrence (c.1805).

*(page 150)*
**Fig. 5 c)**  *Map of the Scheldt Estuary, showing the Island of Walcheren.*

*(page 166)*
**Fig. 5 d)**  *Preparations for the Jubilee, or Theatricals Extraordinary*, after Thomas Rowlandson (published 1809).

*(page 170)*
**Fig. 6 a)**  *Portrait of Major-General John Gaspard Le Marchant*, by Henry James Haley.

*(page 177)*
**Fig. 6 b)**  Page from LETTER 6: 6, dated 30 June 1812.

*(page 182)*
**Fig. 6 c)**  *The Battle of Salamanca*, engraved by T. Fielding (published 1819).

*(page 185)*
**Fig. 6 d)** *Aufstieg und Niederfallen Napoleons (The Rise and Fall of Napoleon)*, by Johann Michael Voltz (published 1814).

*(page 189)*
**Fig. 6 e)** Extract from **6: 10** (a description of part of the Battle of Waterloo, 18 June 1815).

*(page 198)*
**Fig. 7 a)** Page from LETTER **7: 2**, dated 2 September 1820.

*(page 199)*
**Fig. 7 b)** *Portrait of Henry Birch Reynardson as a child*, by Henry Alken (c.1820).

*(page 213)*
**Fig. 7 c)** *Portrait of Charles T. Birch Reynardson* (c.1836).
**Fig. 7 d)** *Portrait of Mrs Anne Birch Reynardson, née Yorke* (c.1836).

*(page 215)*
**Fig. 7 e)** *Portrait of Mrs Mary Birch at her spinning wheel*, by John Frederick Lewis (c.1827).

*(page 219)*
**Fig. 7 f)** *Portrait of John William (Newell) Birch*, attributed to Sir Martin Archer Shee.
**Fig. 7 g)** *Portrait of Diana Bourchier, Mrs John Birch*, attributed to Sir Martin Archer Shee.

*(page 235)*
**Fig. 8 a)** *Portrait of Colonel Edward Birch Reynardson*, by Colonel Cadogan (1854).

*(page 237)*
**Fig. 8 b)** *Portrait of a Spahi*, by Edward Birch Reynardson (June 1854).

*(page 238)*
**Fig. 8 c)** *View of Encampment of Brigade of Guards at Galata near Varna*, by Edward Birch Reynardson (September 1854).

*(page 252)*
**Fig. 8 d)** *Lord Cardigan at the Battle of Balaklava*, by Alfred A. de Prades.

*(page 263)*
**Fig. 8 e)** *The Roll Call*, by Elizabeth Butler (1874).

*(page 264)*
**Fig. 8 f)** *Lives at Stake!* and *Sick & Wounded coming from the front on Cavalry Horses to recruit at Balaklava*, by Edward Birch Reynardson (winter 1854).

*(page 271)*
**Fig. 8 g)** *The Monastery of St George, between Sebastopol and Balaklava*, by Edward Birch Reynardson (April 1855).
**Fig. 8 h)** *Colonel Edward Birch Reynardson*, by Roger Fenton (1855).

*(page 277)*
**Fig. 8 i)** *The Entrance to Balaklava Harbour* and *The Approach to Constantinople*, by Edward Birch Reynardson (May 1855).

*(page 278)*
**Fig. 8 j)** *Four sketches drawn in Constantinople and on board the* Indus, by Edward Birch Reynardson (May 1855).

*(page 283)*
**Fig. 9 a)** *A nineteenth-century view of Adwell*, by Admiral Smythe.

*(page 286)*
**Fig. 9 b)** *Henry Birch Reynardson as High Sheriff of Oxfordshire* (1861).
**Fig. 9 c)** *Portrait of William John Birch Reynardson*, by Countess Karolyi.

*(page 287)*
**Fig. 9 d)** *Théoule on the Côte d'Azur*, by William John Birch Reynardson (1889).
**Fig. 9 e)** *A Continental Lakeside Town*, by William John Birch Reynardson (1889).

*(page 296)*
**Fig. 9 f)** *A nineteenth-century view of the gardens at Adwell*, by Admiral Smythe.

*(page 299)*
**Fig. 10 a)** Dargavel House, Renfrewshire.
**Fig. 10 b)** *Lieutenant Francis Aylmer Maxwell, V.C.* (c.1900).

*(page 300)*
**Fig. 10 c)** *Sketch of the Action at Sanna's Post, 30 and 31 March 1900*, by Frank Maxwell.

*(page 320)*
**Fig. 10 d)** Map of the action at Shaiba, April 1915, by Henry T. Birch Reynardson (published 1919).

*(page 327)*
**Fig. 10 e)** Map of the action at Ctesiphon, 22–24 November 1915, by Henry T. Birch Reynardson (published 1919).

*(page 333)*
**Fig. 10 f)** Souvenir of the marriage of Captain Henry Birch Reynardson to Miss Diana Ponsonby, 14 September 1917.

*(page 334)*
**Fig. 10 g)** Sketch map of Mesopotamia illustrating the operations of the Indian Expeditionary Force between November 1914 and December 1915, by Henry T. Birch Reynardson (published 1919).

*(page 336)*
**Fig. 11 a)** Dickie Birch Reynardson (c.1932).
**Fig. 11 b)** The dressing-up party arranged on board ship by the Prince of Wales (1930).

*(page 340)*
**Fig. 11 c)** Dickie, William, Rosamund and Cynthia Birch Reynardson on Neddy, Adwell (1928).

*(page 343)*
**Fig. 11 d)**  My mother, Mrs Diana Birch Reynardson.
**Fig. 11 e)**  My father, Lieutenant-Colonel Henry T. Birch Reynardson.

*(page 347)*
**Fig. 11 f)**  Adwell from the west (1949).

*(page 351)*
**Fig. 11 g)**  My sister Cynthia's wedding to Humphrey Prideaux, 30 August 1939.

*(page 355)*
**Fig. 12 a)**  The Eton Beagles (c.1941).

*(page 358)*
**Fig. 12 b)**  The members of Loders Club, 1942.
**Fig. 12 c)**  John Joicey.

*(page 366)*
**Fig. 12 d)**  Personal Message from the Army Commander, Lieutenant-General Oliver Leese, May 1944.

*(page 378)*
**Fig. 12 e)**  John Joicey and his crew at Coriano Ridge, 20 September 1944.

*(page 384)*
**Fig. 12 f)**  Lieutenant-Colonel Jack Price.

*(page 387)*
**Fig. 12 g)**  'B' Squadron Officers, Palmanova, 1945.

*(page 388)*
**Fig. 12 h)**  Plan of the final Allied advance (Italy), April 1945.

*(page 398)*
**Fig. 13 a)**  My brother Dickie in the uniform of the Grenadier Guards.

*(page 409)*
**Fig. 13 b)**  Our wedding at St Bartholomew the Great, 29 November 1950.
**Fig. 13 c)**  W.B.R., Inner Temple, 1952.

*(page 410)*
**Fig. 13 d)**  Coronation Day, 2 June 1953.

*(page 413)*
**Fig. 13 e)**  *Holywell House* (early twentieth century).

*(page 417)*
**Fig. 13 f)**  Princess Anne receiving her prize at the Adwell Horse Trials, 1968.
**Fig. 13 g)**  W.B.R. leading the South Oxfordshire Hunt at Adwell.

*(page 419)*
**Fig. 13 h)**  *Double Portrait of Bill and Nik Birch Reynardson*, by Benedict Rubbra.

*(page 421)*
**Fig. 13 i)**  Rosalind Ingrams on the last night of Garsington.

*(page 427)*
Page from *Account of the Battle of Dettingen*, dated 30 June 1743.

*(page 431)*
**III: A**  *Sketch of the Attack upon the French at Zambuiera*, 17 August 1808.

*(page 432)*
**III: B**  *Reference to the Sketch of the Attack upon the French at Zambuiera*, 17 August 1808.

*(page 433)*
**III: C**  *Sketch of the Action between the British and French at Vimiero*, 21 August 1808.

*(page 434)*
**III: D**  *Explanation relating to the Battle of 21st of August* (1808).

*(pages 439–444)*
'Real Home Solves Homeless Children's Problem', from *Illustrated* magazine, 16 June 1945.

# FOREWORD

*by* Sir Michael Howard, OM, MC
Regius Professor of Modern History, Oxford University, 1980–89

There can be few families in England who can trace their ancestry back unbroken to the thirteenth century; even fewer who, having lived in the same two properties for over three hundred years, have been able to preserve a complete historical archive; and fewer still who can show such an impressive record as landowners, lawyers, statesmen and above all soldiers as can the Birch Reynardsons. Their story is that of the English ruling classes: serving on both sides in the Civil War, emerging on the winning side both in 1660 and 1688, then amassing wealth from the land and from the City, improving their estates and liberally patronising the arts, until the present day. But even more than most such families, each generation since the eighteenth century has produced distinguished soldiers; and even more than most such soldiers, the Birch Reynardsons proved highly literate and prolific correspondents.

So although this collection contains a great amount of valuable — and often entertaining — material on family matters, its chief interest lies in the letters written home by its members who served in the Army, from the Napoleonic Wars until the Second World War. In the first of these, Thomas Birch (later Thomas Birch Reynardson) wrote home from the little-known Baltic, Egyptian and Walcheren campaigns, as well as receiving letters, maps and other documents from fellow officers serving in the Peninsular War. From the Crimea, Colonel Edward Birch Reynardson sent back eye-witness accounts of the Battles of Alma, Balaklava and Inkerman, as well as vivid descriptions and illustrations of conditions during the horrible winter of 1854–55. The author's great-uncle, Frank Maxwell, described the action when he won the VC during the Boer War. Other members of the family and friends wrote home both from the Western Front and Mesopotamia in the First World War, while the author of this book and compiler of the collection of letters, Bill Birch Reynardson, did the same from Italy during the Second World War. Finally, the author describes how he and his family have survived and flourished at Adwell into the twenty-first century.

In short, the most general of readers should love this book and military historians will be fascinated by it. I cannot remember enjoying anything more.

INTRODUCTION

# The Three Families

*Before my father died, over forty years ago, he mentioned, without going into any details, that he had done some work on a collection of family letters and documents written between 1680 and the 1950s. Because he made so little of it, I didn't attach much importance to this information and it is only in the last few years that I have had time to read most of the letters myself. I found them fascinating and had no idea that our collection (running to several hundred items) was so extensive or that my father had done so much research, principally into the three main families from which we are descended: the Birches, the Reynardsons and the Newells. Not only had he produced detailed family trees, going back to the seventeenth century and in some cases beyond, as well as notes on the history of each family, but he had had many of the letters typed out, preserving the original manuscripts. So, much of the work had already been done.*

*Initially, I thought that the letters and other relevant documents would be of interest only to members of the Birch Reynardson family and their friends, but as I became more familiar with the vivid personalities of the different writers, I began to feel that their voices deserved to be heard by a wider audience, who could read for themselves how it really felt to live through three hundred years of turbulent English history in times of both peace and war. There are far too many letters to reproduce in their entirety and so I have selected those which contain the main elements of our family's story and, where appropriate, added background information about the letter-writers themselves and the historical events which they describe.*

*Like most families, our genealogy is complicated. It involves a huge 'cast' of characters and is made more confusing by the fact that many share the same name — in the eighteenth century alone, at least four George Birches feature prominently! To understand the way each branch of the family has evolved over the generations does therefore require the study of a family tree. It must be admitted that I have always been somewhat allergic to family trees; it seems to me that they are rather dull affairs which tell us nothing about the characters of the people featured in them. Nevertheless, when I was involved in hunting hounds, my mentor Ronnie Wallace (probably the most famous huntsman over the last hundred years) was talking constantly about blood lines and their importance. 'Now that lovely bitch is by Beaufort Bacher out of Bicester Bertha. Bacher, of course you must know, was by Barbary from the Buccleuch.' So I became quite knowledgeable about the mysteries of hound breeding. The same principles apply, of course, to the whole subject of breeding: some unions work, some don't. It's important to acknowledge, I think, that*

## THE THREE FAMILIES

*genes do seem to crop up in all areas of the animal world; in so far as concerns my family, I inherited the fox-hunting gene from my mother (who in turn had inherited it from her father, Ned Ponsonby) and have passed it on to my own children, especially Clare, and to most of my grandchildren. My passion for painting comes from my grandfather on my father's side and was shared by his grandfather, Thomas Birch Reynardson, and at least one of Thomas's children (see* **Chapters 4** *and* **8**). *And of course, as we shall see, there have been lawyers in both the Birch and Reynardson families in almost every generation going back at least as far as the late seventeenth century.*

*It is for this reason that I think I should deal with my family's blood lines, and the composite family tree* (**Fig. A**) *which shows, in different colours, the three families from which we are descended will, I hope, assist my readers. As can be seen from the family tree, the Birch and Reynardson families did not come together until 1806, when Lieutenant-Colonel Thomas Birch — in many ways the pivotal figure of our family history — married Miss Etheldred Reynardson, and it was another six years before the conjoined name 'Birch Reynardson' was first used, after the death of Etheldred's father* (**Chapters 5** *and* **6**). *Thomas, who rose to the rank of General, was also the first of our direct forebears to serve with distinction in the Army. We know a fair bit about the earlier history of both families, especially the Birches; of the Newells, however, surprisingly little is known, considering that (by a rather tortuous process which is explained in* **Chapter 9**) *we became the owners of Adwell through the marriage of a Birch to a Newell (Thomas's parents) in the middle of the eighteenth century.*

*Thanks partly to research carried out by my father, the origins of the Birch family can be traced back to the mid thirteenth century when, as a reward for faithful service in the Crusades, Matthew de Haversage granted the family (then called 'de Birches') 'the whole land of Hindley Birches'*[1] *in what is now the Rusholme area of Manchester. Birch Hall also originated from this period and remained in the family for eighteen generations until it was sold by Humphrey Wyrley Birch in 1743. The house itself was demolished in 1925 to make way for the new Manchester Grammar School, but the number of streets and parks in the area which were named after the Birches have ensured that the family name lives on in Manchester.*

*The family is said to have been granted its coat of arms, in the name of Birch of Birch, from Edward III as a reward to William de Birches, who is reputed to have saved the Black Prince's life at Poitiers in 1356. The would-be assassin of the Black Prince (the 'snake in the grass' which crawled towards him) is symbolised by the snake entwined in the single fleur de lis of the crest. (After the Birch and Reynardson families were joined in marriage,*

---

1   Herbert Birch, *Memories of Birch. Its Owners and its Ancient Chapel*, 1896 (reprinted with additions from the *Manchester City News*, 4 July 1896).

SURVIVORS

## Family Tree

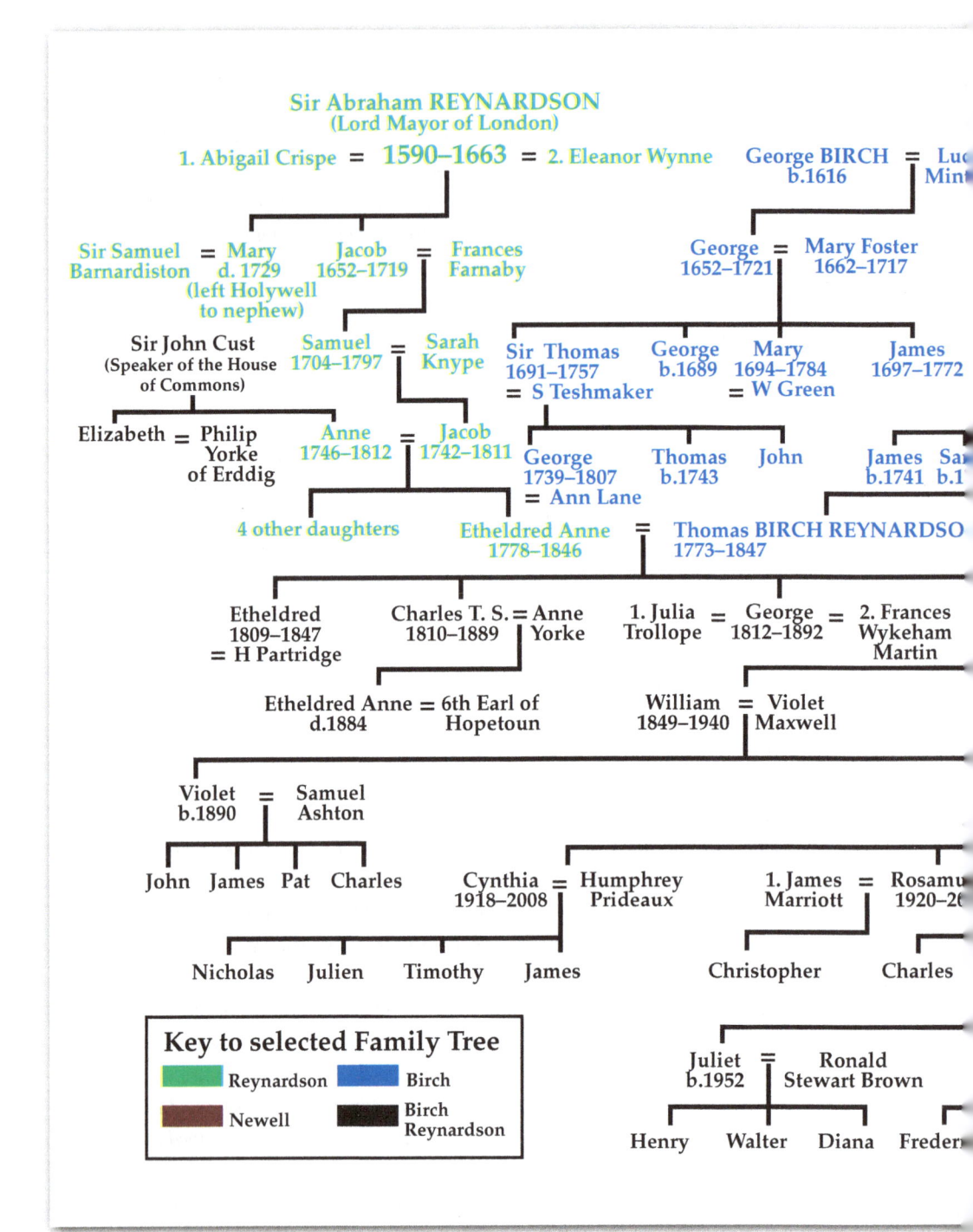

**Sir Abraham REYNARDSON**
(Lord Mayor of London)
1. Abigail Crispe = 1590–1663 = 2. Eleanor Wynne    George BIRCH = Luc
                                                        b.1616        Min

- Sir Samuel = Mary     Jacob = Frances        George = Mary Foster
  Barnardiston  d. 1729  1652–1719  Farnaby    1652–1721  1662–1717
  (left Holywell
  to nephew)

  Sir John Cust    Samuel = Sarah   Sir Thomas   George    Mary        James
  (Speaker of the House  1704–1797  Knype  1691–1757   b.1689   1694–1784   1697–1772
  of Commons)                       = S Teshmaker              = W Green

  Elizabeth = Philip   Anne    = Jacob
              Yorke    1746–1812  1742–1811   George      Thomas    John      James  Sa
              of Erddig                        1739–1807   b.1743              b.1741  b.1
                                               = Ann Lane

  4 other daughters    Etheldred Anne = Thomas BIRCH REYNARDSO
                       1778–1846       1773–1847

  Etheldred        Charles T. S. = Anne    1. Julia = George = 2. Frances
  1809–1847        1810–1889       Yorke      Trollope  1812–1892  Wykeham
  = H Partridge                                                    Martin

           Etheldred Anne = 6th Earl of        William = Violet
                d.1884      Hopetoun           1849–1940  Maxwell

  Violet = Samuel
  b.1890   Ashton

  John  James  Pat  Charles    Cynthia = Humphrey      1. James = Rosamu
                               1918–2008  Prideaux        Marriott  1920–2

       Nicholas  Julien  Timothy  James        Christopher           Charles

  **Key to selected Family Tree**
              Juliet = Ronald
  ■ Reynardson   ■ Birch        b.1952   Stewart Brown
  ■ Newell       ■ Birch
                   Reynardson   Henry  Walter  Diana  Freder

**Fig. A** Family tree showing the lines of descent of the Birches, Reynardsons and Newells.

4

# THE THREE FAMILIES

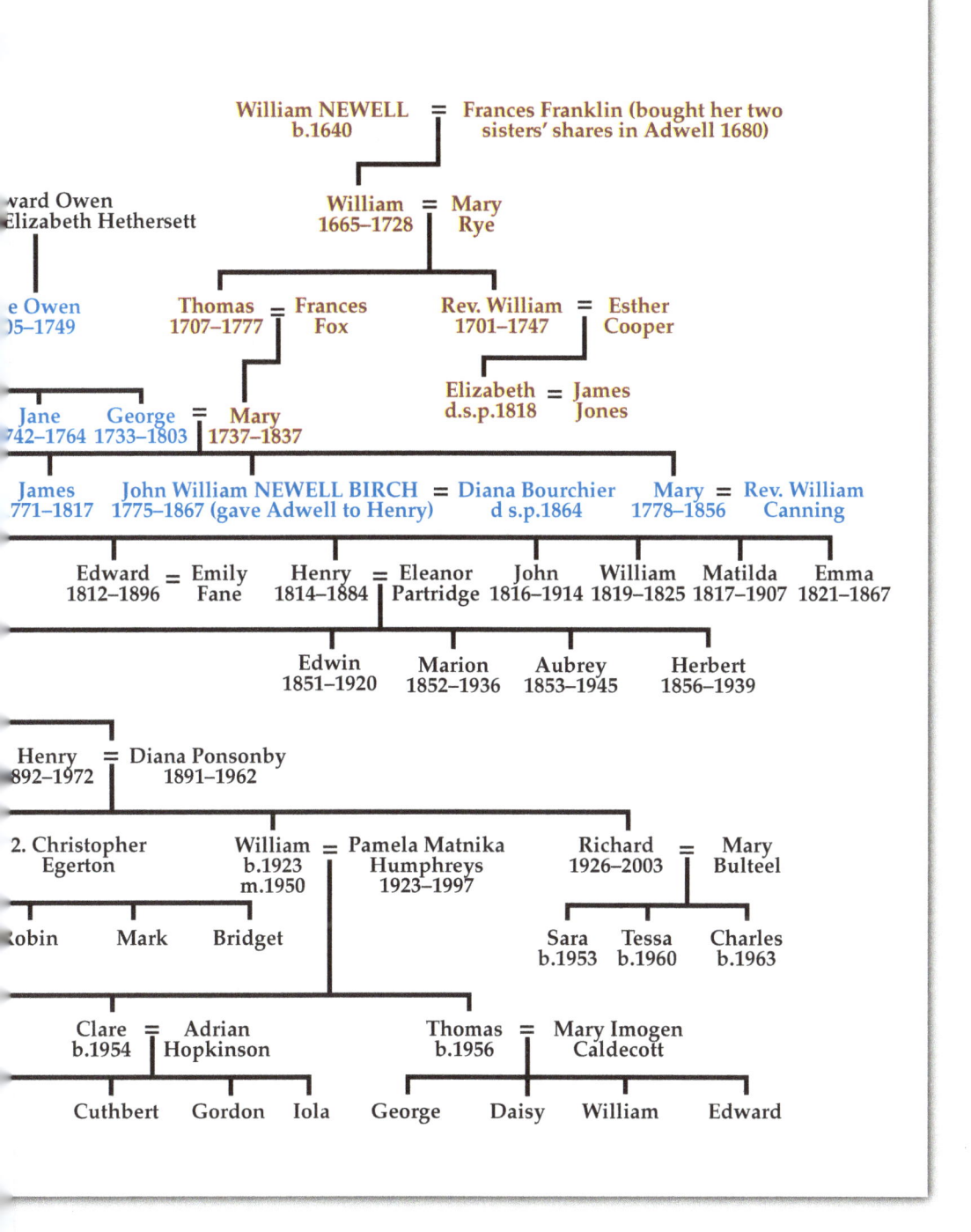

```
                William NEWELL    =   Frances Franklin (bought her two
                    b.1640                sisters' shares in Adwell 1680)
```

ward Owen
Elizabeth Hethersett

                William  =  Mary
                1665–1728    Rye

e Owen
05–1749

Thomas = Frances          Rev. William = Esther
1707–1777  Fox            1701–1747      Cooper

                          Elizabeth  =  James
                          d.s.p.1818    Jones

Jane        George  =  Mary
742–1764  1733–1803  1737–1837

James     John William NEWELL BIRCH  =  Diana Bourchier    Mary    =  Rev. William
771–1817  1775–1867 (gave Adwell to Henry)   d s.p.1864   1778–1856   Canning

Edward = Emily    Henry   = Eleanor     John       William     Matilda     Emma
1812–1896  Fane   1814–1884  Partridge  1816–1914  1819–1825   1817–1907   1821–1867

              Edwin       Marion      Aubrey      Herbert
              1851–1920   1852–1936   1853–1945   1856–1939

Henry    =  Diana Ponsonby
892–1972    1891–1962

2. Christopher    William  =  Pamela Matnika       Richard    =  Mary
   Egerton        b.1923      Humphreys            1926–2003     Bulteel
                  m.1950      1923–1997

Robin    Mark    Bridget                      Sara       Tessa      Charles
                                              b.1953     b.1960     b.1963

   Clare  =  Adrian                  Thomas  =  Mary Imogen
   b.1954    Hopkinson                b.1956    Caldecott

Cuthbert   Gordon   Iola      George    Daisy    William    Edward

5

*the Birch coat of arms was adapted to incorporate the lion and crown crest from the Reynardson coat of arms, which was granted in 1632* (**Fig. B**). *According to Herbert Birch, another member of the family, Ralph Birche, fought at the Battle of Agincourt in 1415.*

*There is a lack of original documentary evidence for the following two hundred years, but we now know that during the sixteenth century different branches of the 'parent-stock' began to migrate southwards; some to Aston, near Birmingham, where there are still schools named Birchfield and Birches Green, and then to Handsworth in Staffordshire, where Thomas Birch (1586–1646) was Lord of the Manor, before settling in Harborne (see* **Chapter 2**) *where he died. It is from this Thomas that we can trace direct descent and from whom other branches spread out: to Coventry and Norfolk in the early eighteenth century and later to Windsor and Oxfordshire.*

**Fig. B** The Birch Reynardson coat of arms. Watercolour, produced by the Royal College of Heralds.

*During the Civil War, two members of the Manchester branch were notable for their support of Oliver Cromwell and Parliament against the Crown. Colonel Thomas Birch (c.1608–78), a Puritan and Parliamentarian 'of a somewhat brutal type'*[2], *took an active part in the Civil War in Lancashire, defending Manchester from being secured by the Royalists in 1642, helping to capture Preston for Parliament the following year and later becoming governor of Liverpool. A cousin, Colonel John Birch (1615–91), played an even more significant role: as a Parliamentarian Army officer he was rewarded with the governorship of Bath and Bristol in return for his help in the capture of Bridgwater and Bristol in 1644 by the New Model Army, and in 1645 was made governor of Hereford Castle after masterminding the storming of the Royalist garrison there. He was returned as M.P. for Leominster several times between 1646 and 1660, and adapted successfully to*

2   William Farrer and J. Brownhill (eds.), *A History of the County of Lancaster: Vol. 4* (Victoria County History, 1911).

*the restoration of the monarchy in that year*[3].

As a Member of Parliament under the restored king, Charles II, John Birch briefly oversaw both the Admiralty and the disbandment of the Army, and was asked to draw up a statement of the debts both of the Navy and the Army. Within a few months of the Restoration, he was appointed Auditor of the Excise for life, with a salary of £500 a year. In this capacity he came into contact with Samuel Pepys, at this time Secretary to the Navy Board, and is mentioned several times in the famous Diary. Pepys did not take to Colonel Birch at first, describing him after their initial meeting on 18 September 1660 (at a Parliamentary Committee to assess the debts of twenty-five naval ships which were to be paid off) as 'very impertinent and troublesome'[4]. Later Pepys revised his opinion and developed considerable respect for the former Parliamentary Army officer; a regard which seems to have been mutual, according to his report of a conversation on 31 January 1668.

> And so away to Whitehall to the Commissioners of Treasury — where waiting some time, I met there with Coll. Birch and he and I fell into discourse, and I did give him thanks for his kindness to me in the Parliament-house, both before my face and behind my back; he told me he knew me to be a man of the old way for taking pains, and did always endeavour to do me right and prevent anything that was moved that might tend to my injury — which I was obliged to him for, and thanked him.[5]

John Birch lived to welcome the Glorious Revolution of 1688, by which time he had moderated his more extreme anti-Royalist and Puritanical views. But it is a strange thought that at the time when he was most vociferous against the monarchy, he could hardly have avoided being known, at least by reputation, to the most prominent member of the Reynardson family: Sir Abraham Reynardson (1590–1660), who was Lord Mayor of London (the first Devonshire man to hold that office) during the eventful year of King Charles I's trial and execution, 1648–49.

Our knowledge of the Reynardson ancestry goes back only as far as Abraham's father Thomas, who is described as a 'Turkey merchant from Plymouth' in the late sixteenth century. His third son, Abraham, pursued the same line of business but on a grander scale; he was a member of the governing bodies of the Turkey and East India Companies and became Master of the Merchant Taylors' Company in 1640. As a moderate Royalist,

---

3   See E. Heath-Agnew, *Roundhead to Royalist: Biography of Colonel John Birch 1615–91* (Express Logic Ltd, 1978)
4   Robert Latham and William Matthews (eds.), *The Diary of Samuel Pepys* (Bell & Hyman, 1970–83).
5   Latham and Matthews (eds.), Diary (as above).

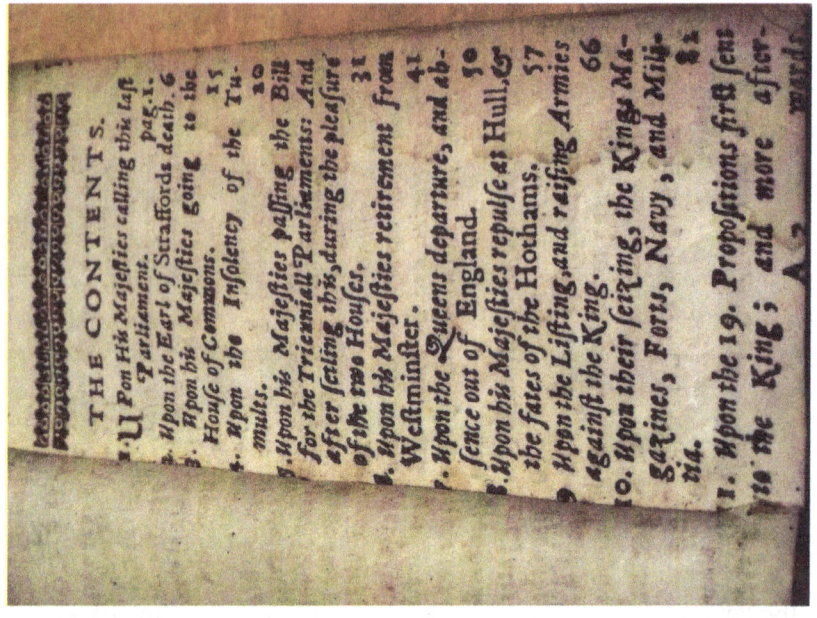

**Fig. C**: Frontispiece (left) and Contents page (right) from Sir Abraham Reynardson's copy of *'The Pourtraicture of His Sacred MAJESTIE in his Solitudes and Sufferings'* (printed 1648).

*Abraham soon came into conflict with the Rump Parliament (which had declared all loyal oaths to the King illegal) by refusing to countenance the act constituting the court for Charles I's trial or (after his execution on 30 January 1649) to read the proclamation of the Act of Parliament abolishing the kingly office. For this courageous act of defiance, Abraham was summoned to the Bar of the House of Commons to answer for his conduct, and after a long debate on 2 April 1649 he was ordered by the House to pay a fine of £2000 (equivalent to between five and six million pounds today), to be committed to the Tower of London for two months' imprisonment and to be deposed from the mayoralty*[6]. *Abraham's copy of a small brown leather-bound book entitled* 'The Pourtraicture of His Sacred MAJESTIE In his Solitudes and Sufferings' (**Fig. C**), *printed in 1648 and listing the chief events of the King's life, is owned by my cousin, Edward Fane (a direct descendant of Sir Abraham), who kindly lent me the book so that I could have the opportunity to examine it.*

*After the Restoration in 1660, Sir Abraham was knighted by Charles II and was formally restored to the office of alderman, but declined, on account of* 'his sickly condition', *the offer of the mayoralty for the first year of the new King's reign. In fact he died later in the same year and, despite having been obliged to pay such a large fine, his fortune at the time of his death is estimated to have been worth (in today's money*[7]*) the colossal sum of nearly three billion pounds! What he did with his wealth is a mystery; we know of only one house owned by him* (**Fig. D**), *in Tottenham, and although the nineteenth-century watercolour shows a handsome building, it is hardly palatial. My father was inclined to regard the Reynardson family as rather 'nouveau riche', as they were (at this time) members neither of the armed forces nor the Bar (the only professions, other than land ownership, acceptable for a gentleman — a view widely held at least until the beginning of the First World War!), but 'in trade'*[8].

*Sir Abraham Reynardson* (**Fig. E**) *was married twice, firstly to Abigail Crispe (daughter of Alderman Sir Nicholas Crispe of Bread Street), who gave birth to two sons before her death in 1632. By his second marriage, to Eleanor Wynne of Shrewsbury* (**Fig. F**), *he fathered six more children and it is from Jacob (see Chapter 1), the third of his four sons from this marriage, that our line has descended. One wonders what Abraham would have thought if he could have foreseen that 150 years later the Reynardson name would survive only through the marriage of one of the last of his line to a member of the*

6    Charles M. Clode, *London in the Time of the Great Rebellion* (1892).
7    Philip Beresford and William D. Rubinstein, *The Richest of the Rich: The Wealthiest 250 People in Britain since 1066* (Harriman House Ltd, 2007). When my brother Dickie read the *Sunday Times* article quoting this figure, he rang me up to enquire, with a touch of aggressiveness, 'Where's the loot now?' I wish I knew!
8    As indeed was Colonel John Birch, who was a wine merchant in Bristol during the years before the Civil War. Newton E. Key, *Oxford Dictionary of National Biography* entry for 'John Birch (1615–91), parliamentary army officer and politician (Oxford University Press, 2004–12).

**Fig. D** Sir Abraham Reynardson's house at Tottenham. From an early nineteenth century watercolour.

**Fig. E** *Portrait of Sir Abraham Reynardson (1590–1660)*, by Cornelius Janssen. Oil on canvas. Private Collection.

**Fig. F** *Portrait of Eleanor Wynne, Lady Reynardson*, by Cornelius Janssen. Oil on canvas. Private Collection. Eleanor Wynne married Abraham Reynardson in 1636 as his second wife.

*Birch family, or that the conjoined name is still going strong into its seventh generation!*

*At the risk of sounding rather like Chapter 15 of the* Book of Genesis, *I do not want to leave my venture into the genealogy of my family without mentioning some members of the present generation whom I would particularly like to thank for their involvement in the preparation of this family history. All are descended directly from General Thomas Birch Reynardson and fall into three categories by virtue of the houses owned by them and their offspring.*

*I refer first to the 'Rushington' family — so called because Rushington Manor in the New Forest was the house to which Thomas Birch Reynardson's son Edward retired after serving in the Crimean War, when he commanded the 3rd Battalion of the Grenadier Guards at the Battle of Inkerman (see* Chapter 8). *Edward's grandson was another Army officer, Lieutenant-Colonel Morgan Henry Birch Reynardson (born 1895). His two daughters, Eve (born in 1943) and Avril (born in 1947), have both been extremely helpful over the preparation of this book. Eve lent me the watercolours of the Crimea, painted by Edward Birch Reynardson and some fellow officers, some of which are reproduced in* Chapter 8. *Avril I got to know very well when she was sent to school near Adwell, following the sad death of her mother who died of a heart attack when riding on the beach in Jersey. We have had long discussions about her branch of the family whenever I stayed with her to shoot in Shropshire.*

*My cousin Edward Fane, whose grandmother 'Buss' was the last member of the family to live at Holywell (see* Chapter 13), *has taken much trouble to brief me about the Reynardsons of Holywell, as well as lending me some original material from his own collection; his wife Suki has also shown particular interest and has, as well as accompanying me in a productive and enjoyable visit to the Lincolnshire Archives, spent much time going through a mass of family papers and lending me many relevant documents.*

*Last, but by no means least, my own children — my daughters Juliet and Clare, and my son Thomas and his wife Imogen, the present custodians of Adwell (see* Chapters 9 onwards) *— have all shown an interest in the whole project and their enthusiasm has encouraged me to continue in bringing it to fruition.*

*Bill Birch Reynardson*

## A note about the original letters

*Many of the letters, especially the ones earliest in date, include antiquated spelling, abbreviations or symbols which are no longer in general use and this can make them quite difficult to decipher. In order to retain the distinctive 'voices' of the writers I have mostly left the original spelling unaltered (sometimes with 'translations' in square brackets). However, to help make the letters easier to read, some punctuation has been silently added and the abbreviations for the most part are written out in full.*

CHAPTER 1

# Two Unsuccessful Courtships

*Family Letters 1680–1728*

'I am prepareing to take the wings of Love to make hast to you'[1]

*Sir Abraham Reynardson's two marriages produced eight children but his two sons by Abigail Crispe both died young. However, all six children from his second marriage to Eleanor Wynne outlived their father and two of them, his fifth son Jacob (1652/3–1719) and one of Jacob's sisters Mary (later Lady Barnardiston), play an important role in our subsequent family history.*

*Jacob Reynardson (**Fig. 1 a**)), the writer of the earliest letter in our collection, was a merchant like his father; later he is recorded as resident in Bristol, where he became Collector of Customs in 1711, but at the time this letter was written in 1680 he must have been working in London. On his marriage to the very pretty Miss Frances Farnaby (**Fig. 1 b**)) of Kippington, Kent, which took place on 11 February in the same year, Jacob's address is given as 'St Martin, Outwich, Middlesex'. His announcement of the arrival of the ship from Smyrna makes it likely that Jacob had continued his grandfather's trade with Turkey, perhaps importing plant-based ingredients of the sort used by apothecaries, as there is a list of these on the reverse of the letter (**Fig. 1 c**)). The reference to other ships 'goeing into Wales' may indicate that he already had business interests in the Bristol Channel area.*

*Although the date, all but the year, has been torn away, it is possible to date this letter quite precisely from Jacob's lively description of the Exclusion Bill, one of at least three unsuccessful attempts by the House of Commons to prevent the King's brother, the Catholic James, Duke of York, from acceding to the throne. On this occasion, the Bill was brought to the House of Lords on Monday 15 November, 1680, and after much heated debate, in the presence of the King (Charles II), it was thrown out. Lord Russell, who was responsible for presenting the Bill, was subsequently executed for his supposed involvement in the Rye House Plot, which planned to depose the King and replace him with the Duke of Monmouth, his illegitimate, but Protestant, son.*[2]

---

1   Edward Owen (junior) to Miss Elizabeth Phillips, 6 November 1699 (**Fig. 1 f**).
2   The Duke of York did indeed succeed his brother in 1685 as James II, but after only three years was compelled to relinquish the throne as the result of the bloodless 'Glorious Revolution', which saw his Protestant son-in-law, William of Orange, and daughter Mary being invited to become the joint sovereigns.

**Fig. 1 a)** *Portrait of Jacob Reynardson (1652/3–1719)*, artist unknown. Oil on canvas. Private Collection.

**Fig. 1 b)** *Portrait of Frances Farnaby (died c.1719)*, artist unknown. Oil on canvas. Private Collection.

**Fig. 1 c)** A hand-written list of plant ingredients (from the reverse of Jacob Reynardson's letter to his brother, November 1680: **1:** 1)

**Letter 1:1 (Jacob Reynardson, London, to his brother, dated 16 November, 1680)**

Lon[don] [part of page missing] ...ber 1680.–

Deare bro'

Your Fryday letter was not brought to our house 'till Sunday night, otherwise [you] may be confident I should have taken due care in sending downe what Mr. Langham should have prescribed with ye oranges which I now doe by this dayes coach, being a little bottle of Phisick & a doz. of oranges. My accountt I received yesterday with your letter, I have not yett examin'd it, but question not but it is right; as to my concerne with Mr. Farnaby[3] I have done nothing in it as yett, if [I] had [I] would have given you an accountt thereof; but this evening shall meett Mr. Nicholls & brother Onslow[4] after which [you] shall heare further from me. I must acknowledge my selfe infinitely obleidg'd for your expressions, and endeavour not only to deserve those past, but acquire new, in confidence of which believe me what I profess to be

Your for ever obleidg'd bro' to love and serve you. —<br>Jacob Reynardson

Goodman Hogg has been with me, & paid 10£ on accountt of rent, he tells me goodman Mallett is dead; & that ye woods at Harlow[5] goe to decay for want of cutting in which pray advise me what [I] had best doe ere ye season be past. — Pray at your leasure send me ye particular accountt of what moneys have [been] received on said landes, and withall advise me what ye rents are, & what remaine behind unpaid for I am a stranger to ye same.

Yesterday ye bill againstt ye Duke of Yorke was carried up by ye Lord Russell to ye Lords' barr[6], ye title of which when read at ye barr, all that went up with him which were a great number[7], made a huge hum, & went away; & ye Lords debated thereon 'till 12 a clock at night, ye King being present, and at last flung it out; which has netled ye house of commons, & this day expect to heare how

---

3   His father-in-law, Joseph (or Francis) Farnaby, Esqr., of Kippington, Kent. The letter is probably addressed to Jacob's eldest brother, Samuel.
4   Jacob's brother-in-law, who married his sister Abigail.
5   One of the properties inherited from Sir Abraham's extensive holdings in Essex, London (Tottenham), Suffolk and Lincolnshire.
6   The House of Lords.
7   It was reported that 'the whole House of Commons' attended, having 'adjourned their own proceedings to indulge their curiosity in observing the progress and event of this.'

some of them will thunder. Now have nothing else of news considerable. Packet boat Scipio from Smyrna arriv'd & ye [...] ships from said porte were goeing into Wales. —

Yr JR

---

*Jacob and Frances Reynardson had several children, of whom Samuel (1704–1797)* (**Fig. 1 d**)) *was the only son and, as one of the six Clerks in Chancery, possibly the first in a long line of lawyers in the Reynardson family (although as we will see there were already lawyers practising in the Birch family). Samuel succeeded to considerable wealth, partly through inheritance from two bachelor uncles and partly through his own marriage in 1732 to Sarah Knype, but most significantly as the principal legatee of his aunt, Lady Barnardiston* (**Fig. 1 e**)). *Mary Reynardson, daughter of Sir Abraham and his second wife Eleanor and therefore a sister to Jacob, had married (as his second wife) the much older Sir Samuel Barnardiston (1620–1707),* 'a Turkey or Levant merchant' *like his father-in-law, although politically he was at the other end of the spectrum, being* 'a strenuous supporter of the Puritans'[8]. *Both of his marriages were childless; Lady Barnardiston survived her husband by twenty-two years, and shortly before she died she purchased on her nephew's behalf, at the cost of £ 11,200, the manor of Holywell with Aunby in South Lincolnshire, as well as making Samuel the trustee of the rest of her large fortune.*[9]

*Holywell, with its beautiful landscaped gardens laid out by Samuel Reynardson himself and its Palladian-style temples, built as a wedding present for his wife, remained the principal family residence for successive generations of his descendants until the 1950s. Samuel's son and heir, Jacob, and his wife Anne Cust (see* Chapter 3) *had daughters but no sons, and as he was anxious for Holywell to continue a Reynardson property, before the end of his long life Samuel arranged for the property to be bequeathed to his eldest granddaughter on condition that her future husband would take her surname. The marriage in 1806 (see* Chapter 5) *of Jacob's daughter Etheldred Anne to Lieutenant-Colonel Thomas Birch ensured the survival of the Reynardson name although the two surnames were not formally joined until Jacob's death in 1812.*

*We do not hear about the Reynardson family again until later in the eighteenth century, and the focus now shifts to a family whose descendants led in a direct line to the other half of the Reynardson-Birch 'alliance' — the Owens of Coventry. During the seventeenth century, the Owens rose to prominence as a wealthy family of cappers and*

---

8 www.thePeerage.com.
9 The Holywell Collection, Lincolnshire Archives (extensive papers deposited with 'Lindsey County Council' in 1934 by Mrs A. Fane).

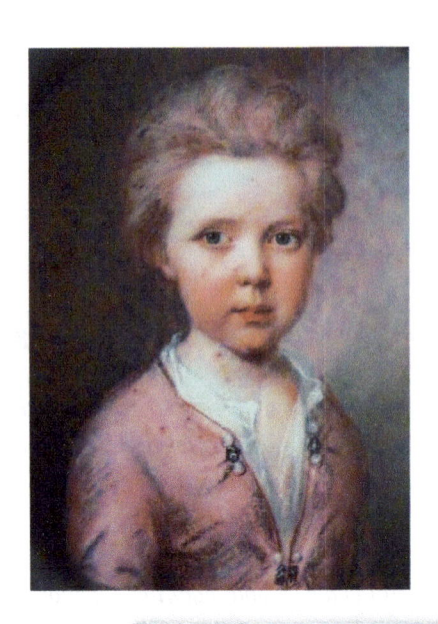

**Fig. 1 d)** *Portrait of Samuel Reynardson (1704–97) as a child*, artist unknown. Pencil and watercolour, c.1708. Private Collection.

*Below right*
**Fig. 1 e)** *Portrait of Lady Barnardiston, née Mary Reynardson (died 1729)*, artist unknown. Oil on canvas. Lady Barnardiston's black servant (just visible on the left of the painting) was reputedly buried in the family churchyard face-down as a non-Christian

*Below*
**Fig. 1 f)** Letter from Edward Owen to Elizabeth Phillips, dated 6 November 1699.

*felt-makers in Coventry. Several members of the family served as Mayors of the city in the seventeenth century, including Edward (sometimes known as Edwin) Owen, senior (1637–1705), who was Mayor there in 1680–81 and again in 1696–97. He was the father of another Edward (1664–1739), who was an attorney in Coventry. At the turn of the century, Edward (junior) had recently been made Clerk to the Corporation of Coventry, but according to a series of letters written at this time he was also making regular visits to London.*

*These letters, of which I have chosen two (**1: 2** and **1: 3**) and reproduced one (**Fig. 1 f**)), written on gold-edged paper in language as flowery as his handwriting, make it clear that the main attraction in London was a Miss Elizabeth Phillips, who seems to have been from the Coventry area originally but by then was living in Holborn. As well as letters to Miss Phillips, both Edward and his father wrote to her mother to assure her of the sincerity of his intentions towards her daughter and of his comfortable financial circumstances, but another rather sinister letter to Edward, signed only with a pseudonym and warning Edward off his intended bride by naming a supposed rival, indicates that all was not well with the courtship. Nevertheless, Edward's letters are so eloquent that it came as quite a surprise to learn, through the recent discovery of a copy of a marriage settlement in*

*Coventry Archives, that only three years later, in 1704*[10]*, Edward Owen, 'son and heir apparent to Edward Owen [senior], citizen and alderman of Coventry', married another Elizabeth altogether — a Miss Elizabeth Hethersett, 'spinster, a daughter of Wormeley Hethersett of Thetford, Norfolk, gent.' It is a mystery as to how Edward's letters found their way back into the possession of the sender, or why he kept them after marrying another woman (to whom no letters have survived).*

---

### Letter 1:2 (Edward Owen [*junior*], Coventry, to Elizabeth Phillips, dated 10 September, 1699)

Coventry Sept. ye 10th: 99.

Madam

You may very well thinke it strange since you received my last, wherein I profest soe much affection for your selfe I have given you before now noe further proofe thereof; I must Confess I was in hopes of being blest with some Casuall oppertunitye of seeing you in some place or other than your home, whereby I might perceive whether there may be any seeming prospect of my being happy in your selfe, before I made any publique appearance; I am not a little carefull Madam how I sett my fortune on a Pinacle to expose it to be the discourse of a Towne, before my intrest is stronge enough to support it from a sudden fall. And thô Madam I am resolved to surmount the highest difficultyes to deserve your heart; Yett if it be my misfortune at last to have all my hopes disapointed & blasted, I had rather to receive my fatal Doome in private, whilst my disigne is a secrett, and thereby free my selfe from the remarkes of this ill natured world, which perhaps (as it's subject to doe) may insult over my defeate, for the perplexing sorrow of looseing your selfe (which heaven forbidd) would be intolerable enough without the addition of other griefes.

But if after all Madam you still Continue to frustrate this method, I will assume a resolution equall to my passion to run all the risques of fate to let you know how much I am yours, & that I can sooner cease to be than to thinke on you and at the same time not to be in Love, tis you alone Madam yt [that] I Love & admire and if you please to owne and Countenance my passion, you will complete all my joy & happiness in this world and I hope make your owne noe less perfect.

---

10  Coventry Archives, Ref. PA 309/85, from a collection of documents presented by Lt.-Colonel H. Birch Reynardson, Wainbrook, Chavel, Somerset, 24 October 1960 (accessed through National Archives). The document is dated 2 March, 1703/4, because the marriage took place before the nominal start of the new year (25 March) under the old-style Julian calendar which was still in use in England at the time.

And let me begg of you to doe me the right to believe the last thinge possible in this world is the least omission of either Kindness or service to you, and wish the whole world was as intirely yours as is

Madam,<br>
Your most humble Servant,<br>
Edw[ar]d Owen jun.

## LETTER 1:3 (Edward Owen [*junior*], Coventry, to Elizabeth Phillips, Holborn, London, dated 1 January 1700)

Coventry   January ye 1<sup>st</sup>: 1699[11]

Madam

I sett out of London on Thursday last about two in the afternoon by the way of Oxford, & arrived here this afternoon, in a melancholy disorder, and the most dejected person living, and soe shall continue unless you prove kind and leave me not to suffer under the misfortune of absence; that there is such a thinge as Love you will not pretend to disowne, and that I am enamoured with your selfe is a veritye more than true, and must needs be soe, unless my heart was either flint or stone and none but your selfe can make me easye under my passion, tho' not abate my zeale?

Deare Madam You and the good Gentelwoman your Mother are the only persons I depend upon and hope you will prevent thinges comeing to any extremitye, for I am soe much concerned for my intrest in you, that I can neaver foregoe it without exposeing that which is most deare unto me (next your selfe) to most imminent danger & hassard; but as I have not behaved my selfe towards you otherwise then [than] a Gentleman soe I doubt not your makeing a returne becomeing a Gentlewoman of your worth and prudence. Mr Hum. Wanley and I dranke your health on Satturday. I communicated my designe to him who exprest a great deale of sattisfaction thereat, & promised me if he could be any ways serviceable to me he will come over to Coventry if I send for him at a day's warneing. I have not yett beene anywhere in towne to understand how much my designe is yett a secrett or published, but standing at my father's door Mr. Olds the

---

11  Under the new-style Gregorian calendar, already used at this time in parts of Europe but not adopted in England until 1752, the year date is 1700 (see footnote 10).

Mercer comeinge by, asked me softlye, but with a great assureance how my Mistriss did naming your selfe (he being a friend of mine). I answered him "very well when I left London" & desired him to tell me how he came to the Knowledge of it, he replyed Your Uncle Burton told him on satturday last at Keresley, I then asked him after what manner he discovered it to him; he said "with a seemeing easynesse and pleasure". I enjoyned him to secrecye which I am sure he will observe & upon second thoughts look upon him one of the most proper instruments I can make use of in this affaire whose honestye & integritye cannot in the least be suspected by either sides and I hope this may be a good Omen.

Pray Madam give my most humble service to Madam Phillips, Your Mother [and] Madam Huck's [sic] with thankes for all their favours and kindnesses, And receive my Cordiall Services, heartye wishes, & sincere, & intire, Love, & affection, to your selfe; from him who is and hath solemnlye vowed to remaine

        Dear Madam
            Your Everlasting Lover & Sincere humble Servant
                Edwd: Owen jun.

Pray Madam, Excuse all faults in this rude scrole [scrawl] being very much fatigued with a dirtye journey.

---

*Edward Owen remained in Coventry after his marriage to Elizabeth Hethersett, continuing to practise the law and, like his father, taking an active part in civic affairs. After the Civil War, when Coventry had taken a determinedly Puritan stance, the city acquired a reputation for political volatility and by the early eighteenth century the 'Whig' civic authority was constantly at loggerheads with the two members of Parliament returned by Coventry, who represented the 'Tory' (or 'Country') party[12]. It was the responsibility of the civic authority to organise parliamentary elections and it was in this context that the Owen family came into contact with no less a person than the journalist, and later celebrated novelist, Daniel Defoe, who was at this period active as an election agent and (secretly) a government spy on behalf of the Tory politician Robert Harley[13]. Defoe had come to Coventry in October 1705*

---

12  The reign of Queen Anne, who came to the throne in 1702, saw the gradual polarisation of the two-party system: the Tory party, favoured by Anne herself for its association with the 'old' land-owning gentry class (the country squirearchy) and its adherence to the practices and privileges of the Anglican Church, versus the Whig party, which was associated with the 'new' wealth of the urban financial and mercantile classes, and defended the interests of those dissenting from the state-controlled Church of England.

*to gauge local reactions to the aftermath of an election campaign conducted amid alarming scenes of mob violence[14] and the letter (**1: 4**) he wrote to Edward Owen (senior) afterwards, from the relatively safe distance of Daventry, begins soberly but rises to a hysterical crescendo giving a dramatic impression of the levels of hostility to which he was subjected.*

---

## Letter 1:4 (Daniel Defoe, Daventry, to Edward Owen, Coventry, dated 26 October 1705)[15]

Mr Owen

I can not but with some satisfaction look back on ye conversation you had with the Gentlemen at ye Bull.

Mithinks I see all our English Gentlemen would come to their reason if they would but allow themselves to argue against us without prejudice. I can not but own the sense and parts of both ye Gentlemen with you and I vallue them as such, and it appeared particularly in two things which as they frankly own'd so all ye Gentlemen of that Party would own them also if they were masters of the like understanding.

1. The Dr allow'd that on Extraordinary Occasion the Collective or representative body of This Nation May Limitt, alter or interrupt ye Succession of ye Crown and that ye said body of ye people are ye Judges of the Occasion — and indeed they must allow it or deny ye Queen's Claim to the Crown.

2. The Dr Allow'd it was Scandalous to ye Church of England that ye Non Jurants should joyn and pretend to Defend the Church of England which at the same time they denye to be a true Church and Declare to be scismaticall.

I know but one thing now I could wish of these Gentlemen to bring us all to be of one Mind, and that is that these Gentlemen would practise what they also

---

13 Defoe (c.1630–1731) had not long before endured bankruptcy, three days in the pillory and a brief spell of imprisonment in Newgate for publishing a seditious pamphlet, *The Shortest Way with the Dissenters*, which satirically advocated extermination of all religious non-conformists. He owed a debt of gratitude to Harley (then Speaker of the House of Commons but soon, as Earl of Oxford, to become the most powerful politician of the day in a role equivalent to the yet-to-be-created position of Prime Minister), who paid off his debts and then employed him as an intelligence agent for the Tories.

14 The riots were widely believed to have been provoked by the two successful Tory candidates in defiance of efforts by the civic authority and its Whig mayor to suppress them. The history of Coventry's often stormy parliamentary elections, especially the 1705 one and the part played by Edward Owen (senior), is entertainingly recounted in D. Hayton, E. Cruickshanks, S. Handley (eds.), *The History of Parliament: the House of Commons 1690–1715* (Boydell and Brewer, 2002).

15 This letter exists in the family collection in transcript only, the original having been sold at Sotheby's in 1943, when it was purchased by Bernard Quaritch Ltd, dealer in Rare Books and Manuscripts of South Audley Street, London.

Allow'd to be reasonable that they might live like Christians Neighbours and Gentlemen with their Brethren who differ in some cases and not two Partyes being Eternally Cutting one another's Throates, on chimeras of a Presbyterian Government which I dare undertake to convince men of their sense and candor no Dissenter in his witts can desire, and he that does must act against the intreste of the Dissenters in generall and be fitter to go to Bedlam than to be a Magistrate.

I have thought sometimes these Gentlemen may Expect I shall reflect Publickly on their Discourse when they may learn who I am, their opinion of me I kno' not, but pray assure them I kno' better than to Invade Conversation or to make use of any words a Gentleman may Unwarily let fall when in Company they kno' not, And as I kno' nothing said for which they can be justly reproached ye Conversation above being I hope their natural sentiments I wish all those we call High Church men would act the Gentleman equally with those to whom Pray give my humble service.

Your Humble Servant<br>D. FOE[16]

Daventry Octo. 26
Speaker

Pray also, Mr Owen, remind those Gentlemen that as to the Character they were pleas'd to give of me that night by report vizt. that I owe 3,000£ and have taken advantage of all ye acts of parliament against my Creditors, it shows ym [them] too credulous and too forward to report things they can not be sure of, for that

1. Tis false in fact I never took advantage or indeed made use of any act of parliament against any Creditor tho' to make use of law must be lawfull.

2. If I do owe 3,000£ I presume a great many men that hold up high now if they were to fall into ye hands I have been in would hardly come out less in debt since I can make it appear I lost above 3,000£ in the broil they and all the world kno' of.

3. It is not actually a crime to owe 3,000£ but to owe it and being able to discharge or Omitt or refuse it.

So that if debt be ye objection and ye occasion to [com]plain I think they do me some wrong there and question not but upon reflection they are men of so much sense they will own it.

Your Humble Servant<br>D. F.

---

16  At this time, Daniel Defoe was still writing under his birth name of Daniel Foe, which he adapted soon after to a more exotic-sounding name.

What cowards are these Coventry Whigs that now Barcelona is taken[17], Mr Smith chosen and all the Torys dead hearted, yet they dare not so much as make a benefice — or ring the bell.

Nay there's that Ned Owen is such a cowardly ro... [rogue] that he dares not go to Green's Coffee house and read a balad there. Fye Ned, Coventry Men Cowards! Fye! Fye! If you are so dastardly now what wou'd ha' become of you if B B B Bromley had been chosen?

Courage! Men of blew [blue], the job is done, rouze up Jezu... What a toad is this defoe, he is old Dog at a guess, he said we should have a majority of 60 — and behold 92, which put against 63, which they had of us last parliament makes near ye 120 [which] I computed. And about 25 more recovred by Coutrooiled [sic] Elections secure ye nation, bewilders the Jacks[18], disheartens ye high church and I hope makes an end of all these brangles.

Amen

Daventry, Saturday morning. [...]

---

*Despite the election resulting in a victory for the Tories, albeit with a much reduced majority (smaller than that claimed by Defoe), the 'brangles' rumbled on and Alderman Edward Owen was fully involved in the aftermath. Following a complaint to Owen by one of the defeated (Whig) candidates that his supporters had been physically prevented from casting their votes, an inquiry was instigated by Parliament and less than two years later the election of both Tory members for Coventry was declared void. To what must have been Edward Owen's considerable satisfaction, both of his Whig friends were returned to Parliament at the ensuing by-election in 1707.*

---

17  For almost the whole of Queen Anne's reign (1702–14), England was involved in a prolonged war on the Continent, which became known as the War of the Spanish Succession (its aim being to prevent the unification of Spain and France under one ruler following the death of Charles II of Spain, the last king of the Hapsburg dynasty). News of the capture of Barcelona on 3 October 1705 had clearly reached England by the end of that month, but Defoe did not yet know of the Spanish counter-attack, which resulted in a prolonged siege. Most of the action in this war however took place not in Spain but in the Spanish Netherlands (modern Belgium), where the land forces were commanded by the Queen's friend and adviser John Churchill, Earl (and by the end of the year, Duke) of Marlborough. His spectacular victories on the battlefields of Blenheim in 1704 and later at Ramillies, Oudenarde and Malplaquet earned him enduring fame and glory, and helped to bring about a critical shift in the balance of power in Europe.

18  This is a reference to the 'Jacobite' supporters of the deposed James II (who had died in 1701, before his daughter Anne came to the throne), who sought to reinstate the Catholic Stuart monarchy to England in the person of his son, James Francis Edward Stuart. The birth of the 'Pretender' (as he became known in England — and later as the 'Old Pretender', to distinguish him from his son 'Bonnie Prince Charlie') in June 1688 to James II's second wife, Mary of Modena, a Catholic, had precipitated the Glorious Revolution.

*Edward (junior) was never so involved in national politics as his father, preferring to concentrate on his civic duties as Clerk to the Corporation of Coventry and on his practice as an Attorney in the city. Some years afterwards he took on a young lawyer, James Birch, to deputise for him during his absences on business in London. The letter Edward wrote to him in April 1719 (1: 5) is of particular significance as it is the first time any member of the Birch family has appeared in the collection of family correspondence. It also illustrates the prevailing fear of invasion from Jacobite supporters on the Continent, which was to gather momentum towards the middle of the century.*[19]

---

### Letter 1:5 (Edward Owen, London, to James Birch, Coventry, dated 16 April, 1719)

London 16th of April 1719

Sir

'tho' I had not your last so soon as I expected, yet was not Impatient, since I allways believe yt [that] nothing but Excess of Business occasions those delays, — and as you thereby gain ye more experience, and consequently greater advantage, 'tis in that respect rather a pleasure to me sometimes to waite for a Letter from you.

I suppose you may now think that I have made a better apology for you than I can make for my selfe, since at present I have not ye same Excuse, nor Indeed any other but that of your writing to me for Newes, which for some time past has been, & still is so variable, that one story is never believed two dayes together and I finde the longer I waite for some to be depended on for truth, the less reason I have to Expect it — That there is an Invasion[20] intended, we have been told from ye Throne, and therefore it would not only be absurd, but even Criminal to pretend to disbelieve it, and I have heard that one man was committed to Newgate, for saying it was only a trick of ye Government to keep up a standing Army, but when or where ye Invaders Intend to Land is still a secret, except to those at ye Helm of State, we sometimes are told, they are Landed in Cornwall, sometimes in Wales, then in Scotland, and sometimes in two of these places at

---

19 'The Pretender' was only twenty when he made his first unsuccessful attempt to invade Britain in 1708, landing in Scotland but being forced to make a hasty retreat when the French fleet supporting him was defeated. A more serious Jacobite rising (the 'Fifteen') took place in 1715 in Scotland and soon spread south into England, ending only in the defeat of the rebels at the battle of Preston. Again, by the time James Stuart landed in Scotland to rally his troops, the rebellion had been largely suppressed and he was obliged to retreat back to France.

once, tho' have not yet found any of these reports true, It is unaccountable to repeat what is whispered by ye Enemies of ye Government, as that there has been an Invitation given in which even ye disgusted Whiggs (in order to secure the Estates they have got) have joyn'd, and amongst them an old Warriour too great to be Named, they have likewise ye assurance to say that even Sir George Byng[21] with ye Fleet are gone over to ye Enemy, and ye more modest of them give out that ye King of Spain has offered Sir George £100000, and £10000, to each Captain in his squadron, with many other vain storys, not one word of which I ever believed.

'twas thought there would have been a great struggle in ye House of Commons about ye Peerage Bill[22] but last Night I heard that it will drop & not be carried into ye House, there are two thousand men Landed from Holland which are Quartered in and aboute Rumforde in Essex and such other due preparations made, that I believe the Government is not in ye least Uneasiness on account of ye Spaniards. — I shall always be glad to hear from you, who am

Your affectionate Friend<br>
and most humble Servant<br>
Ed: Owen

---

*Edward Owen and his wife Elizabeth Hethersett's marriage produced just one daughter, Jane, who was born in 1705. It seems that Elizabeth died while Jane was still a baby and although Edward later married again, there were no more children. As the only child and heiress to her father's considerable estate, Jane was much indulged, but in her late teens she began to cause her parents some anxiety by becoming engaged to her first cousin, Richard Bayliss (son of her father's sister). To put some distance between the young couple, Jane was sent to stay with an aunt in London not long before her twentieth*

---

20- During the War of the Quadruple Alliance (1718–20), Britain and France were for once on the same side, allied with Austria and the Dutch Republic against Spain, to prevent the latter from retaking territories in Italy and claiming the French throne. The anticipated invasion probably refers to the plot by the Duke of Ormonde (the 'old Warriour' referred to in the letter – a former Viceroy of Ireland who had fought with William of Orange at the Battle of the Boyne in 1690 and with Marlborough in the War of the Spanish Succession, but who later developed Jacobite sympathies) to invade with Spanish support. His intention was to replace George I on the throne with the 'Pretender', but his fleet was dispersed by a storm near Galicia and the small force which landed in Scotland was easily defeated in June 1719 at the Battle of Glen Shiel.

21 Byng (1663–1733) was Admiral of the Fleet, which had recently scored a resounding victory over the Spanish fleet at the Battle of Cape Passaro. Rumours of his defection to the Spanish were unfounded.

22 Introduced by the Whig politician Charles Spencer to close the House of Lords, fearing the creation of a large number of peers by the Tory Ministry. As Edward Owen anticipated, the Bill was voted down by the House of Commons on 28 April.

*birthday, but if her father hoped that the delights and distractions of the capital would put an end to the relationship, he was doomed to disappointment. As her increasingly defiant and incoherent letters show, over the next three and a half years Jane's determination to marry 'Cos: baylis' only increased as she made elaborate plans for her wedding 'close' and even enlisted her cousin Sarah Barker to plead on her behalf* **(1:12)**.

---

## Letter 1:6 (Jane Owen, London, to her father Edward Owen, Coventry, dated 20 May 1725)

Sir

I thought it proper to write to you before my Cousen comes down, & I beg that you would do now what you can to accomplish it. You may indever what you can to bring him to your tearms [terms]. But if you cannot I beg that you would comply with him; he sertainly will be with you on sabath day night or munday morning without fail. I expect you to return with him, but in ye mean time let me hear from you every post how you go on. I hope my Uncle is well because you sed nothing to ye contrary; as to Cousin Blackmore[23] I cannot tell any thing of for she dose not think fit to accept of me for one of her aquintanc [acquaintance] & I know now [no] more of her then a stranger dose. Miss Webster is very kind & comes to see me very often, my Auant likes her company exceedingly and so do I. I have no more to say now but remain your

        dutyfull and Obedient Dauhter
        J. Owen

My duty to mama & Uncle. I am in prodigose hast as you may know by so many blotches but I beg you would pardon it & burn ye letter as soon as you have red it

Lon[*don*] May ye 20. 1725

Cos: baylis & Mr Orbel must lye in Seperate beds for Cos: never lise with a bedfellow ye are he never likes [*sic*]

---

23  The Blackmores were related to Jane's step-mother.

**Letter 1:7 Jane Owen, London, to her father Edward Owen, Coventry, dated 25 May 1725)**

Lon[*don*]   May ye 25. 1725

Sir

I hope this will find you & mama, my uncle & ye rest of our frens [friends] in helth. Yesterday I saw Jonerthon wild go to tibern with three others[24] (**Fig. 1 g)**). Ye mob was much delited to see him go whear [where] he had sent so many before & with shouts & hosases [huzzas] of ye peple he was caried thear [*two words crossed out*]. Ye [They] used him barbrosly [barbarously,] ye flong stones at him & cut him very much. Ye [They] wated at tibern for the sleges coeming up with ye man that coind[?]. Thear [There] was a great allteration in ye looks of ye peple when he came by for most was sorry for him. I can say no more of this. I am to go to Coart on the berth night[25], but don't think that Mrs Neal interdruces me, for it is Mr Yong that does & I am to go into ye ball room not in ye garily [gallery]. I hope to see you — with my cos: hear [here] ['but' *crossed out*] don't put me off for I want to have your company. Pray write to me next post. I have writ all ye news I can & beg you would accept this from

Your
Dutyful Dauhter
Jane Owen

My duty to mama & Uncle, service to Cos. & Mr Orbel. Pray when you come I beg you would bring my dioment [diamond] ring, ye little one, with you. Don't let this letter be seen.

*Inscribed on flap (in a different hand):*
please to aquaint Mr Baylis the Bill is pd. — £300 —

---

24   Jonathan Wild (1682/3–1725) was one of the most notorious criminals in Britain at an exceptionally lawless time. He held a virtual monopoly on crime in London in the early years of the reign of George I, posing as a defender of the public against marauding thieves (the self-styled 'Thief Taker General of Great Britain and Ireland'), while all the time manipulating his own gangs of criminals. When eventually convicted and sentenced to death, Wild's execution at Tyburn on 24 May, 1725, drew larger crowds than had ever been seen there previously, with special tickets being sold for the best vantage points. Amongst those in the crowd who watched the spectacle along with Jane Owen were the authors Daniel Defoe and Henry Fielding, both of whom wrote satirical accounts of Wild's infamous life. Other literary works directly inspired by Wild's story include The Beggars' Opera (1728), by John Gay, and its twentieth-century reworking by Bertoldt Brecht in The Threepenny Opera. In Sir Arthur Conan Doyle's detective stories, the arch-villain Professor Moriarty is compared by his great rival Sherlock Holmes to a latter-day Jonathan Wild.
25   Jane's twentieth birthday (see **1: 8**).

**Fig. 1 g)** A 'ticket' for the hanging of Jonathan Wild at Tyburn, May 1725.

## TWO UNSUCCESSFUL COURTSHIPS

**LETTER 1:8 (Jane Owen, London, to her father Edward Owen, Coventry dated 29 May 1725)**

Sir

Yesterday I was at Coart — whear I had the pleasure of seeing ye King & prince, princes[s] & all the yong princes[26]. Ye [They] danced for two hours. We staed till it was lite befor we come away. I had from ye kings sideboard claret & champainge to drink. The butter came scafe [safely] & is very good, my Aunt gives her service to my mama and thanks her for it. I hope, Sir, you do not forget what I have writen to you in my former letters abought [about] &c. I exspect a letter from you every post till I see you which I hope will be when my Cousen & Mr Orbel returns that you would come with them. My duty to mama & my love to sisters [*Jane's aunts*]. My duty to my Uncle, & service to all other frens [friends] Concludes this from

Your Ever Dutyfull And<br>Obedient Daughter<br>Jane Owen

London my birthday. 1725
Aetat: 20


**LETTER 1:9 (Jane Owen, London, to her father Edward Owen, Coventry, dated 6 April 1726)**

Sir

I take this opertunity of writing by Mr Edwards to make my aplycation to you for some wedding close [clothes] which I hope you will oblige me in. I am not ambyesious of grandur for my Close, but onely what is decent; too sutes [two suits] of close, one trimed with silver, ye other a wrich [rich] white damusk & a flowerd silk night gound [gown], a brusels lase hed [Brussels lace headdress],

---

[26] The members of the Royal family mentioned here are King George I, the Prince of Wales (soon to be George II) and his wife Caroline of Anspach. In 1725 they had seven living children, of whom the eldest, Prince Frederick, was born and brought up in Hanover and did not come to England until his father's accession in 1727. The 'yong princes' are therefore probably princesses, of which five were born between 1709 and 1724. The Prince and Princess of Wales's other surviving son was Prince William, Duke of Cumberland, born in 1721 (later to be known as 'the Butcher of Culloden').

& a sute of dres[s] night close, these are things I cannot do without, & other things which I must have too tedious to name. I ought to have according to ye fashon 3 full sutes of close, but as I would not put you to any inconvenicy I shall be easy with what you alow. The spring is forward & I shall have time little anouffe [enough] before ye time I must be at Coventry to prapare my things redy, therefore I beg Sir that you will fix ye some [sum] you will alowe me & send me wourd [word] for till then I cannot bye [buy] any thing. As to ye money I have by me [it] will all be spent in clening & making up my old close, & some odd things that I may buy as ordinery sutes & stokins, so that must not be rected [reckoned] in ye alowance. One thing I desire & I beg is that you will not write to have me take money of either my Aunt or Cosen for this purpose: for if you doo I will not have it, neither will I buy any thing more till you send me ye money in hand. I have not any news at presant. My duty to Uncle & mama. Is all from Your Ever

> Dutyfull Dauhter
> Jane Owen

Pray Sir let me have an answar to this by next post. Aunt gives her service & my Cos. his duty to you and my Uncle Owen. I am in good helth. Don't let this be seen by anybody but your self & Uncle, then burn it.

London April ye 6, 1726


## LETTER 1:10 (Jane Owen, London, to her father Edward Owen, Coventry, dated 16 April 1726)

> London  Ap: ye 16. 1726

Sir

I would have writ last post but was prevented. I have well considered ye contents of yours which from an one [own] father I think is harsh and severe — for had I bene acstravigant [extravagant], had I been luse [loose], had I bieen disobedient then it is whot I might have exspected, but I am sure Sir hetherto you cannot Charge [me] with any thing of that sort. My Aunt gives her service to you & my uncle & is sorry there should be any demer [demur]: for had ye lawyer been at home ye writings had bieen drawn, therefore since it is so my Aunt begs you will make all hast posible to town that things may be seteled [settled] as ye

[they] must be. If you don't care to come alone she begs ye favor of my Uncle or any other whom you shall like to come with you for she thinks it is much better [*for*] you & her to tolk [talk] it out then whot can be sed by letter & in a shorter time then wateing post after post for letters. My Aunt [*gives*] service to Uncle & you. With my duty to him & mama

From your DutyfullDaughter<br>Jane Owen

Cos: Service to you & Uncle

### LETTER 1:11 (Jane Owen, London, to her father Edward Owen, Coventry, dated 7 December 1727)

Decem: ye 7. 1727

Sir

Yesterday came mama's maid in order to attend me down. It is strange my Uncle's letter of Thursday did not prevent your sending — I have not seen her, neither do I intend it, as my resolution is still ye same, lett ye consequence be whot it will — that I will not come home. If you don't think fitt to alowe me a maintanance, absent from you, I will hire my self as a survant for my bread. As to my promise I have punctually performed it, and my one desire in seeing Uncle hear, or elcewher it [*is*] all one. I saw you in Norfolk & have reson to remember it, to my great concern. My Duty to Uncle & mama. I am sorry to hear she is ill, that's another reson of my not comeing for as God has provided well for me I will not devest my self of my one write [right] & ye promise I spoke of to Uncle. Without performing it I can never exspect good in this world, nor in ye next. I cannot charge my self with undutyfullness for from ye furst it was by your consent and incurragemen [encouragement]. Is all

From your Dutyfull<br>Daughter   Jane Owen

It was allwas my desire to live as parent and Child but if it cannot be but on ye turms [terms] of comeing home furst, I never will.

## Letter 1:12 (Sarah Barker to her uncle Edward Owen, Coventry, dated 3 April 1728)

Sir

I am afraid you'll think my writeing to you looks too assuming; but what incourged [encouraged] me to do it is this; that very often what is said by a second person is most persuasive, tho' worse spoke. Sir, my intimacy with Cousin Owen has lead me to a perfect knowledge of the great concern she laboures under by your vast change of carrige to her; for you was, Sir, the very fondest of parants & the most passionate in your expressions of affection to her; are now so altered as not [to] give her one kind word to alay her grief or to sweeten the disopintments she has mett with thro' you.

But uncle Owen, that you should denie giving Cousin an alowence suttable to your rank & her future fortune, I prodigously wonder att; for you uest [used] to say she shou'd have any thing she should ask for that your Estate wou'd alow of; & seemed to speak as if you thought it too little for her; this great alteration you must think Sir a very considerable Trial to her; but not more then [than] the former unkindness I was speaking of; only as 'tis a farther marke of your disaffection.

Pray lett me intreat you Dear Sir to let this heavy Cloud of severity vanish & refresh poor Cousin with your former sweetness of behaviour & I am sure she would be obediant to you in every respect that is consistant with her own safety: & a good father wou'd not desire his Child to be exposed to hazards thro' him.

I hope I have not gone beyond the rules of good manners nor transgresst upon Duty but if my pen have bin larger then [than] my intention pardon it Sir as 'tis thro' extreem venneration for yours; & please to think me as I am, Sir your Most

    Obediant Niece & very humble Servant
       Sarah Barker

P S Cousin Owen desires her Duty
May be aceptable to you & Aunt
Owen; and I allso desire mine may be so.

April the 3 / 1728  Pray give cousin's Duty to her Uncle.

## Letter 1:13 (Richard Bayliss, London, to Edward Owen, Coventry, dated 5 November 1728)

London   Novem: 5<sup>th</sup>   1728

Sir:

Your unstable mind is my great concern — when in town you promised on your Daughter comeing all things should be consumated to make us both happy and on which we relyed — As to her bad health you pritty well know is the Crossing her & me in our desires which affect me as much in mind as her in health — As to my affections it is evident yt [that] I never once thought of any other since I made applycation to her whose agreeable temper suits to what I can wish.

Pray Sir: look some years backward and remember you once was in my Cause and if you have promisd too much give what is in your power for I am minded to be easie for what is world to be at variance with one's friend & indeed one's self. Please to give my sincere love to her & wishing both her & you health, I wait a favourable answer

to Your abject Kinsman & Servant.
Ri. Baylis

---

*By the time Richard Baylis wrote this letter, he must already have realised that his cause was hopeless. Evidently in poor health due to the 'Crossing' of her hopes and desires, Jane was back at home with her parents and her romance, which my father described as 'a long, rather shoddy and pathetic story', was at an end. Edward Owen does seem to have shown remarkable forbearance over the whole episode — perhaps reminded of his own unsuccessful courtship a quarter of a century earlier. But before a year had passed, everything had changed. Edward's colleague and protegé, James Birch (who had by this time stepped into his shoes as Clerk to the Coventry Corporation), was already a husband and expectant father at the time that Jane returned from London, but his wife died in the spring of 1729 and just over six months later — probably to Edward's enormous relief — James and Jane were married. Thus, by direct descent through their third son George (1733–1803), the eldest of their four children who survived into adulthood, James Birch and Jane Owen became my great-great-great-great-grandparents.*

CHAPTER 2

# The Law, Farming and 'The Forty-Five'

*Letters from Friends and Family 1721–1750*

'Fear must continue as long as ye young Pretender continues in any of his Majesty's Dominions'[1]

*Given Jane Owen's earlier history, her marriage to James Birch, which lasted for nearly twenty years, seems to have been remarkably successful. As we have already seen, she was James's second wife, marrying him within eight months of the death, probably in childbirth, of the first Mrs James Birch*[2]. *After their marriage in November 1729, it is likely that Jane found herself having to care for her husband's first-born child, a son (also called James) having been born on 13 April 1729, before giving birth to the first of their eight children less than a year later*[3].

At this point I would like to introduce other members of James Birch's family who play an important role in our story. In order to do so we need to go back a few years to James's parents, George Birch (1652–1721) and Mary Foster, who married in 1688. George was a direct descendant of the Birches of Birch Hall, Manchester (see Introduction), but his great-great-grandfather Thomas Birch (1540–1613) had 'migrated' from there in 1559 with his wife Elizabeth Chetham to Aston, near Birmingham, and by 1570 had acquired the manor of Handsworth in Staffordshire, with the manor house of Hamstead Hall as its main dwelling.[4] About fifty years later

---

1   Rev. Dr George Legh, Halifax, to James Birch, Coventry, 22 April 1746 (**2: 6**).
2   James Birch's first wife was called Susannah Hess and is said to have been from Germany. See www.RootsWeb.com, drawing on information contained in John William Birch, *The Birch Chronicles* (privately printed October 2002, printed by Blaby Art & Print, Blaby, Leicester).
3   Of eight children born to James and Jane Birch, four did not survive infancy, their deaths — at ages ranging from four months to three years and two months old — being recorded on gravestones at St Michael's Church, Coventry (later Coventry Cathedral, which was largely destroyed in the Blitz during a nine-hour bombing raid on 14 November, 1940). It seems unlikely that James's only son by his first wife lived beyond the age of twelve, as the name 'James' was also given to James' and Jane's seventh child, born in 1741. It is strange to reflect therefore that if Susannah Birch had survived, our family history would probably have turned out quite differently.
4   A will made in 1570 describes him as 'Thomas Birch of Birch, Manchester, Lancashire, and Handsworth, Staffordshire. Gent.' See John William Birch, *The Birch Chronicles* (as above). The manor of Handsworth continued in the ownership of a parallel branch of the family until John Wyrley Birch (see **2: 8**) died childless in 1775 and left it to George, the eldest son of Judge Sir Thomas Birch.

*his grandson, another Thomas (1586–1646), settled in nearby Harborne, which is now a suburb of Birmingham three miles south-west of the city centre, and by his death was also the owner of properties in Leacroft and Birchfield a little further north. George (James's father) — the only child of his generation — was born and christened at Harborne, as were all seven of his surviving children: five sons and two daughters.*

*George's two eldest sons, another George (born 1689) and Thomas (born 1691), were both admitted to the Inner Temple, one of the four Inns of Court, in 1707 and 1709 respectively. (And here I should mention that this became a family tradition. When I applied for admission to the Inner Temple in 1950, armed with a large cheque for the admission fee from my father, the rather ancient Clerk, hearing my name, disappeared without explanation. He returned a few minutes later bearing a huge book. 'Ah yes,' he said, 'I thought so: George and Thomas Birch, 1707 and 1709.' He then turned the pages, counting the number of Birches and Birch Reynardsons entered in it. 'There are five generations — so you get a large discount on the fee!'*

*George and Thomas Birch were not the only members of their generation to study the law, although James (who was the fourth son) took a different route, attending Pembroke College, Cambridge, before working his way up through Coventry Corporation. Their father also helped to educate a nephew, George Ball[5], through his legal studies — his letter to his uncle, in which he attempts to justify the fact that he has done little work, amuses me as I seem to remember making similar excuses (though in less elaborate language) over 225 years later (see Chapter 13). No doubt much of George's 'strict…Scrutiny…into ye different Characters of Life' was also carried out in the congenial surroundings of taverns and other places of entertainment!*

---

5   I have not been able to establish exactly where George Ball fits in to the family tree, as it does not appear that George Birch (senior) had any siblings. He is described as a cousin by James Birch, who wrote on the letter (**2: 1**) 'Coz G. Ball to Father 31 July 1721'. We do not hear any more about George Ball himself, but a Miss (given the courtesy title of 'Mrs') Elizabeth Ball, who may have been his sister, of Castle Bromwich, was in later years clearly an invaluable member of the family, virtually running the farm and estate at Harborne (see **2: 7** and **3: 2**).

## Letter 2:1 (George Ball, London, to his uncle George Birch, of Harborne, Staffordshire, dated 31 July 1721)

Honoured Sir

The Bill you were pleas'd to procure me, ye former of thirty, & the latter of forty Pounds, came both safe & were paid, the latter at sight. My Cousin [*probably George, junior, or Thomas Birch*] I suppose has already acquainted you with ye Receipt of them, & I thought it proper to mention it again that my own Hand might be a Testimony of the Receipt. Sir, as these Marks of your favour bespeak a true Friend, they entitle you to ye best Esteem & Respect I can pay, & ye Confession of an Obligation, durable as Life.

I am now in a serious Mood, & can't forbear communicating to you some Account of ye Employment of my Time since I came here; — You'll perhaps think me guilty of a great neglect, when I inform you that I have read but little Law; but I don't doubt your Pardon, when you hear ye Reason why I have not.— Every thing in my Opinion requires a Regard in Proportion to its Consequence, and what concerns most, ought first & [fore]most to be consider'd & studied, & ye greater ye Danger of neglecting that which so concerns, the greater Circumspection is requir'd to prevent such neglect. I found it absolutely needful to settle certain Principles for ye Conduct of Life, to walk by some Standard, that I might not act as in a Maze, & be entirely beholding to ye present Flow of Fancy in any Occurrence for my Direction. I have therefore employ'd a great deal of my time in Studying my Self, and framing Rational Rules for my Conduct & Guard, that so no Station, Transaction, Fortune may find me unprepar'd for a Proper Reception of it, or Behaviour under it; and I wish I could say, I had made such a Proficiency as Occasions of Life may possibly require. However, I hope this Self Study may render me a wiser man, & a better Christian, & if that is ye Consequence, I am sure it will prove ye most Profitable Study in ye World, nor shall I ever repent of ye Pains of attaining that Truly inestimable End. —

As a Spectator, I have made as strict a Scrutiny as I am able into ye different Characters of Life, & endeavour'd to search into ye Principles & Motives of Action, the Aims, the Designs they Propose. Happiness, if I judge right as I think I do, belongs to none; I can't find one Station to which that is appendant, and accordingly I envie no Man his Condition; let it be never so seemingly splendid, I am satisfied it neither deserves nor ought to be envied; and, if my Determinations are just as they appear to me, Every thing is Downright Nonsense and Vanity, but Religion. And, if Others have ye same Manner of Reflecting & Reasoning as my self, the Practices of most in all Stations from that of ye Prince to that of his meanest Subject must be direct contradiction to their Reason, their Judgment & their Consciences.

I Fancy I could prove my Conclusions against every Condition of Man I am acquainted with, by Induction of Particulars, But I consider I should far exceed ye Bounds of a Letter should I once enter upon Speculations of that Nature, & indeed I doubt I have done that already, as well as too much transgress'd upon your Time whilst I have been giving a relation of the employment of some part of my own. I therefore Beg Leave to Subscribe my self

Honour'd Sir

Your Dutiful Nephew and Most Humble Servant

Geo. Ball

London  31 July 1721

My Humble Duty to my Aunt; I hope she is, as well as yourself, in perfect enjoyment of health, & desire she would please to accept of ye Tea & Sugar which are as good as I could procure.

---

*George Ball's hopes for the health of his uncle were not fulfilled, as George Birch died later that year and the responsibility for the running of the estates of Harborne and Handsworth passed to his eldest son George, who consequently never practised the law. However the next son, Thomas (1691–1757), went on to become one of the most distinguished lawyers of his generation (see also* Chapter 3*). He was called to the Bar in 1715 and after fifteen years (regarded as the minimum period of professional experience required to be eligible for the award) he was appointed serjeant-at-law in 1730*[6]*. Though their rôle was eventually superseded in the mid nineteenth century by the creation of the position of King's Counsel, at this time serjeants-at-law enjoyed a high status as the most elite group of lawyers from which judges were chosen.*

6  On appointment, the new serjeant-at-law had to leave his Inn of Court and join one of the two Serjeants' Inns in Fleet Street or Chancery Lane. However, in the same year that Thomas Birch was appointed, the Fleet Street lease ran out and so the two societies merged on the Chancery Lane site.

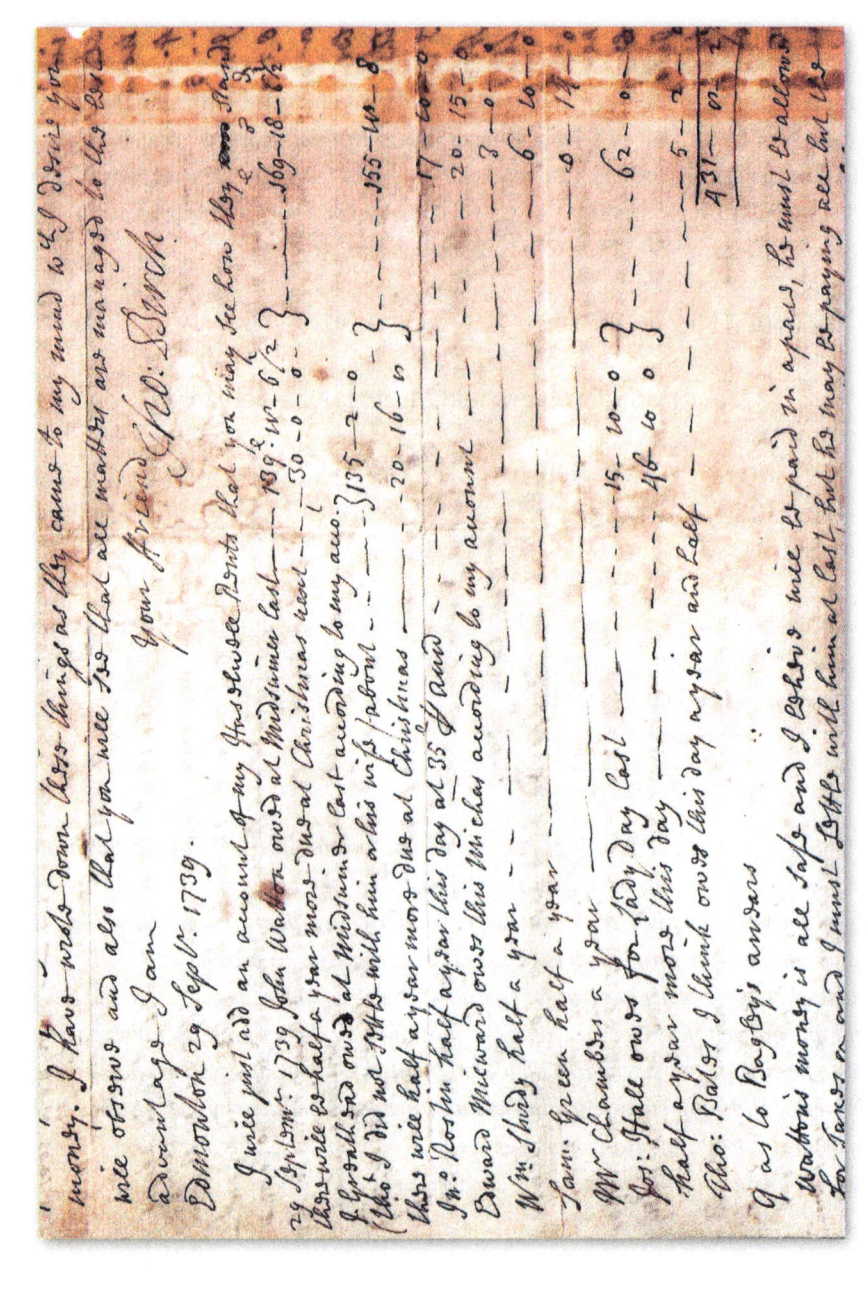

**Fig. 2 a)** A list of Thomas Birch's rents from his property at Hazelwell, from his letter to his bailiff Samuel Pritchett, dated 29 September 1739 (2: 2).

*In the meantime Thomas's brother George died unmarried and relatively young in the 1730s and so Thomas was obliged to take on the management of the family estates in addition to his own legal practice. Although he listed Harborne as his main residence, he did not actually spend the majority of his time there as he needed to be closer to London for his work and had by this time bought a house in the hamlet of Southgate — 'known for its elegant mansions'[7]— in the parish of Edmonton. He left the day-to-day management of the estate to his bailiff, Samuel Pritchett, but as the following letter shows, he took a keen interest in the administration both of the farm at Harborne and of Hazelwell, another estate nearby in the King's Heath area of Birmingham which had been purchased by his father and which passed to Thomas in 1722. This long letter, though written 275 years ago, is I think remarkable for its modernity, reminding me of the sort of letter I used to write to my bailiff in my early days as owner of Adwell. It includes much detail about rents (**Fig. 2 a**)) and instructions about current farming practices[8], about which Thomas seems very well informed — especially in his recommendations of the use of lime and manure ('muck') to improve the soil's fertility, the rotation of crops after leaving land 'fallow' and the clearing of woodland to provide more land for crops and animal fodder. It would appear that Thomas felt exasperated with his bailiff for failing to manage the farm as efficiently and profitably as it could be, or to keep adequate accounts.*

---

## Letter 2:2 (Thomas Birch, Edmonton, Middlesex, to Samuel Pritchett, Bailiff of Harborne Hall, Staffordshire, dated 29 September, 1739)

Sam:

When I sent you to the Widow Philips on Tuesday the 10th Inst., I expected to have seen you again, but as you did not come it is necessary for me to write down some few things:

1. The ffallows must be sown as soon as may be and the ffallow in the Leylands must be limed and mucked, and it will be of service in case the sheep have been put into it.

2. I desire you will get from Mrs Greathead all the Wheat Barley Beans and Oats that she can spare and be sure [to] see that I have just measure and either sell all again imediatly (as I have always told you) or let it be kept safe at Birmingham

---

7 'Edmonton: Introduction', *A History of the County of Middlesex: Volume 5* (1976), pp. 130–133.
8 See Mark Overton, *Agricultural Revolution in England: The Transformation of the Agrarian Economy 1500–1850* (Cambridge University Press, 1996) and M. E. Turner, J. V. Beckett and B. Afton, *Farm Production in England 1700–1914* (Oxford University Press, 2001).

or elsewhere and be sold as soon as may be and I desire to sell the same measure that I buy but no more. I mention these things because I can't afford to loose [lose] 7 or 8 bushels out of 30, if you will take any care about these affairs I may in time be paid the great arrears that are due to me — you must also ask Mrs Greathead for her cheese money.

3. I have often desired you to keep an exact account in writing of my affairs, and yet you keep no regular account of any thing. You shou'd fold up a sheet of paper, and on one side of it set down, Money received on my account and when and of whom and for what, and on the other side set down, Money paid on my account and when and to whom and for what, and always take Receipts (not in your own Book) but upon everybody's Bills for my security and when you have any corn &c from Mrs Greathead or others, when you have seen it measured, set down what you have and at what value, and how and for what values you sell it and when and to whom, I wou'd likewise have an account kept what Grain I thresh and sell from the ffarm in my own hands and what sheep and other Cattel [cattle] are bought in and at what rates, and what are sold out and at what rates — every body does this that looks after other people's affairs and you are upon the spot & can do it with very little trouble.

4. When I observe that every Neighbour I have who rents 14 or 15 acres of land keeps 5, 6 or 7 Cattel, I think as I have in my own hands about 140 acres of land besides the woods & more, I might keep more than 20. I have now as I take it 12 milking Cattel and about 8 more, I believe about 20, reckoning young Calves — Now I desire you will go to one or more of the best ffairs or Markets as soon as is proper and buy me according to the best of your Judgment 5 or 6 or more young Cattel and set down in writing what they cost. I wou'd lay the 2 woods open to the ground belonging to Moor's ffarm, and I believe they and ye other young Cattel may run there [for a] good part of the winter. If ffodder shou'd be wanting, you know I am to provide it, but I beg you will see that the ffodder is not wasted as it was last year.

5. I wou'd have all the sheep sold that can be spared and also the corn, Oats, Beans now in the house and all the grain of this year that can be spared as soon as may be after it is thresh'd — I was at Harborn 3 market days and desired the corn, beans, Oats &c might be imediatly sold, but when I came away nothing was done nor likely to be done.

6. I know very well and every body also tells me that the ffarm in my own

---

9   Equivalent to between about £4,300 and £5,180 in today's money (2005 values).

## THE LAW, FARMING AND 'THE FORTY-FIVE'

hands (if tolerably managed) wou'd keep house for my Mother and produce me £50 or £60[9] a year besides, and as you are upon the Spot and (as a ffriend was lately telling me) may with very little trouble look after my ffarm as well as your own, I did expect under your management and in consideration of the generous allowance I have made you that the ffarm wou'd have been kept in very good order and have produced me a great deal of money, but I am much disappointed as to that, tho' you well know that I placed you at the Welch house on purpose that you might look after my servants & workmen & buy in and sell out Cattel & do all other matters to the best advantage & so manage my ffarm as that it might pay rent as well as other peoples.

6 [*sic*]. John Walton was with me and gave me notice to leave the ffarm at Lady day[10], he said his Brother had a mind to go to Service and that he should not have stock to go on with it. I told him he might do as he wou'd but as the ffarm had long been held by his father and grandfather I wou'd be content to take my arrears by Degrees if he and his Brother wou'd join their stock and hold it on, and as the Overseers of the will and John himself told me that some Muck wou'd be of great use to it I told John I wou'd allow him yearly some muck, meaning perhaps 40s [*shillings' worth*] a year or some such matter for 3 or 4 years. I believe John is not very willing to leave it, and therefore before you hearken to any other Tenant you may talk with John a little about it to know his final resolution. If he is determined to quit, let Sam: Green (my Tenant by Haselwell) and everybody else know it. Sam: Green (tho' I can't well say how he shou'd be able to take such a ffarm) has been enquiring after it and if he can stock it may perhaps be able to pay the Rent — As an abatement of £5.10s per annum has already been made, I am unwilling to abate any more, but I think you had best mention that £5 only has been abated, because I think I ought not to allow the 10s for the poor's levy — If there shou'd be no Tenant to take it at Lady day — you must agree all matters with John Walton as much for my interest and advantage as you can and set every thing down in writing that I may see and know what I am about and John will be paying my arrears [*word illegible*] when he comes to thresh and sell off his stock, of which you may put him in mind, tho' if he goes and I have no Tenant it may perhaps be for my interest to buy such part of the stock as I can have worth my money. I have wrote

---

10  Lady Day takes its name from the Feast of the Annunciation of the Blessed Virgin, which under the 'old style' Julian Calendar fell on 25 March. As the equivalent of the first day of the new year before the adoption of the Gregorian Calendar in 1752, it was the traditional day on which year-long contracts between landowners and tenant farmers would begin and end.

down these things as they came to my mind which I desire you will observe and also that you will see that all matters are managed to the best advantage. I am
>Your ffriend
>>Tho: Birch
Edmonton 29 Septr. 1739.

[…] I may perhaps in a little time send you some account of my Harborne Rents but you know them pretty well —.

---

*We do not know when Thomas Birch married Sarah Teshmaker but the first of their five children (yet another George) was born in 1739. The following year Thomas became King's Serjeant (a serjeant-at-law appointed to serve the Crown as a legal adviser to the monarch) and in 1746 he was appointed to be one of the three Justices of the Court of Common Pleas, a common law court which covered all actions between English subjects which did not concern the monarch[11]. The portrait of him which we have at Adwell (**Fig. 2 b**)) was probably painted around this time.*

*By this time Thomas had also been knighted, receiving 'the honour of knighthood' (according to the Register of his local parish church at Edmonton) 'on occasion of*

**Fig. 2 b)** *Portrait of Judge Sir Thomas Birch (1691–1757), artist unknown. Oil on canvas.*

---

11  For its entire existence of about six hundred years, the Court of Common Pleas sat in the same location of Westminster Hall, together with the Exchequer of Pleas and the Court of King's Bench. By the eighteenth century it was administered by one Chief Justice and three justices. Eventually the jurisdiction of the separate courts overlapped to such an extent that in 1873 they were merged into one body, the High Court of Justice.

accompanying his brethren of the law when they went up in a body to address the … King [*George II*] upon the alarm of an invasion in 1745'. *In this dramatic, turbulent year, the much-dreaded 'invasion' which had the aim of reinstating the Catholic Stuart dynasty on the thrones of England and Scotland — the intention of a number of previous attempts ever since James II had been deposed in 1688, most notably by his son James Edward Stuart (the 'Old Pretender') in 1715 — finally took place.*

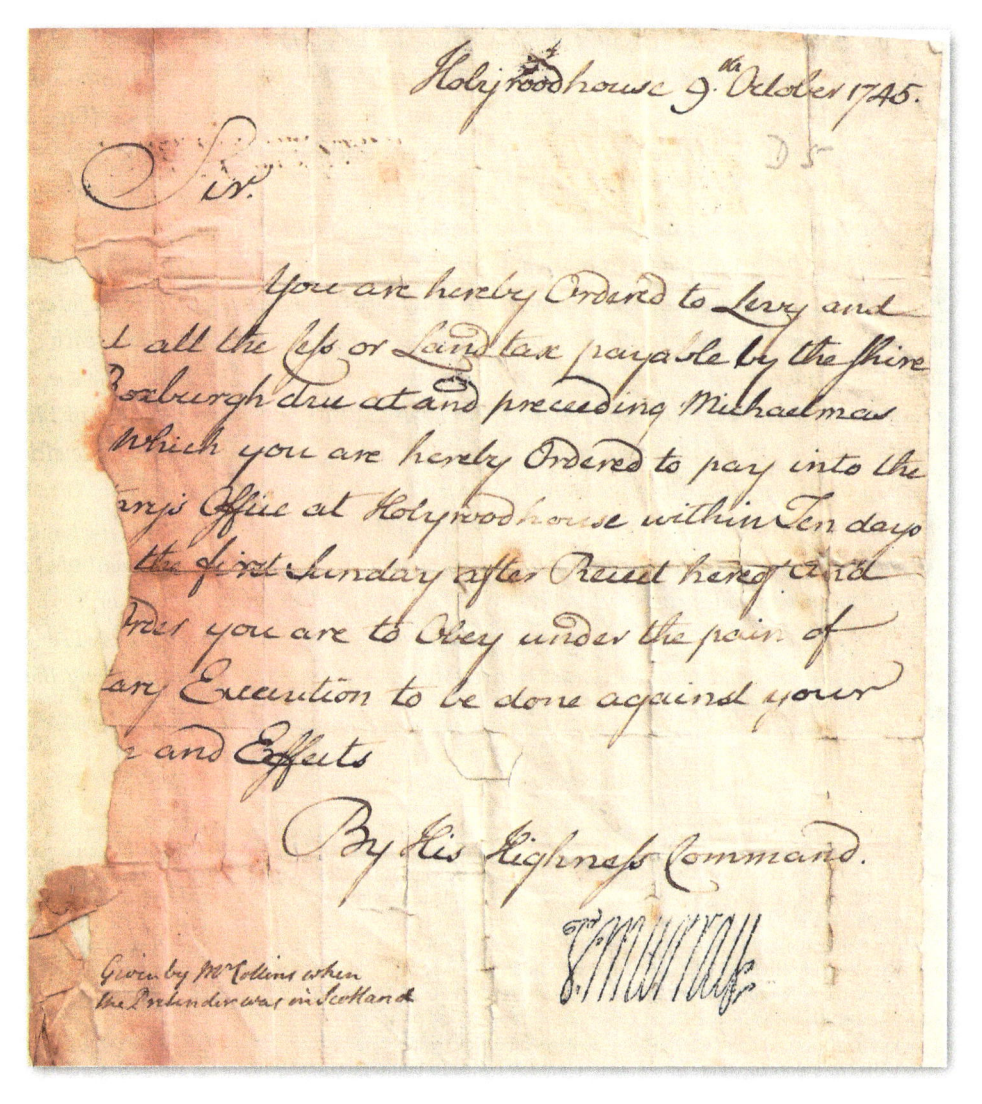

**Fig. 2 c)** Letter from Lord George Murray, Holyroodhouse, dated 9 October 1745.

*Taking advantage of the absence from Britain of much of the army, which was in the Low Countries engaged in the War of the Austrian Succession[12], Charles Edward Stuart — the 'Young Pretender' and grandson of James II, who soon acquired the popular nickname of 'Bonnie Prince Charlie' — landed in Scotland from France in August 1745 with a small army and began to gather supporters from amongst the Scottish clans. Little resistance was offered at first as the 'Jacobites' seized control of Edinburgh in September and proclaimed Charles Stuart's father as King James VIII of Scotland. A few days later a surprise attack planned by Lord George Murray, leader of the 'Jacobite' forces, routed the government army under Sir John Cope at the Battle of Prestonpans near Edinburgh. We have a handwritten document headed* 'Holyroodhouse 9th October 1745' (**Fig. 2 c**)), *which demands the immediate payment of* 'cess and land tax' *from the Shire of Roxburgh with the order* 'to Obey under the pain of Summary Execution to be done against your Person and Effects' *followed by Murray's printed signature.*

*The 'Jacobite' army, which numbered around six thousand to start with but gathered more men as it advanced, then turned towards England. It by-passed government forces at Newcastle and marched south via Carlisle, Lancaster, Preston and Manchester, each of which surrendered in turn, before entering the town of Derby on 4 December. The speed of the advance caused a tremendous wave of alarm and we have several letters in the family collection which illustrate vividly the fear felt by the general population, especially those in the north and east of the country. Some* (**2: 3, 2: 4** *and* **2: 6**) *are to James Birch from his friend Reverend Dr George Legh[13], Vicar of Halifax, whose proximity of his main parish to the path of the rebel army as it marched south, together with his frequent visits to London, meant that he was well placed to receive and pass on the news more or less as it occurred. Another* (**2: 5**) *is from Thomas's and James's sister, Mary Green (1694–1784) in Norfolk, which had also been bracing itself against the threat of invasion along the undefended East Anglian coast.*

---

12  Britain became involved in this conflict in 1742 as the result of a series of alliances — firstly in support of Maria Theresia of Austria's right to be recognised as the rightful successor to her father Charles VI, the last Hapsburg to be Holy Roman Emperor, and later an alliance with Prussia under Frederick II (the Great) against France. The War of the Austrian Succession also produced one of the most intriguing documents in our family collection (see Appendix I). This is an unsigned and anonymous description by a cavalryman who took part in the Battle of Dettingen in June 1743, an event which is now largely remembered because it was the only time in modern history that troops have been led into battle by a reigning British monarch (George II).

13  Rev. Dr George Legh (1693–1775) was Prebendary of York before becoming Vicar of Halifax (Minster) in 1731. His friendship with James Birch seems to have come about through his first wife, Mary Avenant, who was originally from Coventry and had a connection with the Owen family. Rev. Dr Legh was well known as a leading Evangelical cleric, who had allowed John Wesley to preach at his parish church following the latter's courtesy visit in 1742. Wesley subsequently described him as 'a candid enquirer after the truth'.

## Letter 2:3 (Rev. Dr. George Legh, London to James Birch, Coventry, dated 1 October, 1745)

London. 1 Oc.

Dear Sr.

Mr. Odian is as yet in Suffolk; at least I was told so last Saturday.

Your Letter to him, which is a new Favour to your Friend, shal be deliver'd by yt [that] Friend in person, when he comes.

The late Step taken by ye Merchants[14] so unanimously & spontaneously is such a Suport to Public Credit as greatly strengthens ye Government & greatly disappoints it's (sic) Enemies. — In all parts of England. Both Whigs & Tories seem to unite in their Loyalty; which is likewise another Strength to ye Government, & another Disappointment to its Enemies.

Colonel Gard'ner's dying Speech to ye young Pretender is reported to be this: "Sir, you are fighting for a Temporal Crown; But I for an Eternal one."[15]

Ye Number of <u>Officers</u> taken prisoner amounts to 82 or 84.

Respects as in last conclude
Dear Sir.

Your sincere / & obliged<br>Geo: Legh

*Postscript on flap:*
The King of Prussia [*Frederick the Great*] & our King are on ye best Footing imaginable.[16]

---

14  This may refer to the refusal by the Whig burgesses (or merchants) of Glasgow to pay the full amount of tax demanded of them, which 'Bonnie Prince Charlie' required to equip his army.
15  Colonel Gardiner, a senior Hanoverian commander who stayed close to the scene of battle to assist Sir John Cope's inexperienced army, was mortally wounded in a final heroic skirmish of the short-lived battle, in which hundreds of government troops were killed or wounded and 1500 taken prisoner in the course of fifteen minutes. (Battle of Prestonpans 1745 Heritage Trust website)
16  In August 1745, George II promised through the Convention of Hanover to negotiate peace with the Prussians and abandoned his support for the Austrians.

**Letter 2:4 (Rev. Dr. George Legh, London, to James Birch & Stephen Smith, Coventry, dated 15 October, 1745)**

London. At Mr.
Pearson's near
Exeter Exchange in
ye Strand. Oct. 15.
1745.

Dear Sir.

Your Lady I'm obliged to for her kind Invitations &c, And to Bath both You & I & all her Welwishers are obliged for her Recovery. And we are equally obliged to Bristol, I hope, for ye Recovery of Mrs Smith.

To ye Barrel of Oisters[17] intended for You & Mr. Smith, Mr. Hunt & Mr. Secker, (Carriage paid) I hope there wil be no Dissentients, as there were to ye Address. When our Enemies of different Denominations are writing all against English Protestants as such, surely Protestants of <u>different</u> Denominations, And à fortiori Protestants of ye <u>same</u> Denomination, should <u>all</u> unite against those Enemies, that such a Union at Home may be tantamount to that Strength, which we want from Abroad.

Sir John Cope & Col. Lasc—s [Lascelles][18] are arrived. The Latter, 'tis sd., is under an Arrest. I supose Both will undergo a Parliamentary Inquiry.

An Act for A Suspension of ye Habeas Corpus Act[19] is talk'd of, And that it will pass on Saturday. — In ye Eye of my Disposition, which is all Diffidence

---

17   Oysters in the eighteenth century were not the expensive luxury they have become today; indeed by Victorian times they were regarded as the staple diet of the poor in London and other cities. Sam Weller in Dickens' *The Pickwick Papers* remarks that 'Poverty and oysters always seem to go together'. George Legh's gift to James Birch and his colleagues is likely to have been of green oysters, a speciality of Essex around Mersea and the estuaries nearby. These oysters, which had green beards of harmless algae, were preserved after gathering for six to eight weeks in pits dug into the salt marshes, giving them a dark green colour which was much admired at this time.

18   Colonel Peregrine Lascelles was in command of the 58th Foot at Prestonpans. As his lines were overrun, he slipped and fell, and was disarmed by the surrounding Jacobites, who however failed to capture him, leaving him to escape the field of battle while they pursued other fleeing redcoats. Lascelles walked through the enemy lines, procured a horse and rode off. His story was vindicated at the inquiry held the following year, and his memorial tablet (in St Mary's Church, Whitby) described him as a 'brave and Gallant Officer' who 'remained forsaken on the field' after 'a fruitless exertion of his Spirit and ability / at the disgraceful rout of Preston pans'. (Battle of Prestonpans 1745 Heritage Trust website)

19   The suspension of the Habeas Corpus Act duly took place, providing for those suspected of high treason to be detained without bail. The Act suspending Habeas Corpus remained in force until 19 April, 1746, when it was renewed.

& Timidity, things look very dark & threatning; — to such a degree that I'm sometimes considering to what Business I must apply for a Livelihood, & to what Place for a Retreat, ye Vicar of Halifax being determined not to be ye Vicar of Bray[20], but to give up all his Substance rather than his Conscience, And to desert his Country rather than his Religion i.e. ye Bible, for ye Bible wholly; ye Bible only he owns as his Religion.

Haste concludes

Dear Sir. (I'm here speaking to Each of You, i.e. to Mr. Birch, Mr. Smith, Mr. Hunt, Mr. Sec.)
Your sincere
Geo: Legh

Compliments to your Lady & all friends.

*James Birch forwarded the letter to his colleague Stephen Smith with the following covering note:*

Mr Ste. Smith  17 Oct. Sir, I have just received a gift from Dr. Legh with a Barrel of Oysters directed to you & Mr Secker, Alderman Hunt & myself, if you will favour me with your Company at my house, nothing remains but to appoint a time, but if any other place be more Eligible, then both time & place are to be settled, which I will endeavour to attend & am Sir your humble Servant. — Ditto to Mr Secker & Ditto to Alderman Hunt.

*Written in a third hand, the anonymous writer (probably Stephen Smith, to whom the letter was forwarded) seemed to regard the Rev. Dr Legh's present with a certain amount of suspicion:*

Dr Legh  15. Octr 1745 —
A Good 400£ per annum & 12 Chappels or Patronages, a Justice & prebend of Yorke & a House fit for a Bishop. [21]

---

20  A reference to the well-known anonymous eighteenth-century song about a time-serving parson who boasts that he has accommodated himself to the religious views of five successive monarchs from Charles II to George I, and that 'whatsoever king may reign', he will remain the Vicar of Bray.
21  Perhaps this addendum questions the Rev. Dr. Legh's sincerity in vowing 'to give up all his Substance rather than his Conscience', in view of his considerable wealth.

**Fig. 2 d)** *The March of the Guards to Finchley*, by William Hogarth. Oil on canvas, 1750. © Coram in the care of the Foundling Museum, London.

*Mary Birch, the elder of George Birch (senior)'s two daughters, had moved to Eccles Hall, near Thetford in Norfolk, on her marriage to William Green, whose family was formerly from Staffordshire. By 1746 Mary had been widowed for about nine years and her letter (which is addressed to her 'Sister' but was almost certainly to her sister-in-law, James's wife Jane) shows that Molly, one of her three children, had been living for some time with her aunt and uncle — probably to relieve some of the financial burden on her mother but perhaps also to help look after her young cousins, as we know from Rev. Dr Legh's letter (**2: 4**) that Jane had been ill and had recently been to Bath to take the waters.*

*In the event, the 'Jacobite' army progressed no further south than Derby (only about forty miles north of Coventry, which would explain Mary's concern for her relations). At a hastily convened meeting there of a council of his generals and aristocratic supporters on 5 December 1745, 'Bonnie Prince Charlie' had been all for pressing on immediately towards London, convinced that the English 'Jacobites' would come out in force to aid his capture of the capital. His advisers were more cautious, pointing out that two British armies — one of them commanded by the Duke of Cumberland*[22]*, who had been recalled* *hurriedly from the Continent after the 'Jacobites' marched into England — blocked their way to London* (**Fig 2 d**)); *that the promised French reinforcements had not materialised; and that little active support had been forthcoming from the English. Charles was overruled and eventually, unwillingly, bowed to the Council's decision to retreat, but fears of a renewed attempt (see* **2: 6**) *persisted for some time.*

---

LETTER 2:5 (Mary Green (née Birch), Eccles, Norfolk, probably to her sister-in-law, Jane Birch (née Owen) and to her elder daughter, Molly Green, dated 3 February, 1746)

Dear Sister

I shou'd write oftener to enquire after your health but that Mrs Barker[23] is sometimes so kind as to communicate your letters to me. I heartily pitied you when you were so terified with the Rebels — indeed we begun to be pretty much afraid here for 'twas expected when they had escap'd ye Dukes Army that they wou'd come this way in hopes of ye Ffrench landing upon our coast[24], & as here were no preparations made for our defence we were forming Schemes to escape them. Willy[25] who values ye horses very much thôt [thought] them too good for the Rebels; he purpos'd to carry me & his sister up to Town with them & then to join ye Kings Army himself & to make him a present of ye horses. Mrs Hull

---

22  William Augustus, Duke of Cumberland (1721–65), the King's second and favourite son, had been in the Army since 1741 and first saw active service in Germany two years later during the War of the Austrian Succession. Despite his youth and inexperience, he became Commander-in-Chief of the allied British, Hanoverian, Austrian and Dutch troops in Flanders in 1745. Cumberland pursued the retreating 'Jacobite' army after it withdrew from England back into Scotland, eventually engaging the rebels at the Battle of Culloden on 16 April 1746, when the Stuart forces were completely routed (see the postscripts to **2: 6**).

23  Jane Owen lived with her Aunt Barker in London between 1725 and 1728. Shropham Hall, very close to Eccles Hall, was built in the 1720s for the Barker family, which had owned property in the area since the seventeenth century.

24  Mary Green's apprehensions of a French invasion on the coast of East Anglia were not unfounded as an invasion fleet, sent by Louis XV of France, did embark after the French learnt of the progress of the Jacobite incursion into England, and was only prevented from reaching British shores by heavy weather and the intervention of Admiral Vernon.

25  William Green, son of William and Mary Green, who later became Rector of Eccles. The manor of Eccles, which also included the living and rectory, had been purchased in about 1712 by Mary's father-in-law, William Green of Stafford. According to the records of Eccles church, two of Mary's brothers were granted the living in the 1720s: John Birch, A.M., served as Rector for sixteen months from June 1720, and Samuel Birch, A.M., from 1723 until his death in 1732. The latter's memorial tablet, erected by his sister, in the church reads: SAMUEL BIRCH, A.M. Harborniae in Agro Staffordiensi natus, Oxoniae, in Collegio Pembr: Educatus, Hujus Ecclesiae per Novum fere Annos, Pastor dignissimus, Vir vere Reverendus, et doctus, et pius, et admodum obdormit, obijt duodecimo die Decembris, Anno Redemptionis humanae, 1732° Aetatis suae 32°. / Posuit, Maria, Uxor Gulielmi Green Armigeri, Soror amantissima.'

said she never work'd harder in her life than she did for 2 days that week [*when*] we expected ye Rebels in packing up & hiding her plate, linnen & china[26] — I believe I have not so much to lose, nor am quite so soon affrighted for I did not move any thing but got a box ready in which I thôt [*thought*] to put ye Tankard & 2 or 3 other things in case they had approach'd us — I think we had a happy deliverance that they turn'd their backs, & am truley sorry for all who suffer'd by them — we join in wishing you & yours many happy years — I am

Your Affectionate Sister M Green

Eccles   3d Feb: 1745[27]

Dear Molly I received yours together with your Uncle's, I like your writing very well, & I find no fault with your spelling least I shou'd thereby hinder your writing, ye oftener you write the better, tis observation & practice that must make you spell — as you have a good ear, if you speak proper & observe ye sound you cou'd not spell amiss — both Mr Grooms dyed within a week of each other & left a large Estate which their heirs are at Suit for, & that occasions Mr Dove a journey to London who forwards this letter thither. Mr Searles of Attleboro [Attleborough] is dead of a consumption — Becky Foster is marryed to Mr Marner one who was apprentice with Watson & is an Apothecary & Chirurgeon at Kenninghall. I & Jenny thank God have had very good health but your Brother has had a good deal of tooth ach & such a swell'd face as has come to a sore these two winters & Mr Marner has been forc'd to lance ye outside of his cheek which he heald again with very little blemish — the family at Shropham were well this morning. Mrs Barker had a mind her sons shou'd practice their dancing when they were at home in ye holidays & was so obliging to ask us to Shropham to meet ye Redgrave family & some other friends where we din'd & suppd. I think of no other news at present, your Brother & Sister join with me in love to you & service to all friends —

I am Your Affectionate Mother<br>M.G.

26  This reference to hiding valuable household items to prevent their falling into the hands of 'ye Rebels' reminds me of the occasion during the Second World War when my mother put all her jewellery into a large cake tin which was then buried by us in a deep hole near the entrance to the graveyard at Adwell — and indeed of the difficulty in finding the tin at the end of the war!

27  See letter **1: 3** and footnotes 10 and 11 in Chapter 1 for explanation of the dating system under the old-style Julian calendar, which was still used in England up until 1752.

**LETTER 2:6 (Rev. Dr. George Legh, Halifax, to James Birch, Coventry, dated 22 April, 1746)**

Dear Sir.

This salutes You & Your Lady after ye Rebellion; or rather after its short vacation, for I greatly fear 'twil return. Fear must continue as long as ye young Pretender continues in any of his Majesty's Dominions. Sure when Things take a good turn ye Govt. will make Reformations in Scotland.

I have a Relation there ['in Scotland' *crossed out*] of ye Episcopal Church (ye Dep. Comptroller of ye Custom house at Edinburgh) who writes thus, "The Episcopal Clergy have been hitherto with Impunity allow'd to preach Treason & promote Rebellion. The Establish'd Clergy have behav'd with Universal Applause. They abdicated their Churches upon ye Surrender of ye Town. Nor could all ye Promises of Protection ever bring ym [them] back during ye Abode of ye Highland Army. At its Departure they resum'd their Pulpits, and by ye Loyalty of their Discourses & Example ye whole Country took up Arms in Defense of their Religion & Liberties."

How do your little ones? Shal I have ye pleasure now of ye Visit intended me last year? Let me know soon, And you'll oblige

Dear Sir,<br>
Your & Your Lady's Sincere<br>
Geo. Legh

Halifax. 22 Apr.
1746

PS. Thro' my utter Weariness of Court Attendances I could never get an Answer from ye Duke; but suppose you've rec'd one. He might probably be under Engagements at that time; And may be so stil. All I should desire therefore at present is what I scarce think he can refuse to such a Letter as he had from his own Corporation, Vizt. To have your Name enter'd in ye Lord Chamberlain's List such as I supose is kept in ye Office with Memorandum of ye time of Application, & sufficient Incouragement to hope for ye thing being done as soon as a Vacancy offers after his Grace has fulfilled all prior or dearer Engagements. You'll say I'm a very languid, uncourtly Supplicant. To speak Truth I could not Supplicate or Attend in ye usual, low, selfish, sordid way a Fortnight together, if sure that doing so would purchase ye Archbishoprick of Canterbury.

Please to present my Compliments as in last.

*Before sealing this letter, Rev. Dr Legh heard the news of the victory over the rebels at the Battle of Culloden, which he hastened to add, writing it on the folded side flap:*

Ye Alderman who hands this will tell you ye good News gone to London from ye North, by Express carry'd by Lord Bury[28].

*Written on the outside of the folded letter is a copy of James Birch's reply:*

Dear Sir. 27 Apr 1746. I am favoured with your obliging Letter ye day & most heartily rejoyce with you upon ye great & glorious Success of our Shining young Hero ye D of C[29] against ye Rebels, in Honour of whom we have kept a publick day here with all possible demonstrations of Joy; Considering ye apprehensions we were under from ye Rebels & ye deep Impressions ['made' *crossed out*, 'still remaining' *crossed out*] on yt [that] account upon our minds, you could not well expect we should once think of venturing so far north as Halifax; we might indeed with safety venture now, but have for some time fix'd for a Visit to my wife's relations in Norfolk, who are impatient to see her & ye Children after ye Small pox to rejoyce with us on their happy recovery which I thank God they are now safely & favourably over with them all; we still promise ourselves much pleasure in a visit to you, & hope it will be [*word illegible*] & joyn in [*two words illegible*] to you from [*three words illegible*]. We have never heard one word from ye Duke or Mr Odiam on any Account whatever since your application [but] when such an opportunity offers I will not fail to remind ourselves of ym [them].

---

*After Sir Thomas Birch was appointed as a Justice of the Common Pleas in 1746, he was not able to visit Harborne so frequently and so placed the day-to-day administration of the estate*

---

28 George Keppel, Lord Bury (later the third Earl of Albemarle) was aide-de-camp to the Duke of Cumberland at Culloden, and carried the dispatch of the news of Cumberland's victory to London, reaching the capital on 23 April (the day after George Legh's letter was written).

29 In the euphoric days after Cumberland's victory there was no mention in England of the brutal slaughter of those Highlanders — up to 1,000 — who remained wounded on the battlefield, which earned the Duke the sobriquet of 'The Butcher of Culloden'.

*in the hands of his kinswoman Elizabeth Ball, to whom he even left the decision of the number of windows to be blocked up to avoid paying too much tax after the Window Tax*[30] *was raised early in 1747. As well as sitting in London, Sir Thomas was also required to spend periods travelling about the country on what was known as 'the Circuit' to carry out his judicial functions. The following two letters refer to the assistance he received from members of his family in obtaining good horses for this purpose — an essential requirement given the rough state of the highways in the mid eighteenth century.*

*One of Sir Thomas's most sensational cases as Judge of the Court of Common Pleas involved his travelling to Sussex to preside (with two other judges, representing the King's Bench and the Court of Exchequer respectively) over the first of three trials of* 'Fourteen Notorious Smugglers', *charged with the brutal murders of a customs official and a shoemaker. This case became a* cause celèbre *of its day and permission was granted by the king (George II) for the seven worst offenders to be tried at a special assize in Chichester, close to where the crimes had been committed, in order to make* 'public examples of such horrible offenders'. *Having been found guilty at the conclusion of the three-day trial from 16 to 18 January 1749, all seven were sentenced to death and were taken to the gallows the very next day. An account of all three trials in the early part of 1749*[31] *was first published, in graphic and gruesome detail, by an anonymous author named only as* 'A Gentleman of Chichester' *(widely believed to be Charles Lennox, the Duke of Richmond, who had led a crusade against smugglers because they were believed to assist the 'Jacobite' cause) and ran into numerous editions.*

---

30  The Window Tax was originally introduced in 1696, to make up for losses caused by the clipping of coinage during the reign of William III. A banded tax based on the number of windows in a house, it was raised six times between 1747 and 1808. Though the tax was easy to assess and collect, as early as 1718 it was noticed that there was a decline in revenue raised due to windows being blocked up (as Thomas Birch advises Mrs Ball to do) to avoid going into a higher band. The tax was eventually repealed in 1851 after campaigners argued that it was a 'tax on health' and on 'light and air' which placed a disproportionate burden on the middle and lower classes.

31  The gruesome story, under the title *Sussex Smugglers* (originally it had a much longer title), is now available as an e-book from www.smuggling.co.uk/ebooks/sussex_smugglers.

**Letter 2:7 (Thomas Birch, Serjeants Inn, London, to his cousin Mrs Ball[32], Birmingham, dated 14 March, 1747)**

Madam —

I am favour'd with your's of the 11th Inst. I troubled you with a letter last post and I wrote at ye same time to Mr. J. Birch. I hope the Coach horse is not much hurt by the bruise you mention, I am obliged to Mr. Birch for lending me his horse for ye Circuit. — I cannot exactly tell what day I shall get from off the Circuit to Southgate, but I do not expect to reach Southgate before the 28 or 29th of April and I wrote somewhat to this effect to Mr. Birch. — I shall take care of the hogshead of wine for him. I think (as Mr. Birch says) you had best if you please to send S. Pritchet and Ezekiel Gray with the Coach horses and saddle horses on Wednesday next (being the 18th Inst.) without fail, let 'em go directly to Southgate.

I see by the act for the Window Tax, every house is to pay 2s [*shillings*] and 6d [*pence*] per window where there are 10, 11, 12, 13 or 14 — and 9d per window where there are 15, 16, 17, 18, or 19, and 1s per window where there are 20 & upwards. I think you will do well to stop up lights wherever you think proper, this is doing I believe in most places more or less.

I thank God we are all well and join in duty love & service, I am

    Madam, your affectionate kinsman and humble servant
      Tho: Birch

Serjts Inn —
Sat: 14 March 1746 [*sic*]

---

32  Thomas Birch directs this letter to be left for collection by Mrs Ball 'at Mr. Spooner's in Edgebaston (*sic*) street in Birmingham, Warwickshire'. Abraham Spooner was his brother-in-law (married to his younger sister Elizabeth) who is described as an ironmonger in an earlier document drawn up at the time of the marriage of James Birch to Jane Owen, Abraham being one of the trustees of the marriage settlement (Coventry Archives, PA 309/118, dated 5 November 1729).

## LETTER 2:8 (John Wyrley Birch[33] to Mrs Ball, Harborne, Birmingham, undated, probably 1747)

Madam

    I have bought you a pair of Geldings which I think promise for being good one's. The Price is twenty five Pounds ten Shillings which is the price for Coach. One of them has just threw out a fore of nearer Legg [?] before but will not signify anything I believe. I shall go towards St Albans on Wednesday next and if that was to your Convenience to send the horses up at the same time I will see they are taken care off, or you are welcome to let [them] be at Hamsted till I go if you approve of it. They are deliver'd to me to morrow but are fitt for work being bought out of a working team (so of Consequence not very fatt which is the better for the Circuit). If you please to have them under any other regulation you will communicate your thought to me. I will write to the Judge next Saturday. I had like to forget Mrs Birch's & Miss Lane's complements to you, which also accept from

        Madam, your most
            Obedient Humble Servant
                J W Birch

Rec of Sam: Pritchard [sic]. £1 on acct of the horses —

---

*As the decade ended, both the Rev. Dr Legh and his friend James Birch became widowers, in each case for the second time. Jane (Owen) Birch died in May 1749, apparently from a 'Consumption', leaving four surviving children — three of whom were under the age of ten. Only six months later James received a letter from Dr Legh, telling him of his own wife's desperate illness and painting such a ghastly picture of the practice of medicine at the time that it is no wonder that poor Mrs Legh was reluctant to let her husband seek another medical opinion. Happily in due course both men remarried, although Rev. Dr Legh also outlived his third wife Elizabeth by ten years.*

---

33   A cousin of Sir Thomas Birch, who owned the manors of Hamstead (by family descent since the sixteenth century), Handsworth and Witton (since 1736), all in the environs of Birmingham. John Wyrley Birch died childless in 1775 and left his entire estate to Sir Thomas's eldest son George (1739–1807) and his wife Ann (née Lane — herself a great-granddaughter of John Wyrley's grandfather). George also inherited Harborne Hall and Hazelwell when his father died in 1757. Around 1801, George Birch moved to Wretham Hall, near Thetford in Norfolk, only a few miles from where his aunt Mary (Birch) Green had lived in Eccles.

LETTER 2:9 (Rev. Dr. George Legh, Halifax, to James Birch, Coventry, dated 21 November, 1749, with James Birch's copy of his replies, the first undated and the second dated 14 January, 1750, both written on the same sheet of paper)

Halifax. 21. Novr. 1749

Dear Mr Byrch,

Before now I was in Hopes of Waiting upon You again, But was prevented by my Dearest Dear's Feavr [fever] (given her I [do not] doubt by ye New Buildings I made purely to please her) in Shropshire; where ye Apothecary suppos'd it to be Nothing but Cold & Want of Appetite, proceeding from a foul Stomach; and made Applications accordingly. But when we got hither about ye Beginning of last Month, it appear'd in all ye Shapes of a Feavr, of a very malignant ling'ring Kind; Under which She has languish'd ever since; as she does stil; tho' a very judicious, vigilant, tender-hearted Physician, attends her twice a Day; as he has done above a Month together. Her great Addictedness to Vomiting he has remov'd; And abated her Purgings. But by the Hectic Cough attending her, & by her Want of Appetite, She's so emaciated that her Body (always thin & a little Consumptive at ye best or Dispos'd that way) is reduced exceeding low: In so much that this Circumstance, Accompanied with ye Cough, tho' abated, gives me 10 thousand Fears. Which Fears if they had no Circumstance to intermix Hope with ym [them], would overcome me, for a more sincere Affectionate Wife never existed. The only kind Symptoms are her Not Spitting, nor finding any Pain or Load within; whence ye Dr collects that her Lungs are untouch'd. I would fain call in another, tho' not nearer yn [than] 12 or 14 Miles. But this she opposes with such Importunity I dare not contend with it, Lest ye Consequence She fears should be a real one, — that instead of forwarding her Cure he should backward it thro' ye Height of her Aversion, grounded on her Belief that a new Physician wil bring such new Physic as shal bring her again into her Vomitings &c. The present one, She says, understands her Case thoroughly, & has apply'd properly; as She feels; And that a better cannot be found, as a worse may in looking for a better. Asses Milk (with Crab's Eyes), Water-Gruel, Thin Chocolate, & Jellies are her only Food; Fig & Raisin — Liqorice Water with an Acid along with it, are her Physic; ye Bark being left off.

Excuse my dwelling thus long on a Subject yt [that] monopolizes ye Head & Heart of

Dear Sir
    Your afflicted
        Geo: Legh. […]

*As before, James Birch kept a copy of his reply to the news of Mrs Legh's illness, written on the outside folds of Dr Legh's letter, together with the text of another note which he must have sent a few days after hearing of her death:*

Dear Doctor Leigh (*sic*) I rec'd the favour of your Letter last post containing a melancholy account of your dear Ladie's Case, your pathetic description of it excites in me the sincerest sympathy, & revives in me the tenderest sentiments of Grief for the loss of one, in my Esteem, the dearest best creature upon Earth. I dread the thôt [thought] of a Consumption, my poor Dear's crept upon her so slowly & imperceptibly for about 2 years together that no one had the least suspicion of it, till it was declared to be a lost Case. The Regimen you mention, as well for food as physic seem to be extremely well adapted to your Ladie's Case and if it shall please God to spare her till Spring, the waters of Bristol have sometimes done wonders in such Cases. I pray God restore to you in health so inestimable [a] Blessing, a Treasure whose price is far above Rubies. […]

I am Dear Sir your very affectionate & most obedient humble Servant \_\_\_\_

4 Jan. 1749/50} This day Master Ottley rec'd an account from the Doctor of his dear Fanny's death.

Dear Doctor Legh — 14 Jan. 1749/50. I think myself so much concerned in sentiments of grief & affection for you yt [that] I cannot omit Master Ottley's kind offer of joyning with him my friendly mite of Condolence of your loss of so dear & valuable a Companion, a loss I too well know by sad Experience to be the greatest a man can sustain, but you are not only too sensible a man but too good a Christian to repine & grieve as one without hope even in circumstances fullest of affliction; Death is a Debt due to Nature, which sooner or later (as providence shall judge fittest for us) we must all one day pay. Yours I hope, for your own sake as well as for your friends will be reserved to a much later day. — The death of your dear Lady could be no great surprize to you who have long [*fore*] seen her dying daily. ['I pray God' *crossed out*] may we all be preparing for such a change & enabled thro' divine assistance to expect & submit to it as becomes Christians. I know too well the tenderness of your heart to say anything more on this melancholy subject, further than recommend you to the all wise disposer of all Events, Sincerely wishing this Dispensation of his providence may have a due & happy Effect upon you & all your affairs now & hereafter. I am, Dear Sir, your very affectionate & most obedient humble Servant.

CHAPTER 3

# The Three Thomases

*Letters and Diary Extracts 1759–1796*

'I have sent you a hare…'[1]

*Sir Thomas Birch practised for just over ten years as a judge in the Court of Common Pleas, his time in office coming to an end only with his death on 15 March 1757. His standing amongst the judiciary was sufficiently high for the Lord Chancellor[2] to write to George II in the previous month to alert him that 'Mr Justice Birch … is dangerously ill, and it is thought cannot recover.[3]' As Sir Thomas's wife Sarah had also died three years earlier, the guardianship of their orphaned children passed to their uncle James Birch, who was also responsible for their education as all five were still under twenty at the time of their father's death. The three boys — George (born 1739), Thomas (born 1743) and John (Jack) — were pupils at Dr Newcome's academy in Hackney, a privately-run school kept by a Dissenting minister and 'Whig of the old stamp'[4], with a reputation for producing leading politicians; during the latter half of the eighteenth century, twenty-six members of the House of Commons had attended the school including four of the Lord Chancellor's sons, which is perhaps why Sir Thomas favoured it for his own boys. However, within two years of assuming responsibility for the upbringing of his brother's children James Birch received an unwelcome letter from Mary, the elder of his two nieces.*

---

1  Thomas Birch (born 1743) to his godmother Mrs Ball, 4 November 1764 (**3:2**)
2  Philip Yorke (1690–1764), created first Earl of Hardwicke in 1754, lawyer and politician who held the office of Lord Chancellor from 1737 to 1756, serving under four successive Prime Ministers from Sir Robert Walpole to the Duke of Newcastle.
3  G. Harris, *The Life of Lord Chancellor Hardwicke*, 3 vols. (1847), quoted in Oxford DNB.
4  L. Narnier, J. Brooke (eds), *The History of Parliament: the House of Commons 1754–1790*, (Boydell & Brewer, 1964). Accessed on www.historyofparliamentonline.org

## Letter 3:1 (Mary Birch, Southgate, to her uncle James Birch, Coventry, dated 2 March 1759)

Southgate March 2<sup>nd</sup> 1759

Honoured Sir

I am sorry to be Obliged to write to you upon an affair that I make no doubt will give you Concern & much surprize you. My Brother Thomas (who has always Behaved very Prudently & quite beyond the Generality of Boys of his age) has been drawn in by some of his School Fellows to Behave in a very improper Manner to Mr Harry Newcome.

The Case is this, Mr Newcome the Head Master being gone for two or three Days to his Country House, the School was left in the care of Mr H Newcome who is second Master. On Tuesday Evening, one of the Gentlemen upon the first Form being very Impertinent, Mr H. N. struck him, & the Boy returned the Blow, upon which Mr H. N. told him he insisted upon his not coming into School any more. When the Boys went up to Bed they agreed to stand by the Boy & resent what their Master had said, so on Wednesday Morning, as soon as they came down, the Offended Boy at the Head, & six of the biggest Boys fell upon him & hit him 3 or 4 blows, & then all took their Hats & Run away to their Friends.

Mr Newcome came home post [*haste*] as soon as he heard of it. I have been to wait upon him, he gives Tom an extream [extremely] good Character as to his former Behaviour, but is Determined never to admit any one of the seven again. Tom is under great Uneasiness & very sorry for what has happened, he is the 5<sup>th</sup> Boy in the School & a good Scholar & would have left Hackney next Xmas & have gone to Cambridge.

I must beg to know where you will think Proper he should be, till he does go to Cambridge, he is but 16 years old & I fancy it will not be right for him to go thither sooner than was intended. I have wrote by this post to my Uncle John. I hope you & he will be so good as to consult about it & let me know your Opinion. Jack is at School & very well & so happy as to be entirely out of the scheme. I am

Sir, your Dutifull Neice<br>M Birch

*Thomas's uncles do not seem to have been convinced by Mary's argument that at sixteen he was too young for university, as according to Alumni Records of the University of Cambridge he was admitted as a 'pensioner' at Queen's College only four months later, although he did not matriculate until 1761. In the same year he followed in his father's and uncle George's footsteps by being admitted to the Inner Temple. His early disgrace clearly did him no harm, and may even have opened opportunities for his path through life. We hear of him next (**3: 2**) in North Wales, at the house Erddig which is now one of the National Trust's most visited properties. This letter is of particular significance, as for the first time it introduces the family whose name comes up repeatedly over the next century in connection with the Birch Reynardsons, in the form of a man who — perhaps more than any other individual — would play a major role in bringing together the two separate strands of my family.*

---

LETTER 3:2 (Thomas Birch, Erthig [Erddig], near Wrexham, to his godmother, Mrs Ball[5], dated 4 November, 1764)

Erthig [*sic*] Nov: ye 4th 1764

Honoured Madam.

I am now at my Friend Mr Yorke's. We came hither from Cambridge, by way of Leicester, and Litchfield, therefore had it not in our Power to call upon you, however I will certainly do myself that pleasure as I return.

I have sent you a hare, I am ignorant whether you have plenty of Game, or no; if you have not, it will be welcome, and if you have, I hope you will take the will for the deed.

I will now take the singular pleasure I have in subscribing myself your very Dutyful Godson and much obliged humble Servant

Thos. Birch

P. S.
I hope you will accept of my Duty & the best Compliments of my Friend. The Hare is hunted, & therefore will not keep long.

---

5  Presumably the same Mrs Ball on whom Sir Thomas Birch depended to oversee his estate at Harborne (**2: 2** and **2: 3**).

'Mr Yorke' — *Philip Yorke of Erddig (1743–1804)*, who shared the same name as his father's cousin, the recently deceased Lord Chancellor — had been friendly with Thomas Birch, his exact contemporary, since school days in Hackney. It is likely that Philip was one of those who had drawn Thomas in to behave 'in a very improper manner'[6] and may even have been the instigator, as he left Dr Newcome's academy at the same time and a few weeks later entered Eton, where he spent his final year of schooling. He soon made friends with another boy of a similar age — Brownlow Cust, the only son of Sir John Cust, the Speaker of the House of Commons; the two boys continued to see much of each other when they both went up in the same year to Corpus Christi (then known as St Benet's College), Cambridge, where Philip also renewed his friendship with Thomas, already a student at the university.

In 1766 the death of his father left Philip Yorke, at the age of twenty-three, the owner of Erddig. As he was at the beginning of his flourishing legal, and later political, career (he was called to the Bar the following year), Philip was unable to oversee the estate from London and so delegated the responsibility firstly to his mother, and then increasingly to his friend Thomas Birch[7] — who, like Philip, was a member of one of the Inns of Court but unlike him did not become a barrister. A delightful book[8], published exactly 150 years after Thomas's letter from Erddig was written, telling the story of those families which had lived there through letters written over three centuries, includes many from the second half of the eighteenth century in which Thomas is mentioned frequently in the most flattering terms. It is clear that he soon became absolutely indispensable to the family through his successful running of the estate. 'What a privilege it would have been to have been acquainted with that excellent man Mr Thomas Birch! Shrewd, business-like, yet with a keen sense of humour, and such a warm heart for his friends. [...] What would Philip and his mother have done without faithful Tom Birch, his school friend? And the history of two families [*actually three families, counting my own*] would have been entirely changed, had not Philip [...] become

---

6 As the only son of an eccentric father and a much younger, adoring mother, Philip is described as having been 'a precocious child, who knew his own mind' (www.uktourist.tv/ website entry for Erddig). He is said to have declared himself a vegetarian at the age of five, although presumably this had lapsed by the time Thomas was hunting hares on his land.

7 Through his wife's interest, Philip Yorke became Member of Parliament for Helston, Cornwall, serving in this capacity until 1781, and later obtained the seat of Grantham (formerly his father-in-law's seat) which he relinquished to his eldest son Simon in 1793 after only a year. He was known as a good conversationalist and keen amateur actor (one of his good friends was the actor David Garrick), but all these activities kept him away from Erddig and his real interests, which were classical literature and antiquities, and later (after he married his second wife, Diana Meyrick, in 1782), Welsh history and genealogy. To be able to entrust the management of his home affairs to someone as dependable as Thomas Birch was therefore all the more valuable.

8 A. L. Cust Wherry, *The Chronicles of Erthig on the Dyke*, 2 volumes (John Lane, Bodley Head, 1914)

intimate with Brownlow Cust.⁹'

*Brownlow had two sisters, Anne and Elizabeth, whom Philip Yorke is likely to have met when visiting his friend at his father's country home, Belton House in Lincolnshire, which is also now owned by the National Trust. Philip soon fell in love with the younger sister, but the courtship was protracted and marred by threats of disinheritance by his wealthy but dissolute uncle, though it is hard to understand what possible objection there could have been to the match[10]. It was not until 1770 that Philip was able to marry Elizabeth Cust, and the wedding took place very quietly as her father had died only a few months earlier[11]. There are two fine portraits of the Cust sisters by the fashionable painter and pastel artist Francis Cotes (1726–70), which must both have been painted before Elizabeth's marriage; the one of Elizabeth as a shepherdess is still at Erddig* (**Fig. 3 a)**), *but sadly the portrait of Anne* (**Fig. 3 b)**) *is known only from an old black and white photograph.*

*Erddig is famous today for its collection of portraits, in written and pictorial form, of the family's servants and it was during Philip's tenure that the tradition first began. Many of the improvements and decorations in the house, still in evidence, were also set in motion when the young couple took up residence there, although Elizabeth lived to enjoy little more than eight years of marriage, dying in January 1779 after the premature birth of their seventh child. During these years there must have been much coming and going between Wales and Lincolnshire as the two sisters remained very close to each other — Elizabeth said of Anne, 'I am nothing without her'[12] — and as Lady Cust had died before Anne's intended marriage in 1777, Elizabeth and her husband stepped in to offer their own home for the wedding. Thus it was that the marriage of my great-great-*

---

9 Brownlow Cust (1744–1807) was MP for Ilchester from 1768–74 and Grantham from 1774–76, when he was given a peerage (see footnote 10). He reappears in our story in Chapter 4, visiting Mrs Birch in Windsor with his family (**4: 18**). It was his grand-daughter Albinia who wrote *The Chronicles of Erthig* (these extracts are from Vol. 2, pp. 225 and 239).

10 Thomas himself appears to have played a part in reconciling Philip's mother's brother, James Hutton, to his nephew's marriage, witnessing the will in which the bulk of his estate was left to his sister in succession to her son. As a result, the fine collection of pictures, china and furniture Hutton had acquired is still to be seen at Erddig.

11 Sir John Cust was not regarded as a great success in the role of Speaker, as he lacked the forceful personality needed to cope with the stormy exchanges in Parliament during the 1760s. In a eulogy of Cust at the election of his successor, the new Prime Minister, Lord North, stressed his 'amiable character, a positive disadvantage for the post'. Worn out by lengthy debates and ailments brought on by long periods of confinement in the chair (a rule introduced immediately after his death allowed for 'the Speaker to depart the Chair whenever the usual calls of nature should require his absence … The want of so provident a regulation is thought to have hastened the death of the last Speaker' (*London Evening Post*, 27 January 1770), Sir John quite literally gave his life to the service of the House, collapsing in the Chair on 12 January 1770 and dying twelve days later. In 1776 his son Brownlow Cust was created first Baron Brownlow of Belton in recognition of his father's service in the Speaker's Chair, honouring a deathbed promise made to Sir John. (*Oxford Dictionary of National Biography*, Oxford University Press, article 6974)

12 Cust Wherry, *Chronicles of Erthig*, Vol. 2, p. 118

**Fig 3 a)** *Portrait of Elizabeth Cust, later Mrs Philip Yorke*, by Francis Cotes. Oil on canvas, c.1770. Erddig (given to the National Trust in 1973 by Philip Yorke III). © National Trust / Susanne Gronnow.

**Fig 3 b)** *Portrait of Anne Cust, later Mrs Jacob Reynardson*, by Francis Cotes. Oil on canvas, c.1770. Present whereabouts unknown.

great-grandparents, Anne Cust of Belton House and Jacob Reynardson, who had grown up nearby at Holywell Hall, took place at Erddig in Wales.

After the wedding, at which 'They all behaved very well — no tears shed[13]', the couple honeymooned for a month at Erddig and then left 'to make a visit to the Old Gentleman at Holywell' — Jacob's father Samuel, who must have been too old and infirm to make the journey to Wales, although he did survive for another twenty years, dying in 1797 at the age of ninety-three. While Samuel Reynardson was still alive, his son and daughter-in-law lived in London, perhaps to escape the old man's dismay as, instead of sons to continue the family name, Anne produced '<u>only</u> five daughters'! The eldest, Etheldred Anne (her distinctive first name came from her maternal grandmother, Etheldred Payne) was born in 1778; she and her sisters, Katherine, Jemima, Elizabeth and Lucy (who died at the age of four in 1789, the only child not to live to adulthood) were all baptised in the church of St George the Martyr, Queen Square, just round the corner from Great Ormond Street where the family lived.

13   Letter from Lady Brownlow (wife of the newly-ennobled Brownlow Cust — see footnote 10) to her mother, 26 September 1775 [sic], (*Chronicles of Erthig*, Vol. 2, pp. 192–3). The date of Jacob's and Anne's wedding, and also of this letter, is incorrectly given; other letters quoted in the book make it clear that Anne was still unmarried in 1776, and a label on the reverse of the photograph of her portrait at Erddig states that she was married there in 1777.

*The Reynardsons were never as assiduous in their letter-writing as the Birches (or if they were, the letters have not survived), so we know about their married life largely through the testimony of others and cannot be certain exactly when they first became friendly with my ancestors on the Birch side. However it does seem likely that the catalyst was Thomas Birch, whose friendship with both the Yorkes and the Custs would have meant that there would have been many family occasions providing opportunities for members of the younger generation to meet.*

*Thomas's own connection with the Yorkes remained close: he continued to help the family in many ways, securing seats in the Chester Fly for the Yorke boys travelling between Wrexham and school at Eton in the 1780s, and writing chatty colloquial letters to his friend's motherless children, including one in 1784 describing his awe on his first sighting of a hot air balloon.[14] According to A. L. Cust Wherry's book, Thomas also married and by the early nineteenth century (when the household is mentioned in John William Birch's letter, **4:5**) he had moved to Newman Street, London. A letter from there to Philip Yorke's eldest son Simon, dated 5 January 1808, jokes about the infamous Lady Hamilton (lover of the late Admiral Lord Nelson) and tells an anecdote about his recently-deceased brother George Birch, late of Hamstead Hall[15].*

\* \* \*

*Thomas's cousins, the four surviving children of James Birch after his wife's death in 1749, do not appear to have caused their father so much anxiety. The eldest, my great-great-great-grandfather George (born 1733), was the first of his generation to take the well-trodden path of Cambridge followed by admission to one of the Inns of Court (in his case, the Middle rather than the Inner Temple). His brother James entered the church and thereafter, like his married sister Sarah, disappears from our family history; the youngest child, Jane (known as 'Jenny'), died in 1764, aged only twenty-two.*

*In 1751, the same year as his son George matriculated, James Birch was appointed as Receiver-General for Warwickshire and Coventry, an ancient office which is now defunct in the UK (although it still exists in Canada) but which in the eighteenth century carried numerous responsibilities. Chief amongst these was the collection of taxes or rents on behalf of the government; documents presented by my father to Coventry Archives in 1960[16] include lists of separate commissions made by James between 1754 and his death in 1772 totalling many thousands of pounds, and ranging from bonds for taxes to help with the completion of the building of Somerset House, to the collection of houses, windows*

---

14 Cust Wherry, *Chronicles of Erthig*, Vol. 2, p. 226
15 Cust Wherry (as above), p. 275
16 PA 309.

*and lights taxes. Another of his responsibilities, according to* **3: 3** *and* **3: 4** *below, seems to have been some involvement in the financing of parliamentary elections.*

*The election of 1761 was the first to be held in the reign of the new king, George III, who was keen to put his own stamp on his government and bring to an end the decades-long Whig monopoly. He therefore lifted the conventional proscription on the employment of Tories in government, and before the spring election he prevented the Prime Minister, the Duke of Newcastle, from using public money to fund the election of Whig candidates. This did not achieve the desired effect, as Newcastle simply used his private fortune to ensure that his ministry gained a comfortable majority.*

*The election has been described as one of the most undemocratic in British history, with only about a hundred (out of a total of 558) seats being contested. One of these was Coventry, which at the time returned two members. The Hon. Andrew Archer (1736–78), son of Thomas Archer, first Baron Archer, who was at the time Recorder of Coventry, was invited to stand, but as the seat was to be contested, he decided to hedge his bets by also standing for the constituency of Bramber, which had earlier been held by his father. In the event, he was returned for both but chose to sit for Coventry, and held the seat until 1768 when he succeeded his father to the peerage as Lord Archer.*

*It is not altogether clear whether the two letters written to James Birch are from Lord Archer or from his son, the newly-elected Member of Parliament*[17]; *the address makes the former more likely, as Thomas (Lord) Archer was a nephew of the Baroque architect of the same name and may therefore have inherited the house in Grosvenor Square which was designed and built in the 1720s by his uncle. As well as containing much of topical interest, both letters reveal the intriguing information that James Birch must have married again, for the third time, at some stage in the intervening twelve years since Jane's death in 1749*[18].

---

17   It was a busy year for the younger Archer, as earlier in the summer he married Sarah, the daughter of James West, the Whig member for St Albans and one of Newcastle's most loyal supporters.
18   We have no record of any remarriage in the family papers. However, the record of James Birch's death, which took place on 11 December 1772 in Wolston, Warwickshire (a few miles from Coventry), is consistent with an entry in the Victoria County History for the same parish, in which it is stated that 'In 1760 Elizabeth Baker presented [the rectory and advowson of Wolston] in trust for Susanna, wife of James Birch, who is probably identical with the Mrs (Susanna) Hubert named as patron about this time.' L. F. Salzmann (ed.), *History of the County of Warwick: Vol. 6: Knightlow hundred* (Victoria County History, 1951), accessed on British History Online.

**LETTER 3 :3** (Thomas, Lord Archer [*or his son, the Hon. Andrew Archer*], Grosvenor Square, London, to Mr (James) Birch, dated 18 August, 1761)

> Gros: Square
> 18 Aug: 1761

Dear Sir —

I did not hear till very lately, that Mr Corbitt had not paid you the last hundred pounds, that you furnished him with, & was very much surpris'd at it, this I attribute to his having been very ill since the Election, & scarce fit for buisness [*sic*]; if you will be pleas'd to let me know who I shall pay it to, I will forthwith do it, with great thanks.

I came to town yesterday about some buisness [*sic*], to find every body mad about the King's wedding & the Coronation, it is supposed that the wedding will be next week[19].

Peace is little talk'd of but may not be farr of [?far off], but I hear that the French agree to nothing but that the Rivers St Laurence [Lawrence] & Missisippi shall be the Boundaries of our Territories in North America & that we are to restore everything else. I can't think those terms will be agreed to[20].

I hope this will find you, Mrs Birch, & all your family in perfect health, & desire their acceptance of my best compliments. I am

>> Dear Sir
>>> Your Obedient Humble Servant
>>> Archer

19  After George III's accession to the throne in October 1760, the search for a suitable bride for the twenty-two year old King began. Colonel Graeme, an envoy sent to various European royal courts, reported the charms of Princess Charlotte of Mecklenburg-Strelitz (aged seventeen). Although he had not met her, George announced his intention to marry her to his Council in July 1761 and the Lord Chancellor (Lord Hardwicke) was despatched to Mecklenburg to solicit her hand in the King's name. The notion that the wedding would take place before the end of August was premature, as the party (which included the future General William Harcourt, then aged seventeen, accompanying his father, the first Earl Harcourt) which would escort the Princess to England had not yet arrived in Germany.

20  The Seven Years' War (1756–63) is generally regarded as the first 'world' or global war. In Europe, the alliances which had prevailed in the War of the Austrian Succession (see Chapter 2) were reversed, as Britain, Prussia and Hanover took sides against France, Austria and Russia. The related hostilities in North America and India were more to do with Britain's determination to protect its colonies and seize those belonging to France, and to eliminate France as a commercial rival. By 1761, the British forces were firmly in the ascendant in Canada, following the shattering defeat of the French at the Battle of the Plains of Abraham outside Quebec in September 1759, when the British army's heroic commander, General James Wolfe, was mortally wounded. As Archer predicted, the terms put forward by the French to conclude the war were not deemed acceptable and before peace could be agreed, France was compelled to relinquish its interests in Canada to Britain. However, when the American colonies rose in revolt against Britain twelve years later, it was with French military support that they eventually gained their independence.

**Letter 3:4 (Thomas, Lord Archer [*or his son, the Hon. Andrew Archer*], Grosvenor Square, London, to Mr (James) Birch, dated 1 September, 1761)**

> Gros: Square
> 1st Sep: 1761

Dear Sir —

I herewith send you the Bank's receipt for the hundred pounds, that I have placed to your account in their Books, which I should have sent sooner, but Mr Hoare's people[21] did not transmit it to me, before this morning.

The town is very full, in expectation of seeing the King's Wedding, & our intended Queen who, it's apprehended, suffers greatly by the tediousness of the Voyage[22]. Most people are of [the] opinion that Lord Anson got out to Sea on Friday morning, when the wind was fair; if that was the case, it's thought he would not return to Stadt [*Stade*], tho' the wind changed that night, but that he would endeavour to land in England or Scotland, at the first place he could, so we may soon hear of her in the north.

I hope this will find you, Mrs Birch, & all your family in perfect health, & desire yours & their acceptance of mine & Mr Archer's best compliments, I am

> Dear Sir
> Your Faithfull & Oblig'd Humble Servant
> Archer

*At least one of James Birch's children went to London for the Coronation of King George III and Queen Charlotte, an occasion of such excitement and celebration that it was said that London did not sleep for several days. We know of Jane (Jenny) Birch's presence in the capital at this time through her entries in a pair of cashbooks* (**Fig. 3 c**)) *which include*

---

21 C. Hoare & Co is the oldest bank in the UK, having been founded in 1672, and claims to be the sole survivor of the many private deposit banks which were established in the seventeenth and eighteenth centuries. It has been run by eleven successive generations of the Hoare family, since 1690 in premises on Fleet Street.

22 Lord Anson (1697–1762), Admiral of the Fleet, who had sailed to Germany with a squadron of British yachts and warships to escort Princess Charlotte to England, encountered such bad weather that the voyage took nine days instead of the usual three. Although all her attendants were seasick, the Princess herself enjoyed the voyage, amusing herself by playing the harpsichord. Anson eventually decided to anchor off Harwich instead of going on to Greenwich as planned; after landing the next morning (7 September) the Princess was taken in easy stages to St James's Palace and the wedding took place the next day. The even more eagerly anticipated joint Coronation was held a fortnight later in Westminster Abbey.

Left: **Fig 3 c)** A page from one of Jane Birch's cashbooks, September 1761.
Right: **Fig 3 d)** Tailor's Bill (William Drake, Tailor, to James Birch, Esq.) for Servants' Livery, March to May 1770.

*her expenditure for the whole of 1761. Evidently Jenny was normally a more frugal and careful girl than her mother at the same age (see* **1: 6** *to* **1: 10**) — *in a typical month she would spend no more than a pound on items such as 'a yard of ribon' (£0-0s-7d) and 'for washing a Gown' (£0-1s-3d), or on good works: 'for ye Sacrament' (£0-2s-0d) and 'to a pore Woman' (£0-0s-6d) — but in September 1761 she threw caution to the winds. Her carefully itemised list of expenses conveys something of the gaiety of the time, in which we can picture her donning her new 'Hatt' (£0-5s-0d), 'a fan' (£0-12s-0d) and 'a pair of Earrings' (£0-9s-0d) and adorning herself with flowers (£0-10s-6d), before sallying forth to enjoy 'two Plays' (£0-10s-6d) or the opera, equipped with 'an Opera book' (£0-1s-6d), going to hear the 'Showman' (£0-2s-6d) and attending the famous pleasure gardens at Ranelagh (£0-2s-6d). To watch the Coronation procession itself cost her a shilling. In total Jenny spent well over three pounds on Coronation-related expenses alone, which would have far exceeded her means if her father had not been prepared to indulge her: at the end of August, she records receiving 'of Papa' the sum of £1-11s-6d; a slightly more generous amount followed at the end of September; and on 23 December, presumably as a Christmas present, she was given 'a Banknote' to the princely value of £20-0s-0d. Her modest expenditure contrasts with the amount her father needed to spend on servants' livery alone* (**Fig. 3 d)**), *in order to maintain the standards expected of a man in his position.*

*It is sad to reflect that Jenny was to live for only two more years and would never know any of her nephews and nieces. James himself lived long enough to see his elder son George married to Mary Newell*[23] *in 1770 and the birth of at least one grandchild (George and Mary's first-born son James in 1771). But he died the year before the birth of the third Thomas Birch to feature in this chapter, who is in many ways the pivotal figure of our family history. Not only did this Thomas produce the whole Birch Reynardson dynasty through his marriage to Etheldred Reynardson (eldest daughter of Jacob Reynardson and Anne Cust) in 1806, but we have more letters and other documentation associated with him than for any other member of the family, including records of his service in the Army throughout the long period of the French Revolutionary and Napoleonic Wars.*

\* \* \*

*Thomas Birch (later Thomas Birch Reynardson) was born in 1773, the second son of George and Mary Birch. In addition to his elder brother James, he had three younger*

---

23  The history of the Newell connection, and the complicated process by which their family home of Adwell came into our family, is explained in Chapter 9.

*siblings: John William, born in 1775; George Edward, who was born the following year and died at the age of eighteen in 1794; and Mary, born in 1778. We know that near the beginning of their marriage George and Mary settled in St Leonard's Hill, close to Windsor, where their neighbours included General Harcourt (brother of Earl Harcourt and commander of the 16th Light Dragoon Guards in the American War of Independence) and the King's brother, Prince William of Gloucester, but comparatively little else is known about Thomas's early life; at some stage after 1814 he jotted down a summary of his life and career up to that point, but his record differs puzzlingly in a number of ways from other documented information. In Thomas's account, he states that*

> Between 7 & 8, I went to school with a Clergyman who took a few Boys —
> there I remained 7 or 8 years —
> Next I went to a French House for a year —
> Afterwards to the University at Glasgow for 2 Sessions.
> At 19 went to Oxford — for a Year.

*The Register of Pupils of Eton College however tells a different story, recording that, like his brothers James and John (but not George), Thomas spent several years there as a pupil, a detail inexplicably omitted from any of his later recollections or memoranda. Perhaps his experience there had been unhappy; it is certainly true that, when the time came to select a school for his eldest son Charles, it was Charterhouse, not Eton, which was his first choice (see* Chapter 7*). The Eton College records do not mention his further study at any university, but this is hardly a detail which Thomas would have invented and the dates given by Eton for his attendance there (1790 to 1793) must surely be incorrect as that would imply that he did not leave the school until he was nearly twenty, allowing no time for him to have attended university before enlisting immediately after the outbreak of the French Revolutionary War.*

*If we take Thomas's version of events to be the more accurate, it does indicate that neither the Army nor the Law (unlike James and John, both of whom were admitted to the Middle Temple in 1794 and 1795 respectively, though John later migrated to the Inner Temple) was his first choice of profession. Perhaps he had intended to enter the Church, the traditional path for a second son, but if that were the case the University of Glasgow would have been a curious choice as since the beginning of the century it had been required to conform to the newly-established Presbyterian Church of Scotland. Thomas's mention of his year in a 'French House' is intriguing because of its timing; given his age, his stay must have taken place very shortly before the French Revolution in 1789 or may even have coincided with it. Events on the Continent unfolded with*

**Fig 3 e)** *Portrait of Thomas Birch (1773–1847) in the uniform of the 16th Light Dragoons,* artist unknown. Oil on canvas.

*frightening rapidity during the early 1790s. Britain and the Dutch Republic had initially maintained a neutral policy towards the revolution, but that was to change with the execution of the deposed French King Louis XVI on 21 January 1793. France's declaration of war on Great Britain and the Dutch Republic, which followed on 1 February, galvanised Thomas into an immediate decision and by the end of that month he had enlisted as a cornet in the 16th Light Dragoons (**Fig. 3 e**)). Britain and France were to remain at war with each other for an almost unbroken twenty-two years.*

*From early in 1793 onwards, a coalition of states consisting of the Dutch Republic, Imperial Austria, Great Britain, Prussia, Hanover and Hesse mobilised military forces all along the French frontiers with Flanders, with the intention to invade Revolutionary France and unseat the French First Republic. Despite beginning with some early successes, the outcome of the Flanders campaign was disastrous for the Allies; though greatly outnumbered, the French armies had revolutionary fervour on their side and over the summer of 1794 forced the Dutch, Austrian and Anglo-Hanoverian forces into retreat. By October, the King's son the Duke of York[24], who had commanded the British forces since the outbreak of hostilities, was recalled, to be replaced by General Harcourt. It was around this time that Thomas left for the Continent to join his regiment, which by now had retreated into Westphalia in the northern Rhineland region. Over the icy winter, as Holland was taken over by revolutionaries who proclaimed the pro-French Batavian Republic, the British army retreated further into Germany, eventually reaching Bremen from which they were finally evacuated in the spring of 1795, with the exception of a smaller force which remained in Europe in the service of the Prussian King.*

*It was generally felt that the campaign had exposed serious weaknesses in the British army after years of neglect. There are no surviving records of Thomas's thoughts after his first experience of active service, but some conclusions may be drawn from the decisions he took with regard to the development of his professional role and from the admiration he was later to express repeatedly for those responsible for modernising and reforming the army. However, we do have the diary he kept during the next phase of the campaign. The main purpose of the expedition which returned to the Baltic in September 1795 seems to have been the evacuation of the part of the British army which had been left in Bremen five months earlier[25]; if there was an underlying intention to open a new front from the east, it was never put into operation and no attempt was made to engage the French.*

---

24  The nursery rhyme *The Grand Old Duke of York* is sometimes said to have originated from this campaign, unfairly stigmatizing the Duke of York as an incompetent dilettante.

25  Prussia, one of Britain's original allies in the First Coalition, had in the intervening period withdrawn from the conflict with France under the terms of the Peace of Basel; this may have made the continuing presence of a British army in the region of Hanover (which bordered Prussia) not only unnecessary but actually dangerous, since Prussia had also secretly recognised French control of the west bank of the Rhine.

*Thomas was not nearly as eloquent in his diary as he was to become in his letters (see those from Egypt in Chapter 4 and from the Netherlands in Chapter 5) and so I have only included a selection of his brief and matter-of-fact entries from the beginning and end of the expedition and have omitted nearly the whole of his record of the army's encampment and exercises during its three-months' stay on the German mainland. Those entries which remain provide a valuable record of everyday army routine. At the age of twenty-two, Thomas demonstrates leadership qualities beyond his years and his particular concern for the well-being of the horses in his care is already evident. His daily obsession with recording the wind and weather conditions is a reminder that armies and navies alike were at the mercy of the elements, and that — as Thomas found during his last weeks in the mouth of the Elbe, when a court martial or the discovery of an 'improper' verse left anonymously on deck must have been welcome distractions — the necessity of waiting for exactly the right wind direction could cause monotonous delays of weeks or even months.*

---

### 3:5 (Selected extracts from the diary of Captain Thomas Birch, 16th Light Dragoons, written during expedition to north-west Germany, August 1795 to March 1796)

27th August 1795, Thursday. Sail'd on board ye Mary Ann with 2 Horses for Hamburgh* (*on facing page:* *We had 4 Cabin passengers & 30 Hanoverian Soldiers, who had been Prisoners in France & were sent to Chatham, most of them had been wounded.) Anchor'd at ye Nore [...]

28th. Friday. Return'd at 6 O'clock [...] on Board — sail'd at 11 O'clock in company with 24 Merchantmen bound to ye Baltic under convoy of a Frigate & two smaller Ships of War. The Wind blew fresh & owing to some mismanagement in ye Stables a most disagreeable circumstance happen'd. The Horses slip'd off their feet, kicked most violently, broke thro' the Stables & one fell backwards on ye Deck. We conceived they must have been overboard & I had given them up, but the Dragoon I had on Board, with great activity & resolution, caught his halter & turn'd him round. This Horse recover'd his legs & from fear stood quiet. The other lay for some time in a dangerous posture but after much exertion he got up. — The Carpenter refitted the Stables & we got ye Horses in again in a better situation than they were before. [...]

29th. Saturday. At 2 or 3 in ye Morning [I] thought my horses were kicking, got up [&] went on Deck — it was a false alarm — so return'd to bed & slept well till 7.— [...] At 12 O'clock got under weigh [...] A French brig Privateer came in sight with national colours below ye English, as she seem'd to be a Prize just taken. The Frigate fired a Gun to bring her to [...] — A Fresh breeze sprung up from ye South [...] remarkably fine night — at 11 O'clock pass'd Orfordness light houses on ye Coast of Suffolk. [...]

30th. Sunday. [...] out of sight of Land. On board Ship one is too apt to disregard Sunday. One of ye Convoy took an American prize, laden with Lump & Iron bound to France. [...]

31st. Monday. The day passed in perpetual anxiety thro' fear of an Enemy, every fresh sail creating fresh alarms, but our Frigate got intelligence that ye Russian Fleet was out, which in a great measure eased our Apprehensions. [...]

2nd [September]. Wensday [sic]. Strong gales from ye East directly against us, which obliged us to tack without gaining a point. I was very ill & in bed the whole day. Indeed this sort of travelling did not suit any of us, for ye Poor Hanoverian Soldiers were no less Sufferers.

4th. Friday. [...] in ye afternoon the wind changed to ye South West & for ye first time for 5 days we made some way towards Hamburgh.—

5th. Saturday. This morning we were much rejoiced at seeing Hyling Land [?Helgoland], a very small Island about 8 Leagues from ye Elbe [... *where*] it is usual to take Pilots into ye Elbe, ye Passage being at certain seasons very dangerous.

6th. Sunday. [...] A Packet pass'd us for Yarmouth & I made an attempt to put a letter on board but ye stupid German I had given it to neglected it. The wind was right fair for England & this opportunity lost might make a delay of a week or more. [...]

7th. Monday. This morning the tide carried us within 5 Miles of Gluckstadt where we were obliged again to Anchor till ye next tide. The day being particularly fine, I prevail'd upon my Friend, [...] a German, [...] to go on Shore & accompany me thither on Foot, that I might see ye Country; to set foot on any land, after being what I thought too long on board Ship, would be pleasant. [...] I was much struck with ye neatness & comfortable appearance of ye Farm Houses [...] [&] had occasion to go into one of them. It was ye height of ye Harvest Season & the Peasants were at dinner; I partook of what was going & was pleased with ye cleanliness of ye Inhabitants. [...]

The Town belongs to Danemark & is Garrison'd with Danish Troops; it is not handsome in appearance, but ye Inhabitants look cheerful & happy. It is in ye Province of Holstein. [...] In ye Afternoon went on Board a Danish Frigate, from thence to our Ship which was obliged to Anchor within 5 Miles of Staade [Stade] […]

8th. Tuesday. At Staade we landed ye Hanoverian Soldiers, & it occurred to me that it would be better to disembark my Horses here […]

9th. Wednesday. […] Disembarked my Horses at 6 […], well, but much bruised. Lodged them at a Farm House. Went afterwards to Stade, found the Town full of Troops of every description & all Nations. […]

13th. Sunday. […] Set off for Bremen in a post waggon, which answers to our post chaises, & is worse than any one could have conception of. […] Here one must not expect to meet with ye comfort of an English Inn — But One Englishman is generally remarkably well received, amid the Smoke of this […] Lazy people, who are always lounging about with their pipes in their mouths.

14th. Monday. Arrived at Bremen, went to Head Quarters at Delmenhorst to dinner with Col. Don & Capt. Harcourt[26].

16th. Wednesday. Came to Camp at Teddinghausen [Thedinghausen] about 18 Miles from Bremen, where ye Light Brigade & 2 Regts of Hussars are encamp'd. Slepd [slept] on a temporary Straw bed. […]

27th. Sunday. […] Paid a wager with Butler of 5 Guineas that the Light Brigade were not in England by Xmas day. […]

7th [*October*] Wednesday. […] Foot Parade & exercise in ye Morning. Afterwards I ran my Highflyer[27] against Capt. Payne's Mare & beat her.

14th. Wednesday. Fair. The Light Brigade gave a Dinner to Ld. Cathcart on ye Establishment of ye Lt Brigade Club to be held in England. 58 Officers were present — I was one of ye 4 Stewards. We had 2 Bands of Music […]

15th. Thursday […] A Field Day in ye presence of Genl. Dundas[28], Commander in Chief. The officers had rather it had been any other day […]

20th. Tuesday. […] I agreed to be off ye Bet with Butler about going to England. […]

---

26 Colonel George Don, later General Sir George Don (1756–1832), was amongst those who remained in Europe after the evacuation of the bulk of the British army in April 1795. He was seconded to the Prussian court as a liaison officer and may have co-ordinated espionage activities against France during this period. Captain Harcourt was General Harcourt's son (see Chapter 4).

27 See Chapter 4 (**4: 18**).

28 General David Dundas (1735–1820) remained in Bremen as commander of the British forces (mainly cavalry) left behind in April 1795 after the rest of the army had been evacuated. He was a strong advocate of officer training in the British Army well before the establishment of the staff training college in 1799 and wrote many manuals on the subject. At the age of seventy-four, he was appointed Commander-in-Chief of the Forces, holding the office from 1809 to 1811 during the Duke of York's period of disgrace following a scandal caused by the activities of his latest mistress, Mary Anne Clarke.

22nd. Thursday. […] Ye Regiments were mustered, rec'd intelligence that ye French had cross'd ye Rhine. […]

28th. Wednesday. […] The 7th & 11th Regiments march'd into Cantonments [*temporary winter quarters*] across ye Weser. The 15th & 16th had a Field day, & were review'd by General Count Walmoden[29] who express'd himself much pleased with their Conduct. […]

Novr. 1st. Sunday. Very fine. Unlike ye Custom in England, we went out with ye Hounds, belonging to a Gentleman at Hoya; not much to our credit as Sportsmen. We had Hounds & Greyhounds, Poynters [pointers] & 7 Guns, according to ye Custom of ye Country. […]

2nd [*December*] Wednesday. Thaw. […] received orders to March for Stade & embark ye 5th Decr.

5th. Saturday, hard frost. I march'd with half ye Regiment at 4 O'clock thro' Stade to embark at Twelingfleth [Twielenfleth] — we arrived at ye above place at 9 by ye worst roads I ever saw, began embarking about 10 & were all on board before 12. — I dined with Captain Popham [*see* Chapter 5] & returned on board ye Lynx Transport at Night.

8th. Tuesday. Wind north east. In ye afternoon we drop'd down ye River about 2 leagues.

13th. Sunday. Frost. Wind E. N. E. Ye Signal was fired from ye Commodore for all Ships to be ready to get under Weigh […]

23rd. Wednesday, Wind W., blew hard. This day was mark'd by a Melancholy circumstance.— A Master of a Ship with 4 Men (belonging to ye Fleet) were overset in our sight by carrying too much sail in ye boat. The Master & 2 Men were drown'd. […]

25th. Friday. Wind N. W. by N. Blew hard. We little expected to pass our Christmas day in ye Elbe, & much less wish'd it. The Wind was so high that our boat drifted in ye Morning towards Stadt but luckily return'd at night. […] I dined with ye Master & Mate of ye Ship.— The Moon was at ye full & we went to bed in hopes of a favourable change of wind.

29th. Tuesday. Wind W: very heavy Gales. The Wind blew so hard to day that we did not venture from ye Ship. […]

2nd. [*January 1796*] Saturday, Wind S. W. Squally. This Morning went to Gluckstadt for Provisions; in going, a sudden squall had nearly laid ye boat into ye Water & upset it, but luckily ye Sheet was let go in time. — I heard to day

---

29  Johann von Wallmoden-Gimborn, the Hanoverian military commander.

ye Melancholy news of ye Master & [*7 crossed out*] 3 Hands (Lt Dragoons 11th Regiment) belonging to ye Kingston being drown'd close by their own ship last night after leaving ye Frigate. […]

4th. Monday. Wind W. […] Received an order to send to ye Commanding Officer an account of all ye Provisions that had been deliver'd above ye printed instructions. Ye Captain of ye Ship got drunk & behaved extremely ill.

6th. Wednesday. Wind W. […] We smoked ye between decks & wash'd ye Horses' mangers with Vinegar. Tho' above a Month on board, ye Horses were all well.

11th. Monday. Wind S. E. Clear. This Morning a Gun from ye Frigate to prepare to sail. I went on Shore, the Frost broke — in ye Evening Wind to ye South.

13th. Wednesday. Wind W. This Morning I left ye Fleet […] on board ye Friendly Cutter for Hamburgh. We got to Altona about dark — & had great difficulty in finding an Inn to lodge for ye Night.

14th. Thursday. Fine weather. This Morning we walk'd from Altona to Hamburgh, about 17 Miles. […] We got lodgings at ye London Hotel, good but extravagant.— We dined at Theodore's (a Restorative [*sic*]) & were much amused at ye French Play in ye Evening.

15th. Friday. We walk'd about ye town to buy Articles that ye Town was famous for — received an account of ye taking of Ceylon. Dined at Theodore's & to ye Play in ye Evening.[…]

18th. Monday. This Morning we left Hamburgh but could fetch no further than Blankinasse [Blankenese]. Went on Shore & with difficulty got put up for ye Night.

19th. Tuesday. […] The Wind being contrary, we remained at Blankinasse. Walked a few Miles into ye Country which is beautiful, in particular Situations from one Hill you can see 20, 30 & 40 Miles — N; E; S; & W; which is very uncommon — The River Elbe from Hamburgh further than Stade — Hanover & Danemark. […]

22nd. Friday. […] The Wind at Night was South E; & gave us hopes of getting off.—

23rd. Saturday. Wind S. W. The wind return'd to its old Quarter. I stay'd on board ye whole day. […]

31st. Sunday. Wind S. & S & by E. This Morning on going on deck I found a Song nail'd to ye Stern of ye long boat of an improper tendency. Went on board ye Prince of Wales & about ye fleet to discover ye Authors of it. […]

5th [*February*]. Friday. Wind S. S. E. This Morning a Signal from ye Frigate as preparation for sailing. I went on Shore to purchase Sea Stock. […] Received £6–5s from ye Paymaster on my Troop Account, which was expended in ye town ye same day.

6th. Saturday. Wind S. S. E. Owing to some circumstance unknown to us we did not sail this Morning tho' the Wind served. […] I attended a Court Martial on board ye Catharine from 8 O'clock till three. […] Captain Lane express'd his intention of sailing ye next Morning as ye Wind promised fair.

7th. Sunday. Wind S. E. This Morning at 4 O'clock ye Night Signal was fired from ye Frigate for ye Fleet to unmoor — at 7 another was fired for ye whole fleet to get under weigh, which we did at 8 O'clock — The Fleet consisted of upwards of 70 Sail of Transports — under convoy by ye Astrea & Vestal Frigates. We had but little wind & anchor'd off Cuxhaven at 4 O'clock.

8th. Monday, Wind S. E. Frosty. Our Ship drove about a Mile in ye Night but no bad consequence ensued. […]

10th. Wednesday. Wind N. E. During ye Whole Night it blew a violent gale of wind & tho' everything in ye Cabin had been lash'd, the Morning exhibited a Scene of ye greatest Confusion, almost every thing broke or out of its place. […]

11th. Thursday. Wind N. E. We drove all ye preceding Night during a most Violent gale of wind, the Ship rolling all ye time so that one could not stand, sit or walk.— most of ye Soldiers were sick.— but about six O'clock we were relieved by ye Wind abating […]

12th. Friday. Wind S. W. About 9 O'clock & very unexpectedly the Wind began to blow hard from ye S. W. & increased towards morning; […] we made ye Floating light of ye Coast of Norfolk about 7 O'clock. We […] drove till we came off Hasbro' [Happisburgh] where we came to an Anchor […] hoping for a change of wind to make Blackwall. We parted with ye Vestal Frigate in ye Morning, & miss'd some of our own Ships belonging to ye Fleet. […]

13th. Saturday. Wind W. The wind being directly in our teeth we made but little way during ye night […]

14th. Sunday. Wind N. W. We got under way about 9 O'clock & made ye Nore at 3, brought up off Southend at 5. Many English Ships of War & some Russian lying at ye Nore.

15th. Monday. Wind N. W. […] Anchor'd within a league of Gravesend, ran aground in ye night & were obliged to turn out all ye Men to heave ye Ship off. In the Morning we were stop'd at Gravesend with Orders to disembark there, instead of going on to Blackwall. […]

16th. Tuesday. This Morning at 6 O'clock we disembarked & began our March for Woolwich, Greenwich, Deptford & Lewisham at 1.— The Horses were so extremely fatigued that they fell by ye road & were obliged to be left […]We did not arrive in Quarters till 8 O'clock. From ye time of Embarkation in ye Elbe to ye time of our disembarkation, we had been 3 Months, all but three days.

* * *

*Thomas's first postings abroad had been uneventful, but not long after his return from Germany his career took a new and unconventional turn. A young officer, John Gaspard Le Marchant, who had commanded the 2nd Dragoon Guards in the field during the disastrous campaign in the Low Countries and then purchased a majority in the 16th Queen's Light Dragoons (Thomas's own regiment), had been appalled by the poor performance of the British cavalry in Flanders and by the professional ineptitude of staff officers. During the last few years of the century, Le Marchant designed a lighter, curved sabre for use in his regiment, which was soon widely adopted, and devised a more effective system of cavalry sword-exercise which he demonstrated to regular and reserve units throughout the country, insisting on rigorous training and mastery of tactics. At this time, no institution for the education of military officers existed in Britain, apart from the specialist instruction school for artillery officers at Woolwich. In 1798 Le Marchant began drafting a scheme for a national military college, despite initial lack of encouragement from the Duke of York (commander-in-chief of the army), who advised 'I can hardly recommend you to sacrifice your time and talents to a project which seems so very unlikely to succeed'.*[30]

*Nevertheless Le Marchant persisted in refining his ideas for 'An outline of a plan for a regular course of military instruction' for infantry and cavalry officers, and in May 1799 part of his plan became a reality with the opening of a staff training college, established at High Wycombe, with Le Marchant himself as commandant, and Thomas Birch amongst the first intake of trainees. This college was before long (see* **Chapter 4***) to become the nucleus of the Royal Military Academy at Sandhurst. It is an interesting reflection that when I attended Sandhurst for eight months in 1943, my training in military instruction and the responsibilities of an officer — which included physical fitness and man management, map-making and map-reading, efficiency with weapons, and combat strategy and tactics — was on very similar lines to that undergone by my great-great-grandfather at the National Military College in its very first year of operation.*

---

30  *Oxford Dictionary of National Biography* entry for John Gaspard Le Marchant (1766–1812), quoting from D. Le Marchant, *Memoirs of the late Major-General Le Marchant* (1841).

*Thomas is unlikely to have met Le Marchant during his earlier postings abroad, but would have known of him through the wide circulation of Le Marchant's treatises on sword exercises and cavalry tactics. They had shared a commanding officer in the person of General Sir William Harcourt (soon to be the first Governor of the Royal Military College after it received its warrant in June 1801), who was also a near neighbour of Thomas's parents in St Leonard's Hill, so it is probable that the initial contact came about through Harcourt. Thomas soon formed a lasting friendship with Le Marchant, with whom he corresponded until the latter's death, and never failed to acknowledge the professional debt he owed to him. Within months of completing his training at the staff college, Thomas was* 'the first Officer sent from that Establishment on Active Service'[31]*, when he was posted overseas to take part in a campaign which he later came to regard as the most formative experience of his life.*

---

31  From an undated memorandum by Thomas Birch Reynardson, reviewing his career from 1793 to his retirement from the service in 1814.

CHAPTER 4

# The Egyptian Campaign

*Letters and Maps 1800–1801*

'Our Success in this Country is a Miracle; [...]
this Army has gained immortal honor.'[1]

*As a member of the army which left England's south coast in the autumn of 1800, Major Thomas Birch (he had received his promotion in June 1799, just after the National Military College was opened) was well aware that its ultimate destination was widely rumoured to be Egypt. The Egyptian campaign of 1800–01 is not much mentioned in general accounts of the French Revolutionary and Napoleonic Wars, perhaps because it has been overshadowed by a succession of celebrated British naval victories during the 1790s and early 1800s[2]. In my view, the operation has been sidelined undeservedly, as the Battle of Alexandria in March 1801 was up to that time the most decisive British military victory of the war which had begun eight years earlier; the conclusion of the campaign later in 1801 succeeded in its objective of driving the French forces out of Egypt, which they had occupied since 1798, and in restoring the country to Ottoman rule.*

*Thomas was not to return to England for about fifteen months. We have a large collection of letters which Thomas wrote to members of his family in England, as well as some of their replies, during this period and although it is clear from their content that there were many more which have not survived (or which never even reached their destination), those which remain provide a remarkably complete account of the way the whole campaign was conducted. Of equal interest to me are the letters he received from military colleagues which eventually reached him in Egypt, notably those from Lt. Colonel John Le Marchant (**4: 11** and **4: 12**), the founder of the College, and from General Sir William Harcourt (**4: 22**), Thomas's former commanding officer.*

---

1  Letter from Thomas Birch, near Rosetta, Egypt, to his brother James Birch, 3 August, 1801 (**4: 21**).
2  In 1798 Napoleon invaded Egypt, seizing Alexandria and defeating the Mamluks (the Ottoman military caste) at the Battle of the Pyramids. Napoleon's aim to protect French trade interests and undermine Britain's access to India by establishing a foothold in the Middle East received an abrupt setback at the Battle of the Nile in August 1798. In this epic naval battle, fought at night, only two ships of the line and two frigates out of a total of thirteen French ships which had carried the invading army to Egypt escaped Nelson's relentless assault in the Bay of Aboukir. Although the French remained in possession of Egypt, without a fleet Napoleon's army was stranded. Napoleon himself soon returned to France, leaving Egypt under the command of his deputy, General Kléber. Within a few months, Napoleon overthrew the Directoire and was elected as First Consul, making him effectively the ruler of France.

*His first few letters show that the Egyptian campaign began uneventfully with a long sea voyage hampered by autumnal gales, a trying experience for Thomas who was no sailor, as could be seen from his diary (3: 5) five years earlier. The troop ships put in at Gibraltar, home port of the Mediterranean fleet, and then at Malta, whose two-year occupation by the French had ended less than four months earlier after a determined blockade by the British navy, and whose inhabitants were only too ready to have a chance to revenge themselves against their oppressors. On the first day of 1801, the fleet which had left England in mid-November dropped anchor in the Bay of Marmorice off Turkey and began the frustrating and nerve-wracking wait, extending to several weeks, for reinforcements and equipment with which to make their landing on Egypt's coast.*

---

### LETTER 4:1 (Thomas Birch, at Plymouth, to his brother John William Birch, London, dated 7 November, 1800)

Stonehouse, Plymouth Docks, November 7th 1800

My dear John,

[...] Our orders are at last come for embarking the Troops here & sailing immediately but it blows so hard a gale of wind from ye S.W. that nothing can be done. It is a sad time of year for a Sea Voyage but a few days will take us into another Latitude & we shall at least have it warmer. [...]

Entre nous it is disturbing to hear how Ferrol[3] is talk'd about & the Captains of the Navy with whom I am in ye habits of living talk'd about it without disguise, indeed I have seen many who were there — they tell you the Spaniards never meant to defend it, & that they were walking about with the keys in their hand to deliver to any body who might ask for them. I do not take for Gospel all they say — Sir J. P.[4] it seems is to be tried & then we may form a just Opinion.

10th Novr. / Since I began this letter I have rec'd yours & my Mother's joint performance. The wind has moderated & we expect to sail today or morrow. [...]

I am your Affectionate Brother
<u>In haste</u>, T. Birch

3  A reference to the failed British attempt to capture the naval station of El Ferrol, N.W. Spain, from the Spanish in August, 1800. It was followed by an equally unsuccessful expedition against the port of Cadiz on the south coast.
4  Lt. General Sir James Pulteney was the army commander in charge of the attempt to effect a landing of troops.

**Fig. 4 a)** *Portrait of Sir Ralph Abercromby*, by John Hoppner, RA. Oil on canvas, *c.*1787. National Galleries of Scotland.

Novr ye 14th, Saturday —

I open this letter again to say as we have not sail'd you may as well have it, we have been detain'd to carry stores to ye Ships to ye Mediterranean which have suffered but not to ye extent mention'd by the Papers.

Lord Craven is arrived, he has been here some days & brings intelligence that the Armies have separated — that Sir Ralph[5] [**Fig. 4a)**] is gone up ye Mediterranean with all ye Troops for general service, & that Sir J. Pulteney is gone to Lisbon. We are waiting for ye Wind now & nothing can be [a] more provoking experience — pray write me a line — by return of post. It appears to me from the arrangement with Sir Ralph that we must be going to Egypt — God bless you.

5   Sir Ralph Abercromby (1734–1801), commander of British troops in the Mediterranean.

**Letter 4:2 (Thomas Birch, at Gibraltar, to his mother Mrs Mary Birch, at Windsor, dated 29 November, 1800[6])**

Gibralter [*sic*] Novr. 29<sup>th</sup> 1800.

We sail tomorrow morning, therefore in haste tonight —

[…] After a passage of about 12 days we anchor'd here this Morning, tho' we did experience a violent gale & <u>some</u> of ye horrors attending with most of ye <u>inconveniences</u>, — but how much were we repaid on anchoring in Gibralter bay this morning. The Climate much as in May, not a Cloud to be seen, & the grandeur of ye Scene with a quietness & calmness at ye same time that fill'd ye mind with a Sensation that few situations can occasion. We got on shore about 9 with the disposition to enjoy everything that occurred; but indeed I can say with truth that my mind was doom'd to be damp'd; the very first person we met told us of a sad event, that they had this morning lost a fine young Man — yes my dear Mother, Col: Houstoun whom you have often heard me mention dyed here this Morning, he came here with ye Army of Sir J. Pulteney, & has been ill past all hopes since, I say nothing of ye <u>circumstances</u> of his disorder, but poor fellow they originated in himself, & neglect of it […]. He was a very fine young man & a good Officer, & had just got ye Command of ye Rifle Corps which he enjoy'd — it was a damper indeed. — But enough of so melancholy a subject, the variety of ye scenery every moment created new Ideas, the rock is wonderful; the Inhabitants many of them, what one had not seen. I call'd on ye Governor General O'Hara, with whom I dined, & walked in a garden of <u>Orange</u> Trees, Grapes, &c &c […]

You will like to know that Frank[7] is to me a <u>valuable</u>; he is a good & faithful Servant & shall not repent it, please God! I have it in my Power to reward him; [*he*] has begged, today, that I would request you would advance to his wife part of his wages.— he thinks of her as he should do.

[…] God bless you all.
Your Dutiful Son<br><u>T Birch</u>

You will be kind enough to mention me with proper respect to General & Mrs Harcourt, & tell ye General that General O'Hara ask'd after him.

---

6  A Foreign Office stamp on the letter indicates that it arrived in England on 1 January, 1801.
7  Frank Burnham, his soldier-servant, who continued in his service long after both had retired.

**LETTER 4:3 (Thomas Birch, at Malta, to his brother John William Birch, London, dated 20 December, 1800)**

Malta. 20th December 1800

My dear John,

Having a little more time than I at first expected I will give you a more particular Account of our Situation as a military point of view & nothing else.

The Army is on board & to sail from here the first wind, to rendezvous in ye Gulf of Macri off Marmora & near Rhodes, opposite Alexandria & within 3 days sail of it, it is a very safe harbour. The Army will amount to about 14,000 men including 3 foreign Corps & exclusive of them 6 or 700 Maltese raised here to act as Pioneers to save our own Troops, [*the Maltese being*] inured more to ye Climate & go with Joyful hearts to attack their inveterate & detestable Enemies the French — We don't know ye exact strength of ye Turkish Army. [...]

Genl Kleber's[8] last letter to ye Directory gives a sad account of the State of the French Army in point of Cloathing & Arms &c. Oct. 7. 1799 —

They occupy a great extent of territory from Cairo to Alexandria, having Posts at [...] Ramanhal, & Rosetta, Aboukhir, & indeed at Suez. Their force is estimated from Statements we have at within or about 14000 men, including Auxiliaries, they have about 1000 mounted on Dromedaries — Certainly 6000 Men have sail'd from France & it is supposed have attempted Egypt [...]. They [...] must know by this time that ye English are coming. They have fortified Alexandria & 2 hills behind Pompey's Pillar very strongly which must command every thing near it — we know that when they really set to work they are no despicable Foe — Officers are gone from this Army to communicate at Constantinople.

I should think we shall endeavour to strike a hard blow at first, as the Climate must be against delay.

Good Maps of Egypt are not to be got here & are in great request. I have been very busy with Capt. Leighton who is with me in copying ye best that can be procured, as a ground work for <u>our</u> Operations.

We are in orders appointed Assistant Quarter Master General by <u>order of HRH, Commander in Chief</u>. — Sir R. Abercrombie understood our duty was to be confined to ye Field.

---

8  Kléber lasted less than a year after Napoleon's departure from Egypt had left him in charge of the French forces there, having been assassinated in Alexandria in June, 1800.

Our staff Pay altogether is 15 s. a day, which I think a secondary consideration but is not inconvenient […]

Yr Affectionate Brother<br>T Birch

The Fleet is getting out of harbour at this moment — & a fine sight it will be from so grand a Place as this.

**Letter 4:4 (Thomas Birch, near Marmorice, Turkey, to his mother, Mrs Mary Birch, Windsor, dated 31 January, 1801)**

Camp near Marmorice — Coast of Caramania<br>Turkey in Asia — <u>January 31, 1801</u>.

It is whisper'd that a Ship is about to sail for England, I get my letter ready as you know my dearest Mother, I never miss an opportunity of giving you intelligence of me.

We are still here but expecting to sail to Egypt as soon as ye Convoys arrive from England, Smyrna &c […]

I was sent round to ye Bay of Karagatch abt 3 or 4 leagues off to encamp some Troops — the scenery of much ye same nature as here — wooded & surrounded by high Mountains […] We slept in ye Cabin with Italian & Maltese Officers who commanded ye Corps. It would have been dreadful to have lived in this filth for more than 3 days — […] we […] returned on Foot about 8 miles across ye Mountains to Marmorice, Frank following with my Bear Skin upon his shoulders, as we always move with our <u>beds</u> at our backs.

On my return to ye Dido I received an Order to purchase Horses for ye Cavalry of ye Army. In consequence of this & to be on ye spot I came on Shore to take up my Quarters.

On my return to Marmorice [I] was much surprised & pleased to find my Friend Wilson [see **4: 18**] arrived from England, having left it before we did & passed thro' Germany & Italy, a much pleasanter mode of travelling than we experienced. As I was coming on Shore he kindly begged I would partake of his Hut. — Imagine us then thus situated — In a Hut about 6 yards long & 4 broad, 3 or 4 high, made of longe reeds such as ye fishing rods, covered with branches of

Bay tree & Myrtle, fire places cut out of Earth. At first taking up our abode here we had torrents of rain which made its way into our Apartment without much difficulty thro' ye roof, this was […] followed by most violent wind which took ye same liberty: but it agrees very well tho' not what one should chuse.

We breakfast on Honey & coarse bread, & goat's milk with our tea, which is scarce, bad & dear — butter if you can eat it, made of sheeps' tails which are sold exclusively for ye purpose; but sheep are <u>very</u> scarce & goat's meat is <u>in request</u> in consequence. […] Fowls <u>were cheap</u> & plenty but ye demand has altered both. Game would be abundant but for ye numerous customers — Raisins are plenty & make with coarse flower [flour] very <u>good puddings</u> — Figs, Oranges, Citrons, Lemons, Walnuts, Chesnuts, in abundance.

We lay down our beds in two corners of ye Hut & certainly fare in every respect as well as our neighbours, but know this: that nobody who has not been put to shift at a distance from home where many of your wants could not be supplied knows what real comfort is […]

It will seem strange to you to hear that every night near ye Camp, we hear ye yells & howling of Wolves & Jackals […], ye chief Inhabitants of this part of ye World. They come in droves from ye Mountains […]. Bourchier[9] went with me the other night & shot 2 Jackals at a shot, I have got one of ye skins & shall have a Muff made of it for my dear Mary. Wilson […] writes a long letter by this Ship to Mrs Wilson. She […] is coming to Windsor. I hope you will endeavour to see a good deal of her, I think she & Mary would suit very well. — but I never need make observations of this sort to you […]

[…] Marmorice is just like your Farm yard at St Leonards surrounded with houses; open stalls where every thing is exposed to sale. Bullocks, sheep & goats kill'd & cut up under your nose, the entrails never thrown away & the whole making such a stench as would bid fair to breed a plague were we to stay much longer. […] Every Turk smokes his Pipe & every Englishman will do the same, they say it is wholesome & I hope it is –

The Commander in Chief lives on board Ship & no Troops are landed but those who are sickly. Ye Army is in general Healthy — Sir Sidney Smith[10] [**Fig. 4 b)**] is just come. I paid a visit one day to ye Turkish Admiral on board his Ship, it is curious to see ye different manners of nations — tho' ye almost

---

9   James Bourchier, later to become Thomas's brother-in-law when John William Birch married Diana Bourchier in 1821.
10  A British naval officer who served in the American War of Independence as well as throughout the Napoleonic Wars, Sir Sidney Smith (1764–1840) was at this time captain of HMS *Tigre* in the Mediterranean fleet. His good relations with the Turks were crucial to the success of Abercromby's bid to defeat the French in Egypt. Napoleon later said of him: 'That man made me miss my destiny'.

**Fig. 4 b)** *Sir Sidney Smith* (study for *The Landing of British Troops at Aboukir* [**Fig. 4 c**), page 94]), by Philip James de Loutherbourg. Pencil and watercolour, 1802. National Galleries of Scotland

impossibility of making oneself understood is dreadful. I have [*been*] busy these some days hand drawing a Plan of ye Country for ye Quarter Master General, & gave it him to day. We are in anxious expectation of some Ships from England — as we are so totally shut out from all Intelligence of what is going forward — we are fearful that the news from Germany & Italy will be dampers.

[…] We are much imposed upon by ye Turks, they are difficult about money & that is difficult to be got. They will take nothing but Spanish Dollars […] I do not like to beg, borrow or steal, ye middle I have been obliged to do where I could get it, not having rec'd one farthing of Pay of any sort since I came out […] I don't quite understand it, this Entre nous, an Army of 16000 Men must run away with something particularly so far from home. Such an immense Fleet too. […]

[…] Pray remember me to General & Mrs Harcourt & I hope ere long to send him some intelligence that may authorise my troubling him with a letter […]

## Letter 4:5 (John William Birch, London, to his brother Thomas Birch, in Egypt, dated 23 March, 1801)

5 King's Bench Walk. March 23rd 1801.

My dear Tom,

Your letters which we all received at the same time[11] gave us great satisfaction, their voyage was not indeed quite so expeditious as yours as we did not receive

---

11  John's letter was probably in reply to letters Thomas wrote from Malta and just after arriving in the Bay of Marmorice, although Thomas believed that the ship carrying them had been intercepted (**4: 6**). Letters from Turkey and Egypt took on average about eight weeks to reach England; those from England to the troops in Egypt tended to take considerably longer.

them till the 14th of March. Franck Austen[12] brought them to England, whom my Mother was so lucky as to see at Steventon, where she was for only 2 days. She will of course give you an account of all domestic proceedings, since you heard last, & of consequence will leave little interesting to be told by the rest of the family.

Of myself I can only say that I am settled in my chambers, which have indeed cost a good deal, but are very comfortable & eligible in every respect, and I am beginning to get just enough business to prevent my Spirits from drooping, & excite my hopes of more. — My Aunt & all the family in Newman Street are well, I see them almost every day, & their kindness contributes most materially to my comfort & Happiness. I have got Sam Newell a Situation in the office of my friend G. Frere, an Attorney […] Anna Maria Newell is going to be governess in the bishop of Bangor's family. In giving you this little account I endeavour to fill up what may probably be omitted in my mother's intelligence, & in some hope that the constant succession of new & foreign objects & events which you must have witness'd of late, will give you an interest & variety to the humble account of family occurences, which it might otherwise want […]

[…] you must by this time have trod classic ground & sacred ground too, & if the public accounts of today are to be depended upon have approached very near to the celebrated plains of Troy — But the rumours in the papers are so wild & contradictory, & have sported with the expedition so capriciously, at one time sending you to Egypt, at another to Asia, then back to Malta, & lately placing you at Smyrna, one day defeating you with great loss, the next expressing the most sanguine hopes of success, that they assure us of nothing but their ignorance of all that relates to it, & have us in a state of painful anxiety. These observations apply to the foreign journals as well as our own, which […] prove this at least, that there never was an expedition that […] fix'd the attention of Europe more universally than the Egyptian campaign at the present moment. […].

I touch lightly on domestic politics for fear of Accidents. Pitt & some of his friends are out & have given place to Addington, who is removed from his office of Speaker to that of Prime Minister[13]. Mr J. Mitford is made Speaker, & Sir

---

12  Frank Austen (1774–1865), later Sir Francis Austen, a naval officer who served with Nelson and other commanders during the Napoleonic Wars and became Admiral of the Fleet. He was a brother of the novelist Jane Austen (whose family, then living at Steventon, was friendly with Thomas Birch's mother — see Chapter 7) and probably the model for the character of William Price in *Mansfield Park*.

13  Henry Addington, later 1st Viscount Sidmouth (1757–1844), became Prime Minister in March, 1801, in succession to William Pitt the Younger, who had been Prime Minister since the outbreak of war in 1793 presiding over a broad coalition of Tories and Whigs. Pitt's unexpected resignation was ostensibly over the refusal by King George III to remove existing political restrictions, including the right to sit in Parliament, from Roman Catholics in Ireland following the Act of Union of 1800 (see footnote 27). The sensitivity of this issue may explain John's reluctance to go into details in his letter to his brother. Addington was widely regarded as a very inferior substitute for Pitt, as a contemporary couplet indicates: 'Pitt is to Addington, as London is to Paddington'.

Edward Law, Attorney General. The King has been so unwell as to be unfit for business, but has recovered his health & usual capacity for business[14].

We are involved in a war with the Northern powers, & are in a state of some anxiety about a fleet that sail'd for the Baltic about a week ago with Troops on board. Upon the whole (considering the Union & all) public affairs have assumed entirely a new appearance. — I hope you keep a journal of all that happens, & will impart from time to time all that you can with safety communicate, that you think may interest us [...].

I shudder to think of the dangers you may be exposed to at the moment I am writing this letter [...]. Believe me, my dearest Tom

Your very affectionate Brother
J. W. Birch

PS.
Tell James Bourchier with my love that his brother was well a few days ago. Remember me to Franck. [...] I hope my Mother will not omit one extraordinary piece of intelligence, as the marriage of Mrs Watts to H. Brooksbank, aged 24 — She is 45 —

---

*Sir Ralph Abercromby's army set off from the Bay of Marmorice around the end of February, but the weather was against them and it was nearly ten days before they could land at Abukir* (**Fig. 4 c**)), *a journey which should normally have taken no more than three days. Thomas's two letters about the landings, written in great haste and in terse prose, are in stark contrast to his eloquent descriptions of Turkish customs and scenery which had preceded them.*

---

14 Just after the change in the ministry, George III suffered a sudden recurrence of the illness which had incapacitated him for weeks in 1788 and included symptoms of temporary insanity. The King's illness is referred to several letters during the spring of 1801 (**4: 11** and **4: 13**). It was given out in bulletins that the King had recovered and was carrying out his business as usual, but very few people outside the inner Court circle knew that for several weeks around the time of John's letter their monarch was being kept as a virtual prisoner by his physicians at the White House, Kew, and was forbidden to leave the palace or to see any members of his family. See John Brooke, *King George III* (Constable and Company Ltd, 1972).

**Fig. 4 c)** *The Landing of British Troops at Aboukir, 8 March 1801*, by Philip James de Loutherbourg. Oil on canvas, 1802. National Galleries of Scotland

**LETTER 4:6 (Thomas Birch, near Alexandria, to his mother, Mrs Mary Birch, at Windsor, dated 16 March, 1801)**

Camp before Alexandria.<br>March 16<sup>th</sup> 1801

My letter must be short my dearest Mother, but you are the first person I think of in any communications I have an opportunity of sending to England. This will accompany the dispatches […] You will see a statement of ye Actions of ye 8<sup>th</sup> & 13<sup>th</sup>. In the former the British Army effected a landing before an Enemy strongly posted & with every advantage of ye Knowledge of Country, tho' inferior in numbers. I am sorry to add our loss was serious — the result was glorious to ye British Army.

We advanced on ye 11<sup>th</sup>, skirmished with ye Enemy's advance Posts & encamped within about 4 miles of Alexandria on ye 12<sup>th</sup>. — On ye 13<sup>th</sup> we attacked at 6 in ye Morning, drove ye Enemy from a Strong Position but seeing it impossible from the Strength of their position to gain the heights of Alexandria we took up ye Position the Enemy had left in ye Morning. — We were very superior in Cavalry & Artillery.

The Action was over about 11 or 12 tho' we did not get off our horses till dark […] I feel a satisfaction in having been chiefly employ'd in a Plan of ye Operations [*see* **Fig. 4 d)**] to be sent home with ye dispatches to ye Duke of York — my time's all taken up, but a few minutes I have to write upon my knee, in a hut, made of Palm trees with ye Candle blowing out.

I wrote to you, my Father, James & John from Malta & Marmorice. I hear the Ship was taken & am sorry for it as I had taken pains to amuse you all when I had more time. […]


**LETTER 4:7 (Thomas Birch, near Alexandria, to his brother John William Birch, London, dated 18 March, 1801; date of delivery in England stamped on 16 May, 1801)**

Camp at Alexandria. 18<sup>th</sup> March <u>1801</u>

My dear John,
　I have just 10 minutes to write — but you will like a line from me, & will

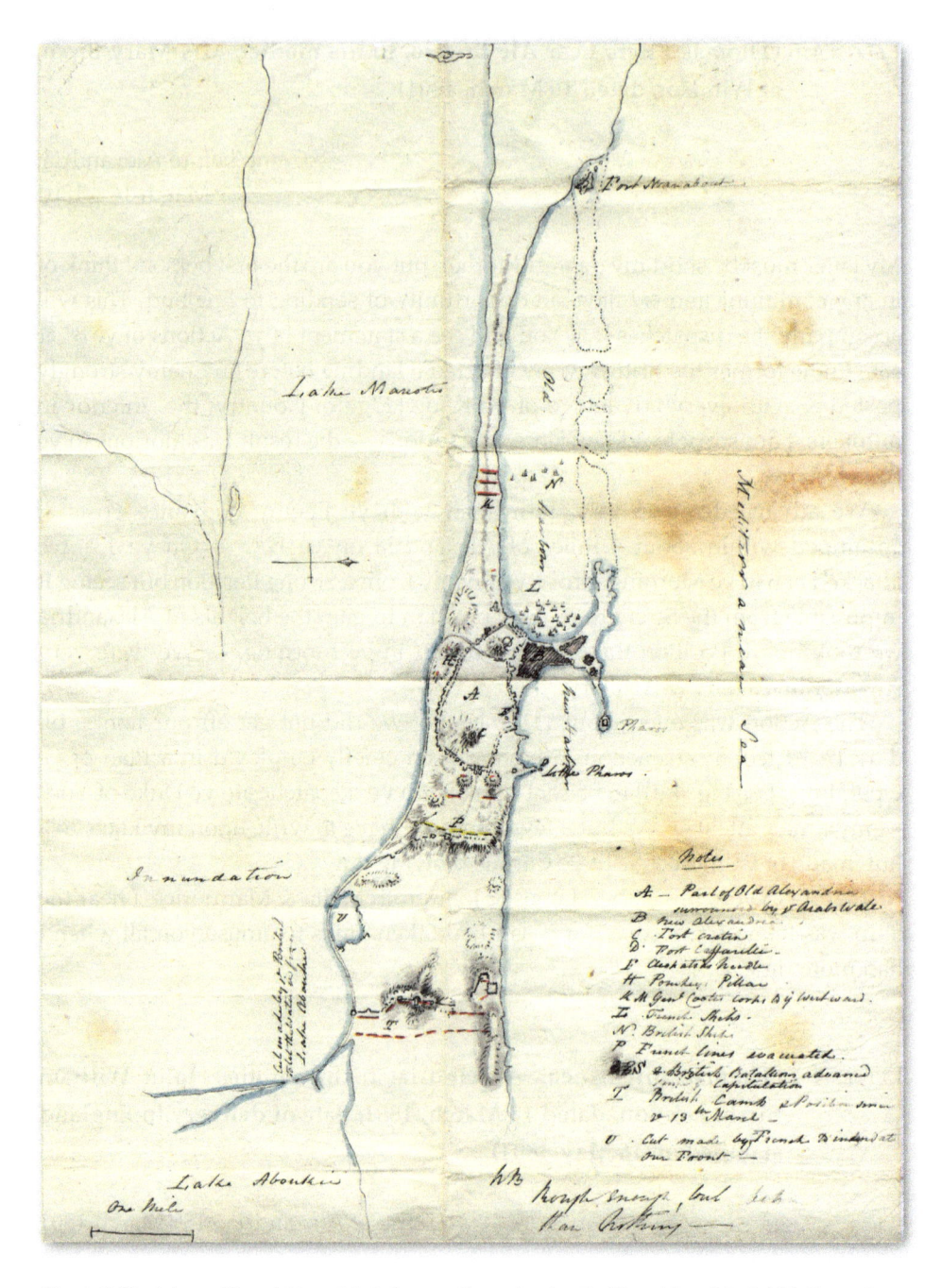

**Fig. 4 d)** *Hand-drawn Plan of Alexandria & Surroundings, showing the Disposition of the British Troops & Enemy Lines*, by Thomas Birch. March, 1801

communicate it to James to whom I wrote from Marmorice.

Our landing at Aboukir was brilliant on ye 8th & the loss was severe.

Since then we have advanced within 3 miles of Alexandria. On ye 13th at 6 in ye Morning we attack'd ye Enemy strongly posted. We had little Cavalry or Artillery, they had both & were driven to ye heights of Alexandria with great loss — Ours was very serious, 1300 men & many valuable officers —.

The French are now strongly posted & it remains with us when we have our heavy Artillery to attack. We have been deceived in our Ideas of Alexandria —

I pray God we may be successful. We expect 10,000 Turks, who will be of little use I fear —

You will be glad to hear I have sent officially a Plan <u>of Operations</u> since landing as far <u>as Alexandria</u> to HRH ye Duke of York. […]

Love to all<br>
Affectionately your Brother<br>
<u>T Birch</u>

I have not had a moment to myself —

*Thomas's request to John to share the information with James was carried out, as both brothers' reactions are written on the same sheet of paper. John wrote as follows:*

I'll thank you to return it when you have read it, that I may send or carry it […]
Yours, J. W. B.

*James Birch replied:*

The account is the most welcome imaginable. I always anticipated he would live & triumph. The next dispatches I expect will be sent by him — if Providence fights for us, who can be against us?

Yours ever affectionately<br>
J. B.

I send you his last to me, which, as I have not yet answered, I wish return'd soon.

**Fig. 4 e)** *The Battle of Alexandria, 21 March 1801*, by Philip James de Loutherbourg. Oil on canvas, 1802. National Galleries of Scotland

*The successful landings at Abukir and the actions there on 8 March and at Mandora on 13 March forced the French to retreat towards Alexandria itself, near which the combined British armies attacked before dawn on 21 March (see* **Fig. 4: e)**). *In three separate letters, Thomas describes the ensuing Battle of Alexandria — the most significant British military victory of the war to date — in markedly different ways. To his mother* (**4: 8**), *he is sparing in the details he gives of the battle itself, dwelling instead on the slaughter of so many men, including some whom she knew personally, and especially on the death of Sir Ralph Abercromby, whose loss threatened to overshadow the emphatic victory which had been achieved. Thomas's account to General Harcourt* (**4: 9**), *the former commander of his regiment, is strictly factual, with great attention to detail. It is perhaps in his letter to his brother James* (**4: 10**) *that we find the clearest indication of the way the action affected him personally.*

---

**LETTER 4:8 (Thomas Birch, near Alexandria, to his mother, Mrs Mary Birch, at Windsor, dated 29 March, 1801)**

Camp near Alexandria  29th March 1801

Tho' I am told the chances may be against your ever receiving this letter, it is my duty as well as strong inclination to write as I well know my dearest Mother how your anxiety will be alive when ye sad news which accompanies it becomes public.

Lamentable to tell we have this day lost our good Commander in Chief Sir Ralph Abercromby, he died of his wounds received in ye last Action of the 21st. — Glorious to ye British Army tis true, but dreadful the afflictions that accompany such Glory — he remain'd too long in the Field after being wounded & refused that assistance which might have caused a favourable turning.

He was shot in the thigh, rode & walked afterwards & did not leave the Field till ye Enemy retreated which he seem'd anxious about, but was in good Spirits when carried off upon ye Bier. I was with him at the time[15]. His son went with him & must suffer indeed; he went on board Ship immediately.

Thus died this excellent Old Man [...] — beloved & respected by the whole army; he had the satisfaction of seeing it behave under his command with

---

15  It is a family tradition that Sir Ralph Abercromby was carried off the field wrapped in Thomas Birch's sash, which was afterwards kept at Holywell.

steadiness & bravery almost unexampled, beating the Enemy in three pitched battles, by dint of intrepid conduct, as we were very inferior in Cavalry & Artillery. [...] The Action lasted about 5 or 6 Hours & the Enemy retreated to their old Position near Alexandria with ye loss of near 4000 killed, wounded & Prisoners [...].

It will not bear reflexion that any thing like satisfaction should arise to one in counting the dead bodies of our fellow creatures but war will not bear reflexion <u>at any rate</u>. It could not be expected that in such slaughter of ye Enemy our loss should not be serious. It was indeed! [...] Thank God! I am spared to my Family this time, tho' I almost feel it too great a happiness to look forward to the embracing them all again [...].

Fancy not from ye Sentiments & Observations I have express'd to you my dearest Mother that I am dissatisfied in my Situation. I have reason for ye contrary & have not once repented the Profession I have chosen, but if amidst ye scenes one has been familiar with lately, the loss of Friends & acquaintances one has been in ye habit of seeing every day, the mind can entirely divest itself of reflection it must be made of very different materials from mine. — Poor Col. Erskine, eldest son of my Friends at Cardross [...] everything that human nature could boast was in him — Col. Brice whom you may have seen, gone — I liked him much. I will not go on — I must talk to you always from my heart & should think it an insult to your strong mind to screen my real feelings & situation from you for fear of making you low spirited. Thank God I have hitherto had my health & tho' literally sleeping with my blanket on ye sand & always with my Cloaths on, sleeping soundly. [...]

[...] Poor Frank has been unwell but is getting much better — he is always assured of what care I can give him — where we are encamped now is deep sand [...]. We see Alexandria, Pompey's Pillar & Cleopatra's Needle — God bless you all [...]

Your Affectionate & Dutiful Son,<br>
<u>T Birch</u>

**LETTER 4:9 (Thomas Birch, near Alexandria, to General Harcourt, dated 31 March, 1801)**

Camp near Alexandria  31 March 1801

My dear Sir

Ere you receive this, official accounts will have reach'd England of the operations of the Army of Egypt. I wish'd to have written to you with the last dispatches but at that time had scarcely a moment to myself, being employ'd in making a rough plan to illustrate the movements of our Army to be sent to H R H the Duke of York.

After a tantalizing view of the Coast of Egypt for near 10 days, during which time the weather was too squally to attempt a landing, a favourable change took place, the morning of the 8th was taken advantage of & the Troops were in the boats before day break. I am particular in this as no other opportunity would have occurred for many days afterwards so great is the swell in Aboukir Bay.

The Enemy to the amount of about 2000 Men with 7 pieces of cannon & about 150 Cavalry occupied the strongest Position imaginable, a strong high steep sand hill on their centre & left having numerous smaller hillocks with Palm trees & bushes on their right.

The Boats containing the Reserve & Brigade of Guards under Generals Moore & Ludlow amounting to less than 5000 Men, pulled into the shore, under the heaviest fire of Grape & Musquetry were order'd not to load till out of the boats — This was conducted with the greatest regularity. The Troops […] gain'd the steep ascent on hands & <u>knees</u>, drove the Enemy from it & took 6 pieces of cannon, their cavalry made one attack without success, & the whole retreated towards Alexandria. The Action lasted from 9 till 12, the loss amounted to about 400 Men, ours about 500 […]. We advanced about 2 miles & took up our Position at night in a wood of scatter'd Palm Trees, on the sand hills our right close to the sea, our left upon the Lake Aboukir.

The Army remain'd in this Position till the 12th when it advanced between 5 & 6 miles & came up with the Enemy strongly posted within 3 miles of Alexandria.

The Order was to attack the next morning at day break. We advanced against this position with hardly any artillery to cover us & very little Cavalry, across a plain under heavy fire from their Artillery which was remarkably well served. Their Cavalry ought to have done more, but was repulsed in one attack by the steadiness & intrepidity of the 90th Regiment — it is impossible to form a higher idea of the good conduct of Troops than was evinced by ours, on this day; our cannon was chiefly dragged by sailors & soldiers who tho' they exerted themselves could not bring it forward so rapidly as might have been wish'd — the Enemy was driven from this position & retreated across the Plain to the immensely strong heights of Alexandria, & during their retreat they suffer'd severely. We advanced about a mile & half beyond that which they had occupied in the morning but finding their position much too strong for any attempt [...] it was determined on taking up the position which we occupy at this moment.

Our loss amounted to about 1300 Men. That of the Enemy to more, according to their own account, with 2 or 3 pieces of cannon. Their force in this action might be from 7 to 8000 men, some accounts say more. [...] The various reports of Sheiks of Arabs who came forward as Friends, gave us to understand that we were to be attack'd at night, by General Abdullah Menou[16] with his whole force; much credit was not given to this, but before day break on the 21st this menaced attack was made upon the whole line. It began by a feint upon our left, the Regiment was surprized & a gun in a redoubt turn'd upon it, but which was retaken; upon the whole, this had the good effect of getting the line sooner under Arms than they otherwise would have been. In the meantime 2 strong columns of Infantry with a large body of Cavalry advanced upon our right as close as possible [...]. They were received steadily by the Regiment of Reserve, under Lt General Moore & in a moment the action was severe, their Cavalry advanced & charged, & was repulsed with great slaughter by the 28th & 42nd Regiments [...]. They then attempted our centre, the 2 Battalions of the Guards advanced, & behaved in a manner that does them honor with the loss of 200 Men. — We have since heard that General Menou order'd Genl. Regnier to charge with the Bayonet[s] which was refused. Unable to make any impression, about 9 o'clock they began their retreat across the Plain they had advanced over with so much confidence, & suffer'd dreadfully. It is ascertained, they lost over 4000 men, in kill'd wounded & prisoners — General Menou only arrived the night before, brought his whole force (excepting that left in Garrisons) amounting to between 11 & 12000 Men, 24 pieces of cannon. He urged the Army to attack again the following night, but such a defeat did not promise success for another attempt, he is reported to have torn his hair & wept, different deserters have agreed in this.

The Action cost us very dear, 1500 Men kill'd & wounded, in that list are included 5 General Officers & I wish I could stop here, but the lamentable News of the death of our good Commander in Chief will accompany this. [...] Very sincerely regretted by this Army, he consider'd the wound trifling — to a young

---

16  Leader of the French forces in Egypt by seniority after the assassination of General Kléber.

## THE EGYPTIAN CAMPAIGN

Man it might have been; but the anxiety of mind which it is known he suffer'd, indeed ever since our landing here, added to pain of body, overcame him. — The command devolves upon Major Gen. Hutchinson [...]. At present we are healthy & thus situated: occupying a very strong Position naturally, & made stronger every day; the Enemy occupying the heights of Alexandria, very strong exclusive of ye Forts within the old Walls. Our out Posts [are] close to each other. They have a Regiment of Mamalukes & Hussars together, it is suppos'd ye former to be a check upon the others who have occasionally shewn inclination to desert.

Genl. Menou & his Army don't seem to agree, I believe his object is to remain in the Country, theirs to return to France. Such difference of opinion may be favourable to us. — Should affairs in Egypt be settled by negociation it seems it will suit the disposition of every one as well as undertaking ye siege of Alexandria. — Rosetta & Cairo I should think must fall, without great difficulty, the Vizier is making towards the latter place. The Captain Pacha[17] is here with the Turkish Army [of] 6000 Men, to cooperate; but I should be sorry to trust much to their cooperation.

Our Position is favourable for provisions, plenty of fresh meat, & vegetables are brought to Market in Camp from the Interior — we have the Sea on our right & ye Lake on our left, by this a constant communication is kept up with our fleet in Aboukir Bay, for every supply that may be wanted, the Lake swarms with fish enough to supply the Army. [...]

Sir Sidney Smith is very active with us, & is at home with the Turks. I see a great deal of him, he begged his remembrances & Compliments to you & Mrs Harcourt.

The Plans we have had of this Country have given us not the <u>smallest</u> idea of it; we conceived all was a plain, instead of which there is much strong Ground tho' totally uncultivated; here 'tis true we eat & drink sand & literally sleep in it, a few scatter'd Palm Trees is the only verdure. The days are at present not too hot & always a breeze, the nights cold & damp, but intense heat we must expect soon.

I lament that I really have not time to send you a sketch of our Operations without which I fear that my hasty account will be unintelligible, but I hope I may be allow'd to look forward to ye time when I may be able to explain the whole more satisfactorily to you [...] believe me my <u>dear Sir</u>

Yr Obliged & Faithfull <u>T. Birch</u>

---

17  The Grand Vizier and the Captain Pacha were the two most important leaders of the Ottoman armies.

April 3rd

A Detachment of British & Turkish Troops have just march'd to take possession of Rosetta — it is not strong & expected to fall [...]

**Letter 4:10 (Thomas Birch, near Alexandria, to his brother, James Birch, dated 3 April, 1801)**

3rd April. Camp near Alexandria —

My dear James,

Tho' I wrote to my Mother it was another in haste, & I will endeavour to amuse you with what is passing here, as I can talk to you without restraints. The actions of the 8th & 13th I enter not into ye particulars of [...] the papers will have given a better account — On the last action of the 21st we were attacked an hour before day break. To give you an idea of it, we were awoke[n] when quite dark by a firing on our left & as we never pull cloaths off, were out in a minute & the action soon commenced along the whole line. [...]

We were on this day great sufferers [...] to the sorrow of the whole army our excellent commander in Chief Sir Ralph Abercromby is since dead of his wounds; [...] He had the Satisfaction of dying gloriously after having beat the enemy in three Actions, he was delighted with the conduct of the troops, which without an exception was gallant to a degree. — He mention'd he looked upon the landing at Aboukir the handsomest thing he had ever seen done in the course of his Service.

[...] I have lost, my dear James, some friends, & many acquaintances [...] & many, many wounded [...]. I only wonder that so many escaped — on the 13th I led the left column on which was the chief Brunt of the action [...] A Field of Battle is a dreadfull Sight, & calls you to wonder how such means should ever have been invented to torture fellow creatures — it's enough to break your heart [...]. Alexandria is a strong place [...], if we besiege it will be a tough job. The French are not in a Situation to give it up, but we hope diversions may be made in our favour. The French wish to quit Egypt; Menou does not — it is a great object with Buonaparte. [...] A force of British & Turks have just march'd off to Rosetta & I think it must fall, which will give us a fine Key to the delta. This army is at present [...] occupying a strong position & strongly entrenched [...] in sight of the French army [...], our vedettes near enough to hold conversation. — A Mamaluke has come in to us today as a deserter from the French. Our private comforts are not great, sleeping in a blanket on sand half way up your legs, & eating & drinking it in every thing [...]

We have had a Splendid Sight today, the Captain Pacha has review'd the army, he answers to Lord High Admiral, is the 3$^{rd}$ person in ye Empire. Such magnificence of dress & appearance one has heard of & seene in Pictures, but I never expected to see it really [...]

Individually I feel the loss of Sir R., he gave me a general invitation to his table. No longer so, tho' I know his Successor Genl. Hutchinson very well. [...] Some Men have got the Opthalmia, also blindness at night [...] Anxious that my dear Mother should hear from me as soon as possible. I wrote a letter by way of Constantinople, & I fear the letter was not put in that bag, by which means she would have got it earlier, it very probably will go by the same conveyance as this — I only wish her to know that I had written to her, & that she is always the first Person I think of.

---

*The news of the decisive victory at the Battle of Alexandria did not reach London until early May, but was the subject of much favourable comment in Parliament* (**4: 12**). *Thomas received several letters of congratulation for his part in the action and particularly for the detailed Plan of Operations (a speciality of the 'Wycombites'), which he had made following the landings but before the main battle took place. The letters which gave him most satisfaction (he made careful copies and was still quoting from them towards the end of his life more than forty years later) were from Lt. Colonel John Le Marchant, the commandant of the National Military College. As Le Marchant was quick to acknowledge, the positive benefits of professional military training and instruction could hardly have been demonstrated in a more propitious light or at a more opportune time for the future of the British army. Only three years after he had first proposed the establishment of a staff training college and had been discouraged by the Duke of York (see* **Chapter 3**), *the achievements of the army in Egypt were being discussed, in the House of Commons and with the King, in terms 'most flattering...to the Establishment'. The following two letters were written on successive days, as the news of the full extent of the army's success had not reached Le Marchant until after he had written the first letter.*

## Letter 4:11 (Lt.-Colonel John Gaspard Le Marchant, High Wycombe, to Thomas Birch, in Egypt, dated 9 May, 1801)

High Wycomb 9th May 1801

Dear Birch,

Many thanks for all your letters — the last was dated the 16th February off Marmorice.

Accept my most hearty congratulations on the very handsome manner Col. Anstruther speaks of you & the Wycombites — in his last Dispatches he says "The Officers sent me from Jarry's are of infinite use, & the Details of the several actions fought by this Army are accompanied by plans in Drawing executed by Major Birch & the Officers from Wycomb in a Style of Perfection that does them great Credit." I saw this encomium on you & my friends at the Secretary of State's. [...]

[...] Brown & Montalembert will join you with reinforcements said to be ordered amounting to 5000 Men — Two Major Generals & one Lieut. General. Genl. Floyd conveys this to you: he is a warm Friend of the Establishment. At my recommendation he takes Stewart as his First Aide De Camp, who will keep him in mind of all the Assistance he may be able to render you and our Views of ye General Staff. [...] The Establishment is improving in Science Daily. I have some very intelligent officers here at present — & Government is so sensible of the advantage to the Country the Establishment is of — that it receives the greatest possible encouragement. The moment an officer is qualified to belong to the Staff he is immediately appointed. Any who have reasonable claims to promotion are attended to; in short we are in full feather & the Credit which the world is willing to allow to the College exceeds my most sanguine Expectations.

In regard to my progress in establishing it as a National Institution, I have been equally fortunate. This week it is to be Brought before Parliament and the Secretary of War assures me he does not expect the smallest opposition to the measure: & indeed your conduct joined to those of the Establishment with you have materially contributed to fix the opinion of the Public, as to its utility to ye Services.

We have purchased for the College the Mannor of Sandhurst; it contains five hundred acres & is situated to the right of the road & by the Turnpike as you enter into Blackwater beyond Bagshot. The Situation, Circumstances of ground & water are all peculiarly adapted to the objects of the institution. Wyatt[18] the

---

18 James Wyatt (1746–1813) was probably the most sought-after architect of his generation. Many of his earlier buildings were in the fashionable neo-classical style, but he later became celebrated as a neo-Gothic architect.

Architect is expected daily to [?]discourse in the Plan of Building, which is to be of Stone & of Gothic architecture. Stone Bricks &c we have on the spot. The Barracks Department are to Build on Wyatt's design. We hope to begin our Building immediately that the money is voted.

The Poor King's Illness — join'd to the unexpected Change of Ministry threw me back for the moment. But I set to work with such expedition, & found the trend of the new Government so well disposed towards my Plans that I experienced no difficulty.

[…] The Classes — Progress of Studies &c are all better arranged than when you were here: But notwithstanding the Establishment is more difficult to conduct. Fine gentlemen cabal together & divide the members which must be the case until I have a Book of Statutes confirmed by His Majesty, which must shortly be the case. […]

We see no immediate Prospects of Peace, therefore you have a fine Game to Play, recollect all I have told you on the need of exertion — for it is by <u>doing</u> what others <u>do not</u>, that you are to build your hope of Preferment. […]

Mrs Le Marchant is not very far from being confined, so that my Family will keep me low let my Endeavours to Rise be what they may […]

Believe me, Dear <u>Birch</u> very truly your Friend
<u>J. G. Le Marchant</u>

Ps. We had an Anniversary Dinner at the Thatched House Tavern at which the Duke of York, Dundas & all the General Staff of Head Quarters were Present, it was Magnificent & the whole were highly pleased.

### Letter 4:12 (Lt.-Colonel John Gaspard Le Marchant, High Wycombe, to Thomas Birch, in Egypt, dated 10 May, 1801)

Wycomb 10th May

My Dear Friend,

I have this moment received your Friendly letter dated Alexandria the 16 March.

I have infinite Pleasure in acknowledging its receipt & congratulating you on the Honor you have acquired with the Army, & individually the Credit which your personal exertions have earned in the opinion of Ministers, and all about Head Quarters.

Before the Dispatches were rec'd, Col. Anstruther wrote very favourably of you & he did you justice in Regard to the Plans which he said were <u>drawn by you</u>. Persevere in your Plan of Conduct, your Merit forces itself into notice. Your intelligence is equal to the Exertion, & I have no doubt you will arrive at the head of your Profession. [...]

[...] By this day's post Col. Calvert writes me that he heard Mr Pitt & Addington speak of the Officers sent to Egypt from Wycomb in a Style the most flattering & Honorable to you as to the Establishment.

Had you not succeeded — I should have shut up shop & walked off to my rest. But as it is I shall cheerfully persevere in completing a work so happily begun that ultimately [it] will prove the Glory of our Profession.

I anticipated your views — by obtaining leave for Brown & Montalembert to go out: The anxiety you express for More, will <u>make</u> me exert myself with additional zeal to get them away. [...] [*Inscribed in pencil in the margin, in Thomas Birch's handwriting, is the comment:* Does not this show that he felt all depended upon him?] If I had more fit for Service you should see them out by this opportunity; but none others will be qualified till Autumn. We have a Rising Set soon of Exceeding good Soldiers.

[...] The following is a copy of a few lines just rec'd from Calvert: "Major Birch has transmitted a Plan of the operations of our Army in Egypt, which gives great Satisfaction. Several copies are making of it in the Quarter Master Genl's Office. Pray remember me to Genl. Jarry, tell him I congratulate him sincerely & participate with him in the Satisfaction I am sure he must derive from the Credit gained by his Eleves [pupils] on service.

"Mr Addington [*the new Prime Minister*] desires to know what officers the College has furnished — to the Staff — on what services — & how many are now fit for the Genl. Staff."

You may judge from this how you have paved your own way — & that of the Establishment.

[...] Once more Adieu. Believing me with all under this Roof your Sincere Friend

JLM

## Letter 4:13 (John William Birch, London, to his brother, Thomas Birch, in Egypt, dated 16 May, 1801)

My dearest Tom,

This morning brought me a letter from Egypt, which arriving at the moment of the account of the victory gain'd by the British Army on the 21$^{st}$ of March I hoped contained a detailed account of the battle: for all fears for your personal safety had been allay'd by not seeing your name in the list of those, who suffered on that day. [...] My mother got your letter dated the 16$^{th}$ of March as soon as she heard of the action of the 13$^{th}$, that is with the government dispatches — for we had heard of the landing & that action (of the 13$^{th}$) from the French accounts some time before, which corresponded exactly almost with our own account except in considerably overstating our loss in the landing. [...]

We had a variety of rumours of the action of the 21$^{st}$ before the authentic accounts arrived. The first from France, but merely a loose report — then some accounts from Constantinople, among which one from Lord Elgin stating that Menou had joined the Garrison of Alexandria with 2000 cavalry & had been repulsed with loss in an attack he made on the 21$^{st}$ was considered at most entitled to credit [...] — I can not tell you the constant anxiety which these accounts kept us in; [...] subject however to this anxiety I feel infinite satisfaction in your being engaged in an expedition so very important, so much the object of general attention & interest I had almost said over the whole Globe, all over Europe, & India & the greatest part of Asia it is so undoubtedly, & above all that has hitherto been attended with circumstances so glorious to the British name & arms. [...] A friend of mine was dining in company with the Secretary at War a few days ago (this was before your plan arrived) & he talking of the Expedition to Egypt said there was one Major Birch who had been of great service, & had much distinguish'd himself . [...] I really don't know if I ever heard anything which gave me so much pleasure, as I consider your advancement & reputation as my own.

[...] I have been so entirely engrossed by Egypt & its concerns both on national & personal accounts, that I forgot that others may be more interested about domestic affairs. [...] Suffice it to say that every thing at home goes on very quietly with the new Ministry. The King is still an invalid, but convalescent.

I told you in my last which perhaps you never received of the sailing of the Northern fleet under the Command of Parker & Nelson for the Baltic in consequence of a dispute with the Northern Powers; after a severe action fought with the Danes in the harbour of Copenhagen[19] in which 18 of their ships were taken or destroyed, & the town exposed to Bombardment, which was followed by an Armistice with that power, & by the fortunate death of the Emperor Paul, which happen'd just at the same time, that dispute is I trust in a fair way of being accommodated — & Egypt engrosses the public attention.

My Mother, Father & Mary are in Duke Street, Manchester Square, for 6 weeks & are mixing in the dissipations of the gay world with reasonable vivacity. My Father has been at a rout or two, & an opera, those who see him in public say he is as well as ever [...] You will I am sure be pleas'd to hear that I am getting a little business [...]

Let me intreat you at your leisure to give me a detail'd account of the battle of the 21$^{st}$ & tell me particularly what you had to do in it [...] — how you felt when first in action &c. We have had all the letters you have written, infinite amusement they have afforded to the circle which is always collected to hear your dispatches; but the interest, which attended your first communications has now become anxiety as the circle has been drawn closer, the nearer you have approached the scene of danger. [...] When I think of the hardships & dangers you are exposed to it sometimes makes my heart ache, but when I consider you as engaged in the exercise of an honourable profession with credit to yourself & benefit to your country, no inconveniences which are accrued to your situation can deprive you, I should think, of the solid satisfaction it must afford. A fine speculation this you'll say for a man who is going to a comfortable bed & surrounded with every convenience of life, which would vanish before the prospect of sleeping on the sand at night, & rising to a breakfast of bayonets & cannon balls in the morning [...] What idle nonsense I am talking [...] but one day is much like another & every thing goes on so much as usual, that I really don't know how I can amuse you. [...]

Yours affectionately<br>J. W. Birch

Saturday — May the 16: 1801.
5, King's Bench Walks.

[19] Several of Thomas's correspondents mention the Battle of Copenhagen, which saw a British fleet under the command of Admiral Sir Hyde Parker overcome a Danish-Norwegian fleet anchored off Copenhagen on 2 April, 1801. The main attack was led by Vice-Admiral Horatio Nelson, who is famously reputed to have declined Parker's instruction to withdraw at his discretion by holding the telescope to his blind eye (lost at the siege of Calvi on 10 July, 1794) and claiming not to see the signal. The Emperor Paul referred to here and in other letters was the Russian Tsar, whose formation of a League of Armed Neutrality (consisting of Denmark-Norway, Sweden, Prussia and Russia) to enforce free trade with France was seen by the British as a serious threat, and the Tsar's death by assassination on 23 March, ten days before the battle, as providential.

*Le Marchant's letters, which were delivered in person by a fellow officer, General Floyd, reached Thomas some time in July, by which time the next objective in the campaign — the capitulation of Cairo — had already been accomplished. Thomas received a batch of family letters in June, but these had all been written before they knew that he had even landed in Egypt, let alone anything about the experiences he had undergone since then. He continued to write as regularly as possible from each stage of the campaign, but it is clear from the content of his letters that he found the lack of return communication disheartening and felt that the army in Egypt, so many thousands of miles from home, had been forgotten. He was also suffering badly from the effects of the climate, to an extent to which he was not prepared to admit until after he had left Egypt and was recovering on the long journey home.*

*The longed-for letters were not finally delivered until mid-September, almost six months after the Battle of Alexandria; they included enjoyably gossipy missives from his mother and his brother John (**4: 18** and **4: 19**), but significantly none from his father, an omission on which Thomas commented reproachfully (**4: 25**).*

---

**Letter 4:14 (Thomas Birch, at Rosetta, to his brother, John Birch, 1 May, 1801)**

Rosetta. May 1st 1801

My dear John,

[…] By the last Ship that sail'd I wrote to my Mother & a very long letter to James & to Genl. Harcourt [**4: 8** *to* **4: 10**], giving an account of our Operations from our landing since that time. The British & Turkish Army combined have march'd into Rosetta, one of ye Keys to ye Delta. A small part of ye Garrison retreated to Fort St. Julien which held out about 4 or 5 days. I came here a few hours before ye surrender. — The Prisoners who were taken said that however glad we might be to get in they were as glad to get out.

Here then you find us possessors of Rosetta, looked upon as the most beautiful town in Egypt. It is close on ye banks of ye Nile which is here about as broad as the Thames at Westminster Bridge […]. Pray don't believe Savary[20], his descriptions would make you believe it a Paradise, but to those who have lived upon, or seen even, the lovely banks of the Thames feel it otherwise — all is by

---

20  The first edition in English of the French writer Claude Etienne Savary's *Letters on Egypt* was published in 1786. It was regarded as essential reading by Napoleon and his army when they invaded Egypt.

comparison. We had cross'd a sandy desert for some miles, after that the sight of a fine River & ye smell of Orange & Lemon Trees may be imagined delightful [...]. The Country on either side flat as in Essex, fertile in corn & clover fields but without the advantage of any hedges — Dykes, Ditches & Canals intersect the Country every where & when you have seen one mile with little variety you have seen 20. [...] The numerous villages on ye banks of ye River & in ye Interior appear pleasing at a distance from the multiplicity of Mosques in & about them, but enter them & all is ruin & filth, the Inhabitants — men & women — naked all but a thin dirty robe thrown indifferently about them [...] The Musquitoes, flys & fleas are torments you are strangers to in England. With nets we keep off ye former with difficulty.

The British & Turkish Army is posted with its left on ye Nile about 4 Miles off, about to move on soon. I made a Patrol yesterday in ye Delta; about 12 Miles on front I saw from ye top of a Mosque the Enemy's Out Posts. We do not suppose them to be very strong there in numbers tho' they may be strongly posted. We expect they will make a stand at Rahmanie about 37 Miles on — it has appear'd that they have been endeavouring to pass all their Treasures & Valuables to Alexandria. The Inhabitants of ye Country like ye Sight of us. I don't know how they feel towards the Turks. — Our Army here is about 10,000 Men, half & half Brits & Turks. I think it is their turn to have ye brunt of ye next Affair. — [...] The Captain Pasha visits the Army in great Style now & then — the Pomp & parade of that nation is beyond any thing. I often think how extraordinary a thing it is for a British Army to find itself in Egypt fighting in conjunction with the Turks.

The Grand Vizier is certainly not far from Cairo, & Amurad Bey is on his march[21]. We have reason to believe too that a force is on ye point of being landed at Suez.

Believe me my dear John, never will an Army rejoice more to return to their own Country [...] it is very different, be assured, from war in Europe. The Climate hitherto has favor'd us thank God, but we have had a Specimen of what we may expect. I pray something decisive may be done ere that — but we are far distant here & can't communicate with our own Country so quickly as would be agreeable. [...] I want to see Cairo & ye Pyramids & a few other curiosities & then I don't care how soon I see dear England.

I forgot to tell you that a long meditated Plan has been carried into effect of cutting the Canal of Alexandria & letting ye water into ye Country on ye other

---

21 Thomas Birch was unaware that Murad Bey (1750–1801), leader of the Mamluk élite military force, had died of bubonic plague about three weeks earlier while marching towards Cairo.

side from Lake Maadie [*possibly a misspelling of Mareotis*] which communicates with the Sea, it has inundated many many miles & broke down the canal which months & perhaps years can't repair & the fresh water when the present supply is gone will be cut off from Alexandria. [...]

Your Affectionate Brother<br>T Birch

I am inclined to think ye sad accounts in our Gazettes will make People think of Egypt a little.

## Letter 4:15 (Thomas Birch, near Cairo, to his mother, Mrs Mary Birch, dated 17 June, 1801)

Camp on the Nile: within 1½ miles of Grand Cairo<br>17th June,<br>1801

We are just apprized that a ship is about to sail for England, it gives me an opportunity of returning to you my dearest Mother my earnest & heartfelt thanks for your letters, one dated 16th January, one 16th March, one 22nd March & one 21st Ditto[22] from dear Mary, how differently were we employ'd on that day! Oh! did you know the real happiness I have experienced in reading all your letters (from those I most value in the world indeed) you would never conclude them by saying "but you have too much upon your mind to attend to my trifling chat" or something of that sort [...] had you been as remote from those you love best in the world as I am from you, [*you*] would feel that every incident & the most trifling domestic circumstances that placed you for however short a time in the company of such dear Friends were precious [...]

[...] My dear James was the first to write to me [...] I hope John got my letter about send[*ing*] ye newspapers; you have not an Idea what treasures they are. I am always obliged to write in a hurry & am perhaps called away in the middle of my letters so they must be unconnected. — Mrs Watts' [*see* **4: 5**] second extreme certainly surprised me not a little. The late & present upon an average will bring it even[...]

22  None of these letters has survived.

[...] We are encamp'd within 1½ miles of Grand Cairo apparently an immensely large town & at this distance presenting a very grand view. The R. Nile passes by our left. [...] we occupy the Ground about Imbaba where was the famous battle of ye Pyramids[23] between Bonaparte & ye Mamalukes. Our bridge is just finish'd & we move on immediately to ye siege of Cairo [...] I have little time to write to any body but you [...] indeed this Climate fatigues me too much to do what allows me to exert myself to ye extent of my Wishes & tho' I have felt it a little [I] am getting quite stout again [...]

[...] I am glad to hear of your Idea of going to Town, that must be all over by this time. I hope dear Mary enjoy'd a pleasant time [...] as your comfort I am well aware must have depended upon it — having her delightful & agreeable friends the Reynardsons[24] will have been a great point [...] I say nothing of how much I should have enjoy'd being of the party [...] You & Mary delight me riding my Horse; to think I should have given you any thing that may have contributed to your health as well as pleasure, is a Satisfaction indeed [...]

[...] How differently are we employ'd. With us this is a Critical Moment on ye Point of commencing ye siege of Cairo: should we carry our point we may take a favourable view of ye termination of affairs in this Country, tho' Alexandria will still remain which in such circumstances will hardly hold out long. We must hope & pray for success. Should we meet with it, this Army will return with honour & credit [...]

### Letter 4:16 (Thomas Birch, near Cairo, to his father, George Birch, Windsor, dated 28 June, 1801)

Camp before Cairo. 28th June 1801.

My dear Sir,

Dispatches of an event which must be consider'd of consequence in the affairs of Europe are on the point of sailing for England. I feel a pleasure in thinking you will have a gratification in receiving the earliest intelligence of it; could I be assured you would feel a Satisfaction in communicating it how happy it would make me.

Grand Cairo has capitulated — No sooner had the British & Ottoman Armies

---

23 In July 1798.
24 This is the first mention in Thomas's correspondence of the family to which he was soon to be united by marriage and whose name he adopted (see Chapter 5).

invested it than Genl Belliard sent to ye Commander in Chief of ye British Army for a conference, some difficulties have attended the arrangement but all is now settled. — The Armistice has continued 4 days — The Terms required by ye French were exorbitant & they have been in part only granted, the <u>French</u> Army to the amount of 4000 Men […] is to march out with every honor, Arms, Battalion guns &c […] to be allow'd 12 days in Cairo previous to their departure, it is supposed they will take off a great deal of treasure. Whether they have been granted too good terms is not for me to determine, but it is a great point to get them out of the Country & without the loss of lives which must have happened in [*the*] case of a siege.

Alexandria still remains a strong hold, but it is not improbable that General Menou, cut off from all hopes of recovering the Country, may follow ye example of Genl Belliard, the obvious difficulty appears in regard to ye Shipping; he will want it & we shall not give it him. — I think we may hope that more blood will not be spilt in driving the French from this Country & that we certainly are much nearer the time when we may turn our faces towards our own. […]

During ye Armistice the other day a British & a Turkish Officer from ye Grand Vizier's Army were appointed to settle ye line of demarkation & arrange ye outposts. I went on ye Part of ye British with an Officer from ye Grand Vizier with a flag of truce & met a general Officer on ye part of ye French. — This settled I returned to ye Grand Vizier & sent ye Enemy with him smoking & drinking Coffee & Sherbet, he desired to see me next Morning & invested me with a Pelisse[25]: so much for my honor rec'd from the Grand Vizier. — The Turks in all have an Army of above 30000 Men, sadly disciplined but eager to get into Cairo & Plunder […]

Your Affectionate & Dutiful Son
<u>T Birch</u>

PS The Nile is beginning to rise & ye Plague which I now tell you has raged this year to such a degree that they say 22000 have dyed [*sic*] at Cairo is over.

---

25  A short fur-trimmed jacket often worn by Hussars.

## Letter 4:17 (George Holme Sumner[26], of Hatchlands, Surrey, to Thomas Birch, in Egypt, dated 4 July, 1801)

My dear Friend

I have received with very particular Satisfaction and pleasure, three Letters from you […] & it is doubly gratifying to my feelings at once to know that I stand so high in your Regard, that you can find time to give me news of you, amidst the arduous Toils & Dangers of the Field […]

[…] We have had great Political Changes in this Country since you left it […] I never can believe the Catholic Emancipation to have been the real Ground of Mr Pitt's Secession — but whatever may have influenced his mind to such a measure that Mr Addington should have been look'd to to fill his Place or that He should have resign'd one to which his Abilities were so equal & well suited — for one so arduous & so beyond the usual powers of Mens' Minds is beyond my Comprehension […] The Consternation prevalent on the first News of it, & arising I conceive from the persuasion long impress'd upon the Minds of the Country that Mr Pitt was alone capable of extricating us from the Labyrinth of Difficulties in which we have so long been involved, is now a good deal abated & the Apprentice Ministers as they are call'd by Opposition, seem rather to be obtaining Confidence. […]

While you have been extending our Country's Glory over the hot Sands of Africa, the Gallant Nelson has made it scarce less conspicuous on the Shores of the Baltic than he did at Aboukir. The Battle was hard & well fought but it is much believed that the Gallant Commander distinguish'd himself as much by his prudence as by his Valor & that we owe not less to the former than to the latter, the fame of our Arms in this new Scene of their Action. […]

I don't always think the Devil's at play because I don't see Him at work — but the people here, think that is the Case with Bonaparte — He certainly has appear'd to be doing very little since the Conclusion of Peace with Austria — but I suspect such a Mind as his, can never know repose, & if his Situation at Home is not more thorney & difficult than we are taught here to believe, I fear we shall be surprised with some new & daring Effort against the weakest but certainly one of the most important Branches of this Empire. I mean our new associated

---

26  Member of Parliament for Surrey, and a Colonel in the Royal Surrey Militia, Sumner owned Hatchlands (now National Trust), at East Clandon, Surrey.

Kingdom[27]; if they were as united at Home as we are, I should have no fears for aught the daring Corsican could do to us at home or abroad — but with internal divisions the Enemy must be always dreadful. They say there are 26 Sail of the Line ready to sail from Brest, but whether for Egypt or Ireland each man calculates according to his Opinions. I believe they'll not get out, & if they do they must have good luck to get to either Destination […]

[…] I am if any thing a greater Farmer than ever — & thank God the appearance of the Crops upon the Ground is such as to give us reasonable hope of that sufficiency if not abundance of Grain that we have been greatly distress'd for the want of these two years — the Importations have put us beyond the Apprehensions of starving this year, but Wheat is still £40 per load — & Meat at a proportionately high price […]

[…] We were as usual at the Ascot Races this year, & had the Pleasure of seeing your good Mother & Sister who look'd very well—they talk'd a good deal to Mrs H. S. but did not recognize me in my new Farmer's Garb of a crop, without powder […]

> Believe me Dear Birch
> Very sincerely & faithfully yours
> G. Holme Sumner

---

*It is a great pity that only one of Mrs Mary Birch's many letters to her son in Egypt has survived. Mary (1737–1837) was clearly a lovely personality who lived through a century of dramatic events, captured in her delightfully chatty letters to a variety of correspondents[28].*

---

27 Two Acts of Union, passed respectively on 2 July and 1 August, 1800, combined to unite the Kingdom of Great Britain and the Kingdom of Ireland as the United Kingdom (UK) of Great Britain and Ireland, coming into force on 1 January, 1801.

28 After Mrs Birch's death, a few months short of her hundredth birthday, members of her family published a book of her selected letters written in the last couple of years of her life, some of which are included in Chapter 7.

## Letter 4:18 (Mary Birch, Windsor, to her son Thomas Birch, in Egypt, dated 5 July, 1801)

St. Leonards July 5<sup>th</sup> 1801

My dearest Tom,

Never having heard a word from you since the action of the 21<sup>st</sup> your dear letter dated the 29<sup>th</sup> of March & that to James dated the 3 of April which arriv'd yesterday was most truly welcome indeed, we never know how to make enough of them but read them over & over fancying ourselves nearer to you. I endeavour not to make myself uneasy as that wou'd imply a distrust of that Providence under whose care & protection you are in all places alike, but you are in my constant thoughts & prayers, & may it please God to preserve your dear & valuable life [...].

[...] Today at Church Mrs Harcourt introduced me to Prince William of Gloucester[29] — who said to me "I hope the Major was well when you heard, indeed Genl. Harcourt probably has heard since you — he had a letter yesterday giving a full & excellent account — & I have heard from Genl. Coote since those accounts & he I'm sure would have mention'd, if any thing had happen'd to Major Birch." [...] Genl. Harcourt sent us your letter to read which is a most clear & clever account & quite brings the action to one's presence — surely with this, you must have got some of our letters — I long'd to send you some money for I can't bear you should want any thing but unless you send me word I can't tell how & it is not plenty enough to be able to lose any without feeling it.

How you contrive to write so very clean, clear & well as to Style & writing I cannot guess — it puts those to shame who are surrounded with writing materials & [...] every comfort of life & nothing to annoy them & yet complain, & are discontented for ever — I hope my dearest Tom if you escape unhurt you will remain well — & if it shou'd (which Heaven avert) be otherwise I trust you will be rewarded for the uniform endeavour you have shewn to make the best of your profession & so reconcile us to it by every affectionate & dutifull attention in your power, for a more affectionate Son & brother cannot exist! Your Father is high in commendation of your letters & sends with this, Mary & your dear Aunt, love as sincere as can be sent — your Aunt Molly is keeping a dog for you.

---

29  Brother of George III, a former Army officer and Warden of Windsor Forest (of which General Harcourt was Deputy Warden), Prince William of Gloucester lived at Cranbourne Lodge, St Leonard's Hill, Windsor.

## THE EGYPTIAN CAMPAIGN

Lady Birch[30] sent us a Puppy; I grumbled at keeping it, & therefore your Aunt said she would — Sultan is sold, Mr Rose sold him for us to Sir Thos. Miller for 4 score Guineas, an excellent Master he has got who doats upon him and only canters gently with him a few miles every day — Highflyer Mr Parry did not want, & nobody else seems to stand in need of him so here he is Coughing still — now I will tell you how we are situated […] all ye Family are well — but the country about rather sickly. Mrs Henry has lost her Dairy maid, two grown up Sons & a Daughter with a fever in the space of a fortnight some weeks ago before they came into the Country. I mention it only to shew you maladys & accidents happen here as well as at ye seat of War […]

[…] Mr, Mrs & the Miss Reynardsons came in their way from Town for two days — they are going to ye Sea, Katherine having as usual a pain in her side — but all lively & well. Lord & Lady Brownlow & the Miss Custs & his 4 eldest Sons came for a day to Windsor — & drank tea & spent 2 or 3 hours here. […]

[…] John comes down every Saturday & returns at 6 Monday morn'g; […] he […] was delighted the other day to hear his friend Mr Scot say when he came from the House of Commons that when they were discussing the usefulness of a Military College of instruction being estimated, your Name was particularly mention'd by the Secretary of War Mr Yorke, as having shewn how usefull it was by the service you had been of.

[…] Mrs Wilson […] is now I find Lady Wilson from Major Wilson having been invested with ye order of Maria Theresa[31] for grand action somewhere, but she says she will not be call'd so till Major Wilson returns. She seems a sweet sensible woman & has a delightfull Girl & Boy. — God bless you. — I hardly know how to finish with tenderness enough — I have so much reason to be your Affectionate Mother

Mary Birch

The doubt of your ever getting your letters makes one have no comfort in writing […]

---

30 This reference is rather obscure, as since the death of Sir Thomas Birch's wife in 1754 there was no one in the immediate family with this title. Mrs Birch may be referring to the judge's daughter-in-law, Mrs George Birch (née Ann Lane), the mother of Wyrley Birch — soon to be married to Katherine Reynardson —, as elsewhere she implies that side of the family was inclined to give itself airs. 'Aunt Molly' is probably Sir Thomas's unmarried daughter Mary (see **3: 1**).

31 Thomas's friend Robert Wilson (1777–1849), whose hut he had shared in Turkey before the Egyptian landings, was one of eight British officers awarded a special gold medal by Emperor Francis II for their part in the Anglo-Austrian victory over the French at the Battle of Villers-en-Cauchies in April 1794, since at that time the Military Order of Maria Theresa — the highest military honour conferred by the Austro-Hungarian Empire — was not given to foreigners. After a change in the Order's statutes in 1801, the same officers were created Knights Bachelor (*London Gazette*, No. 15370).

**Letter 4:19 (John W. Birch, London, to his brother Thomas Birch, in Egypt, dated 8 July, 1801)**

5 King's Bench Walks, Temple —
July 8th

My dear Tom,

I cannot think how it happens that you have never heard from England, & cannot help thinking there must have been negligence somewhere among those in official situations, who ought to have establish'd some communication with our Brethren in Egypt. We have written several letters all of us, perhaps they may have been taken, & may give Bonaparte an opportunity of retorting the publication of an intercepted correspondence; <u>individually</u> I hope not so, for mine would make a sorry figure in print. Among other things we sent some newspapers which contained an account of some important political events which have occurred since you left England, as the Union, the change of administration, & the war with the Northern powers &c which after the glorious victory at Copenhagen is in a way of being terminated by an amicable adjustment. — […] Active negotiations are at present carrying on for peace with France, & we wait with patience for the results; in the mean time Buonaparte is making most formidable preparations all along the coasts to invade England, whether with a view to alarm us, or with a design of making a Serious attempt is uncertain: if the latter Be assured the Spirit & confidence which has been inspired by the glorious victories in Egypt will afford us the best security against the attacks of the enemy by giving us a proper dependence on our own exertions.

[…] Your Plan has been engraved & publish'd [**Fig. 4 f)**]; […] Faden who published it had it of Col. Calvert that with your excellent letter to General Harcourt [*it*] enables us to accompany the movements of the army with great exactness.

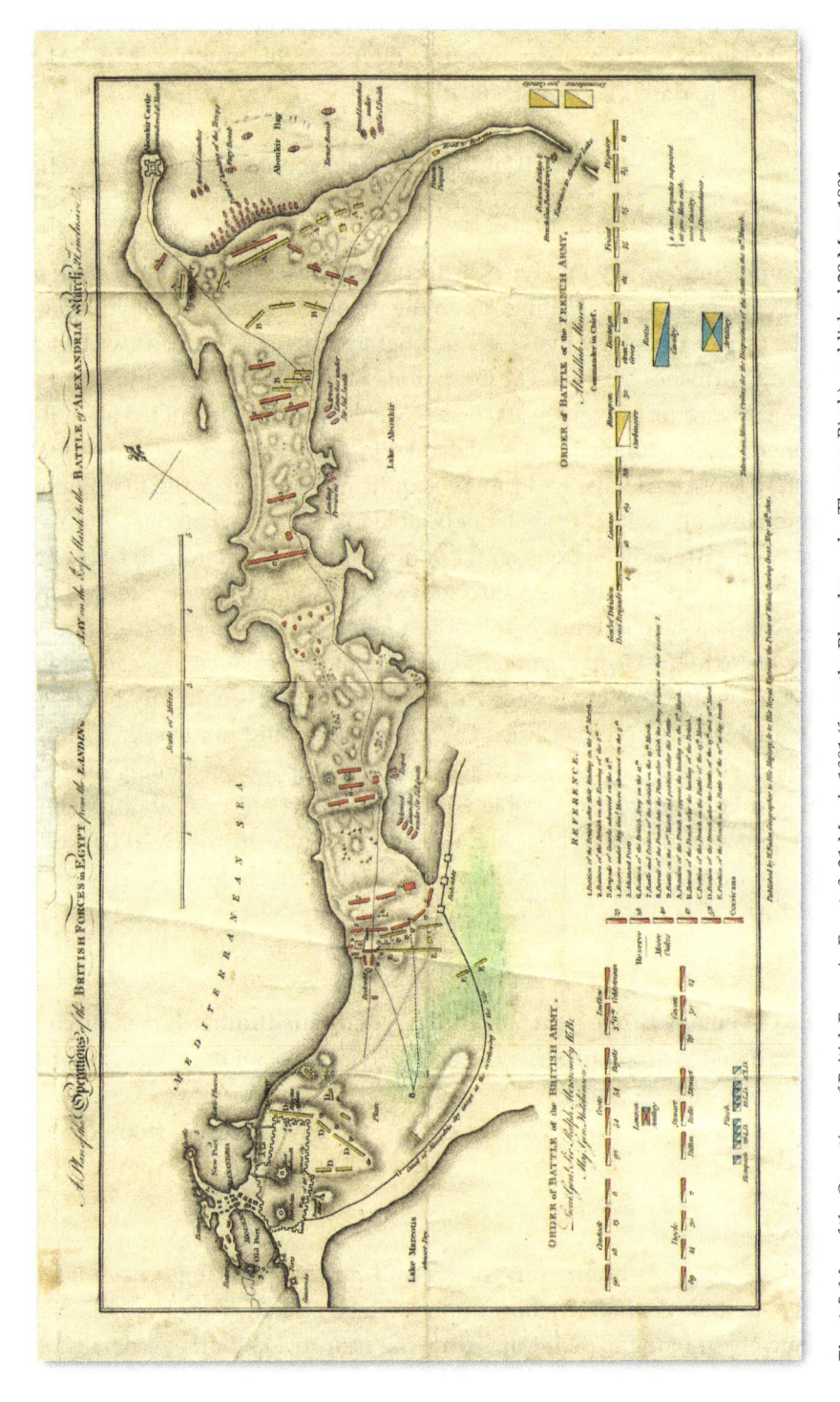

**Fig. 4 f)** *Map of the Operations of British Forces in Egypt, 8–21 March, 1801* (from the Plan drawn by Thomas Birch), published 28 May, 1801

## Letter 4:20 (Thomas Birch, near Rosetta, Egypt, to his mother, Mrs Mary Birch, dated 1 August, 1801)

Camp on the Nile about 8 Miles from Rosetta.<br>
1<sup>st</sup> Aug. 1801

It will be some time since you have heard from me my dearest Mother; various are the reasons for it & I don't think upon the whole bad ones; to tell you that I had not the proper use of my Eyes for a fortnight particularly as far as writing & drawing goes furnishes one […]. The Opthalmia or blindness is dreadful, tho' the Sight after a time returns; you see 100 or 150 Men of each Regiment led about by their Brother Soldiers totally helpless. I cannot boast of anything so bad as that, but for a few Mornings have had my Eyes quite closed. This is the first night I have written by Candle light & shall not be able to go farther than the bottom.

I have been extremely anxious about poor Frank, & after a month's absence he is returned to me […] before Cairo he was very ill, fell away, ate nothing &c & so weak that he could not help himself. Some advised me to send him to Rosetta by water to the Hospital, others said he could not bear ye passage, which is 3 or 4 days, without ye greatest attention; I was anxious to do my duty by a good & valuable old Servant & Friend who I fear'd would not live, & […] put him on board a boat myself about 5 Miles from ye Camp, got an awning made & every thing as comfortable as possible with strict injunctions to a careful Man to pay him every attention & so I left him satisfied that whether he lived or died I had done my duty by him […]. I was indeed happy to find him yesterday quite recover'd […]

## Letter 4:21 (Thomas Birch, near Rosetta, Egypt, to his brother James Birch, dated 3 August, 1801) *(Letter in transcription only)*

Camp on the Nile, 8 Miles from Rosetta<br>
3<sup>rd</sup> August, 1801.

My dear James,

Since I last wrote to my friends in England important changes have taken place in the situation & affairs in this Country, which give one reason to hope that the ultimate object of the Expedition is drawing near to a favourable conclusion.

[...] A few days after [*the capitulation of Cairo*] the French sent to require a conference; an Armistice [...] ensued [...] till the terms of the convention were agreed upon finally. I send them for you & John to look over at leisure; [...] tho' I suppose when you receive this it will be old news. Whatever may be the opinion of the terms at the first view, tho' by some they may seem too favourable, I fancy when a just statement of the force of the French fit to bear arms in defence of Cairo is ascertained, it will appear as a measure that has saved the lives of many valuable Troops, deserving of credit to those who have authorised it.

[...] The French army have marched in formidable force from Cairo, encamped daily within 3 miles of ours [...]. They are nearly all now on board, it is an extraordinary event in the annals of war. [...] A French Col. commanding 9th D. Brig. told me the other night that they should embark 14000 Men fit to bear arms, that they had 13000 ready to fire a musket behind the walls of Cairo tho' not to bring into the Field, & they draw rations for 16000 souls, so from this you may form an Idea of their strength.

My dear James, our success hitherto in this Country is a miracle; had the force of the French at the beginning of March been thoroughly known, we should not have been authorised to have ventured upon a Landing; had the proper measures been taken by the Enemy to have prevented it, it could not have been effected; judge for yourself: besides the Troops above mentioned, they have 4000 at Alexandria & we have killed or taken prisoner as many more. We hear from England that this Army has gained immortal honor; that is a great reward but it deserves some thing after a tedious fatiguing Campaign which it has borne cheerfully under many inconveniences of Climate [...]. We have lost many valuable officers & men by disease, but the plague & dysentery have ceased [...]

The much talked of Mamalukes came fully up to my expectation; they are mounted on the most beautiful horses dressed in robes of the most brilliant colours & greatest variety with large turbans on their heads; desperately armed, their dexterity in the management of their horses is surprising. Every Bey has his Mamaluke; every Mamaluke his servant [...] dismounted & constantly by his side, the latter always runs by him to carry dispatches &c. [...]

Alexandria remains; they say Menou will stand a siege perhaps to retrieve his character which must have suffered from the bad disposition he has made in this Country. I am inclined to believe he will be glad to quit the Country with his treasure when he finds himself pushed, but I hope then it will be too late [...]

I am, your very affectionate Brother,
T Birch

## Letter 4:22 (General William Harcourt, Windsor, to Thomas Birch, in Egypt, dated 13 August, 1801)

St Leonards 13<sup>th</sup> August 1801

Dear Birch

I avail myself of the opportunity of Capt. Harcourt's [*the General's son*] departure for Egypt, to return you my best acknowledgments for the two very satisfactory accounts of your Operations; much do I wish that your next letter may convey to us, the news of the final completion of a Service, which has reflected so much credit upon the Army, for its valour and unremitted exertions.

Capt. Harcourt will inform you of the present State of Affairs in this Country, which I thank God have been in a gradual State of improvement ever since that most Fortunate event, the death of the Emperor Paul; and tho' Buonaparte has run the whole of his force to act against us, and has made preparations to invade us from every Port of the French, Flemish, and Dutch Coasts, from Brest to the Texel; I trust that the measures which have been taken to oppose him, supported by the general spirit of the People, will have [*been*] sufficient to repel any attack he may make against this Country.

As I know you are in correspondence with Col. Le Marchant, I conclude you will have heard that the Military College, to which without flattery your labours in Egypt have done much credit, is now organizing [...] as fast as possible; Parliament having given a very liberal Grant for creating a College upon an extensive Plan, near Blackwater; with such allowances to the Officers of this College, the Professors, and Masters in the various Services, as promise to put this most useful Establishment upon the best possible Footing; a very well digested Code of Regulations, compiled & put into form by Le Marchant [...] has been approved of by His Majesty, who has also been so gracious to appoint me to be the Governor, Le Marchant Lieut-Governor, and Genl. Jarry Superintendant and Instructor of the First Class, with such Appointments as fully satisfy the wishes of a Man who is certainly the Main Spring of the Institution, and whose merits cannot be too amply rewarded [...]

> [...] Very sincerely and truly Yours
> William Harcourt

**Letter 4:23 (Thomas Birch, near Alexandria, to his father, George Birch, dated 1 September, 1801 (Fig. 4 g))**

Camp before Alexandria, 1st Sept. 1801

My dear Sir,

   As one of the most important events in <u>my military</u> career, I feel the utmost satisfaction in having an opportunity of making you acquainted with it; & an event of the most extensive <u>national importance</u> too, I have a right to claim as I have in your congratulations. Alexandria is ours; and the Once <u>invincible French Army of ye East</u> has surrendered Egypt to a British Army, that deserves any Name its country chuses to bestow upon it. […]

   […] We don't calculate very deeply on our prize money. Soldiers are so little in the habit of profiting by it but I suppose something will be forthcoming by & bye.

   The next step is the Embarkation of the Army for Malta, Minorca & part probably [*for*] England. The Staff I have reason to believe will be broke up, my object is to get to Malta & compleat as far as circumstances will admit of it the Plans I have been endeavouring to arrange for HRH the Commander in Chief […]

   […] The Ottomans are intoxicated with joy in having a Country restored to them which so much extends their consequence & Power. […]

   You will excuse I'm sure my not saying more tonight […]. Distribute the only present I have which is the most sincere affection for all my Family.

I am, my Dear Sir,<br>Your Dutiful Son<br><u>TB</u>

*The letter was re-opened after sealing for Thomas to add the following news:*

   The Grenadiers of the British Army took Possession of the French lines & works yesterday — & we have Picquets at <u>Pompey's Pillar</u>.

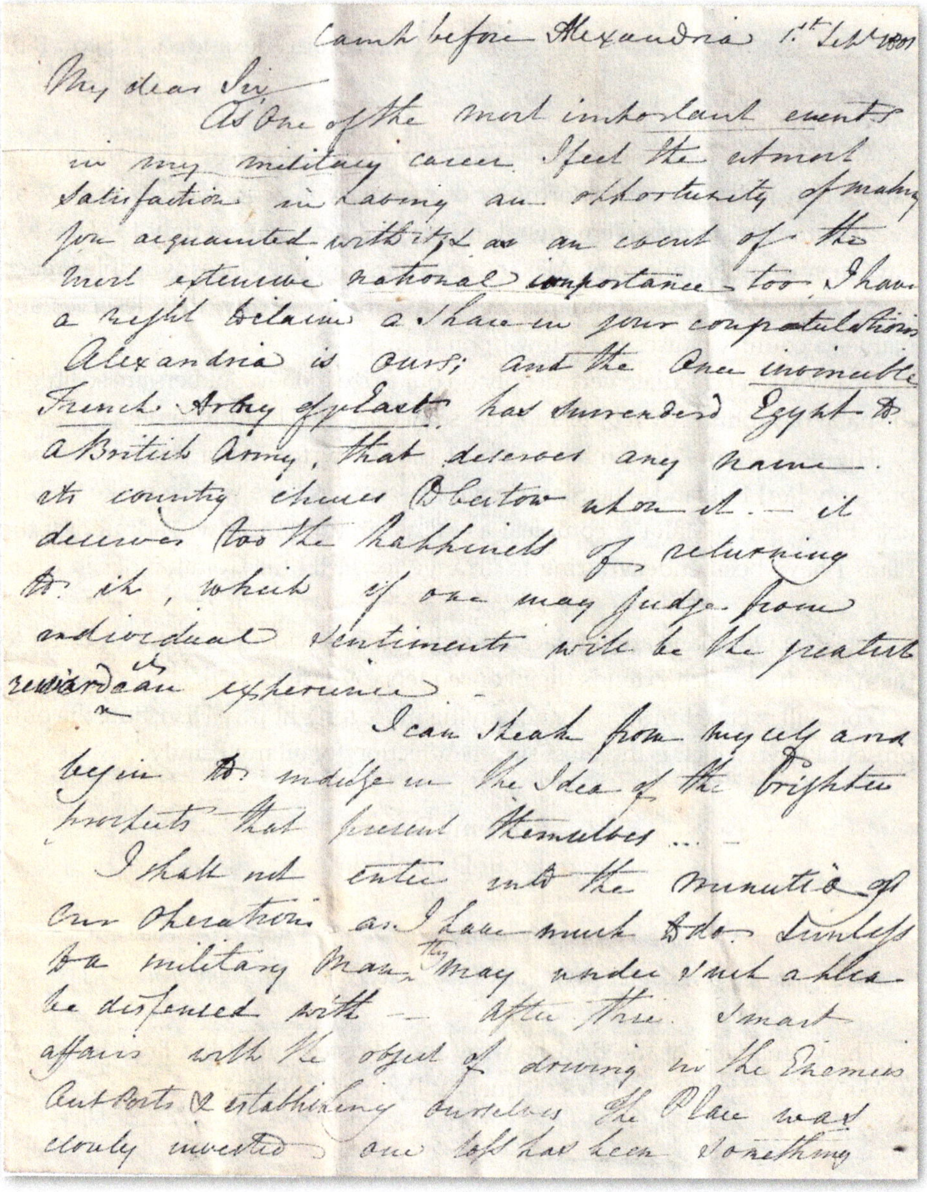

Fig. 4 g) A page from Letter 4: 23 (Thomas Birch to his father, George Birch, dated 1 September 1801)

## Letter 4:24 (Thomas Birch, Alexandria, to his brother, John William Birch, dated 9 September, 1801)

Camp to the Eastward of Alexandria
9th September 1801

[...] It strikes me that it is your turn my dear John as I wrote by the Ship that took the dispatches 9 days ago to my Father [...]. My Mother I have hardly ever missed writing to.

You will scarcely credit it but I have not received a line from any part of my Family since [...] March & I'm sure you must all have written to me. From Col. Le Marchant I rec'd a letter dated 10th May. I know he wrote many others; so whether they have contributed to the amusement of the curious or are gone to the bottom of the Sea will probably remain a Secret. — Some letters that I wrote by the Swiftsure[32] will of course not be received as she was taken by the Enemy.

Six months ago, my dear John, & in what a different Situation we felt ourselves then; we stood in a dreadful uncertainty & now the great task is perform'd — [...] when I have given you a Statement of the French force in the Country [...] it will appear next to a Miracle. [...]

[...] Genl. Menou thought it adviseable to send in his Proposals [*after Alexandria had been retaken successfully*], which were arranged & conducted with a good deal of firmness on the Part of Genl. Hutchinson — The Shipping to be given up; the Public Stores, & the antiquities & Curiosities[33] amass'd since the landing of the French in this Country — all Plans &c, which they endeavour to keep snug & I don't know as yet whether we have got at any.

Genl. Menou is indignant at the conduct of Genl. Belliard, [*he*] is an oldish Man & seems firmly attach'd to the cause [&] says one or the other shall have their heads upon a Pole, on his return to France[34].

[...] I conclude my letter with a statement of the French force in this Country

---

32   HMS *Swiftsure*, a 74-gun third rate Royal Navy ship, played a prominent role in the Battle of the Nile in 1798 and, as part of Lord Keith's Mediterranean fleet, helped to cover the landings of the British troops at Aboukir in March, 1801. She was captured by a French squadron on 24 June, while on her way to Malta as a convoy escort, and for the next few years was taken into service by the French navy until she was recaptured at the Battle of Trafalgar in October, 1805, and towed into Gibraltar for repair before returning to England.

33   Amongst these was the Rosetta Stone, an ancient Egyptian tablet inscribed with three distinct texts which have provided the key to understanding hieroglyphics. It was discovered in 1799 by a soldier in Napoleon's invading army, but passed into British possession after the capitulation of Alexandria and was transported to London, where it has been on display in the British Museum since 1802.

34   It was said that Napoleon was much attached to Menou, despite his dismal record in Egypt; he avoided the fate he feared, and ended his career as Governor of Venice, before his death in 1810.

at ye time of our landing —

The total embark'd & to embark including Men, Women, Children, Employees, Sick &c [...] amounts to:

31,412 Souls — of which 23,900 were effective Soldiers —

Accounted for: 3,500 (embark'd according to Lord Keith's return [...])
         9,500 March'd from Cairo & embark'd
         3,000 Kill'd, disabled, dead of Plague
         6,000 Effective at Alexandria
         1,900 Marines
         ———
         23,900 [...]

## Letter 4:25 (Thomas Birch, Alexandria, to his father, George Birch, dated 19 September, 1801)

Camp before Alexandria.
19th Sept. 1801

It is incomprehensible to me my dear Sir that almost all the letters written lately from home have come to hand <u>excepting yours</u>; the same direction that brings the one would bring the other, but no matter, <u>you will know</u> how to account for it, I have only to suppose they were written & to return you all the amusing intelligence I can from this quarter of the Globe.

Yes indeed my dear Sir, in the receipt of letters from those I love best in the world, about 3 nights ago I received pleasure & heartfelt satisfaction I had been a stranger to for over 4 Months [...]: 1 from my Mother, in London <u>without date</u> [...], another 5th July, St Leonards, from Ditto — 1 from John, 16 May, amusing & satisfactory <u>in ye extreme</u>, 1 Ditto 8th July — Oh! What a treat! You are not in Egypt away from every Soul who can have a real interest for you, nor have you ever been my dear Sir in a Situation to experience feelings such as mine.

From Friends too I had two or 3 other letters; it is pleasant not to be forgotten, Mr Sumner wrote me a very long one full of good nature, good sense & political information [4: 17]; Montalembert wrote expecting to join me daily but that I should think would not take place; at all events it would be "<u>a day after the fair</u>" — For thank God, the arduous task in <u>this</u> Country is completed, & wherever next our Services may be called for, I pray the Climate may not be included as an Enemy; [...]

An entire new distribution has been made of this Army since the last dispatches. Those Regiments which have most suffer'd go directly to England; some to Malta &c — about 4000 Men remain in this Country & an Expedition under Major Genl. Coote is on foot — but at this Moment all breathes peace & tranquillity <u>with us</u> […]

[…] I have litterally only had my saddle bags with a Change of Cloaths for these 6 Months, my small trunks having been left on board Ship — I hope they will come to light some time or other […]

I am my Dear Sir — Your affectionate & Dutiful Son
<u>Thos Birch</u> […]

**LETTER 4:26 (Thomas Birch, on board the *Lord Duncan*, to his mother Mary Birch, dated 8 October, 1801)**

On Board the Lord Duncan Transport   October 8th 1801

This letter will surprise you all; if I judge right too it will be read with no small degree of pleasure & I shall fancy your congratulations from my own feelings on my having quitted the Egyptian shore after an <u>existence</u> of seven Months mark'd by circumstances that have taken too strong a hold of my mind to be easily forgotten & which may probably furnish the most remarkable events of my life.

Yes my dearest Mother I embark'd yesterday Evening. This Morning [*I*] saw the last of Egypt <u>7 Months</u> exactly [*since*] I set foot on Shore. <u>That day</u> will not be forgotten — I thank God that I have escaped plague, pestilence & the sword […]; tho' I cannot say the Country or Climate agreed with me, I hope the being on board Ship may work changes & improvements or I fear I shall not do credit in appearance to my Egyptian expedition.[…]

10th October.

[…] Among the saddest tales I have to relate is ye loss of my Baggage […] — my two small Trunks with almost all my Cloaths & in short every thing I did not absolutely want on Shore at landing was left on board; has since been overhauled from Ship to Ship & I may probably never hear of it again. — My Sketch books were among the Valuables.

You were so good as to be alarm'd about Money. That has never cost me a thought & if I don't return richer than I came out I shall have been working very hard for nothing — tho' making money is certainly one of the last recommendations to our Profession.

October 17th. [...] I find myself much better than when I came on board, & chiefly want Strengthening & fattening & as that is the case I don't mind telling you that I have not been quite well. My Bones are actually so near ye <u>edge</u> of my Skin that I am sore by ye Motion of the Ship & in leaning against ye sides & chairs in which we have not been in the habit of indulging in lately. It is a great Satisfaction to think, I stand a chance of being renovated by a little English <u>Flesh</u>. [...]

[...] The Day before we left Egypt afforded a grand Spectacle. The General Officers & heads of ye Staff waited on ye Captain Pacha & rec'd presents sent from Constantinople by ye Grand Signor. — Sir John Hutchinson rec'd an Aigrette[35] & all of them <u>Diamond</u> presents in different Shapes, were invested with most sumptuous Pelisses [...] & the Commander in Chief's Horse was cover'd with a most Splendid coat of Mail of Gold [...]

October 25 — Malta — on Board.

[...] We yesterday came to an anchor & are in quarantine for some days but how long I know not, perhaps may not go on Shore at all. It is too tantalizing after having been for some time on board. — This place abounds with the finest Vegetables & Fruit which they bring off to us [...]

## Letter 4:27 (Thomas Birch, in Milan, to his father George Birch, dated 25 December, 1801)

[...] You may be glad my dear Sir to know I am got so far on my Road home. We had come a little out of our road to see Milan & mean to proceed immediately thro' Turin & Lyons to Paris[36] without stopping longer than it is absolutely necessary.

I have experienced the greatest amusement & of course variety in the course of this journey which was no inconsiderable undertaking at this time of ye Year. — The Appenines were tremendously cold but beautiful. Florence exceeds any description I have ever met with, & the towns of Bologna, Modena & Parma &

---

35 A headdress made from the tufted crest of the egret, often used with diamonds and rubies to decorate the turbans of Ottoman sultans.
36 The Treaty of Amiens, which brought about a brief period of peace between France and Britain, was not signed until 25 March, 1802, but as its provisional terms had been negotiated the previous November, it was possible for returning British combatants to pass safely through France.

Placentia are all worth attention with the intervening Country which is a perfect Garden. We stopp'd a short time to look at the famous bridge at Lodi, & in short from having pass'd thro' this very military Country we shall feel greater interest in the Campaigns.

We feel very forcibly the change of Climate, Sicily was delightful & here the ground is cover'd with snow, but we must reserve all our courage for ye Alps. I confess I shall congratulate myself when we have cross'd Mont Cenis — we have now about 600 Miles to Paris.

[…] I thank God for ye perfect restoration of my health […]. We live luxuriously in this very beautiful Country, & I must think we have a right to indulge a little after the privations we have experienced for many Months past — Instead of a skeleton, which indeed I have been, I hope to present myself to you in <u>better condition</u> or as good as when I left England; I cannot feel too thankful for it considering the very reduced State I was in some Months previous to my quitting Egypt.

It would have added to my happiness could I have spent <u>Xmas</u> day with my Family, I fancy you all now happily assembled at home. With what pleasure do I look forward to our meeting […].

      Adieu & God bless you all.

CHAPTER 5

# The Peninsular War (1) and the ill-fated Walcheren Campaign

*Letters and Diary Extracts 1802–1809*

'It is quite impossible to ride thro' the town &
not feel deeply impress'd with the Horrors of War.'[1]

*Thomas Birch was one of many who visited the Continent during this time, taking advantage of the brief period of peace between the end of the War of the Second Coalition (1798–1801) and Britain's renewed declaration of war against France in May 1803*[2]*. Soon after his return to England, Thomas was rewarded for his services in Egypt by being promoted to the rank of Lieutenant-Colonel. His responsibilities in Egypt as Assistant Quarter Master General had included the supply of equipment, provisions and munitions to the army, as well as intelligence gathering and surveying the land ahead of the marching troops. When war broke out again in 1803, Thomas was appointed to the permanent staff of the Quarter Master General, which was confirmed in a letter from General Robert Brownrigg, Quarter Master General to the Forces (in which capacity he would later be Thomas's superior officer in the Walcheren campaign). The letter makes it plain that even before the war against France had resumed, Thomas had already been commissioned to carry out another assignment on behalf of his former training college, when he was* 'placed in the Command of Officers selected from the Royal Military College to make a Military Survey of ye Coast of Kent'[3], *in anticipation of invasion from France.*

---

1 Letter from Lt.-Colonel Thomas Birch, Tergoes, South Beveland, to his wife Etheldred, at Holywell, 19 August, 1809 (**5: 12**), describing the aftermath of the bombardment of Flushing.
2 The flood of British tourists to France and Italy, taking the first opportunity they had had for nine years, included a large number of writers and artists. For the next twelve years, after the resumption of hostilities in 1803, there would be few chances of private visits to the Continent. The war would this time go on until 1815, ending only with the victory over France by the Allied armies under the Duke of Wellington (Britain) and Marshal Blücher (Prussia) at the Battle of Waterloo (see Chapter 6).
3 From an undated 'Memorandum' in his own hand, reviewing his career with the army from 1793 to 1814.

LETTER 5:1 (General Robert Brownrigg, Horse Guards, London, to Lt.-Colonel Thomas Birch, dated 2 May, 1803)

Horse Guards
2nd May 1803

Dear Sir

I have sincere pleasure in acquainting you with your appointment to the situation of Assistant in the Department to which I have the Honour to belong, an arrangement that I trust will prove as satisfactory to you, as I am persuaded it will be advantageous to the Service. It cannot I am sure fail of being gratifying to you, as proving in the most flattering way, the Approbation of His Majesty and the Commander in Chief, of your merits and past services.

To myself your appointment is every way acceptable, and I hope to render it as pleasing to you, as circumstances can possibly admit. — There is at present no reason to suppose that it will affect the Service you are intended to be employ'd upon in conducting the Survey to be undertaken by the Officers of the Royal Military College[4].

I am, Dear Sir, your faithful and very humble Servant
Robt. Brownrigg

---

*Following his appointment, Thomas was soon placed in charge of the Quarter Master General's department in the Eastern District, not far from the East Anglian coast (its headquarters being at Lexden, near Colchester in Essex). Around this time he also began to occupy his free time more pleasantly by getting to know his sister Mary's 'delightful & agreeable friends the Reynardsons' (4: 15), and especially the eldest of Jacob Reynardson's and his wife Anne Cust's four daughters, Etheldred (generally known simply as 'Ethel'). By the summer of 1805, Thomas and Etheldred were engaged and the two families appear to have celebrated by holidaying together at the seaside resort of*

---

4   The military Survey on which Thomas was engaged concentrated on the coast of Kent, one of the areas where an invasion was thought most likely to take place. In response to Britain's renewed declaration of war, Napoleon, who was by 1803 the virtual ruler of France (he had been named First Consul for life in 1802 and would be proclaimed Emperor in 1804), mustered his army on the north coast of France and began to assemble a fleet at Boulogne. Deployments of British troops were moved close to the southern and eastern coasts where the French army was expected to land and Martello towers were built along these coasts to give advance warning of any approaching enemy fleet.

*Southend, made newly fashionable by recent visits from Princess Charlotte, George III's eldest daughter, and from his daughter-in-law, Caroline, Princess of Wales. Putting his artistic skills to good use, Thomas recorded one of their holiday expeditions in a charming watercolour signed 'Chaperona fecit'* (**Fig. 5 a)**), *also writing a poem about the occasion which he called 'The Angels on Horseback'* (see **Appendix II** *for full text).*

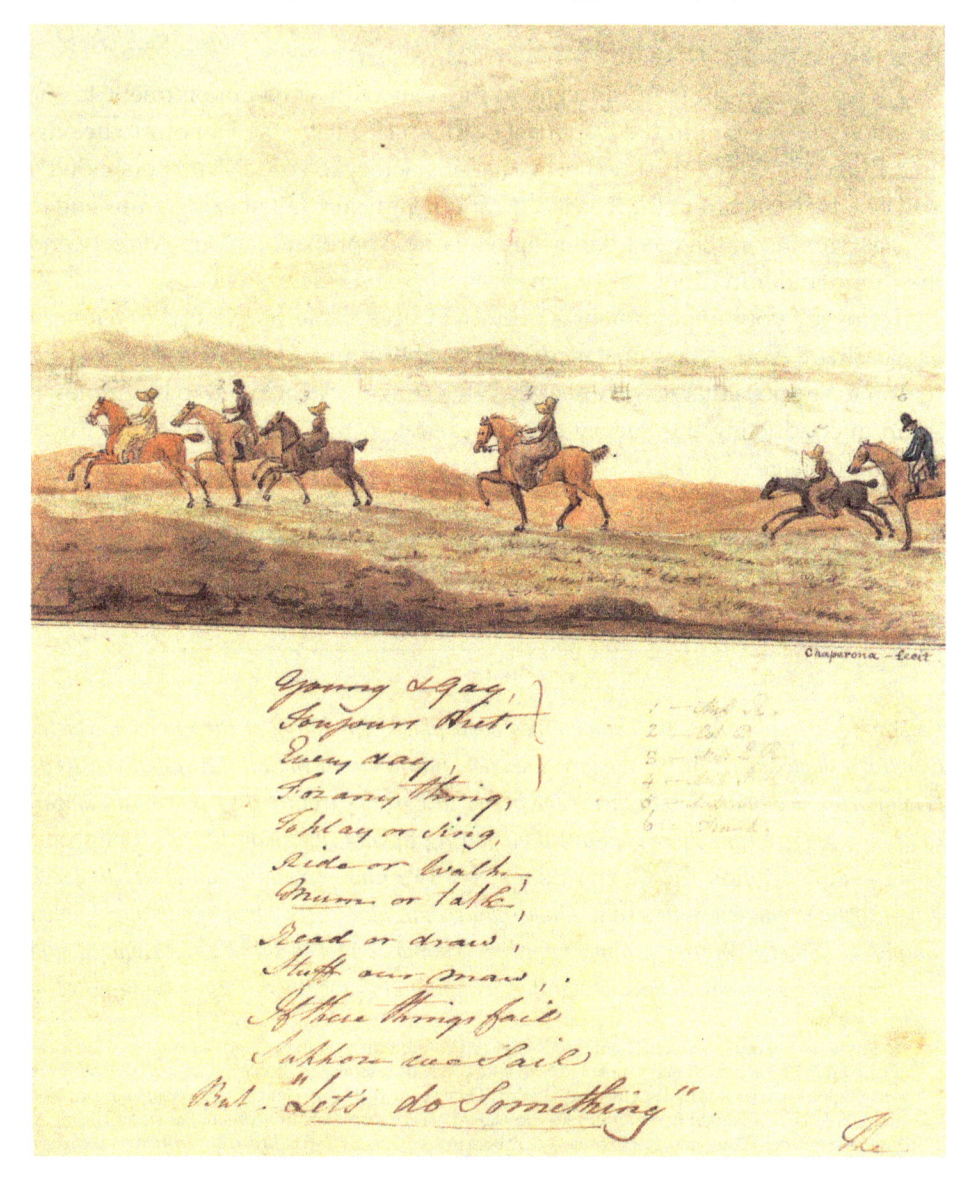

**Fig. 5 a)** *A Riding Party at Southend*, by Thomas Birch. Watercolour, July 1805.

*My great-great-grandparents Thomas and Etheldred were married on 3 June 1806 and settled in their first home, a cottage close to the military encampment on Lexden Heath. They were not the first members of the Birch and Reynardson families to marry, as in 1804 Thomas's second cousin Wyrley Birch (grandson of the judge, see* Chapter 2*) had married one of Etheldred's younger sisters Katherine — she of the perpetual pain in her side* (**4: 18**)*. However, as the eldest daughter and heiress of the family home of Holywell, it was on the insistence of her father Jacob (the last male member of the Reynardson family) that Etheldred added her surname to that of her husband, which took place following Jacob's death in 1812.*[5]

*In spite of his newly married state, it seems that Thomas still hankered to return to active service, even though the immediate danger of invasion had been averted by Nelson's emphatic victory over the French and Spanish fleets at the Battle of Trafalgar in October 1805*[6]*. He wrote for advice to his old friend and mentor, Lt.-Colonel John Le Marchant, who at this time was still lieutenant governor of the Royal Military College. Le Marchant's reply makes ironic reading in view of his own fate a few years later (see* Chapter 6*).*

---

### LETTER 5:2 (Lt.-Colonel John Le Marchant, High Wycombe, to Lt.-Colonel Thomas Birch, dated 3 October, 1806)

Private<br>High Wycombe  3<sup>rd</sup> October 1806

My Dear Birch,

You ask my opinion on the propriety of soliciting employment abroad. There was a time when my advice would have been to exert every endeavour to get on

---

5   There is a licence of this date (Holywell 110/14), allowing 'Thomas Birch, Esqr., to take the name Thomas Birch Reynardson and to bear the arms of Reynardson and Birch quarterly', in the Holywell Collection, Lincolnshire Archives, deposited in 1934 by Mrs Agatha Fane who grew up and lived at Holywell and was, like me, a great-great-grandchild of Thomas and Etheldred.

6   Napoleon's attention next turned towards Austria, Russia and Prussia, which were successively defeated, giving the French Emperor domination over most of Europe. By maintaining naval superiority, Britain had withstood invasion, though the sense of danger remained acute in the country as Napoleon's territorial ambitions spread more widely across the mainland of Europe. A comparison can be made with Hitler's decision not to invade Britain, having failed to establish air superiority during the Blitz in 1940–41. As Napoleon had done, Hitler then looked eastwards towards Russia and his subsequent attempt to invade had consequences as disastrous as Napoleon's campaign 130 years earlier.

service, because at that period you had neither Military Rank, fortune or home, but at present you are in the enjoyment of all these comforts, therefore as much as I should have thought it to your advantage to solicit employment before, I consider it would be folly to do it at present. Do you not see the Politician out of Place a Patriot, and when in office as interested as all against whom he ever declaimed? In short my dear friend I begin to perceive that we are a Set of Selfish Animals, who think & act but for our Selves, whilst those who purchase their experience late, are the dupes of such as acquired their knowledge sooner. I do not mean by this that a man should drive away every finer sentiment, but that he should see the <u>world as it is</u>, and not mislead himself in <u>thinking it</u> what <u>it ought to be</u>. If Service was proposed to you, of course you would not hesitate in accepting it, but even then without friends to sound your praises at home but little is got in return for hard blows. [...]

---

*Thomas's mother also expressed her own opinions on the matter. Mrs Mary Birch, who was over seventy when she became a grandmother for the first time on the birth of Thomas's eldest child, was already a widow, her husband George having died in 1803. In many ways however, at least to outward appearances, her life carried on much as before: she remained in the house she had shared with her husband, Barton Lodge at Windsor, with her sister moving in to live with her; she moved in the same social circles and kept the same company; and she continued to write copious and affectionate letters to friends and family, particularly to her children. The two letters from Mrs Birch (**5: 3** and **5: 4**) which I include here are characteristic: the first bemoans the fact that her daughter Mary, who was then approaching thirty, is not yet married; and the second praises her son for his professional success but also offers him advice of the sort which only a mother can give!*

---

LETTER 5:3 **(Mrs Mary Birch, at Windsor, to her son Lt.-Colonel Thomas Birch, at Colchester, 15 December, 1807)**

December 15 (at night)
1807

My dear Tom

I feel glad to see your dear hand writing again, I see but little of any of my children but my dear Mary & if I cou'd have her well married & know she was as happy as you are, that reflection wou'd prevent my regretting the want of her society, as much as it does the want of yours, tho' I may with truth say in my estimation, such is hardly or rarely to be met with. So far from grudging you John's company, I enjoy'd the idea of the dear trio, being together that loved each other, & that I loved so well — he was as much pleas'd with his visit as you were — "they look remarkably well & happy, Ethel growing fat, & in high beauty, Tom without a cold & not quite so thin" — company at dinner &c ... "dinner substantially good, well dress'd, & elegantly put on", — I think you like to hear his sentiments. [...]

Why Patty [*Frank's wife*] chuses to leave the Country she is in, & come so far to lie-in, I can't guess. I shou'd think she wou'd run some chance of losing her child on its journey, but she must manage for herself.

My dear Sister & I are now alone — [...] — Melly [*Mrs Birch's niece*] & Mary gone to Mrs Reeve to the Chalfont Ball — & to stay till Friday. Your aunt & I take a dirty walk every morning & knit & read alternately in the Evening [...] Mr & Mrs Weyland [...] are now enlisted into Mrs Harcourt's suite making constantly part of her parties (circle would read better) which circle [...] never falls off, & is seldom now at all brilliant. Mrs, & Col. Le Marchant were there on Monday, the first time she was ever ask'd; I was ask'd to meet her — Mary went in my stead — some [...] were curious, she said, but poor Mrs Le Marchant managed very well[7] – Sir Home[8] & Lady Popham were there also [...] — as to Gentlemen they

---

7   Mrs Marie Le Marchant (née Carey) was the Guernsey-born wife of Lt.-Colonel John Le Marchant. Her rare appearance at the Harcourts' parties may be due to the fact that she and her husband produced ten children during their marriage of twenty-one years, so she must have been perpetually either pregnant, recovering from childbirth, or nursing children. See Letters 6: 2 to 6: 7.
8   Admiral Sir Home Riggs Popham, K.C.B. (1762–1820) entered the navy at the age of sixteen, and served under Admiral Rodney in the American War of Independence as well as throughout the French Revolutionary and Napoleonic Wars. Despite a career marked by a number of questionable actions (see footnote 11), Popham held several commands and was promoted to Rear Admiral in 1814. At the time of this letter he was M.P. for Ipswich, which he held until 1812.

are rare in this part of ye world, not one to be seen.

As I have nothing out of my own mind to amuse you I will transcribe some excellent sentiments of John's out of a letter sent me on my birthday. "For all our sakes I wish you many returns of the 24th of November — & join in thanks to God for having preserved you to us, in the enjoyment of health, & your faculties, till this period, & may each of us shou'd we attain the same age, have the same enjoyment of the present, the same reasons to look back with satisfaction, and forward with hope. That you're interested about your earthly habitation, & are not indifferent about ye comforts of this world, is a proof that your faculty for enjoying them is unimpaired —. [...] If old people usually grow indifferent about these things it is oftener to be placed to the account of indolence or infirmity than of any sound principle of wisdom or religion."

In a letter since, he says "Not having much business, I feel low spirited, & desponding & stupid which has call'd for the constant exercise of my religion & philosophy to counteract it, by reminding one that in the enjoyment of health, of good friends, & competent circumstances, with the absence of bodily pain, I enjoy comforts which are withheld from thousands, & ought therefore to excite gratitude in the few comparatively, to whose lot they fall."

[...] I thought those sentiments of John's excellent & better than any thing we met with in the letters in Beattie's Life[9], which we have been reading & which is a heavy performance I think. God bless you both — I am my dearest Tom your very affectionate Mother

M. Birch

Your dear Aunt begs her love —

I have always forgot to tell you — I use the glass you had in Egypt constantly, it just looks in my face & suits my wrinkles & having a scarcity of glasses is of use & it constantly reminds me if I stood in need of such a memorandum of the dangers you have escaped & the sufferings you have undergone — & my reason for gratitude & thankfulness for such mercies —

Don't forget my most affectionate love to dear Ethel.

---

9 Sir William Forbes, *An Account of the Life and Writings of James Beattie, LL.D, late Professor of Moral Philosophy and Logic at the Marinchal College and University of Aberdeen* (published 1807).

## LETTER 5:4 (Mrs Mary Birch, at Windsor, to Lt.-Colonel Thomas Birch, at Colchester, dated 26 July, 1808)

July 26th 1808

My dear Tom

A letter just now of a few lines from dear John to tell me his tooth was out, that kept him in misery the whole of the two last times he has been here — & also to tell me you cou'd not help feeling chagrin at not being appointed to the staff, & yet at the same time being assured the gnawing in your loss as wou'd have been ten times worse if you had, when the parting with your dear Ethel had come to the point, wou'd it not? & what hers wou'd have been, perhaps I can tell better than any one — but your feelings are natural […] — and therefore not to be supprest wholly but regulated — […] it is owing no doubt to the goodness of the Almighty, that you are so situated as to have military duties to perform of high responsibility that do not interfere with those of domestic import — & from your not having been remov'd from them is a strong proof of your giving entire satisfaction in the line in which you are placed. What more can the bravest & greatest soldier require? You have seen the hardest Service, have acted in a most satisfactory manner & gain'd all the credit a Man cou'd do — & to make ye satisfaction still more compleat have been within an ace of paying your life for it. — And yet still have a hankering for seeking "that bubble reputation in the cannon's mouth"[10].

I do not blame, but think those feelings belong to a Man who likes his profession, & so far I am gratified because I might be in some measure instrumental to your adopting ye profession. Your not going does not augur your being set aside & forgotten at all — but where hundreds are suing to be appointed & pressing it continually & have no tye to make it inconvenient, but many reasons to make them perhaps wish to quit this Country, 'tis no wonder they did not send for you. — You must excuse me if upon reflection you suffer any thing further than a little military ardor not to say (vanity) to disturb you after the first moment — when you ought to be thankfull to Heaven for every circumstance of your Life — & particularly for your being at this time so placed that your dear Wife & myself & your Brothers & Sister also have no reason to fear for you — […] that ought

---

10  'The soldier', from Jaques's 'All the world's a stage…' speech in Shakespeare's *As You Like It* (Act 2, Scene VII).

to make you as thankfull as I am not to say rejoic'd — and if you for a moment encourage any <u>other</u> <u>feelings</u> but acquiescence & gratitude to the wise dispenser of all things you are not so good a Christian as I was in hopes you were.

[…] Just when they are <u>shouting away</u> at going: & when they return with the <u>Dollars & Laurels</u>, a little original Sin will stir in your mind — but depend upon it, few men have less reason to envy any one — or more reason to be contented & happy than yourself. I am sorry to say that sort of chagrin at an idea of being set aside is a part of my nature — & I fear my Children may inherit from me, but I pray God to strengthen their minds — & enable them all to think more justly & care less for the fleeting uncertainties of this world & root out all envy & hurtfull ambition. Half these people may never return, & if they do may be call'd to account. Think of Whitelocke[11]— & many great & clever Men who have been ill thought of for doing well —

While you are so <u>blest</u> in your domestic life — be easy & contented — lest worse shou'd happen — God bless & preserve you — & I must add how happy I am you are not gone — Love from dear Mary to Dear Ethel & Eliza[beth][12]
    & believe me my <u>dear</u> Tom
        Your very affectionate Mother
           M. Birch

---

*The date of Mrs Birch's second letter makes it clear that Thomas was disappointed not to be called upon to go to Portugal, where another theatre of war had opened. In the autumn of 1807 Napoleon had moved his troops through Spain to invade Portugal and in the following spring, he created a new enemy by usurping the throne of Spain in favour of his brother Joseph. The popular uprising in Spain which followed was the start of the Spanish War of Independence, better known as the Peninsular War. Britain saw an opportunity to acquire a new ally in Spain and to support Portugal, its historic ally, and in June 1808 it agreed to send an expeditionary force, under the command of Lieutenant-General Sir*

---

11  John Whitelocke (1757–1833), a British army officer, had recently been dismissed from the service after being found guilty by a court martial for surrendering to Spanish colonists following a failed expedition, of which he was the commander, to seize Buenos Aires. Mrs Birch's apparent belief that Whitelocke had been harshly treated may reflect her knowledge that her acquaintance Sir Home Popham had been fortunate to escape the same fate after an equally unsuccessful attempt on Buenos Aires a year or so earlier.
12  Probably Etheldred's sister Elizabeth, who is referred to several times in letters at this time and seems to have been a general favourite with Thomas, as well as being his sister Mary's particular friend.

THE PENINSULAR WAR (1) AND THE WALCHEREN CAMPAIGN

*Arthur Wellesley[13], to the Iberian peninsula. It was this campaign with which Thomas desperately wished to be involved, especially as a number of friends from the Royal Military College and fellow officers and commanders with whom he had served in Egypt had already been (or soon would be) chosen to go.*

*It must have been of some compensation to Thomas that, although he was not able to take part in person in the campaign, he received a number of letters, maps and first-hand accounts from former colleagues who were fighting in Portugal and Spain. Over time Thomas built up a collection of Peninsular War memorabilia, including plans and eye-witness accounts of the first two battles in the conflict (at Roliça on 17 August, 1808, and Vimiero four days later — see* **Appendix III**)*, which bear all the hallmarks of someone trained at the National Military College with its emphasis on map-making and the importance of using the terrain to advantage in battle conditions. We know that one of Thomas's correspondents around this time was Major Peter Carey[14], John Le Marchant's brother-in-law, who wrote to Thomas early in 1809* (**5: 7**) *about the* '**Operations**' *of the British army in Spain since the previous autumn. As it mentions General Fraser, to whom Carey was Aide-de-Camp, he may also have been the author of the unsigned letter* (**5: 5**) *about the terms of the Convention of Cintra[15], the controversial ceasefire agreement signed at the end of August 1808.*

---

13 Sir Arthur Wellesley (1769–1852), later the first Duke of Wellington, had been destined for a career as a soldier since the age of seventeen, but his military genius, which would see him by 1815 the world's most admired soldier who had never been defeated in battle, was little known at the start of the Peninsular War. See Peter Snow, *To War with Wellington* (John Murray, 2010).
14 Peter Carey (1774–1852), who was, like his sister Marie (Mrs John Le Marchant), from Guernsey, was clearly a close friend of the Birch family and is mentioned in several letters (see also **6: 6** and **6: 7**). He was much the same age as Thomas, and their lives and careers evolved along similar lines. They attended the staff military college at the same time, got married and produced their first child (in both cases a daughter) in the same years, and both served in the Walcheren campaign. Peter, who attained the rank of Major-General in 1820, is remembered chiefly as an instructor of the cavalry, to which he taught a new kind of sword exercise which had been first introduced by his brother-in-law.
15 The ceasefire was signed only a few days after the two emphatic victories secured by Wellesley. The Convention of Cintra offered such generous terms to the defeated enemy that it provoked outrage at home and all three generals (Wellesley and two higher-ranking officers, Sir Harry Burrard and Sir Hew Dalrymple — the latter two thought to be well past their prime by their troops, who nicknamed them 'Betty' and 'Dowager') were recalled to London to appear before a court of inquiry.

## Letter 5:5 (Writer unknown[16], possibly Major Peter Carey, in Lisbon, dated 30 September, 1808)

Palace of Queluz[17] Sept. 30<sup>th</sup>

On my return home from my usual morning ride I found that Sir Harry [*Burrard*] is on the point of sending his letters for England & Head Quarters, therefore have seized [*the opportunity.*]

— You will have heard immediately after your letter that our commander was recalled, & I cannot help saying however unguardedly perhaps that the convention has at least produced <u>one</u> good effect, whatever may otherwise be its demerits — The dispatches arrived yesterday, & in a few days Sir Hew [*Dalrymple*] will be off — I never had any opinion of him as an officer & the little we have seen of him has fully confirmed it — he does not possess a single Military idea — unfortunate for him & the army, that he ever was placed in a situation to which he was wholly inadequate. […]

As for the treaty itself there is no doubt it was bad & such terms ought never to have been granted, but he will make out a stronger case than the public are aware of […] I confess I was not a little surprised to see Sir Arthur's name to the Preliminary treaty. By the papers it would appear that his friends are endeavouring to screen him, & say that he was order'd & was against the whole thing, far otherwise is the fact, & tho' the [?]Head is no doubt responsible, the Treaty (between ourselves) may be called his quite as much[18]. He often declared at their meetings (this is what now comes out) that the first object was to get the French out of the country for they certainly had it in their power greatly to protract things & that it was of the greatest consequence to have our force fully at liberty to act elsewhere — This was the language, I understand, & which he cannot deny.

There will be a good deal said about it, & I dare say much ill blood in consequence — I fear Sir Arthur will take another turn, (tho' quite a different

---

16  The letter has been written by a close associate who knew he could rely on the recipient's discretion; it is revealingly disparaging about the Convention of Cintra and highly critical of the commanders responsible (the fact that the letter does not suggest that Burrard should bear equal responsibility may be because the letter was to be included with his own despatches).

17  The eighteenth-century Rococo palace of Quelez, Lisbon, had been the official residence of the Portuguese Prince Regent, John VI, until he and his family fled to Brazil in 1807 following the French invasion of Portugal. The French occupational forces took control of the building and their commander, Marshal Junot, made several alterations to the building.

18  Although the court of inquiry cleared all three generals, it was widely felt to be a whitewash and Wellesley's protestations that he had been over-ruled by Dalrymple and Burrard were seen as less than convincing.

question) & say "had I been permitted to follow up the enemy on the 21st all this would not have happen'd" — [...] But upon reflection it does not appear so certain that it would have been so admirable [...] The enemy's cavalry had not even been engaged, at least very little, and they could soon have brought up considerable reinforcements from the immediate neighbourhood of Lisbon — [...] We had no cavalry & little artillery (very difficult to bring on from the want of horse), the country stronger than earlier conceived, & no doubt we should have fared ill in regard to supplies — Moore's force had not arrived, & all the naval people expected that it would be a most difficult operation to land them. [...] The event would have been the same, tho' it cannot be denied that it might have been attended both with loss & trouble. I do not mean to say the convention was well judged, far otherwise my friend, but you see they will get out of it better than the world imagines. We certainly had the means of humbling a French force & it's a great misfortune it was not done. [...]

The Portuguese army must not for a moment be mentioned for a more dastardly lot I never saw & they would have done us more harm than good — they themselves & the peasantry, never could have got the French out of the country. Junot must have embarked about 22,000 Soldiers, a greater force than was imagined either here or in England no doubt. If Sir Hew had entered into Particulars as he ought to have done, certainly the country would not have been outrageous, tho' they could not be pleased any more than ourselves. [...] Sir Arthur having before heard that the treaty would not be well received immediately sailed for England, where no doubt he will make out the best story he can.

All this is extremely unfortunate — for the business of the 21st[19], certainly brilliant, will now be quite forgot, & nothing heard of but abuse — and altho' the army has nothing to do with the errors of its Commanders, still it suffers, & so it always must be. [...] The business of the 17th [Roliça] was by all accounts dreadfully bungled, we ought to have taken every man, whereas if the truth was known, I believe we lost more in killed & wounded than the enemy. I do not see where we can act. The North of Spain is certainly just now the only point, but Cavalry & Artillery are more wanted than Infantry — [...] If Buonaparte pours an immense force into Spain, there will be the struggle & God knows what will be the event of it — I think as I always did that we shall remain idle here for a

---

19  The Battle of Vimiero (see Appendix III), which took place on 21 August, 1808.

considerable time. Where can Baird[20] be going? He will remain at Falmouth, as you say the north of Spain only can he get to, unless we really mean to collect a large force in the Mediterranean.

We are magnificently lodged in a palace lately fitted up by Junot for Buonaparte & Beauharnois, who was to have been King of Portugal. [...] Genl. Fraser, & Hill are here also — Moore opposite in the Marquis of Pombal's house. We have about 12,000 men encamped here — beautifull ground — but we must soon get into cantonments, lest the rainy season should come on suddenly & which is to be dreaded. Genl. Hope is gone towards Elvas, the Spaniards having refused anything but an unconditional surrender to the Garrison of Fort La Lippe. Sir Hew has judged ill in risquing a quarrel with the Spaniards, & I hope the event may not prove so.

---

*After Wellesley, Burrard and Dalrymple had been recalled to face an inquiry, Lieutenant-General Sir John Moore* (**Fig. 5 b**)) *took command of the British forces in the Iberian peninsula[21]. As a close associate of General Sir Ralph Abercromby, Moore was well known to Thomas, who had served with him in Egypt (see* **4: 9***); after the war resumed in 1803, Moore was put in charge of the defence of the coast against invasion from Dover to Dungeness, where Thomas may well have encountered him again. The news of Moore's death in action at the Battle of Corunna in January 1809 therefore came as a particular blow to Thomas, although his despair was somewhat offset by an account he received from Major Peter Carey of the heroic way in which the army had conducted itself in halting the French advance and the knowledge that, thanks to Moore's skill and exemplary leadership before he was fatally wounded, most of the British force managed to escape by sea.*

---

20 General David Baird (1757–1829) joined the army at the age of fifteen and served in India for many years. He was sent to Spain in 1808 in command of a considerable force to co-operate with Sir John Moore, to whom he was appointed second in command.
21 In the face of a massively reinforced French army of 200,000 men, led by Napoleon himself, Lt.-General Moore drew the French northwards while the British army retreated to the north-west coast of Spain and the embarkation ports of Corunna and Vigo.

**Fig. 5 b)** *Portrait of Lieutenant-General Sir John Moore, (1761–1809)*, by Thomas Lawrence, RA. Oil on canvas, *c.*1805. National Army Museum (1966-07-22).

## LETTER 5:6 (Lt.-Colonel Thomas Birch, near Colchester, to his brother John William Birch, London, 24 January, 1809)

Lexden January 24th 1809

I write to you with a heavyish heart My dear [Mother *crossed out*] John. But I must not allow Public Calamities[22] to preclude private attentions & indeed talking on any subject that gives one uneasiness, I think rather tends to alleviate it. I could not read the papers this Morning without a bleeding heart & if <u>my</u> Eye was full on reading the account of some of those that have fallen, what must be the feelings of those more nearly & dearly connected with them; but the General Sufferings of our Army seem to have been excessive — Poor Sir John Moore! he is indeed a public loss & as such is to be lamented; individually I can only feel it among the Many who may have received kindness & may have been allowed to consider him a Military Friend; I keep a few of such letters as I may have had from Eminent Characters more as a Satisfaction <u>to myself</u> that I have been worthy of their friendship & acquaintance, than from any other Motive.

Among these I found one from Poor Sir J. Moore. — Ethel was surprized that I knew him so well. — Sir David Baird (who I hear is since dead)[23] has spent a life of toil in the Service, & Poor Anstruther I am led to lament excessively as having been under his immediate direction & having received from him attention, & been flattered by his good Opinion, he has left a Wife & 4 Children to bewail his loss, & the Public service is deprived of one of its best Officers — he was Adjutant General in Ireland & an officer, who saw him the night before he left that Country for Active Service, observed to me that he was much out of Spirit at going.

It may be remark'd, that of the Personal & immediate friends of Sir Ralph

---

22 The Battle of Corunna had at first been represented in the newspapers as a humiliating defeat for the British, preceded by their epic retreat across northern Spain in harsh winter conditions pursued by the French under Marshal Soult. Both armies suffered severe losses, but the British success in holding off the French long enough for the bulk of its army to get away has since come to be seen as a tactical, though not a strategic, victory.

23 Thomas was misinformed; Baird succeeded to the supreme command after Moore's death, but shortly afterwards his left arm was shattered and the command passed to Sir John Hope. Baird lived for another twenty years, but was not employed again in the field.

24 In view of his admiration for Lt. General Sir John Hope (who succeeded to the title of fourth Earl of Hopetoun in 1816), Thomas would no doubt have been gratified if he had known that their families would one day be linked through marriage, when his granddaughter Etheldred (daughter of his eldest son Charles) married the General's grandson John, sixth Earl of Hopetoun, in 1860.

Abercromby in Egypt (Moore, Hope & Anstruther), Hope[24] only remains & in him, according to my Estimation, I see most of the Requisites of a General combined. Fortunate that such a Man is left.

Moore was most unfortunate, constantly on Service; in Action always wounded; in Sicily, in the Baltic & in Spain & no opportunity of distinguishing himself (except perhaps on the march – which I can be no judge of) till the day of his death, while others, of little or no <u>merit</u> have gain'd honours with little trouble.

What next is to be done, what can be done in Spain against the Power of France? We may try Cadiz & other Points, but we must be outnumbered, & the Spaniards will be afraid to act if so disposed. — People will <u>now</u> say, why did we trust a British Army in the Heart of Spain — how far it may have been prudent at <u>the time</u> the order was given is a question — & it's hardly fair to judge from Events. It has just struck me that Moore, worn out with disaster, may have exposed himself too much —, this is merely what comes across me. — I had intended this Letter for my Mother, but my train of thought seemed more calculated for you.

Ethel's love. Ever yours Affectionately<br>
<u>TB</u>

This letter will not be amusing, but indeed I have not been myself to day [...]

### Letter 5:7 (Lt.-Colonel Thomas Birch to his brother, John William Birch, dated 12 February, 1809)

12<sup>th</sup> February

My dear John,

Carey having, very kindly indeed, sent me a Sketch of the Operations of the Army since Salamanca[25], I forward it to you, knowing that it will afford you a real

---

25  Not the famous battle which took place there in 1812, but one of the agreed rendezvous in Spain to which the large number of British troops remaining in the peninsula after the Convention of Cintra were ordered to make their way in the late autumn of 1808. The documents about the 'Operations' of the army between then and February 1809, which had been supplied by Major Carey, have not come to light and were probably not returned to Thomas after they passed from him to his brother John and then to his father-in-law, Jacob Reynardson.

treat. — I request, after you have satisfied yourself, that you will get your Friend Mr G Harrison to pass it to Mr Reynardson. — if you like to shew the letter to Harrison, do by all means. Private Opinions are, I know, safe in his hands.

Carey was Assistant Adjutant General with General Frazer [sic]. — I really think for a hasty Sketch he has said a good deal, & it is pleasant to have an account from an authentic Source — notwithstanding our great loss in officers, I can't help feeling that the action & conduct of our Troops before Corunna was the salvation of the Character of our Army, & the most fortunate event that ever happened. — Without making allowances for the situation in which the Army was placed & the <u>impossibility</u> of preventing it, what a discreditable impression would such a <u>flight</u> have left. — Three Hours fighting turned the Scale of things, & in the midst of almost unparalleled disasters, we left the Country crowned with laurels, earn'd under the most untoward circumstances. — <u>One day's</u> delay in the order for the retreat & God knows what would have become of them all —. The Coolness of our Troops & the recovery of their Spirits on the immediate prospect of action is beyond all praise & proves of what Stuff a British Soldier is made.

I must mention one anecdote — the 4th, 50th & 49th (Lord William Bentinck's brigade) were form'd in line & necessarily exposed to the fire of a French Battery, which had got the exact range; Sir J. Moore was at the Head of the 42nd Regiment. The shot struck the line or near it every time, one shot took off a file exactly & knocked their Bonnets into the air; Sir J. Moore for some time said, "don't move, don't move" (the French were advancing under cover of their Guns), he then said, "now move on & fire" — which they did, to some effect as the Sequel proved. Sir J. then went to the right, & fell immediately — our fellows reserved their fire till the French came near them. My informant, as I believe I before told you, had his horse shot, a shot thro' his hat & the cape of his Coat. — he dined with me yesterday & I pumped him (for he is a modest man) at the Expense perhaps of another Friend or two when dining with me. [...]

*[remainder of letter missing]*

---

26 Peter Hicks, *Walcheren — the Debacle*, online article for The Fondation Napoléon, first published in *Trafalgar Chronicle*, 2010. For many years it had been a pet scheme of Lord Castlereagh, who proposed it again when he became Secretary of State for War in 1807, although it took another two years before he could persuade the War Cabinet of the desirability of carrying it out while French attention was diverted elsewhere against the resurgent Austrian army.

*Thomas did not have to wait much longer before being recalled to active service, although in the event his spell of duty abroad, from the end of July to mid September 1809, lasted only six or seven weeks before he returned to England. The campaign[26] to seize control of the island of Walcheren and its port of Flushing (Vlissingen), together with South Beveland and other islands in the mouth of the River Scheldt (**Fig. 5 c**)), was conceived mainly to prevent Napoleon from reconstructing his navy at the port of Antwerp, some fifty kilometres further inland, and to protect British national security.*

*The commander chosen for the expedition was John Pitt, Earl of Chatham[27], the elder brother of William Pitt, the recently deceased former Prime Minister. The expeditionary force which crossed the short distance from the Thames estuary to the island of Walcheren on the Netherlands coast at the end of July 1809 was the largest ever to leave the British Isles, consisting of a total of 618 vessels (in two waves) carrying 35,000 infantry and 1,900 cavalry, a larger force than that serving in the Peninsular War, from which many officers and troops had been diverted. Despite all this, the Walcheren campaign was catastrophically unsuccessful. Described by the newspapers of the time, notably* **The Times***, as 'a national disaster', the failure of the expedition has subsequently been put down to a combination of disease, which claimed the lives of 4,000 men (far more than were killed in action) during the short campaign and left three times as many permanently weakened, and of poor leadership[28].*

*We have six long letters and a diary entry in which Thomas records in detail this brief but disastrous episode, and because so little has been written about the Walcheren campaign since that time, I think that they make extremely interesting reading. Much had changed over the eight years since he was writing home from Egypt. All his letters are now addressed to his wife, from whom he could expect a reply in days rather than the months he had to wait in Egypt for any communications from England. However, it appears that some sort of censorship had been introduced and it is noticeable that Thomas is somewhat circumspect about the political turmoil at home (of which he knew from newspaper reports) and charitable about the shortcomings of the senior leaders of the operation* (**5: 14**).

---

27 John Pitt, second Earl of Chatham (1756–1835) was a very different proposition from his energetic brother. His reputation for indolence and dilatoriness was already widely known before he was appointed to command the Walcheren expedition, and his indecision in failing to capitalise on the initial military gains was seen as one of the main reasons for the operation's lack of success.

28 There was an immediate knock-on effect on the British Government. Most of the Cabinet resigned, including the ailing Prime Minister, the Duke of Portland; Castlereagh and his former ally, the Foreign Secretary George Canning (who had objected to so many troops being sent to the Netherlands instead of to the peninsula), fought a now famous duel; and the government was only saved from falling completely by a closely-fought vote and the reluctant agreement of the new Prime Minister, Spencer Perceval (1762–1812). Perceval was Prime Minister for less than three years (1809–12) and has the dubious distinction of being the only British Prime Minister to have been assassinated whilst in office.

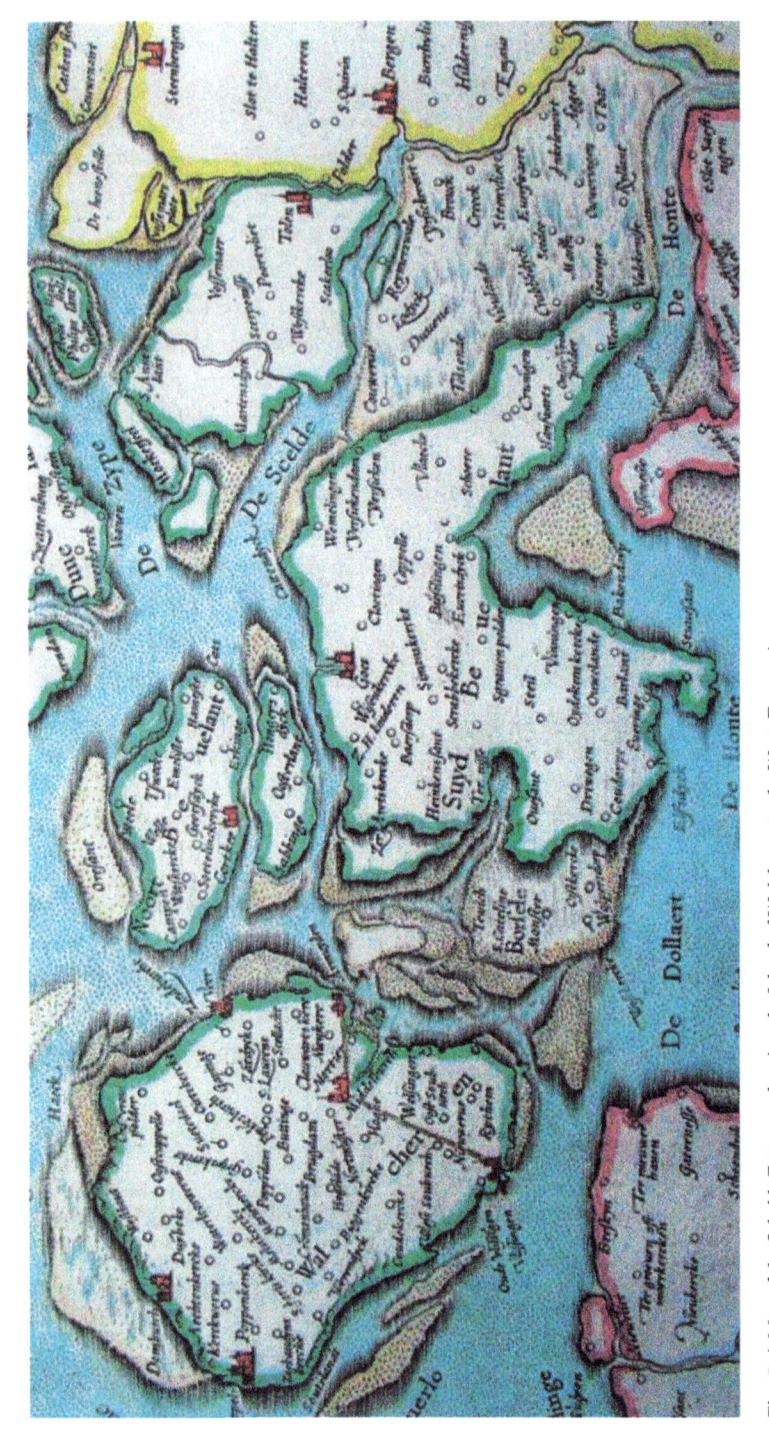

**Fig. 5 c)** *Map of the Scheldt Estuary, showing the Island of Walcheren to the West. Engraving.*

## 5:8[29] (Extracts from the diary of Lt.-Colonel Thomas Birch, on board HMS *Venerable*, 28 to 30 July, 1809)

HMS Venerable – 28th July 1809.

After delays usually attendant on conjoin'd expeditions, the Signal was made at 6 O'clock this Morning to get under weigh […] Having sail'd in Transports & Troop Ships, (altho' comfort to a Landsman is in my Opinion out of the question) I certainly drew a comparison, very favourable to a Ship of War, of this size (74 Guns), from its cleanliness, spaciousness & order preserved throughout.

The sameness to us is tedious tinctured with sickness headaches &c, tho' I am upon the Whole Stout on board — Any variety hitherto has been [*of*] a distressing nature; a sailor was yesterday crush'd to death by the lowering of a water cask — & this Morning, the Ship going 9 or 10 Knots an hour, a sailor, while heaving the lead fell overboard — but almost miraculously clung by the rope of the lead, tho' the sea wash'd over him & he was nearly exhausted, till the Boat was lower'd & he was picked up. I never remember feeling a stronger sensation of anxiety, as we expected every moment he would have gone down.

I resume my Pen in the course of the Evening & indeed my intention is to take it up from time to time as opportunity offers — at about 4 O'clock we made the fleet, which had been detach'd from the Downs under the command of Sir Richard Keates in case the Enemy's fleet should attempt to get out of the Scheld — about 2 Hours after we made the island of Walcheren. So far […] our prospects were favourable — all were in good Spirits, the band of the King's Own playing "God Save the King" & "Rule Britannia" as was daily the practice after dinner — our Commander in Chief, on seeing the Dutch Coast from the Cabin Window, chearfully drank Success to the Expedition […]. I wish I could close this Evening without adding another accident to those already mention'd & melancholy as the first. — We had come to an Anchor, the sailors had almost finished reefing the Sails, when one Man fell from the Main Yard upon the Deck & was killed upon the spot — an old & valuable Sailor. This caused a gloom throughout the Ship. […] Friday night.

Saturday 29th […] The Fleet from the Downs which followed us yesterday Evening appeared in sight. It was determined to land the Reserve under Sir J. Hope on the Island of Walcheren to take possession of the Enemy's Gun boats

---

29  These seem to be the only surviving pages of the 'slovenly sort of journal' Thomas mentions in **5: 9**.

in the East Scheld & to secure a safe Anchorage in that River. The detachment of the Fleet for this purpose sail'd about the middle of the day, Sir Home Popham accompanying it — about 10 O'clock at Night, we had the satisfaction to receive intelligence from Sir J. Hope that the ships with ye Reserve had reached their Anchorage unmolested & as the debarkation must necessarily be deferred till the ensuing morning, a proposal was submitted by Sir J. Hope & Sir R. Keates, upon the Suggestion of Sir H. Popham, that that part of the armaments should proceed higher up ye River & effect its landing near Goes in South Beveland — this measure was approved & to be adopted the next morning, while the Part of the army under Sir Eyre Coote was to carry into execution the Original Plan for the Attack upon the Island of Walcheren. […]

Sunday 30th The Army effecting their landing this Evening about 6 O'clock — with no other opposition than the exchange of some shots, between the Haak Battery & the Gun boats. The Troops establish'd themselves on the Sand Hills, after a little Skirmishing with the Enemy's light Troops — We made a good many Prisoners. The 71st Regiment […] lost about 20 Men. The Haak Battery being evacuated on our approaching Head Quarters were established there that night in a small house within the Battery — I should have observed [*that*] the Commander in Chief landed with the 1st Division of the Army [*on*] Sunday night.

## LETTER 5:9 (Lt.-Colonel Thomas Birch, at Middleburgh, to his wife Etheldred, at Holywell[30], Stamford, 2 August, 1809)

Middleburgh 2nd August 1809

My dearest Ethel,

As dispatches are on the point of being made up for England, my first thought is of course directed to satisfy the kind anxiety you will feel to hear tidings of us, & you may judge how I am press'd for time, when I must request you to be the Channel of any information, to those who have a claim upon my affections; my Mother of course among the first — A most slovenly sort of Journal which I have not been able to revive will take you to the Night of our setting foot on this Island, it is so bad that you had better keep it to yourself or selves […].

It is quite unnecessary to relate the difficulties & inconveniences an Army is put to on landing in a foreign Country without the means of conveyance for baggage or almost anything else, bordering on Comfort (an Idea, that so great a Soldier as Lord Harcourt, would never allow to enter the head of a Soldier, altho' he had his Sposa with him). Sleeping with Cloaths on 20 in a room, wet feet, fleas, & other vermin were all accompanyments to our first night on shore [...] We moved on in the course of the day about 7 Miles to Griepskerken [Griepskerke] — (I should say that, not till the day after our Landing did Sultan[31] get on shore & happy I was to see poor Frank mounted on the beach, tho' himself very ill indeed, & almost dangerously so, with a most dreadful breaking out in his face & throat, all the time he had been on board ship.[...]

The next morning (Monday) the Army moved forward to invest Flushing [Vlissingen] & after carrying some batteries on establish'd ourselves within a proper distance of the town, but not, I am sorry to say, without the loss of a considerable number of men kill'd & wounded, I believe about 300. — & this must always be the worst part of my history! — The necessary arrangements are making for the Siege, which I fear will hold us a tug.

Middleburgh, which is Head Quarters, is one of the most beautiful towns I ever beheld & certainly furnishes an opportunity of arguing upon the Variety of a Soldier's life in a short space of time, three nights ago in a filthy little House which had been just before occupied by the Enemy, here all of us are magnificently lodged. Lord Chatham is in the Palace, a Staad Royale, General Brownrigg[32] in a noble House, & I am at this moment, having a house to myself, writing in a handsome <u>Comfortable</u> room, carpeted all over; Crimson bed curtains & laced Pillow cases. Of this however last night I only enjoyed 3 hours as I was up this Morning at a quarter past 3, but what think you of the Servant bringing me the nicest breakfast possible, before 4 O'clock? — I should have had some trouble in getting this at my own house. [...]

I should have told you that the Enemy lost some men in retreating from this place as did we in advancing. — but the Military news is less interesting to you than the Civic & this in truth is a sad jumble of both for I have no time to put any thing in Shape — [...] at some future time I hope to enter more into description. [...]

This Evening Grosvenor landed with his Division & is gone to take his place in the line — he would be sorry to have missed the Operation of landing with

---

30   While her husband was away on active service, his wife Etheldred, who had given birth to their first child (a daughter, also called Etheldred) earlier that year, returned to live at Holywell, the family home.
31   In her letter of 5 July 1801 (**4: 18**), Mrs Birch tells Thomas that his horse Sultan has been sold, but he must have purchased him back soon after his return from Egypt, as the horse appears in **Fig. 5 a)** (being ridden by Thomas's fiancée Etheldred) as well as accompanying his master on active service to Walcheren.

the Army at first. I am thank God quite well, have had time to say more than I expected, but as it is past 11 & I had only 3 hours sleep last night, I know you would allow me rest but I indulge till 6 tomorrow. Do copy this letter or part of it, & send it directly to my Mother & John […] Don't fancy I forget the dear little Darling, but kiss it for me — & distribute my love as you know I wish. My Mother will be aware I could not have written two letters therefore they will all take this as amongst them.

Ever my dearest with constant prayers for your health & happiness,

Your most affectionate — TB

Thursday 4th

I reopen this to say that no letters whatever go to England with the dispatches but those which are sent from the Commander in Chief himself.

Sir Eyre Coote[33] was as near as possible being taken Prisoner this morning, entirely from imprudence which gained him no Credit, & Lord R. Manners in accompanying him, I believe against his own Judgment, had his horse Shot, it will teach them better.

PS

I just learn that letters are positively prohibited, except to immediate Friends thro' the interest we have at head Quarters — Even my Lord Lowther's despatch has been question'd. He is good humour'd enough & I could not help smiling at seeing his Lordship looking miserable & dripping wet under a hedge, without a horse, or what we call padnagging.

---

32 See 5: 1. In addition to being Quarter Master General to the Forces, General Sir Robert Brownrigg (1759–1833) had been appointed Chief of Staff of the Army for the British Expeditionary Force to Walcheren, with Thomas Birch as his Deputy.

33 Sir Eyre Coote (1762–1823), second-in-command to Lord Chatham. As the commander of the 'Grand Division', it was Coote's responsibility to take Walcheren, which was successfully accomplished, while the Reserve of the Army, under Lt. General John Hope (with whom Thomas served in Egypt), managed to take control of South Beveland and the fort at Batz by 2 August. A few years later, Coote's tendency towards 'imprudence' was to lead to his dismissal from the service after a scandal involving boys at Christ's Hospital School.

## Letter 5:10 (Lt.-Colonel Thomas Birch, at Tergoes, South Beveland, to his wife, Etheldred, dated 11 August, 1809)

Tergoes — South Beveland<br>
August 11<sup>th</sup> 1809 — 10 O'clock <u>at Night</u>

My ever dearest Ethel,

[…] I trust you have received from me one letter from Middleburgh; I take shame to myself for not having written a second line, but I have lately been detach'd from the Army before Flushing […] & my time indeed has been much occupied, generally, as often between 4 in the Morning & late in the Evening. It is not long since I left England, but really, from the daily Variety & other circumstances it seems an age, you have no conception of the distance of time it seems since we parted, for in your life there is a sameness, in mine there is constant variety. […]

[…] On the 6$^{th}$ of the month circumstances render'd it necessary that I should be sent to this Island to communicate with Sir John Hope (who was in Command of the Reserve of the Army) to make arrangements for the further Debarkation of the Divisions of Lord Huntley & Lord Rosslyn. This measure of force here to the amount of 16000 Men altogether, made it necessary that I should conduct the duties of the Quarter Master General's Department in South Beveland, while General Brownrigg remain'd with the army (in Walcharen) acting before Flushing — as I had been all over Walcharen & with the besieging army, this change has not been unsatisfactory to me, more particularly as I like the people I am acting with & live at Lord Rosslyn's table who commands here, & am quite in his confidence […]

Between this & Middlebourgh the distance is not above 12 miles, crossing a Channel, which makes the communication troublesome. This Island which was taken possession of with such opposition, is about 30 miles in extent, flat but exceedingly rich in Corn, the Houses & farms good & numerous, neat & cleanly to an excess I never before witness'd, & no symptom of poverty, but we are eating up their cattle, even to their milch cows — & I fear as we occupy their Barns & keep 2 or 300 Waggons in requisition, that their harvest may suffer — but war was never supposed to improve the state of individuals.

The Chief point of our Operations here is at the Eastern Extremity of the

Island where we occupy the battery of Bathz [Batz] commanding that part of the Schelt where the Eastern & Western Branches divide or nearly so — it is about 21 or 2 Miles from this place. I have twice rode there & back to dinner & today am not long returned after excessive heat almost Equal to Egypt. Sir Home Popham had just arrived with some Ships of war & 40 Gun boats — the French Flotilla & fleet & Antwerp are plain in the distance — Bergen op zoom & other places on that part of the Continent. The first day (Tuesday 8th) I went there with Sir John Hope — a very brisk Cannonade was kept up for about two Hours between their Brigs (27 in number) & the Fort, but the fire of the latter made them withdraw & they have not molested us since. Col Rainsford of the Guards had a narrow escape, a shot came thro' the window of his rooms thro' his bed, dressing gown & door & in to the street — no harm done however. A Minister, not far from the Fort, who had the like salutation met us & said "on m'a déjà fait un Compliment j'avais un boule dans ma Chambre".

Upon the whole, I must say we are at present a good deal out of harm's way here — before Flushing, previous to my leaving Middlebourgh we had lost a good many Men & some have fallen since from a vigorous sortie made by the Enemy, in which however they also lost about 600 Men. The Troops engaged in that Siege will I fear suffer much from the weather which has been dreadfully wet, every drop of rain goes to one's heart, as the ground is naturally wet & they have very indifferent cover. The Batteries are to open tomorrow & a few days will give us some idea of what we have to expect from that part of the Operations, but I am sorry to say, the Enemy has Opportunities of getting reinforcements into Flushing from the opposite side, which may protract the business — they are beginning too, to inundate the country, which may be a serious check to that part of our operations. The Troops however it must be allowed have behaved remarkably well, & it is to be hoped will be rewarded by the Completion of this part of the business (the reduction of Flushing).

Further than this, John knows, I have never looked forward to, & the certain intelligence which has just reach'd us, that the Enemy is collecting a force at & near Antwerp, Bergen [op Zoom] &c will I trust decide upon stopping before it is too late & thereby saving the Credit of your Army & lives of your Men, which are indeed valuable. I shall not enter further on this subject, or into particulars that may be more safely talk'd about than put on paper — much as I should rejoice in the prospect of further success to our Army, & in bearing a share in promoting it I may tell you that I am of Opinion that our Operations are drawing towards a conclusion, how distant must depend upon a variety of circumstances. […] I shall now close the military part of my letter, which you may make what use of you like […].[34]

I saw Espinasse today, quarter'd at a village on this Island & laid up with the gout, for which I should much pity him but that he makes one sick with his nonsense & chatter, talking that he wishes to be led against the Enemy — & march, sink or swim he would be at them.

[…] Poor Frank I left at Middlebourgh for hospital attention, he is much better & has join'd me here today. — […] Both my Horses are treasures, Sultan never better, & I know you will be glad […], for when I have to be so long on Horse back it is every thing to ride in a great Chair.

[…] As I am stealing this time from sleep after my long hot ride, I know you would rather it was so appropriated — I have not time to read over my letters, so make allowances accordingly. Say every thing affectionate for me to all under the Holywell roofs. I am not unmindful of Mrs Partridge's attention to our dear baby, & pray say so — say everything for me at Hamstead, write to my Mother, John &c. […]

I send you some lace which I got at Middlebourgh. I have no business to be a judge of it — they said it was, tho' not the best Brussels, as you will be quite aware of, "bien travaillé & brillant". My Hostess bought it for me — I had no time to look out for anything & was hurried off at an hour's notice. […]

Ever most affectionately
TB

**Letter 5:11 (Lt.-Colonel Thomas Birch, at Tergoes, South Beveland, to his wife Etheldred, dated 15 August, 1809)**

Tergoes — S. Beveland
August 15th   1809

My dearest Ethel,

Flushing, after being on fire in several places & a heap of ruins, surrendered this Morning at 2 O'clock # [*at the foot of the page:* # What joy to some, what misery

---

34 Although Thomas is cautious about the details, the knowledge that the French were mobilising in great numbers indicates that he must have realised that the British operation was losing the initiative.

to others!], which will be productive of another Dispatch, consequently, I hope, of another opportunity of my writing to you. The Dispatches will furnish you better with the Details of the Operations of the Siege & surrender of the place, than you can look for from the Pen of an individual; it is to be lamented that we have lost upon the whole a great many brave fellows, but War was never invented for the happiness of the human race, tho' I suppose it is necessary — I am very glad the Siege is over, as it will release the poor Men from the wet & uncomfortable situations they have been exposed to [...]

As every body speaks out & all have a right to an opinion, there can be no harm in giving you mine, which has been long since form'd & has been much corroborated by repeated intelligence since my last letter. — The Enemy is not likely to have been inactive since our arrival in this Country & have certainly assembled such a force between Antwerp & Bergen op Zoom, as must in my mind make any further attempt most hazardous, on the other side [of] the water, & I trust as what has been yet done has been well done, we shall know when to Stop — The Fleet too & the Enemy's gun Boats & flotilla are I fear gone too far up the Scheldt to make an impression, tho' we are all getting as forward as we can with that view.

I mention'd that I had been detach'd, with Lord Rosslyn's, Lord Huntley's & Sir John Hope's divisions, about 17000 Men, in South Beveland. We are expecting Lord Chatham here to morrow, when he will in all probability read dispatches from England — so quick are communications made to & fro that Montalembert told me to day, he wrote a letter to England on Wednesday last & got an answer to it yesterday (Monday), but this is extraordinarily expeditious.

I had a long & harrassing day yesterday, with Lord Rosslyn in reconnoitring the Islands of Wolvers Dyke & North Beveland — both excessively rich in corn, much intersected with Dykes having 3 or 4 Rows of trees on each side of them [...]; the Villages & houses excessively neat & the inhabitants, females in particular, the most extraordinary figures you ever saw, with their skimming dirk, broad brimm'd hats (straw), their immoderate long waists & bottoms & in short all round, sticking out like the little wooden figures you may have seen in the Shops — not surprizing when 8 & 10 Peticoats are common, but what they have in Number is taken from the length, which does not exceed half way their legs, or much below the knees. Close Caps, held fast by gold earrings, fixed on as if they grew into their faces, not forgetting a silver bracelet on one arm, which I could not prevail upon a woman to sell the other day.

[...] We are none of us anxious to spend the Autumn here as that Season is not reported healthy, & I am induced to hope that that information will weigh with his Excellency the Commander in Chief — if nothing active is going on.

[…] I have just got a magnificent house here for Lord Chatham, the bed that King Louis Bonaparte slept in, with <u>Cambric sheets</u>, what a temptation to indulge.

I quite forgot to beg you to save all newspapers from the time of my departure as one likes to hear what people have been doing & what we have been doing ourselves, as the newspapers are always the best judges — I forget whether they read & burn immediately at Holywell. […]

> Ever my dearest
> Yours with all possible Affection
> <u>TB</u>

**Letter 5:** 12 (Lt.-Colonel Thomas Birch, Tergoes, South Beveland, to his wife Etheldred, dated 19 August, 1809)

> Tergoes 19$^{th}$ August,
> South Beveland <u>1809</u>

I omitted to number my other letters, my dearest Ethel, as you desired (very properly, as it would be a means of ascertaining whether all came safe to hand), but this, I think, should be No. 1. — I hope you received my Packet with the Lace enclosed. […] I have received only Nos. 1 & 2 from you & am waiting anxiously for further accounts, not that I think you have been deficient at all, quite the contrary, but we have rec'd no letters from England since the first mention'd. — You know in absence, it is one's greatest Source of pleasure & comfort, — from those we love.

I went on the 17$^{th}$ to Middlebourgh, from thence to Flushing; it is quite horrible to think of the Devastation committed by the Bombardment on that town — burnt in many places, & <u>riddled</u>, thro' & thro', with shot & shells, many of the Inhabitants buried in the ruins — it is quite impossible to ride thro' the town & not feel deeply impress'd with the Horrors of War. Carey & I riding together yesterday in Flushing, he remarked, how very unlike our quiet scenes at Lexden!

Yesterday Morning was the time appointed for the French Garrison to march out of Flushing, Prisoners of War & lay down their Arms [...] The French General Monnet was in conversation with Lord Chatham during the whole time of the procession — the Number of Troops, with so large & brilliant a Staff, form'd a Grand & interesting Sight. The French were marched across the Island to be put on board Ship, & if you have any curiosity to see them, I dare say you may give them the meeting in Norman Cross[35] — [...] They deceived us in the first instance in point of numbers, which were stated by them as less than they have since turned out to be, the Garrison consisted of 5,800 or thereabouts, & they are stated to have lost one way & another about 2,400 — in killed, deserters, Prisoners etc. This will be the first French Army, I think, that has ever found its way prisoners to England — & I hope will please John Bull.

On my return from a <u>Morning's</u> Ride of <u>about 42 Miles</u>, I find your letter No. 3, more grateful to me than any thing else I could have received — only 6 days from Holywell, which really alleviates absence excessively. The pleasure I experience from your letters, which are so full of domestic incident & therefore so interesting to me, is not to be told [...] [*They*] are without compliment what letters ought to be. I like to know exactly, who composes your parties, where you go & how you employ your time, & in short any thing that may tend to make me feel one amongst you. This cannot be the case with you in regard to me — as all here must be strange to you. [...]

I can give but a poor account of my domestics. Frank however is mending fast, but James[36] is very poorly — & till his disorder comes to a Crisis will not be better. The weather here is uncertain, one day excessively hot & Oppressive, another cold & again very wet. I told you I had been a little bilious, but have benefited by a proper directive.

[...] I see very often your friend Espinasse & I assure you he writes often to the Hon Mrs Espinasse; he has been laid up with the gout ever since he has been in the Island, but in his usual ridiculous style, pants to meet the Enemy, because I suppose he does not expect it. — I have no idea of a fellow talking so much about it.

[...] We have plenty to eat here but no Money which is all very well — not that this has been absolutely the case with all, as Lord P— laid out £70 in Gs[37]

---

35 A prisoner-of-war camp for French and Dutch soldiers and sailors was built during the Napoleonic Wars at Norman Cross, Cambridgeshire, only a few miles from Holywell. Between 1796 and 1816 it held around 10,000 prisoners, of which nearly twenty per cent died and were buried in the camp cemetery. Several thousand English troops were also stationed there to guard the prisoners.
36 Another man-servant, 'lent' to Thomas by his father-in-law to take care of his second horse.
37 Probably guilders, the official currency in the Netherlands since the seventeenth century.

at a Middleburgh fair; he bought I am told 12 Doz. Boxes of eau de Cologne. This I could not venture upon, as I have neither time to look after it or means of carrying it which for your sake I am sorry for. Query — has Lord P— bought it for his Wife? [...]

What a sad sad list from Spain![38] We can't afford such victories — Lady Brownlow will be happy in the safety of Peregrine. Some are fallen that I knew intimately & lament much — but an Officer dined with us today (Montague Wynyard) who gets his Lieutenant Colonelcy upon the death of Lt. Colonel Ross, of the Coldstream, & in a soldier's phrase says, "Yes, I'm a very lucky fellow". [...]

Monday Morning, 21st — I have time to add a little. So true it is that no life experiences such Varieties & extremes as that of a Soldier, we live like Princes or Pigs, drink the best wines when we can get them, or content ourselves with water, which is bad enough here, sleep on the floor with our Cloaths on, or (in this Country) in the softest beds — After Egypt however, nothing appears hardship. — The General Rule is to live while we can — & at this moment I can't complain. [...] I live at Lord Rosslyn's table where daily is Claret, Hock &c &c — indeed on the Score of <u>foraging</u> I have no trouble, as General Brownrigg considers me as a constant guest, & I am included in Lord Chatham's (<u>his Excellency's</u>) number whenever I like it. I hear Complaints of Fleas, bugs & Musquitoes & that the latter are formidable in the villages, there can be no doubt — one made an attack upon me the other night to remind me of Elizabeth — A little after 7 & I am going to breakfast. I seldom get up later than 6 on <u>days of repose</u> & generally earlier.

Master Negrond [*probably his wife's dog*] would find plenty of Associates here as this place is full of Pugs & Poodles. I appear to write so much <u>stuff</u> that my letters are only fit to be between Ourselves.

---

38  This probably refers to the Battle of Talavera, a victory for the combined British and Spanish armies under Sir Arthur Wellesley and General Cuesta, against the French under Napoleon's brother Joseph Bonaparte, but a costly one, the British contingent losing a quarter of their troops. Thomas's former regiment, the 16th Light Dragoons, was in action in this battle, which took place on 27 and 28 July, south-west of Madrid. The Hon. Peregrine Francis Cust (1791–1873), referred to above, was the fifth son of Etheldred's maternal uncle, Brownlow Cust, first Baron Brownlow (d. 1807). He served in the 3rd Dragoon Guards in the Peninsular War between 1809 and 1814, after which he went onto half pay.

**LETTER 5: 13 (Lt.-Colonel Thomas Birch, South Beveland, to his wife Etheldred, dated 27 August, 1809, with additions both dated 28 August)**

Fort Bathz [Batz]<br>
South Beveland 27<sup>th</sup> August 1809

My dearest Ethel,

Since I finish'd my last letter no opportunity has offer'd of sending it, you will therefore receive two at the same time. I was vex'd when Carey told me a Messenger had gone the very Evening I had finish'd my letter but no opportunity offer'd of communicating [...]

I conclude you have ere this got my letter by Bradford; he arrived in town on the Saturday, started again on Monday & reached us here on Thursday which was a long passage; he passed our Chateau at Lexden & reported Captain Vernon walking & picking flowers in the Garden. Bradford brought me a large Packet & I think you will allow, the most mortifying one I could have experienced, for there was not <u>one</u> letter for me of any description, only for those who had taken advantage of my Situation to ensure their Arrival – I begg'd Sergeant Sewell to send me the 6 last papers, so what does he do, but sends me 6 of <u>the same date</u> (the 21$^{st}$) which, tho' the latest & valuable, 'twas not what I wanted [...]

Nothing active has taken place since I closed my last letter dated Tergoes. Lord Chatham & Staff have moved forward to this point, the most eastern one of the Island of South Beveland. From the Fort in which we are all (Head Quarters) stationed with the Grenadiers of the Guards, we plainly see Antwerp & the French Fleet — & I think here we must end with a <u>Veni</u>, <u>Vidi</u>, & <u>Vici</u> if you please, as far as relates to past Operations, but this very day a Council of War of all the Lieutenant Generals[39] has been assembled here which will decide upon the hazard of any further attempts & when we know that the Enemy is in such

---

[39] At this meeting General Brownrigg advised the commanders of the many difficulties involved in continuing the expedition, not least the rapidly rising level of disease afflicting all ranks of the army, which is also mentioned in this letter. This came to be known as 'Walcheren fever', which was mostly malaria — already known to be prevalent in Walcheren's swampy terrain — but probably also complicated by the sort of highly contagious illnesses, including typhus and typhoid fever, which were common at the time in troop encampments. The decision by Monnet, the French commander in Flushing, to impede the besiegers by cutting the dykes and flooding the already swampy land occupied by the troops (the 'inundation' which Thomas refers to in **5: 10**) exacerbated the insalubrious conditions. As a result of Brownrigg's presentation, the lieutenant generals agreed that the siege of Antwerp, which had been the ultimate object of the expedition, was now 'impracticable'.

force on the side of Antwerp. I confess I have always leant this way myself & think Lord Chatham has shewn the greatest good sense in declining to prosecute an operation which offer'd the most serious obstacles & almost certain disasters, & in this I do not believe any body has differ'd with him.

Our Movement now will be Retrograde, & no doubt when the next dispatches, in answer to those on the point of being transmitted, arrive from England, arrangements will be made for part of the Army to return to [England *crossed out*] Home. How this will affect me I don't know, but I need not say what my wishes dictate, as inactivity on a foreign station I shall never court…& when active duties do not absolutely call upon me, there are those at home who have a prior claim to every other feeling — Some Troops will of course be left in the Island of Walcharen, but I am not ambitious to represent the Quarter Master General there during the Winter, particularly as, if the Enemy does not molest you, which I think likely, the climate is bad […] Every body smokes here to keep off the Ague & fever, to which that custom & Port Wine are the Chief antidotes. Our Army only having the benefit of the former, will I fear fall off a good deal — which certainly is but poor encouragement to retain possession of these Islands.

[…] I write a sort of Military letter to John as he is so great a Soldier. I will beg him to send it to Mr Reynardson.

[…] I am eat up in this Fort every night with fleas, James kills in the Morning a certain proportion so I hope the Stock will be reduced. […]

Postscript<br>
Fort Bathz, 28<sup>th</sup> August,<br>
11 <u>at Night</u>

My dearest Ethel,

Since my letter of this date, arrangements have been making for the Embarkation of some of the Troops & to proceed to England. — I have had the offer from Gen. Brownrigg to remain Deputy Quarter Master General of the Island of Walcharen — <u>Carey strongly recommends it</u>, therefore you will weigh in your mind whether you like to join me at Middlebourgh — a beautiful Town & where you would inhabit a much handsomer house that I could afford you in England, with an increased salary, allowances &c — & where your Daughter may learn Dutch for Nothing.

I am to give him my Answer tomorrow Morning. No my dear, when I have a Choice, without its touching my honour, you may be quite sure of the decision, & that my Cottage at Lexden will be preferable to me under present circumstances, to a palace at Middlebourgh.

Let not the prospect of my return alter your Plans tho' I should hope now it would not exceed a fortnight or 3 weeks […]. I conclude they will give me a Month's leave of Absence […]

Ever your affectionate<br/>TB

I write a Duplicate of this & send it to Hamstead. Should your Party be gone to Wales[40], it will not disappoint me to join you at the above place where I feel assured of a good reception […].

TB

## Letter 5: 14 (Lt.-Colonel Thomas Birch, Middelburg, Zeeland, to his wife Etheldred, dated 12 September, 1809)

Middleburgh 12<sup>th</sup> Sept <u>1809</u>

Still the same date my dearest Ethel, altho' two letters (very short ones)[41] which I trust you will have received, may have announced our intention of sailing ere this. But there is such a thing as a foul wind, which in '94 [sic] detained us in the Elbe for more than two Months[42]; however, as our passage is short we shall put to sea the Moment it changes at all in our favour as 24 Hours may bring us up. […]

We have newspapers up to the 8th. They will I am aware create anxiety among those who are nearly & privately interested for us here; at the same time I must

---

40 Etheldred's uncle, Philip Yorke of Erddig (see Chapter 3), had died five years earlier but this reference suggests that there was still plenty of contact between the Reynardson, Birch and Yorke families.
41 These do not appear to have survived.
42 Thomas has misremembered the year when the fleet carrying the British Army from Germany back to England was held up for weeks in the Elbe waiting for the wind to change: it was in the winter of 1795 to 1796 (see the extracts from his diary, **3: 5**).

tell you, that many of the public prints contain misrepresentations which are distressing, & which state circumstances that are not founded on fact.[43]

In the first place the most perfect unanimity has prevail'd among all the Generals, & between the Naval & Military Commanders; Sir Richard Strachan has dined here this very day & has unequivocally declared in my hearing that he thought nothing further could be done. I mention this because his dispatch, which you may have seen, has been adverted to in the papers, & has misled the public by giving an impression that the Navy were ready, while we were not. […] I should not mention this now, but that people will talk — & you are quite welcome to quote me, who from my Situation may be allowed to judge.

If I stay here much longer I shall spend all my money, in Pictures & other trifles, fine work for you to chase them up; I have bought seven, good & indifferent — if I thought your father would like to have any of them or all at Holywell he should have them, that we shall see; I have bought one or two with a View to your Copying […].

I have not forgot a <u>little</u> present for our dear <u>little</u> Darling — I am burning to collect some good specimens of China for your Father, but really must give it up as there is such a difficulty in packing & bringing home.

I ought to be most thankful in continuing so well, when I consider that the Sickness of this Army has exceeded any former instance of the kind even in the West Indies — both in Officers & Men. Our Medical Aid & accommodation has been totally inadequate to the sudden pressure, I believe about 10,000 have been on the sick list, or nearly so at a time[44]. All Lord Chatham's <u>Grooms</u>, Servants, & Col. Carey's, have been totally incapacitated. Poor Carey is labouring under his old Complaint but desires kind remembrances.

God bless you all with my kindest love —
Ever your most Affectionate
<u>TB</u>

---

43  The British press had become increasingly critical of the management of the expedition from mid August onwards, reaching a crescendo in early September. Rumours of dissension between Chatham, who was perceived as having dragged his feet all along, and Sir Richard Strachan, who was in charge of the naval element and was reported to be still anxious to press on to Antwerp, were repeated constantly, and Chatham in particular was cruelly lampooned in caricatures (**Fig. 5 d**).

44  In total, around 4,000 men died during the Walcheren campaign, nearly all of them from disease, and of those who had survived illness almost 12,000 were said to be still unfit in the following February. Many of these were nevertheless sent back to the Peninsular War to join Wellington's army (against his wishes), causing a permanent doubling of the sick lists there.

**Fig. 5 d)** *Preparations for the Jubilee, or Theatricals Extraordinary*, after Thomas Rowlandson. Hand-coloured etching, published by Thomas Tegg, 24 October, 1809. (British Museum, No. 1868,0808.7877). The satirical print shows a group of workmen putting the finishing touches to a row of entertainment booths, each with a different placard. In addition to 'Ld Cheatham's Booth — A Comedy call'd Delays and Blunders', the print also makes reference to the duel between Castlereagh and Canning. The 'Jubilee' in question was to mark the fiftieth anniversary of George III's accession to the throne.

My servants are fortunately both well, excepting poor Frank's neck again returned; he will, with my horses, require a course of Physick, & I believe I must send him to his <u>wife</u> as they are the best Nurses. […]

CHAPTER 6

# The Peninsular War (2) and the end of the Napoleonic Wars

*Letters and Eye-witness Accounts 1810–1815*

'What extraordinary events since you were here
& what an anxious moment!'[1]

*Thomas's service with the Walcheren Campaign was his last active experience of 'the Horrors of War'. Having turned down the offer to remain in the Netherlands (postscript to **5: 13**), for a while he resumed his previous role of running the Quarter Master General's department in the Eastern District, and the family returned from Holywell to their cottage in Lexden, where their second child and heir, Charles Thomas Samuel, was born in 1810. In an undated **Memorandum** (probably written soon after 1814 since that is as far as he lists each appointment and posting of his career to date) Thomas also mentions having been offered the position of Deputy Quarter Master General at the Cape of Good Hope. There is no evidence that he ever went to South Africa so it must be assumed that he declined the offer, but he did have one final posting when in 1811 he accepted the position of Deputy Quarter Master General to the Forces in North Britain (as Scotland was widely referred to after the Act of Union in 1801).*

*The wording of the letter from General James Gordon, who had just succeeded General Brownrigg as Quarter Master General to the Forces (a position he held until his death in 1851) suggests that Thomas himself had applied to him for employment. The advantage of a position within the new United Kingdom was that his growing family could accompany him to his new posting; we know that Etheldred and the children did go with him to Scotland as in 1812 she gave birth to twins there — Edward and George. But in the same year their lives changed for good when Etheldred's father Jacob Reynardson died, followed soon after by her mother, leaving their eldest daughter to inherit Holywell, and Thomas to become the first to bear the combined surname of Birch Reynardson — now into its seventh generation.*

---

1    Letter from Thomas Birch Reynardson, at Holywell, to his brother John William Birch, 19 March, 1815 (**6: 8**), following the news of Napoleon's escape from the Isle of Elba.

## THE PENINSULAR WAR (2) AND THE END OF THE NAPOLEONIC WARS

Letter 6: 1 (General James Gordon, Quarter Master General, Horse Guards, London, to Lt.-Colonel Thomas Birch, Colchester, dated 4 September 1811)

Horse Guards, September 4, 1811.

Private

Dear Sir,

In acknowledging your very modest letter of the 1st Instant, the only answer I have to make upon the subject is that I am quite sure that the necessary accuracy and precision will attend every service upon which you may be employed.

Having, upon my appointment to this Office, found the situation of Deputy Quarter Master General in N. Britain vacant, it occurred to me that it could not be better filled than by yourself, and I therefore ventured to name you accordingly to the Duke[2]. — His Royal Highness entirely coincides with me as to your fitness for this station, and your appointment to it will therefore, now, wholly depend upon yourself. — I should observe to you that this appointment would necessarily remove you from the permanent Staff of this department, and you know that on obtaining the rank of Major General, you would no longer be able to retain it. — I mention these points that the whole matter may be fairly under your consideration, before you make your decision upon it.

On being removed from this department, I understand that you will be placed upon half pay as Lieutenant Colonel, but be enabled to receive your halfpay together with the pay of your Office.

I remain with great regard, Dear Sir, Your most faithful Servant,

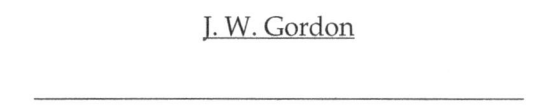

J. W. Gordon

---

*The change in Thomas's family circumstances came only a few months into his new posting and so the Birch Reynardsons, as we must now call them, did not move into Holywell immediately. Instead, Thomas completed two years' service in Scotland — during which time another son, my great-grandfather Henry (who was to inherit Adwell), was born — before being promoted in 1814 to the rank of Major-General, which*

[2]  The Duke of York, Commander in Chief of the Army.

*appointment, as he says, 'necessarily removed me from the Staff & I came to reside at Holywell'.*

*Around this time Thomas was much concerned with the misfortunes which had befallen his mentor John Le Marchant (see Chapters 3 and 4). For ten years Le Marchant had served as lieutenant governor of the Royal Military College* (**Fig. 6 a)**), *until in June 1811 he was without warning relieved of his command, apparently as the result of a joint*

**Fig. 6 a)** *Portrait of Major-General John Gaspard Le Marchant (1766–1812), first Governor General of the Military College at High Wycombe,* by Henry James Haley. Oil on canvas. Joint Services Command and Staff College, Defence Academy of the United Kingdom, Shrivenham. The portrait is a copy of the original (artist unknown) which hung at Chobham Place, the family home of Le Marchant's eldest surviving son, Denis.

*decision by the new Prince Regent[3] and his brother the Duke of York who considered that Le Marchant's recent promotion to the rank of Major-General was incompatible with his responsibilities at the Royal Military College. Within two months Le Marchant left England to sail to Portugal, where he was to join Wellington's victorious armies as the head of a Brigade of Cavalry in the peninsula, from which he would never return as he was killed leading a cavalry charge at the Battle of Salamanca on 22 July 1812.*

*I have very mixed feelings about the letters on the subject which were exchanged between Le Marchant and my great-great-grandfather, and am including extracts from them here with some reservations. They add nothing to our own family history and Le Marchant's tone strikes me as self-pitying and unnecessarily complaining about what, after all, is the duty of a serving Army officer. But Thomas himself made it quite plain where his sympathies lay. He had known Le Marchant well for around fifteen years and was a close friend of his brother-in-law, Peter Carey, and so was bound to feel keenly Le Marchant's reversal of fortune, and the succession of disasters which then befell his family. Thomas kept the letters he received from Le Marchant together in a wrapper on which he later wrote 'I consider his removal from the College a Circumstance of great Hardship as well as of real disadvantage to the Service & that Establishment particularly.'*

---

### Letter 6: 2 (Major-General John Le Marchant, High Wycombe, to Lt.-Colonel Thomas Birch, Colchester, 24 June, 1811)

High Wycombe 24 June 1811

My dear Birch

I have always found you most friendly, in taking a lively interest in my welfare, especially on trying occasions, of which unhappily I have now experienced a greater number than falls to the share of most men of my standing in life.

My removal from the College was most unexpected, not only that I believed the Lieut. Governor to be a <u>permanent</u>, & not a Staff appointment; in the next place, having founded the Establishment, I looked upon it as my home, unless removed to a better thing.

The first intimation that I had to the contrary was a fortnight ago, by a letter

---

3   In October 1810, the King (George III) suffered a recurrence of his mental illness which this time proved to be permanent. The Regency Act was passed by Parliament in February the following year, allowing the Prince of Wales to reign in place of his father.

from Calvert, stating that the Regent & the Commander in Chief considered my present Rank in the army incompatible with the appointment of Lieut. Governor at the College, & that H. R. Highness intends employing me on the Staff. I send you a copy of the letter that I wrote in reply, which I request may be your guide whenever you may have occasion to speak on the subject, as no doubt it will be spoken of.

I live in hopes that my services will soon or late be acknowledged & done justice to; in the meanwhile I am prepared to act with zeal & integrity wherever the Commander in Chief may think proper to employ me. To my Wife and family it is a terrible break up. I cannot express with what little fortitude Mrs Le Marchant bears up against it — perhaps her situation & approaching her confinement may have something to do with her want of nerves. My Income will suffer a diminution of £500 per annum at a time when I am least able to bear with the loss, owing to my family, adjoining to those fears that lye with Education. In this respect I shall be badly distressed — and what to do I know not. Denis [*one of his sons*] was going to Cambridge: now I cannot afford it without spending from my capital.

As there is no seeing into futurity, it might be of consequence, if not to my self, to my children when I am gone, to have some written testimonials of my exertions in the early formation of this institution. — You, my good friend, were a witness of my endeavours as well as difficulties, and in many instances were in the secrets of what was passing. If you would turn the subject in your mind, & at your leisure write me a letter, as being done at my own request, stating such things as come under your observation in proof of my having made all the arrangements that were requisite to the establishment going on, and the innumerable difficulties & prejudices against which I had to struggle. I shall write to others of your standing at the College to the same effect.

I did not expect that it would ever have been necessary to provide myself with such proofs of my exertion & I trust that in possessing them, I shall have no occasion to bring them forward, by the government doing justice to my pretentions when an opportunity offers.

When my destination on the Staff becomes finally fixt (which it is not) I will again write to you.

Remember me to Mrs Birch in which Mrs Le Marchant joins in kind regard […]

Believing me Dear Birch ever truly yours<br>
J Le Marchant

*As stated above, Le Marchant enclosed a copy of the letter he wrote to Henry Calvert, Adjutant General from 1799 to 1820, who had been amongst those on the Board (which also included the Duke of York and Brownrigg's predecessor as Quarter Master General, the future Field Marshal Sir David Dundas) when the National Military College was first set up in 1799.*

---

My dear Sir

Allow me to thank you for the early intimation that you have had the goodness to give me of my intended removal from the M. College. […]

I had certainly (tho' without sufficient consideration) looked forward to my continuance at the College as the more natural course that my military life would have taken, under the particular circumstance of my having given rise to an Establishment which is admitted to have been of essential service to the army, & of my having devoted my best military years to its advancement & improvement, during which time I have unavoidably lost every opportunity of distinguishing myself in common with those of my own standing, by active service in the field. But as the appointment of Lt. Governor is deemed incompatible with my present rank in the army, I hope that I need not say that these thoughts shall never occupy me a moment, & I shall thank you to assure H.R.H. ye Commander in Chief that I never can have any other object in view as to my professional employment, than that of showing myself worthy of that situation (whatever it may be) in which H.R.H. may be pleased to think my humble service may be most useful & acceptable.

Of course I do not know whether it is to you alone that I am indebted for this early communication of what is intended, if so, pray allow me to repeat my best thanks, but if you have done it with the permission of H.R.H. may I beg that you will express in the strongest terms my humble acknowledgment of this mark of his consideration & kindness.

JLM

**Letter 6: 3 (Lt.-Colonel Thomas Birch, Colchester, to Major-General John Le Marchant, 12 July, 1811)** [*This letter must be a copy, as it is not in Thomas's own hand.*]

Colchester 12th July 1811

My Dear Le Marchant

I was really sorry to hear of your removal from the College & regret it the more because you seem to feel it so sensibly yourself; but I am no stranger to the anxious interest you have always taken in this institution from its Birth — Circumstances no doubt, which you are unacquainted with, have made the change expedient & when you have got over the first impulse of feeling & disapointment, I dare say you will reconcile what appears now, rather in the light of a hardship. I admit however, that it is natural you should take it a little to heart.

You call upon me for my opinion as to the conduct of the Establishment, Generally, as far as it came under my observation; I am glad you have done this, because I perhaps, more almost than any other person, had an opportunity of witnessing your exertions & the innumerable difficulties you had to struggle with, in the progress of it; &, as we have always lived upon friendly terms, it was not unnatural that you should communicate with me confidentially on what was passing.

I question very much whether it is generally known, that the first arrangement for carrying on the Duties of the College owes itself entirely to you; and that altho' General Jarry was there to instruct, he troubled himself very little as to how the instruction was to be conducted & indeed I may say that the College [was] so composed at the outset that he could not have put things in a proper train — with Officers of various standing in the army (some of them very young) who came to the College more as a release, or change if you please from Regimental duty, than from a desire to benefit by the intention of the establishment, a certain degree of control was quite necessary, much alteration was required, and upon this hinged many difficulties.

To recommend the removal of Officers was not a popular measure, but I know that you thought it essential to the well being of the Establishment, & it was accordingly in some instances done, & I do not hesitate to say that if this decisive step had not been taken, that the Establishment would in all probability at an early period have got into disrepute. I wish to repeat that whatever merit there might have been in the system of instruction that was at first established &

for the most part pursued at the College, you are entitled to it; & the same may be said in regard to every other regulation, & I firmly believe, from my own knowledge of circumstances, that nothing but unremitting attention on your part & a perseverance against difficulties & prejudices, would have continued the Establishment to the public advantage.

If I were to be asked whether General Jarry had nothing to do with these arrangements, I should say that he had not; and with respect to the Instruction, altho' every advantage was to be derived from his Military knowledge & experience & no doubt there has been to a very great extent, the Information was extracted from him, in a great degree by your pains and attention — General Jarry was a most entertaining & instructive Companion & communicative to those who seemed anxious for information, provided he took a fancy to them; he kept however a good deal aloof, & rather avoided than courted the society of the Officers in General. — He was old, which might be a fair excuse for his inclination to be idle, but well as I know, that unless he had been frequently urged by you in regard to communicating his instruction at the College or in the field, there would have been reason for complaint & much of his information would have lain dormant; I mention this to shew that you exerted yourself more perhaps than you were called upon to do, & some times I have thought, even risqued General Jarry's displeasure, in order that justice might be done to the Establishment.

I cannot speak stronger than by repeating it as my firm conviction, that, to your unremitting attention, perseverance & judgment the College, while you had more immediately the direction of it, owed every good arrangement both in regard to instruction & the Military Government of it & that your zeal for the Good of the Establishment [&] conscientious discharge of your duty superseded every other consideration.

I shall be happy at all times when an opportunity offers to give this as my opinion as indeed I have before done.

Believe me &c &c &c<br>T Birch

## Letter 6: 4 (Major-General John Le Marchant, High Wycombe, to Lt.-Colonel Thomas Birch, 27 July, 1811)

High Wycombe<br>
27 July 1811

My dear Birch,

From day to day I have postponed writing to you, in expectation I should find time to say all that I feel, & could wish to express in return for your friendly letters, but so far am I from being more at leisure, the pressure of business is greater as the moment of my embarkation approaches.

Allow me to thank you most sincerely for your judicious advice, & well timed letters, which I shall not lose sight of, but bear in recollection their contents as they justly merit.

My removal from the College & the appointment of so flattering a Command, as a Brigade of Cavalry in Service, has I trust nothing but ultimate good to issue from it. At present I suffer a considerable loss of income by the change, & were my past service not in some way or other speedily taken into consideration, my family would feel it heavily, as I should find it difficult to continue the education of my children as my Rank entitles them to expect, & which has been my aim for so long to accomplish.

Mrs Le Marchant is on the point of being confined. At first she bore the change in regard to my removal very ill indeed, alarmingly so, but I think that she appears to recover, and I trust her good sense will dispose her to view things favourably[4].

I go to Town on Monday, whether to proceed direct to Portsmouth, or to return here for a day or two, I do not yet know. [...]

Believe me my dear Friend<br>
Ever truly yours<br>
J. G. Le Marchant

---

4    In fact, Marie Le Marchant died after giving birth to her tenth child (the baby, a boy named Thomas, survived) just after her husband had left for the peninsula, and their children – with the exception of Carey, the eldest, who was in the Mediterranean after completing his own training at the Royal Military College – were distributed amongst relatives. The four younger girls and the baby who had cost his mother's life were taken in by Marie's sister, Sophy Mourant, who lived in Guernsey, while their uncle, Thomas's great friend Peter Carey, took charge of the elder children so that they could finish their education in England, as Le Marchant had always been committed to educating his daughters to as high a standard as their brothers.

*Thomas described the last two letters that he was ever to receive from Le Marchant* **(Fig. 6 b))** *as* 'very Interesting to me'. *The cavalry commander's ten months in Portugal and Spain coincided with the turning point of the Peninsular War as the combined British-Portuguese-Spanish force under Wellesley (by now Viscount Wellington) advanced into Spain.*

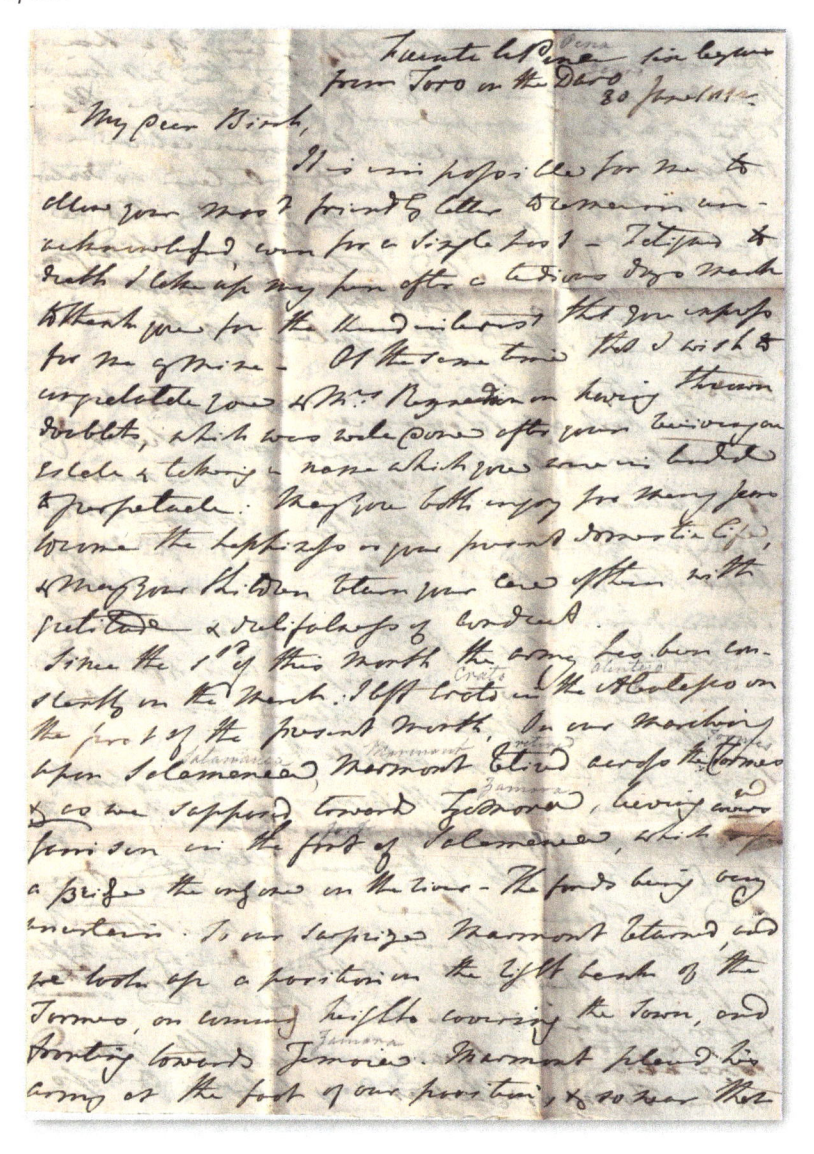

**Fig. 6 b)** Letter from Major-General John Le Marchant to Lieutenant-Colonel Thomas Birch Reynardson, describing actions near Fuente la Pena, Spain, dated 30 June 1812 (6: 6)

## Letter 6: 5 (Major-General John Le Marchant, Alentijo, Portugal, to Lt.-Colonel Thomas Birch, N. Britain [*Scotland*], 10 March, 1812)

Alentejo. Borba 10th March 1812.

My Dear Birch,

I am satisfied of your friendship for me, therefore your silence needed no apology.

Your kind letter reached me about a fortnight ago. I assure you that it gave me great pleasure to hear from an old friend, & in particular to learn that you had recently inherited so considerably, altho' I regret the loss that you experienced in the death of a valuable Friend[5].

May you & your Amiable Wife enjoy your very ample fortune with every degree of happiness that this life affords. […]

From Carey you will have heard how my poor Children have been disposed of, it is impossible to express what I owe to his friendly care of them, added to the unexampled kindness of his Sister Mrs Mourant. Whenever I allow myself to think of my Family in their present dispersed & dependent state, I am made truly wretched.

Whatever may be my lot, I feel that I shall have done my duty to my Country & to my Family, & if I have not been more successful, it will not be owing to any want of exertion on my part to merit a more fortunate issue. But I will not my dear Birch dwell on this gloomy topic: you know already every thing that relates to my most private Concerns, & I am confident no one participates more than yourself in my grief.

I have now been six Months in Portugal, during which I have constantly been on the March. I am now just arrived here from the North, having been present at the Storming of [*Ciudad*] Rodrigo[6], the most spirited enterprise that has been undertaken this War — and nothing could exceed the good order & judgment with which it was carried on.

The Troops are collecting fast on the left banks of the Tagus with a view to

---

5   This refers to the death of Thomas's father-in-law, Jacob Reynardson, and his inheritance of the Holywell estate.
6   After a siege lasting from 7 to 20 January, 1812, the Anglo-Portuguese army under Viscount Wellington (who was created Earl of Wellington after the news reached London) succeeded in seizing the fortress town of Ciudad Rodrigo from its French garrison before Marshal Marmont, who had been appointed by Napoleon to command his forces in Spain, could arrive with reinforcements. The capture of Ciudad Rodrigo opened up the northern invasion corridor from Portugal into Spain, and allowed Wellington to proceed to the more strongly fortified town of Badajoz, 150 miles further south.

the Attack of Badajos[7]. It is expected that we shall find the works considerably strengthened since we last sat down before it, added to the probability of a General action.

I am in command of (what is considered) the finest Brigade of Cavalry in this Army, consisting of nine large squadrons — Rely upon it, they will make a hole wherever their exertions are directed.

I expect my son Carey to join me from Cadiz, I have not seen him since his tour in the Mediterranean; it is two years since we parted: What unforeseen events have occurred since we parted!! [...]

I meet with great kindness from old quarters — not a single controlling hand from any in this army; and I have reason to hope & believe that I shall make it out well with all whom I have any concern with, which is no small degree of consolation & comfort. In the course of a few days it is supposed that the Cavalry will be pushed forward beyond the Guadiana as far as Villa Franca. I am told it is a fine country for the movements of that arm, where it probably will have much to do.

I congratulate you on the flattering appointment that you hold, the more so from the manner [in] which your promotion took place. [...]

Ever Truly Yours
JLM

P.S.

I shudder at the Narrow Escape that Miss Newell had of being murdered[8]. There can be no doubt of the intention. — I hope that the fellow will be Delicted.

Remember me to your Mother and Sister, as well as to Mrs & Miss Newell. [...]

---

7   Although Wellington's army was ultimately successful in taking Badajoz (besieged between 16 March and 6 April, 1812), it was at the very heavy cost of 3,000 allied soldiers killed in the last few hours of the siege alone, as well as many earlier casualties. The occupying French garrison was well prepared for the siege, as Le Marchant had anticipated, and defended the fortifications fiercely as the British and Portuguese attempted to breach the curtain walls, which were in some areas also mined with explosives. The aftermath of the Siege of Badajoz is remembered as 'one of the worst orgies of military indiscipline in British military history' (Peter Snow, *To War with Wellington*, p. 151).
8   Tantalisingly, we have no further information about this incident. The Miss Newell in question was presumably one of Mary Birch's relations, a member of the family who lived in Newman Street (see **4: 5**).

## Letter 6: 6 (Major-General John Le Marchant, Fuente la Pena, to Lt.-Colonel Thomas Birch Reynardson, Scotland, 30 June, 1812)

Fuente la Pena, six leagues<br>
from Toro on the Douro<br>
30 June 1812.

My dear Birch,

It is impossible for me to allow your most friendly letter to remain unacknowledged, even for a single post — Fatigued to death I take up my pen after a tedious day's march to thank you for the kind interest that you express for me & mine. At the same time tho' I wish to congratulate you & Mrs Reynardson on having thrown doublets[9], which was well done after your receiving an estate & taking a name which you were in budlet to perpetuate. May you both enjoy for many years to come the happiness in your personal domestic life, & may your Children return your care of them with gratitude & dutifulness of conduct.

Since the 1$^{st}$ of this month the army has been constantly on the March. I left Crato in the Alentejo on the first of the present Month. On our marching upon Salamanca, Marmont[10] retired across the Tormes & as we supposed towards Zamora, leaving covers and Garrison in the fort of Salamanca [...] To our surprize Marmont returned, and we took up a position on the right bank of the Tormes, on commanding heights covering the Town, and fronting towards Zamora. Marmont placed his army at the foot of our position, & so near that the two armies were within half the range of a six pounder, perfectly in view of each other, there not being a tree or single impediment to their view. The outposts were in constant communication.

As you may suppose we could entertain no doubt of a sanguinary conflict: on the first day that he took up his ground, I had thirteen horses killed from a Cannonade in two of my corps, without a man having suffered, the singularity of the case leads me to mention it.

The Fort at Salamanca contrary to all expectation held out; Marmont on the second day of his return retired his left flank. [...] The day succeeding he

---

9   This refers to the birth of twin boys, Edward and George, to Thomas and Etheldred earlier in 1812.
10  Auguste de Marmont, first Duke of Ragusa (1774–1852), a Marshal of France, had been hastily summoned to the Iberian peninsula in July 1810 to succeed Masséna as commander of the French forces there. Although he had considerable success, he was not a match for Wellington and after he was wounded early in the Battle of Salamanca the command passed to Bertrand Clausel. After Napoleon's abdication Marmont allied himself to the restored Bourbon monarch Louis XVIII, with the result that the word taken from his ducal title, *'raguser'*, has come to mean 'to betray' in French.

made a movement on our right, in which had he not failed, would have given him a complete view of our disposition, & facilitated his Attacks; the affair that followed was short but sharp — we lost some valuable officers.

Before day break both armies were constantly ranged in order of Battle opposite to each other, the Band & trumpets of the Enemy playing — ours observed a solemn silence! On the third day when the morning set in, to our astonishment we found Marmont had retired during the night & upon pursuit, it was found that he had taken up a position two leagues on our right [...] on the Tormes, & the next day he began to cross considerable bodies of troops by a ford, having for <u>its</u> object to compel Lord Wellington to leave his position in order to protect his line of operation, our resources being mostly drawn from Rodrigo. In proportion as Marmont detached, Lord Wellington did the same, for his Lordship was on a height that commanded the Ford of Alba & Tormes, & the Enemy could not make a single movement without its being distinctly seen. His attempt to draw us off failed of success — he was not in force on the left bank to obtain an advantage, & to fight with the Tormes to his rear was risking more than he chose to do; the Day therefore passed off in a Cannonade of the Cavalry in which we lost a few men & horses, & at night the Enemy returned to his position on the right bank where he continued to make demonstrations for a couple of days further when he commenced his retreat in Two Columns, one towards Toro, the other Valladolid. Tomorrow we come up with him, or he will cross the Douro; I rather think it will be the latter.

What Lord Wellington's movements may be beyond the Douro, no one but himself knows.

Adieu my dear Friend. I would say more but I am too much fatigued to do more than offer you & Mrs Reynardson my best wishes.

Believing me My dear Friend Ever truly yours

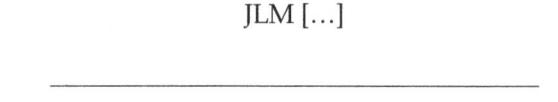

JLM [...]

———————————————

*Within a month of writing this letter, Le Marchant was dead, having contributed substantially to the crushing victory over the French through his leadership of the charge of the heavy cavalry at the Battle of Salamanca on 22 July 1812*[11] (**Fig. 6 c)**). *Thomas annotated Le Marchant's final letters with the comment 'This Excellent Man & Officer & his most promising Son*[12] *have since fallen in battle.' He also kept copies (of which I include an extract from one of them) of letters written by Le Marchant's son Carey, who had fought by his side as his aide-de-camp, to his uncle immediately after his father's death.*

**Fig. 6 c)** *The Battle of Salamanca*, from the series *The Victories of the Duke of Wellington*. Lithograph, engraved by T. Fielding, published 1819.

11 For a description of the decisive role played by Le Marchant in the battle, see Mark Urban, *Generals* (Faber & Faber, 2005). The dashing Major-General 'fell in his hour of glory'; Wellington lamented 'the loss of a most able Officer' and the Duke of York is said to have wept on hearing of Le Marchant's death.
12 Carey Le Marchant saw further action at the Battle of Vitoria, and in the Pyrenees and, as the Peninsular War was coming to an end, at the siege of San Sebastian. However, he received a bullet wound to his instep at the Battle of the Nive on 13 December, 1813, and although he appeared to be making a good recovery, he died of gangrene poisoning on 12 March, 1814, aged twenty-three.

## Letter 6: 7 (Carey Le Marchant, Salamanca, to his uncle Lt.-Colonel Peter Carey, 23 July, 1812)

Salamanca 23<sup>rd</sup> July 1812

My Dear Uncle

I know not how to inform you of the great loss we have had; how you and my poor brothers & Sisters will bear the shock I know not, All we have to do is to trust in the Almighty from whom all comfort is derived, — this melancholy letter will inform you that my poor beloved father fell by a Musket shot yesterday evening after breaking a column of Infantry and in the act of charging another, he was wounded in the groin and expired on the field. I missed him, but I understood he was on the left; from the few killed, I little expected the great loss I had sustained — after searching some time I found the Corpse on the field, which some Soldiers were carrying away. — O my God what a sight, the most beloved of Parents, the best of men (though he did not appear very religious, he had religion at heart), he prayed fervently and regularly to his Maker, which was the reason of his being so cool on entering Action; he always told me that it was from that cause and from never committing an evil action, his feeling so secure in respect of entering the next world, where we all meet sooner or later, when the Almighty chuses to call us.

On account of the Army's advance, the funeral will take place this Evening, it shall be secret and quiet — I shall get a Chaplain and with him deposit the remains, of the best of Parents, a kind friend, pattern to his rising family, and a brave and good soldier, in the cold earth whence we all return, poor Mortals when the Almighty pleases.

[…] To lose two of the best of Parents whose only pleasure was in the care of their children, in the course of twelve short months, appears, and is, a stroke that requires all the resignation one possesses; it is a trial few have experienced — Oh what changes in so short a period! To find myself obliged to take the part of a Parent in respect to my wretched brothers and Sisters, and if it were not for your & Sophy's kind assistance (and I may add Parental affection) I know not what would become of us — Poor children, they little know the great loss that we yesterday sustained […]

I intend applying this day for leave of absence to come to England to settle the affairs of the family and to see you all; it is now two years since I left England — Oh, how altered every thing will appear. […]

Believe me My Dear Uncle
Your most Affectionate Nephew
(signed) Carey Le Marchant

\* \* \*

*By the time Thomas came to live permanently at Holywell, having retired from the service in 1814 with the rank of Major-General, it must have appeared that the long years of European conflict, which had dominated his life since the age of sixteen, were finally over[13] (**Fig. 6 d**)). Within a few years, Thomas acquired a collection of documents and memorabilia about the Napoleonic era, including a copy of the letter written by Lieutenant-Colonel Neil Campbell who had been nominated as the British representative of the four Allied powers to escort the deposed Emperor to Elba, and an unsigned account of an 'audience' with Napoleon during his ten months' exile there (see Appendix IV). But we hear from Thomas next just after events had taken a dramatic and alarming turn: Napoleon had escaped from Elba in February 1815 and was making his way up through France, gathering support all the way. Given the fevered atmosphere of fear and apprehension which must have prevailed, Thomas's thoughtful views about the right of the French to choose their own leader and the desirability of a negotiated peace without the necessity of resorting to more conflict (**6: 9**) are striking and seem ahead of his time.*

---

13  The previous two years had seen Napoleon's invasion of Russia, followed by his army's disastrous retreat from Moscow over the winter of 1812–13. In that year, the allied British, Spanish and Portuguese army under Wellington gradually forced the French into retreat in Spain and after victories at Vitoria in June and Sorauren in July, the Allies finally crossed the border into France in the autumn. By the spring of 1814, following the combined onslaught of invasion over the Rhine by the Austrian, Russian and Prussian armies which had driven Napoleon out of Germany, and Wellington's advance from the south, Napoleon was forced to abdicate. The Treaty of Fontainebleau, signed at Paris on 11 April 1814, confirmed the end of Napoleon's rule as Emperor of France and sent him into exile on the island of Elba.

THE PENINSULAR WAR (2) AND THE END OF THE NAPOLEONIC WARS

Fig. 6 d) *Aufstieg und Niederfallen Napoleons (The Rise and Fall of Napoleon)*, by Johann Michael Voltz. Hand-coloured engraving, 1814.

## Letter 6: 8 (Major-General Thomas Birch Reynardson, Holywell, to his brother John William Birch, dated 19 March, 1815)

Sunday Evening. 19<sup>th</sup> March 1815

My dear John,

What extraordinary events since you were here & what an anxious moment! I own I was quite desponding at the Newspaper accounts, till today. A private account from Montalembert[14] who is Secretary to the French Ambassador has rather relieved me & it is the immediate motive for my writing, he says: "I have but a Moment to say, the news of the day is Excellent, depend upon it, we shall ultimately prevail & if we have a civil War, it will do us a great deal of good, in enabling us to get rid of a Set of traitors, unworthy to belong to our Nation — Bonaparte had not left Lyons on ye 15<sup>th</sup>, his Followers were not numerous — D'Erlon (alias Drouot) has been arrested as well as several other Traitors, the King is firm & never had any idea of quitting Paris."[15] This news appears to be so good (from such a Source) tho' perhaps it may be as well not to give up his name, but I could not help sending it to you.

I have a long pleasant letter from my Mother today. — Mary is going to Town, it seems to the Reynardsons for a few days — We have, with Mrs Kelly, been reading the last part of Granville Pen[16] which really one can apply very closely to the present times — Mrs Kelly says, she hardly knows how to hope they will cut off Bonaparte's head as by Gran: Pen's account there wou'd be an end of us — With our united Love I am

Your Affectionate Brother
TBR

Mrs Kelly is reading The Romance of the Pyrannees[17] [sic] because you recommended it to somebody having an opinion of your Judgement[18].

---

14  Marc René de Montalembert (1777–1831), who fought under Condé and subsequently in the English army. He trained at the National Military College just after Thomas, and is mentioned in several of his and Le Marchant's letters. Montalembert returned to France under the restoration in 1814 and later (1826) served as Ambassador to Sweden.

15  In fact on the same day as this letter was written Louis XVIII, who had seriously underestimated the level of support for Napoleon, left Paris for exile again after the army encamped outside the capital had defected to his opponent.

16  Granville Penn (1761–1844), British author and scriptural geologist (his best-known work, *A Comparative Estimate of the Mineral & Mosaical Geologies*, was published in 1822). The work referred to here is probably *The Bioscope, or Dial of Life, Explained*, published in 1812.

17  A Gothic novel by Catherine Cuthbertson, first published in 1803, then serialised in *The Lady's Magazine* from February 1804 after a warehouse fire had burnt most of the printed copies of the novel.

18  The following letter makes it clear that Thomas means his wife Etheldred.

LETTER 6: 9 (Major-General Thomas Birch Reynardson, Holywell, to his brother John William Birch, at Warwick, dated 4 April, 1815)

Holywell 4th April 1815

My dear John,

Your letter finished the 31st March reached Holywell only this day — it strikes me you may not have received my last letter, in which I mention'd how highly Ethel valued your opinion, saying she had rather have it than any body's she knew, this was when we were talking of the times, Granville Pen &c. I quite agree in what you say, of the declaration of the Allies, they have committed themselves — but Bonaparte is the choice of the French Nation after many years experience of him & can the Allies, with any justice, say he shall not sit on the French Throne? Why then, what do we fight for? It must be for peace at last, & if it can be confirmed, to the satisfaction of Europe, without war, will it not be so much the better?

I have two letters to day besides yours, full of the Subject, one from Col. Thornton, the other from Carey. Thornton who is much at the House of Commons & with Torrens, says, "The Military Secretary (Torrens) is this moment set out for Belgium with the result of a Cabinet council deliberation & to arrange Military Matters with Lord Wellington in case of war, which event, it is still said is very uncertain — Should Buonaparte agree to giving us up Lisle & some of the Frontier Garrisons as a guarantee of his adherence to the Paris Treaty, there will be no War."

Carey speaks very sensibly on the subject & says how the deliberations of the wisest statesmen, for months past have been overturned by one Man. — that even the greatest sceptic must allow, that God is in it if any Truth, & that it sets all human wisdom at defiance. — Think of that Rascal the Duke de Feltre[19], going over to Boney after his conversation with the Prince Regent — this beats any thing, this is the man I dined with at Florence. [...]

The William Booth Greys, that is, he, is an old acquaintance of mine — I am having my House again full of Company, Mr Buckley [&] Lady Georgiana &

---

19 Thomas seems to have been misinformed that Henri-Jacques-Guillaume Clarke, Duc de Feltre, had changed his allegiance back to Napoleon. Clarke, a French politician of Irish descent, had been Minister of War under Napoleon, but was one of the generals pressing for Napoleon's abdication in 1814 as the allies approached Paris. He was rewarded by a peerage by Louis XVIII and when Napoleon returned to France to reclaim the throne in March 1815, Clarke followed the Bourbon king into exile in Ghent. Thomas must have met Clarke in Italy when he was returning from Egypt overland in the late autumn of 1801 (see Chapter 4).

a Son come to us tomorrow; Mrs Fane & 2 sons also — Vere Fane[20] going to be married to Miss Chaplin & to live <u>on Love</u> — poor Diet, be assured. — I am going over to General Grosvenor's to breakfast tomorrow morning & will get him to frank this, if I can. From thence we go to Croxton Park Races. — I have not heard very lately from my dear Mother & Mary.

Mrs Kelly just left us, you are high in her Estimation & she thinks her Opinion worth having — indeed she is a remarkable woman.

[...] Mrs Reeve I fancy comes in about a fortnight, I can't see why My Aunt & Melly should not come, as we shall like much to see them, altho' I am aware it might be as <u>pleasant</u> to be here at different times — I will learn if I can how long Mrs R means to stay. — It is past 12 so God bless you & with our united love I am most

Affectionately Yours<br>
<u>TBR</u>

---

*Thomas's fascination with the character of the man who for a generation had dominated European history long outlasted Napoleon's defeat at the Battle of Waterloo and the terms of the Congress of Vienna, which redrew the political map of Europe[21]. For many years, one of our more unusual possessions which had been handed down through the family was a lock of hair which purported to be from Napoleon's head, said to have been given by him to one of his guards on the island of St Helena, his final place of exile where he died in 1821. The final document in this chapter however has a more direct connection with Thomas Birch Reynardson, as the aspect of the Battle of Waterloo which it recounts is annotated with comments and corrections in the name of 'Cust'* (**Fig. 6 e**)) — *almost*

---

20  This comment makes amusing reading in retrospect, as the daughter of the marriage in question, Emily Fane, born in 1822, was to marry General Birch Reynardson's son Edward in 1847.

21  The Congress of Vienna was set in motion after Napoleon's abdication in 1814 and negotiations continued despite his return from exile and resumption of power in France during 'the Hundred Days' between March and July 1815. Its objective resulted in the redefinition of the boundaries of many European countries, including Germany, the Netherlands, Italy and of course France itself, and the settlement, with some later changes, formed the framework for European international politics for the next century until the outbreak of the First World War in 1914.

# THE PENINSULAR WAR (2) AND THE END OF THE NAPOLEONIC WARS

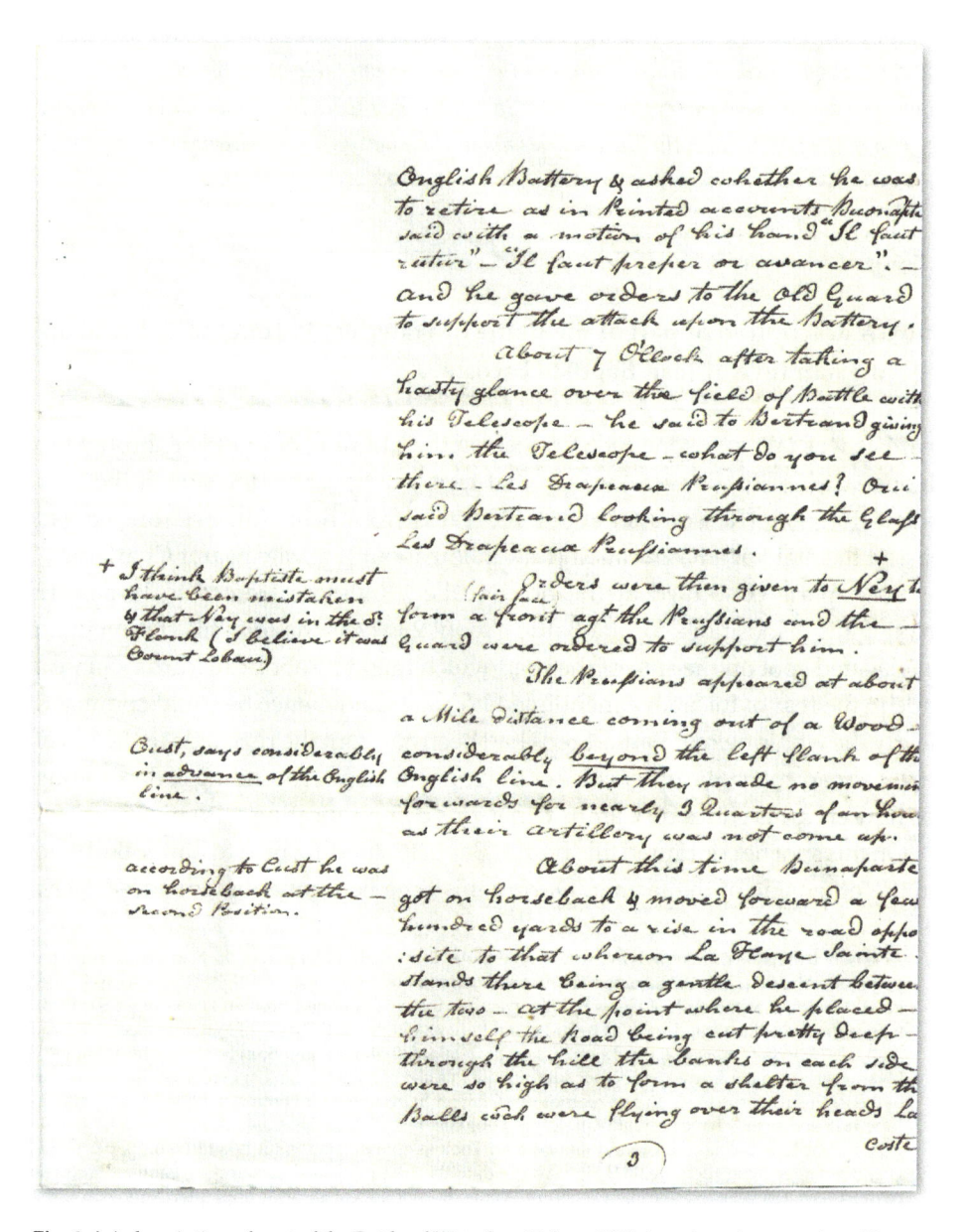

English Battery & asked whether he was to retire as in Printed accounts Buonaparte said with a motion of his hand "Il faut retirer" — "Il faut preper or avancer". — and he gave orders to the Old Guard to support the attack upon the Battery.

About 7 O'clock after taking a hasty glance over the field of Battle with his Telescope — he said to Bertrand giving him the Telescope — what do you see there — Les Drapeaux Prussiennes? Oui said Bertrand looking through the Glass Les Drapeaux Prussiennes.

+ I think Baptiste must have been mistaken & that Ney was in the 2d Flank (I believe it was Count Lobau)

(his face) Orders were then given to Ney to form a front agt the Prussians and the Guard were ordered to support him.

The Prussians appeared at about a Mile distance coming out of a Wood — considerably beyond the left flank of the English line. But they made no movement forwards for nearly 3 Quarters of an hour as their artillery was not come up.

Cust, says considerably in advance of the English line.

according to Cust he was on horseback at the second Position.

About this time Bunaparte got on horseback & moved forward a few hundred yards to a rise in the road opposite to that whereon La Haye Sainte stands there being a gentle descent between the two — at the point where he placed himself the Road being cut pretty deep through the hill the banks on each side were so high as to form a shelter from the Balls wch were flying over their heads La Coste

(3)

**Fig. 6 e)** A description of part of the Battle of Waterloo, 18 June 1815, based on the narrative of Jean Baptiste Lacoste (**6: 10**).

189

*certainly one of Etheldred's cousins, sons of her uncle Lord Brownlow[22]. I like to picture the cousins gathered late at night around the dining-room table at Holywell, poring over maps and accounts of the various battles in which they were involved and entertaining the rest of the family with thrilling stories about their active service during these exciting years.*

---

## 6: 10 (A description of part of the Battle of Waterloo, 18 June, 1815, based on the narrative of Jean Baptiste Lacoste[23])

Baptiste was taken Prisoner at 6 O'clock on the Morning of the 18th & brought to Buonaparte — He (Baptiste) was at that time at a house on the side of the road called Roussom [Rossomme] about 400 Yards from Belle Alliance. But he had passed the night at a Farm called [Le] Caillou about ½ a Mile nearer Charleroi.

Buonaparte continued at the house called Roussom from 6 to ½ past 12 making his dispositions for the Battle. About 2 O'clock he took his station upon an elevated spot on the side of the road which might be about 10 Yards square a little in the rear of the above mentioned house, from whence he could command nearly the whole field of Battle. Steps had been cut from the road side to the top of this & a road cut on the other side for the convenience of ascending & descending for himself & his Aides de Camps & persons communicating with him.

On this spot he continued till about 4, Baptiste standing next to him & Bertrand on the other side of the farmer. During this time he frequently advanced a few

---

22  At least two of Baron Brownlow's five sons served in the Army in the latter part of the Napoleonic Wars; the youngest, Edward (1794–1878), joined Thomas's own former regiment, the 16th Light Dragoons, as a cadet in 1810 and rose to the rank of General. However, it is the next youngest brother, Peregrine (1791–1873), who is the more likely candidate, as he did claim to have fought at the Battle of Waterloo. See R. Thorne (ed.), *The History of Parliament: the House of Commons 1790–1820* (Boydell and Brewer, 1986). The accounts of his war service in the Army Lists do not substantiate this claim, but it is true that Peregrine Cust, a veteran of the Peninsular War (see **5: 12** and footnote 38, Chapter 5), resumed his commission for a brief period in June 1815 and so may have been at Waterloo as a volunteer.

23  It is unclear how this account found its way into Thomas's possession. As it is written on paper which is watermarked with the date 1814, it may pre-date the first published accounts of Baptiste Lacoste's narrative, as it is believed that his version of events did not appear in print until after Napoleon's first volumes of his own memoirs were published posthumously in 1823. Jean Baptiste Lacoste was a Walloon in his early fifties who kept a small tavern on the road between the farm of Rossomme and Belle-Alliance. By his own account, he was taken prisoner on the morning of the Battle of Waterloo, and compelled to act for Napoleon as a native guide to the local terrain. He was by Napoleon's side throughout that day and in particular is said to have observed closely the Emperor's reaction on first sighting the arrival, which he was not expecting, of the Prussian advance guard under Marshal Blücher at about 7 in the evening, whereupon 'he [Napoleon] shook his head and turned quite pale...' Quoted in Harold T. Parker, *Three Napoleonic Battles* (Duke University Press reprint, first published 1944).

paces, looked thro' his Telescope then at his Map — asked Baptiste from time to time what were the name or situations of different places — or walked backwards and forwards with his arms cross'd. Baptiste said he had an air & a manner <u>très vif</u> — but no appearance of agitation.

Aides de Camps were frequently coming & going & Buonaparte directing — reinforcements to be sent to the different stations.

About 4 he moved to another spot something similar to the last about 300 Yards in advance of the former & exactly on the opposite side of the road to Baptiste's house. During the whole time wounded Men were continually passing on the road and cried as they passed <u>"Vive l'Empereur"</u>! — He was dressed in a long Coat, a sort of great Coat, Grey or rather Pepper & Salt — <u>Violet</u> coloured <u>blue</u> Waistcoat, White Pantaloons & short Hussar Boots — He was dressed Baptiste said <u>en Bourgeois</u> — He had a small short sword. The Horse he rode was <u>rouge</u> — probably chestnut.

An English Officer wounded was brought to him — after 20 or 25 questions relative to the force of the English army — as in printed account, he said <u>Mon Ami</u>, il faut retirer.

An Officer came to report to him that he was unable to maintain his position in consequence of the fire of an English Battery & asked whether he was to retire as in Printed accounts. Buonaparte said with a motion of his hand "Il faut rester" — "Il faut presser ou avancer." — and he gave orders to the Old Guard to support the attack upon the Battery.

About 7 O'clock after taking a hasty glance over the field of Battle with his Telescope — he said to Bertrand, giving him the Telescope — "What do you see there? Les Drapeaux Prussiannes?" "Oui," said Bertrand looking through the Glass, "Les Drapeaux Prussiannes[24]."

Orders were then given to <u>Ney</u>* to form a (fair face) front against the Prussians and the Guard were ordered to support him.

[*Marginal note:* *I think Baptiste must have been mistaken & that Ney[25] was in the other Flank (I believe it was Count Lobau.)]

The Prussians appeared at about a Mile distance coming out of a Wood considerably <u>beyond</u> the left flank of the English line. [*Marginal note:* Cust says considerably in <u>advance</u> of the English line.] But they made no movement

24 'The Prussian flags'.
25 One of Napoleon's most trusted and experienced commanders, Marshal Michel Ney (1769–1815) fought throughout the French Revolutionary and Napoleonic Wars, notably in Austria, the Peninsular War and Russia (where he commanded the rear-guard during the retreat and became anecdotally known as 'the last Frenchman on Russian soil') as well as Waterloo. After Napoleon's final defeat, Ney was tried for treason by the Chamber of Peers and was executed on 7 December 1815.

forwards for nearly 3 Quarters of an hour and their artillery was not come up.

About this time Buonaparte got on horseback *[Marginal note:* according to Cust he was on horseback at the second Position.] & moved forward a few hundred yards to a rise in the road opposite to that whereon La Haye Sainte[26] stands there being a gentle descent between the two — At the point where he placed himself, the Road being cut pretty deep through the hill, the banks on each side were so high as to form a shelter from the Balls which were flying over their heads. La Coste upon this could not help ducking his head — upon which Buonaparte said — "Don't be afraid, tenez vous droit — There is as much chance of your being hit, when you duck your head, as when you hold it upright."

While he was in this situation some Aide du Camp (I think La Coste said Bertrand) *[Marginal note:* Cust said not Bertrand but some other A.D.C. came & said "Si vous restes ici un quart d'heure de plus, <u>vous</u> serez entourez ou entonnoiriés par des Prussians."[27]] came & said to him — "Si nous arretons ici un quart d'heure nous serons tournés par les Prussians." "Où sont ils?" said Buonaparte. "Ils ont passies Planchanoit [Plancenoit]" said the Aide du camp.

The attack was now going on which ended in the compleat defeat of the French & from the situation in which he was he could see his own Troops falling back in disorder & the English Cavalry following them from the top of the opposite hill on both sides of La Haye Sainte. Upon seeing this Buonaparte said to Bertrand "Je crois que nous de vous non sauver Pourquoi [sic]." Said Bertrand "Ils sont tout melis emeniable [sic] La Cavalrie au l'Infantrie." Or "Les fantassins [*foot soldiers*] approches La Cavalrie Anglais en masse qui sont tombie sur la Cavalrie & fantassins Francois, qui descendoit de la Montagne en déroute [*in a rout*]" & il dit — "C'est fini à présent; il faut nous sauver[28]. Sauvons-nous." And immediately he turned his horse and with the Farmer & Bertrand set off full gallop. They soon left the road & went over the fields to the right of it, leaving it & Le Caillou a little on their left hand — at the time they set off the Prussians had nearly advanced to Le Caillou on one side and the Belgic & Brunswick Troops had arrived beyond Mont Plasis or nearly at the Observatory on the other, so that in a very short time the Retreat of Buonaparte would have been cut off. They continued galloping till they came to Quatre Bras, when finding they had got the start of the rest of the Army, they drew up & went on less rapidly to Charleroi, then went on a little way further into a Meadow near Marchinnes where they

---

26 The farm of La Haie Sainte on the Charleroi road, which had been captured by the French on the afternoon of 18 June.
27 'If you stay here another quarter of an hour, you will be surrounded or funnelled by the Prussians.'
28 'It's over now. We must save ourselves.'

stopped two hours & a quarter & gave the Farmer their Horses to hold. They had before this been joined by 4 other persons, a sort of attendants not in regimentals & Lacoste* held all their horses.

[*Marginal note:* *And as he was removed to a little distance off them he did not hear what passed.]

Buonaparte now took a little Wine, having eat & drank nothing the whole of the preceding day. He then dismissed the Farmer & Bertrand gave him a Napoleon. The Farmer bowed to him on quitting him & he from his Horse bowed to the Farmer — the Farmer walked home along the Road & filled a horse's corn bag which he carried along with him, with the spoils which he picked up on the road as he went along.

CHAPTER 7

# The General's Family

*Family Letters 1816–1847*

'Formerly I have been within these Walls [Horse Guards], with <u>palpitating heart</u>, upon my own Account; now & henceforward, I shall be here with no less anxious feeling on Account of my Sons…'[1]

*During the relatively peaceful three decades which followed the Battle of Waterloo, Major-General Thomas Birch Reynardson, now retired from active service, settled into a comfortable way of life on his estate at Holywell. He and Etheldred completed their large family with the births of their four youngest children: John (the first of the children to be born at Holywell), in 1816; Matilda Caroline, in 1817; William (the only one of the nine children who did not survive to adulthood[2]), in 1819; and the youngest, Emma Lucy, born in 1821. By all accounts, Thomas was a loving and involved father who was much concerned with the upbringing of his children. In particular he took the education of his sons very seriously, as the following three letters demonstrate.*

---

**Letter 7: 1 (Major-General Thomas Birch Reynardson, at Holywell, to Rev. William Wilkinson[3], South Croxton, dated 14 August, 1819)**

Holywell — 14th August 1819

My dear Sir,

In sending my little Boys to you, I hardly wish to consider it at first, in the light of <u>going to School</u>, but rather as placing them in a Situation, where they may have all the comfort of home in little matters, with the advantage of a strict adherence to such rules as may secure early habits of Obedience — a Friend, with a kind heart, will accomplish this better than a Parent, who […] is still liable to be

---

1   Letter from Thomas Birch Reynardson to his mother Mary Birch, 13 May, 1828 (7: 5)
2   An account of Holywell and its occupants, written in 1844, records that 'this darling child died October 1825 of a fractured skull, occasioned by the kick of a horse, after lying seven weeks in patient suffering — he was a child of the greatest promise.'
3   Rev. William Wilkinson, BA, was Rector of South Croxton, Leicestershire, where he also ran a small school.

influenced (improperly) by affection, at a Moment when firmness might be of the utmost consequence. — In all the conversation I have had with you, if I mistake not, I see this Friend. — I commit my Children, therefore […] to your guidance, wishing that you would watch & check in the bud, any thing that you may see wrong, in their tempers & dispositions & even minor matters such as tricks or bad habits of any sort.

It is a great matter to establish confidence at the same time that one commands respect — I am no friend to government by fear. […] If I have ever known they have been guilty of any fault, rather than ask any question in a way to catch them out in a Lie, I have always preferr'd reminding them that altho' I knew they had committed a fault, how right it was to tell truth […] & I have pursued this plan, with a view to <u>leading</u> them to a sense of truth & in order to establish a confidence between us & to shew them their advantage in it.

Adverting to my own Children, it may be gaining time, to endeavour to give you a little insight into their dispositions & I may at the same time take this opportunity of remarking upon anything I may have observed of my elder Boy Charles, as to his progress in Learning & his conduct generally. — He seems to have gain'd as much ground in his Delectus & Latin grammar as I could have expected & to have a good idea & recollection of his declensions & configurations […]. — I cannot at all find fault with his English reading generally, & when he pays attention […] there is no reason why he should not read very well […] — He generally seems to know what he reads about & to retain what he reads — I do not think him much improved in writing, but that will no doubt come by regular attention & is a secondary object. — […] If you will kindly look to this & take it as a private hint, without telling his writing Master that I had observed upon it, I should be obliged to you.

In justice to this little Boy I must say he is sensible of your kindness to him — His affectionate disposition is very engaging & counterbalances a little occasional irritability, which I could wish otherwise, & which should be seasonably check'd — & I should be particularly obliged to you to guard against it towards his little Brothers, who in fact are too near his own age to come under his protection.

George — From all I have observed of this little Boy, I think his intellects promise well & that habits of attention in him will be easily acquired — His disposition, I believe to be mild & amiable, tho' with much spirit & energy in all he undertakes — As to his acquirements, I may just observe, that he has been once to the end of the conjugation of regular verbs, & was going over this part again — He has a pretty notion of Summing, as far as Multiplication, Subtraction, long division &c, his little weak fingers require time & attention in his writing — English, he reads tolerably, & will, without difficulty, improve by common practice.

Edward — Like most other Boys, he prefers play to Books — poor little fellow, he labours under a natural disadvantage, in a hesitation in his Speech — We must hope however that, by patience & perhaps by not paying too much attention to this little defect, he may in a degree get the better of it. — It strikes me that, at first, nothing too difficult should be attempted, & that, if possible, he should be encouraged to <u>make friends</u> (as it were) with his Books. — He will require constant watching to keep his attention <u>at all</u> fixed; but it will be a main point to arrive at this. — He has kept pace with his Brother in his Grammar, tho' he has got thro' it with more difficulty. — Summing too is harder work to him, & he should be exercised in his multiplication table […] In English, reading too, he will require much patience & attention, tho' I think when he may find that he is <u>obliged to attend</u> & that others about him do it, it may make a great difference — He is a very pleasant, good temper'd Boy, & generally makes friends & has a good deal of fun about him.

He would, I should think, be ready enough to catch hold of improper words, if he heard them, & will not be <u>less likely</u> than others to get into dirt, if it is to be met with, & might be a little slovenly, if he had his own way. — The little Tricks of sucking his fingers & picking his nose, & always having his handkerchief in his mouth, should be attended to — all these appear little things, but he is but a <u>little Boy</u>, & early tricks become lasting habits, if not guarded against […].

After having said this much, it is but fair to add, that I think you will really have no difficulties to encounter, in regard to the dispositions of these Children, they are all amiable & tractable — You will oblige me very much by encouraging as much as possible, harmony & goodwill against these little Brothers, & pray put a stop to any little bickerings & disputes that may arise, & above all I am desirous that strict obedience to all you may say, or wish, should be enforced as much as possible, […] — I am fully sensible of your kind disposition towards them & that all your regulations are temper'd with kindness — I hardly need apologize for having troubled you so minutely on the subject of my Children; they are very near my heart, & I am sure you will make allowances for my feelings. — Believe me Dear Sir

Yours &c<br><u>TBR</u>

**Letter 7: 2 (Henry Birch Reynardson, Holywell (aged nearly six), to his father Major-General Thomas Birch Reynardson, dated 2 September, 1820) (Fig. 7 a))**

[*in Thomas Birch Reynardson's hand*] Sept 2$^{nd}$ 1820

My dear Papa

    I thank you for the book you have sent me, and I like it very much. I think the story of the poor girl is very pretty. Frank takes me out riding every day on the grey Pony, and I dine with Mama. Battle is gone to London. I have been a clean Boy eleven days, and I do not mean to wet myself again by playing at the water. I was giddy with eating green fruit, and took some medicine. Ethel[4] has caught a Greenfinch and it is hung out of doors to see whether the old bird will come to it. Belton has nearly finished the greenhouse, I am sorry because he brings me Pears. Ethel saw two Foxes in the hungry wells. I remain your dutiful Son

Henry Birch Reynardson

**Letter 7: 3 (Henry Birch Reynardson (Fig. 7 b)), Holywell, to his grandmother, Mrs Mary Birch, dated 4 September, 1820)[5]**

Holywell September 4$^{th}$ 1820

My dear Grandmama

    I think you will like me to write to you because you can read my large letters without your spectacles. I shall be six years old tomorrow. If I am a good boy I am to have a half holiday and I intend not to get into mischief or play at the water. I wrote to Papa yesterday to thank him for the pretty little book he sent me. Frank takes us out in the Donkey cart to Castle dykes to get nuts. […] The greenhouse is nearly finished. Mama says that I write so finely that she will ask Uncle John[6] to get me made shorthand writer to the House of Lords. Give my love to him and I wish he was here to row me in the Boat. Ethel sends her love to you and wishes she was at Barton Lodge to rub your leg. Mrs Hawkins sends

---

4    Thomas's eldest daughter Etheldred, born in 1809 (see Chapter 5).
5    Letter in transcription only.
6    For some years, Thomas's brother John William Birch had held the position of Clerk Assistant to the House of Lords.

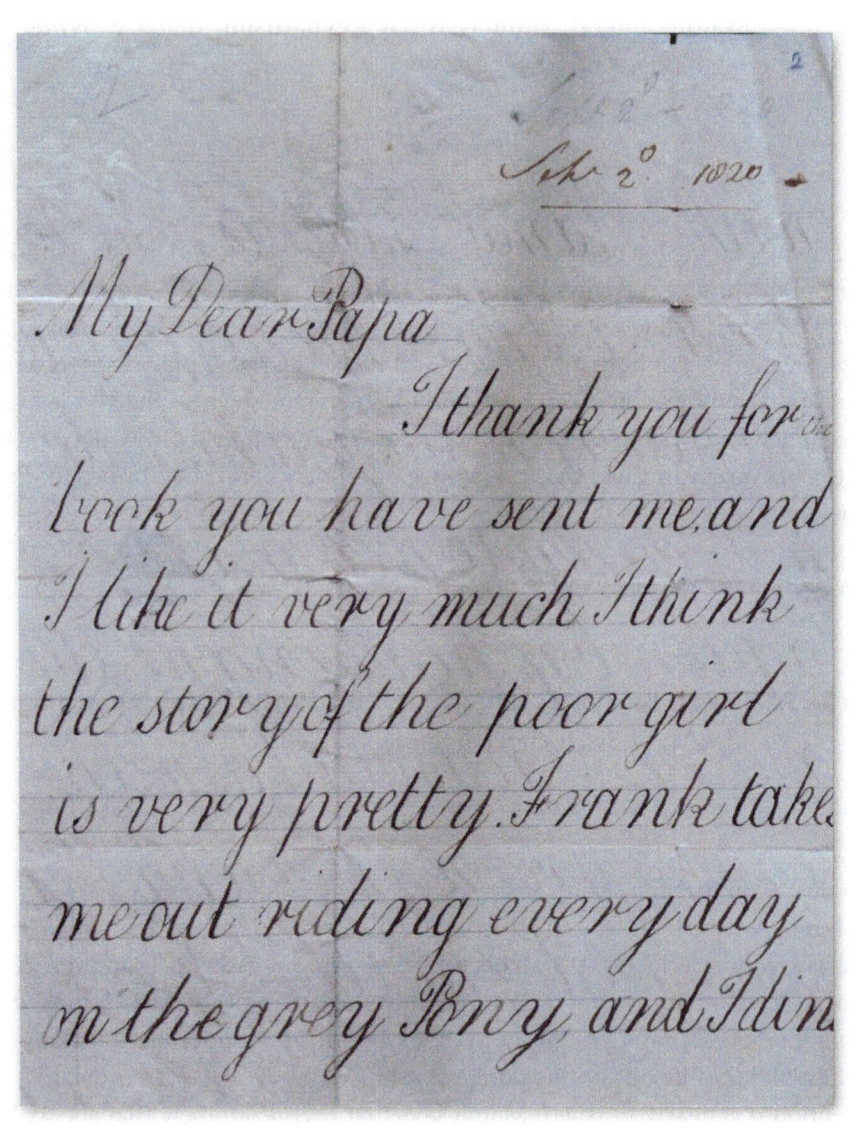

> Sept 2d 1820
>
> My Dear Papa
>
> I thank you for the book you have sent me, and I like it very much I think the story of the poor girl is very pretty. Frank takes me out riding every day on the grey Pony, and I din

**Fig. 7 a)** Letter from Henry Birch Reynardson (my great-grandfather), aged nearly six, to his father, Major-General Thomas Birch Reynardson, dated 2 September 1820 (7: 2)

**Fig. 7 b)** *Portrait of Henry Birch Reynardson as a child*, by Henry Alken (1785–1851). Watercolour, *c.*1820. A friend of the Birch Reynardson family, Alken is mainly remembered as a painter and illustrator of sporting subjects, especially hunting scenes. This rare example of portraiture shows my great-grandfather as a small child, at much the same date as his two letters (**7: 2** and **7: 3**) were written.

her compliments to you. Remember me to Liles. I remain dear Grandmama your affectionate little grandson

Henry B. Reynardson

---

*Thomas's choice of Rev. William Wilkinson as tutor and guide to his three elder sons was clearly a good one, as he continued to take a fatherly interest in his pupils after they had left his school, writing to Charles a well-meant if rather portentous letter of advice as his former charge was about to go to Charterhouse (7: 4).*

---

### Letter 7: 4 (Rev. William Wilkinson, South Croxton, to Charles S. Birch Reynardson, Holywell, Stamford, dated 27 January, 1823)

My dear Reynardson

[…] Though you have left me, I feel an earnest desire for your welfare, — and an interest in you […] You are now about to enter on a new scene of life, — and to mix with a vast Variety of Characters, where much will be left to your own resolution & good sense […] Allow me therefore to offer a few words of advice, which I hope you will accept as a tribute of kind regard.

1. Be courteous & obliging to all, — but do not form an <u>intimacy</u> with any Boy, until you are well acquainted with his Character & disposition; it is easy to form, but not pleasant to break off a connection.

2. Do not choose as your intimate Friend & Companion any Boy who is profane, coarse, or indecent in conversation or conduct — however in other respects lively & pleasant. […] You will probably hear some Boys swear or use the name of God […] in their common conversation; pray be very much upon your guard against contracting such a habit; — it is not merely <u>unmeaning</u> & foolish but <u>exceedingly wicked</u> […] I have thought it right to say so much upon it, because I have frequently observed how soon young Gentlemen contract this habit.

3. Never be ashamed of what you know to be right, nor let any idea of <u>false shame</u>, induce you to do what you know to be wrong. By adhering to this

principle you may incur the jeer of the thoughtless, but […] in the end some will be brought over by your better example, and the wise and good will attach themselves to your society. If I may specify one or two particulars, never be ashamed of <u>kneeling</u> down to your prayers — morning & evening — nor ever be laughed out of a respect for the Sunday, and preferring such books on that day, as have a useful & moral tendency. […]

Again — suffer me as a Friend to warn you against the risings of <u>Pride</u> or <u>anger</u> when you are <u>reproved,</u> — and be willing to feel & own your errors. I name this, because I have perceived the workings of these dispositions in you; — but are not <u>they</u> your <u>best</u> Friends who faithfully tell you of your defects? […] — Let none persuade you to any act, or words <u>disrespectful</u> towards any of your Masters. Not only would this be an ungrateful return for their labours, but […] such things generally reach their ears sooner or later, & will materially injure your <u>character</u> […]. Nor ever make a mock of the <u>infirmities</u> of any of your Masters; this is very common, but […] quite contrary to the golden rule.

I have one subject more to which I beg your attention — […] and that is — <u>Resolve</u> to overcome that <u>trifling</u> state of mind which accompanies you in all your studies. All your Tutors […] have greatly lamented it. — […] The habit is so fixed in you that it will require <u>firm determination</u> on your part to overcome it, but think […] of the <u>anxiety</u> of your […] Parents — who have spared no cost in your education, — and of your own usefulness & credit in Society. […] Do not therefore disappoint the just expectation of your Friends, nor prevent your future […] advancement.

And now my young Friend I must beg you to excuse this (I fear) wearisome epistle, but be assured arising from an earnest desire for your welfare […] I have only further to request that after you are quite settled at Charter House, you will write to me — and tell me how you are going on. Pray […] believe me
   My dear Friend
    Affectionately yours
     <u>W Wilkinson</u>

S. Croxton  27 January 1823.

I hope I need not add how much pleasure it will give us to see you here.

*Unfortunately Charles's experience at Charterhouse was not a success. In the first of his two books of reminiscences[7] written much later in his life, he recalls that*

> After having been bullied and knocked about, roasted and toasted, tossed in a blanket till I touched the ceiling and burst a hole through the blanket, and was nearly killed by coming in contact with the floor of the long bedroom in which some eight or ten of us slept, I was taken home very ill and was supposed to be going to die. This however I did not do; and, much to my delight, was taken away from the horrible prison and sent to that seat of sound learning and religious education called Eton.

*When their time came to leave Rev. Wilkinson's establishment, it was decided that George and Edward, and later Henry, should follow their brother on to Eton, which with its proximity to Windsor and to their adoring grandmother must have seemed a much more attractive proposition. (Oddly, John was in due course sent to the school where his eldest brother had been so badly bullied, to Mrs Birch's implied disapproval* **(7: 6)**). *Charles has left vivid descriptions of the journeys he and his brothers made to and from school by stage coach, on which the boys insisted on travelling outside, whatever the weather.*

> The snow is on the ground, the wind blowing piercingly cold, for it also freezes hard, the stars shining brighter than the brightest diamonds, and the morning, except for the light of the stars, as dark as pitch. It is six o'clock a.m., as they say in these days, in the month of February 1824, and no chance of reaching the 'George and Blue Boar', Holborn, before nine or ten o'clock at night — a pretty look-out for the three little boys who are now mounting on to the 'Regent' coach at Stamford on their way back to school, wrapped in their long drab great-coats. The coach is piled up with luggage till it is loaded like a stage-waggon, and one only wonders how such a heavily loaded conveyance ever reached its destination without breaking down or being upset.
>
> The three little fellows have mounted up to their seats on the roof of the coach, and, though they have been told by their anxious parents to be sure

---

7   *Down the Road: Reminiscences of a Gentleman Coachman* (Longmans, 1874); and *Sports and Anecdotes* (Chapman and Hall, 1887).

and go inside, persist in going, one on the box with the coachman, and the other two behind him, and declare manfully that they are not cold and never feel the cold. They have each got some straw; not new straw, for that is cold stuff, but straw out of the stables which has been a little used and trampled by the horses; and having shoved their little feet into it, instead of on to a hot foot warmer, as in the present day, feel as cheery as possible.[8]

\* \* \*

*It was Thomas's dearest wish that at least one of his sons should follow him into the Army, which necessitated purchasing a commission. His mother, Mrs Birch, had already claimed some credit for easing his entry into the 16th Light Dragoon Guards through her friendships with her Windsor neighbours, notably General William Harcourt; now, at the age of ninety, she was called upon again to use her influence on Charles's behalf. Over twenty years earlier she had moved from her St Leonard's Hill home in the centre of Windsor to Barton Lodge on the other side of Windsor Great Forest, about four miles from the Castle, and fortuitously her neighbours here, with whom she was on terms of the greatest intimacy, included William Wellesley-Pole, first Baron Maryborough (1763–1845), an elder brother of the Duke of Wellington and father-in-law of Lord Fitzroy Somerset (1788–1855), at this time the Duke's Military Secretary.*

---

### Letter 7: 5 (Major-General Thomas Birch, Horseguards, London, to his mother Mrs Mary Birch, Windsor, dated 13 May, 1828)

Horseguards 13 May 1828

My dearest Mother,

If all my time in London was as agreeably appropriated as in writing to you, I would not quarrel with it, but you know what London is & will enter into the feelings of a quiet Country Gentleman come from the retirement of a delightful place, where he certainly is of some consequence,to one where he is nobody; but to enjoy the former thoroughly, tis well to have the comparison — Mrs Reynardson & Ethy [*Thomas's eldest daughter*] like their Quarters, so that's very

---

8   *Down the Road: or Reminiscences of a Gentleman Coachman* (see footnote 7).

well — as my object in coming was to give Ethy an Opportunity of seeing a <u>little of life</u>, our views are <u>mainly</u> to be directed to that End — Plays, Operas, Parties, Balls & so forth; how to get at these things, will probably occupy our thoughts & Mornings & when all that shall be run out, I shall be glad to give a draft for my Bill at the Hotel & shall hope to pay you a visit. [...]

I am so very glad, you decided <u>not</u> to come to Town. It is fuller, than any thing ever was, & will be hotter, I think, in a day or two. [...] Altho' tis difficult to see any body in London, I shall of course leave my card at Lord Maryborough's; Ethel doubts whether she might not be thought to be taking a liberty, having been only introduced at the <u>Church Doors</u> — I am here doing the proper thing, that is, to make my bow to Lord Fitzroy Somerset, unfortunately, I believe I am not, or hardly, known to him, which is unlucky when one has Sons looking forward to the Army. The first, I must think about is Charles & my Object will be to get him into the Guards — the Duke of Wellington's Regiment, & as I am known to him, I think this may be managed & that he might listen to a Wish of ye Sort — formerly I have been within these Walls, with <u>palpitating heart</u>, upon my own Account; now & henceforward, I shall be here & with no less anxious feeling on Account of my Sons — only think of it!!!

I have no sort of doubt that feeling as Lord & Lady Maryborough do by you, & connected as they are with the Duke of Wellington & Lord Fitzroy Somerset, that if you <u>express'd a Wish</u> to get your eldest Grandson into the D of Wellington's Regt, which is the Grenadier Guards, that the thing would be <u>done at once</u>; the way has been <u>already paved</u> & it is not like a favour to be ask'd of the King such as a <u>Canonry of Windsor</u>[9] but merely a <u>Personal</u> favour, but I merely mention this now; it does not press. I am sure it would only be following up the D of York's [...] kind intentions.

PS — 4 O'clock. I just add a line to say that I have had an interview with Lord Fitzroy Somerset & was received very kindly, & not the <u>less</u> pleased was I from his say[ing]: I believe I have the pleasure of knowing your Mother, a delightful woman — & many good humour'd things he said about the Cannings &c — it has been a great point his receiving me in this way — you being the <u>innocent</u> cause I believe.

---

9   A pointed remark, as Thomas's brother-in-law, Rev. William Canning, had just been appointed as a Canon of Windsor. See also footnote 12.

[...] Ethy, I believe, is going to Epsom races with her Aunt Jemima. I have no fancy of the sort — time was, when I could not say so —

[...] Your Most Affectionate & Dutiful Son
T Birch Reynardson

---

*If Mrs Birch did put in a word to Lord Maryborough about her grandson, her efforts would on this occasion have been fruitless. At some point between his father's visit to London in May 1828 and the autumn of that year, Charles suffered a 'bad accident' to his leg, and the next we hear of him (**7: 6**) he is in Switzerland, where he has been taken for treatment to help him recover. Although other members of his family had different theories about the cause of his injury (Mrs Birch attributed it to the effect of his having slipped on the ice in Ditton Park many years before, while my grandfather William was later told that the injuries his uncle Charles had sustained at Charterhouse had left him crippled), Charles himself made it quite clear that a fall from his horse when out hunting was responsible for his permanent lameness, putting an end to his hopes of an Army career.*

---

**LETTER 7: 6 (Mrs Mary Birch, Barton Lodge, Windsor, to her grandson John Birch Reynardson, at Charterhouse School, dated 21 November, 1828)**

Barton Lodge
Novr: 21 1828

My dearest John,

I really have often felt quite ashamed of myself for never having written to you since you have been at the Charter-House, I have often intended getting a Frank & then writing, but now I will write ready for a Frank if my neighbors Lord Harcourt or Maryborough come in my way, or if they do not come, I may do by you as I do by Edward, pay the postage to Sandhurst to him, & to London to you which is just the same (6d). When I write to Charles which I have once only done, I pay 2s.3d postage[10]. Poor fellow he has been laid up with a sprain'd knee ever since he has been there, a great part of the time kept in bed — between ourselves, I think it will be the only chance he will have of not being lame all his life from the sprain of his hip which was done sliding upon the Ice in Ditton Park a long time ago — & for which perfect quiet is necessary. He is with an excellent family [...] and there is an excellent Surgeon attending him. He is now I find wheel'd in a Chair & sat by a Window, where he can see the Alps & a beautiful view, but that perhaps he may have told you. The place he is at in Switzerland is Yverdun[11] — poor fellow, I hope he will with all this care recover of his lameness.

Dear George & Henry [...] were well when I heard from them. — I expect your Aunt Canning[12] this Evening for two or three days before Mr Canning goes into <u>Residence</u>, report says the King is going to reside at the Castle on Monday — Windsor is so enlarged by buildings it is nearly as big again as it was[13]. I hope ere long you will be able to come and pay me a visit & see it. I am thank God still in existence & having so few responsibilities, enjoy my health & faculties, the latter diminishing by degrees, a little deaf & a little blind & forgetfull — but I walk round my grounds, & talk to my friends when they are so good to call — with

10  The complications of the postal service at this time were considerable. Letters were charged by distance and by the number of sheets of paper they contained, and the charge was normally paid by the recipient. Postage costs were at their highest after the Napoleonic Wars, having been designed as a tax to raise revenue. However, all members of both Houses of Parliament, as well as others in public positions, had the right to frank and receive a number of letters free, which they could also do on behalf of others on request — hence Mrs Birch's suggestion that she should wait for her neighbours Lord Harcourt or Lord Maryborough to call, when she would ask them to frank her letters for her. Proposals for reform of the system were first put forward in 1837 by Rowland Hill, who recommended pre-payment of postage at a much lower cost. His plan was eventually adopted and the world's first postage stamps, the Penny Black and the Twopence Blue, came into use in 1840. Postal reform was an immediate success, a dramatic rise in the number of letters sent being followed soon after by a rise in revenue. (Information from The British Postal Museum & Archive).
11  Yverdon-les-Bains, on the shores of Lac de Neuchâtel.
12  Mrs Birch's only daughter Mary (1778–1856) had married in 1818 the Rev. William Canning (1778–1860), whose living was at Heslerton, Yorkshire. He was one of four sons of Stratford Canning (1744–1787) and first cousin to George Canning (1770–1827), the politician and (briefly in 1827) Prime Minister, who grew up in his uncle's house following the early death of his own father. Rev. Canning became a Canon of Windsor under George IV (a part-time appointment when the King was in residence at Windsor). One of his brothers, Charles Fox Canning, was Aide-de-Camp to the Duke of Wellington and was killed at the Battle of Waterloo; his youngest brother, also Stratford Canning (1786–1880), was a British diplomat and politician who became the first Viscount Stratford de Redcliffe, and is best known as the long-serving British Ambassador to the Ottoman Empire in Constantinople (see **7: 15** and footnote 34).
13  Windsor Castle had been much neglected during the long twilight years of George III's final decline (from 1811 until his death in 1820), and after the Prince Regent came to the throne as George IV he began to think about modernising the Castle which up till then had changed little from its medieval origins. Between 1824 and 1828, the new King's architect, Sir Jeffry Wyatville, transformed the whole character of the Castle, raising the Round Tower by thirty feet, replacing the small drawing rooms and music rooms with a series of State Apartments, and building the Waterloo Chamber as a fitting setting for the portraits of Allied sovereigns, statesmen and soldiers which the Prince Regent had commissioned from Sir Thomas Lawrence after the end of the Napoleonic Wars. Mrs Birch's letter is written just at the time that Windsor Castle was ready for occupation by the King.

tolerable Energy still. By living comfortably, using exercise & endeavouring to keep myself in good humour which my faithfull friend & excellent servant good Liles assists me in by doing every thing she can to comfort & assist me, I am as happy as most people — & by the account I have of your temper & disposition I trust you have as good a chance of as long a life[14]. If I live till next Tuesday, I shall be ninety-one, & too thankfull I can't be to Heaven for all the blessings I at this time enjoy, among them I reckon yourself, your dear Father & his family, tho' long in the Army he never gave me cause to find fault with him, & of your Uncle John & Aunt Canning I may say the same; & by the account given of you, my dearest John, I trust you will add to the good list. I can't help wishing the Charter-House was in a pleasanter place[15] — but it makes you enjoy every other more than you would otherwise do — & it is right to draw what good we can from every situation.

May it please God to bless & preserve you is the constant Prayer, my dearest John, of your ever
Affectionate G: Mother<br>M: Birch

---

LETTER 7: 7 (Thomas Todd[16] and Charles Birch Reynardson, Yverdon, Switzerland, to Charles's brother John, Charterhouse, London, dated 28 February, 1829)

Yverdun ___<br>February 28th 1829

Dear Johnny

[…] I have been so much confined with your brother who has been very ill indeed, I have not had an opportunity of seeking for what I promised you [*see Charles's letter below*]. […] Your brother has been obliged to keep in bed for 9 or 10 weeks constantly, that is poor going abroad, is it not? Much worse than being shut up in the Charter House, I should think: at present, he cannot walk at all, without crutches; & I have been obliged to dress & undress him like a child. You

---

14  See footnote 42.
15  Charterhouse was at this time still on its original site near Smithfield, London. The school did not move to its present site at Godalming until 1872.
16  Thomas Todd appears to have been a tutor to the Birch Reynardson children.

see how necessary it is for every person to take care of their limbs, as much as possible. […]

We begin to splutter French with the people tolerably well now, but I can assure you it was no easy matter at first. The winter here has been very cold, the snow is at present melted on the plains, but the Alps at a distance are quite white, and look like monstrous pieces of Lump sugar, or Salt; most of the mountains are so high that the snow will not melt, even in the heat of summer; I should like to go up some of them, but […] this is not the season, I should very likely be upset by a large mass of snow as big as St Pauls, which in the Spring rolls down the sides of the mountains. […]

Your brother has bought the skin of a roebuck, & got it tanned; he is very busy now, cutting it up, & squaring it out; I do not know what he intends to make of it; whether a fur cap, boots, gloves &c. There are a great many foxes about here, but the people do not hunt them as in England, they shoot them, one man shot three in one night near a house in this town; sometimes they hunt wolves in the winter, but there are not many, and none have been heard of near here this winter. A year or two ago, a wild Bear was seen in the mountains near this place, and the people hunted him, & killed him, & afterwards took him in the town to shew him, as something rare. […]

I must leave a little room for your brother to add a little postscript. […]

>  I am dear Johnny
>    Yours sincerely
>        <u>Tho: Todd</u>

My dear Johnny,

I am much obliged to you for your letter written from Harley St. I could not guess at all at first who it was from, it was so much better written than usual. You will be glad to hear that my leg is better, I have had a very unpleasant time of it since I came into Switzerland, but I hope now it will go on well.

I am afraid I shall not be able to get you any stones, the seaside is the place for shells, but we are far enough from it here. I hope I have succeeded in getting Henry some butterflies, but I do not know how they will bear the journey home.

The man who burnt the York Cathedral[17] was a cool hand, I think. I go out in a little one horse carriage sometimes, and my favourite drive is by the side of the lake, it is full of ducks, sometimes I see 2 or 300 together, and often long to be well enough to shoot them. […]

As you pay for your own letters you […] must set the postage of this letter down to Papa, bully him a little for me when you see him and tell him that I had 3 pound of my gunpowder taken away by the custom house officer in France because it was packed up in a box by itself. Pray give my love to Aunt & Uncle & remember me to all the Bourchier family […]

        Your Affectionate Brother
          C. T. S. Birch Reynardson […]

---

*The 1820s must have been a worrying decade for Thomas and Etheldred, beginning with Charles's unfortunate experiences at school, followed by the tragedy of little William's death in 1825, and continuing with the prolonged anxiety over Charles's health. He describes having 'limped about on crutches for two or three years', after which, the family 'not knowing what to do with me', he was sent to Trinity College, Cambridge, where he seems to have done very little work and came down without sitting his degree. His time had not been entirely wasted however, for while he was an undergraduate Charles's frequent journeys between Cambridge and Stamford gave him regular opportunities to indulge in coach-driving, an activity which he had enjoyed since childhood and which did much to compensate him for being unable to ride or hunt.*

> It has been, I own, a sad privation, but matters might have been worse; and I feel thankful that … I have been able to drive coaches, shoot, and fish in a moderate way, and enjoy many amusements which did not require that I should be actually on the top of a horse.[18]

---

17 On 1 February 1829 Jonathan Martin, a former Wesleyan preacher with a history of mental illness, set fire to the woodwork in the choir of York Minster. The resulting blaze was then the most spectacular arson in British history, and when it was extinguished it was found that much of the medieval cathedral had been completely destroyed, including the whole of the roof of the central aisle and most of the woodwork in the interior. Jonathan Martin was tried and found guilty of arson, but escaped hanging on grounds of insanity. An onlooker remarked that the spectacle of the burning Minster was worthy of the brush of the celebrated painter John 'Mad' Martin — an ironic observation as the arsonist was in fact John Martin's brother, though there is no record of his having painted the scene.

18 *Down the Road* (see footnote 7).

*A few years later, by contrast, there was much to celebrate. Thomas's third son, Edward (the younger of the twins who had been born in Edinburgh in 1812, when their father was posted to 'North Britain') had obtained a commission in the Grenadier Guards and was beginning his distinguished career which was to culminate in the Crimea twenty years later (see Chapter 8). There is a charming letter (7: 8) to Edward from his mother (the only surviving one in her hand), full of maternal advice as he left home to start on this new life. I particularly like Etheldred's encouraging postscript about the best way for Edward to cope with the 'hesitation in his speech', from which he had suffered since he was a little boy.*

---

## Letter 7: 8 (Mrs Thomas (Etheldred) Birch Reynardson, Holywell, to her son Edward Birch Reynardson, 1830)[19]

<u>1830</u>

My dear Edward

I am very glad your Horse arrived safe and that you are pleased with her. I hope you will have many, many pleasant rides & enjoy yourself. — I am rejoiced you find me so good a Jockey, I expected you would have been undutiful enough to have <u>smiled</u> at least at my presumption. — We are very happy you are so settled and comfortable [...]. I hope you will like your new line of life every Day better & better, and that you may in time become an <u>ornament</u> to it by your good conduct and <u>Example</u>, tho' we may not live to see it.

But the purport of my Letter is this; I am going to make a few observations to you from the great anxiety I feel, as a Mother, <u>for you</u>, my dearest Edward, at <u>this Moment</u>, more than for any other of my Children, only because you are the <u>One</u>, who is now making his <u>debût</u> in the World, and you are in a Manner separated (not <u>estranged</u>) from the parental Roof. [...] Convinced as I really am of your excellent principles & disposition and the genuine goodness of your Heart, yet I should never cease reproaching myself, were I not at this time to lay before you a few plain rules & observations [...].— You are now entered on a State of trial, & you are aware that your happiness in this World & the next, depends on your conduct [...]. With every wish to do right you must never be unmindful, that the <u>greatest Sins</u> generally begin from mere trifles, & from being

---

19  The original letter is in the Holywell Collection, Lincolnshire Archives (Holywell 110/17a and 17b).

taken off one's Guard; watch therefore & never let yourself be tempted to do what your conscience tells you is wrong, or that you would feel ashamed to do, if you thought your Father or I were looking at you. […]

You will have a great variety of Characters, tempers & dispositions to deal with amongst your Companions; study each of them, that you may not be misled in your Friendships, nor trust too much to any one, before you are <u>sure</u> of him.— Never commit yourself by talking too <u>freely</u> & <u>heedlessly</u> before a Stranger. You never were given to say ill of any one — do not fear being a little laughed at, by silly <u>young Fellows</u>, because you do not join with them in doing what <u>you feel</u> is wrong. […] Above all, never use Oaths, or <u>any</u> <u>kind</u> of profane words or language whatever, because they do & you may fancy it sounds Knowing; depend upon it, you will be more <u>respected</u> for your forbearance, than if you followed the <u>bad</u>, I may justly say, <u>Wicked</u> example […].

Be constant in praying Night & Morning for God's protection and blessing, & in returning thanks for the Mercies he has been graciously pleased to bestow upon you […]. Perform all your religious duties as strictly as you please, but also as privately. It is not good or becoming to make a show of religion.

Should you at any time through <u>Misfortune</u>, or even your own <u>Fault</u> get into any Scrape or difficulty, never be afraid to apply to your kind & indulgent Father, or to myself, who will ever be willing & anxious to relieve, comfort & advise you.— Could you, my dear Edward, know and feel the affection & extreme anxiety of Parents towards their Children, you would think you could never do enough, <u>for your own good</u>, to oblige them.

Whatever you do, strictly avoid being <u>Selfish</u>, that one vice comprehends more vices than I can describe.— do not think that I mean in any direct, or <u>indirect</u> way to charge you with Selfishness; no indeed I do not, only I have so frequently seen the ill effects of it that I caution you against it.

[…] I did not intend to have written so much on this serious Subject, but having done so I must now make you my Excuse which is the truth, my love & zeal for you have run away with my discretion, and still add a line or two more. — I beseech you […] employ well your leisure moments; read […] a chapter in the Bible and the Psalms every morning, […] — then take up some entertaining French Book to keep up your readiness in that Language, or read a little German. […] Draw pretty constantly; there is an endless fund of amusement in that & you have a nice opportunity of Sketching at Windsor […] — Try to improve yourself in Geography, a very useful knowledge for a Soldier.

And now, at last, my dearest Edward, with the blessing & fervent prayers of your most truly affectionate Mother, for your present & everlasting happiness, believe me, my beloved Child, most tenderly yours

Eth[eldre]d A. Birch Reynardson

When you hesitate, think of me, stop! — and speak out slowly —

---

*In 1834 Thomas's eldest daughter Etheldred (Ethy) married Henry Champion Partridge, of Hockham in Norfolk — a neighbouring village to Shropham, where Thomas's great-aunt Mary had moved a century earlier when she married William Green (see Chapter 2), and close to Wretham Hall, where the descendants of Judge Sir Thomas Birch still lived. The marriage took place at Holywell, where both the children of the couple (Etheldred Mary and Henry Thomas) were later christened. The following year Charles also married; his bride was Anne Yorke of Erddig (**Fig. 7 c**) and **Fig. 7 d**)), indicating that the family connections, which had begun with Judge Birch's son Thomas's friendship with Philip Yorke back in the 1750s and continued with the marriage of Charles's grandparents at Erddig in 1777, remained as strong as ever. Charles and Anne's first daughter, yet another Etheldred, was born in the summer of 1836 and so would have been around four months old when the next letter, describing some of the tribulations of a country squire, was written.*

---

LETTER 7: 9 (Lt.-General Thomas Birch Reynardson, Holywell, to his son Henry Birch Reynardson, Trinity College, Cambridge, dated 6 November, 1836)

Holywell 6 Nov 1836

My dear Henry

[…] My time lately has been much occupied with Poachers & all yesterday I spent in Bourne Town Hall, so many game cases were never known to come before the Magistrates in one day — 5 or 6 Convictions […] but the most Audacious act seems to have been one at Holywell; you […] will not be surprised at my annoyance, upon my returning from Hunting ye other day

THE GENERAL'S FAMILY

**Fig. 7 c)** *Portrait of Charles T. Birch Reynardson*, artist unknown. Watercolour, *c.*1836. Erddig (given to the National Trust in 1973 by Philip Yorke III). © National Trust / Susanne Gronnow.

**Fig. 7 d)** *Portrait of Mrs Anne Birch Reynardson (née Yorke)*, artist unknown. Watercolour and bodycolour, *c.*1836. Erddig (given to the National Trust in 1973 by Philip Yorke III). © National Trust / Susanne Gronnow.

(Thursday) with Edward, when I was cold & wish'd to have stretch'd myself comfortably in my Arm Chair before ye fire, at finding that Herring & <u>Tim</u> had got two Chaps in hold, having eased them of their guns [...] they had no time to get away, Tim demanded the guns, which being refused, he dashed at one of the Fellows like a <u>Bull Terrier, down'd him</u> & took it away, & both were brought to Holywell — The Examination in my room was Capital, the fellow produced his shot, but said he had no powder, however Charles slipping his hand down his shooting Jacket, <u>unkennel'd</u> a powder Horn — declared he had no copper caps, however a little further search produced these.

We find they are Notorious Characters from North Witham [...], that they make a trade of this occupation [...] — there are 3 summons out against them. Therefore, altho' they seem to have done well in their <u>vocation</u>, I should think <u>this Shot</u> would hit them too hard — & they may probably spend the Winter in Folkingham Gaol. [...]

— Charles & Anne left us yesterday for Gaddesby on way to Wales, Edward came to fetch them — dear little Emma [*Thomas's youngest daughter*] starts on Tuesday with Miss Pitt for Harley St — to the anticipated joy of Ethy [...]

[...] I shall be anxious, most anxious, about your approaching degree, not as to any <u>difficulty</u> you will have in passing, but I want a little more. I shall be <u>gratified</u> & so will your Uncle, in seeing you in a <u>respectable</u> place [...] Pray therefore keep my feelings in mind & make this a first Object.

I dread the prospect of this Winter, as I see the snow under the Hedges waiting for more.

      Love to dear John & most Affectionately your Father & Friend
      T Birch Reynardson [...]

\* \* \*

*At the end of March 1837, just a few weeks before the death of the old King, William IV, and the accession of the eighteen-year-old Queen Victoria, Mrs Mary Birch reached the end of her long and remarkable life. Her passing, though not unexpected at the age of ninety-nine years and four months, must have seemed like the end of an era to her family, to whom she continued to write until within a few days of her death, dispensing a characteristic mixture of loving benevolence and bracing advice to all, regardless of age. Fortified by a strong and unwavering faith, her main pleasure in life was her family;*

THE GENERAL'S FAMILY

**Fig. 7 e)** *Portrait of Mrs Mary Birch at her spinning wheel*, by John Frederick Lewis. Oil on panel, *c*.1827

*she suffered the loss of her son James in 1817 but was cheered by the late, but extremely happy, marriages of her daughter Mary and her youngest surviving son John[20], and by the arrival in the last year or two of her life of her first great-grandchildren who were duly brought to her to be admired. Although she was a copious letter-writer throughout her life, few of her letters now survive and most of those which do are from her very last years. Over a hundred of these, written between late 1835 and March 1837, were turned into a book soon after her death, which has as its frontispiece a lithographed detail from the portrait of Mrs Birch at her spinning wheel* (**Fig. 7 e)**), *painted when she was about ninety but showing her clad in the high-necked costume with lacy collar and mob cap*

20  See footnotes 12 and 27.

*which was fashionable for elderly ladies more than thirty years earlier.*

*I have chosen two of these letters (**7: 10** and **7: 11**) to illustrate her charmingly discursive style, which could be gossipy but was never malicious or judgmental; for instance she was able to mention her dear friend Lord Maryborough and express warm approbation for Lord Winchilsea in the same sentence, without making any reference to the fact that a few years earlier the latter's intemperate and insulting language[21] about the Duke of Wellington's Catholic Relief Bill of 1829 caused the Duke — Lord Maryborough's younger brother and Prime Minister at the time — to issue a challenge to a famous duel. Neither was injured in the encounter and Lord Winchilsea subsequently apologised, but it must have led to temporarily strained relations between the two families!*

*The letters are tantalisingly short on details of her earlier life and reminiscences; although she lived through a century of enormous changes and dramatic events, she preferred not to dwell on the past, and avoided anniversaries that 'lead to recollections in the end that may be painful[22]' (perhaps adverting to the deaths of two of her sons in infancy). A rather gruesome exception was when she wrote about the winters of her youth, recalling that*

> The <u>very hardest frost</u> in my time began, I think, February 1745, and I was born in 1737; and I have heard then the head of a poor woman, who sold pippins on the Thames, was cut off by the breaking of the ice, and <u>it</u> still kept crying "<u>Pippins</u>" on the ice. [Letter No. 96, 3 February, 1837]

*Of possibly her most interesting friendship, there is no mention in Mrs Birch's surviving correspondence. Mary was the only child of Thomas Newell, an attorney in the firm of Cooper's in Henley, and as a girl growing up at his house Henley Park (later the country home of her son John), one of her closest friends was the daughter of the rector of nearby Harpsden, a Miss Cassandra Leigh.[23] A couple of years younger than Mary, Cassandra nevertheless married earlier than her friend and settled with her new husband, the Rev. George Austen, in the village of Steventon, Hampshire. She went on to have eight children, of which the seventh, a second daughter called Jane, was born in 1775, the same year as Mary Birch's fourth (but third to survive) son, John.*

*Although by the time their children were born, the childhood friends can have met only infrequently, Mary Birch and Mrs Austen maintained their friendship until the*

---

21 Lord Winchilsea wrote that the Duke of Wellington, 'under the cloak of some coloured show of zeal for the Protestant religion, carried on an insidious design for the infringement of our liberties and the introduction of popery into every department of the state'.
22 Letter to her son John William Birch, 26 November, 1835.
23 I am indebted to Miss Deirdre Le Faye for providing me with information about the connection between Jane Austen and Mrs Mary Birch.

*latter's death in 1827. None of their letters still exist, but there are frequent references in Jane's own correspondence which indicate that the friendship had carried on to the next generation and that Jane's affection and regard for Mrs Birch was as warm as that of her mother. In describing to her sister Cassandra a meeting with a mother and daughter of their acquaintance, Jane declares that 'I like the Mother, 1st because she reminds me of Mrs Birch & 2ndly because she is cheerful & grateful for what she is at the age of 90 & upwards.'[24] An earlier letter offers Cassandra something to look forward to, after she has been obliged to pay a duty visit to some family friends:*

> To make you amends for being at Bookham, it is in contemplation to spend a few days at Barton Lodge in our way <u>out</u> of Kent. The hint of such a visit is most affectionately welcomed by Mrs. Birch, in one of her odd pleasant letters lately, in which she speaks of <u>us</u> with the usual distinguished kindness, declaring that she shall not be at all satisfied unless a very <u>handsome</u> present is made us immediately from one quarter.[25]

*Further intended visits to Windsor are mentioned in May 1813 and August 1814, by which time Jane Austen had achieved some measure of fame through the publication of 'Sense and Sensibility' (1811) and 'Pride and Prejudice' (1813). It is frustrating not to know whether Mrs Birch, who was a great reader of morally improving and philosophical books but not necessarily of novels, ever read anything written by her old friend's daughter — and it is also tempting to speculate on whether she was the inspiration for any of the characters in Jane Austen's novels. While most of Jane Austen's biographers have maintained that she* 'drew from Nature…never from individuals', *the choice of name for the place of sanctuary in which the Dashwood sisters and their widowed mother set up home in 'Sense and Sensibility' may have been intended as an oblique tribute — it is called 'Barton Cottage'.*

---

24  Jane Austen to Cassandra Austen, from letter of 11 October, 1813, quoted in R. W. Chapman (ed.), *Jane Austen's Letters to her sister Cassandra and others* (Oxford University Press).
25  From letter of 10 January, 1809, quoted in Chapman (ed.), *Jane Austen's Letters.*

## Letter 7: 10 (Mrs Mary Birch, Barton Lodge, Windsor, to her daughter Mrs Mary Canning, Heslerton, dated 6 September, 1836)

6th September 1836

My dearest Mary,

This showery weather, one minute dark and another sun, is not favourable to my eyes, which are very dim; hearing very deficient, so I am rather unable to try at writing at all, though just finished a letter to the General to thank him for three brace of young partridges and one young hare; making up for last year, when I had hardly any from anybody.

I hope you and dear George[26] will continue to like each other as much as you say you do him; they are all deserving, from the little I have seen of them, of the good opinion of all who know them […]

Dear John and Di[27] (**Fig 7 f)** *and* **Fig. 7 g)**) are set off to Southampton, in order to go to Lymington; both well and in good spirits. This is a showery day, therefore I fear I cannot take a drive to cheer men; though from being so deaf, and not hearing common conversation, I lose much of the pleasure of having any friends with me. When alone I find a well printed old book, and try to read, and sometimes puddle, picking up what I throw down. When fine, walk a little, or crawl round the field, the wheat and oats being in the fields I let to Pasmore; and go the old woman's drive in the horse chair, as usual. I have made no visits lately. […] Now here is wet again. I have a fire, for it is cold. I thank God we are all well; and with love to Mr Canning and George, I am, my dearest Mary,

Your truly affectionate Mother,
M. Birch

---

26  Thomas's second son, George (twin to Edward), had been ordained and had just taken up the position of curate to his uncle Canning in Windsor.
27  John William Birch was the last of Mrs Birch's children to marry, in 1821 when he was forty-six. His wife was Diana Bourchier, the younger sister of Colonel James Bourchier, who had served in Egypt with Thomas (see Chapter 4).

**Fig. 7 f)** *Portrait of John William (Newell) Birch (1775–1867)*, attributed to Sir Martin Archer Shee, PRA. Oil on canvas, undated.

**Fig. 7 g)** *Portrait of Diana Bourchier, Mrs John Birch*, attributed to Sir Martin Archer Shee, PRA. Oil on canvas, undated.

## Letter 7: 11 (Mrs Mary Birch, Barton Lodge, Windsor, to her son Lieutenant-General Thomas Birch Reynardson, dated 15 December, 1836)

15 December 1836

My dearest General,

After tarrying so long in this world it is not surprising I should have found out the rapidity of time & therefore after having had a comfortable night's rest with as little interruption from sleep as I could expect & endeavor'd to be thankfull for it, & read a delightfull Epistle of St Paul's & read Prayers to my family, I have eaten a good Breakfast, read your delightfull letter so fraught with affection & comfort of every sort, that I will not doubt whether I shall thank you now, or at some future opportunity for it as it deserves my earliest attention, & gratitude, & which together with the fine day cannot fail of being excited — & soon if the day will allow of it I will try to walk round my beautifull <u>grounds</u> or take my airing in my new Chair & I hope be thankfull for being able to do so [...]

I am looking forward to seeing dear Aunt Canning for I am sure you will not object to her being foremost in <u>my</u> list of worthies nor can she be far from any who know her as well — as all those connected with her — & happy is it that this is and must be a united opinion — & I will not leave out among the worthies Mrs Liles who will come in, in a few minutes, & hope I will not lose the day in writing but try & get a little air. She is much oblig'd to Miss Emma for thinking of her, & of course & with truth thinks her a very sensible young lady, so grown & improved: to her & dear Matilda & dear Ethel, Mrs B. R; Mr & Mrs Birch, dear John &c, say every thing affectionate for, my dearest General, your affectionate Mother,

M. Birch

I must add a word or two for dear Lady Maryborough — whose uniform attention & kindness to me, is above all praise!! & Lord Maryborough also, & it is not in my power to say how they are, & will be miss'd here — I know not when I have felt more real satisfaction than in the approaching union of dear Miss Bagot & that Excellent Man Lord Winchilsea, by all I know of Miss Bagot & have heard of Lord Winchilsea, they with the blessing their good minds have every reason to expect, must be as happy as the Union of good & religious minds may reasonably hope for. In this state of things without a constant endeavor to the contrary we may always find enough in every state of life to prevent <u>comfort</u> & <u>extasy</u>, but if we have good health, if we could keep our tempers & minds with all <u>diligence</u> as our dear friend David recommends, things would not so often vex us — for there generally are two ways to look at events & circumstances & a habit of looking at the best would keep us oftener right than we are apt to be […].

* * *

*In the early autumn of 1838, a small party consisting of John William Birch, his wife Diana (see Chapter 9), her sister Miss Emma Bourchier, and John's nephew and protegé Henry Birch Reynardson, who had recently come down from Trinity College, Cambridge, and was soon to be admitted to the Middle Temple, embarked on a short tour of Switzerland and parts of Germany. Henry was a particular favourite with his uncle and aunt, who seem to have found him an agreeable companion. The slow progress necessitated by Miss Bourchier's poor state of health and by the still-antiquated modes of travel[28] did not prevent Henry from enjoying several mountaineering expeditions (7: 13).*

---

**LETTER 7: 12 (John William Birch, Donaueschingen, Germany, to his brother Thomas Birch Reynardson, Holywell, Stamford, dated 17 September, 1838)**

1838.
Donaueschingen. 17 September

My dear Tom,

Here we are still out of the Boundaries of Switzerland, detained by Dear Emma's indisposition. Tomorrow we may hope please God to get to Schaffhausen — But Emma is less able to bear the continued travelling than we had calculated. I sent my last letter from Offenburg, where we were at a very comfortable Inn & did not therefore regret being detained a day. […] The Master of the Inn a considerable person, Landowner & wine merchant, sends much of his wine to England, & upon the strength of many of the letters he shewed me from

---

28  Continental travel was becoming much more popular at this time but the great expansion of the railway network would not take place until the 1840s, so getting about was laborious and often uncomfortable.

Gentlemen in England, who had had & approved of his wine, & giving further orders (viz. Lord Albermarle, Mr Drummond &c &c) I have ordered a cask. The original cost £12.— & with duty, carriage & all &c it will come to £24.— It is a sort of Hock (Klingelberger), if you like to go halves in this, you shall.

From Offenburg we came by the beautifull vallies of the Kinsig, & the Gutach to Freiburg (not Fribourg which lies in another road). Slept there, & saw a beautifull waterfall of the Gutach, & came on yesterday by the valley of the Breg (one of the sources of the Danube) to Donaueschingen.— This is a part of the Black Forest, which few English have yet traversed, indeed there is no post road through it, except the first part, yet, but one will be established next year.

[…] Yesterday & today the weather very fine — […] We shall see all we can see of Switzerland without fatigue, or hazard of Illness & then turn our steps homewards, as soon as the state of the weather & season dictates the prudence of such a step — we shall make a tour in Switzerland, but certainly not a tour of it. I have offered Henry to go where he likes, & when he likes, & not to consider himself tied to our party longer than he wishes & will advance him the means of moving independently of us when he desires it […]

We have been amply repaid for our exertions & expenses by the very interesting Scenery we have already passed through […] & shall return satisfied even if Switzerland should afford but a scanty taste.— After Lucerne we shall make our next Head quarters at Thun […] & shall probably close with Geneva.— If we allow about a week to Paris we may hope to set our foot on old England again the beginning of November. […]

We have met now & then with Gagliani's [sic] Messenger[29], & this has supplied us with a few patches of the History of England, since we left it. I see among other things […] that Mr & Mrs Harcourt have been dining at the Castle!! — and that poor Mrs Vere[30] is dead. All the countries we have passed through have appeared to us flourishing & improving, particularly Belgium. Liege quite astonished me by the extension of more works, of recent establishments, & of Handsome Streets since I saw it before — People well clothed, chearfull & industrious — & few beggars — and we have hardly seen one acre of ground, which is not in a state of High cultivation.

Schaffhausen — Septr. 19th — We reached this place yesterday from Donaueschingen. A pleasant road & fine day. Emma bore her journey well, & we

---

29  *Galignani's Messenger* was founded in Paris in 1814 as a daily paper for English residents all over Europe, as stamp duty and postage rendered London journals expensive. At this time one of the writers for the *Messenger* was William Thackeray.
30  The wife of Vere Fane and mother of Emily Fane, who was later to marry Edward Birch Reynardson.

have this day visited the falls of the Rhine, & were much delighted. I had seen them before, but was much more struck with them now. […] We have met with good accommodation at almost all the Inns we have stopped at — English habits & tastes understood & consulted & in many English spoken. […]

> Ever your affectionate
> J. W. Birch […]

**LETTER 7: 13 (Henry Birch Reynardson, Chamonix, to his father Thomas Birch Reynardson, Holywell, Stamford, dated 11 October, 1838)**

> Chamonix. Oct: 11. 1838

My dear Father

My Uncle I believe wrote to you from Lausanne, to which place I did not go. […] I suppose he told you that Switzerland is in arms, collecting from all points[31]. If the French come into Switzerland which I think they will not, they will find it a tough job, they are to my mind playing a very bullying part, the Swiss always ask what will they do. When Louis Bonaparte is in England they ought to demand him of it as well as of us. […]

Oct 5. I started at 5 from Berne to Solothurn and ascended the Weissenstein, a high point of the Jura, it is an extraordinary thing that this is not more known, very few English go up there. The magnificent view quite surprised me […] in front is the whole chain of mountains from Schweitz to beyond Mont Blanc, the finest view of the mountains in all Switzerland, besides the Lakes of Neuchatel, Murten & Bieler & the windings of the Aare. Returned to Berne the same day, a long day's work.

6. From Berne by Thun to Kandersteg up the Simmenthal, a very pretty valley at the foot of the Niesen, this I did in a small voiture […].

7th. Walked over the Gemmi, a good day's work. […] The descent to the Baths of Leuk [Leukerbad] is certainly very wonderful, the whole path cut in the solid rock which is quite perpendicular so that in most places you might drop very

---

31  The trip to the Continent coincided with a threatened invasion of Switzerland by the French, which seems to have alarmed Henry much more than it bothered his uncle (who does not mention it in his letters). Switzerland had been an independent country since the end of the Napoleonic Wars and all the signatories to the Congress of Vienna had agreed to guarantee its neutrality, so it is likely that John Birch saw the French show of force as mere sabre-rattling which did not pose a serious threat.

nicely to the bottom of the valley. Of course the whole is zigzag. Met 5 chamois hunters coming up to stop at a chalet on the top for three or four days. I slept at the Baths of Leuk which were quite deserted, no stranger but myself there, in short I met none from Thun to Martigny. The water comes steaming out of a fountain in the middle of the street, very convenient as at the source they say you may boil a chicken in it.

8. Walked from the baths through part of a forest & then up a most curious sort of path, being no less than a perpendicular rock which I mounted by eight ladders, the pass is called "Les huites echelles". The rounds of the ladders are sometimes at rather an inconvenient distance apart; it is very much like an ant creeping up the greenhouse at Holywell. [...] At Martigny I found my Uncle & Aunt who had come in a voiture from Lausanne [...]

10. Ascended Montenvers & went on the Mer de Glace, we met Dr Buckland[32] the famous Geologist coming down, he told us it was a <u>trumpery thing</u> & not worth seeing; he is a great man & no doubt must know better than I, but I must presume to call him a great ass for his pains, as more wonderful & indeed magnificent sight than the Mer de Glace & the Aiguilles rising above it can in my poor opinion hardly be conceived.

11th (today) We have been up the Hegére opposite the Montenvers so as to get a view of all the Pics & Aiguilles of Mont Blanc, the Mer de Glace & glacier du Bois, Argentieres, Bossons &c, & afterwards went to the source of the Aveiron which I saw also yesterday. [...] My Aunt is a capital Mountaineer, is quite at home on the Mule's back up the mountain & on her own down it. [...] Was rather horrified at my Uncle's having candles lighted last night just as the sun was beginning to set on Mont Blanc & the other mountains, this evening I saw it well. [...]

Oct. 13th (Geneva) Yesterday we left Chamonix & visited the Glacier des Bossons on our way, I went up to it & having put on a pair of Grimpons (iron spikes fixed under the shoes), with the aid of a boy who cut steps in the ice [I] crossed the Glacier & returned the same way. [...] A storm of wind & rain in the night & in the morning a deep snow almost down to the village nearly a mile lower than before, so adieu to the mountains for this year. Today it was very cold & rained nearly all the way, but we have had such fair weather we cannot complain.

---

32  William Buckland (1784–1856) was an eminent and eccentric geologist and palaeontologist, as well as being an Anglican priest and Canon of Christ Church Cathedral, Oxford. His theories were not universally respected; he claimed at one stage to have proved the existence of the 'Universal Deluge', which caused his detractors to accuse him of 'reducing the science to buffoonery'. He later came to a compromise view, believing the landscape of Britain to have been formed by a combination of glaciation and floodwater. At the time when Henry met him, Buckland had recently published *Geology and Mineralogy Considered with Reference to Natural Theology* (1836).

[…] I am sorry to say that Miss Bourchier does not seem at all well, & the journey from here to Paris is no joke if it continues cold, I hope she will be better in a day or two.

It looks very much like war here, young men of all degrees working on the ramparts, cannons planted & sacks of earth on the top of the ramparts &c — which you understand better than I do. We are at the Hotel des Etrangers some way outside the town which is quieter for Miss Bourchier as the other hotels are full of soldiers, they say that all the English families have left not liking the idea of a siege. […]

Give my love to all, & believe me<br>
Your affectionate Son<br>
Henry

We expect to be in Paris in about 10 days.

---

*My great-grandfather Henry seems to have spent much of his twenties travelling. In 1840 he was again on the Continent, this time also visiting Italy, where his uncle wrote to him.*

---

**LETTER 7: 14 (John William Birch, West Heslerton, Yorkshire, to his nephew Henry Birch Reynardson, Milan, Italy, dated 25 September, 1840)**

West Heslerton — 25 September 1840

My dear Henry,

I begin a letter without knowing whether you will get it. But in your last from Munich you say direct Venice so I conclude you will leave there directions for forwarding any letters which may arrive after you may have left it. I wrote to you at Inspruck [Innsbruck] calculating upon your being there about the 7th or 8th when I now find you were at Munich, so I hope tho' a bad hand at shooting flying, I may have hit you by shooting rather before my bird.

We have been spending our time pleasantly here. Your Aunt Canning has had two attacks of Headach, but rallies in the intervals surprisingly & is now

I thank God well. [...] Your Uncle Canning is going next week to Windsor to attend the funeral of the Princess Augusta[33], who died last Tuesday. There have been great rumours of war, the French being angry with us for the part we have taken on the eastern question, that is supporting the Porte, & against Mehemet Ali whom they befriend — They are making great preparations for war, but I do not find that <u>we</u> are making any.

[...] George will be going to Holywell when his Uncle returns from the funeral at Windsor, till they go & take up their more permanent residence at Windsor towards the latter end of October. He & I have a good deal of discussion upon matters connected with his profession & he does the duty very well. I do not think they are much annoyed by the Wesleyan Chapel now. Your Uncle wisely does not set himself against them, & everything seems to go on harmoniously enough.

All our loves to you both, & believe me Ever<br>
Your Affectionate Uncle,<br>
J. W. B.

---

*Two or three years later, this time in the company of a cousin, Robert Cust, Henry went to Turkey where his uncle-by-marriage, Sir Stratford Canning[34], had resumed his earlier role as British Ambassador to the Ottoman Empire. Henry was present in Constantinople at a volatile time for the Ottoman Empire[35] so it is a pity that his letters from Turkey have not survived. When writing to Henry in Constantinople his sisters, Matilda and Emma, do not comment on the political situation there, being rather more interested in the exotic goods their brother had offered to bring or send home, especially the 'otto of roses[36]'.*

---

33  Princess Augusta Sophia (1768–1840) was the second daughter of George III.

34  See also footnote 12. Sir Stratford Canning (1786–1880) served two terms as British Ambassador to the Ottoman Empire, the first from 1825 to 1828. He held other diplomatic and political positions, before being offered the Constantinople embassy again in 1841 after Sir Robert Peel became Prime Minister, this time holding the office until 1858 (with a brief hiatus in 1852, when he was disappointed not to be offered the Foreign Office under the new government of the Earl of Derby). One of the leading figures in Constantinople, in 1852 Sir Stratford (by now Viscount Stratford de Redcliffe) became caught in the midst of a dispute between Napoleon III of France and Tsar Nicholas of Russia which was to lead to the Crimean War.

35  In 1840 the Ottoman sultan, Mahmud II, had been murdered following the unsuccessful invasion by the Turks of Egyptian-controlled Syria in the continuing dispute with the ruler of Egypt, Mehmet Ali. For some time war seemed inevitable, between French-backed Egypt and an alliance including Britain, Austria, Prussia and Russia which agreed to support the Ottoman Empire. After intense diplomatic negotiations, war was averted and Mehmet Ali agreed to settle for a position as hereditary ruler of Egypt. The earlier stages of this dispute are referred to in **7: 14**.

36  Turkey was one of the main suppliers of attar of roses, an essential oil distilled from fresh rose petals and a valuable ingredient in perfume, liqueurs and ointments.

**Letter 7: 15 (Matilda and Emma Birch Reynardson, Holywell, Stamford, to their brother Henry Birch Reynardson, Constantinople, dated 19 October, 1843)**

Holywell Hall October 19th<br>Thursday[37]

My dear Henry

If our letters had duly arrived at their destinations you would have received a joint one from Papa & Emma in answer to yours received on the 12th, we always write the same day or the one after we get yours. […] We have nothing to relate that can make our letters as interesting as yours, but I know you like to hear all we are doing. How can I write when Mamma & Mapperson are talking so fast about beds & Ticking! We have Winter in Earnest now, such sharp frosts & on Tuesday there was Snow, indeed it is cold enough for any thing.

Your letter of this Morning & account of Constantinople is delightful, so interesting, it makes me wish myself in your place. Papa is glad you went to Sir S Canning's & only regrets you could not avail your selves of his second invitations. […] You are a Good Boy for getting Otto of Roses. I am so sorry the Stupid Man lost your Tortoise, tho' perhaps it has saved you much trouble & anxiety on his behalf — but it would have been such an amusing Pet & your having picked it up your self would have added to his charms. There was one at Erddig they had had for years. Robert Cust sent home some of the Coffee cups you describe, they are very pretty. I can fancy you both enjoying your Pipes under the Trees. […]

Think of Dan O'Connell's[38] being arrested. I only hope he will be kept quiet for a year or two. There are plenty of Troops now in Ireland to keep the peace […] John Yorke[39] is just ordered off there which is rather annoying as he was looking forward to getting some leave in the Winter. Emma has a little say for you so I shall give this to her, & only add […] best love to you. I am glad to hear you are both so well, pray keep so.

Ever dear Henry, your very affectionate Sister Matilda

---

37 Matilda added next to the date: 'I ought to say thanks for your letter received this Morning, the 2nd we have had from Constantinople.'

38 One of the most prominent Irish political leaders in the first half of the nineteenth century, Daniel O'Connell (1775–1847) campaigned for Catholic Emancipation and for the repeal of the Act of Union combining Great Britain and Ireland. He became known as 'The Liberator' for his success in helping to achieve the former, but was arrested after calling off a huge demonstration against the Act of Union, charged with conspiracy, and imprisoned. His term in prison seriously weakened his health and he died less than four years later.

39 See Chapter 8, footnote 47.

*Emma's letter is written on the same sheet:*

My dear Henry, I am sorry to find that the <u>family Document</u> never came to hand; we <u>all</u> had a word in it, that is Pa, Ma, Mat, & I. Fancy what a many things you have seen, that we <u>Petticoats</u> are never likely to set Eyes on, & must therefore think ourselves lucky to have had the good description you sent us; <u>rather</u> a pretty compliment. [...]

    My Uncle & Aunt John talk of coming here some time if Mr Bourchier continues the same as he now is, he had not been quite so well. [...] Edward goes to the Lover on the 29 or 30 of this month, he is now out hunting. [...] Poor George cannot settle the <u>Dilapidation</u>[40]. Old [*name illegible*] is so crafty & shabby — there is no getting on with him in a gentlemanlike way. I am sure the Rector will soon be come to fiddle things.

    [...] All the Dahlias &c are done brown — & winter is coming, but the leaves are still on the trees so I will not grumble. Charles was here for 3 weeks shooting, but has returned for some Salmon Fishing with Mr Watkin Wingfield, in Wales — much good may it do him, this cold weather. He was not well when here, & grown much thinner — which is very becoming — they all come here in December. [...]

        Adieu dearest Henry, your ever Affectionate Sister
                                Emma

---

[40] In ecclesiastical terms, 'dilapidation' means 'impairing of church property by an incumbent, through neglect or by intention'.

## THE GENERAL'S FAMILY

*By the mid 1840s the busy household at Holywell, which not long before had thronged with children, was much diminished. Only the two youngest daughters, Matilda and Emma, still lived at home. Etheldred, the eldest daughter, and Charles were both married; 'Ethy' lived mostly in Norfolk, while Charles seems to have spent a good deal of his married life travelling, his only son (also named Charles) being born in Milan in 1845. There were plenty of family weddings during the second half of the decade. After serving as 'Uncle' Canning's curate in Yorkshire for some years, George took the living of Eastling in Kent, and around this time married Julia, the daughter of Sir John Trollope, who lived nearby at Casewick, Stamford, and was a second cousin to the novelist Anthony Trollope[41]. From Emma's letter above, it would seem that in 1843 Edward was already courting his future bride — Emily Fane, daughter of Vere Fane whose marriage to the impoverished Miss Chaplin in 1815 Thomas commented on disparagingly (**6: 9**) — though the marriage did not take place for another four years. By this time Henry had already pipped his elder brother to the post by marrying, in 1847, his brother-in-law's sister Eleanor Partridge, thus becoming the third member of the Reynardson family to ally himself with this Norfolk family.*

*Sadly Thomas did not live to see the last two marriages, as he died on 31 January, 1847, only three months after being promoted to General in the previous November. Perhaps his demise had been hastened by grief at the double loss of his wife Etheldred earlier in 1846 and the death, only a month before his own, of his eldest child 'Ethy', aged thirty-seven. Thomas himself was in his seventy-fourth year — not a bad age for the times, but paling into insignificance besides the astonishing longevity of many members of his family. Three of his sons lived into their eighties, his daughter Matilda was ninety when she died in 1907, and most impressive of all, his son John — born the year after Waterloo — lived until he was ninety-eight[42]. John also took holy orders and for seventy years, from 1844 onwards, he served as rector of Careby as well as being the incumbent of the tiny parish of Holywell itself; each morning, while his parents were still living, he would take prayers for the whole household in the hall of the big house where my father remembered him well from his childhood visits there.*

*The last two letters we have in Thomas's own hand make affecting reading. The first (**7: 16**) I have included as an example of how nothing much changes — it is a copy of a letter he sent to the secretary of the London & York Railway company (soon to be re-*

---

41 Disappointingly, it is unlikely that any of the clerical relations on this side of the family were used as 'copy' for Trollope's Barsetshire novels, as he spent little time in England before starting to write them in the 1850s and probably barely knew his cousins in Lincolnshire.

42 See **7: 6**, in which Mrs Birch prophesied that her grandson would have a long life. John Birch Reynardson's obituary in the *Stamford Mercury* (May 1914) pays tribute to 'one of the most venerable personalities in the county [...] a public-spirited benefactor [...] [whose] life seemed largely devoted to alleviating the lot of the unfortunate, both inside and outside the parochial circle.'

*named the Great Northern Railway), objecting to the proposal to drive the new line across part of his own land and through the nearby countryside and villages. Thomas's protests went unheeded; the line went ahead as planned and indeed still exists as one of the main lines between London and the North, going via Peterborough and Doncaster to York, though Thomas died well before its completion.*

*The other letter (**7: 17**) is to Lord Fitzroy Somerset, the Duke of Wellington's Military Secretary, and reads at first like the complaint of a disappointed man. On reflection, however, there seems some justification for the points Thomas makes. Even at the time, almost half a century earlier, Thomas held the view that the armies in Egypt had been forgotten, being so far beyond the normal reach of communication that despatches took months to be delivered and had usually been superseded by events by the time they did arrive. Nothing had happened in the intervening years to make him change his mind. The veterans of the Peninsular War and of Waterloo had deservedly had honours heaped upon them, but little official acknowledgment had ever been paid to those who had served in Egypt. Two hundred years later, it is an aspect of the Napoleonic Wars to which reference is hardly ever made. In addition, Thomas still felt very strongly that the contribution which John Le Marchant had made in founding and administering the first staff military college for the training of officers, leading to the establishment of the Royal Military Academy at Sandhurst, had never received the recognition he believed it deserved.*

*Whatever Lord Fitzroy Somerset thought privately about this letter, he replied graciously (**7: 18**) in a short note written on black-edged paper which, by a poignant coincidence marks his mourning for his father-in-law, Lord Maryborough, Mrs Birch's much-loved friend. Eighteen months later, Thomas Birch Reynardson received his promotion to the rank of General, but by that time he had less than three months of life left in which to appreciate the gesture.*

LETTER 7: 16 (Lt.-General Thomas Birch Reynardson, Holywell, Stamford, to Mr J. R. Mowatt, Secretary, London & York Railway Company, dated 29 August, 1844)

Holy Well Hall Stamford<br>29<sup>th</sup> Aug. 1844

Sir,

    I beg to acknowledge your printed letter & map of "London & York Railway". In reference to the subject I may observe that, on the same day that I received the letter & Map alluded to, Persons came upon my property at Aunby, Careby &c to make their observations […] without any notice to me or communication whatever.

    In the present stage of the business, I do not know what steps are to be taken further than to state, that the proposed Line thro' the Valley & even Village of Careby is so objectionable to me, that I hope it will not be persisted in or I must endeavour to oppose [it] by every Means in my power.

    I heard <u>by accident</u> that Mr Locke[43] was at Stamford one day this week, but I had no Opportunity of seeing him.

        I am Sir
           Your Obedient Humble Servant
              T B R.

---

43  The renowned surveyor and civil engineer, Joseph Locke, carried out the initial survey.

**Letter 7: 17 (copy of letter, in his own hand, from Lt.-General Thomas Birch Reynardson, Holywell, Stamford, to Lord Fitzroy Somerset, dated 6 May, 1845)**

Holywell Hall<br>Stamford<br>6 May 1845.

My dear Lord

If I am taking a great liberty in writing to you, I must trust to your indulgence & shelter myself under the sort of fancied priviledge of the "Age of Man" & 52 years in the Service.

As an Old Egyptian Officer I trust I may be excused for quoting part of a speech of Sir Henry Hardinge last year in the House of Commons, in which he says: "What should be said again of the Officers of the Egyptian Army who had met the veterans of Napoleon flushed with their achievements in Italy & had dealt to them the first decisive blow they received […]?" Connected then with these remarks […], I venture to send you an Extract of a letter, which […] I find from my lamented Friend General Le Marchant at High Wycombe addressed to me in Egypt. He says (May 10, 1801) "I have infinite pleasure in acknowledging your letter from Alexandria & in congratulating you on the Honor you have acquired with the Army & individually the Credit which your personal exertions have earned in the Opinion of Ministers & all about Head Quarters. […] I saw this Encomium upon you & my Friends at the Secretary of State's."[44]

All I ask then is, the favour of you to read this Extract as marking the approbation of my Early Services & which were acknowledged at the time, by the Appointments to the Situations I filled upon the Quarter Master General's Staff after my return from Egypt […] As you could not possibly have become acquainted with the circumstances I have stated from any other quarter, I have ventured to hope you would allow me the satisfaction of making you acquainted with them […].

> I have the Honor to remain
>     My dear Lord
>         Yours faithfully
>             T Birch Reynardson

---

44  See **4: 11** for the full text of this letter.

**Letter 7: 18 (Lord Fitzroy Somerset, Horse Guards, London, to Lt.-General Thomas Birch Reynardson, Holywell, Stamford, dated 13 May, 1845)**

Horse Guards<br>May 13. 1845

My dear General

I have had the pleasure of receiving your letter of the 6$^{th}$ instant.

I was aware that you had served in Egypt and that wherever you had been employed you had established a high character but of course I had no means of knowing that your Services in Egypt had been particularly noticed by General Anstruther. I here therefore forward the Extract to which you have drawn my attention with much satisfaction.

Believe me My dear General
        Very faithfully yours
                Fitzroy Somerset

CHAPTER 8

# In The Crimea

*Letters and Diary Extracts 1854–1856*

'How I escaped God only knows…'[1]

*By 1854 Lieutenant-Colonel Edward Birch Reynardson was forty-two and had already retired from the Army to his home Rushington Manor in the New Forest, where he lived with his wife Emily and their young daughter. But early in that year he was recalled from retirement, to take part in the conflict which soon became known as the Crimean War. Despite having spent nearly a quarter of a century as a soldier, this was to be Edward's first experience of actual combat, in which he would distinguish himself when he was called upon unexpectedly to take command of the 3rd Battalion, Grenadier Guards, after the death of his colonel.*

*After a period of nearly forty years during which no major conflicts had taken place in Europe, during the 1840s Edward would have been aware of the rising tide of revolution, both at home and abroad[2]. In particular, through his family connection with the Ambassador to the Ottoman Empire, Sir Stratford Canning (see Chapter 7), Edward must have known about the growing dispute between Russia[3] and Turkey over access from the*

---

1 Colonel Edward Birch Reynardson to his brother Charles, 8 January 1855 (**8: 14**), referring to the Battle of Inkerman on 26 October 1854, in which he commanded his Battalion.
2 The year 1848 became known as the 'Year of Revolution' or the 'Spring of Nations', as a series of political upheavals spread throughout Europe and parts of Latin America. The ruling classes, to which the Reign of Terror which followed the deposition and execution of the French king Louis XVI after the French Revolution was still comparatively recent history, feared the consequences of another wave of revolutions. Governments fell and many regimes tottered as working-class revolutionaries rose up against reactionary monarchies or repressive political leaders. In Great Britain, which escaped outright revolution, there was still much unrest; in April 1848, the Duke of Wellington was called out of retirement to organise a military force to suppress a large gathering of Chartists, who were campaigning for political reforms.
3 Tsar Nicholas, the autocratic ruler of Russia since 1825, had spent much of his reign crushing rebellions at home and in neighbouring countries in order to maintain the balance of power in Europe. He believed, mistakenly, that Europe would allow it a free hand in its dealings with the Ottoman Empire and that Britain, its former ally in the Napoleonic Wars, would continue to side with Russia against France, as it had done in an earlier dispute in 1840 which is referred to in Letter **7: 14**.

Black Sea to the Mediterranean, via the narrow Dardanelles Straits[4]. As a leading trading partner of Turkey, Britain was not in favour of Russian control of the Dardanelles, fearing that its dominance of that region could also damage British access to India, and entered into a diplomatic alliance with France[5], with the aim of resisting Russian expansionist ambitions towards the Ottoman Empire.

'Uncle Stratford' Canning, by now Lord Stratford[6], played a central role in the crisis of 1853 which escalated rapidly into war. Acting on behalf of the British Prime Minister, Stratford convinced the Sultan of the Ottoman Empire, Abd-el-Mejid, to resist granting responsibility to either France or Russia for the protection of the 'holy places' of the Orthodox Christian Church, on the grounds that it would compromise the independence of the Turks. In retaliation for the Turkish rebuff of the diplomatic mission of Prince Menshikov (soon to command the Russian forces in the Crimea), Russia occupied the Ottoman-controlled Danubian Principalities of Moldavia and Wallachia (modern-day

**Fig. 8 a)** *Portrait of Colonel Edward Birch Reynardson* by Colonel Cadogan. Pencil and watercolour, 1854.

4   Much of Russia's naval fleet was based on the Baltic seaboard, from where it could defend its northern coast during the ice-free summer months from any attempt at invasion by Allied naval forces. The smaller part of its fleet, based in the Black Sea, could only gain access to the Mediterranean by passing through the Bosphorus and the Dardanelles (together known as the Turkish Straits), both of which were at the time controlled by the Ottoman Empire.
5   The new leader of France (who was the former Emperor's nephew and heir), Louis-Napoléon Bonaparte (1808–73) was elected by popular vote in 1848 as the first President of the French Republic. He initiated a *coup d'état* three years later and in December 1852 he ascended the throne as Emperor of the Second French Empire, taking the title of Napoleon III and ruling until September 1870, when his empire was overthrown during the Franco-Prussian War. He died in exile in England in 1873.
6   In 1852, Canning had hoped to be offered the position of Foreign Secretary under the minority government of his old ally, the Earl of Derby. Instead he was raised to the peerage as Viscount Stratford de Redcliffe, and when Derby's ministry fell, to be replaced by a coalition government led by the Earl of Aberdeen, Stratford returned to Constantinople for the fifth and final time (his fourth as Ambassador), where he served throughout the Crimean War, eventually leaving Turkey in 1857. As the most experienced of British diplomats, he had the reputation in Turkey as the 'Great Elchi', the ambassador *par excellence*. (Trevor Royle, *Crimea* (Little, Brown and Company, 1999), pp. 31–32.)

Romania) in July 1853. Britain sent a fleet to the Dardanelles, where it joined another sent by France, although both countries — together with their allies Austria and Prussia — still hoped for a diplomatic compromise. But matters were taken out of their hands in October, when the Sultan declared war on Russia; the following month, the Russian Black Sea fleet destroyed a Turkish squadron at Sinope; Britain and France issued an ultimatum to Russia to withdraw from Moldavia and Wallachia, and after the ultimatum expired, both countries declared war in March 1854.

Returning to the service with the brevet[7] rank of Colonel (**Fig. 8 a)**), Edward sailed from England with his fellow officers and men in the spring of 1854. Over the next eighteen months he wrote home by almost every despatch, numbering each letter and sometimes accompanying them with illustrations. Most of these letters have not survived and some are known only from typed transcriptions; it is intriguing to compare those which still exist with better-known published accounts of the Battles of the Alma, Balaklava and Inkerman, as in some letters Edward's version follows the 'official' line and in others contradicts it. He also kept a diary, of which only fragments remain, describing the bitter winter of 1854–55 (**8: 15**).

Edward may well have been amongst the first shipment of Grenadier Guards which departed from Southampton in February 1854, even before the declaration of war. He was certainly with his battalion by the time they sailed from Malta on 24 April to anchor in the Dardanelles and then encamp at Kadikoi, near Scutari[8] on the opposite (Asian) side of the Bosphorus from Constantinople, where they spent six weeks in training. The commander-in-chief of the British army in the field, Lord Raglan — Edward's father's old acquaintance Lord Fitzroy Somerset (see **7: 17** and **7: 18**), who had, like Lord Stratford, been made a peer in 1852 — also set up his headquarters at Scutari, while the army moved up the western Black Sea coast to disembark at Varna in Bulgaria. Between June and the end of August the army was encamped at several sites inland, which were also occupied by divisions of the French army[9] and the colourful Spahis (elite Arab cavalry regiments) (**Fig. 8 b)**). While the allied forces were at first favourably impressed by the lush and verdant encampments away from the main port area (**Fig. 8 c)**), disease soon began to be a serious problem for all ranks of the army. By the end of the summer, many men had died or been incapacitated by the effects of typhus, dysentery and especially cholera, the latter

---

7   Edward's promotion was confirmed on 20 June 1854. The term 'brevet' was applied to the temporary higher rank given to those being recalled from retirement.
8   Soon to be the site of the British Military Hospital, where Florence Nightingale arrived in November to take up her appointment as Superintendent of the Female Nursing Establishment.
9   Marshal Jacques Leroy de Saint Arnaud was commander-in-chief of the French army at the beginning of the Crimean War. He was already extremely ill with stomach cancer, but remained indefatigable almost to the end. At the Battle of the Alma on 20 September, he was so weak that he had to be lifted bodily into and out of the saddle. He resigned as commander-in-chief on 25 September and died four days later.

**Fig. 8 b)** *Portrait of a Spahi, taken at Varna, June 1854,* by Edward Birch Reynardson. Pen and watercolour.

*believed to have been introduced through the French transport ships. Small wonder that Edward was so relieved to depart from Varna, that 'detestable place'.*

### LETTER 8:1 (Colonel Edward Birch Reynardson [*unsigned*], Battschuk [*Balchik*] Bay, to unknown recipient, dated 5 September, 1854)[10]

On board [...] Man of War[11]
Battschuk Bay [*sic*]
Sept. 5. 54

[...] We got here by 9 o'clock and with a lovely day the leaving Varna with so many Vessels in our wake was a splendid sight — and when we got here we found the whole Fleet at anchor, and all the Light Division in one long line at anchor. We form behind it — the 2nd, 3rd & 4th; you can scarcely picture a fairer sight, such fine

10  Letter in transcript only (No. 18, *Family Letters*, Vol. 2).
11  No name for the transport ship is given in the transcript, but it is likely to have been the *Simoon*. The Grenadiers embarked at Varna on 29 August, waiting there for the rest of the fleet to assemble before sailing across the Black Sea to Balchik Bay, off the western coast of the Crimean peninsula.

**Fig. 8 c)** *View of Encampment of Brigade of Guards at Galata near Varna, Sept 1854* by Edward Birch Reynardson. Watercolour, dated September 1854.

vessels and so many of them, nearly 300 in all — even now our destination is not known and we are supposed to move on somewhere tomorrow morning. There seems no one who is not glad to turn their back on Varna — a more detestable place never was and I for one never care to see it again. The Battchuk [sic] Bay is larger than I expected and holds the Fleet without any appearance of their taking up much space. I can see out of my window about 100 vessels. The French I believe are already advanced, where to I know not, it struck me that many were remaining behind at Varna for we could see 4 or 5 encampments.

Sept. 6. Still in Battschuk [sic] Bay all ready to start. The Wind being against us, we are waiting for a change. I have made a copy of the order of Anchorage and when we get near our Destination we shall move up in Column, the Light Division landing first — the 1st (Ours), 2nd, then 3rd, 4th — It will be a grand sight, I have no doubt.

IN THE CRIMEA

*The Allies had originally intended to confront the Russian armies in the occupied Danubian Principalities. Over the summer of 1854 the plan changed, as Russia called the Allies' bluff by unexpectedly agreeing to an Austrian ultimatum to withdraw from Silistria, on the southern border of Wallachia and Bulgaria. It was then proposed by the Duke of Newcastle (Secretary of State for War) and endorsed by the British cabinet that the new Allied target should be the port of Sebastopol, the base for the Russian Black Sea fleet at the southern tip of the Crimean peninsula; the intention was to besiege Sebastopol and destroy the Russian fleet. It took several days to convey the Allied armies across the Black Sea and when they disembarked, much of the army's equipment, including tents, food and cooking utensils, was left on board: inefficiency over supplies, mentioned several times in Edward's letters, being a problem which was to recur during the early months of the war.*

---

**Letter 8 :2 (Colonel Edward Birch Reynardson** [*unsigned*]**, Kamishla Bivouac, to unknown recipient, dated 17 September, 1854)**[12]

Kamishla Bivouac
Sept. 17 / '54

We still remain in our first place on landing, as the sea has not allowed us to get on shore much of our ammunition & other necessaries. Yesterday we were given a few tents for our men & sailors. But the numbers were very short & not enough for the men's comfort, they being 16 in a Bell tent. We agreed to give up some of the tents of the officers whose allowance was very small — only one for 3 or 4 which they did not like. So Hood — always wishing to oblige & set a good example — in which I am sure you will feel I was not backward in forwarding his views — took 6 into his tent. So we had last night Prince Edward, Hamilton, Higginson, Kinloch, Hood[13] & self all under what Mrs Heneage thought "a small tent". It was dark before we all settled down on our bed of weeds (which I made

---

12  Letter in transcript only (No. 19, *Family Letters*, Vol. 2).
13  It was a distinguished gathering which squeezed into the little tent. Prince Edward of Saxe-Weimar, a British military officer born to German parents, was the nephew of Queen Adelaide, wife of the late King William IV. Colonel Sir Frederick Hamilton later became the official historian of the Grenadier Guards (*The Origins & History of the First or Grenadier Guards*, 3 vols., John Murray, London, 1874). Colonel the Hon. F. G. Hood was commanding officer of the 3rd Grenadier Guards. When he was killed a month later (see **8: 7**), as the officer next in seniority Edward Birch Reynardson took over in temporary command.

myself for all) & we did not know where to put all our swords, revolvers, boots etc, as you may imagine. Well! In the middle of the night when we were all fast asleep the horrid sound of "To Arms!" Pitch dark, we rushed for our boots & swords & pistols, having everything else on luckily & each took wrong swords & boots at first, tho' I had put mine ready for an emergency of this sort. I in vain tried to put on one of Hood's, but we soon exchanged & got right & in an incredibly short time we were formed, ready for action & on our horses. The bugles sounding all through the Regiments & the clashing of arms was the most exciting thing I ever saw.

We had expected Cossacks as it was thought they had got through our lines, but we hear now it was caused by some enemy firing a battery on our outposts, who gave the alarm.

Horace Cust made me laugh for in the hurry, having two pairs of trousers under his head, he put one leg in one & one in the other!

---

*Within a week of disembarking, still desperately short of equipment, the Allied armies advanced south towards Sebastopol and encountered the Russian army near the river Alma. Though inferior in numbers, the Russians occupied a natural defensive position, but in the action which followed — the first battle of the Crimean War — the Grenadier Guards distinguished themselves by forcing the Russian infantry retreat and capturing their strongly-held redoubt. The Battle of the Alma was the first in which the new powerful Minié rifle was used by the British, a critical factor in securing the decisive Allied victory.*

---

### Letter 8:3 (Colonel Edward Birch Reynardson [*unsigned*], Balzanack River Bivouac, to unknown recipient, dated [?]20 September, 1854)[14]

20 Sept. Balzanack River Bivouac.

We left Kannishale [?*Kamishla*] yesterday morning at 7 a.m., having turned out at 4 a.m. & as we sent our tents back again to the vessels, we bivouacked. Last Friday we got to the above after a long & tiring march [at] about 10 o'clock & let

14 Letter in transcript only (No. 20, *Family Letters*, Vol. 2).

the men halt & get water: but finding the Russians in force a mile beyond, we set to work & our artillery drove in their outposts, losing 3 men wounded & 5 horses killed. What the Russians lost, I don't know. Our men fell out a good deal — but others more — not being in condition. The French killed a few Russians who got near their flank. We fired the first shot & in 2 hours the Russians retreated, & we lighted fires & got water & bivouacked on the ground for the night. We got up at 4 in the morning & were under arms for 2 hours: then breakfasted & started again towards the Alma River at 7, & then the whole Army moved off in column. […]

It is now late: our two Armies are close together & I expect we shall soon be in action. We got a hurried scrap of food at night & fried a scrap of meat over a lamp & boiled a couple of onions I had brought in my haversack — although tough as a board, we thought it a luxury. I also had a good night's rest though the dew wetted everything. I put on two nights back an extra pair of drawers & a flannel waist band & have not had time to take them off — & at 11 o'clock it is very hot.

All the way here from the Landing Place has been one vast plain with scarcely a tree to be seen — plenty of corn about & hay, which is all burnt before we come up. Though our men straggled badly yesterday we were all in this morning & I have no doubt will get on well today; though they wanted food badly yesterday, they bustled up well when the firing began.

Thursday, 21st Bivouac

One line to say that after a most severe action here I am, thank God, quite well.

We found the River Alma strongly fortified & a great force of the enemy with their guns planted behind the trenches & their strong positions. The Light Division suffered a good deal & we followed them crossing the river at Buirluk [*Bourliuk*]. Our fellows behaved most gallantly & their cool determined front carried the day. The action was begun at 10 o'clock & the firing upon us began at 2.30 & didn't cease till ½ past 4 when we drove the enemy away, sweeping all before us. We* [*at foot of page:* *His company] have only 3 officers wounded — Burgoyne, Percy & young Hamilton. The first through the ankle, Percy through the flesh of the arm, and the last a side grazed. The others have had more casualties, but I cannot now enter into that for fear of making mistakes.Poor Horace Cust** [*at foot of page:* **His cousin] had a bad wound in the leg which was amputated & I am grieved to hear now that he is dead. I had just put on my spectacles when a ball knocked off my cap & my mare got a slight wound in the hock. We are in high spirits: & I never felt more in command of myself than yesterday — & we can't have a more severe day.

The Duke of Connaught[15] came up to Hood & shook hands after the action & then did the same by me. Hood led us capitally, & I hope his first Major's# [*at foot of page:* #Himself] exertions were not without their effect! The Duke complimented us very much indeed & so have officers of other Regiments, which is most satisfactory. I could not have supposed that under such a scene & of so severe a nature I could have felt so composed & excited to do my duty, & thank God for it, as I know there is no credit to myself. What made it more severe was the Russians had erected large crosses of which they had got the various ranges & could without our being aware of it pepper us unmercifully. But they have learnt a lesson. General Brown says, they say, he never saw anything so sharply contested in the Peninsula.

I rode back to the battlefield & looked up our poor fellows — such a scene, such a mixture of English & Russians. I did all I could of course to relieve & assist, & got back in the dark. I found our Battalion had moved to this place I date from, & all getting there in the dark. We had to cook a bit of meat & lie down in our cloaks all night on the bare ground — most uncomfortable after a hard day's work. But I am quite well & ready to go ahead.

The Zouaves[16] took a fort, most gallantly, & the French gave us due credit for our performance. In fact all behaved nobly indeed. We call the action The Passage of the Alma. Some Regiments got into a position opposite the big guns & I fear have suffered sadly. The Fleet reached some of the Russians from the sea, & I hope will have still more power of helping us if we have anything to do between here & Sebastopol.

---

15  The Duke of Connaught was not in the Crimea, and this is probably a mistake in transcription for the Duke of Cambridge. Prince George of Cambridge (1819–1904) was the son of Prince Adolphus, Duke of Cambridge (the seventh son of George III). He was a professional army officer who was at this time commander-in-chief of the 1st Brigade (the Coldstream, Grenadier and Scots Fusilier Guards) although his state of health obliged him to return home before the end of the campaign. Prince George inherited the title of Duke of Cambridge in 1850 from his father; after his death in 1904, the dukedom fell into abeyance and was not revived until Queen Elizabeth II awarded the title to her grandson Prince William on 29 April 2011, the day of his marriage to Catherine Middleton. Their first child, born on 22 July 2013, is only the second to bear the name of Prince George of Cambridge.
16  Members of French light infantry regiments from French North Africa, mainly Algeria. The Zouaves were noted for their dashing and distinctive battle dress of short open-fronted jackets (which became a fashionable style of costume for British women during the 1850s), baggy trousers, and often sashes and oriental headgear.

## LETTER 8:4 (Colonel Edward Birch Reynardson [*unsigned*], Heights of Alma, to unknown recipient, dated 21 September, 1854)17

Written by firelight, Bivouac on Heights of Alma, Sept 21 / '54

We got under fire first about 2 o'clock & were peppered for nearly 3 hours. It fell to our lot to support the Light Division which attacked a post to the right of the Russian position. We accordingly advanced through a most murderous fire of shell, shot & rockets and, as we got nearer, grape & cannister & musketry. We crossed the stream in front of the entrenchments & pounded up the hill. Meantime the Light Division had taken the entrenchments but were driven out & retired in great confusion & carried the F[usilier] Guards away bodily. The Coldstreams were too far to the left to give any assistance, & we remained the only unbroken Battalion. The men stood like rocks, advancing slowly but not firing a shot as the 95th were straggling all over our front. As soon as we were clear we opened a splendid fire & advanced slowly, the Russians fighting like men: but they could not stand the Minie rifle & the bullets which were whistling past their ears, & at last bolted into the entrenchments. We almost ceased firing & quickened our pace & were into the place & out of it in as little time as it takes to write this scrawl, the Russians tearing up the hill best pace & not giving us a chance with the bayonet. The 95th — or such as were left of the brave fellows — formed round the Colours & followed us cheering & shouting "Brave Grenadiers — you've saved the day for us."

---

17  Letter in transcript only (No. 21, *Family Letters*, Vol. 2).

*The speed with which the news of the victory at the Alma reached England is an indication of how much had changed over the fifty years since Edward's father was fighting in Egypt (see Chapter 4). Then, despatches took a couple of months to be delivered and letters from home could take even longer to reach the soldiers on the front line. The Crimea was even further away from England than Egypt by the sea route, but by the 1850s travel was much faster. Sailing ships were giving way to steam, and a network of railways across Europe meant that servicemen returning from the Eastern Mediterranean no longer had to go via Gibraltar and beat up the Bay of Biscay, but could disembark in the south of France or at an Italian port and make the rest of the journey by train. Other forms of communication were even quicker: the first official reports of the battle were published in England less than three weeks after the event, but Edward was anxiously aware that his wife Emily would already have heard something about the battle, and the very heavy casualties, via the electric telegraph. This had been invented as recently as the 1830s and was being used in wartime conditions for the first time. Early on in the war, submarine cables reached only as far as Varna on the coast of Bulgaria; by the spring of 1855 however the submarine cable was extended to Balaklava in the Crimea, and a further underground cable laid to link up with Lord Raglan's headquarters at Khutor, seven kilometres from Balaklava. This enabled government officials to communicate with the commanders in the Crimea within twenty-four hours.*

---

### Letter 8:5 (Colonel Edward Birch Reynardson, the Katcha Heights, to his wife Emily, dated 23 September, 1854)[18]

> Sept 23 — 54. The Katscha [*Katcha*] Heights
> over the River [...] by Marnashai
> Village
>
> Saturday

[...] We are now halting having cross'd the above River [*Katcha*] — which we find <u>unopposed</u> to us by the Russians — who no doubt after their good Defeat we gave them at Alma [...] It was a splendid action — very severe [...] & attended a success that nothing but British arms could have sustained & much to the confusion of the Russians — who meant to have held it for 3 weeks —

---

18  Letter in transcript only (No. 22, *Family Letters*, Vol. 2).

instead of only 2 Hours & ¾! The whole army engaged have gain'd immense credit — and I am happy to say none more marked than the Grenadiers who have added a name to their former Laurels, which they will long be justly proud of. [...] We hear Lord Burghersh[19] is going home with dispatches today and if so I shall send this by him. How I have felt for you dearest knowing how long you would be hearing after the Telegraphic dispatch. The army have had a severe loss but not considering the very strong position taken which since I have looked it over appears a marvel to me how it could ever have been done, and we only had the Light Division and the 1st (Ours) and part of the 2nd engaged. There is a strong place between here and Sebastopol to be taken we hear, but they think the Russians have gone back to Sebastopol — had we not had such a poor supply of cavalry we should have cut them up to a much greater extent and made no end of Prisoners — as it is we have very few prisoners except their 2 Generals, who think we are Red Devils! and were sure we should take Sebastopol with comparative ease. I have no doubt it will not be so bad as we expected.[20]

I must try to write to Col. A. Cust as I could not do what I wished about his son, being regularly ordered off on Duty — his horse was shot thro' the shoulder, the ball came out by the flap of the saddle and thro' the poor fellow's thigh — cutting his revolver in two — the leg was obliged to be unluckily performed upon twice and he sank from exhaustion.[21]

We hear today that the Russians don't mean to even dispute the next River and are gone into Sebastopol — expecting us shortly. I don't think a siege will be half so bad as what we underwent the now-famed 20th of Sept. They say 4 vessels are sunk at the mouth of the harbour to prevent our ships going in, but that

---

19  Lord Raglan's official despatch, written the day after the Battle of the Alma, was brought to London by one of his aides-de-camp, Lord Burghersh, whose steamer arrived in Marseilles on 7 October. After travelling up through France by train to Paris, a special train was arranged to take him to Boulogne to cross the Channel. Raglan's text was published in full in *The Times* on 10 October.
20  The Allies failed to follow up the advantage they had gained through the victory at the Alma, and did not pursue the Russians back to Sebastopol. Even the Russians, who were expecting a direct attack on the port, were convinced that the fall of Sebastopol was imminent. However, the advice of Sir John Burgoyne (the leading strategist of the British army) was that the city could only be taken by a formal siege. Accepting this advice, the Allies marched around the city to besiege it from the south, allowing the Russians time to fortify the city, and to stage two flank attacks from their field army, based in the central Crimea. The siege of Sebastopol was to drag on until September 1855.
21  'Of the officers killed, none had more sincere mourners than Captain Cust, Coldstream Guards, A.D.C. to General Bentinck. He expired immediately after the amputation of the thigh on the evening of the 20th. Cust was no common man, he had all the attributes of the good soldier. He was acute, energetic, and of a singular bold, independent spirit. He abhorred meanness and chicane. [...] He was a frank enemy, as a friend he was true as steel. [...] Is it so surprising that Horace Cust's memory should be held so dear?' Extract from Captain C. T. Wilson, *Our Veterans of 1854 in Camp & before the Enemy* (Street, London, 1859), quoted in Michael Springman, *The Guards Brigade in the Crimea* (Pen & Sword, 2008).

will not much signify — it will be managed somehow. I shall not be surprised at their capitulating. The French have just got a good reinforcement of troops, some infantry and cavalry — <u>and it was light</u> — to sea today. The French <u>army</u> alongside of ours both cheering each other and the French General crying Vivre les Anglais. Sir Colin Campbell told me today that not only had he heard the Grenadier Guards' conduct praised by many Regiments — but by two or three old & good officers who said nothing could exceed it. Of course a most flattering General Order has come out, so we are all men and officers in the highest spirits. What a change from when we were rotting under canvas at Aladyn & Gevrelek[22] !! & it repays us much for the Dangers we have undergone & I think you will feel yourself as <u>one of us</u> — and be proud of undergoing discomforts in such a cause or for such results. If I can I mean to send by Burghersh to you a sketch of Hood's of the Battle Field which you must forward to her [?Mrs Hood] directly please — they are numbered 1.2.3.4.5. from right to left. The number of killed and wounded is great — viz. 2,780 Men killed & wounded, 107 Officers killed & wounded (28 killed), & 1400 French. The Russians loss very severe but we don't know numbers.

These flowers were picked from the Battle Field where our success took place — close to the Battery.

### Letter 8:6 (Colonel Edward Birch Reynardson, outside Sebastopol, to his wife Emily, dated 14 October, 1854)[23]

Before Sebastopol<br>Octr. 14 — 54.

My dearest Em,

We are still where we were when I sent the 65. We stay till the Trenches are all done which we expect every day — it's always <u>tomorrow</u> we shall begin, and then when it comes, the next day — however we are getting very forward now & have got strong batteries close to the Town. It is quite marvellous to see how few casualties have happened in our working parties considering the incessant shelling and roar of cannon from the enemy's big guns. They generally go over or fall short of our parties and if they do fall amongst them & they lie down flat

---

22  Two camps inland from Varna. Cholera was rife in both camps.
23  Letter in transcript only (No. 23, *Family Letters*, Vol. 2).

they generally escape. We have had two or three small outpost encounters with Cossacks and killed a few but they seem not to dare to come and face us in the open. […]

13th [*sic: actually 15*] Sunday. We are terribly hardly worked now, no day without either being in the Trenches as working party or else to furnish a large armed party for them. I was up almost all last night and have now got to go there for 24 hours again. I shall be heartily glad when we really begin operations — as being fired at all day without returning it and bobbing under trenches and falling on our faces to avoid shells is but poor fun at the best.

16th. I did not go after all last night as they have now put the Brevet Colonels on another duty with larger Commands, indeed I have from my rank escaped much annoying work which might otherwise have fallen upon me. The firing is more incessant than ever as we begin to get our guns into position. The delay has been caused I believe from the difficulty of breaking up the hard ground. Fancy our having been in the Crimea actually a Month! I hope we may soon smash the place when we begin and then be sent off somewhere to winter quarters — anything sooner than staying here — which I can't think is likely myself. We only want to destroy the fleet and damage the Town when I have no doubt most of the Russians would Evacuate the place. I hear all the inhabitants have, and deserters tell us they have not at all a large force in the Town. I hope therefore for their own sakes they may capitulate.

No. 48, Sept 22, is the last letter of yours I have received. We hope to get letters today. I fear the next will find you in great anxiety at the news of the Battle not knowing how things were going on. We have been having very fine weather for our night work but it is very hard work — our men are generally in good form now, tho' with sickness and wounded we are much reduced in numbers. I heard poor Lord Clinton[24] has died of his wounds. I see W. Partridge* [*at foot of page:* *A cousin — R.N.] now most days. He has given me a little paper, Ink, and some needles and thread, all of which are most useful as I had nothing we required with me[25] — we now and then can buy a little Potted meat as a change from a ship — but very dear, and candles — about 3/- a lb. However I have never used one since I landed (for a Month) till 2 days ago — we have had an extra blanket served out to us — but the nights are cold & ground very hard — so I have got a large biscuit bag and mean to fill it with branches (there are only a few bushes, a

---

24  No one of this name is recorded in the Crimea; probably a mistake in transcription for Captain Lord Chewton, who died of his wounds a few days after the Battle of the Alma.
25  Edward's comments are an indication of how much better prepared the Royal Navy was in terms of supplies, by comparison with the Army.

bush some way from here, no such things as trees to be seen except in one or two small ravines) and so place it where I feel the ground the most — we now have tea — a little Rice & Sugar & occasionally coffee — biscuit & saltmeat, I fear the fresh is now done or nearly so — these we get served out daily in different lots — and with an extra allowance of grog during our hard work we can scratch on pretty well. Hood & I generally go and look at some of the Works which extend a long way. [...]

Just got your dear letter No. 49 — Sept 27 [...] — with little time to answer it. We have had a <u>tremendous</u> cannonade on our Works today — oddly enough they have done little damage. 13 men of the whole 1000 men on that duty wounded, 4 killed, and I regret to say poor Capt. Rowley of my Regiment killed — a shot struck a stone and ricocheted up into the air falling upon him as he was lying on his back and he died very soon afterwards — it was a curious thing to happen and occurred before the great firing began. I believe the Artillery and Navy are to begin to fire at the Town tomorrow and we hope the Town will surrender in the course of a few hours.

---

*By the time he wrote his next letter two days later, the situation for Edward had become much more serious. The death of his commanding officer, Colonel Hood, on 18 October meant that by order of seniority Edward would have to assume the command of the 3rd Grenadier Guards until a relief officer could come out from England. In this capacity, Edward led the 3rd Grenadier Guards not only in the Battle of Inkerman on 5 November, but also in the less well-known action which had taken place nine days earlier, which was termed the Combat of the Lesser (or Little) Inkerman.*

---

### Letter 8:7 (Colonel Edward Birch Reynardson, outside Sebastopol, to his wife Emily, dated 18 October, 1854)[26]

18 Oct. 54

My dearest Em —

Since sending off my letter, I have had the task of writing to poor Hood's\*

---

26  Letter in transcript only (No. 24, *Family Letters*, Vol. 2).

[*at foot of page:* *Commanding 3rd Grenadiers.] friends to announce his death this morning at 9 a.m. He was killed in the Trenches while looking over the Trench which I fear was an imprudent thing to do. I need not tell you what my loss is — and all of us I may say — oh his poor wife. The Command devolves upon me now — and as I am very well I trust in God to enable me to do my Duty properly, tho' I shall but ill fill his place. I write in this hurry for fear you should know it from any other quarter and fear I am too late after all.

  Ever your most loving
    Husband
      EDWARD


**LETTER 8:8 (Colonel Edward Birch Reynardson, outside Sebastopol, to his wife Emily, dated 21 October, 1854)**[27]

            Before Sebastopol
              Oct. 21. 54
              Saturday.

I must write a few lines tho' I am as you may suppose much more occupied than before I had the melancholy task of taking poor Hood's place in this Temporary Command of the Battalion which just now is a very responsible situation. We are worked very hard and most of us tired out almost — as a great deal is night-work. His loss to me as a <u>friend</u> is not to be replaced — and so good an officer as he was it makes it more difficult for me to follow him tho' all our Fellows will assist me in every way I am sure. The siege is going on daily very sharply — and has been now for 5 days, as we began last Monday, & for 2 days we have been trying to fire the Town, but being all stone we can't do much before it is put out. The French have failed us a good deal having had their works blown up several times, once by the Russians and once or twice by themselves from putting their powder away insecurely.

 A Merciful Providence seems to help us in distress — so don't be at all uneasy about me as I shall no doubt fall into my new place better than I expected — Ridley will have to come out to take the Command — Elwine came yesterday but he stupidly left my [*word missing*] at Scutari, however I suppose he had put it

---

27 Letter in transcript only (No. 25, *Family Letters*, Vol. 2).

away with other things and could not bring any more with him. I cannot say how I feel for poor Mrs Hood. I was on duty all day and 2 nights at the same place as poor Hood — and was told that had he not rather imprudently gone to look with his glass at an exposed place it would not have happened and that one of the Engineers begged him to come away — just as the accident happened. I tell you this but don't wish you [to] mention it — poor fellow, he heard a report of Russians leaving the Town so went to see — he did not suffer a moment.

I was much distressed that duty took me away — so as not to be <u>possibly</u> at his funeral — but I left the whole in good hands and have consol'd myself feeling all was done for him that could be and that a good Christian as he was has been taken away from us without a moment's suffering. Post had left here or I should have announced more fully this sad Event, but had not time. The Duke of Cambridge rode up here and condoled with me on our loss & I had the melancholy satisfaction of telling him how great a loss all had sustained in him as an Officer.

The incessant firing & attack & rouses at night are very tiring and bothering. I was ordered out last night at ½ past 12 o'clock and after the Battalion had gone ½ a mile in the Dark were told to return home, keeping our accoutrements on till Morning — this constantly happens so I am oblig'd to be much on the alert & am now resting on my couch of Cloak & Branches in my Tent and writing at the same time & so kill two birds with one stone. We most of us have to catch sleep when we can […] — This is a grand undertaking but I hear Lord Raglan is in good spirits as to the ultimate success. The Town must have suffered very much from the number of shots fired into it.

22nd. Siege going on as vigorously as ever. We hear from Deserters that the Russians have lost great numbers and the streets full of killed and wounded. I do hope it will not last much longer. We are told letters go tomorrow early and will not be received till probably the day after — Lord Dunkillin was taken prisoner last night, having missed his way with a party of men & seeing troops (tho' his men thought they were Russians) he went on ahead by <u>himself</u> to see and of course he was taken. However I believe they treat their Prisoners very well.

I suspect this has been a much tougher job than was expected — but I hope as the French are working well now & we have a good supply now of ammunition I am told. […] I have not yet seen the Picture in Punch[28] — some like it, others [*not*]. I should, I think, but have no time for reading. In case I have no more time I will

---

28  This probably refers to the cartoon captioned *Bursting of the Russian Bubble* (depicting an exploding Tsar Nicholas), which appeared in *Punch* on 14 October 1854.

conclude this. Kiss the Darling & with love to all, Believe me

Your ever most loving Husband<br>
EDWARD

---

*Soon after writing the above letter, two separate engagements of great significance took place on consecutive days, 25 and 26 October 1854. The first of these was the Battle of Balaklava which ended with the legendary Charge of the Light Brigade led by the Earl of Cardigan[29]. Edward described the battle as* 'a most disastrous day to us' (**8: 10**), *though he does not seem to have actually witnessed the Charge itself: his regiment was in action at Balaklava only in a reserve capacity. He was not alone in regarding the conclusion of the battle as a catastrophe (not least because of the loss of so many horses) but more recent historians have been less damning in their assessment. The actual number of casualties was relatively small and the Russians were said to have been so frightened by* 'the cold courage of the British troopers [*that*] they never again dared face them in the open field'[30].

*I have a strong personal interest in this epic event as I am very lucky to have stayed often at Deene Park in Northamptonshire, the ancestral home of the Brudenells (the family name of the Earls of Cardigan) since 1514. I first went to Deene to attend my friend Edmund's twenty-first birthday Ball over sixty years ago. Lieutenant-General James Thomas Brudenell, seventh Earl of Cardigan (1797–1868) — Edmund's forebear who achieved fame in the Crimea — died without leaving any legitimate issue (there were plenty of illegitimate ones!) and the Earldom passed to his second cousin, the Marquess of Ailesbury. Edmund's father, George Brudenell (1880–1962), who inherited Deene through the third Earl (1692–1732), was old-fashioned and eccentric and was undismayed by the shabbiness and inconvenience of the house, which had neither electricity nor heating and only two bathrooms. I still remember the state of the house and its extreme cold when I first went there.*

*But thanks to the wonderful taste and extraordinary energy of Edmund Brudenell's wife Marian (whom he married in 1955 and who sadly died in 2013) and indeed of Edmund's ability as a landowner of many acres, the house is now a model of beautiful and most comfortable rooms. In the dining room hangs the famous painting by de Prades of Lord Cardigan at the Battle of Balaklava* (**Fig. 8 d**)), *riding his charger Ronald (whose*

---

29  Whole books have been devoted to the analysis of this battle alone, perhaps most notably Cecil Woodham-Smith's *The Reason Why* (McGraw-Hill Book Co., 1953).
30  Andrew Lambert, BBC History website (The Crimean War).

*stuffed head is in the hall). I am most grateful to Edmund, who has kindly allowed me to reproduce the picture and to include the following extracts from an article in a bound book in his library, written by a participant in the battle whose account begins:*

> It was my great good fortune in early life to become an actor in an event which has been more commended than many others […]

**Fig. 8 d)** *Lord Cardigan at the Battle of Balaklava,* by Alfred F. de Prades. Oil on canvas. Collection of Edmund Brudenell.

## 8: 9 (Extracts from article by W. H. Pennington, May 1887)

[…] At daybreak the enemy was seen advancing in force towards the redoubts which intervened between them and the British position at Balaclava.

[…] The redoubts were held by the Turkish Artillery […] which were carried early in the day by the Russians in what candour compels one to describe as a somewhat feeble resistance, the Turks unfortunately retiring without spiking the guns.

Encouraged by their success, the enemy advanced […] towards Balaclava. Their passage was contested by […] the Highland Brigade under Sir Colin Campbell […] and the Heavy Cavalry Brigade, which advanced to meet the Muscovite horsemen.

As the ranks of the British and Russians intermingled, the great numerical superiority of the enemy was painfully palpable […] and for a space the issue appeared doubtful. The wings of the enemy enveloped the flanks of our 'Heavies' […] but the courage and discipline […] of our men in the end prevailed […]

The gallant regiments comprised our Heavy Brigade of Cavalry, the Royal Dragoons, Scots Greys, the Irish Dragoon Guards, the Fifth Dragoon Guards and the Enniskillen Dragoons. The guns of the British corvette, which was moored broadside at the head of the harbour, would have swept every Russian from his saddle [*had the battle developed as planned*].

The scene was witnessed by the Commander in Chief and by the General Staff of the Allies from a position commanding every movement of the combatants. Hence, it seems impossible to find an excuse for the miserable blunder that was shortly to be perpetrated.

The valley at the head of which the Cavalry Brigade was drawn up […] was surrounded by a high chain of hills. The Regiments of the Light Brigade were posted on the left […] At the base of the cliffs our brave French comrades' Artillery occasionally shot at the enemy.

From the elevated plateau above us Lord Raglan and his staff must have viewed every part of the field. The Heavy Cavalry Brigade commanded by Sir J. Scarlett, the Light Brigade by Lord Cardigan, with Lord Lucan directing the movements of the whole Cavalry Division. The Heavy Cavalry Brigade, though opposed by heavy odds […] behaved magnificently and there was a pause in activities after the capture of the redoubts.

In the meantime the Brigade of Guards, under the Duke of Cambridge, […] moved to support the Cavalry and Highland Brigades should the enemy […]

resume his offensive. Aides de camp were galloping from all parts of the field [...] and it became clear that something was imminent.

At the bottom of the valley we could see, a mile distant, a line of field pieces pointed towards the brigade. Captain Nolan (15th Hussars), who was on the staff of Lord Raglan, reined up his charger by the side of Lord Cardigan and pointed in the direction of the guns [...] We didn't know what was said, but Lord Cardigan cried in his deep full tones 'The Light Brigade will advance!' [...]

---

*It is noticeable that, while Edward's account concurs with Pennington's as far as the early part of the battle is concerned, he gives a very different impression of Cardigan's readiness (or otherwise) to lead the Light Brigade into a charge against such superior numbers and without back-up or reinforcements.*

*In contrast to the Battle of Balaklava, the combat of Little Inkerman the following day (see* **8: 10**) *was misleadingly celebrated as a resounding success for the British, who did not realise that the Russian action was a reconnaissance to discover the layout and strength of the British defences. Having gleaned all he needed to know about the right flank of the Allied line on the Inkerman Heights, Prince Menshikov used this intelligence to launch his main attack on the same position a few days later at the Battle of Inkerman.*

---

**LETTER 8:10 (Colonel Edward Birch Reynardson** [*unsigned*]**, outside Sebastopol, to unnamed recipient, probably his wife Emily, dated 26 October, 1854)**[31]

Before Sebastopol — Oct. 26, 1854.

The papers with Lord Raglan's dispatch[32] have arrived & are so quickly devoured I can't get a peep at them. All agree that this is a good & true & modest account whereas the French seem to attribute all the day to themselves & are most bombastic. This is anything but what was really the case for though they did their part well we had the chief of the work to do.

5 p.m. 26th. Just come home from being all day in an attack upon us by the

31 Letter in transcript only (No. 26, *Family Letters*, Vol. 2).
32 This must refer to the newspaper reports of the Battle of the Alma on 21 September.

Russians of which I'll write later, as I have just had the great pain & pleasure of receiving your two last letters. Yes — I was busy late at night sorting our wounded from the others when a ball came close by me — they said it was from a wounded Russian & that they often did it & had done so several times that week wounding one of our men in that way. [...] Thank God I had not to take life but should have done so had I seen a man shoot at those others as I describe; there are times when it can't be avoided.

I have been out all day & have commanded the right flank of our line. The column of Russians made an attack on the Front with guns & Infantry & Drove in our Picquets in the 2nd Division after a good deal of fighting, gave them a handsome dusting following them to the walls almost of Sebastopol when they being short of ammunition, & through Harbour & ships' guns opening on them, they were obliged to retire. A Lancaster gun & our Rifles & 2nd Division killed a great many; some say a 1,000 but perhaps not so much. [...] We have lost but a few more & taken a good many prisoners, amongst them the officer whose Party took Lord Dunkillin prisoner. He says he is living with Menschekoff & very comfortable & a very nice young man!

We had a sharp engagement yesterday & were out all day till night; & I am sorry to say a most disastrous day to us. The Russians under Guchikoff[33] [sic] came to attack Balaklava & finding our redoubts were only manned by Turks made a vigorous attack on them. The Turks ran away to a man, letting our guns be taken & would not wait till we came to support them — an unfortunate order came for the cavalry to take the Russian guns. Lord Cardigan remonstrated & said he had no support & that it was madness & asked the A.D.C. to put it on paper. This he did: the consequence was the A.D.C. Nolan was killed first off, & the cavalry coming into a crossfire of shell & grape shot from masked batteries was literally cut to pieces & though they took the guns could not hold them, having no reinforcements to back them up. I hear the French Cavalry never offered to assist & ought to have gone to the Front. The Turks bolting did all the harm. Though the charges of Cavalry were beautiful they could not do impossibilities against the guns. The 13th Light Dragoons had only 32 men left at the last & three officers out of 7 killed. The 4th [?]Light [?]Dragoons the same. The 17th sadly cut up & the Greys I am sorry to say a good deal worsted. John Yorke's Regiment has got off fairly well — he is not hurt. But we are now done for Cavalry — I wonder

---

33 The Russian commander was Lieutenant-General Pavel Liprandi. Edward seems to be confusing his name with that of Gorchakov, the name of two of Russia's most senior military commanders. Prince Michael Gorchakov was soon to replace Prince Menshikov in overall command of the Russian army, but neither he nor his cousin General Paul Gorchakov was in action at Balaklava.

who will be blamed for so sad a blunder.

It was pitiful to see the wounded officers & men, & I fear many are taken prisoner. The Russians today taken, some of whom were where, said they would not have attacked the guns had the English commanded them, but seeing Turks, they advanced. A Marine who helped the Turks fired 6 shots himself after they had bolted & the 2nd officer in command of the Turks was seen hiding in a vineyard. When the Turks first saw the Russians many ran into Balaklava with all their traps on their backs, crying "Turco-ship-oh! Johnnie Ship Turco."

This disaster made the Russians bold today & they have paid dearly for it. We were not engaged yesterday but reinforced others & drove the Russians back again.We were not in reserve at Alma but had the hottest of it as you have heard by this time.

We are all amused at seeing in <u>large</u> letters in the Chronicle "Gallant conduct of Fusilier Guards & Zouaves." I don't want to say anything, but all agree that it is a pity it ever was put in; as the former happened to be rather unfortunate & in consequence suffered more than otherwise would have been the case.

Thank your Father for his letter & tell him I find my mare has been quite unsteady in the two last affairs from (I suppose) being wounded: but spurs soon bring her right. The shells terrify her sadly. I wonder when this place will be taken — shells, shells, rockets, rockets all day. The place is full of killed & the town much knocked about. The Governor is killed, I hear, & we are getting batteries nearer to the walls — but the ships fail us as they can't get near enough for shallow water.

I hear that Lord Raglan in his Home Despatch mentions the name of poor Hood honourably. Oh! how I hope it may produce something to the benefit of his poor wife.[34] She must be badly off — very, I fear. I have undertaken the mournful duty of disposing of his things here, as he wished, and I hope successfully.

---

34  Edward's concern for the plight of Colonel Hood's widow was not misplaced. At this time, if an officer who had purchased his commission (as was the usual practice for members of the cavalry, foot guards and infantry regiments) died while on active service or was killed in action, his commission would revert to the Crown. If on the other hand he survived and retired, the sum raised from selling his commission would finance his retirement. This system had existed since the seventeenth century (with the idea of limiting admission to the officer corps to amateur gentlemen of private means, who would be less likely to act like mercenaries or try to exercise political power as had happened with Cromwell's New Model Army), but had the effect of leaving widows of officers who had died on active service in a state of destitution, with no means of support other than could be supplied by the sale of their possessions. The practice was not changed until the Purchase of Commissions was abolished by Royal Warrant on 1 November 1871.

*The Battle of Inkerman, which took place on 5 November 1854, has been remembered as 'The Soldiers' Battle', a tribute to the courage and inspiration of the troops which fought mostly on their own initiative due to the foggy conditions which prevailed throughout the day. Though greatly outnumbered by the Russians, the battle resulted in a stunning victory for the Allies, but at a heavy cost, as Edward reported in a letter to the commanding officer of his regiment (**8: 11**). In particular Inkerman is an iconic battle for the Grenadier Guards, which was the only regiment to take its colours into the battle. Twelve Victoria Crosses[35] were awarded to British soldiers for actions in the battle, including Captain Percy of the Grenadiers (mentioned in Edward's letter) who succeeded in extracting fifty men of his regiment from the midst of the Russians. Although Edward led his troops into battle as acting commanding officer of the 3rd Battalion, his account of his own part in this momentous engagement is characteristically modest, but he would no doubt have been gratified to have known the opinion of Captain Higginson, Adjutant of the 3rd Grenadiers, who wrote*

> Reynardson is far from well but his pluck is indomitable. He is really at the moment of action and danger far more decided, however, and encouraging in tone than when on an ordinary quiet parade.[36]

---

**LETTER 8:11 (Colonel Edward Birch Reynardson, outside Sebastopol, to Colonel Thomas Wood, Regimental Lieutenant Colonel, dated 7 November, 1854)**[37]

Before Sebastopol
Nov. 7th 1854

Dear Colonel

I must write you a few lines in the midst of much business in hand to inform you of a general action which took place on Sunday morning early at ½ past 6

---

35 The Victoria Cross is the highest military decoration awarded for 'valour in the face of the enemy'. It was first introduced at the end of the Crimean War in 1856 to reward members of the armed forces of any rank.

36 Letter to Captain Hatton, Regimental Adjutant, dated 27 October 1854 (letter held in the Regimental records at RHQ Grenadier Guards). Quoted in Springman, *The Guards Brigade in the Crimea*, pp. 82–83.

37 The original letter is held in the Regimental records at RHQ Grenadier Guards. Quoted in Springman, *The Guards Brigade in the Crimea*, pp. 93–96.

a.m. between the Russians, who attacked us in very great force at first our 2nd Division and the Brigade.

The Russians during the night had managed to place a large quantity of guns on a Hill commanding the position held by the 2nd Div and with (they say Polish & Russian prisoners) of 56,000 men, we are told under Prince Constantine, himself; these troops principally from Odessa. Our informant says with provisions for 4 days, and they were certainly well primed with Raki.

When we got to the scene of action which was about an hour after it commenced we were under a very severe fire of shells and some shot from the overwhelming force of Russian artillery & as we had not got into position, they were doing great mischief on crowning the height. We found one of our redoubts taken by a very large force of Russians, who were pouring a tremendous fire into us as we advanced. There was nothing to be done than to take this position from them, which our Gallant fellows did in very good style; the fire now was worse than Alma & our poor fellows began to fall.

Sergeant-Major Algar amongst the first shot through the head! He died next day — a sad sad loss to us. (Sergeant Norman takes his place and Powley next to him.)

At this time my charger was shot from under me, four shots in her neck and chest & I think in the girth — and another in the loins, so I had to go thus the rest of the day on foot — all our horses were soon <u>told off</u> — and the staff being [*word(s) missing*] from loss of horses, and themselves wounded, amongst them General Bentinck in the arm, we were pretty well left to ourselves. Once from the overwhelming forces of Russians and their turning our flank from such insufficiency of support, we were <u>obliged</u> to retire behind the breastwork and the redoubt was retaken by the Russians.

However we soon went at them again and after a very sharp fire, and when short of ammunition, pelting them with stones, we succeeded in driving them down the Hill. I ordered the Grenadiers to charge with the bayonet, but not to go down the Hill after them on any account. However they were so flushed with success, they did overdo it[38], and the consequence was we were <u>almost</u> outflanked again, and were obliged to retire behind the breastwork again to refresh ourselves from the fatigue and get a fresh store of ammunition, for we

---

38  Edward refers to a less edifying aspect of the battle when after taking, losing and then retaking the Sandbag Battery, guardsmen of the Scots Fusilier Guards and, to a lesser extent, the Grenadier Guards, became out of control, stabbing and slashing the Russians with their bayonets; it is clear from Edward's account that this was contrary to his specific orders, but without a horse he was powerless to prevent behaviour which was described by observers as a temporary madness.

had long been without it in some parts of our line.

I cannot speak <u>too highly</u> of the <u>individual conduct of all</u> the officers, who were important in their endeavour to keep up a good front and nobly as our gallant fellows behaved, it would have been no <u>help</u> to have attempted to hold the position much longer, had not our reinforcements come up, and in which the French rendered very great assistance.

I grieve to say that in this attack we have lost three officers — Lt. Col. Pakenham, Sir R. Newman & Capt. H. Neville; wounded, Sir J. Ferguson, Percy, Tipping, Barford — contusion, Hamilton — contusion. How any escaped is to me a perfect marvel.

A spent ball hit my arm and went through my cloak and a shell smashed my Grenadier Cap, as it did at the Alma. So I have indeed to thank God for his Mercies to me.

I have just seen General Bentinck, who is going away for three months. Upton [*Coldstream*] has the Brigade of course.

We have just found some of our missing men were killed, which will be in the return. We are now 5 Companies of 30 files each!!!! So your 80 men will be of little reward to us. [*If we*] have any more loss we shall soon be wiped out of the list altogether. As yet we have had to bear always a heavy share of the work.

Sir G. Cathcart was killed by too free exposure of himself I fear. […] Wounded: General Adams, Dr Osmond and General Bentinck; Upton not much hurt, but the staff also have suffered very much.

I told Percy I should not forget the gallant manner he tried to rally our men and did rush up almost single handed and unbacked [*by men*] to the redoubt, and was the means of returning them to the assault, where he got a blow over the head.

However I must say all behaved admirably and it is difficult to particularize. I made Palmer [*later awarded the VC*] a N.C.O. from the gallant manner he followed Sir C. Russell [*also later awarded the VC*], who offered to lead them at a critical time, if they would follow him. He [Palmer] was the only man who was near and bayoneted a Russian who would have otherwise killed Sir C. R. Russell. Higginson [*Adjutant*] has seen your letter.

We seldom have any rest and as all our men & officers suffer more or less from the horrid bowel complaint of this country, if we cannot get less work and more rest we shall soon be a sorry lot.

The Coldstream were a good deal cut up. The Fusiliers very little in comparison. Poor Blair [*Scots Fusilier Guards*] died this morn; Walker [*Scots

*Fusilier Guards*] was also wounded slightly in the neck; there seem to be few who escaped altogether. I can't remember the names of the 8 officers of the Coldstream who were killed. Just been told we are to be in readiness to turn out, and having sent a party to bury the Dead have just 100 men!!! disposable.

I expect John Bull has overrated our powers and thinks we are invulnerable; whereas the Russians can supply their army I fear to any amount. I am so glad Nicoll is coming out as we are sadly short of medical advice. Poor Bradford [*Lt. Colonel*] is so rheumatic, he cannot crawl about scarcely; he is most plucky and does his best but could not get on in the Affair the other day, as he had no horse. I must recommend him to get leave for a few days or weeks, and that may entail a medical board, but he is of very little use.

I am believe me yours most truly<br>
Ed. Birch Reynardson.

I hear I am to congratulate you on the birth of a daughter. I hope doing well.

P.S. Late tonight Laurence (Assistant Surgeon) & 1 Sergeant & 32 men just arrived, after buffeting about in the sea for a fortnight; their clean appearance are a strange contrast to our tattered fellows here, who many of them have hardly trousers to cover themselves.

My last return says:

| Officers | Sergeant | Drums | Corporals | Privates | |
|---|---|---|---|---|---|
| 3 | 4 | 1 | 4 | 66 | Killed |
| 6 | 6 | 1 | 11 | 127 | Wounded [*or*] Missing |
| 9 | 10 | 2 | 15 | 193 | |

Just had a turnout & false alarm; it seems we are never to sleep with our uniforms off. I have done so once since we landed at Eupatoria.

8th. We expect to move our ground today nearer to Lord Raglan to give us a little rest & change […]

## Letter 8:12 (Colonel Thomas Wood, London, to Colonel Edward Birch Reynardson, in the Crimea, dated 28 November, 1854)[39]

Orderly Room
Guards
Nov 28th

My dear Reynardson

I must address a few lines of congratulation to you upon your own escape, and upon your good fortune in having commanded the old third Battalion at the moment of its <u>greatest peril</u>, in the most <u>severe battle</u>*[40] perhaps of modern history. Thank you for your excellent account of the battle, which has been for some days at Windsor and which will be much appreciated by the Prince & Queen.

I had great satisfaction in communicating the mode you spoke of Percy's conduct to Lord Beauley. In reply he very truly says that the approbation of one's brother officers, at a time when all acted so nobly, is the <u>highest</u> honor, & so it is. Although you all deserve & I expect will receive other rewards. It seems that we repeated the splendid error of [*word(s) missing from transcript*], charging too far; but as you say how could you stop them, being unhorsed?

But now for the sad loss – Pakenham! quite irreparable. Neville! Where are we to find his equal? Poor Sir R Newnham and alas Sergeant Algar! You will be glad to see Neville's brother's name in the gazette as coming in to the regiment. Be assured everything shall be done for Sergeant Algar's widow. I have already taken steps on her behalf.

Thank Higginson for his letter to Hatton and tell him how I rejoice not only for his own sake but that of the Battalion at this moment that he is unhurt. His letter, being more dramatic & calculated for effects than your plain statement (which however is not a <u>whit the less valuable</u>) I read to the reinforcement, 400 men, which we dispatched on Friday from the Wellington Barracks. The men were quite delighted; and gave you all such hearty cheers which I know they will repeat whenever they join you before the enemy. I shall address the business part of what I have to say in a separate letter to Ridley which you will open if he has not arrived & taken the Command. If so take a little rest, & take care of your

---

39 Letter in transcript only (No. 27, *Family Letters*, Vol. 2).
40 Unaware that Edward's letter to Colonel Wood (8: 11) had been preserved in the records of RHQ Grenadier Guards, my father wrote on the typed copy of Wood's reply: '*This refers to Inkerman. E.B.R.'s letters at this date are missing.'

health. I assure you when I think of what you all go through, both officers & men, I could cry.

> Believe me
>> Sincerely yours
>>> Thomas Wood

What do you do for a horse? Horses can be sent out free of expense.

---

*Edward's superior officers and his family alike (**8: 13**) were justly proud of the part he had played at Inkerman, but in the aftermath of the battle it came to be felt (as Edward himself had already suggested) that the undoubted victory achieved by the Allies had been gained at too heavy a price. William Howard Russell,* The Times *correspondent, wrote that*

> We have nothing to rejoice over, and almost everything to deplore, in the battle of Inkermann. We have defeated the enemy indeed, but have not advanced one step nearer toward the citadel of Sebastopol. We have abashed, humiliated, and utterly routed an enemy strong in numbers, in fanaticism, and in dogged resolute courage [...] but we have suffered a fearful loss, and we are not in a position to part with one man.

*The pitiful state of the ragged soldiers and the walking wounded after the battle is vividly portrayed in the painting 'The Roll Call' (**Fig. 8 e**)), by Elizabeth Thompson[41]. Despite being painted nearly twenty years after the event (it was the sensation of the Royal Academy Exhibition of 1874, where it was exhibited under its original title of 'Calling the Roll after an Engagement, Crimea'), it nevertheless included recognisable portraits of members of the Grenadier Guards, including the mounted adjutant, though Edward Birch Reynardson himself is not amongst those depicted[42].*

41 A remarkable female success in a field of art then entirely dominated by male artists, Elizabeth Thompson (1846–1933), later Lady Butler, was only eight when the events which were to inspire her first major success, 'The Roll Call' in 1874, took place. There was intense competition amongst buyers to purchase the painting from the Royal Academy exhibition, but when Queen Victoria made it known that she wanted it for her own collection, all prospective purchasers withdrew. The Queen did allow engravings of 'The Roll Call' to be made, which sold in large numbers.
42 Edward's non-appearance in the painting may be explained by the fact that immediately after the battle he was transferred to take over temporary command of the Guards Brigade (see footnote 48).

# IN THE CRIMEA

Fig. 8 e) *The Roll Call*, by Elizabeth Thompson. Oil on canvas, 1874. Collection of H.M. the Queen.

# SURVIVORS

**Fig. 8 f)** *Lives at Stake!* (top) and *Sick & Wounded coming from the front on Cavalry Horses to recruit at Balaklava* (bottom), by Edward Birch Reynardson. Pen and watercolour, 1854.

*In addition to the loss of great numbers of horses, most of which were already in poor condition (**Fig. 8 f**)), matters were made harder still by the onset of winter, which turned out to be severe even by Russian standards. Only a few days after the Battle of Inkerman, a terrible storm (which Edward and many others who experienced it described as a hurricane) hit the Crimean peninsula and raged for three days. Many ships in Balaklava's crowded harbour were lost and there was great loss of life amongst their crews; to the men waiting on shore for the delivery of winter supplies as they dug themselves in to the hills surrounding Sebastopol, the worst loss was that of thousands of winter uniforms and boots, as well as much-needed medical supplies, which had gone down with the steamship* Prince, *leaving them ill equipped to face the harsh conditions.*

*Once the bitter winter had set in, it was clear that no further attempts to take Sebastopol could be made before the spring and that the Allied armies must prepare for a long siege. Thanks largely to the efforts of Lord Raglan and the ambassador Lord Stratford, supplies of warm clothing were beginning to come through, but distribution to the troops in the field remained chaotic and it was also a different matter when it came to providing adequate shelter. Many accounts of the conditions in the Crimea during this terrible winter state that officers suffered less than the lower ranks from the appalling conditions, but Edward's own testimony (see **8: 15**) makes it clear that he at least shared the privations of his men to much the same extent.*

---

**LETTER 8:13 (Emma Birch Reynardson, in Rome, to her brother Colonel Edward Birch Reynardson, in the Crimea, dated 9 December, 1854)**

Rome — December 9
1854

My dearest Wardy,

The mails for Malta are sent on the 11th so I will write you a line, & <u>most</u> thankful I am that such is possible, for after that dreadful Battle of the 5th & <u>so</u> many lives lost, ought we not to feel deeply grateful that the one so dear to all of us is spared & unhurt. A merciful Providence indeed seems to watch over you, my beloved Brother. The rumour of the Engagement reached us, from the Various papers before we could hear any particulars of you, or anything.— The thoughtful Henry, however, tho' he had the same day sent off a letter, on the

Gazette coming out, hurried 3 lines to say your name did not appear; then we saw you were one who had had your Horse killed under you, (your poor Mare). We feared there might be a mistake & that you were not unhurt, but Thank God, there was not.

Emily has most kindly copied me a little of your letter; which of course interests us so much. We feel the distance from tidings of you, & losing parts of your Charming letters; a great loss — but it cannot be helped; & we are grateful for any <u>stray fragments</u>. Henry tells us of the Duke of Cambridge riding up & congratulating <u>you Grenadiers</u> … it does one good to hear all these fine, & touching, particulars. I hope ere this the much needed reinforcements have arrived to your aid, tho' I could have wished that after having borne the "burden & heat of the day" <u>you</u> had continued, now you are accustomed to it, & feel confidence in it, to have the responsibility & command in poor Col. Hood's place. You would feel his loss in every way, I know.

Emily writes in <u>comfortable</u> Spirits & I hope she & the darling are well; they seemed to like Henley Park, & the young Lady, she tells me, was made much of there. How I wish we had been in England when things were being sent out to you — it would have been such <u>real</u> pleasure to have added our mite of Comfort in some warm shape. I almost envy Eleanor[43] knitting you muffetees, only I know the pleasure it gave her. Well, one thing is certain you will not doubt our good wishes; & particularly at this Season — it is long now since we have spent a Christmas together. I trust you will not have very severe weather, or if you have that some means will be provided to supply you, & all "the brave fellows," with as many Comforts as possible, this seems now to be the earnest wish of all & I hope active steps are being taken to send them out.

Bob[44] is very keen reading the newspapers — & takes the greatest interest in all. We are getting on very well. He enjoys this place I think, & I hope it agrees with him. Just now, & indeed ever since we came it has been raining & cold; he has had neuralgia & I have more or less cold & cough — but when fine, I think it will agree. There are such endless scenes of interest, Ruins, Statues, pictures, &c, &c. I only want strength to enjoy them to the full; but somehow, even at a grand ceremony at St Peter's, at which we looked in for a short time, my <u>heart</u> was not there; & you were not out of my thoughts for a minute hardly — it only proves

---

43 Henry Birch Reynardson's wife (and my great-grandmother), Eleanor Partridge, whom he married in 1847.
44 It appears that this is a reference to Emma's sister Matilda's husband, Robert Stopford. They had married in 1853, so it is unlikely that they were in Rome on a wedding tour. Perhaps Emma had accompanied her sister and brother-in-law for her health, but it is odd that she makes no mention of Matilda.

how dearly you have been & are still loved by us, & in proportion as we look back on past days with pleasure & affection, & regret your absence, as great will be our gratitude if we are permitted to welcome you back again. <u>How</u> like you finding another Horse on the field, having to <u>repair</u> its nostrils would be quite in your line. I hope it was not claimed after your cutting its Mane & Tail — what little Willy would call a good "dodge" — but you can be up to a trick or two. […]

John tells me Charles & the Girls have at last returned to Holywell; <u>none</u> of them ever put pen to paper in our service. Indeed we know nothing of them, except that Ethie & Pollie had, as usual, colds. […] New days for Holywell, but whether happier or better remains to be proved.

General & Mrs Drummond are here, he as usual rejoicing in a pet grumble. Sir Coutts Lindsay is here, I believe. Really there are such <u>Hairy</u> Swells of Englishmen with turned down Collars, & just a little ribbon round their necks, going mincing about the Streets & at Church, we said what good the Crimea would do them. I long to ship them off. You are a "<u>Hairy Swell</u>" enough I know, but it is an <u>honour</u> in your case, I fear you have not time to <u>wax</u> & <u>curl</u> your Moustache & comb out your beard.

(December 10th). I hope it may be true that Austria has settled to join the Allies – we anxiously look out for the report being confirmed. In that case Old Nick[45] will feel himself rather "Alone in his Glory" – & perhaps come to terms after his severe lessons & great losses – how many lives he has to answer for. The conduct of the Russians on the field is most revolting in killing the wounded men.

I feel to have so little to say to interest you in your present position. You must have so much to do & think of, but you like a letter & it is a pleasure to write. I am becolded today & am trying to get rid of it by keeping in bed – so adieu dearest Wardy, with affectionate Love,

    Your very affectionate Sister
        <u>Emma S. B. Reynardson</u>

---

[45] Tsar Nicholas, here equated with the Devil. The Tsar died three months later, from a chill he picked up in the Crimea which turned to pneumonia.

## Letter 8:14 (Colonel Edward Birch Reynardson, outside Sebastopol, to his brother Charles Birch Reynardson, dated 8 January, 1855)

Camp before Sebastopol   January 8. 55.

My dear Charles,

Tho' I have little time for letter writing from Constant interruptions — and finding it impossible to make a <u>practice</u> of answering letters — from my always sending a letter each post to my dearest Wife (who is never out of my thoughts as you may imagine) — still I must write you a letter to say how glad I was to see your hand writing — for I could not account for never having, amongst the numerous letters received […] any from you most particularly after the two great Events! The success of which I am sure you must acknowledge & value with the rest of the world and am certain from your heart congratulate me on my <u>extraordinary</u> preservation. How I escaped God only knows — particularly when my Mare fell with 6 Balls in her — & tho' hit twice on the Grenadier Cap and once in the arm with a spent Ball, I escaped unhurt.

The Congrats from all sides, of the Manner in which I have been spoken & mentioned by Lord Raglan and the Duke of Cambridge particularly in the last affair when I commanded the Regiment, is most satisfactory to me and tho' I only did my <u>duty</u>, I cannot help feeling proud of the circumstance, [*word illegible*] it not only affects me but my Family — whose Name I hope never to disgrace. — tho' I confess such scenes of horror and carnage are most revolting and known only to those who witness them.

Then we have undergone up to this time a Campaign of great hardship and such as few armies have been exposed to & are now all under Canvass in snow 1 foot deep — and the thermometer has been as low as 18° [*minus 8° Celsius*]. You can scarcely conceive the discomfort after the breath on my blankets — perfect <u>Icicles</u> & tho' I have a bit of Charcoal fire in my Tent, the Inside is white frost and the water I get for my teeth freezes while I am washing my face &c! Many men have been frost bitten particularly in the trenches at night where they have no covering [*and are*] not able to lie down — unless in Mud, Water — or Snow! & this for 12 hours at a time. Our horses picketed in the open have some of them died. I have lost one, & disabled another. How they stand the cold I know not.

I suppose you saw the account of the awful Hurricane which blew over all our tents and against which at times <u>no man</u> could stand up — such rain, and then snow. I expected we should have died all of us before Morning — but we got over it, and after losing many things [*word illegible*] ourselves. I hope never to see the like again — the misery was too great to endure much longer.

I use your Revolver daily — and have only as yet shot a Horse with it; also Georgey's Lamp has been invaluable out here. Our siege goes on slowly, but today the French are keeping up a fire upon them. I wonder when we shall take the place? It is very strong and they have such lots of Guns, that unless we are well prepared it would be no use attempting it, and [*word illegible*] I suspect they are awaiting reinforcements again.—

The Vote of thanks in the House to the Army is very interesting, I read some parts out to the Regiment today. I hope you have seen the main Speeches. Emily sent me out the times [*The Times* newspaper?] of 14 & 16 — to read them but I cannot get it by snatches. — We have lost an immense number of men what with Battles, and sickness — terrible to think of — and many officers killed, & wounded — besides numbers gone away on the sick list. I was very sorry to hear of poor John Yorke[46] being wounded, I suppose he is gone back to England, I hope much better.

I had the Command of the Brigade[47] for some time but now Ridley is come out, I have got the Regiment again. They say I am certain to be C.B., & probably K.C.B. All this sounds very grand but I own I would willingly give it up to get back to old England again — it's too hard a life to enjoy — a gypsies [*sic*] is nothing to it.

Thanks for offering to send me some warm Clothes — but of such things I shall have <u>plenty when</u> they all get here. I have no doubt you felt if you wrote that a letter might not reach me, but recollect if I am non-effective my letters are returned; so pray write for it costs nothing and everything amuses a poor

---

46　Lieutenant-Colonel (later General) John Yorke (1814–90), of the 1st Royal Dragoons, had a double connection to Edward. They were cousins, their grandmothers (Elizabeth and Anne Cust — see Chapter 3) being sisters; and John's sister Anne had married Edward's elder brother Charles in 1836. At the Battle of Balaklava John was so seriously wounded that he was disabled for life. In endeavouring to cope with 'the painful feelings of despondency when every pursuit in life is so suddenly snatched away, while just in the prime of manhood', he took up sculpture in ivory and became so proficient in this medium that his work was exhibited at South Kensington (precursor of the Victoria and Albert Museum) and elsewhere. In 1863, during a tour of Norway and Sweden, he was received by King Charles XV of Sweden, to whom he presented a carved ivory cup. The charming letter of thanks he received from the King is still in the family collection. Towards the end of his life John Yorke recorded his recollections in an unpublished book entitled 'The Memories of a Cavalry Officer during Four Reigns'.

47　Both the commanding officer and his deputy of the Guards Brigade (Major-General Bentinck and Colonel Upton) were wounded at the Battle of Inkerman, so Edward was transferred in temporary command. He continued in this capacity until 1 December, when Colonel Ridley arrived from England to replace Hood and took over as Acting C.O. of the Guards Brigade. Edward resumed as Acting C.O. of the 3rd Grenadier Guards until 15 January 1855, when Colonel Upton returned as Acting C.O. of the Guards Brigade, relieving Colonel Ridley who in turn took over the 3rd Grenadier Guards and thus relieved Edward of the command.

banished Soldier. I have not seen [?]Francis Wykeham Martin, tell George, and only two of the Tryons — the naval one & one in the 7th — the other poor fellow you know was killed. We are a long way apart & could only meet by accident. W. Partridge I see occasionally.

I hear about your dear Girls every now & then & Carlo from Emily & John; I hope they will like Holywell as we did, what would I give to be there, I may almost say in a Cottage at Aunby [...] I suspect we have much more before us, but may remain idle for some time. Thank George for his letter or send him this as I cannot write. I hope his Chicks are well again. He wanted to know about how I fared at the Hurricane? I thought Emily would have sent a short Circular about it but I suppose she did not, & now I must close this with love to all of you from

Your very Affectionate Brother,
Edward

---

*Amongst the many ways in which the campaign in the Crimea differed from all previous conflicts is that it was the first to be recorded by 'official' war artists and photographers. Towards the end of his time in the Crimea Edward met two of the best-known to depict the war from the British perspective: the artist William Simpson and the photographer Roger Fenton. Both men had been engaged by commercial galleries (respectively Colnaghi's and Agnew's) which are still flourishing today. Simpson (1823–99) arrived in the Crimea the day after the hurricane and three weeks after the Battle of Balaklava; nevertheless, his first task was to produce a pictorial record of the Charge of the Light Brigade, making three attempts before his efforts satisfied Lord Cardigan.*

*At the time that Edward met him* (**8: 15**) *Simpson was working on a drawing which showed part of the Battle of Inkerman and was later published as a coloured lithograph under the title 'Second Charge of the Guards, when they took the two-gun battery at the Battle of Inkermann'. Simpson's watercolours were published (as lithographs) later in 1855 in a book entitled 'The Seat of the War in the East'. One of his more picturesque views, of the Monastery of St George, is so similar in its viewpoint to Edward's own sketch* (**Fig. 8 g)**) *that one wonders if the two men could have been there at the same time, sitting side-by-side as they drew.*

*Roger Fenton (1819–69) is perhaps even more celebrated for having produced many of the most memorable images of soldiers and battlefields (though not views of actual*

IN THE CRIMEA

**Fig. 8 g)** *The Monastery of St George, between Sebastopol and Balaklava*, by Edward Birch Reynardson. Pencil and watercolour, dated 27 April 1855

**Fig. 8 h)** *Colonel Edward Birch Reynardson*, by Roger Fenton. Photograph, March to May 1855

*combat*[48]*) in the Crimean War. He did not arrive at Balaklava until March 1855 and left the Crimea less than four months later with an astonishing collection of over 350 usable large format negatives, including one of Edward Birch Reynardson* (**Fig. 8 h**)) — *the earliest photograph in existence of any member of my family. We do not know exactly when or where this photograph was taken, but it must date from before Edward's own departure from the Crimea, towards the end of May 1855.*

---

**8:15 (Extracts from Edward Birch Reynardson's *Diary*[49], 2 to 5 January 1855, copied by W. D. Fane. Copy in Lincolnshire Archives, Ref. No. Fane 6/10/7/C/7)**

E. B. R. 1855

Jan. 2. Nine of us dined together last night & had a capital dinner to begin the new year — Soup — Welsh leg of mutton (such a treat) — turkey — chicken — gooseberry pudding, plum pudding — [...] peas & potatoes — then coffee & cigars. We had a little punch also.

Our new draft are [...] finer than the other regiments — however I am sorry to say they are dwindling off fast into hospital & some dying — it is sad work. In these few days (they have only been on shore a fortnight) I have today 74 sick — & now they begin to do work they will be daily more & more — several of our Doctors are also on the shelf, particularly the new ones — others will be sent to us from the Staff to fill their places. — My horse I think is English — tall — bay with tan muzzle & long bay tail.

Now for answers to [?]W'son's queries — how did I know where to take my battalion at Inkermann? On finding the Russians had taken a redoubt on the right of the hill looking over towards Inkermann Ruins, I was ordered to advance & retake it, & after a sharp attack soon drove the enemy away. It was here when urging on the men to flank the redoubt & so kill more men at each discharge that my mare was shot within 20 yards of the redoubt, on the left of it as we looked down the hill to the Ruins. The firing then was terrific, & no doubt officers were all picked out.

48 Because photographic material of the time required long exposure periods, Fenton could only make photographs of non-moving objects and people.
49 Although the transcribed copy is recorded in the Lincolnshire Archives as extracts from Edward Birch Reynardson's *Diary*, it is actually written in the form of an extended letter, presumably to his wife. The transcriptions were made by Emily Birch Reynardson's cousin, William Dashford Fane.

The most advanced part <u>we</u> got to was half way below the hill towards the plain in a charge. We ought not to have gone down, but I could not keep my men back, they were so elated at seeing the enemy fly before them — a common error but one never to be controlled […], tho' I went in front of them & held up my sword & revolver & tried to keep them back — I could not blame them. There was a breastwork behind the redoubt […] behind which we reformed. The Inkermann road was to our left a little — these were in front & rather on the right of <u>the 2$^{nd}$</u> Division. The Inkermann road W. F. may mean may be from Sebastopol to Inkermann. <u>I</u> mean the one through the 2$^{nd}$ Division to the Ruins. We were on the right arm of this & nearer to the Inkermann Valley — the former road being <u>much</u> to our <u>left</u> .

When we charged we drove the Russians down the hill into the valley on the right of the Ruins, having the Tchernaya close on our right, when they tried to outflank us, & were beaten back by our <u>right</u> flank. They also tried to do so on our left & would have cut us off had not the 4$^{th}$ Division come to our support — the Coldstreams were on this flank & most of our guns. My tent & hut were situated so as to see the 2$^{nd}$ Division on left — ¼ of a mile from the windmill (Majegni) to our left rear, & about 200 yards from the ridge looking over the Tchernaya Valley & Canrobert Redoubt, which is not far from the Woronzoff Road leading down the Tchernaya Valley to Balaklava. When I get his map I will copy it & mark plans out.

My hut is to be our kitchen & smoking room or place of rendezvous if our tents fail — our wooden houses are not come up yet, nor do I expect to get one: but we are now [?]converting our tents to the dry soil, which makes them larger & more comfortable. I have a double tent one over the other & by cutting out windows from the outside one manages to get more light. <u>We</u> are 2 miles from the town — & the 3$^{rd}$ & 4$^{th}$ Divisions [?]march within almost shelling distance, but under the brow of the hills, from whence you look upon the town. The most <u>advanced</u> trench is in front of Gordon's Battery or Frenchman's Hill, towards the South — the former are about 500 yards from the walls of the town, so we get shelled there day & night, but are so well protected from the height, they seldom do us any harm; a few of the working party are killed now & then & sorties are made at night which have been well repulsed hitherto. The chief battery here is about 300 yards from the advanced one. Then there is the Chapman's Battery, a very strong one towards the East, & nearer to the French Battery […]. Hood was killed at Gordon's Battery. The Russian Picquets are very near, within 200 yards of our advanced battery, & we are always picking each other off. No shelter over our heads in the batteries, or place to lie down on, & in wet weather a pool of water. I have had none of it lately, & hope may escape that duty. We are on for 12 hours now instead of 24 as before. Our sharp shooters go forward & dig out holes so as to pick off the Russian gunners at the battery guns in the town & the harbour. Many have been killed in this way & very few of our men.—

A Mr Simpson is sketching here & has sent home to Colnaghi's some sketches of Sebastopol, Balaklava, country around — & [the] taking of Inkermann Redoubt by the Guards. My horse is lying down near to Higginson's & the thing is very well done. Another of a party of Officers who dined at Hamilton's tent, but as yet I have not come into any picture.—

Tell Mrs H. I often envy her her bright fire: we can only burn charcoal, but I am warm with it compared to many, so don't mean to grumble. A loaf of her bread also would be a treat here — we can't get [word(s) missing] & then so very very dear, but the biscuit is very good that is issued to us.

3 January. Such a deluge of wet last night. We have snow on the ground & occasionally very heavy falls. I am now well off for shirts & gloves. I have got up some of my things from Scutari. Warm [...] frock & shooting coat & pea jacket. I am afraid to ask about my saddle. I fear it is not come: if so, it has got into the Custom House, where every thing is stolen worth having. I have got a pair of high thigh Russian leather boots — black — & hope they will prove waterproof — also my thick mattress so shall give my thin one to [?]Warren & the Batman.

4 Jan. We have snow a foot deep & hard frost — such a curious scene. Many prefer it to rain — I do not — it makes it hard to get firewood. A most dreary appearance without sun, but with it & working, we keep ourselves warm: the tents are warmer for the snow, but very [?]dabbly work coming in & out. You would think it impossible for us to get on: but we hope if frost lasts to cut out roads & get on well: not so unhealthy as wet, I believe. I have given one of my mattresses to my servants & hope it [will] keep them warm; if we only got Prince Albert's coats for us & the men: why did they not send them off sooner? Also the huts which are so heavy we can't put them up: it takes 20 horses or men to bring up one.

Jan. 5. Our water all hard frozen.

LETTER 8:16 (Copy by W. D. Fane of a letter from Edward Birch Reynardson, headed 'Camp before Sebastopol', dated 16 February 1855. Copy in Lincolnshire Archives, Ref. No. as in 8: 15)

Camp before Sebastopol Feb. 16.

You seem to be in a colder climate than I am as warm S. W. winds have arrived that almost kill us with kindness, or at any rate produce too much contentment[?] as to whether the tents will stand or fall. The Prince & I wake at intervals in the night, bestow an adjective on the wind & go to sleep again. Two nights ago I actually got up & dressed thinking the final [?]march must soon come, & feeling that it would be a great bore to buffet the wind in my shirt sleeves: dressing only implies putting on a coat & a waterproof, after which I turned in again & slept till morning in the happy consciousness of being ready for anything.

I was in the trenches the other night again: our party was sent to the advanced post of the left attack: it is rather near the Russians, their sentries being at night only about 200 yards apart. The Russians behaved like gentlemen & did not fire at my sentries nor [at] me, so of course we let them alone: but might have had a very easy shot at one of their picquets when they all sat round a fire talking, laughing & cooking in a ravine apparently close to us, but in reality about 400 yards off. They were as comfortable as if no Enemy was within 50 miles, & I rather admired their sangfroid. The [?]point is we never annoy them at night, & they never bother us unless they make a regular attack. The French fire all night & get a very rapid return from the enemy. [...] this advanced work is no joke, as the moment a head appears above the parapet some 10 or 12 bullets are rattling at it, & inquisitive gentlemen occasionally pay a heavy penalty for peeping.

I went to the French works in front of our right today by way of a walk. When we got to their advanced trench we found Chasseurs & Zouaves blazing away at a great rate at Russian sentries, who returned a very correct fire — but nobody hit nobody [sic] while we were there. One of our party, who was too proud to walk in the usual way, had a narrow escape from a stray ball: we immediately made him come under cover, telling him it was too bad of him to expose us to the chance of having to carry him home in case he was knocked on the head. Being a sensible fellow he acknowledged the force of the argument at once, & it was with the greatest difficulty we could get him to let us look through the loopholes at the splendid view of Sebastopol, the harbour & shipping. It really was quite a picture to see how those wily rascals have worked & are working at their defence: the whole place is like an anthill, black with little [?]beggars, working as hard as possible. Guns are on our side being brought up very quick & the new French works are getting on fast. They are making an attack on Tour Malakoff or Round Tower, of which the battery will be within 400 yards, close quarters for big guns. General Niel says that is the key of the plan, & that taken the town must fall[50]. They [*the Russians*] have strengthened it very much, any expedient they could think of to make it impregnable has been resorted to, & there will be some broken heads among those who assault. Amongst other dodges the ditches are strewed with broken glass & iron spikes. We hear there is frightful sickness […] where a large part of their army is.

**LETTER 8:17 (Copy by W. D. Fane of a letter from Edward Birch Reynardson, headed 'Before Sebastopol', dated 19 February 1855. Copy in Lincolnshire Archives, Ref. No. as in 8: 15.)**

Before Sebastopol Feb. 19

We have just received tidings of an action at Eupatoria when by the Turkish account an attack was made by about 50,000 Russians on the lines, but they were driven back by the Bono Johnnies[51] with the loss of 400 killed. It appears to have been a satisfactory affair on the whole, but our headquarters imagine 15,800 assailants to be nearer the mark than 50,000. I was at Balaklava today — the railroad has made great progress, & the rails are laid nearly as far as Kadikoi: the navvies are making the line much further on than that, & I dare say it will be used shortly for carrying shot & shell a couple of miles towards Sebastopol[52].

50 The long-awaited storming by French troops of the Malakhov bastion did indeed take place, but not until 9 September 1855, by which time Edward Birch Reynardson was back in England. After this the Russians resigned themselves to defeat and evacuated the city of Sebastopol. The war dragged on, with little activity on either side, until the following spring when peace talks began which resulted in the signing of the Treaty of Paris on 30 March 1856. Under the terms of the treaty, Russia returned southern Bessarabia and the mouth of the Danube to Turkey; Moldavia, Wallachia and Serbia were placed under an international rather than a Russian guarantee; the Sultan promised to respect the rights of his Christian subjects; and the Russians were forbidden to maintain a navy on the Black Sea or to refortify Bomarsund in the Baltic. (BBC History website (The Crimean War).)
51 According to *The Times* journalist William Russell, the Allies called everyone 'Johnny', so the Greeks and Turks began to adopt the nickname and applied it to themselves. (William Howard Russell, *The British Expedition to the Crimea* (London, 1858)). The Russian attack on the well-defended garrison at Eupatoria was a fiasco and led directly to Prince Menshikov being relieved of his command.
52 The extension of the railway from Balaklava made a great difference to the speed of getting supplies from the harbour to the troops in the front line.

# IN THE CRIMEA

**Fig. 8 i)** *The Entrance to Balaklava Harbour* (top), dated 23 May 1855, and *The Approach to Constantinople* (bottom), dated May 1855, by Edward Birch Reynardson. Watercolour.

**Fig. 8 j)** *Four sketches, drawn in Constantinople and on board the* Indus, *28 to 30 May 1855*, by Edward Birch Reynardson. Watercolour.

IN THE CRIMEA

We expect to go to Balaklava very soon, as the 89th which we are to relieve come up here tomorrow morning.

There is a story prevalent that a large French force & one English division are to go to Eupatoria, join the 35,000 Turks & move to the Alma, Katcha & Belbek & invest the north side of Sebastopol. At the same time the English army & the 15,000 Sardinians are to go to the [*name illegible*] to take the lines there in masse, & join the Anglo-Franco-Turco army in their movement on the north side. Canrobert[53] with the French army is to hold our present position. I should think something of the kind will certainly be done sooner or later. Both Niel & [*Brigadier-General*] Jones seem to think the opportunity for taking the place by assault has been lost, & there is reason to suppose that the garrison is short both of food & ammunition, so that if invested they would have to surrender.

---

*After writing this letter, Edward was to spend another three months in the Crimea. We have no more letters from him and so have had to piece together some idea of his movements during this time from other sources. The short-lived coalition government was replaced in early February by a ministry led by Lord Palmerston. Lord Panmure took over at the War Office, one of his first appointments being to give the command of the 1st Division and Guards Brigade to Lord Rokeby in place of the Duke of Cambridge. By the time Rokeby arrived in the Crimea some weeks later, Edward's Division must already have been relieved of their duties and marched to Balaklava for rest and recuperation, where they were joined a little later by the tattered survivors of the rest of the brigade.*

*It is likely that Edward's own health had deteriorated to such an extent that there was no question of his returning to the front although the rest of his brigade returned to the siege in June. We can date Edward's departure from the Crimea precisely from two watercolours on the same sheet of paper (**Fig. 8 i**)), the first looking back at the entrance to Balaklava harbour as he was leaving on 23 May 1855 and the second a view of Seraglio Point and Scutari as his ship approached Constantinople. Another sheet of sketches (**Fig. 8 j**)) shows that he was still in Constantinople on 28 May, when he drew a 'Howling Dervish', but two days later was at sea on board the* Indus *(part of the Mediterranean fleet), by which time we must assume he was on his way home.*

*Edward did not receive the knighthood which fellow officers had predicted (**8: 14**), but he was made a Companion of the Bath and was also awarded a medal with four clasps*

---

53 General Robert Canrobert had succeeded Marshal Saint-Arnaud in command of the French forces after the latter's death in September 1854. He was rudely known as 'Robert Can't' to the British.

*and the Turkish medal for his services. As far as I know, he never wrote or spoke about his experiences in the Crimea after he returned home. He lived out the remainder of his life in retirement at Rushington Manor, where three more children were born to him and Emily. All three of his surviving male descendants followed him into the Army; his elder grandson (also Edward) was missing, believed killed, in 1915, but I knew Edward's son Vere, who died in 1941 aged 76, and Vere's younger son Morgan well, as he lived until 1984. Morgan (always known by his second name Harry) was commissioned into the 6th Inniskilling Dragoons on 10 October 1914 and entered the Indian Army in January 1915. He reached the rank of Lieutenant-Colonel and retired to live on the Isle of Wight. He was often at Adwell. It is to his two daughters, my cousins Eve and Avril, that I am indebted for permission to reproduce their great-grandfather's Crimean watercolours.*

CHAPTER 9

# Adwell

*History, Genealogy and Reminiscences 1850–1900*

'Our grandmother … was still the centre round which Adwell,
in those days, moved very slowly.'[1]

*Suddenly, in the second half of the nineteenth century, the volume of family letters slows down and then, after the return of Edward Birch Reynardson from the Crimea, abruptly ceases. There are no more letters from any members of the family until 1900. After reading so many lively letters written by and about several of the General's children, it is frustrating that no such record exists of the childhood and youth of the next generation — especially as that generation, led by my grandfather William John Birch Reynardson, who was born in 1849, is the first of which I can claim to have personal recollections.*

*This was however a significant period in our history, as it was around this time that the house and estate of Adwell came into our family, in which it has continued through seven generations down to the present day. All that we know about the earlier history of the ancient parish and manor of Adwell is recorded in an undated typescript written by my father*[2]*, and in the relevant volume of Victoria County History, covering the Lewknor and Pyrton part of Oxfordshire*[3]*. Both sources mention that at the time of the Domesday Book (completed in 1086), there was a Water-Mill at Adwell which took its name from the Saxon 'Aedah' (or 'Ead(d)a')'s well, fed by the stream which rises in Spring Covert. The mill 'was presumably where the waterfall now is'*[4]*; it is shown on a map of 1797, but had probably ceased working some time earlier and at an unknown date a little afterwards both the mill and the miller's house were pulled down and the mill stream incorporated into the grounds of Adwell House*[5]*.*

*We also know little about the early history of Adwell House itself before it was virtually rebuilt in the late eighteenth century. According to my father, 'when making alterations in 1935, traces were found of late 16th or early 17th century work'*

---

1 From '*Adwell: Memories for my Grandchildren: Part 1*', by Henry T. Birch Reynardson (**9: 1**)
2 Henry T. Birch Reynardson, 'Notes on Adwell'. The seven-page document was probably compiled between the 1940s and the early 1960s.
3 Mary D. Lobel (ed.), *A History of the County of Oxford: Volume 8: Lewknor and Pyrton hundreds* (Victoria County History, 1964).
4 'Notes on Adwell' (see footnote 2).
5 Victoria County History (see footnote 3). The last known lease of the mill was in 1736.

*and he believed that there would have been 'some sort of house here from very early days', though not necessarily on the exact site of the present house. Of the seventeenth-century house, he says 'there can be little doubt that the main rooms originally faced north: [these comprised] the Housekeeper's room, the Servants' Hall, and possibly the Kitchen on the ground floor; and upstairs my Dressing Room, my Mother's room and the Nursery [...]. Then in Queen Anne's reign, or the reign of George I, the house seems to have been turned around, for the present Drawing-room and Dining-room date from then, [though] the gilt mirrors etc are later [...] and the front door and porch are somewhat later than Queen Anne.'*

*Our family's connection with Adwell commenced in 1770 when George Birch (1733–1803) married Mary Newell (1737–1837), but it was not until their third son, John William Birch (1775–1867), inherited the property in 1846, through a somewhat involved process which is explained below, that Adwell belonged to our line of the family. At the time of his inheritance John William Birch lived at Henley Park, which had been left to him by his maternal grandfather, Thomas Newell. No doubt he often visited Adwell and its estate after 1846 and would have stayed at the house, but it was another few years before any members of the family regularly lived there, after John had given Adwell to his nephew, Henry Birch Reynardson, in 1854.*

*The Newell family was one of the three main families from which the Birch Reynardson line of the family is descended (see* Introduction*), but the one about which we know the least. It is certainly rather curious that we know so little about them. There are no pictures of them at Adwell and very few books. They must have been keen on their food as of the few books which we do have of theirs, three are recipe books. And it seems they may also have been religious, though they were not called upon to demonstrate their faith in a very demanding way. Adwell was a very small parish which never exceeded more than about fifteen households and of the four Newells who served as Rectors of Adwell, Christopher (Rector 1677–78) had been ejected from Bloxham, a few miles north of Oxford, for his nonconformity; John (Rector 1729–31) was killed by a fall from his horse while riding between Adwell and Oxford; his elder brother, William (Rector 1732–47), who succeeded him, combined the living with being lord of the manor; and his nephew, Samuel[6] (Rector 1775–1802), was described as being* 'not quite the character a clergyman ought to be' *but being too old to enter another profession and burdened with eight children and many debts, was allowed to continue in the ministry. After Samuel's time, during which the number of communicants declined from ten or twelve to six or seven, there was never again a resident rector in Adwell and the living was combined with, at different times,*

---

6    Rev. Samuel Newell was the brother of Mrs Mary Birch (see Chapter 7), and it is presumably two of his children, Sam and Anna Maria, who are referred to by John William Birch, their first cousin, in Chapter 4 (4: 5).

*Wheatfield, South Weston (from 1866) and Lewknor (from 1927).*

The ownership of Adwell by the Newells dates from 1680. Before that date it had been farmed by the Franklin family of Bledlow, a village about nine miles from Adwell which it had owned since 1581. On his death in 1663, Henry Franklin, who had no male heirs, left the property in one third shares to his three daughters, the youngest of whom (Frances) had married William Newell, who in 1680 bought the remaining two-thirds' share of Adwell from his wife's two sisters. William and Frances left Adwell to their second son, William (1665–1728), a High Sheriff of Oxfordshire, and in due course the estate passed to his elder son by his marriage to Mary Rye, the Rev. William Newell (1701–47). William and Mary's second son, Thomas (1707–77), another lawyer who practised as an attorney in Henley-on-Thames and lived at Henley Park a few miles north of the town, married Frances Fox and had a son, Samuel (see above), and a daughter, Mary (the future Mrs George Birch) — my redoubtable great-great-great-grandmother, about whom I have written in **Chapters** 3 to 7.

Rev. William Newell married Esther Cooper and they had just one daughter, Elizabeth, who was first cousin to Mary and Samuel Birch. Elizabeth, who was born

**Fig. 9 a)** *A nineteenth-century view of Adwell,* by Admiral Smythe. Watercolour.

*in 1743, is reputed to have been very beautiful and was known locally as 'The Lily of the Valley'; despite this, and despite being an heiress, she did not marry until 1787 when she was forty-four. We know little about her husband, James Jones, except that he came from Stadhampton, was said to have been in the Navy, and became High Sheriff in 1797. However, it was during their tenure that the manor house of Adwell was greatly enlarged and its present appearance dates mainly from that time* (**Fig. 9 a**)). *The stuccoed two-storey south front with its projecting centre bay, the moulded cornice, low parapet and hipped roof, and the marble chimneypieces in the front rooms are all contemporary with the late eighteenth-century house. A notable feature of the interior of the house, the staircase and skylight with Greek Revival detail, appears to have been added in the early nineteenth century[7]. There is no doubt that Elizabeth and James Jones did much to improve the garden and to plant many trees in it. It was probably they who had the wall of the enclosed garden built and, maybe, they constructed the high waterfall in order to make a dam for the garden pool. It was at about this time that Adwell was described by a contemporary writer as 'one of the most remarkable seats in the county'[8].*

*Elizabeth and James had no children, and when she was widowed in 1806 she invited her great friend and distant cousin, Miss Frances Webb of Norton Court, Gloucestershire, to come and live with her at Adwell, accompanied by her brother, Colonel Edward Webb. Elizabeth herself died in 1818 and, as my father wrote, 'instead of leaving Adwell to her first cousin and next-of-kin, Mary Birch (née Newell), she* gave *it to Miss Webb!' He further went on to report the tradition that for many years Elizabeth 'walked' through the house, 'a prey to remorse for her uncousinly behaviour', and suggested that because it is not known where she died (she was not buried at Adwell), she may have passed away whilst staying with her Webb friends in Gloucestershire 'and that towards the end gentle pressure was brought to bear'[9]. In her will dated March 1843, Frances Webb bequeathed the Adwell estate to John William Birch 'in estate tail' and that, failing his issue, it was to go to Admiral Francis William Fane[10] of Bath, who in fact pre-deceased Miss Webb. By the time Miss Webb died in 1846, John William Birch was over seventy and therefore unlikely to have children. A year later John fulfilled one of the conditions of Miss Webb's will by adopting, by Royal licence, the additional name and arms of Newell.*

*For a few years after Miss Webb's death, Adwell was let to a succession of tenants, including a Mr Thornhill, 'a reputed "nabob" from India, with a horde of children[11]',*

7   Victoria County History (as above).
8   Victoria County History, quoting William Brewer's *Guide to Oxfordshire* (published 1819).
9   'Notes on Adwell' (as above).
10  My father thought this arrangement particularly unfair as the Fanes 'were no relation whatever', but in fact, by a curious coincidence, Admiral Fane was a distant cousin of Emily Fane, soon to marry another of John William Birch's nephews, Edward Birch Reynardson (see Chapter 7).
11  'Notes on Adwell'.

*who are said to have done considerable damage to the house. Then, in 1854, John bought the reversionary interest for £21,000 from Miss Webb's niece, thereby preventing the estate from passing out of the family, and gave Adwell to his nephew (my great-grandfather) Henry Birch Reynardson, fourth son of 'the General' and his wife Etheldred. Henry had been married for seven years and had a growing family; they must have moved in to Adwell almost immediately, as in the 1861 census their youngest child Herbert is described as having been born in Oxfordshire (unlike the first four — William, Marion, Edwin and Aubrey — who were born either in Kent or in Lincolnshire).*

*Disappointingly, all is hearsay and we have nothing in Henry's or his uncle's own words about the real circumstances of their acquisition of Adwell, or about their family life there in the mid nineteenth century. All we know about the nearly thirty years of Henry's tenure is that he was High Sheriff of Oxfordshire in 1861* (**Fig. 9 b)**) *(a position later held also by his son, grandson and great-grandson) and that he rebuilt and re-modelled Adwell Church in 1864–5. The earliest part of the church dates from the Norman period, but the only survival of the medieval building is the Romanesque south doorway; alterations were also made in the fourteenth century, when it is thought that the pretty bell-cot with its four slender spirelets was installed. The Victorian rebuilding, designed by the architect Arthur Blomfield, is regarded as 'a competent example of nineteenth-century Gothic in the decorated style'*[12] *and is in my view is a charming and sensitive adaptation of the original medieval church; I am puzzled therefore by my father's disparaging comment that 'unfortunately' Henry also did the same (rebuilt the church) at South Weston, which at the time belonged to Adwell*[13]*.*

*My grandfather William Birch Reynardson (1849–1940)* (**Fig. 9 c)**) *grew up at Adwell from the age of five. I got on famously with him as a boy (he died when I was seventeen) but I do not recall ever having had a conversation with him about his childhood or his memories of his great-uncle, John William Newell Birch. He was educated at Eton and then at Christ Church, Oxford (like my father, my son and me!), and was called to the Bar (Inner Temple, like me) in the early 1870s. However, as was quite usual in those days, my grandfather never had a paid job — indeed I don't think he ever went into Chambers. He seems to have spent a good deal of his time travelling abroad, and produced a large number of high quality watercolours (see* **Figs. 9 d)** *and* **9 e)**)*. Although he inherited Adwell on his father's death in 1884, he did not himself live there between 1889, when he married Violet Maxwell — a rather dour Lowland Scot of Dargavel — and 1906, the year after his mother's death. For the intervening seventeen years the family lived at a house called The Prebendal (no longer standing) on the outskirts of Aylesbury.*

*It has been left to my father, Henry Thomas Birch Reynardson, to provide the most*

12   Victoria County History.
13   'Notes on Adwell'.

**Fig. 9 b)** *Henry Birch Reynardson (1814–84) when High Sheriff of Oxfordshire.*
Photograph, 1861.

**Fig. 9 c)** *Portrait of William John Birch Reynardson (1849–1940),* by Countess Karolyi.
Oil on canvas.

*comprehensive picture of life at Adwell at the very end of the reign of Queen Victoria and into the Edwardian period. He wrote this down many years afterwards as a memoir for his grandchildren, but I think it is of sufficient general historical interest to be reproduced here. As my father was born in 1892 and did not live at Adwell until he was fourteen, his earliest memories recall visits made by his sister Iola (Violet) and him as small children; these are included in this chapter and his later recollections, from 1906 until about 1914, follow in* Chapter 10.

**Fig. 9 d)** *Théoule on the Côte d'Azur*, by William John Birch Reynardson. Watercolour, 1889.

**Fig. 9 e)** *A Continental Lakeside Town*, by William John Birch Reynardson. Watercolour, 1889. This watercolour and **Fig. 9 d)** may well have been produced on my grandfather's honeymoon, as they both date from the year of his marriage to Violet Maxwell.

## 9: 1 ('Adwell: Memories for my Grandchildren: Part 1', by Henry T. Birch Reynardson)

I think I was about four years old, therefore in 1896, when I first remember anything about Adwell. It was winter. We had arrived at Aston Rowan station, Iola and me and our nanny, Nanny Cain, and it was very dark. But I remember the portly shape of the brougham, a lovely leather smell but not entirely innocent of stable flavour.

The rest of the arrival is a blank; but I am sure that before anything else we had our clothes changed and were generally tidied up. In Victorian days children lived almost entirely in the nursery to which very few grown-ups, except their mothers, penetrated. In some cases even the mothers didn't trouble so much about this. Nanny was the complete autocrat of the nursery, with a humble nursery maid to see to the more menial duties. We had all our meals in the nursery, except possibly, as one grew a little older, Sunday luncheon. But otherwise life went on upstairs till after tea. Then, after a tremendous 'spit and polish' we were dressed up in pretty clothes and our hair beautifully brushed. And so we were taken down. This meant brought down to the Drawing Room to show off our nice clothes and nice manners.

Our grandmother, Granny[14], was still the centre round which Adwell, in those days, moved very slowly. To tell the truth I really remember very little about her as a person of character; she was to us a kind of dimly realised institution, which certainly had form and shape, but little definite meaning. I remember what I saw. There was always an audience by candlelight in the early morning, when we were brought into the North Room and decanted onto an enormous great four poster bed complete with curtains and tester. There, propped up on a pile of white pillows lay a bundle of white: white cap, white face, white shawl. Granny. The one large candle stood in a tall wooden candlestick on the left of the bed. The room was always very hot, and smelt of cedar wood, from the burning of cedar spills. We were dumped on the bed and the opening gambit was the presentation to each of us of the most delicious blackcurrant lozenge, round and flat and black, with white sugar sprinkled over it. Then she would show us juvenile coloured picture books, which rather bored me; or perhaps I was too impatient for what was for me the great moment. From under her pillow she would extract a large gold watch; and when she pressed a little knob, it chimed out the hour and then

---

14   Eleanor Partridge, wife of Henry Birch Reynardson.

the half hour in the most melodious, miniature and fairy-like tones imaginable. But of course I have some daytime memories of her, dressed in black silk with jet beads sparkling here and there, a white widow's cap — rather a neat and spry affair — and some sort of soft shawl round her shoulders. I clearly remember her small velvet slippers and there were certainly jet beads on those, resting on a red velvet cushion.

Christmas festivities at Adwell in those days were extensive and remarkable. Father Christmas (my Uncle Aubrey) I will pass over. I thought the whole thing most sinister and am told I used to bellow throughout; I loathed that benign bearded figure. The Christmas tree was, of course, lovely, as all still are. After that came the Mummers. They were also terrifying, but slightly more bearable because I knew that 'King George', although partly disguised by a large hat and ribbon pinned all over him, was really George Bull, for whom I had a great affection and respect. But he was pleasantly terrifying as he came clumping in mumbling "Ere I be, King George a valiant knight, so I be'. The business took place in the servants' hall and the audience cowered beside the big fireplace, leaving the floor to the actors. The Play, if one could call it so, was an odd, muddly affair consisting mainly of unintelligible rigmarole, mumbled or shouted in the broadest Oxfordshire accent.

And now I come to the highlight of Christmas at Adwell, the 'entertainment'. It was held in what in those days was the dining room, and involved most fascinating preparations. Days beforehand there was the tremendous business of erecting the stage. My father, who was a very good carpenter and a terrific gadgeteer, had years before constructed a moveable stage which could be taken apart and put together again, and this was the job for old John Janaway, the Estate carpenter, with sundry helpers. There was a day or so of much hammering and then a couple of days, I think, of rehearsals; but of course I was shut out from these. Then came the day when lo and behold the dining room appeared completely disguised as a theatre, quite different and most exciting.

The 'entertainment' was divided into two parts: first, a contribution by members of the family; secondly, a conjurer hired from Oxford for the occasion. Uncle Aubrey always took the lead in the first part. Coster songs were his strong line, both funny and sentimental. He performed in a rakish peak cap, with 'pearlies' sewn all over his corduroy jacket. He was a very good actor and had a pleasant voice and was always a great success. I never myself saw my mother and father do a turn, but I gathered later that this was due to there having been a debacle when they once did so. Apparently my mother had the character of an ill-tempered wife and my father that of an ill-mannered husband. He was supposed to enter with his hat on while she had to exclaim 'How dare you come into my room with your hat on, Sir!' Well, that was alright; but he had forgotten to put his hat on so it wasn't so frightfully funny.

Then followed the conjurer. I think he could just about manage to produce a faded rabbit out of a top hat, but if so it was the zenith of his performance. Of course I was thrilled by every minute of it and was always furious with Mr Smith, the then tenant of Postcombe, who in a very loud whisper always explained just how each trick was done. He was a great fat chap in a shiny blue serge suit, with a massive gold 'Albert' across his taut waistcoat. He sat in the front row with my mother and Mr and Mrs Neighbour from Radnage, and some other tenants from South Weston. Behind came the lesser lights like Mr and Mrs Constable (the butler and his wife), the Head Gardener (so suitably named Budd) and dear old 'Daddy' Ward, the keeper and his wife, who had a goitre which looked like a dewlap and was a source of great interest to me. Then there were, of course, Mr and Mrs Hall, he was the Bailiff of the Home Farm, with Albert, his podgy son and my devoted friend.

I think everyone enjoyed 'the entertainment' enormously (and the tea later); though in these days of radio and television they wouldn't cross the road to attend such a show! People were so much more simple, of course, in those days, much less sophisticated and more easily pleased. But judging by the laughter and leg pulling and banter that one heard, they were certainly not less happy than people are now. Happier, I believe; though perhaps I think so because it was long ago and I was young then and old now. 'Laudator temporis acti'. But I would certainly except the old and sick. They were a sad case in those days and are without any doubt much better off now and certainly more happy and comfortable.

I won't take you on a tour of the whole house as I think that would be rather a bore; but particulars of one or two rooms may interest you. In the first place the hall. Right up to the time when I came to live permanently at Adwell in 1936 the walls were literally covered with stuffed birds and animals. I thought them quite beautiful. I am afraid none now survive except the herons and the owl. He is the most splendid bird and I hope the tradition will long survive. My grandfather had him in his room at Eton, I suppose in about 1840 and so did my father in about 1865. Strangely, I was never so honoured. But Bill had him in his room and I hope the custom will continue.

The drawing room was very much as it is now, though differently furnished, with pictures from skirting to cornice in the Victorian fashion and there was a big conservatory or winter garden beyond the south window.

I have a feeling that the drawing room wasn't much used in my grandmother's day. I have a much clearer memory of the library, which naturally I think of mostly in the evenings when we were brought down and in candle-light, as of course in those days there were only lamps and candles. In the middle of the library was a big round table covered with a rough tapestry with woolly blobs all round the edges; and in the middle of the table was a solid tall oil lamp with a petticoat shade of red silk. It gave a lovely soft light, created a beautiful warm fug and very often a beautiful smell; at least I thought it beautiful, though the grown-ups used to complain of the horrid smell, and how the lamp smoked.

Upstairs, everything has been so much changed (and improved) that I don't think it's worth describing the rooms as they were. But the attics must have a word; a long passage, generally known as 'Oxford Street' ran more or less the length of the house, with an immense number of rooms leading off on each side, on the south rather pleasant; on the north quite the reverse. […] Iola had a nice fairly big room on the south, then there was a sewing room opposite and the remaining rooms all occupied by servants, of whom there were a good many in those days.

Then I think you should hear about the kitchen; to me, in those days, just about next door to Heaven! On the right, as one came in, was a long trough-like bin, full of flour. It smelt quite delicious and if one were going fishing in the pond one could always find a few mealworms there! Disgusting? I suppose so but no one seemed to think it in the least odd and they certainly did make the most effective bait! Anyhow, that flour (milled in the old windmill at South Weston long ago demolished) made the most wonderful bread. Fred Witney managed the great oven in the back regions; he used to fill it with faggots, light up and then rake the ash out, when the lovely fat dimpled loaves were shovelled in and the ensuing smell was altogether delectable.

But to return to the kitchen again, all the centre was occupied by an enormous table of scrubbed elm, so scrubbed that it was almost polished, with a large oil lamp on pulleys above it; and, beyond, the butt of a biggish elm tree, used as a chopping block. Then there was a colossal 'Eagle' cooking range, again with a pendant oil lamp above it.

I must digress for a moment here to talk about baths, for it was this immense range that produced all the hot water for the house. There were, of course, no bathrooms in those days; everyone had a bath in their own room, and in winter before the fire, which was extremely pleasant. The baths were made of tin, white inside and of a curious mustard-colour outside. There were two kinds: one, a flat saucer-like affair, with turned-up edges; the other, rather like an egg-cup, with a high side against which one leant, dangling one's legs over the edge, and pleasantly roasting one's shins. It doesn't sound comfortable but actually was — extremely so. The bath was always put on a folded blanket, one's towel on a chair within reach. An enormous can of hot water (the can also mustard-coloured) containing about three or four gallons of water stood nearby, and of course cold water as well. Every drop of water, hot and cold, had to be carried to the rooms by the housemaids — also the little brass cans for the wash-stands (all furnished with lovely Coalport china). And every drop carried down again. Unless you are pretty hefty, the emptying of a 'saucer' bath is extremely tricky — as I discovered as rather a puny little fag, my first Half at Eton.

My next haven was the housekeeper's room — or 'the Room', as it was called behind the green-baize doors. This was the holy of holies, the room special to the upper servants — in those days Mrs Bagley, the cook; Mr Constable, the butler; and my Granny's maid — of whom I can remember nothing, except that she existed. I don't think the head housemaid qualified. It was a charming room, sunny although it looked west. My memories of it revolve entirely round those happy occasions when we were invited to tea as guests — though not exactly honoured guests, for though our hosts were certainly grown-ups they were neither too grown, or too up! In some way the gap was pleasantly narrowed. There was more freedom, less restraint; and though manners were expected, they could be rather more elastic. But of course one could never so far forget oneself as to interrupt or fidget when Mr Constable was telling one of his anecdotes — and he often was. He would pour his tea into his blue-flowered saucer and with exquisite skill proceed to balance it on the splayed-out fingers of one hand.

Mrs Bagley I ought to remember far better than I do, for I know she was very kind and cheerful. But all I can recall is a little woman in a white dress covered with lines of blue spots; and that she used to bring up to Iola in the night nursery delicious leftovers from the dining room. This, of course, was most irregular as we had had our teeth washed and were supposed to be asleep and not eating ices and fruit salad. I have a dim idea there was a row about it and the poor dear rather caught it.

Next, the servants' hall, or rather 'the Hall'. I used to think of it as a great big room, now I realise it wasn't at all. Straight in front as one entered was the end of a long table with a dark red table cloth. A wooden seat ran all along the wall on one side of the table and round to the bottom of it, and a moveable bench was on the other side. At the head was a wooden armchair. On the other side of the room was a cavernous fireplace with immense iron 'dogs' to support the logs. To the left of the fire was a tall wooden settle with a very narrow seat and a high back, incredibly spartan and uncomfortable. In this room everyone else ate; I think even the 'uppers' had their main course there with Mr Constable to carve, and then retired for their 'afters' and dessert to 'the Room', but the poor kitchen scullions, being so very junior, weren't allowed even the meagre comforts of 'the Hall'. They had to eat at a little table in the kitchen. Don't ever believe that class distinctions, privilege, prerogative and all such snob stuff were the peculiarities of the far side of the baize doors. I can assure you that it was quite otherwise. Poor scullery maids, they led a miserable existence really, in a scullery which smelt eternally of pig-tub — mixed, in summer, with the scent of roses. Bittersweet, indeed. Yet they had some fascinating jobs, mind you, such as blowing into shiny lengths of pig gut to extend them and then pushing the sausage meat in with their thumbs. Enthralling to watch. Then it was their job to ring the big bell which hung on the top of the house at 8am and 5pm. They had to put a foot through the loop of the rope to give themselves more purchase to help their straining arms on the pull. The rope went up through the ceiling and then reappeared, miraculously, on the wall of 'Oxford Street'. If you timed it just right there and snatched the rope as soon as it moved and pulled like blazes, the poor girl's foot was hoisted up and flat she went on her back! But of course there was a pack of trouble about that and I was warned that the practice must cease, or else!

Outside, the stable yard was very much as it is now, except of course that the inhabitants were horses and carriages. These consisted of the snug brougham to which I have already alluded; a Victoria, an open four-wheeled carriage with a leather hood, with very considerable seating for two facing forward and a seat for barely two (which was remarkably uncomfortable) facing it. Later there was a waggonette for more extensive outings. These equipages were drawn by a pair of horses, with old William Tice, the coachman, and Frank Eborn on the box beside him. Then there was a four-wheeled dog cart, drawn by a single horse, for four passengers: two in front, one driving, and two in the rear facing backwards. There was always a pony cart of sorts, a 'governess cart', which held four small occupants at a pinch and there was also a heavy, rather rough, two-wheeled dog cart in which the bailiff drove to Thame market every Tuesday for general household shopping.

In those days there was nowhere to wash the carriages except in the open yard and varnished carriages had to be carefully washed and leathered as soon as they came in, the water carried in wooden buckets from the iron tank. If there weren't dealt with at once, whatever the time, horribly unsightly white spots would appear on the highly varnished surfaces.

I have an idea that hanging about in the stable yard was not welcomed by old William; anyhow we never did so and my father, who was essentially 'unhorsy', took little interest. But he was very inventive and mechanically-minded and after he bought his first car in 1902, he spent a lot of time tinkering with it. How you would laugh to have seen that first car. It was a four and a half HP single cylinder Oldsmobile, built in the shape of a four-wheeled dog cart in which the passengers sat back to back and was steered with a tiller. It had a curly prow like a Canadian toboggan and could, when all was well, which was seldom, achieve the dizzy speed of 20mph which was the legal limit.

But if not so welcome in the stable yard, matters were very different in the farmyard, where my memories are of the happiest. Looking back, it always seems to have been summer and always sunlit. If William didn't welcome small boys, Mr Hall, the bailiff, certainly did. Although when one is very young most men appear to be tall and old, Mr Hall — though certainly tall — I never thought of as excessively old, I suppose because he was so cheerful.

Mr and Mrs Hall lived in the Old Vicarage. I remember so well how once we had tinned salmon for tea which I thought was wonderful. They had a 'backhouse' or earth closet. Most intriguing as it was a three-seater affair: two large holes for Mr and Mrs Hall side by side and a smaller one in the corner for Albert. It always seemed to me a rather curious occasion for a family party, but still, when one is young one isn't over-critical and if people liked it that way, why not?

There were six Shire horses as a rule, for it is stiff land at Adwell and ploughing up the rise in the Farm Fields was work for four horses and hard work at that. But I do have a dim recollection of a 'steam tackle' ploughing in East Farm field. It was so wonderful as to be almost miraculous. In the first place there were two enormous traction engines, which went, as George Bull said 'of theirselves like'. They puffed up through Stamp Green and took up their positions at each end of the field. Under their bellies they had great drums of heavy wire cable. A three-furrow plough was joined to the cable and the traction engine wound it right up the field; then the process was reversed and the plough was pulled back again.

Then there was the engine on the farm. George Bull was its master and therefore a great hero to me. He was a great tall, thin man who walked with a limp. I was told that I mustn't 'pass remarks', but he had a club foot. The engine lived in a shed opposite the barn door with its funnel sticking up through the corrugated iron roof, and by a series of belts and wheels and shafts drove all sorts of machinery inside the barn: mill, root cutter, chaff cutter and at the appropriate season the threshing machine.

The wood yard was next door to the carpenter's shop, the abode of John Janaway. He smelt of wood with which he worked and of strong tobacco which he chewed, so I didn't really cotton to him much. He was always quite kind in letting one watch but sternly refused to have anything to do with mending toys, etc — 'Ain't got a momint o' time; you take it along to the Squire, 'e'll make it up for you.'

Then there was the shepherd, Mr Croxford, who lived at Postcombe. He was never called Croxford but always 'Shepherd'. He was a nice quiet man who seemed devoted to his (I thought) very dull and stupid charges who looked generally scruffy and caked with mud from being penned on this heavy land.

Before we leave the farm yard I must mention the slaughter house, still standing though no longer in use. In those days, everything except the beef was home-killed, calves for veal, sheep for mutton and pigs for bacon and ham, etc.

Next, the garden (**Fig. 9 f**)). I really have only the dimmest, though very pleasant, impressions of the garden in Granny's day. Lots of smooth grass, cool and soft to my bare feet, interspersed with lots of little 'jam tart' beds; and any amount of gravel paths winding about. There was a fountain on the lawn and at the far side there was a narrow stone bridge which ran from the surrounding pavement to the centre of the fountain where the water jet was; but as two out of three male heirs of Adwell during the last one hundred years have fallen into the water from the bridge and been very nearly drowned, perhaps it is as well that it has been done away with. I can remember nothing about Mr Budd, the head gardener, and there were many under-gardeners to look after, and so many beds of annuals and lots of grapes and peaches. I don't think any of these came our way, except possibly if we were ill. Along the stream at the bottom of the lawn was a broad gravel path and across the stream an impenetrable box hedge, so that one couldn't look into the sunshine and shade of the shrubbery at all: such a pity. But I think the Victorians considered dark and gloomy vistas picturesque and romantic. Down beyond the waterfall there was the most wonderful little fairy-story summerhouse, with a high thatched roof running up into a point. It was six-sided and the walls were covered with rough bark and the floor was made of small round cobblestones. Inside there was a table also covered in bark.

SURVIVORS

**Fig. 9 f)** *A nineteenth-century view of the gardens at Adwell, by Admiral Smythe. Watercolour.*

In those days the 'shrubberies' were beautifully kept up, and all the gravel paths swept and smoothed so that Granny's bath chair and the jennet [*a female donkey*] could use them.

I've only made passing mention of 'Daddy' Ward, the (game)keeper as he never really came my way much as a child. He was always 'Daddy' and seemed by me to be extremely old but that was because he wore a beard, a small tidy little job. Out shooting he always wore a very curious sort of double decker bowler hat and the most lovely moleskin waistcoat with gilt buttons with the family crest on them. This was also the rig on Sundays. He and Mrs Ward lived in London Lodge. Ward had a terrible black curly-coated retriever called Jet. He lived in a kennel just by the farmyard gate. He had yellow eyes and a most evil disposition. Fortunately for me he was always kept on a chain as, whenever I passed, keeping a wary eye on the kennel, he would dash out with a hideous snarl to the limit of the chain.

CHAPTER 10

# The Boer War and the Great War

*Letters and Reminiscences 1900–1918*

'I think the world has gone mad. It destroys all one's ideas on the stability of things.'[1]

*Of all his relations on either side of the family, my father had a particular admiration and affection for his Uncle Frank, one of his mother's younger brothers. The Maxwells were an old Scottish family whose home was originally at Dargavel House[2]* (**Fig. 10 a)**) *in Renfrewshire, where Grandmother Violet's parents were married in 1860. However, the newly-married couple then went out to India, where Thomas Maxwell was a Surgeon-Major in the Indian Army and where their first four children, including my grandmother, were born. After Thomas retired from the Indian Army medical service in 1868, the family came back to England and settled in Guildford, where another seven children were born.*

*Seven of my grandmother's siblings were boys; five of them entered the army, at least three in the Indian cavalry and each of them later commanded their regiments[3]; but it was my great-uncle Frank who had the most distinguished record with the award of the Victoria Cross. Francis Aylmer Maxwell* (**Fig. 10 b)**), *who was born in 1871 and attended the Royal Military College at Sandhurst in 1889, was commissioned into the Indian Army and joined his regiment in India in 1891. He showed his courage early on when he was mentioned in despatches after recovering the body of a fallen comrade under heavy enemy fire, while serving with the Chitral relief force on the Waziristan Expedition in 1895. Four years later he was posted to South Africa, where he was attached to Lord Roberts[4]'s Mounted Infantry regiment, known as Roberts's Light Horse, during the Second Boer War.*

*Although Frank Maxwell served in the army for thirty-six years and reached the rank*

---

1. Robert Cornwallis Maude, sixth Viscount Hawarden, to my father, Henry Birch Reynardson, 2 August 1914 (**10: 6**)
2. Now absorbed into the site of the Royal Ordnance Factory (Bishopton), constructed in the late 1930s.
3. Information from the website of St Mary's Church, Guildford, which owns a chandelier presented in memory of my great-grandmother Maxwell. The inscription reads: 'To the memory of Violet Sophia Maxwell, mother of their Squadron Commander [her youngest son Eustace, who was killed on the Somme in 1916], this candelabrum was given by the Indian Officers and Men of the Mohammedan Squadron XI King Edward's Own Lancers (PROBYN'S HORSE) 1914'.
4. Frederick Roberts (1832–1914), soon to be created the first Earl Roberts, commanded the British troops fighting in the Second Boer War until November 1900, and from 1901 to 1904 was Commander-in-Chief of the Forces, the last to hold the office before it was abolished.

# THE BOER WAR AND THE GREAT WAR

**Fig. 10 a)** Dargavel House, Renfrewshire, my grandmother Violet Maxwell's family home. Photograph.

**Fig. 10 b)** *Lieutenant Francis Aylmer Maxwell, V.C.* Photograph, c.1900.

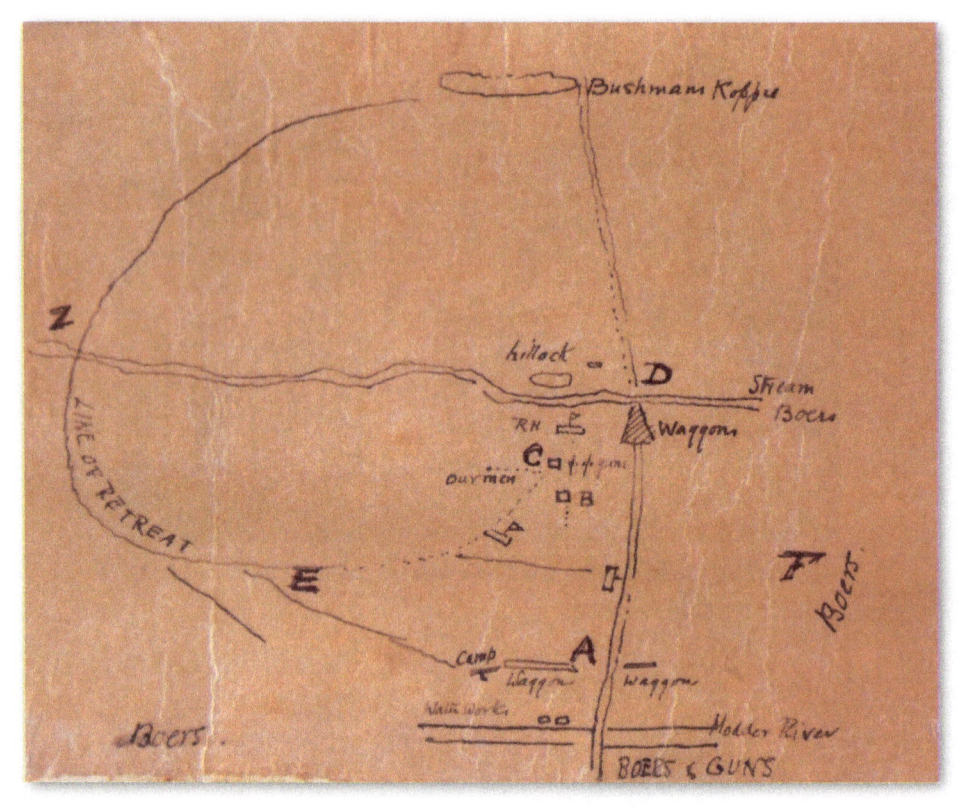

**Fig. 10 c)** *Sketch of the Action at Sanna's Post, 30 and 31 March 1900*, by Frank Maxwell. Drawn in pen and ink on the cardboard back of a notebook.

*of Brigadier-General, we have only one letter from him* (**10: 1**) *about his active service. However, this is the letter describing the action for which he was to receive his V.C., which took place on 30 and 31 March 1900 at Sanna's Post (also known as Korn Spruit), some miles from Bloemfontein, capital of the Orange Free State*[5]. *The sketch plan drawn by Maxwell on the back of a notebook* (**Fig. 10 c)**), *enclosed with the letter, shows how the action developed.*

---

5   Bloemfontein had fallen to the British under Lord Roberts a few days earlier. At that point, the British believed that the war was all but over and were taken by surprise by a new form of guerrilla warfare planned by the Boers to target British supply and communication lines, of which the ambush of the escorted convoy described in Maxwell's letter was their first attack.

LETTER 10: 1 (Lieutenant Frank Maxwell, Indian Staff Corps (British Indian Army), Bloemfontein, Orange Free State, to Mrs Violet Maxwell, his mother, dated 2 April 1900)

Bloemfontein<br>2 April 1900

My dearest Mother

We left here on the 18th, I think, with a couple of batteries [*of the*] R.H.A. [Royal Horse Artillery], the Household Cavalry, & 10 Hussars and about 700 Mounted Infantry under French[6]. [...]. Our object was apparently to watch a large Commando of Boers moving north [...], also to collect any arms from Orange Free State people who wanted to hand them in — our stay was only meant to be a short one: but for some reason we hung on & on with disastrous results [...].

[...] Our advance party ½ way between Thabanchu & Ladybrand saw very large numbers of Boers daily: and one day [...] a few men rode into Ladybrand & collared the Landrost[7] [*sic*], returning with him at full gallop & getting away with a narrow shave. This stirred up the ant heap, which previously was fairly quiet. Pilcher [...] reached us on the morning of the 29th, reporting Boers in great numbers behind him. [...] Early next morning (the 30th), our [...] picquets[8] came into contact with the enemy and at midday all of us were ordered out to stand by while the transport was packed 3 miles back. The Boers meaning business, the transport was ordered back to Modder River some 16 miles back [...].

Then occurred the next grave mistake (in my humble opinion). Knowing that the Boers would be hot on us the Waggons were not ordered back again towards Bloemfontein at daybreak: and at 6.30 there was musketry firing on the Thabanchu side of the river from the Boers. [...] watching with my Field glasses, I could see the enemy's guns coming quietly up. The first gun opened at about 7 am [...]. No order was necessary then to inspan[9] the waggons; the 4th or 5th shell dropped in amongst them & that was order enough, for every mule was in in no time & a real Hades of shouting & yelling of Black boys urged them pell

---

6    Major-General John French (1852–1925) commanded the Cavalry Division during the Second Boer War and was knighted in 1900 in honour of his successes. On the outbreak of the First World War, as Field-Marshal Lord French, he was Commander-in-Chief of the British Expeditionary Force, holding the position until December 1915 when he was compelled to stand down in favour of Field-Marshal Haig. He returned to the U.K. as Commander-in-Chief of the British Home Forces.

7    The Landdrost was the chief magistrate of a district under South African law.

8    In military terminology, a picquet (now spelt 'picket') refers to soldiers or troops placed forward of a line to warn of an enemy advance.

9    ]Originally taken from an Afrikaans word, meaning 'to harness animals to a vehicle' or 'yoke'.

mell to the rear. Our guns did not reply, and now comes the next point which shows a great error — pardonably, I suppose, as the existence of obstacles was probably forgotten. About a mile back was another stream — pretty steep & with a difficult road down & up for waggons. All the transport galloped from 'A' (camp) to 'D' and got crowded into a wedge shape trying to cross by the one road. The Boer guns were a long way off out of the sketch across the Modder, but dropped shell pretty thick into everything [...], hence the continued hurry from 'A' to 'D' of the waggons.

[...] My Squadron was leading, i.e. nearest to 'D', & when about ½ mile from the stream, an excited man galloped up & said the Boers were right in the Waggons, disarming our men (every waggon had 2 or 3 men with it). I at once galloped out with an advance guard [...] up to the waggons & sure enough, without the smallest noise or confusion, [there] were Boers as thick as peas collecting arms from our men. [...]

Back I went full split to the Regiment,[...] told the Colonel & at the same moment a Boer, standing up on the bank of the stream with others around him, shouted to us to go to the waggons — the hillock we could then see was full of Boers. [...] Only then did we fully realize the trap into which we had fallen & the 2nd in Command, Beresford, sang out 'files about', the Colonel shouting ditto. The very moment we turned came the storm — Men & horses on the grass in a second [...] full gallop for most, I think. Don't think me a bragging ass, & trying to make myself out a brave man, but I honestly tell you I was so completely taken by surprise at the whole thing, & most of all at our going files about, which undoubtedly was quite the right & only thing to do — that I didn't hurry back, more fool I, & I think that I was clear enough in my head to see that the chief storm on us was from the stream & hillock, and on the poor gunners from the waggons.

My orderly stayed with me like a brick & [...] refused to gallop off as I ordered him. It never occurred to me personally that I was going to get out of the show, & I just did not care a rap — at which I'm surprised now, but I remember the feeling so perfectly that I know that my imagination isn't going astray. From where we were fired on first to 'C', the first tin hut, was perhaps 400 yards & arriving here, we turned in for shelter. Here there were ½ dozen wounded & dismounted men already [...] As I arrived at 'C', the battery or what remained of it opened fire. There were only 5 guns out of the 6, of those only 3 were worked, & very soon only 2 for in such a hail the gunners went down like flies. Never was anything more magnificent than the way those men fought.

[…] an Australian […] & I ran out to help the Colonel commanding the 2 Batteries to drag a limber[10] up to one of the guns so as to have the ammunition nearer — He thanked us as if in Pall Mall & said he did not require our help any more & we skunked [sic] back to our shelter; the Australian, poor chap, getting badly hit on the way. The Colonel was wounded too, soon after, & all 3 subalterns were, leaving only the Major & the Captain & about 3 men per gun. They were still fighting there when I summoned up sufficient courage (I did not know till then how hard it was to leave cover) to ride out over the ground between 'CA' & 'E' to try & find my squadron. Boers were now swarming up on the side by 'F' & heavy firing [was] going on from the Modder. […]

Meanwhile the cavalry household [Household Cavalry] & 10th Hussars had sloped away by the 'line of retreat' marked on plan […], moving very slowly round […]. As their moving around quickly to Bushman's Koppie & then making a demonstration behind the Boers seemed to be our only chance, this slow movement was discouraging and the last I saw of them was halted under the foot of Bushman's Koppie — anyway they gave us no help whatever; [the] Cavalry seem to have lost any dash or enterprise, if they had any in this war, except during French's ride to Kimberley[11]. […]

When I got back to 'B' the horse gunners & horses, most of them wounded, were crowding about on the left side of it. The order had come 2 or 3 times for the Guns to retire, and as many times the Major, Phipps-Hornby[12], who with his Captain bore a charmed life, sent back to say he could not get away — As often as horses under plucky drivers went out, so often were horses shot. Three guns & limbers were hauled back from 'C' by officers & 1 or 2 gunners to the shelter, [such] as 'B' tin house could afford; the horses were put in (about 2 only instead of 8) and galloped off. The 5th gun could not be got out as there seemed such a beastly hurry to retire; it could have been got out had they not bothered to send out horses. These were shot dead when they were hooked in […] so it had to be left. […] Our battery lost 2 guns & saved 4.

The guns having gone, the people facing 'F' & at 'A' began to retire […]. The Boers were now pressing very hard, galloping like steam as each last lot retired & opening fire: they came on in great numbers from 'F' round to the left

---

10   A two-wheeled vehicle used to tow a field-gun, which would normally be drawn by horses but in this case there was no time to harness them.
11   Major-General French had led the Cavalry Division in the relief of the siege of Kimberley, where a combined force of 14,000 cavalry and mounted infantry overwhelmed a much smaller Boer force on a ridge at KlipDrift.
12   Major Edmund Phipps-Hornby also earned the Victoria Cross in this action, as did Sergeant Charles Parker, Gunner Isaac Lodge and Driver Horace Glasock.

hand bottom corner of the Paper 'O', fortunately not from 'D' (we learned why afterwards). [...] We got back to 'Z' & after this [we] were free of them, but not of their bullets. We all massed quickly under Bushman's Koppie & had a roll call. Our casualties were — killed & wounded & missing: 94 (since reduced to 86 by men turning up), out of about 270 [...]. This included 9 officers: 1 killed, 2 wounded brought back with us, 3 left in the hut & 3 missing. Both my horses were shot, one only a graze, the other, my orderly's, severely & my orderly wounded in the finger. I left him behind when I went back to the hut to save the little horse who was losing much blood [...].

At Bushman's Koppie we heard that a Division of Infantry was at hand from Bloemfontein, sent out at 2 am that morning on account of Broadwood's report the day before of the enemy being in such strength [...] there is much heart burning in our Brigade that they appear to have made no effort to come down towards 'D' & get at the Boers' rear. This may be wrong, for movements away from one's own sphere of action are hard to follow. Still it has never been contradicted yet that [*the Division of Infantry*] was there at Bushman's Koppie & stayed there. However, indirectly it helped us, for the Boers knew they were there & so did not attempt to cut in from 'D' to 'Z', or did so in a very half-hearted way. [...]

At 5 pm we began our 15-mile march back to Bloemfontein. It was a weary long march, as we had had no bite since noon the previous day [...], reaching our goal at 11.15 pm. Here after much delay we got some bully beef & bread — but most of the men were off the saddle & asleep long before it was issued. [...]

And so ended an eventful 36 hours from noon on the 30th till midnight on the 31st, when we reached the Commissariat Camp. Every horse had been under saddle all that time except from 4.30 am till 6.30 am when the battle practically began. Lucky we were to have an enemy who had not the pluck of the proverbial louse, for our whole brigade of MI was under 600, and also an enemy who shot so ill, for heavy though our losses were at that first place, it was nothing to what it ought to have been [...]. There is no doubt that they thought we had discovered their presence at 'D' & were walking quickly up to surrender as they stood & told us to go to the waggons. [...]

[...] Four of our wounded officers are doing well, having been brought into Bloemfontein — & Beresford is going to live all right in spite of a hole thro' his lungs. I have now been made Adjutant & it is a bit too much of a good thing to be this in an irregular corps — especially at a time like this with endless casualty returns, futile attempts to get kit for the men, & endless worries all day about picquet. I'm dead beat, so now I'll turn down onto my flagstone & sleep till 4.30 am.

---

*The announcement of Lieutenant Maxwell's receipt of the Victoria Cross was published in the* London Gazette *on 8 March 1901, in the following words:*

> Lieutenant Maxwell was one of three Officers not belonging to 'Q' Battery, Royal Horse Artillery, specially mentioned by Lord Roberts as having shown the greatest gallantry, and disregard of danger, in carrying out the self-imposed duty of saving the guns of that Battery during the affair at Korn Spruit on 31st March 1900. This Officer went out on five different occasions and assisted to bring in two guns and three limbers, one of which he, Captain Humphreys[13], and some Gunners, dragged in by hand. He also went out with Captain Humphreys and Lieutenant Stirling to try to get the last gun in, and remained there till the attempt was abandoned.

*A year or two later Maxwell was appointed as A.D.C. to Lord Kitchener (Lord Roberts' second-in-command in the Boer War, who succeeded him in overall command in November 1900) and became a favourite of the notoriously socially reclusive General[14].*

\* \* \*

*In 1905 'Granny' (Mrs Henry Birch Reynardson, née Eleanor Partridge) died at the age of eighty-seven and in the following year her eldest son, my grandfather William Birch Reynardson, and his family moved back into Adwell. My aunt Violet (named after her mother and maternal grandmother, but always known as 'Iola') was then sixteen and my father coming up for fourteen. After taking up residence at Adwell, my grandfather became an extremely expert farmer as well as being an outstanding shot (see* Chapter 11*) and life at Adwell before the outbreak of the First World War was dominated by these country pursuits. To the recollections of life at Adwell in his grandmother's time which*

---

13  By an extraordinary coincidence the Captain Humphreys mentioned, whom my great-uncle barely knew, was my future father-in-law (see Chapter 13). He was awarded the D.S.O. for his part in the same action.

14  Herbert Kitchener, first Earl Kitchener (1850–1916), served in the Mahdist War in the Sudan (1884–99) and the Second Boer War, before becoming Commander-in-Chief in India from 1902–09. He rose to the rank of Field-Marshal and on the outbreak of the First World War was appointed Secretary of State for War, appearing on recruiting posters to proclaim 'Your Country Needs YOU' in an image which is still recognisable today. For his relationship with Frank Maxwell, see Thomas Pakenham, *The Boer War* (Weidenfeld & Nicholson, 1979), quoting from letters published by Maxwell's wife after his death (Mrs Frank Maxwell, *Frank Maxwell: a Memoir, and some letters edited by his wife* (1921)).

*he wrote for his grandchildren (9: 1), my father added a shorter memoir about these few idyllic years, after which* 'the "old days", good or bad, depending on how you looked at them, really ended.'


## 10: 2 ('Adwell: Memories for my Grandchildren', Part II, by Henry Birch Reynardson)

When my father took over Adwell, a good many of the old familiar faces vanished: sad, but I suppose it had to be. In due course Mr Constable [*my grandfather's butler*]'s place was taken by a man called Moulden, an awfully nice, kind, silly chap. And considering that he drank like a fish whenever the family was away, he more or less got away with it. My dear mother was very sorry for him and did her best to help him when he fell from grace! Hall [*the bailiff*]'s place was taken by a great character, Graham, from the lowlands of Scotland; he had a charming blue-eyed wife, two tough sons and several daughters.

[...] In my father's small study, off the billiard room, were all sorts of enthralling things: his guns and a motley collection of rook rifles, [*as well as*] what he called 'pea rifles', which I suppose were .22s. There he used to reload his own cartridges, for in those days it was customary to use all brass cases, which were carefully salvaged and then recapped and reloaded with powder, shot and wads, a lengthy and intricate operation. I can only imagine that he did it because it amused him, though of course the cases were used over and over again. There were all sorts of very intriguing little machines employed for these operations, but my orders were 'Don't touch'.

William Tice [*the coachman*] retired to Oxford and his place was taken by an amusing card called Soden. He was a good whip and horseman. We still kept a pair of horses and a single — Peter, of whom more below; but we were going up in the car world and had risen to (as I thought) a proper car — a very nice Argyll. It had a canvas hood which, if you were a conjuror and had five hands, could be erected in about five minutes. If you weren't, and hadn't, it took half an hour and several bleeding knuckles. To care for it arrived Bob Barrett. He had very red hair and very blue eyes and an irremovable grin. His heart was with motors and not with horses; but he was a very nice chap.

Under the influence of my mother's brothers, all in the Indian Cavalry, it was borne in upon us that of course we ought to hunt: and so, somehow, it happened. I don't think my father was exactly enthusiastic but he submitted with great patience, although the arrangements he made were a trifle unsuccessful. Our Uncle Frank (who had the V.C. and two D.S.Os. and was a wonderful character) was the most persistent encourager. Aunt Iola was much braver than me and was always 'in his pocket'; I was much more nervous and until I was seventeen or so really only pretended that I liked hunting. But I must say that I often had a raw deal. I generally had to ride Peter, who was a clumsy and ill-mannered cob. He very seldom agreed to jump anything but if he did, he would buck over the obstacle and somehow manage to land on all four feet together — wallop! [...] Also, if he could reach out and kick a hound, he would; and once the Master — rather an unpleasant man — gave me an awful dressing down for this, and sent me home. I was covered with shame and confusion.

I suppose that my father was told in time that Peter was not exactly suitable, so he made a change. But now he went to the other extreme: he got hold of a horse from the Surrey Union — a very flash chestnut, who stood 16.2 hands and had won four point-to-points, but since those triumphs had poked out one eye with a thorn and so was going cheap. He was most suitably named Cyclops (or perhaps that is what we christened him). As I stood about 4 ft 6 ins and weighed, I suppose, about eight stone, it really wasn't a very suitable buy! [...] He not only jumped as though he were jumping a house but, being blind on one side, always 'screwed' as he took off. I was continually over his head — I should think about one in half a dozen fences put me on the floor. My word! I did hate it. Fortunately my Uncle Frank said he'd 'larn' him — but after three or four fences, he'd had enough too. 'He's an old pig,' he said. And after that poor Cyclops vanished, and Biddy appeared. She was quite a nice little mare, except that she had a curious habit of sometimes refusing to budge, standing stock still for half an hour or more: neither whip nor spur had the slightest effect. [...] I seem to have had the most original horses!

Enough now of my equestrian experiences. Adwell to me at this time was a very happy home, with lots of things to do. I was allowed to have plenty of school friends to stay in the holidays, which was pleasant as boys of my age were very few in that part of the world [...]. We had lots of tennis and bathing (in icy water, as there was no swimming-bath then), and [...] croquet, which my mother adored. She had been an extremely good tennis player until she had the bad luck to crack a tendon in her leg two years running, which put a stop to it — so she took up croquet. Curiously [...] tennis wasn't allowed on Sundays, but croquet —

that most vicious and spiteful game, calculated to arouse all the most unchristian passions — was all right. Was it because croquet didn't demand violent motion, which in some odd way might be judged unseemly for the Holy Day?

---

*1906 was also the year in which my father went to Eton, a few months before his fourteenth birthday. Despite an encouraging letter from his Uncle Frank (**10: 3**), when he was just starting his first half, my father was not happy there. He told me that he was constantly ill and in a poor house with an 'extremely dull' tutor. Perhaps he was a little hard on A.C.G. Heygate, the tutor in question, as a letter written by Heygate when my father left Eton in 1910 (**10: 4**) shows that at least his tutor recognised his abilities in both Latin (one of the subjects he would read at Oxford) and poetry, which seem not to have been acknowledged by other members of staff.*

### Letter 10: 3 (Francis Maxwell, Guildown Grange, Guildford, to his nephew, Henry Birch Reynardson, at Eton, dated 4 May 1906)

Guildown Grange
Guildford

4 May [1906]

My dear old Henry

By the time this reaches you [*you*] will be quite an old Eton boy and feeling no end of a swell. I hear you went there 2 days ago, so no doubt are settling down to your new life. Just at first I expect you felt a bit homsesick, but that very soon wears off once work begins. And now for the next 6 or 7 years you will have a rare happy time, and one which you will all your life look back on with pleasure.

Such a good little chap as you are doesn't want any advice, but I'm going to give you a very short bit.

Work hard, play hard: fight with your fists and not with your tongue (for which purpose learn boxing soon): and above all be <u>straight</u> which means be honourable and straightforward in small things as well as big so that as you begin your life, so you may live it all through and be 'Sans peur et sans reproche'. You know enough French to be able to translate this splendid motto. I think it is the best thing that could be said of any man, don't you? […]

[…] Now old boy, goodbye. Don't answer this, but some time later on write and tell me how you are getting on and who your best pal is etc.

Ever very affectionately<br>
<u>Frank</u>

**Letter 10: 4 (A.C.G. Heygate, Eton College, to William J. Birch Reynardson, dated 22 July 1910)**

ETON COLLEGE<br>
WINDSOR

July 22.   10

Dear Mr Birch Reynardson

There is no need to delay sending Henry's reports, and I take the opportunity to thank you for the sloe gin! I also enclose Henry's certificates, the receipt for which please acknowledge.

[…] He has a cultivated and literary mind, and was thus able to produce, not only several good copies of Latin verse, but an admirable 'Vale'[15] and a Hervey verse poem of great merit. I fear I am not in accord with the official criticism thereof, but I did not see the other competitors' productions.

Henry has of course been seriously handicapped by weak health all through, and a boy loses touch when obliged to miss a half; nor is he of the ordinary school type of mind.

But though these causes have prevented his becoming conspicuous here, I imagine he has derived both pleasure & profit from his Eton time & will look back on it with pleasurable recollections. He is in any case one of the boys whom Eton is proud of, and will, I am sure, make a useful member of Society. I shall always be glad to see him here & hope he will not forget us.

Yours sincerely<br>
A C G HEYGATE

---

15  We still have copies of the 'Vale' (or 'Farewell') and another poem written by my father when he left Eton in July 1910.

*In contrast to school, my father spent what he described as* 'three idyllically happy years at Christ Church' *(Oxford). He graduated with a Double First in 'Greats' (Classics) and his tutor, Robert (Robin) Hamilton Dundas*[16] *described him as the most brilliant student he had ever taught. In 1913 he went to join his regiment in India. The example of his dashing uncles, three of whom were in the Indian Cavalry, must surely have influenced his choice of career, though his regiment — the Oxfordshire and Buckinghamshire Light Infantry — was not a mounted one*[17]. *My father saw a good deal of his uncles while in India and one of his letters written from there around Christmas 1913 gives a flavour of how he spent much of his free time.*

---

LETTER 10: 5 (Lieutenant Henry T. Birch Reynardson, Ahmednagar, India, to his parents, William and Violet Birch Reynardson, Adwell, dated 30 December 1913)

Ahmednagar
Tuesday. Dec. 30

My dearest Mother and Father,

I last wrote to you from the wilds of the jungle! And I got all my Xmas letters in camp there on Xmas eve which was very delightful. Well, as you can imagine I had the very best Xmas I possibly could have considering I was some 5000 miles from home […].

First as to our bag: we got two sambhar [*species of deer*] […] — the first, entirely by luck & not by skill, fell to my rifle & the other to Uncle Law's: one small chinkhara […] I got too; two pigs, tho' we could have killed any amount, to Uncle Law & Cawley; & one Nilgai [species of antelope], […] also to the latter. On the last day I laid out an old crocodile too — horrible beasts. We also got a fair amount of feathered game: sand-grouse, wood-grouse, grey partridge, painted-partridge, quail & bush-quail: the latter when cooked little bigger than a sparrow! There were also a great many pea-fowl about, which when driven make excellent

---

16  Robert (Robin) Hamilton Dundas (1884–1960) was a tutor in Greek History at Christ Church from 1909, a position he held on and off for the next forty-six years. A familiar and idiosyncratic figure of Oxford, his life was posthumously immortalised in a biography by Roger Venables, *D: Portrait of a Don* (Basil Blackwell, 1967). He was distantly related to General Sir David Dundas, commander in chief of the British forces when my great-great-grandfather was in northern Germany in 1795 (see extracts from Thomas Birch's *Diary*, 3: 5).

17  The 1st Battalion of the 'Ox and Bucks' (formerly the 43rd Foot) had been based in India as part of the 6th (Poona) Division since 1903, when the latter was formed following the Kitchener reforms of the Indian Army after the Second Boer War.

'high pheasants', but nice and big so that even I hit the only one I had!

[…] On Xmas night we had an even bigger fire than usual of blazing logs & a pea-cock instead of turkey (and quite as good): of course Uncle Law had brought out mince-pies & plum-pudding. We drank your healths and thought of you all at home & wished that you could either be with us or we at home with you!

On the last day I might have had a panther & I haven't yet got over my disgust at having missed such a chance: he was seen by the beaters standing about two yards behind me watching me. I thought I heard a slight crackle but didn't dare turn round for fear of frightening something in front — so the old panther offed it safely. […]

[…] Uncle Frank has written and asked me to go up to Simla in the hot-weather [*season*] if I can get leave — but that I'm afraid is v. doubtful.

Just before I went to Saugor Uncle Law sent me a cheque for, if you please, £50! Of course I returned it with many thanks & said I couldn't possibly accept such a huge tip. He is the kindest uncle in the world — not just because he's given me £50, tho' you don't meet that kind every day — but being with him a bit one sees & notices in everything he does what a wonderfully good man he is in the best sense of the word. It does one more good to be one day with him than to spend several hours in church! I was too young to realize this when I was last with him yachting.

I'm going to be left here when others go on manoeuvres — it will be a bit 'lonesome' but I've got plenty of work: besides learning my job I'm in for the A Exam., (one's first for promotion) and also for the Lower Standard Hindustani. This last is voluntary & not necessary, but if one does get a job such as A.D.C. etc one gets 250 R [*rupees*] extra per month if one has passed it — not so dusty. I shall also have time too, I hope, to learn to hit the elusive polo-ball. I've just invested in a pony — an Arab 14.1 [*hands*], grey & a top-hole player who knows a good deal more about the game than I shall for several years to come! He cost 1200 R (£80) which sounds a lot for a 10 year old pony but […] this pony is well known & belongs to a fellow in the Regiment who is going home & gave the same price for him three months ago — so I'm not being 'stuck'. […]

Ever your loving<br>
HENRY

P.S. Please let me know all about Grandmamma & how she is in your next[18].

---

18  A letter to Henry from his mother Violet Birch Reynardson (née Maxwell), dated 11 February 1914, apologises for her lateness in sending greetings for his twenty-second birthday as his grandmother had died a few days earlier, having been ill with influenza and double pneumonia.

\* \* \*

*My father had been in India for less than a year when the events which led to the outbreak of the First World War escalated swiftly during June and July 1914. Although the general news, thanks to telegraph and long-distance telephones, travelled much faster than in the days of his great-grandfather (the General) or his great-uncle Edward, letters from home still took several weeks to arrive and so it was the end of August 1914 before Henry received any personal letters from friends or family giving their reactions to this unexpected and cataclysmic development. The earliest letter to reach him was from the man described by my father as 'my great friend at Oxford'[19]. Robert Cornwallis Maude (1890–1914) had succeeded to the title of sixth Viscount Hawarden on the death of his father in 1908, the year he also went up to Oxford. As an undergraduate, he had been a member of the University Contingent of the Officers' Training Corps and so, as a commissioned officer in the Guards, he was one of the first to be mobilised as part of the British Expeditionary Force even before the declaration of war on 4 August 1914. He joined the 3rd Battalion, Coldstream Guards with the rank of Lieutenant and must also have been one of the earliest British casualties of the war; his battalion was involved in the two-day Battle of Mons[20] in Belgium, before withdrawing just over the French border on 25 August to Landrecies, where a subsidiary action took place during which Hawarden received his fatal injuries. By the time Henry received his first letter therefore, his friend had already been dead for two days.*

**LETTER 10: 6 (Lieutenant Viscount Hawarden, Coldstream Guards, to Lieutenant Henry Birch Reynardson, dated 2 August 1914)**

<u>Bank of England</u>
Sunday night, 2nd August

Dearest old Henry

I am here on guard, and I expect it will be the last guard I do for a considerable time. We have not been ordered to mobilize yet, but the order will probably come late tonight or at the latest early tomorrow morning. Really it is a ghastly state of affairs, Henry. A week ago no-one would have dreamt that a war was

---

[19] When I was born nine years later, I was given the second name of Robert in memory of my father's friend. My third name, Ashley, was in honour of my mother's brother, who was also killed in action, on 8 September 1915.
[20] The first battle of the First World War between the British and German armies, fought on 23 and 24 August.

ever possible for England, and now it is absolutely inevitable.

The extraordinary thing is that there is no news. Germany has certainly crossed Luxembourg, and is advancing into France. The special editions, which have been coming out all day, report a German defeat by France, and also a Russian invasion of Germany, but no-one knows anything.

As we are part of the expeditionary force, we shall be the first for it.

Henry, I make a confession to you that I could make to no-one else. I am a coward right through, and I am fearfully afraid of playing the [*word illegible*]; and showing the white feather one way or other. I ought never to have gone into the army. I am not good enough for it. I have the power of bearing calamities pretty philosophically, I think, but when it comes to a pinch, where pluck is wanted on the spur of the moment, I am absolutely hopeless. I have no gallantry at all. And, mind you, it wants a certain amount of pluck to lead a bayonet charge when you have had no food or sleep for 3 days and have got a perfectly damnable chill on the liver, as well.

I think the world has gone mad. It destroys all one's ideas on the stability of things. One can't get any money now you know. No club will cash a cheque for you nowadays. I tried two today. And all this within a week, merely because of a bicker between Servia[21] [*sic*] and Austria. We truly live in stirring times.

If I do play the [*word crossed out and 'coward' substituted in HBR's writing*] you will never see me again, I promise that. It is appalling to think how easy it is for anyone to lose their nerve for a moment. I suppose you will be 'for it' too, in time. I fancy such a colossal show as this must be about over before you can arrive, though.

Well, dear old Henry, this is just to let you know that you are my dearest friend and to wish you the best of luck. You have been more to me than I can ever say.

Well — good-bye
Yours always
Robert

---

21  This spelling, taken from the Greek language, was then sometimes used in relation to Serbia, the Serbs or the Serbian language and should not be confused with the town in N.W. Greece.

## Letter 10: 7 (Lieutenant Viscount Hawarden, France, to Lieutenant Henry Birch Reynardson, dated 18 August 1914)

France August 18th

My dear Henry

I am not allowed to tell you where we are, for fear of the letter getting into the wrong hands. Suffice it to say that we are at present out of the war area, and billeted extraordinarily comfortably in a French village. We and the 2nd Grenadiers are here, while the Irish Guards and our 2nd Battalion are at another village about 3 miles away. They say we shall be here for another week. The French people are giving us a perfectly wonderful reception. The fat of the land is being showered upon us. 'Vivre l'Angleterre' and 'À Berlin' everywhere. The people we are billeted on press coffee & omelettes etc upon us & [*written in pencil from this point onwards*] a great many of them refuse to accept payment. And yet they are making a good thing out of the soldiers, though they are very very honest, and obliging, & will take English money on your word as to what it is worth in their own. It is really awfully like some English country — rather like East Kent, very open and practically entirely arable.

There is a rumour that we may be moved tomorrow, but the general idea is that we shall be here for another week. I had my second anti-typhoid injection, but this time it has hardly affected me at all. The first one in London made me ill for about 3 days. The men have all been done. Most of them have had the two doses in one.

We had a most awful journey from our base — 20 hours in the train — the men sometimes 50 per cattle-truck, — the maximum being supposed to be 40. We got to it in a tremendous thunderstorm and on the way succeeded in losing 3 of our 4 G. S. [*General Service*] Waggons, all the officers' kits being on them. One waggon broke down and the Transport Sergeant told the others to follow the column, but in the darkness they followed another column by mistake, and we left without them. That was now 5 days ago and they have not arrived yet, though we have heard they are on the train. Luckily we could buy spare things at the local shop (soap etc), so we have not missed them like we should have if we had to sleep in the open.

Yours always<br>
<u>Robert</u>

Suppose you are for this too, good luck.

**Letter 10: 8 (copied extract from a letter written by Lt.-Colonel Percy Johnston, C.M.G., Mersey Coast Defences, written 17 October 1915 but referring to events which took place in August 1914)**

Oct. 17th 1915

I met tonight Major Furness, R.A.M.C. [*Royal Army Medical Corps*], who is in charge of the hospital ship 'Lanfranc', sailing tomorrow. He has been for many months a Prisoner of War in Germany. He was taken prisoner at Landrecies, where he was one of the Medical Officers. On the night of the Attack he met Hawarden walking along by himself looking as if he would fall at any minute. Furness stopped him & asked him if he was wounded & offered to put him on a stretcher, but Hawarden said 'No, there are others worse than I am.' However Furness seeing how unfit he was to move, put him on a stretcher & took him to the place used as a hospital & examined him. He found his left arm shattered by a shell which had gone across the body, taking the knife which Hawarden had in his left breast pocket. The blade & corkscrew were sticking in his arm. Furness had to amputate the arm, & then found that the right shoulder blade and part of three ribs had been shot away. The shock of these terrible wounds was too much, & Hawarden succumbed. He is buried at Landrecies cemetery in the same grave as young Windsor-Clive (son of Lord Plymouth), and Major Furness had a cross put over each.

Major Furness has the greatest admiration for Hawarden on account of the wonderful pluck & unselfishness he showed when so frightfully wounded — when he was carried along he said 'I am an awful rotter giving you so much trouble'.

Major Furness gave a terrible account of what the wounded Prisoners suffered through the brutal & diabolical treatment by the Germans. He says he has told the story of Hawarden's unselfishness & courage a score of times — to show how an English officer & a gentleman can behave.

**Letter 10: 9 (Lieutenant Henry T. Birch Reynardson, Ahmednagar, to his parents, William and Violet Birch Reynardson, Adwell, dated 28 August 1914)**

Ahmednaga  August 28 (1914)

My dearest Mother & Father,
   No mail last week but we expect one or perhaps two tomorrow: it ought to be a particularly interesting one as you'll have written just after war broke out — I am anxious to hear from those on the spot how people took it.
   We have been getting a fair amount of news last week & our latest concerns our Expeditionary Force round Mons last Sunday when our papers say they fought all day & did very well — but of course we have no details, except roughly as to the number of casualties which considering the fighting I suppose aren't anything out of the way. It is perfectly beastly being here out of it all & feeling one's doing no good & hearing really practically nothing. I suppose our turn will come, but not for a long time.
   Several more prisoners have arrived — in fact they come in every day now — & Davenport, who is looking after them, has plenty of work. Some of them have been pretty insubordinate & refused to do their tasks etc & have, I think, been treated <u>far</u> too leniently — why are we always so absurdly soft-hearted to our enemies? I don't think we shall find them suffering from the same fault!
   It's quite extraordinary how keen all the men have become even in their ordinary work […]. The men are mad keen to get to Europe & have a go. […]

<u>Friday</u>
Your letters dated Aug. 7th have arrived & […] I had a letter from Bob[22] dated Aug. 2: he said they were on the point of mobilization & were going with the Expeditionary Force — so he's in it all right by now — I hope to goodness he is all right […]. We heard a rumour today that two line regiments and one 'crack Cavalry Regt' — further rumour says 'The Greys' — rather got the knock at Mons last Sunday. […]
   Poor old Iola with Sam[23] gone off to his Yeomanry: but they're sure, anyhow at present, to keep them for internal defence & not ship him off to Belgium — there's no need for it anyhow yet.

22  Henry's friend Robert, Lord Hawarden (**10: 6**).
23  Henry's sister Violet (my Aunt Iola) had married Samuel Edgar Ashton in 1911.

I'm quite sure the Germans are going to get the biggest knock anyone has ever had: but it's no use thinking it's all going to be over in 3 months — it'll be far nearer 3 years before things are quiet again: and of course the Allies are not going to have it <u>all</u> their own way. It's simply a question of whether the Russians can hold the Austrians while they make a dash at Berlin. How queer it seems talking of the 'Allies' in Belgium again — just the same as 100 years ago.

Goodbye now dear Father & Mother — best love<br>
HENRY

---

*My father had hoped that his regiment would be recalled from India and sent to fight on the Western Front, but after another theatre of war opened in the Middle East[24] against the Ottoman Empire (which was allied with Germany) in the autumn, his battalion was moved to Mesopotamia (present-day Iraq) at the end of November 1914. Mesopotamia was defended at first by only one division of the Turkish (Ottoman) Army, much of the rest of its military resources at the time being occupied in Gallipoli, the Caucasus and Palestine, which were seen as taking higher priority. The Indian Expeditionary Force, consisting of the reinforced 6th (Poona) Division of the British Indian Army, scored some early successes against inferior numbers, notably at Qurna in December, helping to secure the city of Basra and the oil fields at Abadan, and only sporadic attempts such as the one described below* **(10: 10)** *were made by the Turks to dislodge them.*

---

24 The Anglo-Persian Oil Company had exclusive rights to petroleum deposits throughout most of the Persian Empire and Britain was concerned to protect its supply of oil, especially for the Navy. The military force sent from India was intended initially to protect the oil refineries at Abadan, and also to uphold the prestige of the British Empire in India by maintaining good relations with Indian Muslims.

## Letter 10: 10 (Lieutenant Henry T. Birch Reynardson, Maserah on the Tigris, to unnamed recipient, dated 21 January 1915)

Maserah on the Tigris: Jan 21/15

We had quite a good little show yesterday against the Turks. The sniping had been getting a bit too thick so it was decided to go & give them a bit of a lesson, the main object being to drive them off some sandhills they were holding about 5 miles N. of this. […]

I will tell you roughly what happened. We assembled N of camp about 4.45 a.m. Very cold, pitch dark, threatening to rain. Half an hour of sort of strange shadow play & whispers. Bodies of men suddenly looming out of the darkness — a shuffle, whispered orders — a suppressed clatter, & one gradually made out that they were formed up next to one. Then perhaps a lantern would flash & there would be fevered whispers: 'Put out those lights; put out those lights'. Then a staff officer like a perturbed ghost: 'Who are you? Oh yes — no — certainly not — where are the Oxfords?' All in whispers. Everyone apparently quite lost! However after about ½ an hour the black mass shook & heaved itself into motion & off we went across the desert — […] Gradually as we shuffled along, the horizon to our right grew grey, & then grey-pink, & the desert along the same bit of horizon grew the same colour, […]. At ½ to 7 we heard the advance guard come under rifle fire & soon after we deployed: as the men swung out of the column into the long thin line of open order the sun came up with a rush above the horizon & immediately the desert became a sheet of gold. […]

Soon we were up to the sand dunes, which the enemy had left to take up a position rather on our left […] — we were on the right & a native Regiment deployed along the […] bank on our left. Then with a rumble & crash & clank our guns came up on our left, swung round, unlimbered, & the teams galloped back — all splendidly quick & in a moment whop! went the guns & s-s-s-h went the shells. Then from their main position some 1¾ miles off came a flash & then a wallop! Just like a man shaking out a big blanket — then a drone, then scroop-scroop-scroop, then a third bang & a great cloud of earth — just 20 yards behind our guns […]. They had got guns too, & were starting in with percussion shell, […] [then] switched to shrapnel. […] They were shooting awfully well & got the exact range of our guns: they were bursting over them nearly every time but luckily rather too high. Then they let us have a few — one shell went plumb into the ground between two men of my Company who were luckily lying rather far apart — threw up a column of earth, covered them, knocked off their helmets & they both got up grinning! — absolutely untouched — it is wonderful what escapes there are — [...] We lay there for about an hour — very cold & absolutely in the open on the desert as flat as your hand. At last we got the order to advance — just as I had got my lot up & gone about 10 yards, a shell came over & burst just behind us knocking spots out of the ground on which we had been lying. So we were lucky. I have got a piece of it now.

We had then to advance across the marshes in front with our guns shooting over our heads [...] half way over [...] we got under rather a nasty enfilade fire from our left. But the men were of course quite splendid. My platoon just walked along splashing & laughing & imitating the whistle of the bullets & making funny remarks — they were A1! We [...] formed a firing line & pumped lead into them at about 900 yards. By this time our guns had set two villages on fire & knocked out, or at any rate silenced, 5 out of their six guns: [...] the retirement began soon after without our even being allowed to take their camp & see what damage we really had done — Everyone was rather sick at this — Except for a few shells from their one remaining gun [...] the retirement was uneventful & we got back [...] in time for a late lunch. So we had a very gentlemanly little battle! Our losses were 9 killed and 60 wounded — 3 rather badly but the rest nothing much. If their shells had been better & their rifle fire more accurate we should have lost a good deal more I think —

Stevens who was A.D.C. to H.E. has a letter from Uncle Frank saying that our chances of going to Europe are practically Nil — it is a gloomy look-out, is it not? — But he says that the Turks have practically given up the idea of invading Egypt & are very likely to come down & try to round us up. We are ready for them.

———————————————

*At the Battle of Shaiba in April 1915* (**Fig. 10 d**)), *the British met much stiffer opposition from a larger Ottoman army augmented by irregular Arabs and Kurds, which was attempting to retake the city of Basra. Three days (12–14 April) of hard infantry fighting, in which — to their disappointment — Henry's regiment did not take part, succeeded in forcing the Ottoman retreat, although there were heavy losses on both sides. As Henry predicted correctly* (**10: 11**), *Arab allegiance to the Turkish army wavered as a result of this battle and later revolts broke out against their Ottoman rulers.*

SURVIVORS

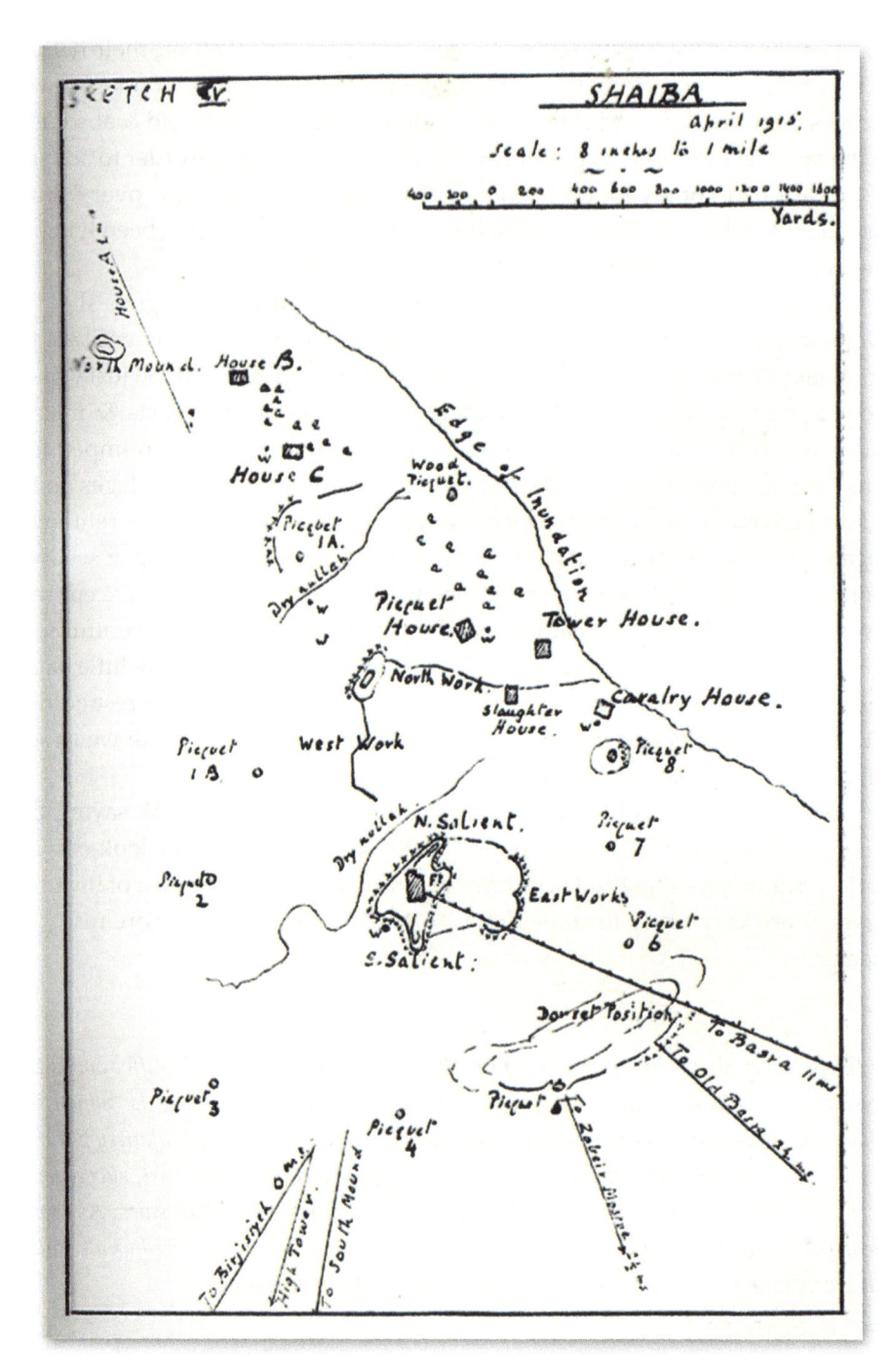

**Fig. 10 d)** Hand-drawn map by Henry T. Birch Reynardson, showing the action at Shaiba, April 1915. From *Mesopotamia 1914–15*, by Captain H. Birch Reynardson (published 1919).

**Letter 10: 11 (Lieutenant Henry Birch Reynardson, Qurna, to his father, William Birch Reynardson, Adwell, dated 20 April 1915)**

Kurnah [Qurna]   April 20   1915

My dear Father

There has been great activity below, this week, at Shaibah [Shaiba]. A big battle in which the Turks got a tremendous rattling and got on the run — they were properly whacked, but at a certain loss to our troops. Of course I need hardly say we were out of it — [...] we're all too sick to talk of it. After one or two small affairs it was made certain that a large Turkish force was about Shaibah & on the 16th a force under General Mellis moved out to attack it. Two Infantry Brigades, one Cavalry Brigade & 3 Batteries, i.e. 18 guns.

The Turks were in a strong position, beautifully entrenched by their German 'advisors' and numbered with Arabs about 23,000 and 30 guns — very long odds. We had to advance over desert — [...] not a scrap of cover & their trenches so well sited that they couldn't be seen 100 yards off: & to top all these was an awful mirage – tho' probably that cut both ways.

They say the Turks shot wonderfully well — tho' whether this referred to their rifle-fire or guns I don't know — probably their guns.

We know no details even yet: but we took the position — it was a really splendid feat, a force of probably under 8,000 attacking a force of 23,000[25] in a prepared position & with more guns & an uninterrupted field of fire.

The Turks stuck it till the last & we had to go in with the bayonet to clear them: then they ran — & as far as we know are still running, as next morning they were out of sight & had evacuated Nokalla — [...]

Our losses were very heavy, 1,276 out of 8,000 — more than 1 in 8. I'm afraid the poor Dorsets[26] got it in the neck again: I know their Colonel & his Adjutant were both killed. [...]

A Turkish officer taken said that they were all utterly dumbfounded at the way our chaps came on — he said 'Why, in the Balkan war it would have taken the Bulgarians three days to make any impression on such a position.' The Turks have a very poor idea of our Indian troops.

---

25  The official (approximate) figures were just over 6,000 (British and British Indian armies) to 18,000 (Ottoman Empire).
26  The 2nd Dorsetshire Regiment, which led the bayonet charge. The other British regiment involved was the 104th Wellesley's Rifles, and the two Indian army regiments were the 7th Hariana Lancers and the 24th Punjabis.

Well, what will happen now we don't know: this was evidently the Turks' big effort to turn us out as they attacked there & at Ahwaz & here — whether they have the guts to try again I don't know. But one thing is quite certain & that is that the Arabs will be very much affected by this — Even before this engagement they were pretty rocky and would not fight for the Turks without payment (& then often 'downed tools' for a rise, we heard) so there cannot be any very acute religious feeling about it. [...]

The parcel from the [Army & Navy] Stores has not yet arrived but no doubt will next mail — the insect powder will be most useful, as fleas are awful here – everyone is a 'mask' of them. [...] I've had a little fever lately, not at all bad tho' & it's gone now: also boils of a kind known as 'Baghdad Boils' but they are getting better & I shall soon be fit. [...]

---

*After the unexpected victory at Shaiba, a change in strategy was put in place by the British high command. Major-General Townshend, commanding the 6th (Poona) Division, was ordered to advance north towards Kut-al-Amara; it was slow progress, as the Tigris was in its seasonal flood and the surrounding land (normally desert) could only be navigated by flat-bottomed boats* (**10: 12**), *and Townshend's army was attacked several times by Ottoman forces trying unsuccessfully to thwart its advance. Amara, a small garrison town on the Tigris, fell in June, as my father reported* 'without a shot', *followed three months later by the greater prize of Kut-al-Amara.*

---

**LETTER 10: 12 (Lieutenant Henry Birch Reynardson, Ezra's Tomb, to his family, at Adwell, dated 4 June 1915)**

Ezra's Tomb   4 June 1915

My Dearest Family

I suppose I must begin at the beginning to tell you all about it.

[...] About the 20th of last month we heard definitely that we had to force [*the Turks*'] positions & go on to Amara: & of course the only way was obviously by boat. Bellums — big heavy canoe-shaped local boats — were sent off & the 'Bellum Squadron', which before had been rather a farce, began to be taken very seriously & there was a tremendous lot of hard work to be done — in fact a month's work had to be got thro' in a week. Morland, of the Regiment, was Brigade Bellum officer & I ran the Regimental Bellums: but without his help I should have been hopeless.

As the day approached the river gradually became filled with steamers & barges mounting heavy guns & it was evident that we were to be helped by a tremendous bombardment. Several of the bellums were provided with steel shields & also machine guns & mounted guns on rafts made by joining two boats together: 2 aeroplanes had also arrived & all our gunboats.

On Saturday night we knew for certain that Monday 31st, 5 a.m. was to see the opening of the ball. [...] Morland [...] had to command his Company & I was taken as Orderly Officer to O.C. Brigade.

Now you know how the land lay & as far as the battle is concerned, I think if I copy out my diary & explain where necessary, it will be the easiest way. [...]

Sunday May 30
[...] Pow-wow at 11, orders etc. At 7.15 p.m. all complete — I am to start tomorrow at 4.30 to flag the course (The route from Kurnah to position of assembly had to be 'flagged' as there were some shallows on the marshes) & report to General [sic] Climo[27].

Monday May 31st
Had flags out by 4.45. Bombardment started at 5, just as sun rose over palms. Bert's (Thompson's) Howitzers led off — 4 lovely lyddites[28] onto Norfolk Hill[29]. Their rifle fire started 6 a.m., gun-fire very erratic at 6.30. Aeroplane appeared 6.15. [...] Our guns firing terrifically — no one can be alive on Norfolk.

They are still on Norfolk now — 7 a.m. — have opened heavy rifle fire on our boats coming in from west: think they have an M.G. [*machine gun*] too. Norfolk taken 7.15 — dear Mike killed: 3 men of my platoon wounded [...].

Tower Hill taken 8 a.m. [...] one gun captured complete [...].

---

27 Lieutenant-Colonel (not General) Climo (1868–1937) came to Mesopotamia in March 1915 as commander of the 24th Punjabis, and was temporarily seconded to command the 17th Brigade in May during the attack aboard boats up the River Tigris which resulted in the capture of Amara. He was promoted to Colonel on 3 June, and also held positions of command when Kut-al-Amara was taken in September 1915 and in the advance to Baghdad, but left Mesopotamia after being badly wounded in November 1915.
28 A form of high explosive composed of molten and cast picric acid, lyddite was much used in shells during the Boer War and First World War.
29 The most southerly of seven main Turkish positions. The rest, from south to north, were Tower Hill; Gun Hill; Bahran; Ratta; Mazeeblah; and Socretia, all except Ratta being on the right bank of the Tigris. On the first day of the bombardment, the objective was to take Norfolk and Tower Hills.

During this I was away on left carrying messages for the General [*Lt.-Colonel Climo*] [...] Took it 11.45 — poor resistance — white flag. 130 prisoners, 1 Turk, 1 Kurd officer, 2 guns (— breech blocks), much gun & rifle ammunition [...]. Miles of Cable evidently connected to mines — tried to cut it but couldn't. [...] back with Regiment at Tower Hill at 4.30 — there they have found another mine control station in charge of officer & 6 men: all connections complete but evidently so stupefied by shelling that they never touched them off. [...]

June 1st
[...] from 5 a.m. bombardment of Bahran very heavy — whole place hidden by dust & lyddite [...] At 8.45 we landed on Bahran & found the place evacuated. They had got their 4 guns away [...]. At 9.15 came a message from [...] Div. H.Q. to say whole Turkish Position [...] cleared out. At 10 Gun boats came up, followed by Transports with [...] Brigade. At 2, Gun boats pushed on & by 3 were past the obstruction (made by Turks in River) & going hard. [...] All afternoon I was on the job for the General — he is a topper [...].

The rest I can tell you better without my diary. That night we embarked & put off next morning at 4 a.m. for Ezra's Tomb. We were frightfully closely packed & the heat was such as I never want to experience again. 11 men went down with heat-stroke. However after two days of rushing about in the sun we were all so beat that we slept.

The next day at 4 we landed at Ezra's Tomb & took up our quarters in the ruined caravanserai attached — where at least there is some shade. We learned that our victory, thanks to the Navy, had been complete: they had pushed on by moonlight & gone full split after the Turks, caught them all except one ship: sunk their 700-ton gunboat at 7,500 yards! & two other smaller gunboats, captured a big river-steamer & the 4 guns from Bahran, 400 prisoners besides many killed & drowned: a whole barge-ful of huge mines & dynamite & tremendous quantities of arms & ammunition.

Today we hear Amara, our objective, has fallen without a shot — 30 officers & 900 men. This show has simply terrified them out of their wits. — it was Neuve Chapelle[30] on a tiny scale but the actual bombardments just as effective, 40 guns instead of 400 but all concentrated on these small island-positions. I can't describe

---

30  A battle fought between 10 and 13 March, 1915, in the Artois region of France, Neuve Chapelle was seen as a tactical British victory but an operational and strategic failure. It is not clear why my father equated the successful taking of Amara with Neuve Chapelle: perhaps he was comparing the relative contributions of the Indian Corps, which provided half the attacking force in the French battle and were conspicuous for their bravery.

what Norfolk Hill was like when Bertie T[hompson]'s big howitzers had finished with it — it was too ghastly. [...]

There is no doubt from a letter written by a German & captured at Bahran that it was a complete surprise: they never knew of our big guns & thought our bellums were being prepared for a retreat, not an attack.

[...] I am sitting on the flat roof with my back against the dome — a gorgeous thing of glazed tiles, which changes with every shadow from sea green to peacock blue — every imaginable shade. [...]

> Goodbye for present.
> HENRY

---

*The period of inactivity which followed the taking of Kut-al-Amara in September extended into the autumn, enabling Henry to take some leave to go back south to Basra for some dental work. By October Townshend received instructions from the War Office to push a hundred miles further on to Baghdad and attempt to seize the capital.*[31] *My father's account of the otherwise uneventful march north also contains the ominous information that 'the remains of the Turks' (believed to be a smallish force) were known to be encamped at Ctesiphon, sixteen miles south-east of Baghdad, 'with an advance position watching us'.*

---

**LETTER 10: 13 (Lieutenant Henry Birch Reynardson, on the Tigris on the way to Basra, dated 17 October 1915)**

Oct. 17th 1915

[...] I wrote last from Kut el Amara which we reached after a horrible week cleaning up round the Battle field — we had hoped for a rest of some time there as it was not a bad place with plenty of trees & a good camp — however we only had about 3 days there and then our Brigade got orders to follow the other 2 up [*towards Baghdad*] — we took it easy the first day and only did 10 miles. [...] it

---

31  There seems to have been some dissent over the advisability of this move. General Sir Archibald Murray (at the time Chief of the Imperial General Staff) and Townshend himself thought the advance was logistically unwise, but were over-ruled by Kitchener (Secretary of State for War).

was rather a nasty shock to hear that evening that we had to press on as far as we could & were to do 20 miles the next day & 22 the day after — we started off at 5.30 a.m. in the dark — terrible trouble with our transport which was almost entirely camel and local donkeys as we were marching light. [...] [*By the end of that day*] we made out that we had marched 25 miles and were told that we had 23 to do the next day, 17 of them without water — but we were too fagged to worry.

We got off next morning about 7 & watered after we had gone about 4 miles. After that we were told that we should not see water again until night [...] We halted near a big Arab camp & the cooks just had time to make tea for the men & us, which I think saved all our lives. [...]

This camp was the first Bedouin one we have met — [...] I went & asked a man what his tribe was and he said 'Shammar', which is the big Bedouin tribe of Mesopotamia. We got about one and a half hours' halt here, [...] practically a repetition of the day before except that at about 5.30 a convoy met us with water & carts for the sick, which helped a lot. [...] At last we got in at about 8 and having filled ourselves with Bully beef and biscuit & tinned pineapple & hot tea [...] we rolled up in blankets & slept like logs. We all looked like scarecrows next morning, covered with dust from head to foot. We couldn't wash until our ship turned up with all our kit.

In the end there seemed no pressing need for us. The camp is on the river bank about 45–50 miles below Baghdad. Not a tree, even a palm, for miles & terrible dust — and there at present we are to [...] 'make ourselves comfortable'. The remains of the Turks are entrenched by the ruins of Ctesiphon, some 25 miles from Baghdad, with an advance position watching us. — However we were told that there was nothing doing, so I put in for leave to Basra to get my teeth looked to. So here I am about half way on my journey some 400 miles by river. It's nice to look at the bank and to think that a month ago we were foot-slogging along it. The river is very low & boats find great difficulty in getting up — we have been aground constantly today but bumped off successfully.

---

*My father's next letter must have come as both a shock and a relief to his family (who had been notified by cable that he had been wounded at the Battle of Ctesiphon), as it was written not from Mesopotamia but from the military hospital in Bombay, where he arrived almost three weeks later after an agonisingly protracted journey. The 6th*

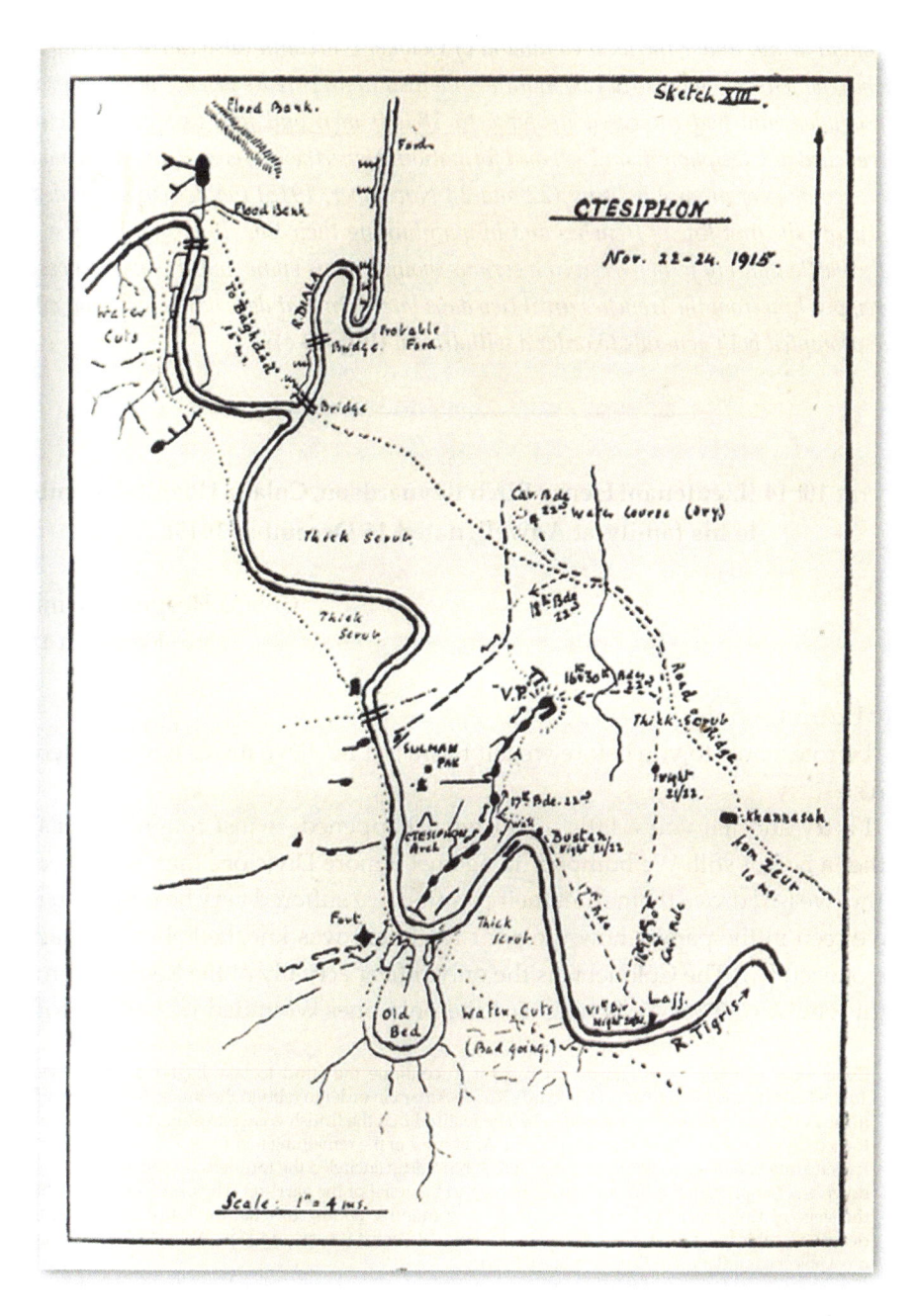

**Fig. 10 e)** Hand-drawn map by Henry T. Birch Reynardson, showing the action at Ctesiphon, 22–24 November 1915. From *Mesopotamia 1914–15,* by Captain H. Birch Reynardson (published 1919).

(Poona) Division, with 11,000 men and two warships, was greatly outnumbered by the Ottoman army, under the local command of Colonel Nureddin (also called Nur-ud Din Pasha), which had had nearly two months in which to prepare its defence of the approach to Baghdad and had increased its force to 18,000 men and fifty-two guns, securely entrenched at Ctesiphon in an L-shaped formation. Nevertheless, even against such odds, over two days of intense fighting (22 and 23 November, 1915) the British succeeded in capturing the first line of trenches and in maintaining their line. It was on the first day of the battle that my father received a serious wound to his spine, but it was not possible to remove him from the trenches until two days later. On that day, heavy losses on either side prompted both generals to order a withdrawal (**Fig. 10 e**))[32].

---

### LETTER 10: 14 (Lieutenant Henry Birch Reynardson, Colaba Hospital, Bombay, to his family, at Adwell, dated 15 December 1915)

Colaba Hospital Bombay
Dec. 15th 1915

My Dearest Family

I wrote a note to you before we left Basra but I believe it was never posted — I'm so sorry.

I'll try and tell you a little about what happened — just roughly as it's all rather a horror still. We bumped up against 2 more Divisions than we expected & tho' we [...] drove them from their position, we suffered very heavily. You will have seen in the papers how the poor Regiment was knocked about — hardly anyone left [...] The Colonel was the only officer actually of the Regiment in the fight who wasn't hit. Foljambe[33] & I the only ones wounded [...] all the killed

---

[32] Concluding that his losses had been too great to continue the effort to take Baghdad, Major-General Townshend decided to retreat back towards Kut-al-Amara in order to rebuild the strength of his army. This turned out to be a disastrous decision: when he realised that the British were retreating, Colonel Nureddin turned his army around and sent it in pursuit. After most of the remaining members of the depleted British-Indian army had taken temporary refuge in Kut, Nureddin encircled the fortified city and sent other forces down river to prevent the British from marching to the relief of the garrison. Thus, on 7 December, began the siege of Kut which was to last for nearly five months, ending in what the historian James Morris described in his book *Farewell the Trumpets: An Imperial Retreat* (Helen and Kurt Wolff Books, 1978) as 'the most abject capitulation in British military history'.

[33] Brevet Major the Hon. Jocelyne Foljambe, son of the Earl of Liverpool. Foljambe's injuries must have been less severe than my father's, as — unluckily for him — he returned to the fray in time to take part in the First Battle of Kut in April 1916, one of a number of failed attempts to relieve the siege of Kut-al-Amara. Foljambe was killed on the second day of the action and three weeks later, Townshend surrendered unconditionally.

except one were our own fellows. I believe about 160 men were left at the end of the fight — & we went over 600 strong, so you can guess what it was like.

[…] I was bringing up my M.Gs [*machine guns*] by hand when I found John Courtis very badly hit: he had been carrying a message from the General [*Townshend*] to the Colonel & I had to take it from him.

I at last found some of the Regiment in a small ditch […] but couldn't find the Colonel or any senior officer. I found poor Kearsley there hit thro' the head but still alive, tho' luckily unconscious — & the remains of 'Q' & 'R' companies, so as the message was by this time unimportant, I took over command. The ditch was nearly full of water & the job was to keep one's head below the top of the bank — & above water! I was trying to get ammunition collected […] when I was hit. A man shouted 'Keep your head down, sir' — I suppose I ducked my head & forgot the rest for I felt a most awful smash on the back & was rolled over into the water. […] I thought I was done for as it had seemed to hit me bang in the spine. We lay there in the water, frightfully cold, for one and a half hours until the redoubt was taken — then they hauled Kearsley out & then me.

We were moved that night into a trench a little way back. In the night Kearsley died — such a good plucky fellow — I am so glad he was unconscious the whole time & can never have felt anything. The next day they dressed me roughly & put me back in the trench. That night the Turks counter-attacked & we had to be left — six of us whom they couldn't move. The Padre & I think a doctor stayed with us — it was beastly as the shrapnel bullets were falling in the trench & the rifle bullets whistling over & we couldn't do anything or get away. The Padre was perfectly splendid. I'll never forget him. They got within 300 yards of us & then the attack failed & they retired — thank God. We had very little water & no food except some tinned milk.

The next morning they did move us — it was very unpleasant. We had to go 8 miles over very rough desert on […] iron carts with iron frame bottoms & no springs — you can imagine what it was like — or rather, I don't expect you can!

We got onto a ship at last — & got to Kut — beyond Kut we were attacked by Arabs […] & had to return to Kut twice before we finally got thro' — it was all pretty beastly. […]

We got to Basra at last on the 7th of Dec. […] & onto the Hospital ship — where there were nurses & food one could eat & beds — simply Paradise.

We got here the night before last. It's very nice & comfortable, tho' rather strict & proper & hospital-ly — & the nurses go about with long faces instead of being jolly & cheery like the ones on the ship.

And yet I haven't told you where I'm hit! I had a wonderful escape — the bullet actually did hit my spine & took away a bit of bone but glanced off, & I'm perfectly all right. I've still got a large hole in my back which has to have a tube put in & taken out every day — which is unpleasant. But I'm getting on like fun & can now with much puffing & groaning pull myself more or less into a sitting position — which is a tremendous improvement. I don't know at all how long I shall be — one doctor (but I think he was a pessimist) said 6 months [...]

Possibly, just possibly they may send me home! Just think of it. Dobbs[34] [...] came & saw me at Kut & said he would cable to his mother who would let you know. I also cabled at Amarah, so I hope you heard all right. I have written to Di[35] of course & cabled her to write here [...] — but I've had no letters for over a month and I can't tell you how I long for a mail. I suppose some nerves have been rattled up [...] my nerve at present is gone & I hate talking & writing about it. The last two nights have been the first that I haven't dreamt it all over again [...] we really did have a pretty bad time that seemed as if it would never end.

I am so anxious to hear how you all are at Home & what your news is — only one's positively frightened of news these days. [...]

### Letter 10: 15 (Lieutenant Henry Birch Reynardson, Colaba Hospital, Bombay, to his father, William Birch Reynardson, Adwell, dated January 1916)

Colaba Hospital   Bombay

My dear Father,

I must write you a line 'on your own' this week and tell you how I'm getting on. My wounds — or rather wound, as one hole has practically healed, is all it should be — very clean & healthy. They still ram in gauze pipes about 3 inches or more, so there is a fair hole still [...] I grew an abscess on my spine but they managed to scotch that pretty quick: however that, I believe, is the cause of the deep hole, which has to be kept open until it heals from the bottom. Anyhow things are going on A 1 now. They can't decide definitely whether they will send me home or not: I've never wanted anything so much but I'm afraid my chances are small. [...]

[...] We had rather a dreary Christmas: all in this ward who could walk,

---

34  Henry (later Sir Henry) Dobbs (1871–1934), an Indian civil servant who served as High Commissioner to the Kingdom of Iraq from 1923 to 1929.
35  This is the first mention of my mother, Diana Ponsonby.

hobble or crawl were asked out and only 4 of us, quite hors de combat, stayed in. However, in the afternoon a lady & gent turned up to sing to us. As she was girt about with a much be-ribboned guitar I thought we were going to have a poor time. But quite otherwise. She — the lady — played and sang beautifully: I had no idea a guitar could produce [*such*] music. She sang Spanish & Italian songs, the former simply splendid — full of fire & dash. Then the man started in: […] without any accompaniment sang like nothing I've ever heard before — an Irish song & 'Annie Laurie'. By jove, it was worth hearing: it just seemed to flow out of him without any effort at all. […] They're coming again this afternoon & I'm looking forward to it like anything. I shall try & get him to sing some more Scotch songs.

It will still be a long time before I can hear from you as to how things are going at Adwell: do tell me — <u>not</u> about the war. […]

## Letter 10: 16 (Lieutenant Henry Birch Reynardson, Colaba Hospital, Bombay, to his parents, William and Violet Birch Reynardson, Adwell, dated 6 January 1916)

Jan 6th 1916
Colaba Hospital   Bombay

My dearest Mother & Father

I have just heard I'm really to come Home & almost certainly sail tomorrow. Also I've just got your letters written when Di was at Adwell — so you can imagine how happy I am. It seems everything has come together. I can't tell you how glad I am that now you both know Di and understand why I love her: it's what I've been longing for for so long — I <u>am</u> glad. […] Thank you so much for your letters — they made me about twice as well as I was before & last night I was told I looked 10 years younger! But I don't think I ever looked very aged!

I don't expect they'll let me come to Adwell at once as I shall be a crock — I've got 3 inches of hole in my back to fill up & I haven't tried to walk yet! — so I suppose it'll mean more hospital somewhere. I wish it could be Oxford — but it's just as likely to be the other end of England I suppose. […]

What a lot we shall have to talk of, shan't we? It seems almost too good to be true that I shall see you all again — perhaps even before this letter arrives. I never thought of that!

A large parcel of tinned meat & chocolate, also some flea-powder & 4 Shakespeares, have come back from the Gulf — for which many thanks. All except the books will be given to men of the Regiment in Hospital.

Goodbye now my dear Mother & Father — I shall see you in less than a month almost certainly! My best love to Iola.

>     Your loving
>     HENRY [...]

---

*This marked the end of my father's active service during the First World War. I do not think that he ever fully recovered from this tragic event. His return to England was followed by months of hospital treatment and he was still confined to a wheelchair when he married my mother, on 14 September 1917* (**Fig. 10 f**)). *His home-coming must also have been marred by the great losses his family had sustained; as well as his best friend and his fiancée's brother, both killed early on, his mother lost four of her brothers during the course of the war, including my father's beloved Uncle Frank (Maxwell), who was killed at Ypres on 21 September 1917, just a week after his nephew's wedding.*

*My father loved the Army and still hoped to make it his life-long career. During his long convalescence he wrote a much-praised account of the campaign in Mesopotamia up to the point at which he was wounded, which was published in 1919 and very soon became required reading for staff officers*[36] (**Fig. 10 g**)). *But he was bitterly disappointed when, after six years of 'office' jobs, his wound failed to respond to treatment and he was obliged to leave the Army in 1922. In recent years, however, I have come to feel that he had a lucky escape. If he had not been wounded when he was, it is likely that he would have retreated to Kut, along with most of what remained of the 6th (Poona) Division (apart from the cavalry, which managed to escape south before the garrison was fully encircled). Despite huge losses to sickness and starvation during the five-month siege, when the garrison surrendered unconditionally on 29 April 1916 there were still around 13,000 combatants of the British and Indian armies left to be taken prisoner by the Turks. Of these, about seventy per cent of the British and fifty per cent of the Indian troops died either of disease or at the hands of their Ottoman guards during their brutal captivity.*

---

36  *Mesopotamia 1914–15: Extracts from a Regimental Officer's Diary*, by Captain H. Birch Reynardson (Andrew Melrose Limited, London, 1919).

**Fig. 10 f)** Souvenir of the marriage of Captain Henry Birch Reynardson, L.I., to Miss Diana Ponsonby, at St Mark's, North Audley Street, London, on 14 September 1917.

**Fig. 10 g)** Sketch map of Mesopotamia, illustrating the operations of the Indian Expeditionary Force between November 1914 and December 1915. Hand-drawn by Henry T. Birch Reynardson. From *Mesopotamia 1914–15*, by Captain H. Birch Reynardson (published 1919).

CHAPTER 11

# The Inter-War Years

*Reminiscences 1918–1939*

'Do you want me to beat you with a cane or with this chair leg?'[1]

*By the end of the War, my parents settled into married life in a large house near Lancaster Gate, London. My two sisters, Cynthia (born 1918) and Rosamund (born 1920), spent their early years there, but although I was also born in London, on 7 December 1923, I have no recollection of the house as I was taken at a very tender age to Adwell, where the family (as well as Nanny Turner) was living at the time with my grandparents. My father, who had recently left the Army after his serious wound had failed to heal, was casting around for a job.*

*My memories of Adwell at this time are also rather hazy, as we left England for South Africa before I was three and although we came home on visits from time to time, the family did not return to England to live until 1933, when I was coming up to ten. My earliest memories are of South Africa, where we all went in 1926 as my father had been appointed as Secretary to the Governor-General, Lord Athlone*[2]. *We (the immediate family, which by this time included my brother Dickie* (**Fig. 11 a)**) *who was born shortly before our departure), together with Nanny Turner and Mrs Walker, our head housemaid) were allocated a charming house in the gardens of Westbrooke, Cape Town, where Government House was situated. My mother and father soon became friends with*

---

1  'Joc' Lynam, son of the headmaster of the Dragon School, Oxford.
2  The first Earl of Athlone (1874–1957) was born Prince Alexander of Teck, the son of Prince Francis, Duke of Teck, and his wife Princess Mary (a granddaughter of George III and cousin to Queen Victoria, popularly known as 'Fat Mary'). His sister was the future Queen Mary. The family had to relinquish their Germanic titles during the First World War in 1917, when King George V changed the name of the Royal Family from the House of Saxe-Coburg and Gotha to the more English House of Windsor, and the earldom of Athlone was created in the same year. In 1904 Alexander (or 'Alge' as he was nicknamed, taken from the first letters of two of his Christian names, Alexander and George) married his second cousin Princess Alice of Albany (see footnote 3). Lord Athlone served as Governor-General of South Africa between 1923 and 1930, and later, in succession to the popular Lord Tweedsmuir (the author John Buchan), as Governor-General of Canada between 1940 and 1946. During the war years, he proved to be instrumental in the Canadian war effort and was an invaluable host to British and American statesmen, including Churchill and President Roosevelt at the Quebec Conference in 1943, with whom he and the Canadian Prime Minister, Mackenzie King, discussed the Allied strategies which would eventually lead to victory over Nazi Germany and Japan.

**Fig. 11 a)** 'I put the smaller ones back!' My brother Dickie Birch Reynardson, c.1932.

**Fig. 11 b)** The dressing-up party arranged on board ship by the Prince of Wales. Photograph, 1930.

*the Athlones, particularly with Princess Alice[3] (King George V's cousin) who I remember loving very much.*

*A few years after our arrival I was enrolled in the junior school at Bishops, the well-known boys' school at Rondebosch, whence I rode every morning on my pony Joey accompanied by Solomon, our charming black groom. Soon after my arrival at Bishops I was taken by my fellow pupils (all of course white, but mostly South African-born) to a small hillock made of stones. I was instructed, firmly, to climb to the top of the hillock which I did with some hesitation. Once there, a large Union Jack was spread out below me. I was told, or rather ordered, to spit on it. Of course I refused to commit an act of such disloyalty. My 'friends' then started to throw stones at me when, most fortunately,*

---

3   Princess Alice (1883–1981) was the longest-lived Princess of the Blood Royal of the British Royal Family and the last surviving grandchild of Queen Victoria, her father being the Queen's youngest son Leopold. She had a double connection to the King and Queen, being first cousin to George V and sister-in-law to Queen Mary. As the wife of the Governor-General, she accompanied her husband to South Africa and then to Canada, where she also supported the war effort through her honorary commandships of women's branches of the Canadian navy and air force.

*the Headmaster Mr Charlton appeared on the scene. The boys ran off and I explained to Charlton what had happened. 'Ah yes,' he said, 'I'm afraid there is a lot of Nationalism around nowadays — they want independence from Great Britain.' (Lord Athlone was keenly aware of the republican aims of the ruling National Party and tactfully proposed a compromise by advancing a flag which was unique to South Africa but which still contained the Union Jack within it.)*

*It was this issue which particularly concerned my father and he quite often had to return to London to report to the Foreign Office, but also to the King. On one occasion, I think early in 1930, he was asked to accompany the Prince of Wales[4] to South Africa as a temporary equerry. The Prince didn't like my father because the latter was constantly trying to make him behave and not ogle the pretty girls on board, etc (the 'etc' covering quite a wide area of activity!). But he liked us children — and I became a particular pal (aged about six) of his. As the future King of England, I reckoned that he must have intimate knowledge of such matters as the locomotion of the ship, the position of the stars, the making of glass and other essential topics. As a result the Prince arranged for him and me to visit the ship's engine-room, to sit on the bridge at night to observe the stars through a telescope and to obtain saltpetre and sand in order to make glass in the ship's hospital, where there was a Bunsen burner. He also arranged for a dressing-up party for all the children on board* (**Fig. 11 b**)*.*

*But the incident which I remember particularly clearly occurred when the ship was about to dock at Cape Town. There we all were on deck as the ship slowly manoeuvred into the harbour, the Governor-General in full military dress with Princess Alice clearly visible standing on an elaborately decorated dais on the quayside. But where was the Prince? Nowhere to be seen. So my father hurried down to his cabin, accompanied by me (unbeknown to him). There was the Prince wearing a cream-coloured silk suit and a Botha hat. My father suggested that it was time for him to change. 'No, it's too hot for uniform.' My father explained that his uncle, the Governor-General, was waiting to welcome him in full dress (as was my father). There was quite an argument but, in the end, the Prince most unwillingly changed into uniform! He was, as a result, in a fearful sulk when he met the Athlones!*

*I am quoting here a letter from Lord Athlone, written just after he had retired from the position of Governor-General, in which he expresses clearly what my father meant to him.*

---

[4] The Prince of Wales (1894–1972), briefly King Edward VIII before his abdication in 1936, undertook on average one trip a year between 1919 and 1935 to various parts of the British Empire on behalf of his father. At the time of this visit to South Africa, the Prince — known by his last name of David to his family and friends — was the most photographed celebrity of the time, due to his rank, good looks and unmarried status.

LETTER 11: 1 (His Excellency the Right Honourable the Earl of Athlone, Salisbury, Rhodesia, to Lt. Colonel Henry Birch Reynardson, dated 16 December 1930)

SOUTH AFRICAN RAILWAYS
GOVERNOR-GENERAL'S TRAIN

Salisbury
Dec. 16<sup>th</sup> 1930

Dear Henry,

I can not sufficiently thank you for the wonderful help you have been to me during the last four years. Smith of course was good but his position made things difficult for him and he could not talk to people in the way a Secretary can. Your speeches have been an example of what a Gov. General's speeches should be, with just enough bite in them to make them worthy of being referred to in a leading article in the newspapers. At first my successor[5] must not criticize but feel his way gradually. He should be civil but not at any time to pander to the Dutch. I want him to see more of Natal than I did and he will have more time to go to out-districts including Vryheid[6], where I never was. I suggest he could do this after his month's stay in Durban. He must give the British a good 50-50 as a (de) Villiers! [...]

It was terribly sad parting from you all and all the way to Krugersdorp we were waving farewell.

Our love to you both and the children.
Yours very sincerely,
<u>Athlone</u>

---

5   George Herbert Hyde Villiers, sixth Earl of Clarendon (1877–1955), who succeeded Lord Athlone as Governor-General of South Africa from 1931 to 1937.
6   A coal-mining and cattle-ranching town in KwuZulu-Natal, South Africa, which had been nominated as the capital of the *Nieuwe Republiek* (New Republic) in 1884 by mercenaries in the aftermath of the Zulu War. 'Vryheid' is Afrikaans for 'freedom' or 'liberty'.

*After Lord Athlone retired, his place was taken by Lord Clarendon who my father served for another three years. When the time came for my father to return to England, he and my mother and sisters embarked on an epic journey from the Cape to Cairo, which resulted in my father's book* High Street Africa *(published in 1933). I was sent to stay with my governess (see* Chapter 12*) Helen Addison's sister and brother-in-law in Bechuanaland (now Zambia) and cannot resist including the only surviving letter from me at this time, written at the age of about eight, as it demonstrates that I showed my sporting prowess early! Evidently my father had asked specifically that I should not be allowed to fire the 12-bore gun in view of my small size.*

---

**Letter 11: 2 (William Robert Ashley Birch Reynardson, Clober Ranch, Bechuanaland, to his family, c.1933)**

Dear Family,

I am so exited [sic] I have just shot my first bird, a blue starling, but better still I shot a Toucan with a shot gun, I hope you don't mind Father but I couldn't help it if I had got it with the Daisy[7] it wouldn't of killed it but any how I got a frightful kick.

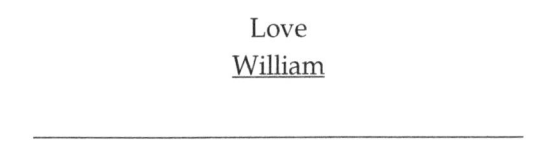

Love
William

---

*My grandparents were still in residence at Adwell, where we stayed on visits home to England* (**Fig. 11 c**)*. My grandfather was an outstanding shot. I well remember one occasion — I must have been about six, I suppose — when there was a shoot at Adwell. I was standing on the drive opposite Spring Covert when he joined me with, to my surprise, a small .410 gun (which I later had as my first gun — not the one with which I shot the toucan!). Suddenly a very high pheasant, which had been missed by a number of the guns, hurtled towards us. Up went the gun and down came the pheasant. He then turned on his heel, without comment, and returned to the house.*

*As we have already seen in* Chapter 9*, my grandfather's main occupation, especially in his later years, was his watercolour painting. He spent much of his time painting abroad,*

---

7   An inexpensive air gun using birdshot or 'BB' pellets.

**Fig. 11 c)** Dickie, William, Rosamund and Cynthia Birch Reynardson on Neddy, Adwell. Photograph, 1928.

*particularly in Egypt, France and Italy. Perhaps he wished to be away from his rather dull Scots wife! I'm not sure that he was a very nice man. Certainly his relationship with my father was distinctly distant and I don't remember many friends being entertained at Adwell. Staying there as a family was not much fun; my parents were always distinctly 'edgy' and found life extremely formal and lacking in affection. Once my brother Dickie and I invited my grandparents to tea in the garden house near the waterfall, preparing tea, sandwiches and scones for them with the help of our Nanny. Imagine our disappointment when, after all this work, we spied a procession coming across the lawn, headed by Mr Sones (the butler) and Walter (a footman) — both carrying tea, sandwiches and cakes on silver trays — followed by my grandparents, he in a tweed tailcoat and she in a blue chiffon dress!*

*Nevertheless I got on famously with my grandfather, much to the surprise of my parents. His headquarters was the Billiards room — the table was piled up with books and various kinds of chemical equipment. He did experiments. Some of them ended in near disasters. He <u>made</u> wirelesses including the various valves (out of electric light bulbs). He had a car (nobody else did). Once, when one of the farm workers came to him carrying his* *left index finger in his right hand (it had been caught in a mangle cutter), my grandfather stuck it back on and bound it with gutta-percha (a strange rubber substance) and it <u>worked</u>. Of course I thought him a miracle worker!*

*My father returned to England in 1933 to find half the Adwell estate sold without his prior knowledge and certainly not with his consent[8]. Our first house on our arrival back in England from South Africa was a dreadful little semi-detached house in Lathbury Road, North Oxford. It was from here that I was introduced, aged nine, as a day boy at the Dragon School in Bardwell Road. Even in those days there were over three hundred boys (no girls, of course, except daughters of masters). I had been at Bishops in Rondebosch when we lived in South Africa and I found the Dragon School much tougher, with frequent beatings for every sort of offence. 'Joc' Lynam (son of the headmaster, 'Hum' Lynam[9]) would call one into his study and, after haranguing you about your offence, would say 'Well, do you want me to beat you with a cane or with this chair leg?' It was an extremely painful proceeding and what made it worse was that Lynam obviously revelled in the event.*

*And another thing of which I gradually became aware was the somewhat affectionate way in which many of the masters embraced their charges! This came to a head when one of them kissed me very warmly when I was returning from swimming. I didn't like this! I went to 'Hum' Lynam and explained what had happened. He told me to come to his house and I was shown into the drawing room, where I'd never been before. There then followed a long (and straightforward) explanation of homosexuality: 'This means that some men like boys and not girls. Many of the masters here like boys; that is why they are such good teachers. But I quite agree that Mr — should not have kissed you and, if he does that again, you must tell me.' The offence was not repeated but the master in question left to run a hotel nearby!*

*Later on in my career as a Dragon School boy, John Mortimer[10] and I attended a 'sex' talk by 'Hum' Lynam, again in his drawing room. The whole subject was so concealed by references to 'birds and bees' that we did not understand one word of his explanation. Nevertheless, neither of us was prepared to reveal this, so when John asked me afterwards 'Could you explain exactly what that was all about?' I was completely flummoxed and had to admit that I had no idea. John then insisted that we return to the headmaster for*

---

8   My grandfather had been advised by his son-in-law Sam Ashton, who was a rather unsuccessful businessman and very amateur farmer, to sell much the best part of the estate for a completely paltry sum during the agricultural depression in the 1930s. He was not in need of further cash!
9   The Lynams had been involved with the Dragon School almost since its inception in 1877 and three members of the family served as headmaster in an unbroken line from 1886 to 1965 (C.C. 'Skipper' Lynam, 1886–1920; his younger brother A.E. 'Hum' Lynam, 1920–42; and 'Hum's' son, J.H.R. 'Joc' Lynam, 1942–65).
10  Sir John Mortimer (1923–2009), a barrister, dramatist, screenwriter and author. His autobiographical play, *A Voyage Round My Father*, recounting his experiences as a young barrister and his relationship with his blind father, was originally broadcast on the radio in 1963 and later became a stage and television success.

*a fuller explanation. It was 'Hum' Lynam's turn to be flummoxed! Many years later, I went to see John's play* A Voyage Round My Father *in which this scene is re-enacted by two teenage boys (representing John and me). It was a hilarious occasion with John sitting behind me in the theatre! The audience did not understand the laughter from Rows 3 and 4 of the stalls!*

*Here I think I should pause to write something about my parents. First then, my mother* (**Fig. 11 d**)*: I adored her and we had a very close relationship — though if I behaved in a way which she considered unacceptable she would certainly let me know! Her religious beliefs were central to her life and, before she married, she wrote two little books of prayers of great depth of feeling. She made a little chapel from a dressing-room next door to her bedroom. We were bidden there most mornings to say our prayers with her. But she never forced her very strong religious beliefs on us; she merely expected us to accept them — no discussion, let alone any argument, was considered necessary. Religious instruction was given by Bible reading. On birthdays we would meet in the chapel when my mother would read the Christmas Gospel of* St John 1. 1 *('In the beginning was the Word...').*

*She sacrificed herself in caring for my father and it was he who took priority over us children. Because he was physically unable to hunt as the result of his war wound, she never hunted again, although she took a great interest in my riding and hunting.*

*Although my mother's family history is not the subject of this book, I should like to digress for a moment to talk about her background. She was born Diana Helen Ponsonby in 1891, the youngest of five children of the Hon. Edwin Ponsonby, who was himself the youngest child of Charles Frederick Ponsonby, second Baron de Mauley, and his wife (who was also his first cousin), Lady Maria Ponsonby, daughter of the fourth Earl of Bessborough. In this way, through both her grandfather and her grandmother, my mother was in direct descent from their grandmother, the beautiful and notorious Lady Henrietta (known as Harriet) Spencer, Countess of Bessborough (1761–1821) — the subject of countless portraits by Reynolds, Romney, Hoppner and Angelica Kauffmann; sister and close confidante of Georgiana Spencer, Duchess of Devonshire; and mother of Lady Caroline Lamb. My relationship to Harriet Bessborough (she was my great-great-great-grandmother) is therefore exactly the same as my relationship to Mrs Mary Birch — two remarkable women in their different ways.*

*My mother's family also overlapped with the Birch Reynardsons in other ways. The wife of the fourth Earl of Bessborough, Lady Maria Fane, was a great-granddaughter of Thomas Fane, eighth Earl of Westmorland, as was Emily Fane, who married Edward Birch Reynardson (see* Chapter 7*). Another son of the third Earl of Bessborough and Lady Harriet, Sir Frederick Ponsonby, was the father of Henry Ponsonby (first cousin to Diana's grandparents), who must have been well known to Edward Birch Reynardson as*

# THE INTER-WAR YEARS

**Fig. 11 d)** Portrait of my mother, Mrs Diana Birch Reynardson (née Ponsonby).

**Fig. 11 e)** Portrait of my father, Lieutenant-Colonel Henry T. Birch Reynardson.

he served in the Grenadier Guards alongside him in the Crimean War when he also held the rank of Colonel. Henry (later the Right Hon. Sir Henry Ponsonby) became a highly esteemed and long-suffering Private Secretary to Queen Victoria, and his son Frederick E.G. Ponsonby (later first Baron Sysonby) fulfilled a similar role, with less tact, for her son Bertie as King Edward VII.[11] Perhaps then the tradition of Royal service in my mother's family had some bearing on my father's decision to apply for the position of Military Secretary to the Earl of Athlone and Princess Alice.

Despite (or perhaps because of) her family background, my mother was the least pretentious person imaginable. She had a strong social conscience (see Chapter 12 and Appendix V) and voted Labour (secretly, so as not to annoy my father) for most of her life. No doubt it was her influence that encouraged me to start the Labour Association at Eton. This was not a huge success. Few boys joined and my Chairman, a senior Eton master, was so close to being a Communist that he was required to leave Eton! When I returned to Oxford after the war, out of respect for my mother's views I refused to join the university's Conservative Association, despite being under heavy pressure to become a member from my great friend Johnnie Dalkeith, who was then its Chairman. But I have to say that I very soon changed my allegiance!

In contrast to my mother, my father (**Fig. 11 e)**) was a distant figure in my life. I feel that I hardly knew him and think that I bored him. He disapproved of my Eton friends whom he suspected (probably correctly!) of keeping me away from my books. Certainly the reading of my school reports each holiday produced an atmosphere of 'Could do better', with little encouragement. I think that he might have approved of my belated efforts to turn the family letters into book form, as he had at least three books published himself. Before publishing Mesopotamia 1914–15: Extracts from a Regimental Officer's Diary, *referred to in* Chapter 10, *and* High Street Africa, *he had, while still a student at Oxford, written a detective novel,* Black Coffee, *as a bet that he would be able to get it published. He also wrote many articles for* Blackwoods *and other similar magazines and some (rather depressing) poetry.*

But we never had a row, though sometimes there were 'rockets'. I well remember two occasions. Once, after an exceedingly wet day's hunting, Audrey Holland Hibbert ('Mrs', of course, to me all my life) told me to ring up and get our chauffeur Jim Hedges to come in a car to fetch me, my pony being left for the night with the Holland Hibberts. This (quite rightly, I suppose) was considered monstrous behaviour and I received a mammoth ticking-off. The punishment was no hunting for a month. An appeal to my mother got this period reduced to a week.

---

11   See Jane Ridley, *Bertie — A Life of Edward VII* (Chatto & Windus, 2012), for an analysis of the respective roles of father and son as members of the Royal Household.

*The other rocket concerned my financial mismanagement. Soon after the beginning of the war I had gone on to an allowance, paid into my bank account monthly. I had, mistakenly, thought that I had a sufficient balance to buy a suit from Austin Reed — very smart, dark blue with a pin-stripe. I was immensely proud of it. I was having my bath after hunting when there was a tap on the door. It was Leslie Jones (our butler), saying that I was wanted by the Colonel in his study. 'Oh, thank you,' I said. 'I'll finish my bath and get dressed.' Mr Jones replied: 'No, Master William, I think that this is a dressing-gown occasion.' So down to the study I went. My father looked at me in a most unfriendly way. 'Why have you overdrawn on your account by two pounds, twelve shillings?' I had no explanation. 'A gentleman never overdraws on his bank account and I am ashamed of you.' As a matter of fact, the suit was a dismal failure. George Holland, the Farm Bailiff (see **11: 3**), who was always impeccably dressed, asked after church where I had obtained it. I told him that I had bought it at Austin Reed. 'Ah, I thought as much. Please remember that your clothes must be made for you by a tailor, as mine are.'*

*I do not want to leave the subject of my father without making it clear that, although our relationship may not have been close, he was nevertheless a charming, intelligent and thoughtful man. He had a crowd of devoted friends. He was constantly encouraging his children and grandchildren with wise advice as they grew up. His kindness as a host was well known throughout Oxfordshire and elsewhere. He was a thoughtful employer, his staff remaining with him often throughout their lives. But, above all, he trusted me as the next custodian of Adwell and made it possible, financially, for me and my family to live here. My father wrote about his childhood memories of Adwell before the First World War and, as I was much the same age as he was when we moved into Adwell (my father was thirteen or fourteen when it became his parents' home after 'Granny's' death and I was coming up for thirteen when my family moved there), I am recording below my recollections of the family home between the wars in a similar way.*

---

## 11: 3 ('Memories of Adwell before the Second World War', by William Birch Reynardson)

Although my parents, my sisters and my brother returned from South Africa in 1933, it was three years before we moved into Adwell in 1936 (**Fig. 11 f**). After we left Lathbury Road, my father bought a rather nice house, called Dove House, in nearby Haddenham. But I do remember the frustration caused by my grandfather's refusal to hand over the management of the Adwell estate to him, let alone to move out of Adwell House. Looking back, I do think he was probably not only thoughtless but selfish. My grandmother was by this time suffering from loss of memory which may have in the end prompted my grandfather's decision to move out of Adwell to a large house in Woodstock Road, Oxford. At this time, England was in a turmoil caused by the rumours surrounding the Prince of Wales (now briefly King Edward VIII) and then his decision to abdicate. We boys were told about this by 'Hum' Lynam at a specially convened school meeting. We were all appalled, though quite excited by the prospect of a new king. Then, within two years, came the Munich Crisis — and, less than a year after that, the declaration of war on 3 September 1939.

So, my father had only three years in which to tackle the mammoth task of re-organising the Adwell set-up before being confronted by war. And what do I remember of these years?

Firstly, of course, I remember the people — those involved in helping to run the house, the garden and the farm. It always used to bore me when I read in biographies how many servants the family had in the house, but now I know the reason. The fact is that, in those far-off days, they ran the show and organised our day. So here goes with the list! First, there were two or three under-housemaids, aged about fifteen or sixteen. They were responsible for calling us in the morning at eight o'clock with hot water, in jugs, for our washbasins (often, in the winter, covered in ice from the nightly frosts!). And they saw that we got up, because they had to be back in our bedrooms at half past eight to make our beds and tidy up. Then there was the head housemaid and two or three housemaids under her. They were responsible for cleaning the house and polishing the floors and furniture (no vacuum cleaners or electric polishers). A few years earlier, they would also have had to maintain all the oil lamps (probably about fifty) which had to be filled with oil and scrupulously cleaned to avoid the evil smell of smoky flames. But the oil lamps were replaced by electric lights very soon after my birth, when an enormous machine which produced rather unreliable 100-

**Fig. 11 f)** Adwell from the West. Photograph, 1949. This view was taken after the war but shows the house much as it was when we moved into Adwell in 1936, before the demolition of the Garden Room.

volt electricity was installed in a coach house. The head housemaid also made my parents' bed and saw to the dressing-room. Lily (who also fulfilled the role of housekeeper) was the charming head housemaid before the war and we all loved her.

The kitchen was run by Mrs Shuttle, who cooked on a huge range, fired by coal. Under her was a kitchen maid and a scullery maid (whose job was to fill the cooking range with coal). I remember that food was a subject which it was considered extremely common to discuss — and just as well as, even to the inexperienced, the standard of cooking was pretty uninspired.

Then there was the butler. In my earliest recollections this was Mr Sones (inherited from my grandfather), but then came Mr Leslie Jones, whom I've already mentioned. (All senior male servants were called 'Mr' — and all senior females 'Mrs', irrespective of whether they were married or single.) He was a completely remarkable man and a wonderful friend to all of us. When we went to shoot in Scotland, there he was with my father. In later years after the war, when my mother became ill, sometimes forgetting to put any clothes on, there he was to dress her. (Sadly, in the end he contracted MS, but he stayed on to see us into the house in 1956.)

However, to go back to my point that it was the servants (never 'staff') who organised our lives, it was Mr Jones who rang the gong at 12.50 every day and announced at one o'clock that 'lunch is served'. At seven o'clock, the gong was rung to remind us to dress for dinner and at 7.45 he announced 'dinner is served'. There was no question of anyone failing to be there or properly dressed (men, of course, in black ties; Jones in a white tie and tails). Jones was assisted by a footman, Wallace Merritt. When I went to Eton, Wallace was assigned to me. He put out my clothes in the evening and made my bed, etc.

Then there were those who worked outside. First, of course, there was George Holland, whom I've already mentioned briefly. He started life as a fourteen-year-old assistant coachman to my grandfather, later to become his close assistant. So when my father arrived at Adwell, he was appointed Farm Bailiff, with his son Michael later assisting him. Mr George was our 'tutor', teaching us how the Home Farm operated (the Evans family rented the Postcombe Farm and lived in Adwell Farm House). He was a remarkably knowledgeable man. Always dressed impeccably in breeches and polished leather gaiters, he was responsible for the stable yard and farm yard employees. Jim Hedges, the chauffeur (in blue suit, breeches, cap and silver livery buttons), maintained the cars and the stable yard; occasionally he also looked after our ponies and my mother's horse. On the farm there were six draught horses[12] under Dick Brown, a herd of (originally) Shorthorn milking cows under Harold Bull and his father George, and a number of young men who were general assistants.

There were, before the war, five gardeners under Mr Wixon. I can just remember the Great Lawn being cut by a row of four gardeners, each with a scythe, walking slowly in line sweeping their scythes at each step. But by the time we went to Adwell, there was a large petrol-driven mower which did the job in half the time with just one man. Nevertheless there was much to be done in the garden. The lawn itself was dotted with small flower beds, filled with annuals. In the centre of the lawn was a large fountain, again surrounded by flower beds. There were peach houses, grapevines and an enormous greenhouse where the tennis court is now. This alone required the sole service of one gardener.

Finally there was the shoot. In those early days no birds were put down so we relied on wild partridges and pheasants. Our keeper was called Wilby and he produced many happy shooting days for us, shooting perhaps fifty pheasants and much the same number of partridges each day. I was allowed to shoot with

---

[12] Before the Second World War it was still not uncommon to see these powerfully-built horses (usually Shire horses in the UK) at work on the farm, pulling heavy agricultural equipment. With increasing mechanisation, they became a much rarer sight.

a single-barrelled .410 on my tenth birthday. I enjoyed it all very much but I do remember getting unbearably cold most days (we weren't allowed to wear heavy coats!). Later, it was Wilby who showed me how to graft roses onto the briars in the hedges. In the end I'd grafted masses of roses, which were all in full flower when we shot the partridges before going back to school in September.

Before leaving the domestic scene, I should perhaps recall two particular institutions, the memory of which, after over eighty years, is still perfectly clear. The first is the extraordinary procedure which occurred every day in the servants' hall at lunch time. Mr Jones presided, sitting on a curved bench with a sort of canopy at the head of the table; Mrs Shuttle (the cook) sat opposite him at the other end of the table. When the pudding was brought in, Mr Jones, Mrs Shuttle and Mrs Turner (then the head housemaid) were served and then, carrying their plates, they filed out of the servants' hall (now the kitchen) and sat down in the Housekeeper's Room (now the small sitting room) opposite. Here they finished their lunch, ringing a bell to have their plates cleared by the kitchen or scullery maid. Talk about class distinction! I believe that this charade went on in many houses in those far-off days.

The second, which I can only just remember, is the morning prayers held by my grandmother before breakfast in the Library. Here again it was quite a performance, with the butler (then Mr Sones) heading the procession of the servants (kitchen and house), who curtsied when my grandmother ended, prayer book in hand. (My father recalled that before the First World War similar customs prevailed elsewhere on the estate, where 'all the children had manners very much drilled into them. When my mother [*my grandmother, Violet Birch Reynardson*] passed in the carriage or out walking, all the little girls would curtsey and the boys took off their caps or touched their forelocks and smiled […] Indeed, Dick Brown […] pulled his forelock as my father [*my grandfather, William Birch Reynardson*] stumped up the aisle in church. But that was too much even for my mother [*Violet BR*], who told Dick that he was in God's house and mustn't take any notice, even if he was the Squire.' These 'becoming civilities' had, according to my father, largely finished by the 1920s.)

When we moved to Adwell, my mother did away with all this and instead had private family prayers in the little chapel upstairs. As I have already said, she disliked anything approaching ostentation, even addressing her own father, the Hon. Edwin Ponsonby (son of Lord de Mauley) as plain 'Mr', which was most unusual and could even have been seen as discourteous in those days. When she arrived in South Africa, my father met her in his car which had a crown on the bonnet (as was his entitlement). She had it immediately removed!

Thinking back, it is clear that my parents felt, quite rightly, that we children should be centred on Adwell, where there was so much for us to do and occupy ourselves. There was never any question of going away for holidays, let alone going abroad. We had a lovely, happy time with our dogs and ponies. We even had a swimming pool (a rarity in those days). No heating or filtering, of course.

The social centre of our lives, before the war, was the Pony Club. It was all great fun and devoid of parental ambition, which is sadly so evident today. The summer Pony Club camps were the main feature of each year. They were held on various South Oxfordshire estates, including Adwell. Run on cavalry lines, there was always 'the Adjutant' (a volunteer cavalry officer, who one year was my future brother-in-law, Humphrey Prideaux). The participating children were divided into troops and the ponies were tied in troop lines. Each troop had an instructor and instruction in equitation was taken seriously.

---

*By 1938, only two years after we had moved to Adwell, we were aware that all was not well. During the Munich Crisis, I can so well remember the visits of the Prime Minister, Neville Chamberlain, to Germany to negotiate with Hitler, and our relief when, as we then thought, the result of their meetings was (to quote Chamberlain) 'Peace in our time'. Despite this, my parents went around with a look of anguish on their faces. My father was convinced that war was inevitable. Having previously forbidden the marriage of Humphrey Prideaux to my eldest sister Cynthia on grounds of age (he was twenty-three, she was twenty), he told them that they should be married as soon as possible, because (as he said) 'You will probably by dead by Christmas.' The wedding took place four days before the outbreak of war, on 30 August 1939* (**Fig. 11 g**)).

**Fig. 11 g)** My sister Cynthia's wedding to Humphrey Prideaux, 30 August 1939.

CHAPTER 12

# Eton, North Africa and Italy

*Recollections and Letters 1939–1946*

'I know that I shall always be glad that I have fought in this war. The difference between good and evil shines like a beacon through the darkness of war.'[1]

*My sister Cynthia's wedding is one of my happiest memories. It was a big affair, with the wedding itself in Adwell Church and the reception in the house with a marquee on the croquet lawn. But it coincided with the first crisis of the war! Just a few minutes after the last of the guests had left, we were relaxing in the library (now the dining room), all rather exhausted, when two double-decker London buses appeared in the drive. 'What the devil are those bloody buses doing in our drive? Damn fools have lost their way, I suppose!' shouted my father. My mother went very quiet. Of course, she had quite forgotten that a year earlier (at the time of the Munich Crisis) she had volunteered to have up to fifty evacuees in the event of war. But she had omitted to consult my father; he took the news badly.*

*There was however little time for recriminations as furniture had to be cleared from four rooms to provide space for fifty children and six 'keepers'. And the cots for the children had been forgotten. Our neighbours were sent for and began to help to clear the rooms, including the removal of the billiard table and other heavy pieces of furniture. My father retired from the scene in a major sulk and my mother took control of proceedings with relaxed authority. Fortunately the South Oxfordshire Pony Club Camp had recently taken place at Adwell and we were able to use the palliasses (filled with straw) as temporary bedding for the children.*

*My mother was not quite so relaxed a few days later when war was declared. We were in Adwell Church when our rector, Canon Henderson, announced: 'I have to tell you that we are now at war with Germany. May God bless us.' My mother was sitting (as she always did) between my brother Dicky and me. She grasped our hands and said 'And may He bless you.' It was the first and only time that I ever saw her cry. After church we went for a walk together through the shrubberies. She was heart-broken. Her beloved brother Ashley Ponsonby had been killed on the Western Front twenty-four years (almost to the day) earlier and she was obviously thinking that I might be next.*

1   From a letter to my mother, 11 May 1945 (**12: 24**).

*The arrival of the evacuee children, all aged between four and six, was of course a major event affecting all of us for the rest of the war[2] (see* Appendix V). *My mother took charge of the whole organisation, assisted by a highly efficient woman called Doris Sayer, and by numerous girl friends of my sisters. My father wisely avoided day-to-day contact with the hubbub by doing a hush-hush job at the War Office!*

*Of course the enormous cost of the war not only nearly bankrupted the country but our family became increasingly stretched financially[3]. In the early days of the war, I was nearly sixteen and had been at Eton for about three years; Dickie had just started there. There had been an alarming suggestion that we, together with our cousin Mary Ponsonby, should be sent to South Africa for the war years. This was strongly opposed by us and the plan was dropped. I was extremely close to my brother, who was three years younger than me and very early on showed his charm. But it must be admitted that at Eton he was something of a liability, his arrival there being rather dramatic. My Tutor, Charles Gladstone, had allocated a 'brother's room' to us (although I was perfectly happy in my single room). The only advantage was that the double room was much larger. Very early on, Dickie produced — to my horror — an air gun with special darts instead of pellets so that they could be removed from the target. The gun was in constant use, firing at a target pinned to the door. Dickie was busily engaged in this activity when, hearing the constant thumping, my Tutor opened the door. Most fortunately the dart missed him and landed on the door jamb. My Tutor was not amused. The gun was confiscated, Dickie was beaten and we were parted. I was rather thankful.*

*Two letters sum up our feelings towards Eton. The first, from Dickie, written at the height of the Blitz, must have caused considerable alarm to our parents. The second one* (**12: 2**) *was written by me as I was about to leave school.*

---

2  It was not until the end of the war that a house was bought in North Oxford — 141, Banbury Road — whence the evacuees eventually dispersed.

3  In December 1940, the Prime Minister Winston Churchill wrote his famous letter to President Roosevelt of the United States, outlining the dire financial situation confronting Great Britain. At the time Britain stood alone against the full might of Nazi Germany; it is unlikely that we would have been unable to continue the fight or indeed to win the war without American economic support. Roosevelt recommended a Lend-Lease programme to assist us in the continuation of the war and the Lend-Lease Act was passed by Congress in March 1941. By April, Britain's reserves of gold and dollars had sunk to £12 million, their lowest point in the country's history. Although the passing of the Act enabled the war to continue, the price was high. In the early days of negotiating the Act, an American warship was sent to Cape Town to recover all the gold bullion which we had accumulated there. The repayment of the enormous War Debt was such that it was only accomplished in 2007.

**Letter 12: 1 (Richard Birch Reynardson, Eton College, to our father Henry Birch Reynardson; undated, but probably January or February 1941[4])**

C.A. GLADSTONE, ESQ.,
ETON COLLEGE
WINDSOR

My dear Father,

Thank you so much for the five /- [*shillings*] but I'm afraid I did not deserve it though.

[...] Bill is all over grins and smiles now because they are going to beagle (**Fig. 12 a)**) one day a week, which realy [*sic*] has made Bill live again. He went to whip in for the Sandhurst beagles and he said it was the greatest fun he had ever had out beagling! Wasn't it grand?

We have started playing the Field Game[5] now, and I love it even more than last year, I suppose it is because I understand it better now than I did before, but we have not got a very good team, as most of the last year's lower boys are uppers this winter.

On Sunday just before chapel we heard lots of guns start blazing away over by Dorney, and I and some other boys saw the Hun flying towards Slough and then we lost sight of it but some people who saw it too said it crashed by Langley, but you can't believe what people say nowadays, can you? We go to the shelter in the day time when the sirens go and miss chapel even when there is a yellow warning, and yet at night when the sirens go and bombs drop within a few miles we just don't bother. I realy [*sic*] think it is a very stupid Idea: if you are going to take any notice of the warnings at all, I think, much as I hate the Idea, that everybody should sleep in the shelter — not just do the job the way it is easiest and in a half-hearted way to make the parents think we are not completely regardless of air raid warnings. But anyway it suits us all right: we get off a sticky construe[6] school in the shelter and at night we have our usual sleep.

---

4    'Oct 1940' is written on the letter in another hand, but other details in the letter make it clear that it was written early in the 'Lent half' (Spring Term).
5    One of two types of football (the other is the Eton Wall Game) devised by and exclusive to Eton College. Although it is similar to football in most ways, the off-side rules are more in keeping with rugby.
6    An analysis of the grammatical construction of a sentence (in this context, Greek or Latin).

Fig. 12 a) The Eton Beagles. Photograph, *c.*1941

**LETTER 12: 2 (William Birch Reynardson, Eton College, to my father Henry Birch Reynardson; undated but probably March 1942)**

C. A. GLADSTONE, ESQ.,
ETON COLLEGE
WINDSOR

Dearest Father,

I hear that you are coming down on Sunday with Mother. How lovely! I wonder when you will arrive. Chapel is at 10.40 in the morning and 5.00 in the evening. I have tried to get tickets for you but have not at the moment proved successful. Do you mind if I ask some people to tea, as we are not allowed to give Leaving Breakfasts any more?

It will be the last time that I will see you as an Etonian. What a thought!

Oh Father — I wonder if you realise what Eton has been to me? I doubt it, you know. I have not achieved any real distinction but I have found in Eton not only just a place where it is 'awful fun', but an atmosphere of pure loveliness. The buildings, the fields, the hounds, old Perkins and all the farmers make up one side of my life here. Music, Art, M'Tutors and my friends make up the educational side. And the two weld into sheer perfection. I will never be able to thank you both in words — that would be too hard, but one day I hope that I will be worthy of your kindness — and worthy of Eton.

I hunted hounds yesterday as Julian[7] went out with the Eight, but scent was practically non-existent — such a pity. [...] Could you possibly send me £5 for our beagling subscription? It is an awful lot, but it is the last time you'll ever have to write a cheque for the E.C.H. [*Eton College Hounds*] for me — how awful! [...]

Your ever loving
Bill

---

*I had been closely involved with the beagles since the start of my career at Eton, together with my inseparable friend Kit Egerton, neither of us being much good at games (though we always enjoyed the Field game). We had a wonderful time with Mike de Chair and Hugh Arbuthnot as masters. The kennel huntsman in our day was Will Perkins, a remarkable man. Not only did he feed and exercise the hounds (sometimes with our help), but he taught us, very tactfully and firmly, the art of venery[8]. Out hunting (always perfectly dressed in his white breeches and Eton brown velvet coat), he would arrive from nowhere when the hounds had checked and whisper a possible (and usually correct) solution. He was a wonderful contributor to all the fun we had in those gloriously happy days when we were welcomed by farmers all over Berkshire, Buckinghamshire and Oxfordshire.*

*At home, too, I was able to carry on with my hunting, which continued after the start of the war on a reduced scale. My choice of horses was actually widened because Sir Robert Fanshawe (Dick Fanshawe's uncle[9]) mounted me on top-class horses sent, for the duration of the war, to his stables at Lobbersdown (formerly a point-to-point venue) by his nephews. I had two glorious seasons hunting with Dick's wife Ruth before I joined the Army, riding a succession of super horses including 'Ginger Rogers', 'Wagon Lit' and 'Koran', the last-named later given to me by Sir Robert.*

*During the summer of 1940, Sir Robert formed a mounted troop of what was then called the L.D.V. (Local Defence Volunteers, to be replaced by the Home Guard). Our Sergeant-Major was Jack Castle, a well-known yeoman farmer who lived in Thame. Sir Robert instructed us in cavalry drill dating back to the Boer War, and my job was to dismount and hold the troop horses while their riders stalked 'the enemy' on foot. We*

---

7   Julian Mond, later Lord Melchett (1925–73), merchant banker, agricultural and industrial businessman, and Chairman of the British Steel Corporation. (*Oxford Dictionary of National Biography*).
8   The practice or sport of hunting game animals.
9   General Sir Robert Fanshawe had been my father's first Colonel, and his nephew Dick was Huntsman of the South Oxfordshire Hounds, and later my instructor at Blackdown.

*drew our Lee Enfield rifles from the Regimental Museum in Cowley. Such was the state of national defence at that time!*

*In my last year at Eton, I remember well the rather distressingly complex discussions I had with my father about my future — particularly whether I should go up to Oxford before joining the Army, or stay on at Eton and go straight into the Army. I was keen on the latter idea because my great friend Bobbie Manners[10], who was Master of the Beagles, had said I could take over from him and hunt the hounds. The plans changed several times for various reasons until in the end it was decided that I should stay at Eton until after I was eighteen and go up to Christ Church for two terms before joining the Army. Julian Mond was nominated as the next Master and I only occasionally hunted hounds after that, one of the biggest disappointments of my life!*

*I went up to Oxford in April 1942 (no question of any entrance exam, just a welcoming handshake from Dean Lowe!) and read General Science with Dr Russell, a particularly charming man, for two terms before going down in December. It was a very happy time with heaps of friends and, I fear, not much work done. My memories of Peter Lothian[11] and lovely Tony Carr[12], whom he subsequently married, Sandy Faris[13] (playing duets with Peter on his piano in Canterbury Quad), Charles Stourton[14], Johnnie Dalkeith[15] and Michael Howard[16] (**Fig. 12 b**)) remain completely clear. It was also during my Oxford days that I first met Lorna Bailie[17] (see **12: 19**) in the summer of 1942 and wrote regularly to her for the rest of the war.*

10 John Robert Cecil Manners, later fifth Baron Manners (1923–2008), of Avon Tyrell, a beautiful Arts and Crafts house on the edge of the New Forest which he presented to the 'Youth of the Nation' after the war.
11 Peter Kerr, twelfth Marquess of Lothian (1922–2004), politician and landowner who was soon to join the Scots Guards.
12 Antonella Newland (1922–2007), who married the Marquess of Lothian in 1943, was an eminent journalist in her own right and founded the annual Women of the Year lunches at the Savoy Hotel. Her eldest son is the former politician Michael Ancram (now the thirteenth Marquess).
13 Alexander 'Sandy' Faris (born 1921) is an Irish composer, conductor and writer, who is particularly associated with the works of Gilbert and Sullivan. As a composer of television and film scores, he is perhaps best known for the theme music of *Upstairs, Downstairs*.
14 Charles Stourton (1923–2006) succeeded his father to the titles of Baron Stourton, Baron Segrave and Baron Mowbray in 1965, and was until his death the premier baron in the English peerage.
15 John Scott (1923–2007), known as Dalkeith from his courtesy title of Earl of Dalkeith, became the ninth Duke of Buccleuch in 1973.
16 Sir Michael Howard (born 1922) served in the Coldstream Guards in the Italian Campaign, during which he was awarded the Military Cross. My contemporary at Christ Church, he became an esteemed military historian and Regius Professor of Modern History at Oxford (1980–89), as well as holding numerous other professorial positions and fellowships.
17 Our correspondence was eventually published under the title *Letters to Lorna* (Wilton 65, 2008). Lorna was doing a typing course at the 'Ox and Cow' (Oxford and County Typing School); as her father and mine had been in the same regiment, Major Bailie had written to my father to ask him to be nice to his daughter. After Lorna's only brother, Douglas, was killed in February 1944, she became heiress to the family home of Manderston, in Berwickshire, which was to cause difficulties between us in the future. In 1950 Lorna married the Hon. Gordon Palmer and, as our lives went in separate directions, we gradually lost touch. It was after Lorna's death that quite by chance I met her son Adrian, who told me that his mother had kept all the letters I had written to her between 1943 and 1948. Sadly, many of those she wrote to me had been destroyed when, on two occasions, my tank was destroyed by fire during the last year of the war.

# SURVIVORS

LODERS CLUB 1942

J. R. SYNGE     D. D. BOLTON     HON. C. E. STOURTON     MARQUESS OF LOTHIAN     W.B.R.
EARL OF DALKEITH

**Fig. 12 b)** The members of Loders Club, 1942. Photograph.

**Fig. 12 c)** John Joicey. Photograph.

358

## ETON, NORTH AFRICA AND ITALY

*It was in March 1943 that I finally began my Army career at Britannia Barracks, Norwich, which was quite a leap into the unknown. There were about twenty-five or thirty soldiers in my barrack room. The other soldiers were extremely nice to me, treating me as an unusual specimen to whom some sort of courtesy was owed. Very soon after joining, our sergeant came up to me and said: 'Yer on boxing tonight; ever boxed?' I had boxed a little at Eton, but I denied this. 'Never mind, yer opponend 'asn't boxed either.' Well, as soon as I got into the ring and saw this huge man opposite me, I knew that he was a boxer. What was I to do? I decided that my only hope was to hit him as hard as I could and try to knock him out before he hit me. I achieved the first objective but not, sadly, the second. I knew no more until I came round in the Regimental Hospital! Soon afterwards my opponent visited me. 'I've come to apologise for hitting you — but you hit me first.' I explained that I was very humiliated at failing so abysmally in our contest and asked him to confirm that he'd never boxed before. 'Well, actually I'm the Police Middleweight Champion.' I felt better after that.*

*I'm not going to recall in any detail my progress towards being commissioned. I followed the normal course of going to Blackdown (Officer Cadet Training Unit — now Deepcut Barracks) at the end of March 1943, then to Sandhurst from July to December 1943, to the 24th Lancers (a holding regiment in Yorkshire) from January 1944 and, finally, joining the 9th Lancers in Algiers in April 1944.*

*But during this year there were a number of special memories which I want to record. First, when I was at Blackdown and next door at Sandhurst, my sister Cynthia and her husband Humphrey Prideaux were living in Camberley (Humphrey now instructing at the Staff College). Having those two near me was a peaceful haven from the rough and tumble of military life. Sandhurst itself was fun, not only because I had many friends there (particularly Johnnie Spencer[18]) but especially because our Company Commander was a particularly charming fellow in the Scots Guards called Reggie Gordon-Lennox, who was an outstanding example of how 'an officer and gentleman' should behave. While at Sandhurst I was still able to get home quite often to hunt and could also make many evening visits to London with dinner (generally at the old Berkeley Hotel in Berkeley Street — the head waiter there, a charming Italian called Galbiati, always whispered when presenting the bill 'Would you like to pay later?' We often had to take him up on his offer!) Afterwards we would dance until dawn in the 400 Club in Leicester Square. I should also mention a memorable dance at Windsor Castle, to which Johnnie Spencer and I were invited by Margaret Elphinstone (later Rhodes), the Queen's niece. I found myself*

---

18  Edward John Spencer (1924–92), Viscount Althorp until he succeeded his father as Earl Spencer in 1975, was the father of Diana, Princess of Wales.

*dancing with the then Queen[19] who asked me, after a pause, whether I could dance a waltz. I was tried out and passed the test. 'Now you must teach my Princesses.' Princess Elizabeth took the lesson very seriously (a lot of '1, 2, 3' etc) but Princess Margaret said she knew it all — and 'none of that 1, 2, 3 business!'*

*At the beginning of April 1944, after a year in training, I finally embarked on the journey which would take me first to join my Regiment in Algeria, then to Italy, where the slow progress to liberate Nazi Germany's former Axis partner — which began the previous summer when the first Allied landings took place in Sicily — would last until within two weeks of the end of the war. I was wounded in November 1944, but my wound was not serious enough for me to be sent home immediately; towards the end of 1945, I came home on leave for a few weeks to undergo another operation on my hand and then in February 1946 I returned to my regiment in Italy, remaining there and in Austria until I was demobbed in August 1946. During this period of two and a half years I wrote literally hundreds of letters, including over 250 to my parents, all of which they preserved in much the same way as Mary Birch had kept all of the letters sent by my great-great-grandfather from Egypt nearly 150 years earlier. While I have found it extremely difficult to select from these letters, my aim has been to extract the most interesting aspects of our active service in Italy and in the immediate post-war period, together with a few letters to, from or about other members of the family or friends to illustrate how we were all affected in different ways.*

*My ship docked in Algiers on 11 April 1944. I well remember being met at the port by John Joicey (**Fig. 12 c**)), who was to become my closest friend in the Regiment, and driven to Blida where the Regiment was living in a farmhouse and neighbouring outbuildings. John introduced me first to my troop, headed by Sergeant Edmunds who welcomed me with an extremely smart salute. He then took me round the tanks to meet each crew member. They were charming and friendly — but I've never been more frightened in my life. They had all fought through the North African desert, ending up at El Alamein, and here I was, aged twenty with no experience, about to command them. I wonder what they thought!*

*After writing a short letter to let my family know of my safe arrival in Algeria (sent by airmail, which typically took only four days to arrive — a far cry from Thomas Birch's experience in 1801!), my next letter, rather surprisingly, was from Morocco. I had gone there with John Joicey and John Goldsmid for a 'swan' (Army slang for a jaunt), which had unexpected consequences when our truck broke down, but did enable me to see a great deal of French North Africa (and, indeed, Gibraltar, where I went in search of a spare part for the truck) in a short space of time.*

---

19   Queen Elizabeth (1900–2002), later the Queen Mother. Princesses Elizabeth (the future Queen Elizabeth II) and Margaret were then aged seventeen and thirteen respectively. They spent the war years at Windsor Castle, the King and Queen having resisted pressure to send them to Canada for the duration of the war.

**Letter 12: 3 (William Birch Reynardson, Morocco, to my family in England, dated 7 May 1944)**

My darling family — I am writing to you all from an R.A.F. station in Morocco. The reason for this rather irregular occurrence I will tell you later, for it is a long story (in fact about a thousand miles long!) I think I told you that John Joicey had asked me to go with him to Morocco [...] We set off in two army trucks with our servants, guns, bedding and general camping equipment on Saturday 29 April after lunch.

The weather was perfect and we drove through the most beautiful country not unlike Scotland [...] round many hair pin bends overlooking great gorges filled with fir trees and looking up from the road [...] the jagged red rocks in the mountains were sparkling as the waterfalls poured down them to the valley below.

We stopped for tea overlooking such a valley and [...] the sun began to set behind the mountains and the frogs began to croak — it was all very lovely. [...] Slowly it became dark but the light of the moon was bright enough for us to drive on quite easily, and after traversing most frightening roads overlooking gullies on each side, we drove into Mascara at midnight. Like most North African towns it has wide streets lined with trees and a large square in the centre. We couldn't all get into the hotel so I slept in the truck on my Dunlopillo sleeping bag (which is growing quite invaluable, Father, and the source of constant envy!). [...] Next morning [...] we came into flat dry country and passed the first camels that I had seen — such proud pompous looking creatures. As we were driving along, I saw a brace of French partridges by the side of the road. The truck immediately stopped and out we jumped. As it was John's gun he had to shoot first [...] It was of course great fun, and when we returned we were rewarded with sarcastic remarks from the soldiers ('Do you want us to take the truck out for the birds, Sir?') and also a 'brew-up'. This, I must quickly explain, is a cup of tea. The soldiers brew up with the greatest regularity whenever the truck stops.

On we went — to Sidi Bel-Abbes. Here we found all the Frogs in tremendous form — bands playing and processions marching with their banners. This town is the Headquarters of the Foreign Legion and we had arrived on their Gala Day. We watched them as we drank the local French beer (odd stuff, somewhat similar to the curious liquid refreshment in vogue when I left Adwell). We arrived at Oudja at tea time with only one stop for a brew-up which we considered quite excellent discipline. [...]

We started off the next morning at about nine and drove to Taza for lunch. Here for the first time I saw some really lovely Arab horses in good condition. They were ridden in bright red Moroccan bridles, with various brightly coloured saddles which looked rather like arm chairs — how I longed to bring a few of them back to Adwell! [...]

By tea time we drove up a mountain and saw Fez. The city is divided into three towns, the Medina (or Native Quarter), the old French town and the modern European town. It is the Moorish capital of North Africa, and as [soon as] we saw it I knew I was going to love it. We stayed at the Palais Jamais, a hotel which used to be one of the Sultan's palaces. [...]

On Friday morning we decided to go to Rabat, the political capital. It is a modern town with wide boulevards and some rather ugly fero-concrete buildings in it — however I really came to see the Sultan's palace and the horses. We drove up there and through some large Moroccan gates guarded by his own soldiers in red and green uniforms who let 'les Anglais' pass without a question. First of all we were shown the gardens. How you would have loved the flowers, Mother — and I know their names in Arabic! Morocco seems to be the gardener's Paradise. And then we asked to see the horses but were told it was impossible [...] [so] we drove up to the stables and looked around ourselves! Oh, they were lovely. Great white fellows (all stallions) standing in their boxes in one huge stable yard. We found a groom up there who showed us the Sultan's favourite horse. [...]

The next morning, Saturday — which was yesterday — we drove to Casablanca[20]. This is a large modern town with a big harbour. We had lunch there but there was nothing really very interesting in it. And then we began our sad drive back to the regiment. We planned to drive to Fez and start at first light today (Sunday) and arrive at the Regiment on Monday night. But this was not meant to be! As we were driving through the cork forests east of Rabat there was a truly horrible grating sound — I leapt out of the truck and found that the differential (the large bump between the back wheels, Mother!) had broken. To go into the technical details the oil seal had gone and therefore all the oil too — and very soon the 'wheels within'!

John Joicey had to get back to the Regiment for an important job so I have had to stay behind with my chap. We are feeling rather depressed as the chance of getting a new differential quickly is remote. And so you see I am writing to you from an aerodrome in Morocco [...]

---

20  Casablanca was the site of the meeting between Churchill and the American President Franklin D. Roosevelt on 14 January 1943 (shortly after the liberation of French North Africa), at which the planned Allied landing on Sicily was agreed for early summer. The first landings actually took place on 10 July 1943, the first Allied success in Europe since the start of the war.

**Letter 12: 4 (William Birch Reynardson, Gibraltar, to my family in England, dated 9 May 1944)**

Gibraltar

My darling Family — and so this long story continues! I think I was at the aerodrome in Morocco when I wrote on Sunday; well, now, as you see, I am in Gibraltar. The fact is that I couldn't find a differential in North Africa so I thought that I would try Gibraltar! So I stepped into an aeroplane — and got here in two hours. [...] But alas! There is not even a differential in Gibraltar so I shall have to try elsewhere — and am now feeling a bit worried as to when I shall get back to the Regiment. [...]

I hope Christopher and Ros[21] are very well and flourishing, send a photograph of her as soon as it is possible (i.e. presentable!)

My love to you all,
WBR

**Letter 12: 5 (William Birch Reynardson, Algeria, to my mother Diana Birch Reynardson, dated 16 May 1944)**

Tuesday 16th May 1944

Darling Mother,

[...] Since I returned to the Regiment we have been pretty busy and have moved out of our comfortable billets into camp. However the servants here are quite wonderful at making us comfortable and I am thoroughly enjoying it. [...] On Thursday night I went to a sherry party given by Daphne and Hermione Llewellyn where I talked to General Wilson[22]. He seemed so nice and [we] had a terrific gossip about Oxfordshire. Then on Saturday night, I was asked to dine at his house in the town, so the Colonel and I drove in to be met by a large crowd who were dining

---

21  My sister Rosamund had married Captain James Marriott in 1943 and their son Christopher was born shortly before I left England for Algeria.

22  General Sir Henry Maitland Wilson (1881–1964), known as 'Jumbo' because of his rotund figure, was Supreme Allied Commander, Mediterranean, from January to December 1944, when he was promoted to Field Marshal and posted to Washington as Head of the British Joint Staff Mission.

to celebrate Dan Ranfurly's return from Italy[23] whence he has escaped. Hermione was of course very happy — I had never met him (though I believe you have) but he seemed a nice sort of fellow. We had a frightfully good dinner and the old general was in the best form and sent his love to both of you. [...]

There is very little doing at the moment, it is rather a case of waiting though I can say no more. But there is nothing to worry about.

## Letter 12: 6 (William Birch Reynardson, on board ship bound for Italy, to my family in England, dated 25 May 1944)

Thursday 25 May 1944

Darling Family,

[...] We are sailing along the coast of North Africa — soon to leave it for good and arrive in yet another new country. But it is so exciting. I did love North Africa though and wasn't I lucky to see so much of it? Of course Morocco was the most beautiful — but Algeria had its own particular beauty too. The miles [...] of vineyards shining in the hot sun, and the oxen slowly ploughing between the rows of vines — the blue wisteria and the dark purple bougainvillea falling over the whitewashed houses and crawling up the trees [...] [and] the smell of orange and tangerine blossom — warm and [...] exotic.

[...] But what of England? What of the green hedges and the lanes — and the sound of the wind in the corn. And the people and the talk and the quiet, just before night. England wins — such apparently small things, not held high for sentimental reasons, but rightly because of its loveliness. I never realised it of course — but I do now. It will be all the lovelier when I come back.

Letters have been arriving from you all very regularly — thank you very much for them. You know how I love them. But I feel that it will be some time

---

23 Daniel Knox, Earl of Ranfurly (1914–88) had married my cousin Hermione Llewellyn (1913–2001) a few months before war broke out in 1939. When her husband, who was with the Sherwood Rangers, was posted to Palestine, Hermione defied the War Office to follow him to the Middle East. Dan was captured at the Battle of Tobruk in April 1941 and imprisoned in Italy, and Hermione vowed not to return home until she was reunited with him. She worked for the Special Operations Executive (as did her sister Daphne Llewellyn) in Cairo, and then became General 'Jumbo' Wilson's secretary in November 1942, moving with him to Algiers early in 1944 and then to Caserta near Naples. After the Italian armistice in September 1943, Dan was amongst those released. He spent several months with the partisans in the Apennines, and managed to escape the German occupation after a series of adventures. Dan's reunion with his wife, and their romantic story, is told in *To War with Whitaker: the Wartime Diaries of the Countess of Ranfurly 1939–45* (William Heinemann Ltd, 1994): 'Whitaker' being the name of Dan's butler, who had accompanied him to Palestine and stayed on to work for the war effort.

now before I get any more — and I shall miss them very much.

[...] In all this time I don't believe that I have really told you much about my regiment which is stupid of me — but somehow there has been such a lot of other things to say! Let me go through them from the top — my Colonel is Stug Perry. He is very frightening but really awfully nice and kind. He took me to dine with General Wilson and we had a bit of a talk going in. The Adjutant is Francis Pym[24]. I am told by him that he is a vague cousin of mine, but no doubt Father will be able to work it out. He isn't a bad sort of fellow, but rather damp and slightly smooth — however he is very good at his job, I believe. (A covert is <u>never</u> blank!)

My Squadron Leader is Derek Allhusen. He is really awfully nice and most helpful and understanding. He is a great horseman and I vaguely remember seeing him jump at Olympia. [...] How I wish I had had a little bit of Army instruction on a horse. After all, anyone can get over country out hunting if they have done enough of it — but it's the real art of horsemanship that I lack so much. [...]

Just before I left I had dinner with Judy Slessor[25]. I would have been furious to go away without seeing her and hearing all her news. She was in such good form too and we had the most tremendous gossip! She is so very nice and perhaps will be joining me in...! (I hope you know where!) [...]

---

*Although the Allies had established a bridgehead at Salerno in September 1943, their advance northwards was slow in the face of determined German resistance. A second Allied landing was made at Anzio in January 1944 but for several months it was still not possible for the two armies to link up or to force a way through to Rome. It was not until the capture of Monte Cassino on 18 May, after a four-month siege and a week-long battle, that the way was opened up for a rapid Allied advance* (**Fig. 12 d**)), *firstly to Anzio and then towards Rome. The Italian capital was entered by American forces on 4 June, the same day as my letter below, although the exciting news had not yet reached us. To satisfy the military censors, I could not give away identifiable details of our location, but it would probably not have been very difficult to work out that we were in Naples, and that the 'famous ruins' nearby were at Pompeii! This letter is significant for recounting my first, overwhelming, introduction to the world of opera, which was to play such an important part in my life later.*

24 Francis Pym, later Baron Pym (1922–2008) became a politician after the war and rose to Foreign Secretary during the Falklands War in 1982. He was a leading member of the 'Wets' (Tory opponents to Margaret Thatcher), which makes my comments about him appear peculiarly apt!
25 A great friend of the family, Judy was the daughter of Air Marshal Sir John Slessor (1897–1979), Commander in Chief RAF, Mediterranean and Middle East from January 1944 and Chief of the Air Staff from 1950 to 1952.

## Personal Message from the Army Commander

Great events lie ahead of us. All round Hitler's Germany, the Allies are closing in: on the East, the victorious Russians drive on — in the West, the British and American Armies are massed to invade.

— Now in the South, the Eighth and Fifth Armies are about to strike.

Side by side with our French and American Allies, we will break through the enemy's winter line and start our great advance Northwards. Our plan is worked out in every detail — we attack in great strength, with large numbers of tanks and guns, supported by a powerful American Air Force and our own Desert Air Force.

The peoples of the United Nations will be watching the Eighth Army. Let us live up to our great traditions and give them news of fresh achievements — great news such as they expect from this Army.

We welcome gladly to our ranks those Divisions whose first fight this is with the Eighth Army. We send a special message to our Polish Corps, now battling beside us to regain its beloved country.

I say to you all — Into action, with the light of battle in your eyes. Let every man do his duty throughout the fight and the Day is ours!

Good Luck and God Speed to each one of you!

*Oliver Leese*

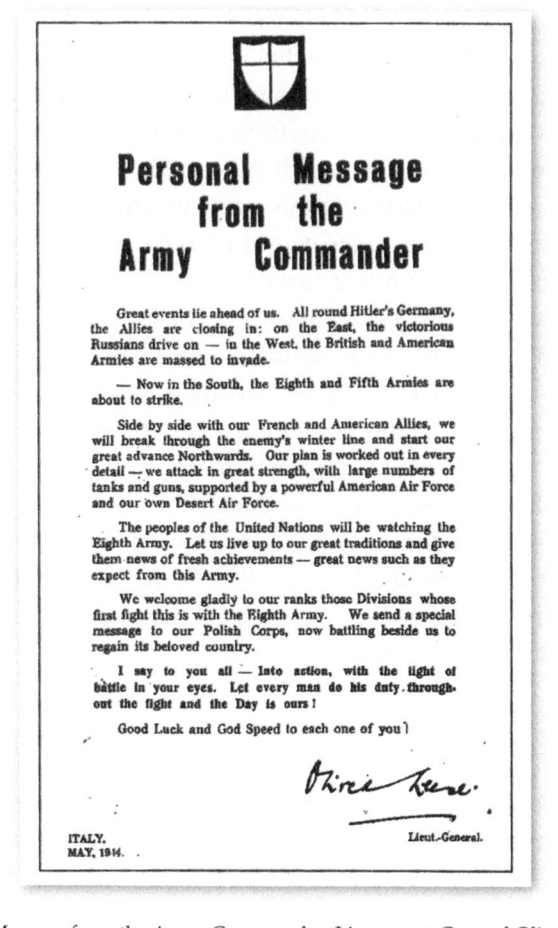

ITALY.
MAY, 1944.                                             Lieut.-General.

**Fig. 12 d)** Personal Message from the Army Commander, Lieutenant-General Oliver Leese, May 1944.

*The reader may draw the impression from these accounts that our Approach March northwards was extremely slow and leisurely, with many excursions to bathe in the sea, visit the Opera and other non-military activities! So I do need to make the point that much of our time was spent in very serious training for the battles ahead. In addition, by the time we came into direct engagement with the enemy, we were in extremely mountainous terrain, the narrow valleys often making it impossible for more than one regiment in the Brigade (and sometimes only one squadron of that regiment) to join battle. This meant that the three regiments in the Brigade (the Queen's Bays, the 10th Hussars and the 9th Lancers) 'took turns' in the fighting, with the result that quite often when we were 'off duty' we were able to go pigeon shooting or exercise our horses instead.*

LETTER 12: 7 (William Birch Reynardson, Naples, to my family in England, dated 4 June 1944)

Trinity Sunday
The Fourth of June 1944

Darling Family,

I have just arrived at a new place and find that we are in very comfortable billets and in a most attractive town built on a cliff overlooking an old village built in grey stone. [...] It has been a very long journey of about twenty four hours from our last camp where we had been for some ten days [...] the journey was slightly gruesome as we all had to travel in cattle trucks. [...] Our beds were put down in rows down the truck, and ten of us lay down to read and write and think. [...] Letter writing [...] is difficult as it is so hard to know what I am allowed to say! Coming through this new country [...] was such fun — new people, new country[side], new architecture: for me, that is what I love. We left the town early in the morning and passed slowly through rather dull flat country, littered with dreary sights of bombing and destruction and poverty — but soon we began to come into the mountains [...] Then [...] through long dark tunnels into the plain. Very flat and highly cultivated with corn and blue flax squares divided from the other fields by poplars standing in the dark against the blue sky. [...]

[As] to my doings of the last week or so, I can't give dates but we arrived not so long ago from North Africa and after a good voyage over, marched ten miles or so to a camp out of the town.

As soon as we had got the chaps settled in, Otto Thwaites and I hitch-hiked into the town. He is a most interesting and charming person. His father is a German and he was educated in Germany and came to England to go to Sandhurst just before the war. Of course he is fascinating to talk to as he knows Goebbels, Goering and the rest personally and the general German outlook on life. But it is difficult for him and often unpleasant. He told me that when he won his Military Cross at [El] Alamein, he wounded a German Officer in a gun emplacement; a few minutes later he was also wounded. While waiting for the ambulance to arrive, all the wounded were collected and there he found that the fellow [he had] wounded had been one of his greatest friends at school. This is just an instance of what he has had to come up against. His uncle is now a Field Marshal in Russia.

By the time we had arrived in the town, the Opera had finished, but we [...]

booked tickets for the next day [...] I went into the magnificent Opera House [&] felt almost sick with excitement. It is a great circular building surrounded by boxes lined in a red plush and faced with white and gilded plaster reaching up to a most beautiful painted ceiling. And from the box (for we were very grand in a beautiful box!) I looked across at the audience, silent and expectant, before the curtain — of dark red, embroidered with gold and silver brocade — rose [...]. We all listened to Susy Morelli singing [*Tosca*] so beautifully and looked at the wonderful scenery [...] I had seen my first Opera, and it had been 'Tosca'[26].

[*The next day*] we [...] saw 'Madame Butterfly'. I didn't enjoy it so much as 'Tosca' — but the singing was very beautiful. After the Opera we all went to dine at a little restaurant the other side of the Bay from the town right on the sea. It was a lovely place and the food, though pretty expensive (but what is £10?) was excellent. Lavinia H[olland] H[ibbert] was also dining there but the party was too large to really have a talk so we made a plan for dinner later on. She was looking so pretty and in very good form. [...]

The next morning I took a party to some very famous ruins not far from the town. They really were fascinating, and the murals were quite beautiful and unbelievably well-preserved. There we saw houses with lovely alabaster baths with hot and cold water laid on — houses centrally heated — public swimming pools in white marble. But I mustn't describe them or it will be censored! [...]

We had a Drill Parade the next morning and [...] [later] went down into the town to hear 'Aida'. This was so different from Puccini's two [*Tosca* and *Madama Butterfly*] that I had seen and I believe I loved it best of all. You have no idea of the scenery, quite fantastic, and of course the singing was wonderful. [...] Clara Jacobs sang Aida's part quite perfectly. [...]

Our last day we spent in town looking at the shops and ending up at the Opera to see Donizetti's 'L'elisir d'amore' — a most amusing and lovely opera to end our 'season'. We went up into the hills again for dinner and hitch-hiked home in the dark. [...]

---

26  Although in my letters I only mention Susy Morelli and Clara Jacobs, I can also remember hearing some of the great names of Italian opera during this period, including Beniamino Gigli, Renata Tebaldi, Gino Bechi and Tito Gobbi — the latter a renowned Scarpia in Puccini's *Tosca* (in which, twenty years later, I was to hear him again, at Covent Garden with Maria Callas in the title role — perhaps the greatest opera performance I have ever been lucky enough to experience). The quality of both the productions and the singing was unbelievable, even though the Germans had only recently left.

*Though Rome was the first Axis capital to fall, there was no prolonged period of rejoicing as less than two days later Operation Overlord — the long-anticipated Allied landings on the Channel coast of Normandy — began. While undoubtedly bringing hope to millions and the end of the war closer in sight, the aftermath of D-Day also brought personal tragedy to our family with the death of my brother-in-law, Captain James Marriott, who was serving with the Oxfordshire and Buckinghamshire Light Infantry (Airborne). He was killed on 10 June 1944, receiving the posthumous award of the George Medal, and is buried at the Herouvillette New Communal Cemetery (between Caen and Cabourg). Two weeks before his death, which left my sister Rosamund a widow at the age of twenty-four with a small baby, Jimmy wrote this letter to my father.*

---

**LETTER 12: 8 (Captain James Marriott, 2nd Battalion, Oxfordshire and Buckinghamshire Light Infantry, to his father-in-law Colonel Henry Birch Reynardson, Adwell, Oxfordshire, dated 28 May 1944)**

Capt. J. Marriott
2nd Battalion Oxford & Bucks. Light Infantry, A.P.O., England

28 May 44

Dear Col. B. R.

Thank you very much for your letter and for the pistol, which is something I have always wanted.

Your letter was very comforting. It is wonderful to feel that I can go away completely confident that my Darling is being looked after and not allowed to worry. I know how marvellous Mother is with her and it makes everything so much easier. It makes me realise how terribly lucky I have been not only in my Wife but in her Father and Mother. Whatever happens I shall never forget all your kindness.

I had not looked at our business in the light that you suggested. It is a kind of crusade and one ought to be very glad and proud to be taking part in it.

When we go I shall do what I can and I believe that we may, God willing, write another page in the Regiment's History.

Thank you again for everything.

Yours
Jimmy

*Britain's mettle was further tested a few days after the Normandy landings with the launch of the new pilotless flying bomb — the V1 (also known as the 'buzz bomb' or 'doodlebug'). These looked like a small plane, weighed two tons when loaded with fuel and were designed to drop 2,000 lbs of explosives, the only warning of an imminent explosion coming when the engine cut out. The first of the V1s fell on 13 June. By 18 June, more than five hundred had fallen on Greater London and the surrounding area — close enough to Windsor for my brother Dickie, then in his last year at Eton, to be well aware of the threat.*

---

**LETTER 12: 9 (Richard Birch Reynardson, Eton College, to our mother Diana Birch Reynardson, dated 18 June 1944)**

My dearest Mother,

We've had quite an exhausting time with these new rocket bombs: the other night the alarm bells went at 11.45 and we did not get to bed again till 7.00: most annoying, and extremely boring as nothing happened at all except for guns at odd times. Apparently one of them hit a hotel in Old Windsor — I wonder if they tried to get the Castle again. I did not have a wink of sleep that night as we had to watch the whole time, and keep the lower boys in order: so we were all very exhausted the next day.

I had a very interesting morning with the Vice Provost [*Lord 'Linky' Cecil*]; he took us all round the Provost's house and showed us all the beautiful pictures. It is rather interesting how the school collected them. In the old days, the Head Master wasn't allowed to accept any fees, so when a boy left, he used to have his portrait painted and gave it to the headmaster. This was the tradition when all the great painters like Romney, Reynolds and Lawrence were alive and all the boys used to have them done by one of these or some other great artist. […] [*There are*] pictures of boys who later became famous Cabinet Ministers, like Pitt, Grenville, Wellington and many others. […]

Your very loving<br>
Dick

*In Italy, the Allies' continued attempts to break through what Churchill had termed the 'soft underbelly' of the Axis met with unexpectedly strong resistance in the German determination to hold their line of defence from Pisa on the Mediterranean coast across the Apennines to Pesaro on the Adriatic — known as the 'Gothic Line'. My Regiment was slowly moving northwards but had still had no opportunity to engage the enemy. One bright spot during this time was the chance to meet up with Helen Addison, who had been our governess during our last two years in South Africa and came to England with us on our return. Helen was extremely pretty and became a great friend of all of us; she had come to Italy as P.A. to a South African General, but by the time I managed to track her down she had become a F.A.N.Y. (First Aid Nursing Yeomanry). The rest of the Regiment referred to her as 'Bill's old governess', until they met her and were then inclined to disbelieve me!*

*In early July I had been admitted to hospital when I spent some time suffering from 'malaria, jaundice and dysentery altogether!'[27], followed by a period of being 'under observation' in a convalescent home at Bari, further south on the Adriatic. It was here that an unwelcome encounter took place; having been quite unwell, I was given a room to myself in the convalescent home, until one day my nurse came in and said that there had been a nasty smash in Yugoslavia and that she would have to put two 'very nice gentlemen' in with me. These turned out to be Randolph Churchill (son of the Prime Minister Winston Churchill) and the novelist and (at the time) war correspondent, Evelyn Waugh! Randolph had been on his way to Yugoslavia as part of a secret military mission to liaise with the Partisans there under the leadership of Josip Broz (soon to be Marshal) Tito, and had recruited Waugh to accompany him, but their plane had crashed on landing, killing ten out of its nineteen passengers. The injured were brought back to Italy for treatment in Bari; Randolph himself was only slightly hurt, reporting in a telegram to his father that he had been diagnosed as having water on both knees and would be in hospital for a week 'with this unheroic complaint'[28], which is how he ended up in my room. It was my misfortune to be between them, in the middle one of the three beds. They never stopped talking (seldom to me!) and drank whisky constantly, day and night. I was glad to move on. (The only good thing to come out of this unenjoyable episode was that when, on my return to Oxford, I became the Chairman of the Chatham Club I got E. Waugh to speak — with Lord David Cecil and John Betjeman — at the Summer Dinner.)*

27  From letter dated 8 July 1944.
28  From records held by Churchill College, Cambridge (CHAR 20/150/75), accessed on www.archives.chu.cam.ac.uk. Another telegram in the same collection (CHAR 20/150/86), sent on 17 July — the same day or the day after the plane crash — is from 'Major Warden' (the codename for Randolph Churchill), addressed to 'Colonel Warden' (Winston Churchill), asking him to inform the wives of Philip Jordan and Evelyn Waugh that they are safe. At the time of the crash, Waugh had just returned to duty after having been granted an extended leave (from January to June 1944), during which he wrote *Brideshead Revisited*.

*By the end of August my Regiment was ready to take part in a renewed attempt to break through the Gothic Line in an offensive code-named Operation Olive. The aim was for the British 8th Army (which included my Regiment) to advance up the Adriatic coast between Pesaro and Rimini, drawing the German reserves from the centre towards the coast which would enable the US 5th Army to skirt round them in a pincer movement and attack from the north west. We had been issued with new (Sherman) tanks, equipped with wirelesses, and before coming into direct engagement with the Germans we had to work very hard in order to be completely conversant with the new wirelesses, guns and engine. My tank was nicknamed 'Foxy' as a pun on my name, by the members of Fourth Troop of which I was now in command, and one of the men painted a large and beautiful fox on the side of it! Over the month of September, several fiercely-contested actions took place; the two with which my squadron was involved were San Savino early in September and the Battle for the Coriano Ridge on the 20th of the same month. During this fortnight of intense activity, I had little time to do more than write a few brief airmail letters (**12: 10** to **12: 12**) in which, although I refer to 'being in action twice since San Savino', the details are sketchy and rather confusing. I can only account for this lapse in clarity by pleading the excuse that we were all somewhat stressed after our first experience of real warfare.*

### Letter 12: 10 (William Birch Reynardson, near Coriano, Italy, to my father Henry Birch Reynardson, dated 7 September 1944)

Dearest Father,

I'm afraid that I have not written to any of you for some time but I believe you know that there is not an awful lot of time for letter writing. I can, of course, mention no dates but we have, at last, had a 'do' with the Hun, a pretty big one which succeeded, but they are holding on to this Italian Line like grim death. Poor Robbie Stuart, having only just joined the Regiment, […] was very badly wounded and I'm afraid has to be counted gone; and Peter Caro's tank was knocked out and we have heard nothing of him since. However, you must know what it is like — no one broods over things like this and we really have had very small casualties. We are now out of battle and resting — though the shelling is pretty severe.

But it is wonderful what terrific form everyone is in — their sense of humour is great. My gunner, Corporal Nichols (who did great work in the battle) is conspicuous. […] The cooking plays an important part, quite naturally; and great inter-tank competitions take place. Lambert (Sergeant Hughes' gunman with a tremendous and hideous Manchester accent) is renowned for Yimkin Dough (pronounced Duff) — Yimkin, as perhaps you know, is Arabic for 'perhaps' — the dainty dish is made of mashed up army biscuits and jam boiled for three hours in any various pieces of cloth. We had some for supper yesterday — it was quite excellent, possibly that little flavour was added by my right pyjama leg in which the biscuits were boiled.

I have as yet seen nothing of John Ashton [*my cousin — see* **12: 18**] [...] You might be interested to hear the general story of our doings. General Leese spoke to us all a few weeks ago — telling us that the object was to get the Hun out of Italy in two months. As you know, we withdrew from the Gothic Line leaving a few [*word missing*] to hold us up. We then fell back to very strong positions in the foothills about seven miles behind it and are holding a line of high ground which we are now fighting on. Coriano is a key town in this line and we are shelling this all the time. I took 38 prisoners — once they are in the bag they lose all the will to fight but are far from passive in the line! I took a very nice pair of binoculars off one and John Joicey got an automatic; we have seen no German aeroplanes or tanks but they are not short of guns and their anti-tank weapons (bazookas) are good at short ranges. [...] It doesn't look to me as if we shall be doing anything for some time anyway.

How different battle is to one's first idea — the excitement and all else is forgotten.

Your loving Bill

**LETTER 12: 11 (William Birch Reynardson, near Coriano, Italy, to my mother Diana Birch Reynardson, in England, dated 11 September 1944)**

Darling Mother,

[...] I can't tell you much about the battle, nor would it really interest you to know. The Squadron got the objective after a stiff battle though and casualties were, considering all things, very light. [...] But let me quickly tell you that one loses one's self in battle and, in the acute concentration and excitement, emotions such as fear or pity go, or seem to, and one returns as from a dream to one's old self after the fighting is done. It is a wonderful thing too — for the vile things of battle are absolutely forgotten and will not mud [*sic*] the mind. [...]

One great advantage of tank fighting is that once the fighting is over, one can get back to normal very quickly as all comforting kit is carried on the tank. [...] But it is [...] vital to remember the good things and to realise the good things when they come along. I have been reading my diary this afternoon — six months ago now we were all dining at the Hungaria after seeing Jack [*Hulbert*] and Cicely Courtneidge[29], wasn't that fun? I wonder where Johnnie Althorp is, and Brian Cumming. They must be in France or I would have heard from them. But there is usually so little time to write.

The mail came up yesterday — letters from both of you. [...] Thank you so much for them. I was glad you liked the scent etc. The next parcel will come from Berlin and not so long from now either! [...]

### Letter 12: 12 (William Birch Reynardson, near Rimini, Italy, to my father Henry Birch Reynardson, dated 26 September 1944)

Dearest Father,

Your letter dated the 20th and mother's too arrived in record time yesterday — just like the old Algiers days when letters took four days! What a long time ago it seems since we were there [...]

You might like to know the situations — about three weeks ago the Brigade went into action against the San Savino-Coriano Ridge. It was a far stiffer job than had (as usual!) been supposed. However, the Ridge fell after a week and we moved up to the next ridge, north-west of Rimini. Although there was comparatively little resistance, the Hun had left a few self-propelled guns behind him as a rearguard in his withdrawal over the River Marecchia. David Gavin's Regiment, the Bays, led the Brigade towards the river and as it moved over the ridge before the river it came under severe fire from three guns. Two Squadrons were very badly knocked about. My Regiment were supporting them, but the decision was made that we were to halt (thank goodness!) and we stayed below the crest for the rest of the day.

That night the Regiment withdrew, leaving me in command of two Troops to hold the sector. Infantry support were, I was told, expected in two hours. As night fell, it rained as you can never imagine! The infantry suffered severe casualties from the heavy shell fire and, in fact, never came up to support me.

---

29  Cicely Courtneidge (1893–1980) and her husband Jack Hulbert (1892–1978) were stage box-office royalty during the first half of the twentieth century, often starring together in musical comedies and revues.

It was, you see, a slightly tricky position for me! However, no Hun attempted to counter-attack, so hard were they running back behind the river — so all was well! The shelling was severe, but one is perfectly safe as long as one does not wander about outside the tank (I never do!)

Derek [*Allhusen — our Squadron Leader*] and I went up to look at the Hun gun position which [had] shot at the leading Regiment [*the Queen's Bays*]. The field of fire was about ten miles long and five wide — so he had a very good stand! No doubt he is proudly wearing the Iron Cross now! General R.H's [*see* footnote 31] short command has now ended — as also has a Brigadier who had particular interests with us. We are all very sad about this. However we have a first class new one […]

Yesterday John Joicey and I went up to the Republic of San Marino. It is a tiny Free State built on the top of a mountain. From here we could see for miles and miles over the loveliest country. Of course, the Boche had all of his Observation Posts there and could see all our movements. But he can't any more!

### Letter 12: 13 (William Birch Reynardson, near Rimini, to my family in England, dated 26 September 1944)

My darling Family,

It is really a very long time since I wrote a sea-mail letter to you all — […] I believe that I have not written a magnum opus since […] the first of August, nearly two months ago and yet it seems two years! […] In those days we were all just south of Bari camping on the coast of the Adriatic. It really was a very lovely place and we spent most of our time in the water or lying in the sun looking out on the blue, blue sea. There was really very little to do in those days — we were waiting (as always!) to do something and no one seemed to want us awfully.

[…] But all this existence ended with rather a bump for us all on August 6th when we began our move northwards.

The journey was very slow and so that we might muddle the Germans (as well as ourselves!) the route was extremely roundabout and included many Leaguering Areas [*encampments of a besieging army*] where we stayed for perhaps as long as a week. […] The first long halt was Ortona, on the Adriatic, for we tried to keep near the sea as much as we possibly could. The town was almost flat[30]

---

30   From earlier bombardment by the Canadian Army and house-to-house fighting during the Battle of Ortona in December 1943.

[*so we*] had difficulty with the food situation! However, with the help of tins of bully beef, soap and cigarettes, I managed to extract quite a number of products from the local inhabitants. It is rather fun going round the farms and collecting eggs from them. Most of the farmers are definitely pro-British and will do anything to help — [...] I found there was need for [...] control in the consumption of local vino which they invariably offered me! We started off again from Ortona after four days and drove on up to Civitanova. Here we got all set for war and there was a certain amount of activity. The guns were all checked and we had great target practices out to sea — the tank engines were overhauled and I took my Troop out map-reading, night and day. I am certain it is essential to be efficient at this. One learns to know the path of the sun by day and the stars by night — and in learning their movements, I came to know their beauty more and more. [...]

Then we began our last hop [...] and arrived for the battle for the San Savino/Coriano Ridge some three weeks ago. The country was really fearful for tanks and as we moved up the road early that morning and Derek told us to look North at our objective two miles away, I must admit I began to wonder. For I could see great hills with gullies below them and horrid heavy plough (which is so inclined to force the tracks off the tanks), but there was no time for a closer look to the ground.

We turned northwards into a field and the Squadron formed up behind Derek; I was on his left, John Joicey was in the centre and Peter Caro was on the right with John Goldsmid in support behind.

Before we had time to make much of a plan we began to get heavily shelled and we decided that it was time to get going! [...] The first look over the crest was appalling! For there below me was a ghastly gully, quite impossible for a tank to get over; so I decided to edge round to the left. Meanwhile everything seemed to be 'coming my way'! However, Corporal Nichols was superb and shot all the guns everywhere and we must have looked so formidable that the chaps stopped and let me get on with the job!

The battle was by now well away and we had got on to the objective and John Joicey was in a first class position to my right flank, while Peter had gone ahead (and without support) to the village.

It surprised me how remarkably clearly one can still think when there is such a noise about — particularly as I was shaking with excitement — or fear, I'm not quite sure which! Anyway it was at least the fear, if that is the word, that one gets when there is a fair devil of an obstacle (water on the take-off side!) ahead — there is such a devil of a lot to think about.

Then we came to a vile place with a steep hill in heavy plough — I told my sergeant to go to the right and my Troop Corporal and I went down the hill. Both our tracks came off. It was a pretty grim moment — I really do think we would have pushed the Hun out of the Ridge but we had had so many casualties, few through enemy action but many through ground. We had to stay for a day and a night under heavy shell fire.

Of course the chaps, as I expected, were quite magnificent. We all lay on our tummies in a Boche trench and giggled. I captured my 38 Germans here [*see* **12: 10**]. It was very interesting talking to them. They are, of course, lost without someone to lead them and they appear to care little what happened to them. [...] There will not be a quick defeat in Italy. The country is against us terribly. One Boche gun can hold up a Regiment for six hours and can do a great deal of damage. They have in fact done this to one of the Regiments in the Brigade.

We are at the moment looking constantly at the sky for signs of the weather breaking. An hour's rain in Italy holds us up for four or five hours, as we get so easily bogged down. And there isn't long before the rain begins in earnest. [...]

We have been in action twice since San Savino — not big days but for shellings they weren't too bad. Our futures now seem to be uncertain. Anyway we shall be doing nothing for some time now as there has been a complete reorganisation which, of course, I cannot write about but which you may already know about when I say that a General we all know personally has lost his Command[31]. Not for one moment because he did not do well, quite definitely not. It is merely bad luck — but I cannot say more.

---

*The Battle of Coriano Ridge on 20 September* (**Fig. 12 e)**) *was altogether a more serious affair than the action at San Savino, involving many more casualties, especially of the Queen's Bays. My regiment was supposed to be supporting the Queen's Bays after they had moved over the ridge. I can remember leading 'B' Squadron to the bottom of the ridge, where we halted to await further orders. After a fairly long wait, Derek [Allhusen] came over to me, looking very white and serious, and called John Joicey to join us. 'Now you two, I want you to climb up this hill but pretend that you're stalking a stag in Scotland*

---

31  This refers to General Dick Hull (a neighbour of ours in Oxfordshire), who commanded the 1st Armoured Division in Italy at the start of Operation Olive. This division was disbanded at the end of September, but in November Hull went on to command the 5th Division, which he led through the final phases of the war in North West Europe. In 1961, as Field Marshal Sir Richard Hull, he became the last Chief of the Imperial General Staff.

*and keep down when you get to the top.' So off we set, crawling much of the way. What was rather odd was that there was no 88mm gun fire and only occasional machine gun fire. Then we very gingerly poked our heads over the top. We saw twenty-four tanks of the Queen's Bays on fire and many soldiers lying dead around their tanks. John and I had a long discussion as to our route. John favoured going over to our left but then I spotted a bit of a hedge line on our right and we agreed that this would be 'best' (rather an odd description of what would have been a fairly desperate move!)*

*We returned to Derek to report on our conclusion. He went very quiet. We waited. In the end, after about an hour, he announced that his wireless had 'broken down'. We never received the order to advance. I have always wondered about that mysterious failure of the radio. I record this in some detail because it was the first time that I felt fear.*

*Although the Gothic Line had been breached in several places during the early autumn, no decisive breakthrough had been achieved by the Allied Armies. The British 8th Army continued to press north up the Adriatic coast and on 5 November captured Ravenna, but with the onset of winter weather, it looked as though any further advance would have to wait for the spring. A few days after the capture of Ravenna a telegram, of the sort which every parent must have dreaded receiving, arrived at Adwell.*

**Fig. 12 e)** John Joicey and his crew at Coriano Ridge. Photograph, 20 September 1944. On the back of the photograph is written 'Coriano Ridge. Waiting to go.'.

## 12: 14 (Telegram from Under Secretary of State for War, to Henry Birch Reynardson, Adwell, dated 13 November 1944)

POST OFFICE TELEGRAM

13th November 1944
3.30 Liverpool O.H.M.S.

Priority

H.T. Birch Reynardson, Esq
Adwell House, Tetsworth

Report received from Central Mediterranean Area that Lt. W.R.A. Birch Reynardson, Royal Armoured Corps, was wounded on 5th November 1944. The Army Council express sympathy, letter follows shortly.

Under Secretary of State for War

---

*I had been blown up by a German Nebelworther multi-mortar, which injured my left hand; I wrote to my parents that 'all my fingers except my thumb were broken but only two have been actually knifed […] I have to be very thankful that it was not worse, as just between us, it was the nearest thing that ever happened! One shell fell so near that the three infantry chaps thought it had fallen on me! In fact it merely blew me conveniently into the nearest ditch and the shrapnel went over my head — one bit actually through the top of my tin hat!' As a result, I had to be evacuated and to undergo an operation, and was out of action for about six weeks, although there was no question of my being sent home. Luckily for my parents' peace of mind, my friends were quicker off the mark than the Army Council and some of their letters offering reassurance may even have arrived before the official telegram.*

**Letter 12: 15 (John Joicey, in Italy, to my mother Diana Birch Reynardson, dated 6 November 1944)**

6th November 1944

Dear Mrs Birch Reynardson

I felt sure you would like to know how Bill is progressing after being wounded. I saw him about half an hour after the tragedy happened — he was very cheerful and walked into the house where he had his hand dressed. He was then rushed to a hospital in Rimini, where the top joints of his fingers were amputated.

David Laurie went and saw him after the operation [...] The doctor said that he won't be disabled at all[32], which is grand news. Bill is a great friend to us and we all hope it won't be long before he is fit again.

[...] Please excuse this awful scribble in pencil [...]

Yours sincerely
John Joicey

---

*I had a thoroughly enjoyable convalescence, at first in a hospital near Ancona before being moved by boat to Bari. Within three weeks, I managed to 'wangle my way to Naples' where there were many people I knew, including my old friend Delia Holland-Hibbert[33].*

---

32  After the war, rather against the wishes of my father, I did go before a Medical Board to make inquiries about receiving some compensation for my wound. At first I was told by a rather ancient Admiral that my injuries (two fingers partially amputated) did not justify compensation. Then I remarked that the disability made it difficult for me to hold a double bridle, particularly when playing polo. The Admiral sat up at this, pulled out his wallet, gave me a (white, in those days) £5 note and nothing further was said!

33  Delia Holland-Hibbert has been a close friend since Pony Club days in childhood and remains so to this day. At the time of writing, she was in the WRNS based in Caserta; when not on duty one of her main occupations was to exercise Field Marshal Alexander's horses! After the war, Delia married Lt. Col. Bill Cunningham, M.C., the Field Marshal's Military Assistant.

LETTER 12: 16 (William Birch Reynardson, 67th General Hospital, Naples, to my father Henry Birch Reynardson, in England, dated 2 December 1944)

I hope that you will have got the cable which General Wilson let me send from A.F.H.Q. [*Allied Forces Head Quarters*] the other day [...] My fingers are healing a treat, but I almost wish that I was more ill, as it is maddening being able to do practically everything except rejoining my Regiment. However, I hope to be back with them all by Christmas[34]. Letters are non-existent here! I suppose that they are following me round every hospital that I have ever been to. Anyway, I have had none since I was wounded which is a pity.

I met someone who left the Brigade two days ago — apparently we have had some more fighting and a particularly successful battle. There have been no casualties. I long to know how my Troop have done. I don't even know who's commanding them now. I have been up to A.F.H.Q. twice since I arrived. Of course the General is far too busy to see me, but Hermione Ranfurly has been as kind as ever and is always making plans for me! They all hate the idea of going to Washington[35], I think, particularly Hermione as both Dan and Daphne are in Italy. [...]

---

*When I returned to my Regiment in January 1945, it was to begin three months of frustrating waiting. The extreme mountainous terrain and weather conditions, together with unexpectedly stiff resistance from the 'soft underbelly' of the enemy, meant that since the previous September, despite the assistance of Italian partisans, the Allies had managed to advance less than a hundred miles northwards. The German army was encamped on the north bank of the River Senio and for some weeks we were in the bizarre position of being within both sight and sound of them, but with no action taking place. That all changed in the middle of April, when the last great push began.*

---

34 I was signed off fit to return before the end of December, and was promptly sent on leave! This was spent in Rome with a couple of fellow officers, with whom I had the great experience of learning to play polo at the Rome Polo Club — 'the best thing in the world for my hand, which is quickly getting more supple'.
35 At the end of November, Lady Ranfurly's boss, General 'Jumbo' Wilson (see footnote 22), was told that he was to succeed Field Marshal Dill in Washington as head of the British Joint Staff Mission and asked her to accompany him as part of his staff. To her great relief (as it would have meant another separation from her husband) the offer was withdrawn at the very last moment when Jumbo's wife objected!

## Letter 12: 17 (William Birch Reynardson, in the Po Valley, to my mother Diana Birch Reynardson, in England, dated 23 March 1945)

[…] We are still Reserve — that is to say my Troop, though I go forward soon now. But even at the front, there is very little on. It is an amazing kind of warfare at the moment. The enemy and our chaps are divided by a flood bank and often one can hear them talking. […] We are all waiting expectantly. We heard at lunchtime that Field Marshal Montgomery had crossed the Rhine and last night that General Patton had. So the news from the Western Front could not be improved upon.

One cannot help but to be optimistic; on the other hand the Germans have little to lose, for so many have been trained to fight and consider this a great chance to prove their [?]worth. They know no other profession. Also they are a tremendously patriotic nation and I am sure that they will fight to the very last for that reason. I cannot see the war finishing before August or September, but I may be wrong. […]

We are all, in different ways, glorifying in the coming of Spring. […] I always go out for a walk before dinner for an hour and yesterday we returned carrying bundles of violets and wild daffodils and cherry blossom, which we have put in the Mess. And Palm Sunday is tomorrow. I shall use your little book as I cannot get to Church.

My love to you all,
Bill

## Letter 12: 18 (William Birch Reynardson, Northern Italy, to my family, dated 15 April 1945)

9th Lancers C.M.F.

[…] Since I last wrote to you the battle has begun — you will have heard that on the wireless. It began with a very big raid with Heavy and Medium Bombers supported by Spitfires in the air — and artillery and flame throwers on the ground. It was no wonder that the River Senio was crossed fairly easily by us. The Bailey Bridge was soon erected and we crossed over at first light. As with all rivers out here there are double flood banks on each side about forty foot high. Therefore the enemy can dig positions in the bank and no tank can get at them. It was amazing to see his implacements [sic]. He had made himself quite comfortable in there during the Winter! Often he had dug in on our side of the Senio — so that our Infantry would hear them talking about twenty feet of earth separating them.

Once over the Senio we cracked on pretty fast over the Santerno up to the Reno. This is a very big river and we were a bit held up with bridging problems and mine clearing (which cover the ground in number). We have advanced through very flat but very close country. The fields are sown with clover or wheat with rows of young poplars (about 50' apart) from which are strung vines. So a Boche can hide quite easily and jump up at you and aim his bazooka. Thank goodness it takes quite a long time to aim the thing!

All the time our air and artillery support has been excellent — and no German aeroplane has been seen. We were all sitting quite close together yesterday standing off our tanks wondering why we weren't being shelled when so close to the Boche, and suddenly the biggest Stonk you ever did see arrived. The speed of our embussing was stupendous and in a very short time at least 100 yards separated each tank! We have all had a lot of laughs — as always.

John Ashton has just turned up — very nice seeing him. He is kept pretty busy at his job now. Charles can't be far away — the chaps that he is with are in Reserve at the moment.

April 16th 1945
Sorry! We moved in a hurry! Everything is going very well which is good — and the whole affair is very exciting. The worst part of this to-do is that we have no spare time — the map setting sessions are quite awful. We have three sets (100, 50 and 25 thousand) and air photographs. You can imagine the chaos in the wind! [...]

[...] There may well now be a gap in my letters — but you will understand.

---

*In fact, as we went into battle just over a day later and achieved our objective by nightfall, it was not long before I wrote again — to Lorna on 19 April and a fuller account to my father the next day. Both letters, naturally, concentrate on the actions of the 4th Troop (my troop) but our Colonel, Jack Price[36]* (**Fig. 12 f)**), *wrote his own more comprehensive*

---

36  Jack Price had taken over as Colonel from Lt. Colonel 'Stug' Perry when the latter caught diphtheria in March. He was a brilliant and inspirational leader during the last dramatic weeks of the war. Less than a year later, he married my friend Judy Slessor (daughter of the Air Marshal — see footnote 25), who thus became the Colonel's wife and had to be treated with considerably more deference and respect!

*summary immediately afterwards of the Regiment's part in the battle, which I also reproduce here* (**12: 21**).

Fig. 12 f) Lt.-Colonel Jack Price. Photograph.

## LETTER 12: 19 (William Birch Reynardson, Northern Italy [near Ferrara], to Lorna Bailie, dated 19 April 1945)

Two lovely letters were brought up to me late last night.

But they arrived at a perfect time. We had a very big battle yesterday — and it was so lovely to come into Leaguer and find them waiting for me. [...] Yesterday [...] was a tremendous experience. We started off at 4.30 am (with a bully sandwich and a cup of tea in our tummies!) At about eight o'clock we met the forward elements of the enemy — I was leading on the left flank and David Wentworth Stanley was on my right.

By lunch time we had advanced some five miles against very heavy opposition and were held up for a short time by a big water obstacle. Cpl Nicholls (my gunner [...]) was shooting very straight and we had by then knocked out an enemy tank and a self-propelled gun. It was intensely exciting and very tiring. [...] The big 'charge' then took place. It was terrific. Under a tremendous hail of fire from two squadrons of tanks (ourselves and 'A') and support from artillery and bombing, we advanced over three miles of very open ground. We knocked out a tank and two guns — and John Joicey got four guns. We took our objective just as night was drawing in. All the farms were blazing and lit the twilight with the setting sun.

### Letter 12: 20 (William Birch Reynardson, Northern Italy [near Ferrara], to my father Henry Birch Reynardson, dated 20 April 1945)

[…] A day has now passed since the big battle of the Argenta Gap. After two days of waiting we moved out of Leaguer before first light on Wednesday. The road was pretty crowded with Armour as we advanced slowly up to the start point and the sun was up before we reached the gap through which the Squadron was to pass.

As usual there was a lot of confusion! We were told that the enemy had retreated to a canal two miles away. However as I took up my position (leading on the left flank) I very quickly realised that the Boche still lurked around as two bullets narrowly missed my hat! The next item was the biggest gun […] which I failed to see. Cpl Probert, who has eyes like a hawk, very quickly got the tank into reverse though, as he shouted down the wireless to me. Thank goodness it had been abandoned and no damage was done.

But that had well taken the sleepiness from our eyes! We advanced pretty quickly down a road and then pulled away left-handed across country — there was at least some cover here as all the fields have these vines stretched across young poplars.

We settled down to some hard shooting then and Cpl Nicholls had to traverse very fast to shoot a Mk IV tank whose gun was wheeling round on us all too quickly at 150 yards range! We pushed on again — all the farm houses seemed to hold Germans and by the time we reached the Canal both my machine guns were red hot and therefore too hot to fire. I looked behind them — every house was ablaze.

[…] By now the Boche were obviously pretty hectic and began coming in, leaving their guns behind. The main road came in sight. If we could get over it and cut it we knew that a good many Boche in the village down the road from it would be in the bag.

So we got our whips well out and galloped across a very frightening bit of open ground and just made the cover of a farm house before they realised what was happening! It was tremendously exciting. And so we really had them on the hop! John Joicey arrived at a farm house and captured the whole officers' mess.

Then 'A' Squadron came up on our right flank and we lined up for a charge on our objective. [...] At the word 'go', twenty eight tanks advanced with infantry in support. The noise was tremendous and the Boche hadn't a hope — and but for the odd gunner who [...] popped up from his trench [...] (causing no damage) — we had little bother. German tanks and guns were lying everywhere. We reached our objective at 8.30 pm.

[...] We have now been resting for a day. It has been lovely in the sun — but there seems to be very little spare time all the same.

[...] Must stop now. This seems to be mostly about Fourth Troop but you will understand. Perhaps Mother would be rather bored with the details; so it is mostly for you.

## 12: 21 (An account of the fighting by Colonel Jack Price, written on or soon after 19 April 1945)

'B' Squadron (**Fig. 12 g)**) on the left had 4th Troop under Bill Birch Reynardson, supported by S.S.M. Huxford in a 105mm tank, and 3th Troop under John Joicey, supported by Otto Thwaites in a 105mm tank, leading, with 2nd Troop under John Goldsmid echeloned back to the left rear. All went in together.

In an area of about 800 square yards they overran a battery of 4 88mm anti-aircraft guns and a battery of 4 150mm field guns as well as 12 20mm ack ack guns. The German gunners put up a very brave show and all went on firing over open sights right up to the end. Luckily the 88s had been sited primarily for ack ack and were taken completely by surprise. They did manage to load with armour piercing and fired a considerable number of rounds at our tanks but they were so cluttered up with camouflage and branches of trees and so plastered with HE [*high explosive*] and browning from our tanks that their aim was very erratic and they only hit Michael de Burgh's tank, whose suspension was holed but he was able to continue. David Whately's tank was hit by a 150mm HE shell but was able to continue although the commander's ear drums were broken.

At the same time as this was going on 'C' Squadron and 'H' Company on the right were having a similar party with a battery of 4 105[*mm*] field guns and a battery of 3 88mm guns which they captured intact. All the time, with all three squadrons, prisoners were streaming in and surprised strong points being routed out by the London Irish. Many enemy vehicles were burning and much equipment, and a large number of houses which had been strong points were on fire, having been set alight by the HE from the tanks.

Just as it was getting dark all squadrons and companies reported that they were on their objectives and were mopping up and consolidating. Further advances were impossible as it was now quite dark and there were still a large number of Germans including many bazooka parties in the area to be dealt with.

R.H.Q. by now had established itself at La Fossa right in the middle of the box formed by the 4 squadrons and companies. When I stepped out of my tank the countryside was a most incredible sight. It was quite dark and we were completely surrounded by a ring of fire. There were 21 houses burning with flames roaring through the roofs, innumerable German vehicles burning and 2 ammunition dumps exploding and sending up every sort of firework.

BACK: W.B.R., JOHN JOICEY, JOHN GOLDSMID, DAVID WENTWORTH STANLEY
FRONT: REX HITCHCOCK, DAVID LAURIE, OTTO THWAITES.
PALMANOVA, ITALY, 1945

**Fig. 12 g)** 'B' Squadron Officers, Palmanova, 1945. Photograph.

*After the success of the Argenta Gap, the Allied advance (**Fig. 12 h**)) was much faster though not, as I reported on 28 April, without some sticky moments. Within a week of the battle, we crossed the River Po; a day or two later, Jack Price wrote a message to us which ended: 'I feel that the 9th Lancers have probably fired their last shot in Europe — and what a shot!' From the armies advancing towards Berlin, shocking reports were coming out as the concentration camps were liberated. Mussolini was captured on the shores of Lake Como on 27 April and executed the next day; his body and those of fellow Fascists were taken to Milan and hung for public display in one of the main squares. On 30 April, in his bunker at the Reichs Chancellery in Berlin, Hitler shot himself, followed the next day by the suicide of his Propaganda Chief, Goebbels. On the evening of 1 May, General Mark Clark, commanding the Allied Troops in Italy, announced that all organised resistance in Italy had ended and the next day Field Marshal Alexander announced the unconditional surrender of all German forces in Italy to the Allies. Berlin also capitulated on 2 May and five days later Germany surrendered unconditionally. VE (Victory in Europe) Day was celebrated on 8 May.*

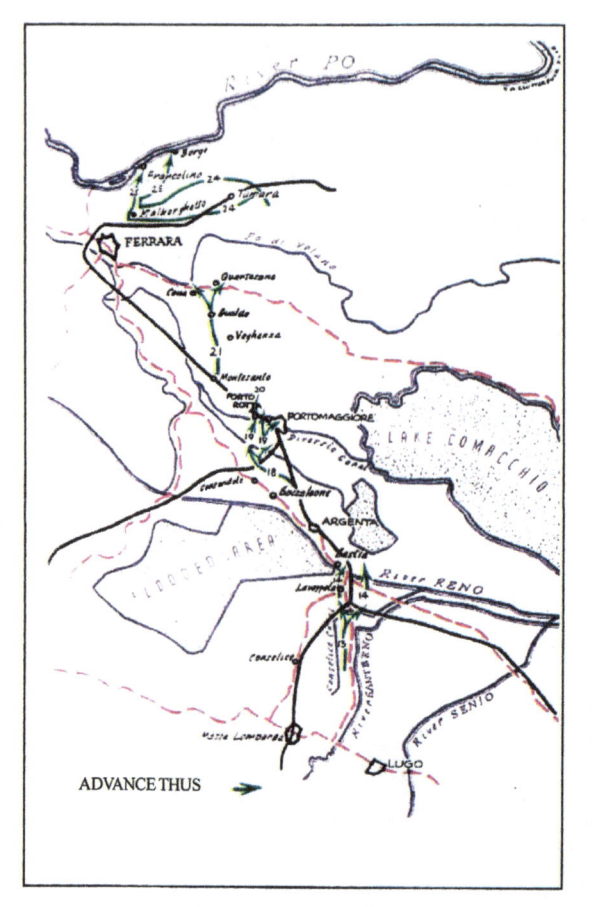

**Fig. 12 h)** Plan of the final Allied advance, April 1945.

**Letter 12: 22 (William Birch Reynardson, Northern Italy [north of the River Po], to my father Henry Birch Reynardson, dated 28 April 1945)**

Dearest Father,

Now, as you will have heard on the wireless, the first phase of this campaign has been accomplished. The Eighth and Fifth Armies have crossed the Po. In a great flanking movement, with Ferrara as the objective, the Germans have been forced to retreat and in doing so a great number of men and a large quantity of equipment has been lost. The advance was so fast in the end that the enemy was forced to destroy much of his armour and wheeled transport himself as they were unable to get them over the river.

The regiment has had an important task and 'B' Squadron has taken part in all the battles. I think that I last wrote to you on the 20th. Since then, of course, we have reached the Po. It really is very exciting seeing the end drawing so close, and it was very much in evidence as soon as Ferrara fell.

John Joicey and I had one very exciting battle when we flushed a covey of Mark IVs. We had really taken them by surprise as they were making off towards the Po as fast as they could go. John was on the left and I was on the right — suddenly I heard John shouting over his wireless that there was a tank coming down the road towards him. He got that one which evidently roused the others and some three crossed my front. Sergeant Edmunds got a right and left and I got the last. Then John got two more on my left.

By this time it was getting dark but we simply had to get on to our objective. We knew that the Boche were running for it so we formed Box formation and moved on in the dark. John had a very unpleasant moment as he was fired on at very close range by an 88mm. The only refuge he could find was a very small signal box and soon he found all three of his tanks there! 'Any moment now the signal box will be hit and then we'll all be very much out in the cold' — that was his message on the wireless. But all was well and the situation ended abruptly by a large explosion — they had 'brewed'[37] the gun themselves! This was the case time and again and they really do seem to be a bit windy!

Our hearts are very high and we hope to be in Venice very soon now! I can't tell you about the actions really now as I feel perhaps one should be security-minded about some of the facts — but when I get back to you I will tell you the whole story!

---

37 'Brewed', short for 'brewed up', means 'set fire to' (or otherwise sabotaged). The Germans often destroyed their equipment rather than leaving it for us to use.

[...] Tonight we heard the news that Himmler had asked for an unconditional surrender from us and the Americans. This is indeed a sound sign of the end. Though, as the Prime Minister said, we cannot forget Japan [...]

## Letter 12: 23 (William Birch Reynardson, Northern Italy, to my mother Diana Birch Reynardson, dated 5 May 1945)

Darling Mother,

I expect that you rejoiced as much as we did when you heard the splendid news on May 2nd. Isn't it glorious! It has been a campaign which has gone according to plan from our original crossing of the Senio on April 10th and the enemy really packed up when we arrived south of the Po on that tremendously exciting night of April 21st — and now the rest of them seem to be following their more than excellent example! This evening we heard that the forces in the North West had surrendered. The end indeed seems very near. We, of course, had a tremendous party when the news that the Italian Campaign was over reached us. All the chaps got frightfully drunk (and deservedly so!). David ordered a royal salute from all the guns in the Squadron. Soon it developed into a battle — everything was firing! The Fourth of June wasn't in it! [...]

We have all been simply horrified and appalled by the reports on these German Concentration Camps. It is very difficult to forgive them for this. It is a proof of the beastly lowness of mind that the Nazis have bowed down to. [...]

We are all very disappointed that we are not up at the kill — it has been rather an anti-climax. However, leave parties have already started in Venice and David and I are going on Tuesday. [...]

## Letter 12: 24 (William Birch Reynardson, Northern Italy, to my mother Diana Birch Reynardson, dated 11 May 1945)

I listened to the Prime Minister's historic speech[38] on the 9th in one of the most beautiful cities in the world. Though we are still sitting on the Po (nothing will move us!), Rex, David Laurie, John Joicey and I drove up to Venice on Tuesday [...]. It couldn't have been a better time to go — we were all so happy and thankful that the end in Europe had really come at last.

But we no celebration had [sic] when the unconditional surrender of Italy was announced, there have been no parties. I think that there are three main reasons: firstly the surrender of the enemy has not come at all unexpectedly; after nearly a year of campaigning in the last phase of the war (beginning at the invasion of France) their defeat has been certain. Secondly the continuation of the fighting against the Japanese and the horrors that we have all heard [about] are not forgotten. And finally the 'tremendous difficulties' that lie ahead in the world are of [...] concern to everyone.

This morning we all went to church in Ferrara to thank God for His help and guidance. It really was a lovely service; and there was a feeling of sincere thanksgiving as we all prayed and sang. I enclose the service sheet, which I should like you to keep if you would. [...]

But to Venice! [...] We drove up most luxuriously [*in a very smart car looted from the enemy at the end of the offensive!*] in about two and a half hours [...]. It really is most impressive driving up the Autostrada leading to the town, with the sea on both sides of us. [*We managed to get*] a splendid room in the Grand Hotel overlooking the Grand Canal. It was so much more satisfying as we weren't allowed to stay there! After lunch we went down the Canal in a gondola in the hot sun. [*Later*] we dined in our rooms [...] and saw the sun setting over the Canal — I think you can imagine the beauty of it as the gondoliers sang their way home under the yellow lights in the gondolas. [...] Oh! It is a lovely place. It was maddening that we only had 48 hours there, but no doubt we shall be back there again soon.

---

38  On 8 May, Winston Churchill made the broadcast announcement of Germany's unconditional surrender, which contained the words: 'The German war is therefore at an end ... We may allow ourselves a brief period of rejoicing; but let us not forget for a moment the toil and efforts that lie ahead.' On the same day, Churchill and his principal colleagues appeared on the balcony of the Ministry of Health, at the lower end of Whitehall, and made two short speeches to the vast crowd waiting below, the first of which I quote in full. 'God bless you all. This is your victory!' (At these words, the crowd roared back, 'No — it is yours!') 'It is the victory of the cause of freedom in every land. In all our long history we have never seen a greater day than this. Everyone, man or woman, has done their best. Everyone has tried. Neither the long years, nor the dangers, nor the fierce attacks of the enemy, have in any way weakened the independent resolve of the British nation. God bless you all.'

We are all wondering what our fortune is — at the moment the War Office doesn't seem to know quite what to do with us. We all hope for Austria, it would be such fun with our horses and the shooting so near. Leave will be generous […] At the moment we spend the mornings with our chaps doing the odd jobs that need finishing off after the battle; then we all go out riding in the afternoon or the evening and back for a late dinner. Bathing is beginning and already the keen water boys have been to Lake Como. So we are really very happy […]

I know that I shall always be glad that I have fought in this war. The difference between good and evil shines like a beacon through the darkness of war.

I must stop now — my brain hasn't quite got accustomed to this new life and as yet I can't really get down to concentrated thinking. […] I believe that we all became very tired during the last battle and it takes a little time to recover.

Bless you all,
Your loving Bill

### Letter 12: 25 (William Birch Reynardson, Northern Italy, to my father Henry Birch Reynardson, dated 14 May 1945)

[…] Now that the first thrill of peace in Europe has passed, we have all been talking and thinking a good deal about our own personal futures. I enclose a letter from Colonel Jack [*Price*] which explains the general situation.

My Release Group number is 50 and therefore I cannot possibly expect to leave the Army for eighteen months. But during that period I might possibly be posted away from the Regiment and my friends. As the Colonel says, it would give him a far better reason to bellyache for me, if I was posted away, if I had passed the Regular Officers' Board. This in no way would force me to stay in the Army. There is no clause about an early release from the Army in order to go to the University. I think that I could probably leave sooner if I wanted to continue with the medical course. But that is the question which I cannot decide […] without talking to you both about it.

I can't think that eighteen months in the Regiment will do me any harm! In fact it will be tremendous fun and a great experience. And in that time I shall be able to think about a profession (having, I hope, been on leave by then and seen you!) I am now twenty-one: before the war I should have been up at Christ Church. I think that I have gained more in the army to prepare me for life than I would have in the comparative isolation of Oxford. The last two and a half years have not been a waste of time — they have been tremendously valuable (and tremendous fun!)

Even if I decide against being a doctor, I should not consider myself educated if I do not go up to Oxford again, as I know that my brain has been forced to work rather differently during my time in the Army and needs a bit of schooling before it recovers again! I propose putting my name down for this Board as there seems to be nothing against it. But I will wait for your reply. […]

---

*For nearly sixteen months after the end of the war — apart from a long-awaited leave home in November, extending into February 1946 as I needed more surgery on my hand — I stayed with my Regiment in Italy. In* Letters to Lorna *I describe this period as an 'extraordinary year of sheer enjoyment'; it was filled by racing, eventing, shooting, trips to the opera and visits to many of the wonderful cities and towns of Italy — a kind of Grand Tour. As I had hoped, we went to Austria more than once: the first time in June 1945 to choose some horses for the Regimental Stables from a huge crowd of horses captured from the German cavalry; on another occasion a year later to take part in the 16th Lancers' show near Klagenfurt, in the part of Austria occupied by the British Army; and finally to attend the Salzburg Music Festival just before I left the Regiment for good in August 1946.*

*But our continued presence in the northern Adriatic area did have a serious purpose. The only threat facing a completely carefree time was Marshal Tito's determination that Yugoslavia should be awarded the port of Trieste by the Allies. It was for this reason that we moved up to within a few miles of Trieste to demonstrate our military strength at the great Victory Parade which took place there in April 1946. I was much occupied during this time with training two successive intakes of raw new recruits to my Troop. Later in the year I was also appointed Regimental Education Officer (see* **12: 26**). *I took my responsibilities seriously and think it all went rather well (which would have surprised my Eton Tutor!)*

## Letter 12: 26 (William Birch Reynardson, Northern Italy, to my father Henry Birch Reynardson, dated 16 October 1945)

[…] My pupils arrived on the 8th, as you know. It was a big day. My staff of learned beaks and I (who do not come in on the teaching side!) had put in a bit of hard work prior to the opening day and it has been worthwhile. I will try and tell you quickly how I have organised it. The army laid down that all men of 28 years of age and service group and under would do at least six hours educational training per week. […]

I sent out a questionnaire to every man in the Regiment in order to get his particulars and also his choice of subjects to be taken from English, French, German, Maths, Book-keeping, Italian and Bricklaying. I found that about 150 men were affected and applications for the various subjects worked out approximately as follows: English 5%, French 12%, Italian 15%, Maths 10%, German 10%, Book-keeping 20%, and Bricklaying 28%. I then had to collect five instructors and a clerk. This was very tricky but the fulltime instructors are paid as sergeants and after a good deal of persuasion I collected the required number.

I was lucky about the building as I found a perfect place with seven small rooms (for classrooms and offices etc), a large Lecture Room and three rooms for the staff. The Colonel was very good and gave me carte-blanche and I had carpenters and plumbers in the place to get it ready in time. I decided to try an experiment with the classes on these lines: every individual comes twice a week, for three hours in the morning. For three weeks he does a course on whatever subject he chooses. […] At the end of his course he is given a test and we shall decide from his results whether he is to go on to a different subject, or not. Of course it all looks fairly simple but after five years of war, many of the chaps find themselves a bit rusty or worse still, completely uninterested. However, everything is trotting along quite well and I think that we will win through despite the difficulties — they are legion!

---

*In most of my letters over this period there is an undercurrent of uncertainty about my future. I knew that I wanted to go back to university, but was less sure about the idea of becoming a doctor, which had been my original plan before being called up. To complicate matters, my father wanted me to stay in the Army and take up the position of ADC to General Paget in the Sudan; I received a number of similar invitations from various distinguished people, but in the end refused them all! Perhaps the great advantage of this thoroughly enjoyable year was that it gave me time to reach a considered decision about what I was going to do next, without undue pressure.*

When I was looking through the collection of family letters, trying to choose which to include in this chapter, I came across an unexpected and sad example of the kind of moral dilemma which war is apt to produce. This was written by Florence Amery, wife of the M.P. Leo Amery and mother of John Amery[39], who was executed for treason late in 1945. It was, I believe, sent in reply to a letter from my mother.

**LETTER 12: 27 (Mrs Florence Amery to (?)my mother Diana Birch Reynardson; undated, but probably written in December 1945 or January 1946)**

John Amery
B[orn] Mar. 14, 1912 — Died for his opinions Dec. 19, 1945

> At end of wayward days, he found a Cause.
> "Twas not his Country's.' Only time can tell
> If this defiance of our ancient laws
> Was treason or fore-knowledge. He sleeps well.
> L.S.A.[40]

We found our darling John in the gloomy prison. He had cast off all the hampering things of life, through which he had ever struggled for the Light. He had found the Light & shone out of those grim surroundings the splendid man we always knew our elfin boy could be.

He pleaded guilty, because he said — 'They tell me fighting Communism was fighting our ally, and that under the Act of 1341, is treason & there is only one sentence. I did fight Communism & tried to get others to do so, to save England

---

39 John Amery (1912–45), the elder son of Leo and Florence Amery, had a troubled early life and became an open Nazi sympathizer, believing that the fascist doctrine of National Socialism represented the only alternative to Bolshevism. He left Britain permanently to live in France after being declared bankrupt in 1936, and before the war travelled to Germany, Austria and Italy to witness fascism in practice. In 1942 he obtained a permit to go to Germany, where he proposed the formation of a British anti-Bolshevik legion (later named the British Free Corps). Hitler was impressed by Amery and allowed him to remain in Germany as a guest of the Third Reich; he stayed there until late in 1944, making pro-German propaganda broadcasts. He was eventually captured in the last weeks of the war, in Northern Italy where he had travelled to lend support to Mussolini. More recently, his relationship with his father Leo was explored in the play *An English Tragedy* (2008), by Ronald Harwood.
40 The initials of Leopold Stennett Amery, John's father. Leo Amery later effectively disowned his elder son, amending his entry in *Who's Who* to read 'one s[on]', but these lines suggest some ambivalence.

& the Europe I loved, after Nov. 1942 when everyone saw Germany could not win. So I am guilty. But at least I can save you the trial. You must not be sad, darling Mother, at Destiny's call — so long as I answer it worthily.' — How nobly, with what calm, sweet selfless courage he answered, thanking those near him at the end, I pray men may one day know. It would help them. <u>He</u> gave us courage for his ordeal. <u>He</u> made our last hour together immortal. He & Leo, his adored father, are close together & understand each other for all eternity. He found in Julian[41] not only a loving brother but a Friend ready to endure anything if it could help. For me, 'I am safe in your love'. He was so alight & young & had such a delicate, beautiful face, utterly unlike the pictures that hurt us so.

Your letter helped me so. John did rise to heights above us all. 'I live again the happy hours of my youth, but above all the sublime hours of these last days, where we seem to have shaken off all the sordidness of life & to have risen so high, all of us — but the example came from you, frail little mother with a lion's courage.' I can write <u>that</u> to you, for I know you will understand.

His lovely smile, his beautiful voice, came clearly through the fourfold wire, the thick glass, through which we saw him. He never complained — he never in all his life did a mean or a greedy thing. He died for his Belief, with such wonderful, sweet Courage. The Mother of Christ must be there & she must understand. He was such a radiant person. They did not do well to take his life. I am so proud of him but oh, the pain.

Florence Amery

---

*By the summer of 1946 I had made up my mind. I had decided to accept my father's advice to* 'go up to Oxford at all costs and get a degree in Law — not necessarily as a career but as a training for any career that I will have decided on by the time I go down.'[42] *My release papers came through unexpectedly early in August and by early September, after a heart-warming send-off by my Regiment (Colonel Price seemed particularly sad to see me go and said some very nice things), I was back in England to start the next phase of my life as an undergraduate and a civilian.*

---

41  Leo Amery's younger son Julian, later Baron Amery (1919–96), also a Conservative politician like his father. During the war Leo (1873–1955) held the position of Secretary of State for India, but at the time of this letter had recently lost his seat to Labour and had retired from politics. My sister-in-law, Jay Humphreys (later Colvile) was his P.A. for some years and spoke of him with affection.
42  Letter dated 16 June 1946.

CHAPTER 13

# The Post War Years

*Recollections and Letters from 1946 onwards*

### 'Can't see why you want to marry my daughter in a butcher's shop!'[1]

*And here the scene changes. The previous chapters have concentrated on my family's survival during more than three hundred years of wars. Now, in the final chapter, I would like to recall more briefly our lives as we adjusted to the start of what has been, for most of us, nearly seventy years of peace.*

*Adapting to post-war life in England was difficult for everyone. You simply can't imagine what poor London looked like after the bombings. The financial situation was, if anything, worse than during the war. In August 1945 President Truman had cut the economic lifeline of Lend-Lease (see previous chapter). Britain had to negotiate new loans from the U.S.A., the terms of which were onerous. Food and clothes were rationed, no one had any money, and our great Empire — of which we had all been brought up as members — was starting to dissolve[2].*

*When I arrived home in September 1946, I found enormous changes. I remember the 'empty' feeling about civilian life after my organised army life and the camaraderie of my brother officers, and longed to be back with them in the Regiment. At the age of nearly twenty-three, I did not have a clue as to my future profession or what I was going to do with my life. But I did know that I wanted to stand on my own feet. Various well-meaning relatives and friends tried to help me by offering me employment in the City, including my uncle's brother-in-law, Lord Aldenham, Chairman of the family bank Antony Gibbs and Son, and were no doubt surprised when, after due consideration, I politely turned down all offers, saying that I had decided to go back to university and read for the Bar — even though I had little idea of what being a barrister entailed!*

*My homecoming was also somewhat muted by the state in which I found things at Adwell. Immediately after the end of the war my father had started to suffer serious*

---

1 My father-in-law, General Humphreys.
2 The four years of warfare which had followed the passing of the Lend-Lease Act involved a vast amount of further expenditure, so that by the end of the war we were victorious but poor. And our serious debt was not assisted by the hugely expensive social and industrial reforms set in train by the new Labour government under Clement Attlee, elected just after the end of the war in 1945. There was insufficient money to pay for Imperial commitments and the dissolution of the Empire commenced with the independence of India (the 'Jewel in the Crown') in 1947. Within twenty years, most of the former colonies of the British Empire had been granted independence.

*depressions, which were compounded by the fact that he had never really recovered from the wound he sustained in Mesopotamia in 1915. He spent much of his time in bed, cared for devotedly by my mother, on whom his illnesses took a tremendous toll. My two sisters were busy with their growing families: Cynthia had recently given birth to her third son, and Rosamund had just married for the second time. Her new husband was Kit Egerton — my old friend from Eton, who was three years younger than my sister but had loved her ever since meeting her on one of the early Fourth of June picnics! My brother Dickie had joined the Grenadier Guards* (**Fig. 13 a)**) *on leaving Eton and was currently stationed in Palestine, and so much of the responsibility for my parents and for Adwell fell onto my shoulders.*

*I was back at Oxford in October 1946 and was given my old room in the Old Library. Again, no entrance exam! Many of my friends had also returned to Oxford after being demobilised, and some eighteen year-olds who had come up for the first time. Tom Quad was full of prams with young wives pushing their babies round Mercury (the fountain in Tom Quad) and there were also many wheelchairs whose occupants had lost legs in the war. In some ways life continued much as it had done in 1942. I was given the responsibility of re-starting the Christ Church Beagles, which I accomplished with the help of Ronnie Wallace[3]. I helped to revive Loders Club[4]. As the College's representative I became partly responsible for the running of the Boys' Club in London (the 'Christ Church United Clubs') near Kennington Oval, then a very poor area. Last, but not least, I hunted*

**Fig. 13 a)** My brother Dickie in the uniform of the Grenadier Guards. Photograph.

3   R.E. Wallace (1919–2002) was certainly the most well-known and brilliant huntsman of the fifty post-war years from 1946 to 1996. I first met him when he was hunting the Christ Church Beagles during the war while I was at Eton (see **12: 1** and **12: 2**). He became not only a great friend but a wonderful tutor in the art of venery. His fame was at its apex when he was Master and Huntsman of the Heythrop Hounds between 1952 and 1977.
4   This rather snobby club, centred on Christ Church, started I believe in the seventeenth century as a Bible-reading society. I'm afraid it deteriorated in its object over the years and its members behaved very badly! I had first been a member in 1942 (see **Fig. 12 b)**).

with the South Oxfordshire Hounds. Not everything was the same, however, as quite a few familiar faces from my earlier attendance at Oxford had not returned. In Christ Church Cathedral there is, on the left side of the entrance, a plaque bearing the names of those Christ Church undergraduates who were killed in the 1914–18 war and on the right side, those killed between 1939 and 1945; it may come as some surprise to learn that the latter includes more names than the former.

I would like to digress for a moment to write about my brother Dickie, who departed to join his Regiment in Palestine (which was administered under a British mandate until 1948) at about the same time as I came home from Italy. My two years at Oxford were punctuated by occasional visits from him when he was home on leave and also by frequent letters. In some of these he writes about the political situation following the Anglo-American Inquiry of 1946, set up in an attempt to reach agreement over the number of Jewish immigrants, mostly refugees from Europe, to be admitted to Palestine, and about the proposals for partitioning the country into independent Arab and Jewish states (which precipitated civil war in Palestine and escalated into the Arab-Israeli War of 1948). I quote a harrowing extract from one of his letters (**13: 1**), illustrating that although the war was over, an acute refugee problem remained.

## Letter 13: 1 (Richard Birch Reynardson, Palestine, to our father Henry Birch Reynardson, in South Africa[5], dated 22 January 1947)

3rd Battalion Grenadier Guards
M.E.F. [*Middle East Force*]

My dear Father,

[...] I was so disappointed that we weren't able to meet down in Port Said: as you probably guessed the old arm was not good and the doctor wouldn't let me leave my bed, much less go down to Egypt. But I can't think what happened to my wire which I sent to explain why I couldn't make it. [...]

I explained to Mamma what happened but if she hasn't passed the letter on, I expect you'd like to know what happened. As you suspected it was a very fair rough house! [...] The ship, about the size of an average tanker, was loaded with 4,000 immigrants from Poland. The majority of them were between the ages of

---

5  Towards the end of 1946, my father had gone on an extended voyage to South Africa and had hoped to meet up with Dickie in Egypt when his ship docked at Port Said. The trip was intended to improve my father's health and so it was disappointing that he relapsed almost as soon as he had got home in the spring of 1947; in one of my letters I say that 'I have never seen anyone so depressed'.

16 and 30, though there were many women and children as well. Most of them had had a terrible time since they were small children in concentration camps; had only known violence and cruelty from anyone other than their own race since they could remember. Moreover they had been perverted by anti-British propaganda from America: therefore they arrived in Haifa — after a journey of appalling hardship and unspeakable conditions — feeling distrustful and already loathing us; and also very tough.

I don't think any of them had any doubt that they might not be allowed to enter Palestine, having come so far under such conditions — and so when they were told they were to be transferred to another ship and taken to Cyprus[6], they just went berserk and mass hysteria broke out [...] it's an awful thing to see women and children even completely out of control, screaming and just like animals: I was appalled.

[...] My Company was there to load all the baggage on to the next ship, and there were a lot of gunners standing by in case there was trouble. Suddenly a leader of the toughest crowd started exciting them to an even greater fervour, and without any warning a hail of bully-beef tins, 7 lb tins of margarine and bottles started to rain down on our heads. [...] They hit any number of troops and there was a regular shuttle service of soldiers being carted off with bloody heads: a broken bottle in the face makes a very nasty mess. [...]

This went on for about 10 minutes and we were obviously getting nowhere [...]. So the gunner commander said they would try to board: we kept up a pretty continuous rifle fire over their heads while a gangway was attached to the side of the ship. At this moment I was laid out by a very hard tin of something on the head so was non-compos for a short time, recovering however in time to see the gunners being fairly effectively routed at the top of the gangway and making a pretty rapid getaway down the gangplank!

So Colonel Peter told Tim Bradley (my Company commander) that we'd have a shot. I must say he is excellent and when I'd got my platoon formed up, up the gangway we went by which time that funny feeling in the stomach had gone and it was all very exciting and our blood was up! Meanwhile we were being rather thinned out as we were going up by these 7 lb tins of margarine which some

---

6  Between August 1946 and January 1949, the British government ran camps in Cyprus for the internment of Jews attempting to immigrate to Mandatory Palestine in violation of British policy (which after the war permitted a maximum of 1,500 per month to settle in Palestine). The majority of Cyprus detainees, most of whom were Holocaust survivors, were intercepted before reaching Palestine, usually by boat. A total of about 51,000 refugees were held in the camps, in which conditions were very harsh with poor sanitation, over-crowding and shortage of clean water; it was considered that German prisoners of war housed in adjacent camps were treated better.

nasty characters were raining down on our heads from the bridge: I thanked the Lord for our steel helmets as these missiles can do a lot of damage. However, we got to the top pretty quickly where I was greeted by some awful thugs who seemed pretty determined we shouldn't get on board. [...] a pick-axe handle proved a very effective weapon and we got on board — or at least I did and then realised to my horror that the others hadn't quite managed to make it [...] and I went down for a bit [...] but managed to crawl away [...] by which time all my platoon had got on and we really began to set about them properly. [...] They didn't last long under the very angry onslaught of 30 very big Guardsmen with very big sticks (we hadn't taken any arms up). [...] We had them under control pretty soon. It was so funny to see the Guardsmen, who were demons a few minutes before, being so gentle to the children and old women who appeared after it was all over. [...]

[...] The next job was to get them off the ship onto the other one which would take them to Cyprus. I can't hope to describe the appalling state the ship was in: but if you remember that there had been 4,000 (or just under) in that ship, and that there were only two latrines in it, you can imagine the smell. [...] The floors of the holds were three inches deep in muck of every description; there were old men and women practically dead from typhus, women in the last stages of pregnancy. It was so hot in the hold next to the boiler room that men and women were stark naked in a state of complete exhaustion [...]; they couldn't go on deck as there was not an inch of room. Everywhere there was rotting food, covered in flies, and the children were covered in horrible sores which were besieged by flies. We found it quite impossible to go down into these holds without a gas-mask on, which will give you some idea of what the stench was like. It was dreadful to see some of these poor old people and small children, who deplored the way the [*others*] had acted. [...] I've never felt so sorry for people. The Guardsmen were quite marvellous carrying men and women who were too weak to walk, and trying to comfort them. This is not an exaggerated account of what it was like, and actually it would take your own eyes to fully realise what a hell-ship this was.

[...] I was very worried as everyone said that two of my chaps had been chucked overboard, and they hadn't appeared again, but thank goodness they had both been fished out — in rather a bad way but still kicking. Five were in hospital and all of us had some sort of mark to show for our trouble. [...] I was taken off to hospital where I was X-rayed and they found a chip of bone was off my elbow, and that otherwise they thought it was all right. However, when it got worse they discovered that one of those blighters had hit me with a sort of club with 1½ inch nails sticking out of the end, and that two of these nails had bored neat little holes into the bone and had infected it. However, after cutting me up twice and giving me all sorts of penicillin etc, I am quite all right now, and the 5 chaps in hospital have all recovered, so all's well that ends well. [...]

---

*Dickie continued in the Army for ten years, serving also in Malaya (**13: 2**), Singapore and Kenya (the latter during the Mau-Mau Uprising in 1956). As he adhered to the pre-war notion that money was a subject that was never discussed in 'civilised' society, my father was very shocked, if not ashamed, that when Dickie left the Army (a gentlemanly profession) it was to become a stockbroker!*

---

**Letter 13: 2 (Richard Birch Reynardson, with the 3rd Battalion, Grenadier Guards, Kuala Lumpur, Malaya, to his family, dated 2 February 1949)**

Since I last wrote we've been very busy again. [...] Of course our doings don't get mentioned much in the papers because they are virtually unimportant: the fact that one spends 4 or 5 days in the jungle under very unpleasant circumstances, and have a small fight perhaps killing two Communists and burning a camp and capturing Communist papers and a few arms doesn't mean to say that it's 'news' for the papers — though to us of course it is more important than a large-scale Brigade operation.

Actually we had an unusual one a few days ago. A very well-kept secret and no one knew where we were going until we got to the Coast and embarked on a destroyer: then we were told we were going to make a landing on an island between the Coast and Sumatra, where it was suspected the Communists had an H. Q. and a wireless station. Well, we embarked at about 6pm, very cramped as there were about 150 of our men and 50 police [...], sailing south down the coast at first to lay a false trail. Meanwhile we got our orders and perused large-scale maps of the island. The plan was to get within 5 miles in the destroyer and transfer into Landing Craft in the dark, and land at Prima Luce. After a very uncomfortable night sleeping on the bare deck [...] we anchored at about

## THE POST WAR YEARS

2am, in inky blackness, soaked to the skin and indescribable chaos trying to sort out one's own men, getting in the way of sailors, loading the weapons etc., and trying to remember the details of where to land and where to go on landing, trying to memorise the map, which of course we couldn't see in the dark. To crown it all there was a heavyish swell and getting into the L. C. was no easy feat in the dark […]. After a few minor accidents we were all aboard and marshalled and set off towards the island. […]

We arrived in the most lovely dawn, just as the first fishing junks were hoisting their sails, to make a perfect silhouette against the rose-coloured sky. Having spotted our individual landing points we glided in towards the shore — only to come to a sickening standstill on the mud 100 yards off; […] we couldn't wade ashore, as the mud was feet deep and it would have taken hours. So one man stripped naked [and] swam off to tow back from the island some sampans, into which we clambered and paddled off. Very tricky little craft, as easy to overturn as a canoe. Our next job was to get to the other side of the island — only 500 yards across […] The whole town is built on stilts about 6ft high above the mud, and at high tide the sea comes in underneath the buildings.

The main street is about 4 yards wide, made of planks, and the shops and houses on each side make it like a perfectly normal Chinese village — but get off the main street and it becomes a warren of houses joined by rickety bridges of rather rotten sticks. The whole place smells quite putrid: a mixture of rotten fish, pigs (which live in the houses quite free to run where they like) and the sickly smell of stale opium. All the rubbish and everything else is just thrown over the side into the water, so that at low tide it's all left on the mud in extreme heat and breeds flies and maggots by the million.

The people are […] riddled with diseases and reduced to shadows of skin and bone by the opium, with no teeth as they live on fish and get no calcium, I suppose. The children are the most extraordinary — they are made up to the eyes, with lipstick and vivid rouged cheeks and waxed hair so that they look like dolls: a very unusual people — […] and I don't suppose there are many towns in the world entirely built on stilts.

As an operation it was rather a flop as there quite obviously was nothing fishy about the place: but we hauled in enough opium and dope of all sorts to make us rich men for life had we decided to run it! And it was an experience I wouldn't have missed to see such a unique place, and these Chinese who have been by-passed by civilization.

*I went down from Oxford in the summer of 1948. A constant refrain in my letters is the statement 'I must go and work' (followed by very little action). At the end of 1947 I told the Kennel Huntsman, Walter Clinkard (a most splendid man and a wonderful help to me) that I wouldn't be able to hunt the Beagles the next Season. 'Why ever not?' he asked. 'Because I must work to get a degree.' 'Oh, never you mind, they always give degrees to gentlemen who hunt the Beagles.' So I was pleased and relieved to be awarded a Third! Few in my year did any better. But we did have fun! When I re-read my letters of this time, I cannot get over the amount of time we spent hunting, dancing (often into the early hours at The 400[7], or some other nightclub), racing and, above all, talking in each other's rooms far into the night. But I did work extremely hard for my Bar exams over the following year and a half. I was determined to get called to the Bar as quickly as possible, and was advised to contact Mr Bob Hart, who specialised in getting people through their exams in double-quick time. He had lost an arm when wounded in the Navy and would use his metal arm to hit me if I couldn't remember some important legal decision! His tactics must have worked, as although it was not fun, I managed to pass my Bar exams in eighteen months instead of the usual three years.*

*In the summer of 1950, an incident occurred which was to change my life. My cousin, Ashley Ponsonby, rang me up and asked me whether I was free to come to a performance of* The Marriage of Figaro *at Covent Garden, for which he had tickets. He explained that the party would consist of Margaret Elphinstone[8], 'a nice girl recently returned from Rhodesia[9]' and the two of us. Of course I should have smelt a rat as Ashley was certainly not an opera buff. Anyway, I accepted with alacrity.*

*On the chosen evening, I arrived at the Opera House punctually at 7.15pm. The lobby was empty. I went to the ticket desk. 'Oh yes, we have a ticket for you, but the performance started at 7.00pm.' I had forgotten that Mozart operas, being lengthy, often begin half an hour earlier than usual. I was allowed in at the end of the first scene and shown to my aisle seat in the dark. 'Why are you late?' whispered my neighbour rather fiercely. 'Kept in Chambers, important case,' I replied, thinking quickly. This was my first introduction to Nik! After the performance we dined at the White Tower in Percy Street and when I got back to Adwell, I told my mother that I had met the girl I was going to marry. I did this six months later on 29 November 1950.*

7   A very important rendezvous for so many of us, not least because it stayed opened till 4.00am, *The 400* was located on the east side of Leicester Square. There was a tiny dance floor and a small bank presided over by 'Snakehips' Johnson at the piano, but the most important person there was Rossi, the head waiter, who looked after everyone. Later in the 1950s *The 400* was a favourite haunt of Princess Margaret's.

8   Margaret Elpinstone (later Rhodes) is the Queen's cousin. She later became Lady-in-Waiting to the Queen Mother.

9   My lovely future wife, Nik Humphreys, was appointed lady-in-waiting to Lady Kennedy, the second wife of Major-General Sir John Noble Kennedy, the Governor of Rhodesia, in 1947. She also served as governess to Sir John's two daughters from his first marriage, Jean and Susan. She was accompanied by her great friend Betsy Dawson, also an old friend of mine, who was killed three years later in a motor car crash.

*My future wife — Pamela Matnika Humphreys, to give her full name, although she was always known simply as 'Nik' — had had an unusually challenging early life. The elder daughter of Lieutenant-General Sir Thomas Humphreys (see Chapter 10, **10: 1**), she spent her first few years in India, where her father was serving at the time. At the age of six, as the result of a riding accident, she contracted tuberculosis and having returned to England she spent the next seven years lying on her back encased in plaster from hip to toe. With the help of two maiden aunts with whom she was living while her parents remained in India, and despite being almost immobile, she mastered a complete range of subjects so successfully that at the age of thirteen she gained entry easily to St Mary's, Wantage, though still on crutches (on which she even managed to play hockey in goal!). By the time she went up to Oxford with an exhibition in 1942 (graduating — unlike me — with a good Second in PPE), she had dispensed with her crutches and managed thereafter with a made-up shoe. Her first job after coming down from Oxford involved looking after Displaced Persons in Germany, which was typical of her lifelong concern for others. Nik brought to everything in life the same brisk, courageous determination with which she had overcome her childhood difficulties.*

*At the time of our first meeting, Nik had not long before returned to England after nearly two years in Rhodesia, where she had gone initially as lady-in-waiting to the wife of the Governor before transferring to the staff of the ill-fated East African Groundnut Scheme[10]. It was not an altogether happy time for her as will be fairly obvious from the following extracts (**13: 3**) but the letter written to Nik's mother by Laura Grenfell (**13: 4**) as Nik was coming to the end of her African sojourn makes it clear how highly she was valued.*

---

## LETTER 13: 3 (Selected diary extracts and a letter from Nik Humphreys, written in Rhodesia between August 1947 and May 1948)

Sunday 3rd August 1947. [*Diary*]

A row from H. E. [*the Governor*] before dinner. He had found my pony in the stables being saddled up by Nevitt's boy. He happened to be saddling it up for Jean, who is always too idle to do it for herself, and my boy had gone off because

---

10  A project of the British government, the groundnut scheme was a plan to cultivate tracts of what is now Tanzania (then called Tanganika) with peanuts. The plan was abandoned in 1951 at considerable cost to the taxpayer when it did not become profitable. Groundnuts require at least twenty inches of rainfall a year; the area chosen was subject to drought.

Nevitt had told him to, but you can't explain these things to a brick wall. Now he is not supposed to come near the place at all, which is a bit boring.

The comic part of it is that the fracas has strengthened the bond between Nevitt and me considerably. Nevitt spends a good deal of his time devising methods of getting round the restrictions or prohibitions and indeed it is almost always he who causes these rows by going one step too far. Obstinacy has driven him to spend much more time over the pony than he ever did before he was forbidden to look at it and I simply cannot keep him away although I keep on saying nervously that he [*the Governor*] may appear at any minute. The idea of H. E. finding Nevitt cleaning out the pony's feet or combing its tail positively sends shivers down my spine. Nevitt thinks it is a huge joke and when I implore him to go away he wrinkles up his face and says 'Do you think I shall get shot, miss?' [...] Having been a coachman he can't keep his hands off the ponies.

The side saddle is rather a success, although the pummels are a bit small.

I haven't told you about my boy, Ben, yet. He is a Nyasaland boy and a very good worker according to Nevitt who has had him before. Unfortunately he knows nothing about horses, but is not at all frightened, which is lucky as most of the Africans are. Having never employed before, I am very proud of him. He has no shirt so I am going to buy him one. He gets 27/6 a month and eats a pound of meat a day together with mealies! He speaks practically no English so I am trying to teach him; we have some funny conversations. He has a great sense of humour, even more than most of them. [...]

27th May, 1948 [*Letter*]

Darling Family,

This has been an eventful week and falls into subjects rather than days. Also I have not been keeping a diary so shall write an ordinary letter.

First you will have got a cable warning you of my departure from here. I had discovered a girl to do lessons with Su [*Susan Kennedy, Sir John's daughter*] so that it was a question of making up my mind rapidly as to whether I should go or stay. [...] The last fortnight since my return has been quite all right. They have both been in good tempers and I am much refreshed after my holiday.

So I went to LK [*Lady Kennedy*] and said 'I think I should warn you that I don't want to stay long after the end of this term.' To which she replied 'I think you must think differently.' So I said 'I'm sorry but I cannot.' After luncheon she came to my room and said 'John says' (which means she says) 'that you had better go at once if at all.' The next morning H. E. sent for me and said he wished me to know how he felt, which was that the staff had been a failure and most disappointing. They had in fact done harm to the regime. He thought I had been better than B [*Betsy, another employee*] or D [*Denis Rowan-Hamilton, A.D.C. to the Governor and an old friend of Nik's*] however and would be delighted if I could reconsider my decision.

I was so shocked at them showing signs of regret at my leaving that I was almost shocked into saying that I would stay. I must say that my conscience was not at all easy at leaving and never was as I don't know that it will improve things for Su. [...] Anyway I said I would think it over, conscience [...] now stabbing at the realisation that they wanted me to stay — not clear from the past two months!

[...] H. E. said that the last six months had been hell for them and although I think they make more fuss than is warranted, and think of things far too much from their point of view entirely, I am sure they really are bothered by these problems. [...] In the end I told H. E. that I would go and he looked most offended, but was civil and said that on personal grounds he was very sorry. I wish I could honestly feel the same. I slightly suspect they know I feel a worry every time they register any sorrow at my departure but it may be an unworthy thought.

Told LK I was off definitely and she said I must pack up and get out at once; very sensible as it is awful having people hanging around. I said I would try to fix my things by the end of the week and get out of Government House, though would have to stay somewhere [...] She took the line that I must leave the colony at once — so I demurred [...] Must see LK this morning on the subject and I am afraid there will be a hell of a row. Don't see how they can expect to give me one week's notice and turf me out on my ears. [...]

I think they are trying to get a woman called Helen Addison [*my former governess in South Africa, with whom I later met up in Italy during the war — see Chapter 12*], who was mixed up with the B-Rs. A good notion as she is about and will be more efficient than B and me put together, but she has quite a mind of her own and may go in for a battle or two. My plans nil at the moment. Never knew I had so many friends. At least ten people have already said come and stay as long as you like.

[...] The view that she [*Lady Kennedy*] takes is so lacking in either responsibility or understanding that it confirms me in the wisdom of my decision. Clearly they put down any unpopularity they may have gained, entirely to us. This is neither fair nor sensible and it is not easy to work on those terms. [...]

**Letter 13: 4 (Laura Grenfell to Lady Humphreys, dated 7 November 1948)**

Dear Lady Humphreys,

Nik left here on the night train last night on the next lap of the journey home. I know you will think I am only saying so because you are her mother, but I would say the same to anyone. In fact I'm having it said to me all the time. Nik has been an unqualified success out here. I just can't imagine what we should have done without her. She has made friends with all and sundry, she's worked like a Trojan and even the people she had to attack only too often in the course of work still ate out of her hand and bore her no grudge — in fact liked her all the more for it. From the work point of view she has been perfect. In roaring good form — far stronger than all the rest of us and I think unique among men and women here, in not succumbing to Kongwa tummy, boils or other ills that beset the rest of us.

My personal feeling towards the scheme is entirely coloured by the fact that it produced the opportunity of getting to know Nik, a bursting of pride and affection and watching her doing so wonderfully well and enjoying it with such gusto. We've had times when things have seemed depressing to a degree, but Nik has always shaken that off and gone forging ahead.

I do hope that she has a really lovely last lap to her very stretched out journey home. I'm trying hard to get used to the idea that she's no longer around but it can't possibly be so much fun without her here and that's contributed quite a bit to my deciding to stay only three more months myself.

I can't tell you how grateful we all are for having had Nik here during these months. She has left a sea of very regretful friends and no one regrets that she's left as much as I do!!

    Yours sincerely
    Laura

---

*Our wedding was, of course, one of the great memories of my life! We were married in London at St Bartholomew the Great in Smithfield* (**Fig. 13 b**)). *My prospective father-in-law, General Humphreys, complained about this — 'Can't see why you want to marry my daughter in a butcher's shop!' (Smithfield Market was in those days the main meat market in the south of England.) It was a great affair — such a glorious church, such a beautiful bride, such a great reception at London House (where I was living) for four hundred people, including dear Princess Alice.*

**Fig. 13 b)** Our wedding at St Bartholomew the Great, Smithfield, London, on 29 November 1950. Photograph.

**Fig. 13 c)** W.B.R., Inner Temple, 1952. Photograph.

*We had a short honeymoon at a 'sporting hotel' in Cumberland (rather ashamed about that) when I shot lots of duck and we played my opera records. It was lovely, but I soon had to return to London to take up my pupillage with Teddy Ryder Richardson in 4 Paper Buildings, Inner Temple. I really enjoyed this and he was extremely nice to me. I worked very hard with him and he offered me a place in Chambers (**Fig. 13 c)**).*

*By this time (another milestone) we had bought our first house, 9 Halsey Street (next door to Peter Jones). The underground to Sloane Square went underneath it. We said, firmly, that we would get used to it! Of course we never did. The house cost £5,000, which we thought a huge amount. I can't remember how we paid this great sum. I suppose there was assistance from our families as, of course, in those days there was no question of overdrawing at the bank or obtaining a mortgage. We had been living there for two or three years when the Coronation — a bright beacon of colour during an otherwise rather drab period — took place on 2 June 1953. I was a Gold Staff Officer[11] and we had a super breakfast at 9 Halsey Street at 4.30am — Nik in her tiara, my*

---

11 The appointment was made through Lord Clarendon (then Lord Chamberlain). There were four hundred Gold Staff Officers, each carrying a stave designed by the Goldsmiths' Company. We were first vetted by the Earl Marshal (the Duke of Norfolk, who bore overall responsibility for the Coronation), to ensure that we were correctly dressed and knew our duties, which were to show guests to their places in Westminster Abbey and attend to their needs.

**Fig. 13 d)** Coronation Day, 2 June 1953. Photograph.

*friend Harry Graham Vivian and my cousin Ashley Ponsonby in Coldstream Guards full dress, Roger Montgomery as an airman and me in Court dress* (**Fig. 13 d**))*!*

A great memory from the year before: Juliet's birth on 20 March 1952. In those days husbands did not attend the births of their children (thank goodness), but I was at the hospital when Nik was wheeled out and her first words were 'Never again!' Despite this, Clare was born on 29 June 1954, followed two years later by our son Thomas. I soon became worried about the expense of bringing up, let alone educating, three children. My fees at the Bar were certainly not great! So, rather reluctantly, I decided to try to find a job which paid me a salary. And I found one! This came about as the result of a chance meeting with Sir Guy Ropner, a well-known Yorkshire ship owner, who was a fellow guest when I was staying with my mother's cousin Will Pott, Chairman of the Belvoir Hounds, to go hunting in Leicestershire. After cross-examining me about my life as a barrister, Sir Guy told me that he was going to be the next President of the Chamber of Shipping and would I be interested in the position of Legal Officer there? We corresponded about it and I was invited for interview with two other candidates. After the interviews had been completed, I was called back in and told that I had been selected. 'Have you any questions?' asked Sir Guy. 'Well, Sir, if it is not an insolent request, may I ask to see the note which Mr Gorick [the General Manager] passed to you during my interview?' The note was produced for me. It read: 'Do you realise that Birch Reynardson is an M.A. and the other two are only B.A.s?' So I got the job on the strength of my payment of £5 to Oxford University to turn my B.A. into an M.A. Not a bad investment!

Before long the house in Halsey Street became a bit small for us. It was Nik who discovered the house which was to be our next home — No. 72, Elm Park Road, between the Fulham Road and the Kings Road in Chelsea — and arranged for me to inspect it on my way home from work. I couldn't believe that she had chosen such an enormous, ten-bedroomed Edwardian house, with basement kitchen, a huge drawing room, study, day and night nurseries and so on, but was soon convinced by her assurance that it was suitable for our needs. By this time (the summer of 1955), our family had been joined by Lorrie Aldridge (later Wollerton), who had trained as an N.N.E.B. nursery nurse and had recently qualified as a Registered Sick Children's Nurse. Lorrie had answered our advertisement, hoping to take a temporary post with a family going abroad. As she says, 'it turned out to be the longest temporary post on record!' for, apart from a couple of intervals, she has remained with us for sixty years.

While Nik, Eileen (the nursery maid) and Mrs Hall (our invaluable daily help) scrubbed and polished Elm Park Road ready for occupation, Lorrie took the children to Adwell to stay with my parents. For Lorrie it was a mercifully brief interlude:

I thought Adwell was lovely for short visits only. It was a sort of time warp in those days; the children were kept behind doors (one of which had a notice pinned to it by the Colonel —known to the children as 'Gramps' — saying 'SLAM IT DAMMIT') and they had to be dressed tidily to be taken down to the drawing room to visit 'Granny' — Mrs Birch Reynardson senior. Amongst the other staff in the house was Mr Jones, the butler, of whom I was very much in awe at first; Mrs Wiggins, the cook, and her daughter Beryl; and Edna, the head house maid.

*However, the whole of the winter and spring following our move to Elm Park Road was spent at Adwell, to keep my mother company as my father had gone on another prolonged trip to South Africa. I commuted to London every day and, as there was a lot of snow that winter, the girls spent much of their time tobogganing in which (to Lorrie's great alarm, as Nik was in the late stages of pregnancy with Thomas) their mother insisted on joining them. Luckily it did the baby no harm and later that spring Thomas was born healthy and strong, the only member of the family so far to bear the same name as my illustrious great-great-grandfather. Thomas's christening, like those of Juliet and Clare, was held at Adwell.*

*It was gradually becoming apparent that my mother's vagueness, which we had all experienced over the years, was taking on an exaggerated form. After a year or two, we had to resort to a full-time companion. Some kind of dementia was diagnosed and in the end she became unmanageable; the only person who could control, and indeed bath her, was our butler, Leslie Jones. After a rather desperate family conference it was decided that my mother had to have proper nursing care and we found a wonderful group of Catholic nuns, the St Joseph's Community, who looked after her until her death in 1962.*

*The late 1950s were a time of change for my family. It was then that Holywell* (**Fig. 13 e)**)*, having been in the ownership of our family for nearly 230 years, was sold. Holywell had passed from General Thomas Birch Reynardson (see* **Chapter 7**) *on his death in 1847 to his eldest son Charles, and the last member of the family to live there was Charles's great-granddaughter, Agatha-Isabel Acland-Hood-Reynardson (always known in the family as 'Buss'), who in 1926 married Mountjoy Fane*[12]*, a highly amusing and larger-than-life character who was in later years recognisable through his piratical black eye-patch. I often stayed with them at Holywell in the late 1940s and always enjoyed myself greatly. But it was clear that Mountjoy was more of a spender than an earner and so, in*

---

[12] The Hon. Mountjoy Fane (1900–63) was the younger son of the 13th Earl of Westmorland and his wife Lady Sybil (who was a member of 'The Souls' and celebrated for her beauty). His nephew David, who became the 14th Earl, was a friend and contemporary of mine at Eton. Aunt 'Buss' was the second member of the family to marry a Fane (her great-great uncle Edward Birch Reynardson having married Emily Fane in 1849).

**Fig. 13 e)** *Holywell House*, artist unknown. Oil on canvas, early twentieth century. Private collection.

*the end, the lovely house and estate of Holywell had to go*[13]. *There is a fund of colourful stories about Mountjoy, of which I include one below.*

> Soon after the outbreak of the Second World War, Mountjoy re-joined the Army and had some sort of staff job which required fairly regular visits to Edinburgh. On one occasion he had his dinner in the Restaurant Car and afterwards asked the steward to bring him a bottle of brandy. 'Brandy, Sir?' said the outraged steward. 'Don't you know there's a war on?' 'Of that I am fully aware and I insist that you bring me a bottle of brandy which I'm confident you will find in your pantry.' After some delay, a bottle was produced and Mountjoy told the steward to leave it on the table. Time passed and eventually the train reached Edinburgh. Mountjoy stayed where he was, an almost empty brandy bottle in front of him.

---

13  Since the 1950s, Holywell has passed through several owners, of whom perhaps the most notable is the Princess Galitzine, who rescued the estate from near-dereliction in the 1990s. The wonderful gardens were restored to designs by Bunny Guinness and are occasionally opened to the public.

The steward came to tell Mountjoy that unless he disembarked quickly, the train would leave with him on board to return to London. Mountjoy merely told the steward to fetch him another bottle of brandy, which he consumed during the return journey.

*After my mother moved into the nursing home, my father decided to leave Adwell and spent an increasing amount of his time abroad. Two stories about 'Gramps' during these years have passed into family legend.*

There are countless stories about his travels. The classic one is about him and Colonel Vere Spencer[14] travelling by train to Venice. When the train got to the border it divided into two, the front end going to Venice, the rear to Milan (or elsewhere). Of course, this operation happened while Gramps and Colonel Vere were having breakfast [...] in the restaurant car at the rear of the train, thereby finding themselves stranded in their dressing gowns without luggage, passports etc, hurtling in the wrong direction. History does not relate how the situation was resolved, but [...] the Italian railway staff [must have] got a roasting from these two intimidating Colonels.

And then there is the story of Gramps having had one of his heart attacks, again [...] in Italy. WBR went out to see him in hospital to find him in an oxygen tent smoking a pipe. When WBR remonstrated that this was very dangerous, he was told to belt up — 'the damn thing draws much better in this tent!'

*Eventually, after many visits to South Africa, to the family's astonishment my lonely father bought a house in the West Country where we thought he knew no one. In fact he chose to live as a neighbour of Frances Straker. Not long after this he announced that he intended to marry her. This he did (I was the only witness at a very gloomy ceremony in Oxford Registry Office) and he purchased a house near Burford. The marriage was not a success. A few years after marriage he went to South Africa and died in 1972 on board a Union Castle Line ship while docked at Durban. After his death, I received the following letter from Princess Alice.*

---

14  Lt. Colonel Aubrey Vere Spencer, DSO (1886–1973) was a friend and neighbour of my father, who lived at Wheatfield, Tetsworth. During the First World War he served with the 3rd Battalion, Oxford and Buckinghamshire Light Infantry. Colonel Spencer held the office of High Sheriff of Oxfordshire in 1959, the year after my father had held the same office.

**LETTER 13: 5 (Princess Alice, Countess of Athlone, Elgin, South Africa, to William Birch Reynardson, Adwell, Oxfordshire, dated 20 February 1972)**

My dear Bill,

It is with real sorrow I heard by chance on arriving in Cape Town of the death of my very dear friend your father. Although for him it is all one could really wish, as his later years have been so full of unhappiness, yet his going so suddenly from you all & far away in Africa must have come as a great shock, & also a great sadness to lose a beloved father.

I do feel so for all of you, for dear B.R. was such a fine personality, & I for one can never forget all he did for my husband during those years we were all together at Government House. Such happy times, mostly. Miss Lascelles happily has your address so I am able to write to you as one of the family to express my affectionate sympathy with you all.

Being here again is a joy & I am reminded of his dear little boy who used to walk off by himself, but could be found in my husband's study eating a chocolate which he produced for the little man!

This goes with all sympathy & kind thoughts from

Yours ever
Alice Mary

\* \* \*

*Nik and I and the children (then aged seven, five and three) moved in to Adwell in 1959. Many of the existing members of staff had been there for years with my parents; Leslie Jones, who was by this time suffering from multiple sclerosis, nevertheless stayed on to help us learn the ropes, and Edna, the head housemaid (and later the cook), was a permanent fixture.*

*The five years I had spent at the Chamber of Shipping were on the whole rather dull, but before we left London I had also met one of the most important people in my life: Cyril Miller, who was Secretary of the British Marine Law Association. He asked me to be Assistant Secretary and when I left the Chamber of Shipping, in order to devote my time to farming at Adwell, I was permitted to retain this appointment. This turned out to be vital for me. Unlike my grandfather, who was very successful at farming, I did not take to it at all. (My children remember this rather anxious period with much more affection than I do!) Financially it was a failure and I was very dependent on the one day a week I* was required to spend in London for the B.M.L.A. My career as a farmer lasted only two years, after which I was very relieved to be offered a job, with a handsome pay packet, by Cyril Miller's brother Dawson at their offices. I started work there immediately in 1962, initially for four days a week while I closed down the farming activities.

And so another new era began, in which I spent the working week in London, mostly commuting daily by train from Princes Risborough, while Nik kept everything going at home. My time at Millers (twenty-five years) involved very hard work, especially after I became Secretary of the British Marine Law Association, which brought me into close involvement with the Comité Maritime International (C.M.I.). In the end I became Vice-President of the latter (with Francesco Berlingieri the President); also Vice-Chairman of Millers in 1976 and finally Chairman in 1982, six years before I retired. I enjoyed both the shipping insurance work at Millers and the maritime law work in the C.M.I. enormously and was lucky to work with nice people in both spheres, but both positions involved almost constant travel abroad. A random glance at one of my diaries (for 1972) gives an idea of my schedule: February — Geneva, Brussels, Yugoslavia; March — Rotterdam; April — Copenhagen, Gothenburg; May — Brussels, Geneva, Genoa; June — Antwerp, Stockholm, Paris, Brussels; July — Gothenburg, Hamburg; September — Stockholm; October — Bermuda; November — Gothenburg, Antwerp, Baghdad; December — Paris, Zagreb. (Naturally there was no travelling in August, as in those days I was always shooting in Scotland then!)

In the early days at Adwell, Nik was uncertain that we could manage financially (not without cause!) and my frequent absences abroad meant that she had to shoulder a large part of the responsibility for running Adwell and looking after the children. But she never complained and set to with wonderful energy. There was much that needed to be done to both the house and the garden, which had fallen into some disrepair during the last few years that my parents were living there.

The happiest memories of these early years at Adwell inevitably involved riding and hunting. In the mid-1960s we started Horse Trials at Adwell which became an annual event, with André and Simone Vaes coming over from Belgium each year to officiate. In 1968, the Adwell Horse Trials were won by Princess Anne (**Fig. 13 f**). The regular Pony Club events were also great fun, especially the annual camps, which owed a great deal to Nik's input. But perhaps above all else were the wonderful days hunting which we all had with Tony Younghusband, when he was Joint Master of South Oxfordshire Hunt of which I was Chairman at the time (**Fig. 13 g**). He was a brilliant huntsman and lived at the Kennels at Stadhampton with his wife and two charming little daughters.

As well as our own shoot at Adwell (for our friends only — never a syndicate), we spent every August shooting in Scotland, at first with the Gawiths at Dalnaspidal, where

**Fig. 13 f)** Princess Anne receiving her prize from Nik at the Adwell Horse Trials, 1968.

**Fig. 13 g)** W.B.R. leading the South Oxfordshire Hunt at Adwell. Photograph.

my father, accompanied as always by Leslie Jones, also shot each year — Jones carrying cartridges, spare coats etc! After the lease of Dalnaspidal came to an end we started shooting at Dougarie on the Isle of Arran, with Stephen and Lavinia Gibbs; and for many years with Jack and Marybeth Whitaker at Auchnafree in the Sma' Glen.

Other memorable occasions from these years were the Ball at Windsor Castle, given by the Queen to celebrate Princess Alexandra's marriage to my friend Angus Ogilvie in 1963, to which we went with my brother Dickie and his wife Mary; and the wedding of John Ambler to Princess Margaretha in 1964 in Sweden, where we lived a very grand life dining with kings and queens (particularly the dinner party on the Danish Royal Yacht).

By the late 1960s I was spending a good deal of my working life abroad, either on Miller or C.M.I. business, so it was quite often possible to combine holidays with work. Nik came with me on our first world tour (one of three) in 1969 when, after the C.M.I. conference in Tokyo, we went with the Berlingieris (one of our most favourite couples) to Thailand and India and I went on to Kashmir (without Nik) with the Berlingieris. After they left me I walked north alone, collecting wonderful plants and bulbs, before returning to Bombay (Mumbai) for some Miller business.

The whole family remembers these years as a round of non-stop activity and entertaining (**Fig. 13 h**)). In 1974 I was High Sheriff of Oxfordshire. This very busy year entailed looking after various judges when they came to sit in Oxford (when I was on duty) and giving dinner parties for them. Then there was the customary Garden Party when 'the County' were entertained. Apart from this, I remember that there was much equitation activity. We went to the Dublin Horse Show and had masses of people to stay that summer. Finally, in the autumn, we went to shoot in Northumberland with the Joiceys at Etal and in North Yorkshire with the Dawsons at Langcliffe.

Our first visit to Australia, again on Miller business, was in 1973. We flew via Hong Kong and Singapore.Then in 1977 Nik and I combined a C.M.I. conference in Rio de Janeiro with a wonderful holiday, starting in Bogota and going down the west coast of South America. Nik had to fly home before the conference started. She was on the County Council and was Chairwoman of the Health Committee; she was also Chairwoman of the Henley and South Oxford Conservative Association when Michael Heseltine was the Member of Parliament. (When Nik died I became Chairman of the Conservative Association.) Most of 1979 was spent on a 'one-off' piece of intensive (and financially important) work entailing numerous visits to Jeddah to draft the Maritime Law Code of Saudi Arabia, which I did with the assistance of Francis Frost, a partner at Millers. We spent the following two summers on John Bute's lovely yacht, **King Duck**. In 1983 I organised a C.M.I. Colloquium in Venice and we took Tony (later a Law Lord) and Jane Lloyd with us on the Orient Express. I remember giving an extremely expensive dinner party at the Cipriani Hotel!

# THE POST WAR YEARS

**Fig. 13 h)** *Double portrait of Bill and Nik Birch Reynardson*, by Benedict Rubbra. Oil on canvas.

*When we were at home, Nik and I spent much time restoring, replanting and extending the garden at Adwell. Perhaps the biggest (and certainly the most expensive!) project was the creation of five half-acre ponds leading away from the garden into the low-lying fields through which the Haseley Brook runs. I had a passion at the time for major operations such as building bridges, making new vistas by felling trees, and other jobs which kept everyone very busy!*

*Although technically I 'retired' from Millers in 1988, I was still a consultant and started doing some lecturing abroad, in Lagos and Yugoslavia and at the United States Maritime Law Association meeting in Florida. My retirement present from Nik was the trip we made in 1989 with our friends Willy and Belinda Bell on the Blue Train from*

Johannesburg to Cape Town. This produced an extraordinary coincidence: the black butler looking after us (in the Honeymoon Suite!) on the train asked me whether my father had been at Government House in Cape Town. It turned out that he had been one of the footmen there, over sixty years previously. As a result he plied us with champagne for the whole journey south! From then on, we went to South Africa most years.

Retirement gave Nik and me more leisure and the opportunity to go to many wonderful concerts, operas and picture exhibitions both in London and elsewhere. In the middle of the 1980s I started painting again, since 1988 with Graham Sproston who is an outstanding painter and teacher and has become a great friend. We went usually to France with him every year and I started to make progress; I owe him a huge debt of gratitude as painting has been a source of wondrous pleasure over the years.

Most of all music, especially opera, has dominated the years since my retirement. For two seasons, in 1979 and 1980, we organised opera performances in the garden at Adwell: the first year with Monteverdi's L'incoronazione di Poppea and the next year with Orfeo ed Euridice by Gluck. Then Nik led a mutiny, saying that all this must stop — otherwise we would be bankrupt! A few years later, Leonard Ingrams (the financier brother of Richard Ingrams, who founded Private Eye), who had been to both of the operas at Adwell, decided to start his own open-air opera festival in the gardens of his home, Garsington Manor, and asked me to help him with the opening season. This has been a wonderful part of my life ever since (**Fig. 13 i)**); I became Chairman after Leonard's death in 2005 and although I have retired from the Board, I still take an active interest in the festival, which since 2011 has taken place at Wormsley Park, the home of the Getty family near High Wycombe.

We had another world tour with the Berlingieris in 1994, this time to California, Bora Bora in French Polynesia, Australia and Singapore. In 1995 I went to Buckingham Palace, with all the family present, to receive the C.B.E. from the Queen, awarded for 'Services to International Maritime Law', and the following year I retired properly (more or less) from the C.M.I. There were some lovely farewell dinners: a special one by Francesco Berlingieri at Brooks and another in Antwerp on 18 May 1996.

# THE POST WAR YEARS

**Fig. 13 i)**  Rosalind Ingrams receiving a bouquet from WBR on the last night of Garsington.

# ACKNOWLEDGEMENTS

*Our happy existence at Adwell came to a sudden end in August 1997 with the death of my beloved Nik, after an illness lasting only a few weeks (Appendix VI). We had been married for nearly fifty years, during which she supported me lovingly and unflinchingly, making life at Adwell possible. But although I have taken my family's story only this far, perhaps I might be allowed by my readers to write just something about the seventeen years thereafter, having survived into my ninety-first year!*

*Soon after Nik's death, I received a letter from Madeleine Devlin*[1]. *She wrote: 'You may not think so, but you will survive without her. But you must be determined to live a new life, don't try to continue the old life.' I have tried to follow her advice.*

*First, I moved from 'the big house' into the Garden House and that, indeed, set me off on the new life. My first task was to create a new garden. Most fortunately I had Roy Smart, who has worked for us for twenty-five years, to help me in this project. And it is the garden that has been my chief pastime, particularly in the spring and summer months. In the winter, since giving up hunting after a bad accident, I have enjoyed my shooting very much, particularly the days at Adwell which my son Thomas has greatly improved since the time that I was in charge. Now I have decided, reluctantly, to call it a day but not before shooting a rather spectacularly high pheasant on my ninetieth birthday!*

*Then, of course, there has been my love of opera. Ever since, at the age of four, I escaped from my nanny, Miss Turner, when on board ship to South Africa, to hear Dame Clara Butt sing, I have been obsessed (I suppose!) with opera. I owe a very great deal to my colleagues at Garsington Opera and particularly to Anthony Whitworth-Jones (whom I selected as Chief Executive when I was Chairman) for all the enjoyment they have given me.*

*Painting — particularly with Graham Sproston — has been another highlight. I have much experience of art teachers and he is not only the best but also the nicest! What glorious holidays I've had with him: generally in France but sometimes in Italy. I'm aware that I have already mentioned him, but I do want to express again my special thanks to him and his lovely wife Carol.*

*My eleven grandchildren have brought me much joy, each of them so different but all very loving. I've tried to watch over them as they grow up. This has not been a tedious duty but the loving occupation of a grandfather.*

---

1  Lady Devlin (née Oppenheimer, 1909–2012) was the widow of Lord Devlin (1905–92), a Lord of Appeal and friend since we were colleagues in my early days at the C.M.I. Patrick Devlin is perhaps best known for his handling of the celebrated Bodkin Adams trial in 1957.

## ACKNOWLEDGEMENTS

*I have been granted the time to do all these things because I have had Lorrie Wollerton to assist and support me and the family for sixty years. My gratitude to her cannot adequately be expressed. And to Thomas and Imogen, who have been the mainstay of my life at the Garden House, my real gratitude continues. In the context of this book, I should like especially to thank my granddaughter Daisy for her practical advice and assistance in helping it into print.*

*The primary object of this book has been to tell the story of my family over more than three centuries, based on the mass of letters and other relevant documents collected by my father during his life. Writing this book has taken over five years. I have, of course, been doing other things as well, but my main occupation, particularly in the winter months, has been reading the letters, choosing those which I thought were of particular interest and then writing commentaries on them. Most fortunately, when I was floundering — and nearly drowning — in a sea of letters and 'first drafts' of commentaries, I was introduced to Kate Dinn. After some discussion she agreed, to my delight, to be my text editor.*

*I couldn't have produced this book without her remarkable assistance. Her general approach to the contents of the book was, to me, not only novel but also correct. She carried out detailed research and made suggestions to my draft text which I almost invariably accepted! To her I owe a huge debt of gratitude.*

*My thanks also go to Sara Rafferty, whose work in designing the contents of my book has been both artistic and highly efficient.*

*Then last, but by no means least, I want to mention my secretary for over thirty years, Linda Hunt. She has typed out most of the text and all the necessary letters relating to it. Again, I am so grateful to her for her efficiency, her patience and, above all, her friendship.*

APPENDIX I

# The Battle of Dettingen, 1743

*Amongst the family papers is a collection of military documents and hand-drawn plans, dating from the eighteenth to the early nineteenth centuries, which seem to have been collected by Thomas Birch Reynardson (see also* Appendix III *and* Appendix IV). *The earliest of these is an eye-witness account of the Battle of Dettingen, which took place on 27 June 1743; an action fought in South West Germany as part of the War of the Austrian Succession, the battle is chiefly remembered today as the only time in modern history that a British Force has been led into battle by a reigning monarch (King George II)*[1].

*The unknown writer was evidently a member of a cavalry regiment (probably the Royal Regiment of Horse or the King's Horse) and of sufficiently high rank to attend the King on foot after both had been unhorsed. I have not been able to find any connection between the writer and the Birch family, or any clue as to how the document found its way into our collection, where it is kept in a wrapper inscribed, in Thomas Birch Reynardson's handwriting, with the words:* Account of Battle of Dettingen. May be Original *(see page 427). The account was written three days after the battle and is of particular interest as it includes details which do not appear in any other published version.*

### Bergen near Frankfort [sic] June 30th N.S.[2] 1743

On ye 27th inst. N.S. the Kg. [*King George II*] gained a battle over the F—ch [*French*] Army who crossed the River Meyne [*Main*] between Hanau and Dettingen, and cut off our communication with Hanau (from whence we had our provision & bread) and afterwards advanced to attack us on our March, on which we immediatly drew up in order of battle, all our English Infantry (except the Brigade of Guards which made the Rear Guard as the greatest danger was apprehended from thence, tho' it proved otherwise).

1   The combatants were an Allied force comprising British, Hanoverian and Austrian cavalry and infantry regiments (collectively known as the Pragmatic Army) against the French. The Allied victory was somewhat unexpected as the French army outnumbered the opposing armies by 70,000 to 50,000. Later in the same year, the victory was commemorated by Handel in his oratorio, the *Dettingen Te Deum*.
2   The initials N.S. stand for 'New Style' and refer to the adoption of the Gregorian Calendar which replaced the old-style Julian Calendar throughout Europe, moving the nominal start of the year to 1 January instead of 25 March (Lady Day). The Gregorian Calendar was not introduced in England until after the Calendar Act of 1750, but was by this time already in use on the Continent.

# APPENDIX I

With a part of the Austrians making the Front Line & part of the Hannoverians & Austrians making a Second Line, the Ground being so narrow between the Mountains and the River Main as not to admit of more than 22 or 23 Battalions in Front with some cavalry (of which my Regiment was a part) so that in some place we had a 3rd Line of Foot, supported by two or 3 Lines of Horse, but our 1st Line of Foot behaved so well [that] we had no occasion to employ ye second, for from the very beginning of the Action, which lasted about 3 hours (occasioned by the woods on our right whence the French were posted) they gained ground on them, forcing them at different times to retire & at last to quit the Feild of Battle & repass the River with precipitation, in which it is said a great many were drowned. What the loss on either side is I don't yet know, only that ours is not very considerable for the length of the action[3], my Regiment having lost more than all the rest of the English Cavalry, being exposed all ye time to a battery of ye Enemies of 12 pounders and towards the end of the action to charge ye Squadrons of the Household of France through which they forced their way three different times, though they were outnumbered in ye first charge 3fold. Yet they thought it much less dangerous than the Cannonade [which] they [with] stood for above 2 hours. My Regiment was sustain'd after the first charge by Lord Stair's Dragoons[4], the Blues & Honeywood's Horse, so that few or none of ye musketeers of the rest of the French Squadrons escaped, above 30 of ye musketeers & officers of Distinction being taken prisoners and the greatest part of ye others being kill'd.

Lieut. General Clayton was kill'd; the Duke of Cumberland[5] who commanded as Major General on the left of ye 1st Line was shot in ye legg & Brigr. Huske in the foot. These were all the General officers of the English that were kill'd or wounded.

Col. Peers is dangerously wounded with several other feild officers, amongst which poor Major Honeywood is of the number having several shots in his body and cutts in the Head, so that I fear much for him. I had one Leiut[sic] and one Cornet killed, and almost all the rest of ye officers wounded, there being now only 5 officers fit to do Duty and about a 3rd part of ye Men and Horses, the rest being either kill'd or wounded. My three Standards are lost, but not taken by

3   The official casualty list for the British was 15 officers killed, 250 soldiers killed, 327 horses killed, 38 officers wounded, 520 soldiers wounded, 155 horses wounded. The French casualties were estimated at around 8,000.
4   The Earl of Stair was in nominal overall command.
5   William Augustus, Duke of Cumberland (1721–65), the second and favourite son of George II, saw action for the first time in this year, fighting alongside his father at the Battle of Dettingen. The leg wound he sustained there was to trouble him for the rest of his life. Within three years he was to become notorious for his role in the brutal suppression of the Jacobite Rebellion in Scotland (see Chapter 2).

the Enemy, they were shatter'd to pieces by the enemy's cannon & trod under foot in ye mud when they charged so as not to be found when the Action was over. One of the men who carried them was kill'd, another wounded and the 3rd, which is Mr Child, Lord Castlemain's brother, had 2 horses kill'd under him, so that my Standards were lost nobly. My usual good fortune attended me having lost only the Horse I rode, being shot close by the King, in ye First fire & not being able to find any of my grooms I attended His Majesty on foot during the whole Action, who had likewise dismounted and put himself at the head of the Foot and exposed his sacred Person more than he ought and was once much nearer the Enemy's Line than ours, but on my taking the liberty to acquaint him with it & how much he exposed his Royal Person & the fate of the Day by it, he retired Back, but kept close to the Front Line during the whole Action which animated our troops to such a degree that double their [*the enemy's*] number could not have beat them. I shall not trouble with a further account of ye Action having but a confused one of it yet myself.

# APPENDIX I

> Col.º Peers is dangerously wounded, w.th several other feild officers amongst which poor Major Honeywood is of the Number, hav.g several shot in his body & cutts in the Head; so that I fear much for him. I had one Lieut.t & one Cornet kill'd, & almost all the rest of y.e Officers wounded, there being now only 5 officers fit to do Duty & about a 3.d part of y.e Men & Horses, the rest being either kill'd or wounded. my three standards are lost; but not taken by the Enemy, they were shatter'd to pieces by the enemys Cannon & trod under foot in y.e Mud when they Charg'd, so as not to be found when the Action was over. one of the four w.o carried them was kill'd another wounded, & the 3.d which is M.r Child Lord Castlemains Bro.r, had a horse kill'd under him; so that my standards were lost nobly. My usual good fortune attended me hav.g lost only the Horse I rode, being shot close by the K.g in y.e 1.st First Fire, & not being able to find any of my grooms I attended his Majesty on foot during the whole Action, who had likewise dismounted & put himself at the head of the Foot & exposed his sacred Person more than he ought, & was once much nearer the Enemy's Line than ours, but on my being so happy to acquaint him w.th it, & how much he expos'd his Royal Person & the fate of the Day by it he retired back, but kept close to the Front Line during the whole Action, which animated our troops to such a degree that double their number cou'd not have beat them. I shall not trouble with a further Acc.t of y.e Action hav.g but a confused one of it yet my self. ———

> Account of
> Battle of
> Dettingen
> [illegible]

Part of *Account of the Battle of Dettingen, 27 June 1743*, dated 30 June 1743, writer unknown, together with the wrapper with an inscription in Thomas Birch Reynardson's hand.

# APPENDIX II

# 'The Angels on Horseback'

*A year or so before his marriage in June 1806 to Miss Etheldred Reynardson, Lieutenant-Colonel Thomas Birch accompanied his future bride and members of her family, together with his own sister Mary, to Southend on holiday. To the watercolour sketch he made of Etheldred and her three sisters riding along the beach (**Fig. 5 a**)), Thomas added the following poem. According to the crib written in pencil under the drawing, 'Betty' (3) is Elizabeth Reynardson, who seems to have been Thomas's favourite of Etheldred's sisters; Mary Birch (5) is trailing a little way behind; and Thomas's manservant Frank Burnham (6) is bringing up the rear.*

"The Angels on Horseback"

A New ballad, sung with much Applause, by the /
Lovely Miss Dakers at a Private Party at South End /
to the Tune of — Down Derry Down —. July 1805

---

All mounted & ready to start from South End,
Say, one to the other which course shall we bend
As all cry at once "'tis the same thing to me,
"Say Rochford or Wakering, & home by the Sea —".
    Derry Down Down Down Derry Down

Aye Aye, by the Sea is the pleasantest ride,
And as we return t'will be just right for tide.
Mammas cry "Make sure that the Riding is Sound,
"God bless you, take care, that you're none of you drown'd".
    Derry Down &c &c &c &c

Before we set forward, suppose I describe,
As near as I can, this Equestrian Ride:
And, altho' some particulars I need not mention
Tout ensemble, suffice, it attracted attention.

## APPENDIX II

       Derry Down &c &c &c &c
Most commonly, leading the Van, might be seen
A Jockey well mounted, in Jacket Nankin,
And as far as one fairly could judge from the <u>pace</u>
She might be quite certain of winning the Race.
       Derry Down &c &c &c &c

No further account could I give if I tried
From a Custom with Ladies their faces to hide*.
True, her plea might be good, to expose it to no Man,
'Tis enough, to know she was attach'd to a <u>Sultan</u> #
       Derry Down &c &c &c &c

My next in succession tho' <u>Least but not Last</u>,
Moves in nice gentle canter & never too fast,
Again comes another, don't think I've forgot her,
Always steady, the dashing along upon Trotter [⸫].
       Derry Down &c &c &c &c

But who's that I see <u>quite the last</u>, some say <u>Least</u>
Striving hard to keep up on a poor little Beast,
Crying out, to those riding before, "'tis not kind
"To gallop away & leave Pony behind."
       Derry Down &c &c &c &c

 "Well well then, Dear Mary, you get on Don Felix."
Mary: "I have half a mind, but supposing that he kicks,
  "Are you sure now Dear Betty that Donny won't shy?"
Betty: "I don't think he will but t'won't hurt you to try:"
       Derry Down &c &c &c &c

# SURVIVORS

Mary: "It is strange & I cannot account for my fears
      "But I don't like it quite when he cocks out his Ears.
      "I'm always afraid that he's going to start."
Betty: "What signifies that, when it makes him look smart?"
                Derry Down &c &c &c &c

    Having summ'd up my Charges permit me to ask
    If as <u>Chaperon</u> I had not an arduous task,
    For tho', as Dragoon, to lead Squadrons my Trade is,
    I never Commanded a Squadron of Ladies.
                Derry Down &c &c &c &c

    Be it so, but in seeking much pleasure to gain
    One must compromise for a small share of Pain
    And tell me, I pray, what in this world could he lack
    Surrounded by Four <u>Chosen Angels on Horseback</u>?
                Derry Down &c &c &c &c

    Just a word if you please ere I finish my Song.
    I'm aware that you'll find it already too long,
    But do not you think t'would be <u>civil</u> to thank
    For all his good Offices the faithful <u>Frank</u> [x] ?
                Derry Down &c &c &c &c

---

[*] Vide — the Straw Bonnets — which completely cover'd ye faces —
[#] Tis Customary with the Fair in <u>Eastern Districts</u> to hide their faces — <u>Sultan</u> was the name of the Horse —
[φ] The name of another Horse —
[x] Servant who had lived many years with his Master —

APPENDIX III

# Peninsular War Memorabilia
(*see* Chapter 5)

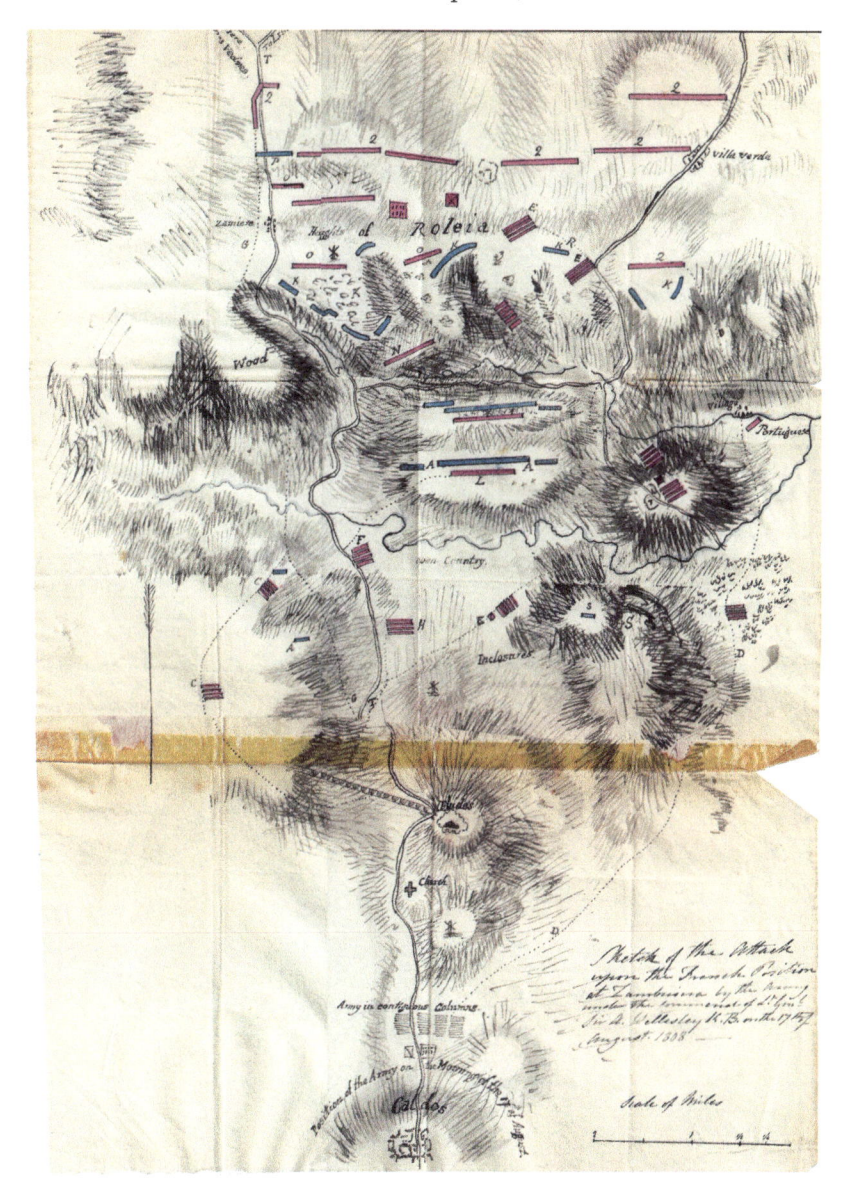

**III: A** *'Sketch of the Attack upon the French at Zambuiera [Roliça] by the English under the Command of Sir A. Wellesley, K.B., on 17 August 1808'*. Pen and ink, unsigned.

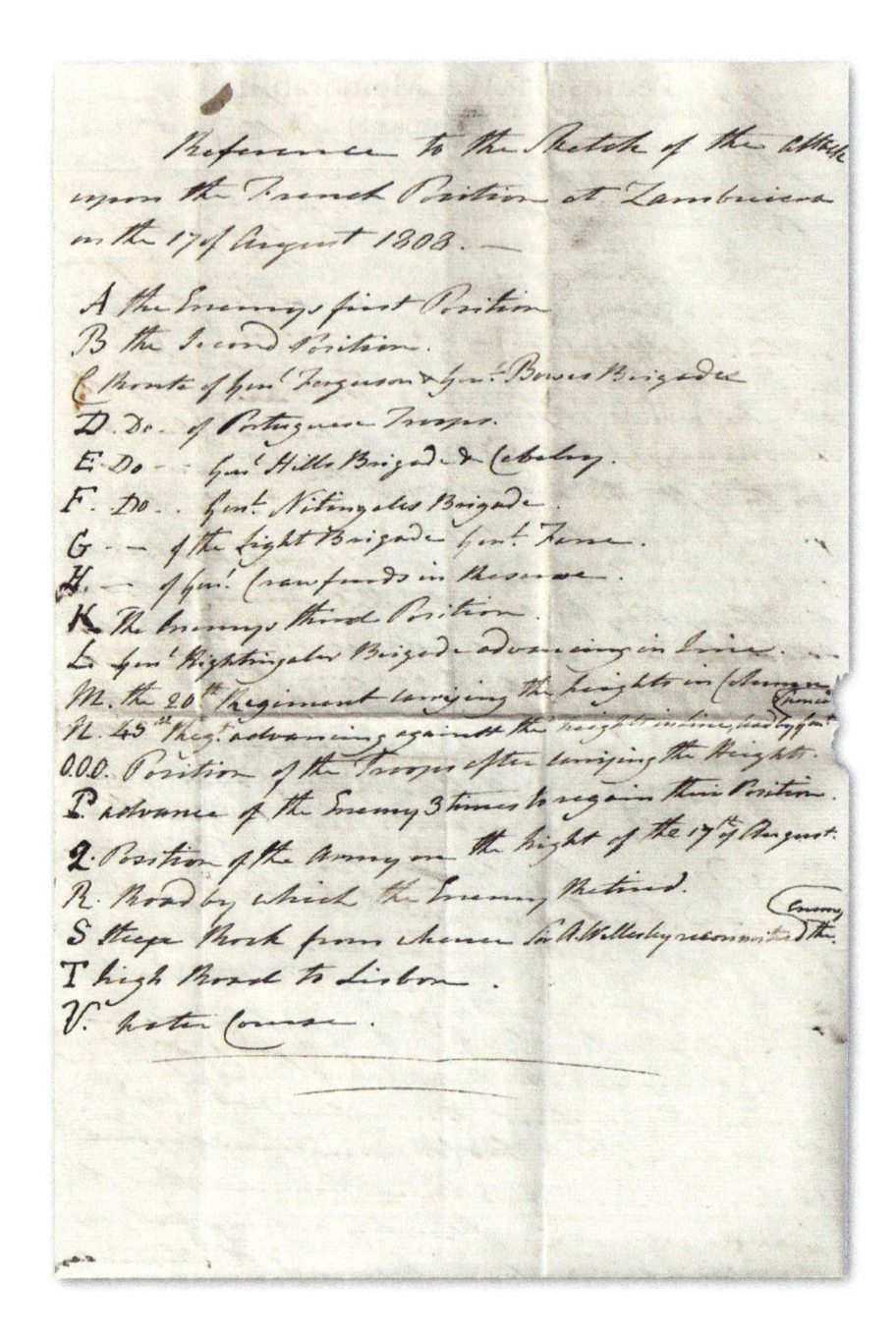

Reference to the Sketch of the Attack upon the French Position at Zambuiera on the 17 of August 1808. —

A the Enemys first Position
B the Second Position.
C Route of Genl. Ferguson & Genl. Bowes Brigade
D. Do. of Portuguese Troops.
E Do — Genl. Hills Brigade & Cavalry.
F. Do — Genl. Nightingales Brigade.
G — of the Light Brigade Genl. Fane.
H — of Genl. Crawfords in the rear.
K The Enemys third Position.
L Genl. Nightingales Brigade advancing in Line.
M. the 20th Regiment carrying the heights in Column
N. 45th Regt. advancing against the heights in line, headed by &c.
O.O.O. Position of the Troops after carrying the heights.
P. advance of the Enemy 3 times to regain their Position.
Q. Position of the Army on the Night of the 17th of August.
R. Road by which the Enemy retired.
S Steep Rock from whence Sir A. Wellesley reconnoitred the Enemy
T high Road to Lisbon.
V. Water Course.

III: B *'Reference to the Sketch of the Attack upon the French Position at Zambuiera on the 17 August 1808'*

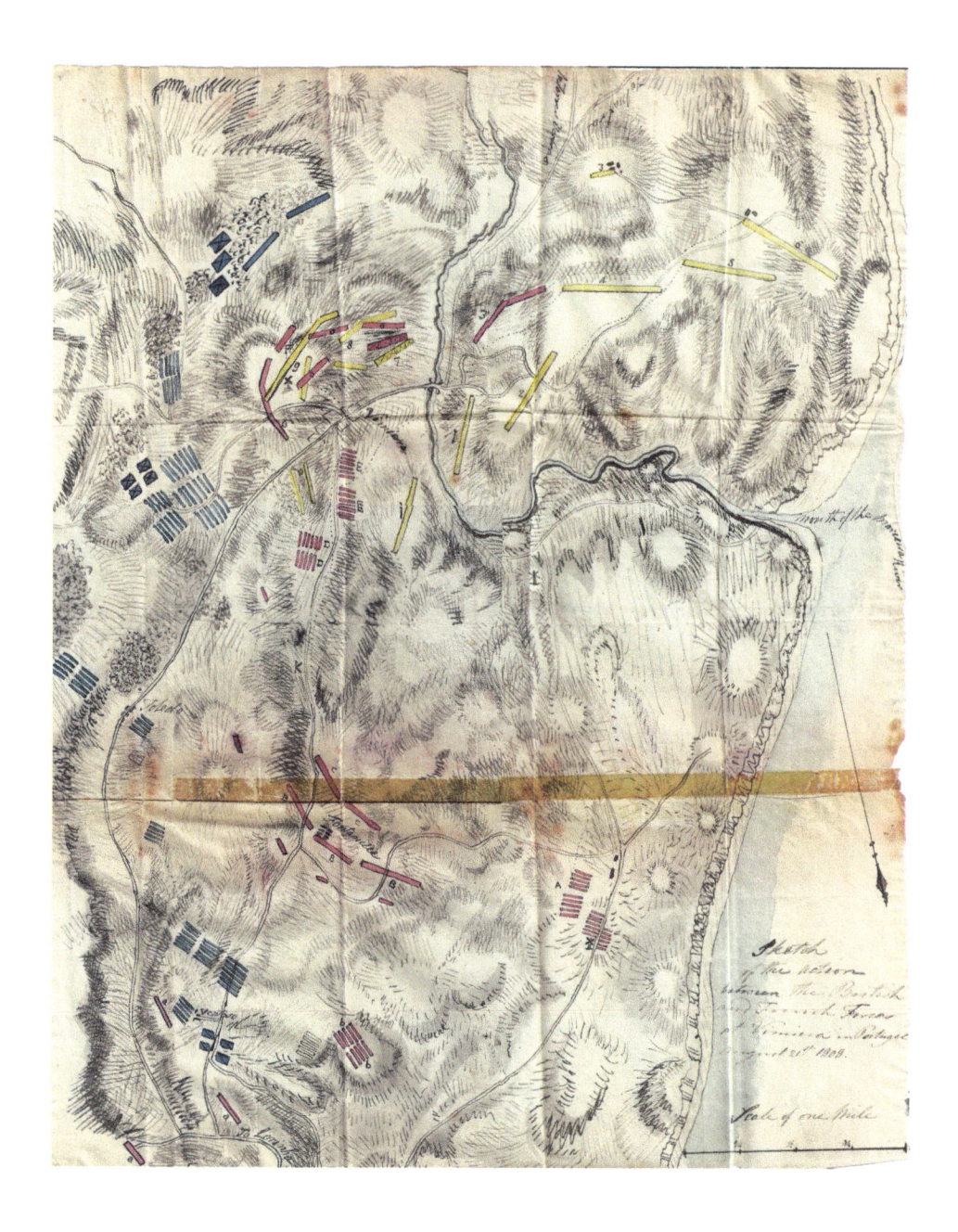

APPENDIX III

**III: C** *'Sketch of the Action between the British and French Forces at Vimiero in Portugal on August 21ˢᵗ 1808'.*
Pen, ink and wash, unsigned.

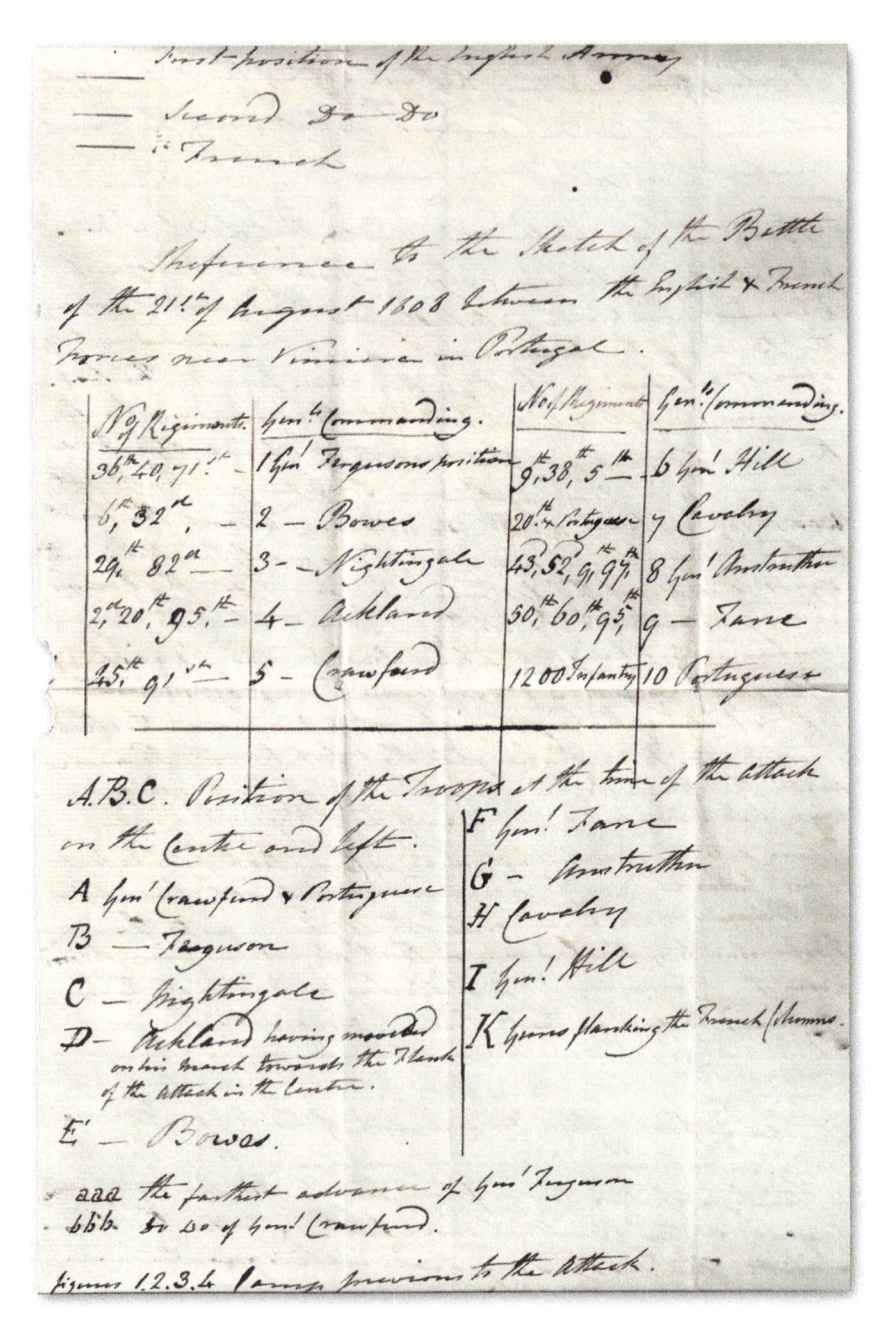

**III: D** *'Explanation relating to the Battle of the 21st of August between the British under Sir A. Wellesley & the French under Genl. Junot'*

APPENDIX IV

# The General's Napoleonic Archive
(*see* Chapter 6)

*It is not known how Thomas Birch Reynardson acquired the two documents included below but it is possible that the copy of Colonel Campbell's letter* (**IV: A**) *was given to him by his mother. Written on the outside of the large folded sheet, in what appears to be Mrs Mary Birch's handwriting, are the words* Anecdotes & Memoranda / of Bonaparte *and* To ask Genl Birch Reynardson if these of any use.

## IV: A (Copy of original letter[1] dated 18 April, 1814, writer unknown)

Copy of Col Campbell's Letter

Private                                                      Palace of Fontainbleau
April 18th 1814

My dear Colonel

I had made up my mind to return to England for rest & recovery from my wounds when Ld. Castlereagh offered me a Mission which was too interesting to decline, altho' it was entirely discretionary — It is to accompany Bonaparte to the Isle of Elba, & even to remain there for some time if required by him & that it appears necessary towards his security & comfort in communicating with the British men of war.

I arrived here the night before last & was presented to him yesterday — The interview lasted a quarter of an hour. He walked quickly to the door to receive me & saluted me with a courteous smile without any formality — He paid compliments to the British nation — and after expressing a hope that a British Ship might convoy the French Corvette destined for his voyage from St Tropsey [*Tropez*] he said he would wish to be conveyed in a British Ship if the other was

---

1   It is unlikely that the copy was made very long after the original letter was written, as it is on paper watermarked with the date 1812, and with the name of the manufacturer, 'C BRENCHLEY'.

not ready on his arrival — He added "Je depends entirement sur vous (meaning the British Government). Je suis votre sujet."

When the negotiations were pending he proposed going to England in case there were objections to the I. of Elba. He told one of his Aid de-Camps that the British Nation was great and generous & he was persuaded he should meet there with liberal treatment — He than added in his quick way "Mais dans mon Isle je suis dans une rue de Londres" — He seems to be quite resigned to his adversity, without dejection — he does not go out & is much occupied with his private affairs — Generals Bertrand & Drouet are the only Officers who go with him. He talks of writing his own Life & employing himself in the study of the fine arts to which he has always been so partial.

He passed great encomiums on Lord Wellington in his conversation with me — also on Genl. Graham in taking of Bergen-op-zoom. He said it was honorable both to the Genl. & his Troops "Car il faut risque[r], il faut de vigeur comme cela dans la guerre." He said however that Genl. G did not think the French Garrison so numerous, & that they were prepared for the attack by information from their Spies.

## IV: B (Probably a copy[2] of an original document dated December 1814, writer unknown)

Heads of a letter from ___ to ___ respecting an Audience with Buonaparte in Decr. 1814 at Porto Ferrago

In a small house, situated on a high Rock, that overlooks the sea on one side, & the town on the other, resides the once Tyrant of Europe, he who so few months ago, gave away Palaces & created Kings, has not now a room so large as your drawing room; ill furnish'd & in all its departments bespeaking poverty — he has not as yet received a farthing of the subsidy from the Government of France & has in consequence been obliged to reduce his establishment, to curtail the salaries of those about him, & to retrench in every possible way the expenditure to which almost as a Gentleman he was entitled.

Mr __, Mr __ and myself had three separate audiences — Napoleon is very low in stature (about 5 feet 6 inches) immensely broad across the chest, altogether

---

2  The document is written on three folded sheets of paper stitched together to form a pamphlet. Two of the sheets are watermarked with the date 1812 and the name of the manufacturer 'GOLDING & SNELGROVE'.

very corpulent but with the appearance of rude health, his Phisiognomy except when animated by some very interesting subject, is not in any way remarkable, not so sallow as generally represented, and a light grey eye approaching to blue — I found him standing by the fire, dressed in a very shabby old uniform with the Grand Cordon of the Legion of honor, & several other small orders, the iron crown &c. — His accent rather blunt, 'd'ou venez vous?' he asked with a sharp piercing voice — 'de la France, Sire,' was the reply, and his tone & manner then changed into the greatest possible affability & good nature, & he asked, 'que dit on de moi dans la France, parlez franchement je vous prie' — Answer; great mass of Population decidedly attached to the Bourbons, yet many to his (Napoleon's) cause, particularly the army — he then began his own history, & went thro' it from his first signalizing himself at Toulon to his campaign in Egypt, on which he debated. In answer to questions addressed to him, he acknowledged that he had authorized the Massacre at Jaffa, but vindicated his conduct on the score of the previous treachery of those Turks, who had been released on parole, had broken it &c. — of his having only 10,000 men with him, of his safety requiring it; he ordered all taken at Jaffa to be shot & 'Je ne m'en repens pas' were his words, 'car dans la Guerre tout ce qui est utile est legitime.'

He admitted that the report of his poisoning his sick, was partly true, partly not; on the eve of a forced march soldiers were reported to be dying of a plague; he sent for Disjeunnettes the head of the medical staff, & asked him if there was the smallest chance of their surviving? was told none — ' "Can they be moved with the army?" "They will infect the rest of your Troops, Sire" — "Alors je lui dis de les traiter comme je voudrais, qu'il me traitat en pareil cas — Enfin qu'il leur donnat une doze d'opium." — Il me repondit "non, mon metier est de guerir et non pas de tuer les Hommes." ' — He (Buonaparte) was silent for a minute & exclaimed, 'Et je crois qu'il avait raison, il faut que chacun remplisse sa destiniée.' He left his men & did not poison them.

'From Egypt' he said, 'I return'd to Paris, where I lived for some time in private.— One day I saw in the paper a decree of the convention, naming Buonaparte Commander in Chief of the Army. I bought the paper & gave three pence for it, not having the least idea it referred to myself, I went to a Coffee house, and began to enquire, who this Buonaparte was, saying that I was not aware of having a namesake.

'No one knew. I walked down to where the convention sat. The doors of the house were crowded — I was soon recognised; the shout was immediately "vive Buonaparte, vive notre petit General &c &c" ' — was then sent in chief command to Italy — gave a short account of his Italian campaigns & of his being afterwards made chief Consul (Buonaparte here forgets his own history, he was made first consul immediately on his return from Egypt & went to Italy after this event). 'Après cette époque,' he said — 'Je trouvais un Trone vaide, personne prêt a le remplir — Je le saisois, avois — je tort [?] mais je suis content. Je repose dans l'idee que j'ai plutôt augmente que diminué le bonheur de la France.'

He then began about the Bourbons. Louis XVIII, 'C'est bien un bon homme que ça — Il a même du talent, travaille-t'il beaucoup' (answer 6 hours a day) 'on peut faire beau coup en six heures — Monsieur est un gentilhomme avec des manieres fort gracieuses. Mais il ne sait pas travailler — Les Ducs d'Angouleme et de Berri ne sont pas grand chose, des Riens!' — seem'd to know little of the Duke of Orleans, seem'd amazingly surprised to hear that he possessed superior talents, firmness, decision &c & betray'd some emotion.

He then talked of the Emperor Alexander — 'ce n'est qu'un leger que ça, mais vous n'avez pas d'idee comme il est fin et faux. Le Roi de Prusse — c'est un bon homme, il se croit sage, mais ce n'est qu'un Imbecile, un Caporal — mais pourtant un bon homme.' Talleyrand he described as a very fiend — 'Ce viellard, cet Evêque qui a epousé une __! It was he who proposed to me to convey the Bourbons from England by means of Smuglers [sic], & to Murder them all — It was he that was the cause of the death of the Duke of D'Enghien; he wore me out with solicitations to have him destroy'd. I at last consented. The young Duke begged to see me, I sent for Talleyrand to arrange the audience, car c'était un brave jeune homme et son sort m'a vraiment touché — to my great surprize Talleyrand told me it was too late. The deed was done, I hated him ever since, for I do believe I should have spared the Duke's life.'

[*Napoleon*] professed himself very friendly to universal toleration, had favor'd the Jews partly on the principle, built Churches for all sects, blamed the restrictions on Roman Catholics in England as 'Indiques d'une grande nation comme la vôtre.' Declared that he murder'd neither Wright or Picheque, 'a quoi bon,' they were in prison & there they died, 'Picheque un homme sans talent, sans tête, Moreau à la bonheur il aurait pu me faire repentir de ma cleménce mais non je ne voudrais pas lui avoir eté la vie.' He then said he had been too Merciful; had he spilt more blood, he might have been now where he was on the throne of France.

Spoke of our English ministers — of both Pitt & Fox he had the highest opinion & Lord Grenville's talents he prized particularly.

# APPENDIX V

# 'Real Home Solves Homeless Children's Problem',
from *Illustrated* magazine, 16 June 1945

## REAL HOME SOLVES HOMELESS CHILDREN'S PROBLEM

Foster-parents can be trained for the full-time, paid career of bringing up this family of 150,000; can give to the unwanted children of this country the home-life and mother-love that so many institutions lack

EVERY young life is of value to Britain today, if our forty-seven millions are to pull their weight in the days ahead alongside the more numerous millions of Russia and the United States.

Healthy, happy childhood is the State's, as well as the parents', affair, far more so now than ever before —especially where it concerns the child whose parents, for a variety of reasons, cannot be entrusted with its upbringing, and the child who has no known parents at all.

The great human problem of the legion of children denied the elementary birthright of proper home life has been enormously aggravated during the last few years. First are the problem-progeny bred of the fleeting friendships formed in the artificial excitement, anxiety and separation of war.

There are the orphans of the blitz; others whose parents have disappeared without trace and may be dead or alive; and those deserted by the contemptible few who vanished to avoid paying billeting charges.

At least a hundred and fifty thousand unwanted or unclaimed children are known officially to have no normal home life—the unofficial figure is estimated to be scores of thousands more.

The Gough case flashed a lurid light on just one sordid aspect of the problem. And now the Home Office committee, headed by Miss Myra Curtis, principal of Newnham College, is touring the country, inquiring into the provisions made for children deprived of normal home life, studying the good and bad of the existing system in order to recommend a new charter of what foster-parenthood should and should not be.

What it can be is illustrated by the picture-story on these pages of a unique six-year experiment in the bringing up, as brothers and sisters of one big family, by one foster-mother, of twenty-one children, most of whom have never known what it is like to have parents of their own.

The joyous life brought about by their change of fortune, and evidenced by their smiling faces, will touch many hearts. More, this constructive story can be an example to authorities and well-wishers of what can be done to help every fostered child to grow up into a valued and useful citizen, instead of into a backward and delinquent one.

The cottage home, with one and the same foster-mother caring for a good-size family of "brothers and sisters," avoids the impersonal and motherless atmosphere of institution life. It offers safer and easier inspection than when odd children are scattered

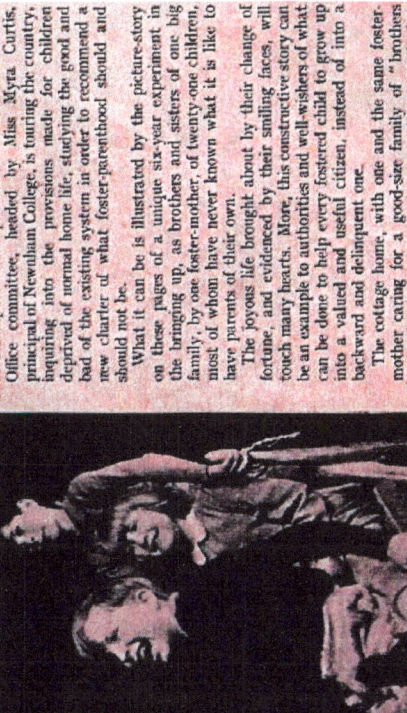

**The Slide.** Gay and grave studies of two "brothers" and a "sister" as one cries excitedly: "Here we go!"

# SURVIVORS

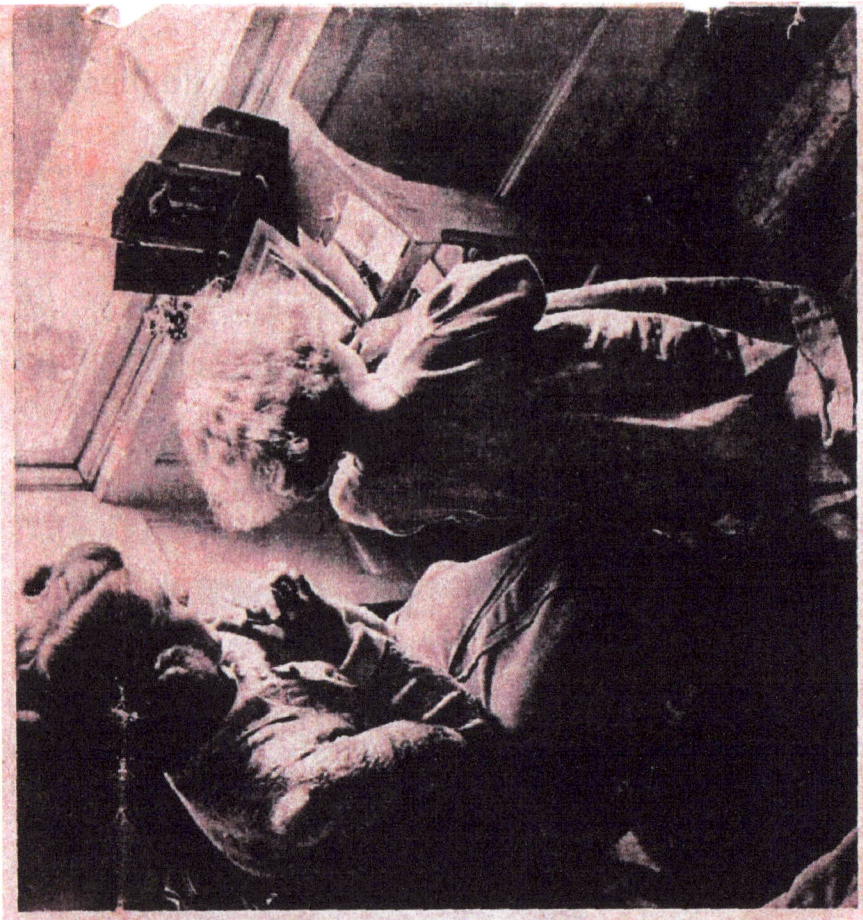

*Prayer Time* in Foster-Mother Doris's room. For children who have never known a real father it is a delight to say "Our Father." They also say another little prayer which has been devised for them. It is: "I want God and God wants me"

among private families, and the motive of profit is sometimes stronger than that of love.

The cottage home as the ideal foster-family unit is, I understand, being urged on the Curtis Committee by some of the most experienced bodies and individuals concerned with unwanted and ill-treated children.

More than two hundred officers of the National Society for the Prevention of Cruelty to Children favour it. They suggest a family of eight or nine, with a mother who is preferably a widow and whose affection for her charges is her foremost qualification.

Affection is rated even higher than efficiency, for the first inborn desire of unwanted children is to feel they are *wanted*.

If the problem is handled the right way there is no reason why they should not enjoy both. But this will come about only if motherhood ceases to be regarded as an amateurish business, and one hears less about choosing "the right sort of foster-mother," instead of a trained and qualified one.

Nobody talks about the "right sort of teacher," where a child's education is concerned. It is taken for granted that a teacher is trained and qualified. Why shouldn't a foster-mother be also?

A child's home life, by which its character and moral outlook are largely formed, is every bit as important as its schooling. And a foster-mother who brings up a family, or series of families, should be following a vocation recognised and paid for as a skilled and noble job.

Such courses of training already exist at the best types of nursery schools, where a potential foster-mother soon discovers whether she loves child-care sufficiently to go on with it as a lifetime career.

Foster-Mother Doris Sayer, whom you see with her charges in these pictures, was not only trained at a nursery school, but is a certificated teacher able to give them their schooling as well. This is exceptional and is not essential. What does matter, if foster-children go out to school, is that they have a mother to come home to—the same one all the time.

This is the reverse of institution life, where they have no one person as mother, and pass through the hands of several if moved from home to home or school to school.

The children you see pictured here at Adwell House, Tetsworth, Oxfordshire, the home of Colonel and Mrs. Birch-Reynardson, have been brought up to know Foster-Mother Doris Sayer as their one mother.

The colonel's wife, who is the presiding genius behind the adventure of this super cottage home with

440

# APPENDIX V

its fostered family of twenty-one, and who throughout the six years has taken her turn with everything from bathing the children to putting them to bed, is regarded as an extra special mother. Five young relatives and friends of the family, who have given their services free throughout the war, take turns as additional helpers.

Now, the German war over, the family is at the parting of the ways. Seven children with homes will go back to them. One has been adopted by the Adwell cook. Thirteen with no homes will, if funds can be found, go with Foster-Mother Doris Sayer into a smaller house and be brought up and schooled by her till they are sixteen.

Friends will provide a house rent-free, and the institutional authority concerned will contribute generously; but the utmost economy still leaves a need for more money, if the thirteen are to enjoy a future as rich in promise as the lives they have led for the last six years.

But thousands of children have never enjoyed such happiness. They have remained in institutions, known only the impersonal life of this system. It is not the fault of the institutions; in well managed ones, everything possible is done for the child. It is the system that is wrong; the cottage home may prove the solution.

With the institutional system should go all the outworn psychological approach to the problem of unwanted children. In some quarters they are still made to feel different from their fellows by being labelled as "waifs and strays." In others the smug words "moral care," creep, in. Elsewhere there is an atmosphere of "pity."

The Ministry of Health has shown daring and enlightenment by decreeing that every unwanted child and its mother shall have all the special medical attention and food allowances that others enjoy. Indeed, as the Ministry official in charge of child-care told me, children without normal home life need if anything more care than those born under a luckier star.

The happy foster-family pictured in these pages have all, since they were toddlers of two or three, been brought up, if not born, under such a star. They are not to be pitied, but envied. They enjoyed what poor little Dennis O'Neill deserved, but did not get, at Gough's farm.

He will not have died in vain if the heart-searchings his death started, and the nation-wide Curtis inquiry now going on, bring about a more humane deal for the Unwanted Child!

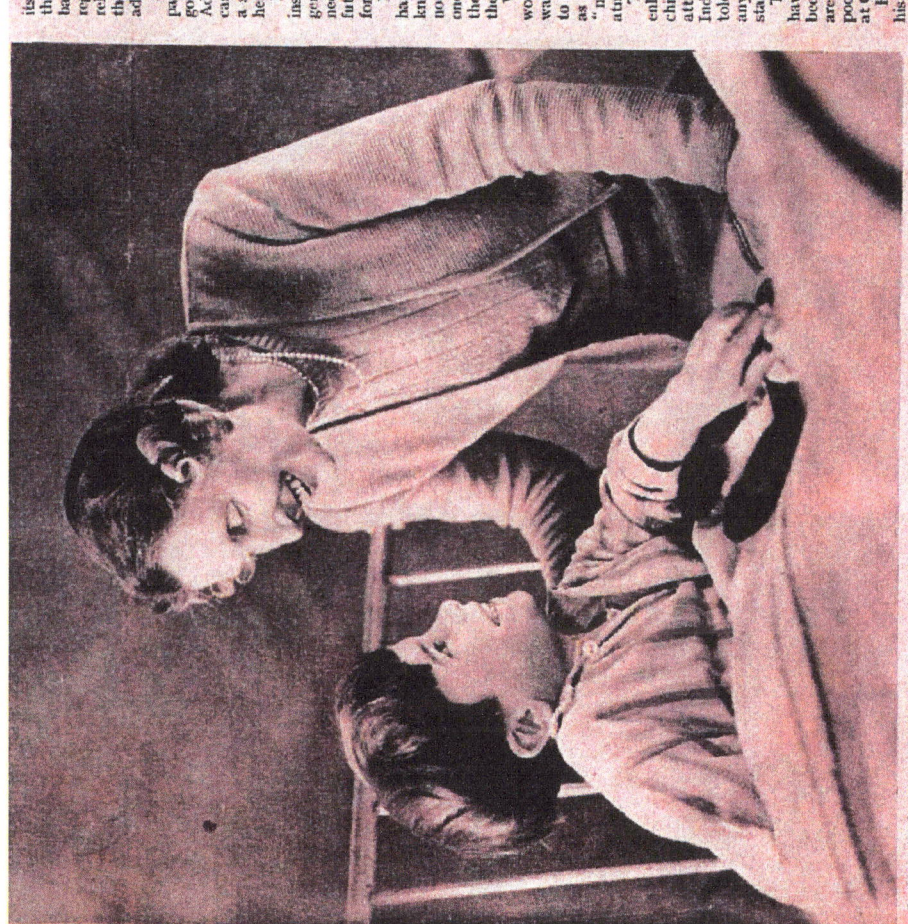

JOHN CASHEL.

**And so to bed.** The Colonel's wife, whom the children call "Mummy Di," bids Brian "good-night." Mrs. Reynardson, herself a mother of four, has a way with children and a deep and tender insight into the psychology of unwanted ones

# SURVIVORS

**High Expectations**—on stilts, a picture symbolizing a real-life fairy story, the rise in the world of a model foster-family—thirteen of them once 'Unwanted Babies'.

**These Children**, some of the twenty-one at Adwell House, Tetsworth, have been brought up as brothers and sisters with one foster-mother; have played together for six years.

June 16, 1945—ILLUSTRATED

APPENDIX V

**HOMELESS CHILDREN'S PROBLEM—continued**

*ILLUSTRATED—June 16, 1945*

**Shaggy Donkey** called Margaret gives rides to the children. Here Sylvia, as girls will, leads Louis, mounted, up the garden path. Children play in surrounding meadows and woods

**Home Farm** at Col. and Mrs. Birch-Reynardson's Adwell House has helped with the rationing and feeding of their big family. The calves are always a popular turn with the children

June 16, 1945—ILLUSTRATED

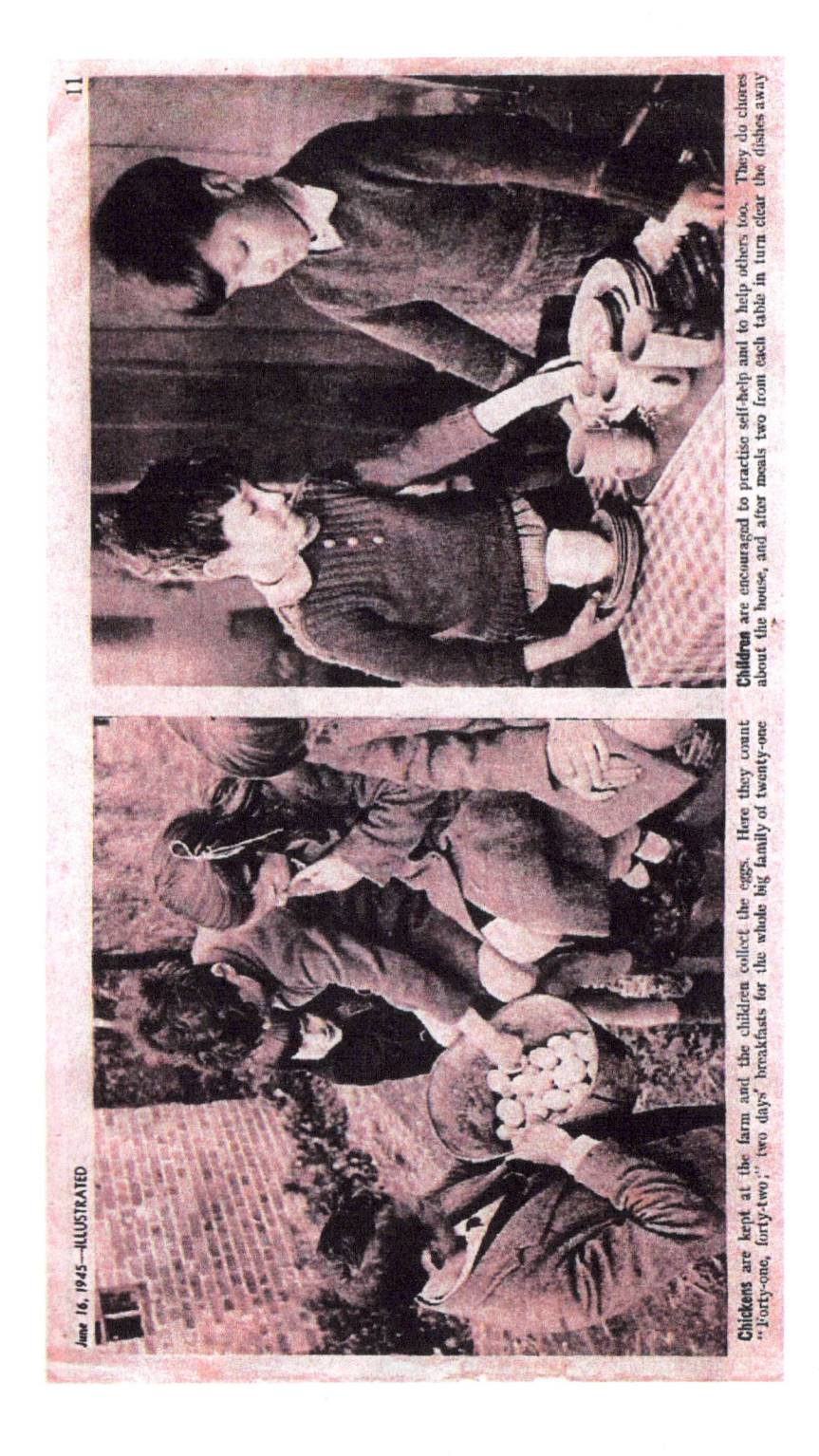

**Chickens** are kept at the farm and the children collect the eggs. Here they count "Forty-one, forty-two," two days' breakfasts for the whole big family of twenty-one

**Children** are encouraged to practise self-help and to help others too. They do chores about the house, and after meals two from each table in turn clear the dishes away

APPENDIX VI

## *From* The Times *Obituaries, 2 September 1997*

# NIK BIRCH REYNARDSON

**Nik Birch Reynardson, former Oxford county councillor and president of the Henley Conservative Association since 1993, died on August 6 aged 74. She was born on June 15, 1923.**

A tireless figure dedicated to the service of the county in which she lived for nearly 38 years, Nik Birch Reynardson could at first sight have been mistaken for a conventional product of the British class system. But that would have been to do her a great deal less than justice. The brisk, courageous determination she brought to every aspect of living was originally reflected in the way as a child she tackled the challenge of tuberculosis.

The elder daughter of Lieutenant-General Sir Thomas Humphreys, Nik Humphreys (as she was until her marriage) spent her early years in India, where her father was serving at the time. At the age of six, as a result of a riding accident, she contracted tuberculosis and having returned to England, spent the next seven years lying on her back encased in plaster from head to toe.

She was first sent to a T.B. sanatorium, where a governess gave her a good general educational grounding. But academic salvation came with her arrival at the home of two maiden aunts living in Kent (her parents were still in India). One of them had beds made up for both herself and her niece in the dining-room and there she taught Nik an almost complete syllabus of subjects ranging from botany to history, languages to geography, music to mathematics.

So well did she do her job that at the age of 13 though still on crutches the young daughter of the Empire passed easily into St Mary's, Wantage, where she spent the next four years, even playing hockey on crutches in goal. Finally, however, she came to manage simply with the made-up shoe that she wore for the rest of her life in order to cope with a faulty hip-bone.

Fortune then once again took a turn for her future. One school holidays the local M.P. came to call at her aunts' home and – struck by her determination and ability – insisted that she should be sent to a crammers to learn Ancient Greek. This she duly did, going up to Oxford in 1942 with an exhibition from St Hugh's

College, where she took a good second in Philosophy, Politics and Economics.

With the Second World War over, she then cast about for a job. It was typical of her lifelong concern for others that the one she chose should have been looking after Displaced Persons in Germany. After that came 12 months in Salisbury, Southern Rhodesia, serving on the staff of the Governor where the atmosphere in those palmy, post war days was presumably rather different from refugee camps in Germany. Her spell in Southern Rhodesia proved, however, to be her last paid job as in 1950 she married a friend she had made at university, Bill Birch Reynardson, a maritime lawyer, who lived near Thame in Oxfordshire.

But the energy that might have gone into a career was now merely diverted into raising her family and into a powerful amount of voluntary work. In 1967 she founded the South Oxfordshire Conservative Women's Advisory Committee, later being elected first for Chinnor and Tetsworth and then for Thame onto the Oxfordshire County Council. A strong supporter of her local M.P., the former Deputy Prime Minister, Michael Heseltine, she eventually became president of the Henley Conservative Association, having served for many years as chairman of its Tetsworth branch. She was, in turn, a member of the Oxfordshire District Health Authority and of the Oxford Regional Health Authority, subsequently becoming a trustee of the Nuffield Medical Trust.

She was a passionate Tory. But she also possessed a gift of listening, and her interest in other people always lay in what they wanted to say rather than in what she felt they ought to be told.

She and her husband lived in a lovely country house which they made into a welcoming family home surrounded by a beautiful garden on which for almost 40 years she lavished great affection.

She is survived by her husband Bill and a son and two daughters.

*This obituary was written by our friend and M.P., the Right Hon. Michael Heseltine.*

# GENERAL INDEX

**Note:** Names given in bold refer to authors and artists whose works are quoted (see also INDEX OF AUTHORS OF ORIGINAL LETTERS, DIARIES AND OTHER DOCUMENTS at end of GENERAL INDEX). Page numbers in bold refer to illustrations.

Abercromby, General Sir Ralph (1734–1801) 86, **86**, 86n5, 88, 90n10, 93, 99–100, 99n15, 102–3, 104, 105, 146–7
Aboukir **94**, 97, 99, 104, 127n32
Acts of Union of 1800 92n13, 117n27, 227n38
Addington, Henry, 1st Viscount Sidmouth (1757–1844), Prime Minister 92, 92n13, 108, 116
Addison, Helen 339, 371, 407
Adelaide, Queen (1792–1849) 239n13
Adolphus, Prince, Duke of Cambridge (1774–1850) 242n15
Adwell
  early history 281–2, 283
  Newell family ownership 283–4
  Birch Reynardson inheritance 282, 284–5
  1896–1906 **283**, 288–97, 305–8
  1920s–30s 339–40, 341, 341n8, 346–50, **347**
  Second World War 52n26, 352, 353, 353n2, **439**, 439–44, **440**, **441**, **442–4**
  post-war years 397–8, 411–12, 415, 416, 418
  garden 295–7, **296**, 348, 419, 420
  Garden House 422, 423
  Home Farm 290, 294–5, 348, **443**, **444**
  Horse Trials 416, **417**
  Pony Club 350, 352, 380n33, 416
  Postcombe Farm 290, 295, 348
  servants 292–3, 346–8, 349
Adwell Church 285, 349, 352
Ailesbury, Marquess of 251
Aldenham, Lord 397
Alexander, Field Marshal Harold (1891–1969) 380n33, 388
Alexandra, Princess, Hon. Lady Ogilvie 418
Algar, Sergeant-Major 258, 261
Ali, Mehmet 226, 226n35
**Alice, Princess, Countess of Athlone** (1883–1981) 335n2, 336, 336n3, 337, 409, 414–15
**Alken, Henry** (1785–1851): *Portrait of Henry Birch Reynardson as a child* **199**
Allhusen, Derek 365, 375, 376, 377, 378
Ambler, John 418
**Amery, Mrs Florence** 395–6
Amery, John (1912–45) 395–6, 395n39
Amery, Julian (later Baron Amery, 1919–96) 396n41
Amery, Leopold Stennett (1873–1955) 395, 395n40, 396n41
Anglo-Persian Oil Company 317n24
Anne, Princess 416, **417**
Anne, Queen (1665–1714) 22n12, 25n16
Anson, Lord (1697–1762) 70, 70n22
Anstruther, Colonel 106, 108, 146
Antony Gibbs and Son 397
Arbuthnot, Hugh 356

Archer, Hon. Andrew (1736-78) 68, 69–70
**Archer, Thomas, Lord** 68–70
Army commissions 256n34
Ashton, Charles 383
Ashton, John 4, 373, 383
Ashton, Samuel Edgar 4, 316, 316n23, 341n8
Aston, Birmingham 6, 36
**Athlone, Prince Alexander of Teck, Earl of** (1874–1957) 335, 335n2, 336, 337, 338
Attlee, Clement (1883-1967), Prime Minister 397n2
Augusta Sophia, Princess (1768–1840) 226, 226n33
Austen, Cassandra (née Leigh, 1739–1827) 216–17
Austen, Cassandra (1773–1845) 217
Austen, Admiral Sir Francis (1774–1865) 92, 92n12, 93
Austen, Rev. George 216
**Austen, Jane** (1775–1817) 92n12, 216, 217
Avenant, Mary (Mrs George Legh) 46n13

Bagley, Mrs 292
Bagot, Miss 220
Bailie, Douglas 357n17
Bailie, Lorna (later Mrs Gordon Palmer) 357, 357n17, 384–5
Bailie, Major 357n17
Baird, General Sir David (1757–1829) 144, 144n20, 146, 146n23
Baker, Elizabeth 68n18
Ball, Mrs Elizabeth 37n5, 55, 56–7, 56n32, 63
**Ball, George** 37–9, 37n5
Baltic campaign 1, 75, 76–82, 147, 164, 164n42
Barker, Mrs 51, 51n23, 52
**Barker, Sarah** 28, 34
Barnardiston, Lady *see* Reynardson, Mary
Barnardiston, Sir Samuel (1620–1707) 4, 17
Barrett, Bob 306
Battle of Agincourt (1415) 6
Battle of Culloden (1746) 51n22, 54, 54n29
Battle of Prestonpans (1745) 46, 47n15, 48n18
**Bayliss, Richard** 27, 28, 35
Beauharnois 144
Beauley, Lord 261
Bell, Willy and Belinda 419–20
Belliard, General 115, 127
Belton House, Lincolnshire 65
Bentinck, General Sir Henry (1796–1878) 245n21, 258, 259, 269n47
Bentinck, Lord William 148
Berlingieri, Francesco 416, 418, 420
Bessborough, 4th Earl of 342
Bessborough, Lady Henrietta 'Harriet' Spencer, Countess of (1761–1821) 342
Betjeman, John 371

Bey, Murad (1750–1801) 112, 112n21
Birch family 3, 4–5, 6, 26, 36
Birch, Ann (*née* Lane) 4, 57n33, 119, 119n30
Birch, Diana (Mrs John Birch) 5, 90n9, 218, 218n27, **219**, 221, 224
Birch, Elizabeth (Mrs Abraham Spooner) 56n32
Birch, Etheldred *see* Birch Reynardson, Etheldred 'Ethel' (1809–1847)
Birch, George (1652–1721) 4, 36, 37, 38–9
Birch, George (b.1689) 4, 37, 39, 41
Birch, George (1733–1803) 5, 35, 67, 72, 73, 110, 136
  letters received 114–15, 125, **126**, 128–9, 130–1
Birch, George (1739–1807) 4, 36n4, 44, 57n33, 61, 67
Birch, George Edward (1776–1794) 73
Birch, Herbert 3n3, 6
Birch, Humphrey Wyrley 3
**Birch, James** (1697–1772) 4
  marriage to Susannah Hess 35, 36, 36n2
  marriage to Jane Owen 35, 36, 56n32, 57
  children 35, 36, 36n3, 57, 67, 72
  as guardian 61
  career 35, 37, 67–8
  marriage to Susanna Hubert 68, 68n18
  letters received 26–7, 46, 47–9, 52–3, 58–9, 62, 69–70, 71
  letters written 54, 59–60
  death 68n18
Birch, James (b.1729) 36, 36n3
Birch, James (b.1741) 4, 36n3, 67
**Birch, James** (1771–1817) 5, 72, 73, 97, 104–5, 122–3, 215
Birch, Jane (Mrs James Birch) *see* **Owen, Jane**
**Birch, Jane 'Jenny'** (1742–64) 5, 67, 70–2, **71**, 72
Birch Colonel John (1615–91) 6–7, 9n8
Birch, John (Jack) 4, 61, 62
Birch, John, A.M. 51n25
**Birch, John William Newell** (1775–1867) 5, 73, 119, 137, 197n6, 207, 216, **219**
  marriage 90n9, 215, 218, 218n27
  tour of Europe 221–3, 223n31, 224
  adoption of Newell name and arms 284
  inheritance of Adwell 282, 284–5
  letters received 85–6, 88–9, 95–7, 111–13, 127–8, 146–8, 186–8
  letters written 91–3, 97, 109–10, 120, 138, 139, 221–3, 225–6
**Birch, John Wyrley** 36n4, 57, 57n33
Birch, Mary (Mrs William Green) *see* **Green, Mary**
Birch, Mary (*née* Foster) *see* Foster, Mary
Birch, Mary (daughter of Sir Thomas) 61–2, 119n30
**Birch, Mary** (*née* Newell, 1737–1837) 5, 110, 117, 435
  family 282n6, 283
  childhood 216–17
  marriage 72, 73, 136
  letters received 87, 89–91, 95, 99–100, 109, 113–14, 122, 129–30, 197, 200, 203–5
  letters written 117–19, 117n28, 137–40, 153n31, 186, 202, 205–7, 214, 215, 216, 218, 220–1
  in old age 206, 207, 214–17, **215**, 218
  death 214

Birch, Mary (Mrs William Canning, 1778–1856) 5, 73, 110, 114, 117, 118, 133, 137, 186, 206, 207, 218, 220, 225–6, 428–30
  marriage 206n12, 215
Birch, Samuel, A.M. 51n25
Birch, Sarah (b.1739) 4, 67
Birch, Susanna (Mrs James Birch) 68, 68n18
Birch, Thomas (1540–1613) 36, 36n4
Birch, Thomas (1586–1646) 6, 37
Birch, Colonel Thomas (c.1608–78) 6
**Birch, Sir Thomas, Judge** (1691–1757) 4, 37, 39, **44**, 44–5, 46, 54–5, 61
  letters written **40**, 41–4, 56
**Birch, Thomas** (b.1743) 4, 61, 62, 63, 64–5, 65n10, 67
**Birch, Thomas** (1773–1847) *see* **Birch Reynardson, General Thomas** (1773–1847)
Birch, Wyrley 119n30, 135
Birch Hall, Manchester 3, 36
Birch Reynardson family 3, 4–5, 11
  coat of arms 6, **6**, 135n5
Birch Reynardson, Anne (*née* Yorke) 4, 212, **213**, 214
Birch Reynardson, Aubrey (1853–1945) 5, 285, 289
Birch Reynardson, Avril (b.1947) 11, 280
**Birch Reynardson, Charles Thomas Samuel** (1810–89) 4, **213**, 214
  childhood 168, 195, 202–3, 205–6
  education 195, 200–3, 205, 209
  hopes of military career 203, 204, 205
  marriage 212, 229
  children 212, 229, 267
  books of reminiscences 202–3, 202n7, 209
  coach-driving 209
  health 205, 206, 207–8, 209, 228
  letters received 200–1, 268–70
  letters written 208–9
Birch Reynardson, Charles (b.1845) 229
Birch Reynardson, Clare (b.1954) 3, 5, 11, 411, 412
Birch Reynardson, Cynthia (Mrs Humphrey Prideaux, 1918–2008) 4, 335, **340**, 350, **351**, 352, 359, 398
Birch Reynardson, Diana (*née* Ponsonby, 1891–1962) 5, **343**
  family 332, 342–3
  marriage 330, 331, 332, **333**, 335, 342, 398
  children 335, 350
  in South Africa 335–6, 349–50
  at Adwell 342, 347, 349, 412, 440–1
  in Second World War 352–3, 353n2, 440–1, **441**
  post-war years 412
  character 3, 342, 344, 349–50
  letters received 363–4, 370, 380, 382, 390–2, 395–6
  religion 342, 349
  death 412
**Birch Reynardson, Colonel Edward** (1812–96) 5, 214, 228
  childhood 168, 196, 205
  education 196, 202
  military career 210, 234, **235**, 236–80, 236n7, 239n13, **271**
  marriage 188n20, 229, 342
  children 266, 280

   in retirement 11, 280
   diary 236, 272–3, 272n49
   letters received 210–12, 261–2, 265–7
   letters written 236, 237–8, 239–43, 244–51, 254–6, 257–60, 268–70, 275–9
   watercolours **237**, **238**, **264**, 270, **271**, **277**, **278**
Birch Reynardson, Edward (d.1915) 280
Birch Reynardson, Edwin (1851–1920) 5, 285
Birch Reynardson, Eleanor *see* Partridge, Eleanor
Birch Reynardson, Emily (*née* Fane, b.1822) 5
   family 188n20, 222n30, 284n10, 342
   marriage 188n20, 229, 342
   children 266, 280
   letters received 244–51, 254–6
   letters written 266, 269, 270
**Birch Reynardson, Emma Lucy** (1821–67) 5, 194, 214, 220, 228, 229, 265–7
**Birch Reynardson, Etheldred Anne** 'Ethel' (Mrs Thomas Birch Reynardson, 1778–1846) *see* **Reynardson, Etheldred Anne**
Birch Reynardson, Etheldred Anne (1836–84) 4, 212
Birch Reynardson, Etheldred 'Ethy' (Mrs Henry Partridge, 1809–47) 4
   childhood 136, 153n30, 157, 165, 197, 203–4, 205
   marriage 212, 229
   death 229
Birch Reynardson, Eve (b.1943) 11, 280
Birch Reynardson, George (1812–92) 4, 270
   childhood 168, 195, 206
   education 195–6, 202
   holy orders 218, 218n26, 226, 228, 229
   marriage 229
**Birch Reynardson, Henry** (1814–84) 5
   childhood 169, 197, **199**, 206, 208
   education 202, 214, 221, 290
   travel 221, 222, 223–5, 226
   law 221
   marriage 229, 266n43
   children 285
   inheritance of Adwell 282, 285
   High Sheriff of Oxfordshire 285, **286**
   letters received 212, 214, 225–6, 227–8
   letters written 197, **198**, 200, 223–5, 265, 266
**Birch Reynardson, Lt.-Colonel Henry Thomas** (1892–1972) 5, **343**
   childhood 229, 286, 288–97, 306–8
   family 298, 340
   at Eton 290, 292, 308–9
   at Christ Church 310, 344
   in India 310–11, 326, 327, 328, 329–32
   in Mesopotamia 319–29, 332
   marriage to Diana Ponsonby 331, 332, **333**
   children 335, 344–5, 350
   in South Africa 335–6, 337–9, 349–50, 399n5, 412, 414, 420
   in Oxford 341
   in Second World War 353
   post-war years 397–8, 399n5, 412, 414, 414n14
   marriage to Frances Straker 414
   books written **320**, **327**, 332, **334**, 339, 344
   character 344–5

   and family history 2, 3, 9, 35, 261n40, 281–2, 284n10, 285
   health 308, 309, 329–31, 332, 397–8, 399n5, 414
   hunting and shooting 307, 310–11, 418
   letters received 308–9, 312–14, 338, 354–6, 369, 372–3, 374–5, 379, 381, 385–6, 392–4, 399–402
   letters written 310–11, 311n18, 316–17, 318–19, 321–6, 328–32
   'Memories for my Grandchildren' 286, 288–97, 305–8, 345
   death 414–15
Birch Reynardson, Herbert (1856–1939) 5, 285
Birch Reynardson, Imogen (*née* Caldecott) 5, 11, 423
Birch Reynardson, Iola *see* Birch Reynardson, Violet 'Iola'
Birch Reynardson, John (1816–1914) 5, 194, 202, 205–8, 229, 229n42, 267
Birch Reynardson, Juliet (b.1952) 4, 11, 411, 412
Birch Reynardson, Marion (1852–1936) 5, 285
Birch Reynardson, Mary (Mrs Richard Birch Reynardson, *née* Bulteel) 5, 418
**Birch Reynardson, Matilda Caroline** (Mrs Robert Stopford, 1817–1907) 5, 194, 227, 229, 266n44
Birch Reynardson, Lt.-Colonel Morgan Henry (1895–1984 ) 11, 280
**Birch Reynardson, Pamela Matnika 'Nik'** (*née* Humphreys, 1923–97) 5, 379, **419**
   childhood 405, 445
   at St Hugh's 405, 445–6
   in East Africa 404n9, 405–8, 446
   wedding 408–9, **409**
   in London 409–11
   Coronation Day **410**, 411
   children 411, 412
   at Adwell 412, 415, 416, **417**, 419
   diary extracts 405–6
   letter written 406–7
   posts held 418, 446
   travel 418, 419–20
   death and obituary 422, (Appendix VI) 445–6
Birch Reynardson, Richard 'Dickie' (1926–2003) 5, 9n7, 418
   childhood 335, **336**, 340, **340**, 352
   at Eton 353–4, 370
   Army career 398, **398**, 399–403
   letters written 354, 370, 399–403
Birch Reynardson, Rosamund (1920–2007) 4, 335, **340**, 363n21, 369, 398
Birch Reynardson, Thomas (b.1956) 5, 11, 411, 412, 422, 423
**Birch Reynardson, General Thomas** (1773–1847) 4, 72–3, **74**, 207
   childhood 72, 73
   in Germany 75–82
   National Military College 82–3
   Egyptian campaign 83n31, 84–131, **96**, **121**, 132
   Military Survey of the Coast of Kent 132, 133, 133n4
   marriage 3, 44, 72, 135
   children 153n30, 157, 165, 168, 169, 194–6, 209
   Walcheren campaign 149–67, 154n32, 168

449

**change of name**  3, 17, 135, 135n5, 168
Deputy Quarter Master General  168, 169
in retirement  194
diary extracts  76–82, 85, 151–2
drawings, maps and watercolours  **96**, **121**, 129, **134**
'The Angels on Horseback'  134, **134**, (Appendix II) 428–30
letters received  91–3, 97, 105–11, 116–17, 118–20, 124, 133, 135–40, 169, 171–2, 176–81, 197, **198**, 220–1, 221–5, 233
letters written  84, 85, 86–91, 91n11, 95–7, 99–105, 111–15, 122–3, 125–31, **126**, 146–8, 152–65, 167, 174–5, 186–8, 194–6, 203–5, 212, 214, 229–30, 231–2
military memorabilia  141, (Appendix I) 424–6, **427**, (Appendix III) **431**, **432**, **433**, **434**, (Appendix IV) 435–8
death  229
Birch Reynardson, Vere (1865–1941)  280
Birch Reynardson, Violet (née Maxwell)  4
family  298, **299**, 332
childhood  298
marriage  285, 287, 298, 339
at Adwell  306, 307, 340
character  285, 289–90, 349
health  346
letters received  310–11, 316–17, 331–2
Birch Reynardson, Violet 'Iola' (Mrs Samuel Ashton, b.1890)  4, 286, 288, 291, 292, 305, 307, 316n23
Birch Reynardson, William (1819–25)  5, 194, 194n2, 209
**Birch Reynardson, William John** (1849–1940)  3, 4, 205, 281, **286**
childhood and education  285, 290
marriage  285, 298
children  286, 305
at Adwell  285, 289–90, 305, 306, 339, 341n8, 346
character  285, 289–90, 339–41, 346
letters received  309, 310–11, 316–17, 328–32
travel  285, **287**
watercolours  285–6, **287**, 339
**Birch Reynardson, William Robert Ashley 'Bill'** (b.1923)  5, 312n19, **419**
childhood  335, 336–7, 339, 340, **340**
in South Africa  335, 420
at Bishops School, Rondebosch  336–7, 341
at Eton  290, 344, 348, 353, 354, 355–6, 357, 359
at Christ Church  357, **358**, 392–3, 396, 398–9, 404, 411
Army service  82, 359–95, 380n32, **387**, **388**, 396, 397
legal career  37, 404, **409**, 409, 411, 415, 416, 418
wedding  404, 408–9, **409**
Coronation Day  409–11, 409n11, **410**
in London  409–12
children  3, 11, 411, 412
grandchildren  3, 422
in retirement  419–20, 422–3
at Adwell  335, 340, 341, 345–50, 398, 412, 415, 418, 419

Adwell Garden House  422, 423
C.B.E.  420
hunting  2–3, 344, 356, 359, 365, 398–9, 404, 416, **417**, 422
*Letters to Lorna*  357n17, 393
letters written  339, 360, 361–5, 367–8, 372–7, 379, 381–6, 389–95
opera  365, 368, 368n26, 404, 420, **421**, 422
painting  3, 420, 422
posts held  416, 418, 420
shooting  339, 347, 348–9, 361, 366, 409, 416, 418, 422
travel  416, 418, 419–20
Birche, Ralph  6
Birches, William de  3
Bishops School, Rondebosch  336–7, 341
Blackmore family  28
Blomfield, Arthur  285
Blücher, Marshall  132n2, 190n23
Boer War  298, **300**, 300–5, 300n5
Bolton, D.D.  **358**
Bonaparte, Joseph  161n38
Bonaparte, Louis-Napoleon (1808–73)  223, 226n34, 235n5
Bonaparte, Napoleon see Napoleon Bonaparte
Bonnie Prince Charlie see Charles Edward Stuart
Bourchier, Diana see Birch, Diana
Bourchier, Emma  221, 222, 225
Bourchier, James  90, 90n9, 93
Bradford, Lt.-Colonel  260
Bradley, Tim  400
British Empire  397, 397n2
British Marine Law Association  415, 416
Brooksbank, H.  93
Brown, Dick  348, 349
Brown, General  242
**Brownlow, Lady**  66n13, 119
Brownlow, Lord see Cust, Brownlow
**Brownrigg, General Robert** (1759–1833)  132, 133, 153, 154n32, 155, 161, 162n39, 163, 168
Brudenell family  251
Brudenell, Edmund  251, 252
Brudenell, George (1880–1962)  251
Brudenell, Marian (d.2013)  251
Buckland, William (1784–1856)  224, 224n32
Budd (Head Gardener)  290, 295
Bull, George  289, 290–1, 348
Bull, Harold  348
Bulteel, Mary see Birch Reynardson, Mary
Burghersh, Lord  245, 245n19, 246
Burgoyne, Sir John (1782–1871)  241, 245n20
Burnham, Frank
Egyptian campaign  87, 87n7, 89, 93, 100, 122, 137
Walcheren campaign  153, 157, 160, 167
in England  197, 428
Burnham, Patty  137
Burrard, Sir Harry (1755–1813)  141n15, 142, 142n18, 144
Bute, John  418
Byng, Admiral Sir George (1663–1733)  27, 27n20

C. Hoare & Co. 70, 70n21
**Cadogan, Colonel**: *Portrait of Colonel Edward Birch Reynardson* 235
Cain, Nanny 288
Caldecott, Imogen *see* Birch Reynardson, Imogen
Callas, Maria 368n26
Calvert, Colonel Henry 108, 120, 173
Cambridge, Duke of *see* George, Prince, Duke of Cambridge (1819–1904)
**Campbell, Lt.-Colonel Neil** (1776–1827) 184, 435–6
Campbell, Sir Colin 246, 253
Canning, Charles Fox 206n12
Canning, George (1770–1827), Prime Minister 149n28, 206n12
Canning, Mary *see* Birch, Mary (Mrs William Canning, 1778–1856)
Canning, Stratford (1744–87) 206n12
Canning, Sir Stratford (*later* Viscount Stratford de Redcliffe, 1786–1880) 206n12, 226, 226n34, 227, 234, 235, 235n6, 265
Canning, Rev. William (1778–1860) 5, 204n9, 206, 206n12, 218n26, 226
Canrobert, General Robert 279, 279n53
Cardigan, James Thomas, Earl of (1797–1868) 251, **252**, 253, 254, 255, 270
**Carey, Major Peter** (1774–1852) 141n14
  family 171, 176n4, 178
  letters received 183–4
  letters written (attributed) 142–4, 187
  Peninsular War 141–4, 147–8, 147n25
  Walcheren campaign 159, 162, 163, 165
Caro, Peter 372, 376
Caroline of Anspach (1683–1737) 31n25
Caroline, Princess of Wales (1768–1821) 134
**Cashel, John**: 'Real Home Solves Homeless Children's Problem' (Appendix V) 439–44
Castle, Jack 356
Castlereagh, Lord (1769–1822) 148n26, 149n28, 435
Cathcart, Sir G. 259
Catholic Emancipation 92n13, 116, 227n38
Cecil, Lord David 371
Cecil, Lord Hugh 'Linky' 370
Chamber of Shipping 411, 415
Chamberlain, Neville (1869–1940), Prime Minister 350
Chaplin, Miss *see* Fane, Mrs Vere
Charles I (1600–49) 9
Charles II (1630–85) 7, 9, 13
Charles Edward Stuart, Bonnie Prince Charlie ('Young Pretender') (1720–88) 25n17, 45, 47n14, 50–1
Charles XV, King of Sweden (1826–72) 269n46
Charlotte, Princess (1796–1817) 134
Charlotte, Queen 1744–1818) 69n19, 70, 70n22
Charlton, Mr (at Rondebosch) 337
Charterhouse 73, 200, 202, 205, 207, 207n15
Chartism 234n2
Chatham Club 371
Chetham, Elizabeth (Mrs Thomas Birch) 36
Christ Church, Oxford
  Beagles 398, 398n3, 404

family members at 285, 310, 312, 344, 357, 392–3, 398, 411
  Loders Club **358**, 398, 398n4
  Second World War 354, 370, 399
Churchill, Randolph 371, 371n28
Churchill, Winston S. (1874–1965), Prime Minister 335n2, 353n3, 362n20, 371, 371n28, 390, 391, 391n38
Civil War 6
Clarendon, George Herbert Hyde Villiers, Earl of (1877–1955) 338, 338n5, 409n11
Clark, General Mark 367
Clarke, Henri-Jacques-Guillaume, Duc de Feltre (1765–1818) 187–8, 187n19
Clarke, Mary Anne 78n28
Clausel, Bertrand 180n10
Climo, Lt.-Colonel (1868–1937) 323, 323n27
Clinkard, Walter 404
coats of arms 3, 6, **6**
Comité Maritime International (C.M.I.) 416, 418, 420
Congress of Vienna (1814–15) 188, 188n21, 223n31
Constable, Mr (butler) 290, 292, 293, 306
Constable, Mrs 290
Constantine, Prince 258
Convention of Cintra (1808) 141, 141n15, 142, 142n16, 143
Cooper, Esther (Mrs William Newell) 5, 283
Coote, Major General Sir Eyre (1762–1823) 118, 129, 154n33
Cope, Sir John 46, 47n15, 48
Corpus Christi College (*then* St Benet's), Cambridge 64
**Cotes, Francis** (1726–70) 65
  *Portrait of Anne Cust* **66**
  *Portrait of Elizabeth Cust* **66**
Court of Common Pleas 44, 44n11
Courtis, John 329
Courtneidge, Cicely (1893–1980) 374, 374n29
Coventry 19, 22–3, 36n3, 68
Craven, Lord 86
Crimean War (1853–6) 234–80, **277**, **278**
  Battle of Balaklava (1854) 236, 251–6, **252**, 269n46
  Battle of Inkerman (1854) 236, 257–65, 258n38, **263**, **264**, 268–70, 269n47, 272–3
  Battle of the Alma (1854) 236, 240–4
  Charge of the Light Brigade (1854) 251, 254, 270
  Combat of Little Inkerman (1854) 254–6
  siege of Sebastopol (1854–5) 239, 240, 245–65, 245n20, 268–79, 276n50
  war artists and photographers 270
Crispe, Abigail 4, 9, 13
Crispe, Alderman Sir Nicholas 9
Cromwell, Oliver (1599–1658), Lord Protector of the Commonwealth 6, 256n34
Croxford, 'Shepherd' 295
Cuesta, General 161n38
Cumberland, William Augustus, Duke of (1721–65) 50–1, 51n22, 54, 54n28, 54n29, 425, 425n5
Cumming, Brian 374
Cunningham, Lt.-Colonel Bill 380n33
Cust family 188–90, **189**

Cust, Anne (Mrs Jacob Reynardson, 1746–1812) 4, 17, 65–6, **66**, 66n13, 119, 168
Cust, Brownlow (*later* Lord Brownlow, 1744–1807) 64, 65, 65n9, 65n11, 66n13, 119, 161n38, 190
Cust, Colonel A. 245
Cust, Edward (1794–1878) 190n22
Cust, Elizabeth (Mrs Philip Yorke, d.1779) 4, 65–6, **66**
Cust, Horace 240, 241, 245, 245n21
Cust, Sir John (1718–70), Speaker of House of Commons 4, 64, 65n11
Cust, Hon. Peregrine Francis (1791–1873) 161, 161n38, 190n22
Cust, Robert 226, 227
Cust Wherry, Albinia L. 64n8, 65n9, 67
Cuthbertson, Catherine 186, 186n17
Cyprus 400–2, 400n6

Dalkeith, John 'Johnnie' Scott, Earl of (1923–2007) 344, 357n15, **358**
Dalrymple, General Sir Hew (1750–1830) 141n15, 142, 142n18, 143, 144
Dardanelles Straits 235, 235n4, 236
Dargavel House, Renfrewshire 298, **299**
Dawson, Betsy 404n9, 407, 418
de Burgh, Michael 386
de Chair, Mike 356
**de Prades, Alfred F.**: *Lord Cardigan at the Battle of Balaklava* **252**
Deene Park, Northamptonshire 251–2
**Defoe, Daniel** (1660–1731) 22–5, 23n13, 23n14, 24n15, 29n23
Denmark 77–8
Derby, Earl of (1799–1869), Prime Minister 226n34, 235n6
D'Erlon (Drouot) 186
Devlin, Madeleine, Lady (née Oppenheimer, 1909–2012) 422, 422n1
Devlin, Patrick, Lord (1905–92) 422n1
Devonshire, Georgiana Spencer, Duchess of (1757–1806) 342
Dickens, Charles (1812–70): *The Pickwick Papers* 48n17
Dobbs, Sir Henry (1871–1934) 330, 330n34
Don, Colonel George (1756–1832) 78, 78n26
Dragon School, Oxford 341
**Drake, William**: Tailor's Bill **71**
Drummond, General and Mrs 267
Dundas, General David (1735–1820) 78, 78n28, 107, 173, 310n16
Dundas, Robert (Robin) Hamilton (1884–1960) 310, 310n16
Dunkillin, Lord 250, 255

Eborn, Frank 293
Eccles Hall, Thetford 50, 51n25
Edmunds, Sergeant 360, 389
Edna (head housemaid) 412, 415
Edward III (1312–77) 3
Edward VII (1841–1910) 344
  as Prince of Wales 261
Edward VIII (1894–1972) 346

  as Prince of Wales 336, 337, 337n4
Edward, the 'Black Prince' (1330–76) 3
Edward, Prince of Saxe-Weimar (1823–1902) 239, 239n13
Egerton, Christopher 'Kit' 5, 356, 398
Egyptian campaign (1800–1) 1, 84–115, 84n2, 120–31, 230, 232
  Abukir (1801) **94**, 97, 99, 104, 127n32
  Battle of Alexandria (1801) 84, 84n2, 88, 95–106, **96**, **98**, 107–10
  Gibraltar 85, 87
  Rosetta 111–13
  Siege of Cairo (1801) 113–15
Eileen (nursery maid) 411
Elgin, Thomas Bruce, Earl of (1766–1841), Ambassador to the Ottoman Empire 109
Elizabeth, Queen (1900–2002) 359–60, 360n19
Elizabeth II (b.1926) 418, 420
  as Princess Elizabeth 360, 360n19
  Coronation 409–11, 409n11
Elphinstone, Margaret (*later* Rhodes) 359, 404, 404n8
Erddig 63, 64, 65, 65n10, 164n40
Erskine, Colonel 100
Espinasse 157, 160
Eton College
  Beagles 354, **355**, 356, 357
  family members at 64, 73, 202, 285, 290, 292, 308–9, 348, 353–6, 359, 370
  Field Game 354, 354n5, 356
  Labour Association 344
  Provost's house portraits 370
Evans family 348
Exclusion Bill (1680) 13, 16

Faden, W. 120, **121**
Fane, Agatha-Isabel 'Buss' (*née* Acland-Hood-Reynardson) 11, 135n5, 412, 412n12
Fane, David, 15th Earl of Westmorland 412n12
Fane, Edward 9, 11
Fane, Emily *see* Birch Reynardson, Emily
Fane, Admiral Francis William 284, 284n10
Fane, Lady Maria (Lady Bessborough) 342
Fane, Hon. Mountjoy 412–14, 412n12
Fane, Suki 11
Fane, Thomas, 8th Earl of Westmorland 342
Fane, Vere 188, 222n30
Fane, Mrs Vere (*née* Chaplin) 188, 222, 222n30
Fane, William Dashford 272n49, 275, 276
Fanshawe, Dick 356, 356n9
Fanshawe, Sir Robert 356–7, 356n9
Fanshawe, Ruth 356
Faris, Alexander 'Sandy' (b.1921) 357, 357n13
farming
  1739 at Harborne and Hazelwell 41–4, 43n10
  19th–20th centuries at Adwell 290, 294–5, 348, **443**, **444**
Farnaby, Frances (Mrs Jacob Reynardson, d.c.1719) 4, 13, **14**, 17
Farnaby, Joseph (Francis) 16n3
**Fenton, Roger** (1819–69) 270–2
  *Colonel Edward Birch Reynardson* **271**

Ferguson, Sir J. 259
Fielding, Henry (1707–54) 29n23
**Fielding, T.**: *The Battle of Salamanca* **182**
First World War (1914–18)
    Europe 312–17, 324n30
    Mesopotamia 317–29, **320**, **327**, 332
Floyd, General 106, 111
Foljambe, Hon. Jocelyn 328, 328n33
Forbes, Sir William: *An Account of the Life and Writings of James Beattie, LL.D.* (1807) 138, 138n9
foster families 439–41
Foster, Mary (Mrs George Birch, 1662–1717) 4, 36
'Fourteen Notorious Smugglers' 55, 55n31
Fox, Frances (Mrs Thomas Newell) 5, 283
Francis II, Emperor (1768–1835) 119n31
Francis, Prince, Duke of Teck (1837–1900) 335n2
Franklin, Frances (Mrs William Newell) 5, 283
Franklin, Henry (d.1663) 283
Fraser, General 141, 144, 148
Frederick, Prince, Duke of York (1763–1827) 75, 75n24, 78n28, 82, 97, 105, 107, 169, 171, 173, 182n11
French, Major-General John (1852–1925) 301, 301n6, 303n11
French Revolution (1789) 73, 75, 234n2
French Revolutionary Wars (1792–1802)
    Battle of Copenhagen (1801) 110, 110n19, 116
    Battle of the Nile (1798) 84n2, 127n32
    Battle of the Pyramids (1798) 84n2, 114
    *see also* Egyptian campaign
Frere, G. 92
Frost, Francis 418
Furness, Major 315

*Galignani's Messenger* 222, 222n29
Galitzine, Princess 413n13
Gardiner, Colonel 47, 47n15
Garrick, David (1717–79) 64n7
Garsington Opera 420, **421**, 422
Gavin, David 374
Gawith family 416
George I (1660–1727) 27n19, 29n23, 31n25
George II (1683–1760) 31n25, 45, 46n12, 47n16, 55, 61, 424, 425n5
George III (1738–1820)
    marriage and Coronation 69, 69n19, 70
    family 118n29, 134, 226n33, 242n15
    politics 68, 92n13
    health 93, 93n14, 107, 109, 171n3, 206n13
    Jubilee **166**
    Regency 171n3
George IV (1762–1830) 206, 206n12, 206n13
    as Prince Regent 171, 171n3
George V (1865–1936) 335n2
George, Prince, Duke of Cambridge (1819–1904) 242n15, 250, 253, 266, 268, 275, 279
Germany 75, 78–81, 221–2
Gibbs, Stephen and Lavinia 418
Gibraltar 85, 363
Gladstone, Charles 353
Glorious Revolution (1688) 13n2, 25n17
Gobbi, Tito 368n26

Goebbels, Joseph (1897–1945) 367, 388
Goldsmid, John 360, 376, 386, **387**
Gorchakov, Prince Michael 255n33
Gorchakov, General Paul 255n33
**Gordon, General James** (1772–1851) 168, 169
Gordon-Lennox, Reggie 359
Gorick, Mr 411
Graeme, Colonel 69n19
Graham (bailiff) 306
Graham Vivian, Harry 411
Grand Vizier 103, 103n17, 112, 115
Gray, Ezekiel 56
Greathead, Mrs 41–2
Green family 50, 51n25
**Green, Mary** (*née* Birch, 1694–1784) 4, 46, 50, 51–2
Green, Molly 50, 51–2
Green, Sam 43
Green, William (d.*c*.1737) 4, 50
Green, William (son) 51, 51n25
Gregorian Calendar 21n11, 424n2
**Grenfell, Laura** 405, 408
Grey, William Booth (1773–1852) 187
Grosvenor, General (1764–1851) 153–4, 188
Guinness, Bunny 413n13

Habeas Corpus Act 48, 48n19
**Haley, Henry James**: *Portrait of Major-General John Gaspard Le Marchant (1766–1812)* **170**
Hall, Albert 290
Hall, Mr 290, 293, 294, 306
Hall, Mrs (Adwell) 290, 294
Hall, Mrs (London) 411
Hamilton, Lady 67
Hamilton, Sir Frederick 239, 239n13, 241, 259
Hamstead Hall 36, 57n33, 67
Handsworth, Staffordshire 6, 36, 36n4, 39, 57n33
Harborne Hall, Staffordshire 6, 37, 39, 41, 42, 44, 57n33
Harcourt, Captain 78, 78n26, 124
**Harcourt, Field-Marshal William, 3rd Earl Harcourt** (1743–1830) 69n19, 75, 83, 153
    letters received 99, 101–4, 118, 120
    letters written 84, 124
    and Mary Birch 73, 87, 91, 203, 205, 218, 222
Harcourt, Mrs 87, 91, 103, 118, 137, 222
Hardinge, Sir Henry 232
Harley, Robert (*later* 1st Earl of Oxford 1661–1724) 22, 23n13
Harrison, Mr G. 148
Hart, Bob 404
Hatchlands, Surrey 116n26
Hatton, Captain 257n36, 261
Haversage, Matthew de 3
**Hawarden, Robert Cornwallis Maude, Viscount** (1890–1914) 312–14, 312n19, 315, 316
Hazelwell, Birmingham **40**, 41, 43, 57n33
Hedges, Jim 344, 348
Hely-Hutchinson, Major-General Sir John (1757–1832) 103, 105, 127, 130
Henderson, Canon 352
Heneage, Mrs 239

Henley Park  216, 266, 282
Hereford Castle  6
**Heseltine, Michael**  418, 445–6
Hess, Susannah (Mrs James Birch)  35, 36, 36n2
Hethersett, Elizabeth (Mrs Edward Owen)  5, 20, 22, 27
Hethersett, Wormeley  20
**Heygate, A.C.G.**  308, 309
**Higginson, Captain Adjutant**  239, 257, 259, 261, **263**
*Highflyer* (horse)  119
High Sheriffs of Oxfordshire  283, 284, 285, **286**, 414n14, 418
Hill, Rowland  (1795–1879) 206n10
Himmler, Heinrich (1900–45)  390
Hindley Birches  3
Hitchcock, Rex  **387**, 391
Hitler, Adolf  (1889–1945) 135n6, 350, 388, 395n39
HMS *Swiftsure*  127, 127n32
**Hogarth, William** (1697–1764): *The March of the Guards to Finchley* **50**
Holland, George  345, 348
Holland, Michael  348
Holland-Hibbert, Audrey  344
Holland-Hibbert, Delia (*later* Mrs Bill Cunningham)  380, 380n33
Holland-Hibbert, Lavinia  368
Holywell, Lincolnshire  **413**, 413n13
    Reynardson family  11, 17, 66, 165, 168
    Birch Reynardson family  99n15, 135n5, 153n30, 168, 169–70, 229, 412
    Fane family  11, 135n5, 412–13
Hood, Colonel the Hon. F.G.  239, 239n13, 240, 242, 246, 248–9, 250, 256, 256n34, 266, 273
Hope, Lt.-General Sir John (1765–1836) 144, 146n23, 146n24, 147, 151–2, 154n33, 155, 156, 158
**Hoppner, John** (1758–1810): *Portrait of Sir Ralph Abercromby*  **86**
horses  51, 55, 56, 57, 76, **134**, 153, 153n31, 157
Houston, Colonel  87
Howard, Sir Michael (b.1922)  1, 357, 357n16
Hughes, Sergeant  373
Hulbert, Jack (1892–1978)  374, 374n29
Hull, General Richard 'Dick'  375, 377n31
Humphreys, Jay (*later* Colvile)  396n41
Humphreys, Nik *see* **Birch Reynardson, Pamela Matnika 'Nik'**
Humphreys, General Sir Thomas  305, 305n13, 405, 408, 445
hunting  2–3, 208, 307, 342, 356, 398–9, 398n3, 404, 416, **417**
Huntley, Lord  155, 158
Hutchinson, Major-General Sir John see Hely-Hutchinson, Major-General Sir John
Hutton, James  65n10

Indian Army  298, 310, 310n17, 317
Ingrams, Leonard  (1941–2005) 420
Ingrams, Rosalind  **421**
Inns of Court
    Inner Temple  37, 63, 73, 285, 409
    Middle Temple  67, 73, 221

Jacobite Rebellions  25n17, 27n19, 45–7, 48, **50**, 50–3, 54
Jacobs, Clara  368, 368n26
James II  13, 25n17
James Francis Edward Stuart ('Old Pretender') (1688–1766) 25n17, 26n18, 45, 46
James (man-servant, 1809)  160, 160n36, 163, 167
Janaway, John  289, 295
**Janssen, Cornelius**
    *Portrait of Eleanor Wynne, Lady Reynardson*  **10**
    *Portrait of Sir Abraham Reynardson (1590–1660)*  **10**
Jarry, General  108, 124, 174, 175
John VI, Prince Regent of Portugal  142n17
**Johnston, Lt.-Colonel Percy**  315
**Joicey, John**
    in Second World War  358, 360, 361, 362, 373, 375, 376, 377–8, **378**, 380, 385, 386, **387**, 389, 391
    in 1970s  418
Jones, Brigadier-General  279
Jones, James  5, 284
Jones, Leslie  345, 347, 348, 349, 412, 415, 418
Jordan, Philip  371n28
Julian Calendar  20n10, 21n11, 424n2
Junot, Marshall  142n17, 143, 144

**Karolyi, Countess**: *Portrait of William John Birch Reynardson (1849–1940)*  **286**
Kearsley (1915)  329
Keates, Sir Richard  151, 152
Keith, Admiral Lord (1746–1823) 127n32
Kelly, Mrs  186, 188
Kennedy, Jean  404n9, 405
Kennedy, Sir John Noble (1893–1970)  404n9, 406–7
Kennedy, Lady  404n9, 406–7
Kennedy, Susan  404n9, 406, 407
Keppel, George, Lord Bury (1724–72) 54, 54n28
King, Mackenzie (1874–1950), Prime Minister of Canada  335n2
Kitchener, Herbert, 1st Earl (1850–1916) 305, 305n14, 310n17, 325n31
Kléber, General  84n2, 88, 88n8
Knype, Sarah  4, 17

**Lacoste, Jean Baptiste**: 'Battle of Waterloo' **189**, 190–3, 190n23
Lamb, Lady Caroline (1785–1828) 342
Lambert (gunman, 1944)  373
Lascelles, Colonel Peregrine (1685–1772) 48, 48n18
Laurie, David  380, **387**, 390, 391
Law, Sir Edward  (1750–1818) 92–3
**Lawrence, Sir Thomas** (1769–1830) 206n13
    *Portrait of Lieutenant-General Sir John Moore, (1761–1809)*  **145**
**Le Marchant, Carey**  (d.1813) 176n4, 179, 182, 182n12, 183–4
Le Marchant, Denis  170, 172
**Le Marchant, Major-General John Gaspard** (1766–1812)  **170**
    army career  83, 177, 178–82, 182n11
    family  137, 137n7, 141, 141n14, 170, 172, 176n4, 178

454

letters received 174–5
letters written 84, 105–8, 127, 135–6, 171–3, 176–81, 177, 232
Royal Military College 82, 83, 106–7, 124, 170–3, 176, 230
death 182, 183
Le Marchant, Marie (*née* Carey) (d.1812) 137, 137n7, 141n14, 172, 176, 176n4
Le Marchant, Thomas 176n4
Leese, Lt.-General Oliver (1894–1978) **366**, 373
**Legh, Rev. Dr George** (1693–1775)
family 46n13, 57–8
letters received 54, 59–60
letters written 46, 47–9, 49n21, 53–4, 58–9
Leighton, Captain 88
letters 12, 281
*see also under names of writers and recipients*
**Lewis, John Frederick**: *Portrait of Mrs Mary Birch* **215**, 215–16
Liles, Mrs 200, 207, 220
Lindsay, Sir Coutts (1824–1913) 267
Liprandi, Pavel 255n33
Llewellyn, Daphne 363, 364n23, 381
Llewellyn, Hermione *see* Ranfurly, Hermione, Countess of
Lloyd, Tony and Jane 418
Locke, Joseph 231, 231n43
*London Gazette* 305
London & York Railway Company 229–30, 231
Lothian, Peter Kerr, Marquess of (1922–2004) 357, **358**
Louis XV 51n24
Louis XVI 75, 234n2
Louis XVIII 180n10, 186, 186n15, 187n19, 438
**Lotherbourg, Philip James de**
*The Battle of Alexandria, 21 March 1801* **98**
*The Landing of British Troops at Aboukir, 8 March 1801* **94**
*Sir Sidney Smith* **91**
Lowe, Dean of Christ Church 357
Lucan, Lord (1800–88) 253
Lynam, A.E. 'Hum' 341, 341n9, 346
Lynam, J.H.R. 'Joc' 341, 341n9

Mahmud II 226n35
Malaya 402–3
Malta 88
Manchester 3, 6
Manderston, Berwickshire 357n17
Manners, John Robert Cecil, 5th Baron Manners ('Bobbie', 1923–2008) 357, 357n10
*Map of the Scheldt Estuary, showing the Island of Walcheren to the West* **150**
Margaret, Princess (1930–2002) 360, 360n19, 404n7
Margaretha, Princess of Sweden, Mrs John Ambler (b.1934) 418
Marlborough, John Churchill, Duke of (1650–1722) 25n16, 27n19
Marmont, Auguste de, Duke of Ragusa (1774–1852) 178n6, 180–1, 180n10
Marriott, Christopher 4, 363n21

**Marriott, James 'Jimmy'** (d.1944) 4, 363n21, 369
Martin, Francis Wykeham 270
Martin, John 'Mad' (1789–1854) 209n17
Martin, Jonathan 209n17
Mary of Modena (1658–1718) 25n17
Mary, Princess ('Fat Mary') (1833–97) 335n2
Mary, Queen (1867–1953) 335n2
Maryborough, Lady 204, 220
Maryborough, William Wellesley-Pole, Lord (1763–1845) 203, 204, 205, 216, 220, 230
Maxwell family 298, 312n19, 332
Maxwell, Eustace (d.1916) 298n3
**Maxwell, Brigadier-General Francis Aylmer 'Frank'** (1871–1917) 298, 307
letters written 300–5, 308–9
military career 298–305, **299**, 305n13, 311, 319, 332
*Sketch of the Action at Sanna's Post*, **300**
Victoria Cross 298, 305
death 332
Maxwell, Lawrence 'Uncle Law' 310, 311
Maxwell, Thomas 298
Maxwell, Violet Sophia (Mrs Thomas Maxwell) 298, 298n3, 301–5, 311, 311n18
Maxwell, Violet (Mrs William Birch Reynardson) *see* Birch Reynardson, Violet
Mellis, General 321
Menou, General Abdullah 102, 102n16, 103, 104, 109, 115, 123, 127, 127n34
Menshikov, Prince 235, 254, 255, 255n33, 276n51
Merritt, Wallace 348
Meyrick, Diana (Mrs Philip Yorke) 64n7
Millers 416, 418, 419
Miller, Cyril 415, 416
Miller, Dawson 416
Miller, Sir Thomas 119
Mitford, Mr J. 92
Moldavia 235–6, 276n50
Mond, Julian (*later* Lord Melchett, 1925–73) 356, 356n7, 357
Monnet, General 160, 162n39
Montalembert, Marc René de 106, 108, 128, 158, 186, 186n14
Montgomery, Field Marshal Bernard, 1st Viscount (1887–1976) 382
Montgomery, Roger 411
Moore, Lt.-General Sir John (1761–1809) 101, 102, 143, 144, 144n20, 144n21, **145**, 146, 147, 148
Morelli, Susy 368, 368n26
Mortimer, Sir John (1923–2009) 341–2, 341n10
Moulden, Mr (butler) 306
Mourant, Sophy 176n4, 178, 183
Mowatt, J.R. (London & York Railway Company) 229, 231
Murray, General Sir Archibald 325n31
**Murray, Lord George** (1694–1760) **45**, 46
Mussolini, Benito (1883–1945) 388, 395n39

Napoleon Bonaparte (1769–1821) **185**
Egyptian campaign 84n2, 90n10, 104, 116, 120, 127n33, 127n34
plans for invasion of England 124, 133n4

ambitions in Europe 135n6
Peninsular War 140, 143, 144n21
Walcheren campaign 149
invasion of Russia 184n13
abdication and exile 184, 184n13, 435–8
resumption of power 184, 186, 187, 188n21
Battle of Waterloo 188, **189**, 190–3, 190n23
exile and death 188
documents and memorabilia 184, 188, 435–8
see also Napoleonic Wars
Napoleon III see Bonaparte, Louis-Napoleon
Napoleonic Wars
Battle of Trafalgar (1805) 127n32, 135
Battle of Waterloo (1815) 132n2, 188–93, **189**, 190n22, 206n12, 230
National Military College see Royal Military Academy, Sandhurst
National Trust 63, 65, 116n26
Neighbour, Mr and Mrs 290
Nelson, Admiral Horatio, Viscount (1758–1805) 84n2, 109–10, 116, 135
Neville, Captain H. 259, 261
Newcastle, Duke of (1761), Prime Minister 68
Newcastle, Duke of (1854) 239
Newcombe, Dr 61, 62, 64
Newcombe, Harry 62
Newell family 3, 5, 179, 179n8, 282
Newell, Anna Maria 92, 282n6
Newell, Christopher (Rector of Adwell 1677–78) 282
Newell, Elizabeth (Mrs James Jones, 1793–1818) 283–4
Newell, John (Rector of Adwell 1729–31) 282
Newell, Mary see **Birch, Mary** (née Newell; 1737–1837)
Newell, Samuel (Rector of Adwell 1775–1802) 282, 282n6, 283
Newell, Sam 92, 282n6
Newell, Thomas (1707–77) 5, 216, 282, 283
Newell, William (b.1640) 5, 283
Newell, William (1665–1728) 5, 283
Newell, Rev. William (1701–47) 5, 282, 283
Newland, Antonella 'Tony Carr' (1922–2007) 357, 357n12
Newnham, Sir R. 259, 261
Ney, Marshal Michel (1769–1815) 191, 191n25
Nicholas, Tsar (1796–1855) 226n34, 234n3, 250n28, 267, 267n45
Nichols, Corporal 372, 376, 384, 385
Niel, General Adolpe (1802–69) 276, 279
Nightingale, Florence (1820–1910) 236n8
Nolan, Captain 254, 255
Norman Cross, Cambridgeshire 160, 160n35
Norman, Sergeant 258
North America 69, 69n20
North, Lord (1732–92), Prime Minister 65n11
Nureddin, Colonel 328, 328n32

O'Connell, Daniel (1775–1847) 227, 227n38
Ogilvie, Sir Angus 418
O'Hara, Governor General of Gibraltar 87
opera 365, 368, 368n26, 404, 420, **421**, 422

Order of Maria Theresa 119, 119n31
Ormonde, Duke of 27n19
Ottoman Empire 84, 226, 226n34, 226n35, 317
see also Egyptian campaign
Owen family 17, 19
Owen, Edward (Edwin, 1637–1705) 19, 23–4, 23n14
**Owen, Edward** (1664–1739) 5, 19, 25–35
and Elizabeth Phillips **18**, 19–22
marriage to Elizabeth Hethersett 20, 22, 27
letters received 23–5, 28–9, 31–5
letters written **19**, 20–2, 26–7
**Owen, Jane** (Mrs James Birch, 1705–49) 5, 48, 50
engagement to Richard Bayliss 27–35
marriage to James Birch 35, 36, 56n32
children 35, 36, 36n3
letters received 51–2
letters written 28–9, 31–3
death 57, 59
oysters 48, 48n17

Pacha, Captain 12, 103, 103n17, 105, 130
Paget, General 394
Pakenham, Lt.-Colonel Edward (1819–54) 259, 261
Palestine 399, 400, 400n6
Palmer (1854) 259
Palmer, Adrian 357n17
Palmer, Hon. Gordon 357n17
Palmerston, Lord (1784–1865), Prime Minister 279
Panmure, Lord (1801–74) 279
Parker, Admiral Sir Hyde (1739–1807) 109–10, 110n19
parliamentary elections 22–3, 25, 68
Partridge, Eleanor (Mrs Henry Birch Reynardson, 1818–1905) 5, 229, 266, 266n43, 288–9, 305
Partridge, Etheldred see Birch Reynardson, Etheldred 'Ethy'
Partridge, Etheldred Mary 212
Partridge, Henry Champion 4, 212
Partridge, Henry Thomas 212
Partridge, Mrs 157
Partridge, W. 247, 270
Patton, General 382
Paul, Tsar of Russia (1754–1801) 110, 110n19, 124
Payne, Etheldred 66
Peace of Basel (1795) 75n25
Peel, Sir Robert 226n34
Peninsular War (1808–13) 140–8, 149, 161n38, 165n44, 171, 177–9, 230
Battle of Corunna (1809) 144, 146n22, 148
Battle of Roliça (Zambuiera) (1808) 141, **431**, **432**
Battle of Salamanca (1812) 171, 180–2, 180n10, **182**
Battle of Talavera (1809) 161n38
Battle of the Nive (1813) 182n12
Battle of Vimiero (1808) 141, 143n19, **433**, **434**
Battle of Vitoria (1813) 182n12, 184n13
Siege of Badajoz (1812) 178n6, 179, 179n7
Siege of San Sebastian (1813) 182n12
Penn, Granville (1761–1844) 186, 186n16, 187
**Pennington, W.H.**: 'Battle of Balaclava' 253–4
Pepys, Samuel 7
Perceval, Spencer (1762–1812), Prime Minister 149n28

Percy, Captain  241, 257, 259, 261
Perkins, Will  355, 356
Perry, Lt.-Colonel 'Stug'  363, 365, 383n36
Phillips, Elizabeth  19, 20–2
Phipps-Hornby, Major Edmund, VC (1857–1947)  303, 303n12
photographs  270, 272, 272n48
Pitt, John, Earl of Chatham (1756–1835)  149, 149n27, 153, 154n33, 158, 159, 160, 161, 162, 163, 165n43
Pitt, William the Younger (1759–1806), Prime Minister  92, 92n13, 108, 116, 149
Ponsonby, Ashley (d.1915)  312n19, 352
Ponsonby, Ashley  404, 411
Ponsonby, Charles Frederick, 2nd Baron de Mauley (1815–96)  342
Ponsonby, Diana see Birch Reynardson, Diana
Ponsonby, Hon. Edwin 'Ned' (1851–1939)  3, 342, 349
Ponsonby, Major-General Sir Frederick (1783–1837)  342
Ponsonby, Frederick E.G., 1st Baron Sysonby (1867–1935)  344
Ponsonby, Sir Henry (1825–95)  342, 344
Ponsonby, Lady Maria  342
Ponsonby, Mary  353
Popham, Admiral Sir Home Riggs (1762–1820)  137, 137n7, 140n11, 152, 156
Popham, Lady  137
Portland, Duke of (1738–1839), Prime Minister  149n28
postal service  205–6, 206n10
Pott, Will  411
*Pourtraicture of His Sacred MAJESTIE in his Solitudes and Sufferings, The* (1648)  **8**, 9
Presbyterian Church of Scotland  73
**Price, Colonel Jack**  383–4, 383n36, **384**, 386–7, 388, 392, 396
Prideaux, Cynthia see Birch Reynardson, Cynthia
Prideaux, Humphrey  4, 350, **351**, 352, 359
Prideaux, Timothy  4, 350
Pritchett, Samuel  **40**, 41–4, 56
*Private Eye*  420
Probert, Corporal  385
Prussia  75, 75n25, 78n26, 236
Pulteney, Lt.-General Sir James (c.1755–1811)  85, 85n4, 86, 87
*Punch*  250, 250n28
Pym, Francis (1922–2008)  365, 365n24

Queen's College, Cambridge  63
Quelez palace, Lisbon  142n17

Raglan, Lord see Somerset, Lord Fitzroy
railways  229–30, 231, 244, 276, 276n52
Rainsford, Colonel  156
Ranfurly, Daniel Knox, Earl of (1914–88)  364, 364n23, 381
Ranfurly, Hermione, Countess of (1913–2001)  363, 364, 364n23, 381, 381n35
Reeve, Mrs  137, 188
Regnier, General  102
Reynardson family  3, 4, 6, 7, 9, 66, 67, 114, 114n24, 133

Reynardson, Abigail  16n4
Reynardson, Sir Abraham (1590–1660), Lord Mayor of London  4, 7–11, **10**, 13
Reynardson, Lady see Wynne, Eleanor
Reynardson, Elizabeth  66, 140n12, 428
**Reynardson, Etheldred Anne** 'Ethel' (Mrs Thomas Birch Reynardson, 1778–1846)  4, 146, 186n18, 187, 203
  engagement  133–4, 428
  marriage  3, 17, 72, 135, 137
  change of name  135, 135n5
  children  153n30, 168, 209
  letters received  149, 152–67
  letters written  210–12
  death  229
**Reynardson, Jacob** (1652/3–1719)  4, 9, 13, **14**, **15**, 16–17
Reynardson, Jacob (1742–1811)  4, 17, 66, 66n13, 119, 135, 148, 165, 168
Reynardson, Jemima  66, 205
Reynardson, Katherine  66, 119, 119n30, 135
Reynardson, Lucy (d.1789)  66
Reynardson, Mary (Lady Barnardiston, d.1729)  4, 13, 17, **19**
Reynardson, Samuel (1680)  16
Reynardson, Samuel (1704–97)  4, 17, **18**, 66
Reynardson, Thomas  7
Richmond, Charles Lennox, Duke of (1701–50)  55
Ridley, Colonel  249, 261, 269, 269n47
Roberts, Frederick, Lord (1832–1914)  298, 298n4, 300n5, 305
Rokeby, Lord (1798–1883)  279
Roosevelt, Franklin D. (1882–1945), President of the United States  335n2, 353n3, 362n20
Ropner, Sir Guy  411
Rosetta Stone  127n33
Ross, Lt.-Colonel  161
Rosslyn, Lord (1762–1837)  155, 158, 161
Rowan-Hamilton, Denis  407
**Rowlandson, Thomas**: *Preparations for the Jubilee, or Theatricals Extraordinary*  **166**
Rowley, Captain  248
Royal Military Academy, Sandhurst
  18th century  82, 84, 105, 106–7, 124, 135, 141, 170–1, 173, 174–5, 176n4, 186n14, 230
  19th century  83, 298
  20th century  82, 359
**Rubbra, Benedict**: *Double portrait of Bill and Nik Reynardson*  **419**
Rushington Manor  11, 280
Russell, Dr (Christ Church)  357
Russell, Lord (1639–83)  13, 16
Russell, Lt.-Colonel Sir Charles, VC (1826–83)  259
Russell, William Howard (1820–1907)  262, 276n51
Ryder Richardson, Teddy  409
Rye House Plot  13
Rye, Mary (Mrs William Newell)  5, 283

Saint-Arnaud, Marshal Jacques Leroy de (1801–54)  236n9, 279n53
Savary, Claude-Étienne (1750–88)  111, 111n20

Sayer, Doris  353, 440, **440**, 441
Scarlett, Sir J.  253
Scot, Mr  119
Second World War (1939–45)  52n26, 346, 350, 352–91
    D-Day landings  (1944) 369
    evacuees  352, 353, 353n2, **439**, 439–41, **440, 441, 442–4**
    Italy  (1944–5) 365–8, 371–91, **378, 387, 388**
    Japan  391
    Lend-Lease programme  353n3, 397
    Local Defence Volunteers  356
    London blitz  370
    North Africa  360–5
    Quebec Conference (1943)  335n2
    VE Day  388, 391n38
    post-war years  397–402, 397n2, 400n6
sergeants-at-law  39, 39n6
Seven Years' War (1756–63)  69n20
Sewell, Sergeant  162
sex education  341–2
**Shee, Sir Martin Archer, PRA** (1769–1850)
    *Portrait of Diana Bourchier, Mrs John Birch* **219**
    *Portrait of John William (Newell) Birch* **219**
shooting  209, 339, 347, 348–9, 361, 416, 418, 422
Shropham Hall, Norfolk  51n23, 52
Shuttle, Mrs  347, 349
Simpson, William (1823–99)  270, 274
Slessor, Air Marshal Sir John (1897–1979)  365n25
Slessor, Judy (later Mrs 'Stug' Perry)  365, 365n25, 383n36
Smart, Roy  422
Smith, Mr (tenant of Postcombe)  290
Smith, Sir Sidney (1764–1840)  90, 90n10, **91**, 103
Smith, Stephen  48–9
smugglers  55, 55n31
**Smythe, Admiral**
    *A nineteenth-century view of Adwell* **283**
    *A nineteenth-century view of the gardens at Adwell* **296**
Soden (coachman)  306
Solomon (groom)  336
Somerset House  67
**Somerset, Lord Fitzroy** (*later* Lord Raglan, 1788–1855)  203, 204
    in the Crimea  236, 244, 245n19, 250, 253, 254, 256, 265, 268
    letters received  230, 232
    letters written  230, 233
Sones, Mr (butler)  340, 347, 349
Soult, Marshal Nicolas (1769–1851)  146n22
South Weston  283, 285, 290, 291
Southgate, Edmonton  41
Spahis  236, **237**
Spanish War of Independence see Peninsular War
Spencer, Lt.-Colonel Aubrey Vere (1886–1973)  414, 414n14
Spencer, Charles  27n21
Spencer, Edward John 'Johnnie', Viscount Althorp (later Earl Spencer, 1924–92)  359, 359n18, 374
Spooner, Abraham  56n32
Sproston, Carol  422

Sproston, Graham  420, 422
St Hugh's College, Oxford  405, 445–6
St Joseph's Community  412
St Mary's Church, Guildford  298n3
*Stamford Mercury*  229n42
Stirling, Lieutenant  305
Stopford, Robert  266, 266n44
Stourton, Hon. Charles E. (1923–2006)  357n14, **358**
Strachan, Sir Richard (1760–1828)  165, 165n43
Straker, Frances  414
Stuart, Robbie  372
*Sultan* (horse)  119, **134**, 153, 153n31, 157, 167, 429, 430
**Sumner, George Holme** (1760–1838)  116–17, 128
Switzerland  205, 206, 208, 221, 223–5, 223n31
Synge, J.R.  **358**

telegraph  244
Teshmaker, Sarah (wife of Sir Thomas Birch)  4, 44, 61
Thackeray, William Makepeace (1811–63)  222n29
Thompson, Bertie  325
**Thompson, Elizabeth** (*later* Lady Butler, 1846–1933)  262n41
    *The Roll Call*  262, 262n41, **263**
Thornhill, Mr  284–5
Thornton, Colonel  187
Thwaites, Otto  367, 386, **387**
Tice, William  293, 294, 306
*The Times*  149, 245n19, 262, 276n51, 445–6
Tito, Marshal Josip Broz (1892–1980), President of Yugoslavia  371, 393
**Todd, Thomas**  207–8, 207n16
Tory party  22, 22n12, 25, 27n21, 92n13
Tottenham house of Sir Abraham Reynardson  9, **10**
Townshend, Major-General Sir Charles (1861–1924)  322, 325, 325n31, 328n32, 329
Treaty of Amiens (1802)  130n36
Treaty of Fontainebleau (1814)  184n13
Treaty of Paris (1856)  276n50
Trinity College, Cambridge  209, 214
Trollope, Anthony (1815–82)  229, 229n41
Trollope, Sir John  229
Trollope, Julia (Mrs George Birch Reynardson)  4, 229
Truman, Harry S. (1884–1972), President of the United States  397
Turkey  89–91, 93, **94**
    *see also* Crimean War
Turner, Nanny  335, 340, 349, 422
Tweedsmuir, Lord (John Buchan) (1873–1940)  335n2

**Under-Secretary of State for War**
    telegram  378, 379
University of Glasgow  73
Upton, Colonel  259, 269n47

Vaes, André and Simone  416
Vernon, Admiral Edward (1684–1757)  51n24
Vernon, Captain  162
Vicar of Bray  49, 49n20
Victoria County History  281
Victoria Cross  257, 257n35
Victoria, Queen (1819–1901)  214, 261, 262n41, 336n3,

Voltz, Johann Michael: *Aufstieg und Niederfallen Napoleons* **185**

Walcheren campaign (1809) 148n26, 149–67, **150**, 168
Walker, Mrs 335
Wallace, Ronnie F. (1919–2002) 2, 398, 398n3
Wallachia 235–6, 239, 276n50
Wallmoden-Gimborn, General Count Johann von (1769–1862) 79, 79n29
Walton, John 43
War of the Austrian Succession (1740–48) 46, 46n12, 51n22, 69n20
  Battle of Dettingen (1743) 46n12, (Appendix I) 424–6, **427**
War of the Quadruple Alliance (1718–20) 27n19
War of the Second Coalition (1798–1801) 132
War of the Spanish Succession (1701–14) 25n16, 27n19
Ward, 'Daddy' 290, 297
Watts, Mrs 93, 113
Waugh, Evelyn (1903–66) 371, 371n28
Webb, Colonel Edward 284
Webb, Frances 284
Wellington, Arthur Wellesley, Duke of (1769–1852) 141n13, 204, 206n12
  in Peninsular War 140–1, 141n15, 142–3, 142n18, 144, 161n38, 177, 178n6, 181, **182**, 182n11, 184n13, 187, 436
  Prime Minister 216, 216n21
  and the Chartists 234n2
Wentworth Stanley, David 384, **387**
Wesley, John (1703–91) 46n13
West, James 68n17
West, Sarah 68n17
Whately, David 386
Whig party 22, 22n12, 25, 27, 27n21, 47, 47n14, 61, 68, 92n13
Whitaker, Jack and Marybeth 418
Whitelocke, John (1757–1833) 140, 140n11
Whitworth-Jones, Anthony 422
Wiggins, Beryl 412
Wiggins, Mrs (cook) 412
Wilby (gamekeeper) 348, 349
Wild, Jonathan (1683–1725) 29, 29n23, **30**
**Wilkinson, Rev. William** 194–6, 194n3, 200–1
William III (1650–1702) 13n2, 27n19, 55n30
William IV (1765–1837) 214, 239n13
William, Prince, Duke of Cumberland (1721–65) 31n25
William, Prince, Duke of Gloucester (1743–1805) 73, 118, 118n29
Wilson, General Sir Henry Maitland 'Jumbo' (1881–1964) 363–4, 363n22, 364n23, 365, 381, 381n35
Wilson, Major Sir Robert (1777–1849) 89–90, 119, 119n31
Winchilsea, Lord (1791–1858) 216, 216n21, 220
Window Tax 55, 55n30, 56
Windsor Castle 206, 206n13, 359, 418
Wingfield, Watkin 228
Witney, Fred 291

Wixon, Mr (Head Gardener) 348
Wolfe, General James (1727–59) 69n20
Wollerton, Lorrie (*née* Aldridge) 411–12, 423
**Wood, Colonel Thomas** (1804–72) 257–60, 261–2
Wretham Hall, Thetford 57n33
Wyatt, James (1746–1813) 106–7, 106n18
Wyatville, Sir Jeffry (1766–1840) 206n13
Wynne, Eleanor, Lady Reynardson 4, 9, **10**, 13, 17
Wynyard, Lt.-Colonel Montague 161

York, Duke of see Frederick, Prince, Duke of York (1763–1827)
York Minster 209, 209n17
Yorke, Anne see Birch Reynardson, Anne
Yorke, General John (1814–90) 227, 255, 269, 269n46
Yorke, Charles (1764–1834) 119
Yorke, Philip, 1st Earl of Hardwicke (1690–1764) 61, 61n2, 69n19
Yorke, Philip (1743–1804) 4, 63, 64–5, 64n6, 64n7, 67, 164n40
Yorke, Simon 64n7, 67
Younghusband, Tony 416

Zouaves 242, 242n16

# INDEX OF AUTHORS OF ORIGINAL LETTERS, DIARIES AND OTHER DOCUMENTS

Numbers given in **bold** (**13:5**) refer to the order of the document within each chapter, followed by the page reference. Original illustrations are indexed in bold (**Fig. 2 a**)), also followed by the page number.

Alice, Princess, Countess of Athlone (1883–1981): **13:5** 415
Amery, Mrs Florence: **12:27** 395–6
Archer, Thomas, Lord: **3:3** 69; **3:4** 70
Athlone, Prince Alexander of Teck, Earl of (1874–1957): **11:1** 338
Austen, Jane (1775–1817) 217

Ball, George: **2:1** 38–9
Barker, Sarah: **1:12** 34
Bayliss, Richard: **1:13** 35
Birch, James (1697–1772) **2:6** 54; **2:9** 59–60
Birch, James (1771–1817): **4:7** 97
Birch, Jane 'Jenny' (1742–64): **Fig. 3c**) 71
Birch, John William Newell (1775–1867): **4:5** 91–3; **4: 7** 97; **4:13** 109–10; **4:19** 120; **7:12** 221–3; **7:14** 225–6
Birch, John Wyrley: **2:8** 57
Birch, Mary (daughter of Sir Thomas): **3:1** 62
Birch, Mary (*née* Newell, 1737–1837) **4:18** 118–19; **5:3** 137–8; **5:4** 139–40; **7:6** 205–7; 216; **7:10** 218; **7:11** 220–1
Birch, Sir Thomas (1691–1757): **2:2** 41–4; **2:7** 56; **Fig. 2a**) 40
Birch, Thomas (b.1743): **3:2** 63
Birch, Thomas (1773–1847) *see* Birch Reynardson, General Thomas (1773–1847)
Birch Reynardson, Charles Thomas Samuel (1810–89) 202–3; **7:7** 208–9; 209
Birch Reynardson, Colonel Edward (1812–96): **8:1** 237–8; **8:2** 239–40; **8:3** 240–2; **8:4** 243; **8:5** 244–6; **8:6** 246–8; **8:7** 248–9; **8:8** 249–51; **8:10** 254–6; **8:11** 257–60; **8:14** 268–70; **8:15** 272–4; **8:16** 275–6; **8:17** 276, 279; **Fig. 8b**) 237; **Fig. 8c**) 238; **Fig. 8f**) 264; **Fig. 8g**) 271; **Fig. 8i**) 277; **Fig. 8j**) 278
Birch Reynardson, Emma Lucy (1821–67): **7:15** 228; **8:13** 265–7
Birch Reynardson, Etheldred Anne (Mrs Thomas Birch Reynardson, 1778–1846) *see* **Reynardson, Etheldred Anne**
Birch Reynardson, Henry (1814–84): **7:2** 197; **7:3** 197, 200; **7:13** 223–5; **Fig. 7a**) 198
Birch Reynardson, Lt.-Colonel Henry Thomas (1892–1972): **9:1** 288–95, 297; **10:2** 306–8; **10:5** 310–11; **10:9** 316–17; **10:10** 318–19; **10:11** 321–2; **10:12** 322–5; **10:13** 325–6; **10:14** 328–30; **10:15** 330–1; **10:16** 331–2; **Fig. 10d**) 320; **Fig. 10e**) 327; **Fig. 10g**) 334
Birch Reynardson, Matilda Caroline (Mrs Robert Stopford, 1817–1907): **7:15** 227
Birch Reynardson, Pamela Matnika 'Nik': **13:3** 405–7

Birch Reynardson, Richard 'Dickie' (1926–2003): **12:1** 354; **12:9** 370; **13:1** 399–402; **13:2** 402–3
Birch Reynardson, General Thomas (1773–1847) 73; **3:5** 76–82; **4:1** 85–6; **4:2** 87; **4:3** 88–9; **4:4** 89–91; **4:6** 95; **4:7** 95, 97; **4:8** 99–100; **4:9** 101–3; **4:10** 104–5; **4:14** 111–13; **4:15** 113–14; **4:16** 114–15; **4:20** 122; **4:21** 122–3; **4:23** 125–6; **4:24** 127–8; **4:25** 128–9; **4:26** 129–30; **4:27** 130–1; **5:6** 146–7; **5:7** 147–8; **5:8** 151–2; **5:9** 152–4; **5:10** 155–7; **5:11** 157–9; **5:12** 159–61; **5:13** 162–4; **5:14** 164–5, 167; **6:3** 174–5; **6:8** 186; **6:9** 187–8; **7:1** 194–6; **7:5** 203–5; **7:9** 212, 214; **7:16** 231; **7:17** 232; **Fig. 4d**) 96; **Fig. 4f**) 121; **Fig. 4g**) 126; **Fig. 5a**) 134; **I:A** 427; **II:A** 428–30
Birch Reynardson, William John (1849–1940): **Fig. 9d**) 287; **Fig. 9e**) 287
Birch Reynardson, William Robert Ashley 'Bill' (b.1923): **11:2** 339; **11:3** 346–50; **12:2** 355–6; **12:3** 361–2; **12:4** 363; **12:5** 363–4; **12:6** 364–5; **12:7** 367–8; **12:10** 372–3; **12:11** 373–4; **12:12** 374–5; **12:13** 375–7; **12:16** 381; **12:17** 382; **12:18** 382–3; **12:19** 384–5; **12:20** 385–6; **12:22** 389–90; **12:23** 390; **12:24** 391–2; **12:25** 392–3; **12:26** 394
Brownrigg, General Robert (1759–1833): **5:1** 133

Carey, Major Peter (1774–1852), attributed to: **5:5** 142–4
Cashel, John: **V:A** 439–44
Cust family: **Fig. 6e**) 189

Defoe, Daniel (1660–1731): **1:4** 23–5
Drake, William: **Fig. 3d**) 71

Gordon, General James (1772–1851): **6:1** 169
Green, Mary (*née* Birch, 1694–1784): **2:5** 51–2
Grenfell, Laura: **13:4** 408

Harcourt, General William (1743–1830): **4:22** 124
Hawarden, Robert Cornwallis Maude, Viscount (1890–1914): **10:6** 312–13; **10:7** 314
Heseltine, Michael: **VI** 445–6
Heygate, A.C.G.: **10:4** 309
Humphreys, Nik *see* **Birch Reynardson, Pamela Matnika 'Nik'**

Johnston, Lt.-Colonel Percy: **10:8** 315
Joicey, John: **12:15** 380

Lacoste, Jean Baptiste: 'Battle of Waterloo': **6:10** 190–3; **Fig. 6e**) 189
Le Marchant, Carey: **6:7** 183–4
Le Marchant, Major-General John Gaspard (1766–1812): **4:11** 106–7; **4:12** 107–8; **5:2** 135–6; **6:2**

171–3; **6:4** 176; **6:5** 178–9; **6:6** 180–1; **Fig. 6b**) 177
**Legh, Rev. Dr George** (1693–1775): **2:3** 47; **2:4** 48–9; **2:6** 53–4; **2:9** 58–60

**Marriott, James 'Jimmy'** (d.1944): **12:8** 369
**Maxwell, Brigadier-General Francis Aylmer 'Frank'** (1871–1917): **10:1** 301–5; **10:3** 308–9; **Fig. 10c**) 300
military memorabilia: **I:A** 424–7; **III:A** 431; **III:B** 432; **III:C** 433; **III:D** 434; **IV:A** 435–6; **IV:B** 436–8
**Murray, Lord George** (1694–1760): **Fig. 2c**) 45

**Owen, Edward** (1664–1739): **1:2** 20–1; **1:3** 21–2; **1:5** 26–7; **Fig. 1f**) 18
**Owen, Jane** (Mrs James Birch, 1705–49): **1:6** 28; **1:7** 29; **1:8** 31; **1:9** 31–2; **1:10** 32–3; **1:11** 33

**Pennington, W.H.**: 'Battle of Balaclava': **8:9** 253–4
**Price, Colonel Jack**: **12:21** 386–7; 388

**Reynardson, Etheldred Anne** (Mrs Thomas Birch Reynardson, 1778–1846): **7:8** 210–12
**Reynardson, Jacob** (1652/3–1719): **1:1** 16–17; **Fig. 1c**) 15

**Somerset, Lord Fitzroy** (*later* Lord Raglan, 1788–1855): **7:18** 233
**Sumner, George Holme** (1760–1838): **4:17** 116–17

**Todd, Thomas**: **7:7** 207–8

**Under-Secretary of State for War**: **12:14** 379

**Wilkinson, Rev. William**: **7:4** 200–1
**Wood, Colonel Thomas** (1804–72): **8:12** 261–2